Lecture Notes in Computer Science 16233

The series Lecture Notes in Computer Science (LNCS), including its subseries Lecture Notes in Artificial Intelligence (LNAI) and Lecture Notes in Bioinformatics (LNBI), has established itself as a medium for the publication of new developments in computer science and information technology research, teaching, and education.

LNCS enjoys close cooperation with the computer science R & D community, the series counts many renowned academics among its volume editors and paper authors, and collaborates with prestigious societies. Its mission is to serve this international community by providing an invaluable service, mainly focused on the publication of conference and workshop proceedings and postproceedings. LNCS commenced publication in 1973.

Romain Laborde · Joaquin Garcia-Alfaro ·
Abbas Yazdinejad · Gregory Epiphaniou ·
Habtamu Abie · Silvio Ranise · Michał Choraś ·
Michał Woźniak · Yuko Hara ·
Jan Tobias Mühlberg · Claudia Greco ·
Kim-Kwang Raymond Choo
Editors

Computer Security

ESORICS 2025
International Workshops

AutonomousCyber 2025, CPS4CIP 2025, DisA 2025, HS3 2025
MIST 2025, Toulouse, France, September 25–26, 2025
Revised Selected Papers, Part III

Editors
Romain Laborde
IRIT, Université de Toulouse
Toulouse, France

Joaquin Garcia-Alfaro
SAMOVAR, Télécom SudParis
Palaiseau, France

Abbas Yazdinejad
Department of Computer Science
University of Regina
Regina, Canada

Gregory Epiphaniou
WMG, University of Warwick
Coventry, UK

Habtamu Abie
Norwegian Computing Center
Oslo, Norway

Silvio Ranise
University of Trento and Fondazione Bruno Kessler
Trento, Trento, Italy

Michał Choraś
Bydgoszcz University of Science and Technology
Bydgoszcz, Poland

Michał Woźniak
Wroclaw University of Science and Technology
Wroclaw, Poland

Yuko Hara
Institute of Science Tokyo
Tokyo, Japan

Jan Tobias Mühlberg
Université Libre de Bruxelles
Brussels, Belgium

Claudia Greco
University of Calabria
Rende, Italy

Kim-Kwang Raymond Choo
University of Texas
San Antonio, TX, USA

ISSN 0302-9743 ISSN 1611-3349 (electronic)
Lecture Notes in Computer Science
ISBN 978-3-032-16164-2 ISBN 978-3-032-16165-9 (eBook)
https://doi.org/10.1007/978-3-032-16165-9

This Springer imprint is published by the registered company Springer Nature Switzerland AG
The registered company address is: Gewerbestrasse 11, 6330 Cham, Switzerland

Preface

The 30th edition of the European Symposium on Research in Computer Security (ESORICS) was held in Toulouse, France, during September 22–26, 2025. In addition to the main conference, 13 workshops were organized and held in the same time period.

This volume includes the accepted contributions to five of these workshops, as follows:

- the 2nd International Workshop on Autonomous Cybersecurity (AutonomousCyber 2025);
- the 6th International Workshop on Cyber-Physical Security for Critical Infrastructurs Protection (CSPS4CIP 2025);
- the 5th International Workshop on Computational Methods for Emerging Problems in Disinformation Analysis (DisA 2025);
- the International Workshop on Hardware-Supported Software Security (HS3 2025);
- the International Workshop on Mobile and IoT Security Technologies (MIST 2025).

While each of the workshops had a high-quality program of its own, the organizers opted to publish the proceedings jointly; these are included in this volume, which contains 34 revised papers. The authors improved and extended the accepted papers based on the reviewers' feedback as well as the discussions at the workshops.

We would like to thank each and every one who was involved in the organization of the ESORICS 2025 workshops. Special thanks go to the respective Program Committees of each workshop, who contributed to making the ESORICS 2025 workshops a real success. We would also like to thank the ESORICS 2025 Organizing Committee for supporting the day-to-day operation and execution of the workshops.

November 2025

Romain Laborde
Joaquin Garcia-Alfaro
Abbas Yazdinejad
Gregory Epiphaniou
Habtamu Abie
Silvio Ranise
Michał Choraś
Michał Woźniak
Yuko Hara
Jan Tobias Mühlberg
Claudia Greco
Kim-Kwang Raymond Choo

Preface to the Proceedings of AutonomousCyber 2025

The *2nd International Workshop on Autonomous Cybersecurity (AutonomousCyber 2025)* was held in conjunction with the 30th European Symposium on Research in Computer Security (ESORICS 2025) in France. Building on the success of the inaugural edition held at ACM CCS 2024 in Salt Lake City, USA, this second edition continued to advance the scientific discourse on autonomous, self-learning, and adaptive cybersecurity systems. The 2025 workshop provided a vibrant interdisciplinary forum for researchers and practitioners to explore the evolution from automation to autonomy in cybersecurity — a paradigm increasingly driven by Artificial Intelligence (AI), Machine Learning (ML), Quantum Machine Learning (QML), and Reinforcement Learning (RL).

The workshop focused on developing and deploying self-improving, proactive, and context-aware defense mechanisms that operate with minimal human intervention. Topics included cognitive modeling for cyber defense, human–machine teaming for resilience, multi-agent coordination, and the ethics and governance of autonomous systems. Through its keynote addresses, peer-reviewed research presentations, and panel discussions, *AutonomousCyber 2025* highlighted how autonomous systems can enable faster, more adaptive, and explainable cybersecurity for next-generation digital infrastructures.

A single-blind peer-review process was adopted to ensure academic rigor and fairness. Each submission was evaluated by at least three independent reviewers based on originality, significance, and technical quality. The workshop received 24 submissions, of which 7 papers were accepted for presentation and inclusion in these proceedings. The final program also featured an invited keynote address, an industry presentation, and a closing panel discussion that fostered dialogue between academia, industry, and policy experts. In total, the workshop attracted more than 40 participants from around the world, both in person and online.

The editors wish to extend their deepest gratitude to all authors, reviewers, and participants for their valuable contributions. Special thanks go to the ESORICS 2025 organizing committee for their guidance and logistical support, and to Springer for publishing these proceedings in the *Lecture Notes in Computer Science (LNCS)* series. We also acknowledge the outstanding efforts of the Program Committee members, whose diligence and expertise ensured the high scientific quality of the accepted papers.

We hope that the papers presented in this volume will inspire further innovation in autonomous and self-resilient cybersecurity, advancing the global effort to build secure, adaptive, and trustworthy digital systems.

November 2025

Abbas Yazdinejad
Ali Dehghantanha
Reza M. Parizi
Gregory Epiphaniou

Preface to the Proceedings of CPS4CIP 2025

CPS4CIP 2025 was a forum for researchers and practitioners working on cyber-physical security for critical infrastructures protection that supports finance, energy, health, air transport, communication, gas, and water. The secure operation of critical infrastructures is essential to the security of nations and, in an increasingly interconnected world, of unions of states sharing their infrastructures to develop their economies, and to public health and safety. Security incidents in critical infrastructures can directly lead to a violation of users' safety and privacy, physical damage, interference in the political and social life of citizens, significant economic impact on individuals and companies, and threats to human life while decreasing trust in institutions and questioning their social value. Because of the increasing interconnection between the digital and physical worlds, these infrastructures and services are more critical, sophisticated, and interdependent than ever before. The increased complexity makes each infrastructure increasingly vulnerable to attacks, as confirmed by the steady rise of cyber-security incidents, such as phishing or ransomware, and cyber-physical incidents, such as physical violation of devices or facilities in conjunction with malicious cyber activities. To make the situation even worse, interdependency may give rise to a domino effect with catastrophic consequences on multiple infrastructures.

To address these challenges, the workshop aimed to bring together security researchers and practitioners from the various verticals of critical infrastructures (such as the financial, energy, health, air transport, communication, gas, and water domains) and rethink cyber-physical security in the light of the latest technological developments (e.g., Cloud Computing, Blockchain, Big Data, AI, Internet-of-Things) by developing novel and effective approaches to increase the resilience of critical infrastructures and the related ecosystems of services.

The workshop attracted the attention of the critical infrastructures protection research communities and stimulated new insights and advances with particular attention to the integrated cyber and physical aspects of security in critical infrastructures. The 6th International Workshop on Cyber-Physical Security for Critical Infrastructures Protection (CPS4CIP 2025) was held in-person. The workshop was organized in conjunction with the 30th European Symposium on Research in Computer Security (ESORICS 2025), at the Université de Toulouse in Toulouse, France, on September 25, 2025. The format of the workshop included technical presentations.

The workshop received 16 submissions that were sent for reviews. After a thorough single-blind peer-review process in which submissions received on average four reviews each, 8 papers were selected for presentation at the workshop. The review process focused on the quality of the papers, their scientific novelty, and their applicability to the protection of critical financial infrastructure and services. The accepted articles represent an interesting mix of cybersecurity innovations for industrial and critical infrastructure, AI-driven security for IoT and cyber-physical systems, and advances in machine learning for secure and privacy-preserving threat detection.

The workshop was supported by projects of the ECSCI cluster, mainly (i) the ECSCI Running projects (AI4CYBER, ATLANTIS, CyberSecDome, DYNABIC, eFORT, ENDURANCE, ESCORT, EU-CIP, EU-HYBNET, HARPOCRATES, HERON, INTACT, IRIS, LAZARUS, MIRANDA, NEMECYS, PATTERN, PHOENI2X, R2D2, ResilMesh, SECANT, SecAwarenessTruss, SUNRISE, TELEMETRY, TESTUDO, TRANSCEND), (ii) the ECSCI completed projects supported by coordinators (FINSEC, ANASTACIA, CyberSANE, CyberSEAS, DEFENDER, EnergyShield, ENSURESEC, FeatureCloud, IMPETUS, InfraStress, PHOENIX, PRAETORIAN, PRECINCT, RESISTO, SAFECARE, SAFETY4RAILS, SATIE, SealedGRID, Secure-Gas, SmartResilience, SOTER, SPHINX, STOP-IT, 7SHIELD), and (iii) the three national projects (NORCICS (Norwegian Center for Cybersecurity in Critical Sectors) project funded by the Research Council of Norway under the Center for Research-based Innovation (SFI), RESTABILISE4.0 (Restabilise and Energy: Specialization of Enabling Technologies for Balancing Energy Infrastructures and Systems) project cofunded by START4.0 - Competence Center for security and optimization of strategic infrastructures, and CybAlliance (International Alliance for Strengthening Cybersecurity and Privacy in Healthcare) project funded by the Research Council of Norway under the INT-PART International Partnerships for Excellent Education, Research and Innovation program). The organizers would like to thank these projects for sponsoring the CPS4CIP 2025 workshop. Their support was instrumental in making the event possible and is gratefully acknowledged.

Finally, the organizers of the CPS4CIP 2025 workshop would like to express their gratitude to the CPS4CIP 2025 Program Committee and the sub-reviewers, whose rigorous and timely evaluations made the workshop possible. We also extend our thanks to the Université de Toulouse, France, for hosting the event, and to the ESORICS 2025 workshop chairs for their valuable support and assistance.

November 2025

Habtamu Abie
Silvio Ranise
Luca Verderame
Enrico Cambiaso
Rita Ugarelli
Isabel Praça
Sandeep Pirbhulal
Manos Athanatos

Preface to the Proceedings of DisA 2025

This volume contains the post-proceedings of the Workshop on Computational Methods for Emerging Problems in Disinformation Analysis (DisA). The workshop was organized as part of the 30th European Symposium on Research in Computer Security (ESORICS) 2025, held in Toulouse, France.

It took place on September 25th, 2025, at the premises of Université de Toulouse. Previous editions of DisA were held at ICCS, DSAA and ESORICS in 2024.

In response to the call for papers, the workshop chairs received 7 high-quality submissions. Each submission was evaluated based on its significance, novelty, and technical quality. The program committee conducted a thorough double-blind review process with submissions receiving three reviews each on average, and selected 4 full papers with the best reviews. The result was a technical program covering a wide spectrum of topics, related to disinformation analysis methods, problems and solutions, challenges, data, and explainability. The presentations were discussed afterwards and many interesting questions were raised and answered.

We would like to express our gratitude to everyone who contributed to organizing the event, including all the members of the organizing committees of both ESORICS and DisA 2025. Our special thanks go to the General Chairs; the Workshops Chair; the DisA Workshop chairs; and all the individuals involved in the ESORICS 2025 organization.

We extend our special thanks to all the DisA Program Committee members, additional reviewers, all the authors who submitted papers, and all the workshop at-tendees.

Finally, we would like to mention that the session was technically endorsed by the IEEE SMC Technical Committee on Big Data Computing, as well by the SWAROG project.

November 2025

Michał Choraś
Xin Jin
Rafał Kozik
Paweł Ksieniewicz
Michał Woźniak

Preface to the Proceedings of HS3 2025

This volume presents the revised papers of the 1st International Workshop on Hardware-Supported Software Security (HS3 2025), co-located with the 30th European Symposium on Research in Computer Security (ESORICS 2025), held in Toulouse, France, on September 25th, 2025.

The HS3 workshop seeks to share experience, tools and methodology on hardware-assisted software security. Combining software and hardware aspects to mitigate new software attacks is becoming increasingly important. For example, hardware vulnerabilities such as Spectre or Meltdown can be exploited entirely through software-level attacks and these attacks can be executed remotely, not requiring physical access to the targeted hardware platform. Effective mitigations to these attacks require hardware/software co-design, in particular when performance impacts are to be minimized. In addition, hardware features can also be used to better detect and respond to traditional software attacks, such as memory corruption. The goal of the HS3 workshop was to provide a forum for researchers and practitioners from academia, industry and government who study the security of software/hardware interfaces in terms of attacks and defenses to develop hardware-supported software security.

For HS3 2025 we were looking for submissions that propose new processor architectures or processor extensions that offer better resilience against software attacks. These architectures typically provide hardware-based security mechanisms to protect the software stack. One of the key challenges in the field is to formally specify and verify the security guarantees offered by such architectures and to better assess the security guarantees provided by existing hardware architectures against software attacks, especially attacks against micro-architectures. This can be achieved by identifying new vulnerabilities using reverse engineering, fuzzing or other attack approaches. HS3 2025 also had a special theme on *Secure Monitoring, Intrusion Detection, and Incident Response* and we specifically invited submissions that present hardware-assisted approaches in this domain.

Given that HS3 is a very young workshop that was running for the first time in co-location with ESORICS, our call for papers attracted significant interest and resulted in 14 submissions. Each manuscript underwent a rigorous peer-review process, with 3 single-blinded reviewers per paper, and guaranteeing that chairs and committee members would not review their own or otherwise conflicting submissions. Ultimately, HS3 accepted 3 regular papers and 4 short papers.

The workshop itself featured 10 presentations (including 3 work-in-progress submissions that are not present in the proceedings), an invited talk, and time for discussion and reflection. With over 30 participants, the workshop was well frequented and promoted lively discussions around recent trends in hardware-supported security and on application-related topics.

We would like to thank our invited speaker, Robert Norton, for delivering an inspiring keynote on *Hardware-software co-design for security with CHERIoT: from memory-safety to software supply-chain resilience*. We further thank the programme committee and external reviewers for their tireless commitment during the advertising and reviewing phase. Most importantly, we thank all our speakers and participants for the great presentations and intriguing discussions during the workshop. Finally we would like to thank the ESORICS organizers and specifically the workshops chair for supporting us throughout the process of preparing and running

HS3. Next year you will have to allocate a bigger room for us!

November 2025

Guillaume Hiet
Yuko Hara
Jan Tobias Mühlberg

Preface to the Proceedings of MIST 2025

The Workshop on Mobile and IoT Security Technologies (MIST) 2025 was held in conjunction with the ESORICS conference and aimed to explore the latest ad- vancements, challenges, and opportunities in securing Internet of Things (IoT) and mobile systems. The workshop provided a platform for researchers, practitioners, and industry experts to discuss emerging threats, innovative defense mechanisms, and the growing role of Artificial Intelligence, particularly Generative AI and Large Language Models, in cybersecurity.

The workshop focused on the unique vulnerabilities affecting IoT and mobile environments, which have become deeply integrated into modern society, from smart homes and healthcare to industrial control systems and critical infrastructure. The discussions highlighted both the potential of AI to strengthen security practices through automation and intelligence, and the risks arising from its malicious use in crafting sophisticated cyberattacks.

A total of 16 papers were submitted to the MIST 2025 workshop. Each submission underwent a single-blind peer review process, with at least two independent reviews per paper. After careful consideration by the Program Committee, 8 papers were accepted for presentation and inclusion in this volume. The accepted contributions covered a broad range of topics, including IoT device security, mobile application protection, privacy preservation, AI-driven threat detection, and case studies illustrating real-world attacks and countermeasures.

The organizers would like to express their sincere gratitude to all authors for their valuable contributions and to the reviewers for their time and constructive feedback. Their collective efforts ensured the quality and depth of the workshop's technical program. Special thanks are also extended to the ESORICS conference for making the event possible.

We hope that the discussions and papers presented at MIST 2025 will inspire further research and collaboration in the ongoing effort to secure the ever-evolving landscape of mobile and IoT systems.

November 2025

Claudia Greco
Kim-Kwang Raymond Choo
Bruno Crispo
Ernesto Damiani

Organization of AutonomousCyber 2025

General Chairs

Ali Dehghantanha	University of Guelph, Canada
Reza M. Parizi	Kennesaw State University, USA
Gregory Epiphaniou	University of Warwick, UK

Publication Chair

Abbas Yazdinejad	University of Regina, Canada

Publicity Chairs

Tooska Dargahi	Manchester Metropolitan University, UK
Tao Li	City University of Hong Kong, China

Program Committee

Ehab Al-Shaer	Carnegie Mellon University, USA
Benjamin C. M. Fung	McGill University, Canada
Andy Applebaum	Apple Inc, USA
Melody Wolk	Apple Inc, USA
Patrick Dwyer	Apple Inc, USA
Vasilios Mavroudis	Alan Turing Institute, UK
Chris Hicks	Alan Turing Institute, UK
Z. Morley Mao	University of Michigan, USA
Derrick Sturisky	Quantum Computing Inc., USA
Mohammad Hamoudeh	King Fahd University of Petroleum and Minerals, Saudi Arabia
Malka Halgamuge	RMIT University, Australia
Andrew Hamilton	Cybriant, USA
Alireza Jolafai	Flinders University, Australia
Vasilis Katos	Bournemouth University, UK
Ryan K. L. Ko	University of Queensland St Lucia, Australia
Georgios Loukas	University of Greenwich, UK

Haider Al-Khateeb	Aston University, UK
Carsten Maple	University of Warwick, UK
Nick Pitropakis	Edinburgh Napier University, UK
Ahmad Ridley	Laboratory for Advanced Cybersecurity Research, USA
Ali Safaa Sadiq Al Shakarchi	Nottingham Trent University, UK
Jeff Schwartzentruber	eSentire Inc, Canada
Andre Weimerskirch	Lear Corporation, USA
Kaiwen Zhang	École de technologie superieure, Canada
Xiaojie Zhu	King Abdullah University of Science and Technology, Saudi Arabia
Venkata Gopi Kolla	Salesforce Inc, USA

Additional Reviewers

Amin Azmoodeh	Mohawk College
Ali Mohammadi Ruzbahani	University of Calgary

Organization of CPS4CIP 2025

General Chairs

Habtamu Abie	Norwegian Computing Center, Norway
Silvio Ranise	University of Trento and Fondazione Bruno Kessler, Italy

Program Committee Chairs

Luca Verderame	University of Genoa, Italy
Enrico Cambiaso	National Research Council (CNR), Italy
Rita Ugarelli	SINTEF, Norway
Isabel Praça	GECAD/ISEP, Portugal
Sandeep Pirbhulal	Norwegian Computing Center, Norway
Manos Athanatos	Foundation for Research and Technology Hellas, Greece

Program Committee

Dieter Gollmann	Hamburg University of Technology, Germany
Sokratis Katsikas	Norwegian University of Science and Technology, Norway
Fabio Martinelli	IIT-CNR, Italy
Einar Arthur Snekkenes	Norwegian University of Science and Technology, Norway
Stamatis Karnouskos	SAP Research, Germany
Reijo Savola	University of Jyväskylä, Finland
Alessandro Armando	University of Genoa, Italy
Federica Battisti	University of Padua, Italy
Alessio Merlo	University of Genoa, Italy
Cristina Alcaraz	University of Málaga, Spain
Giovanni Livraga	University of Milan, Italy
Shouhuai Xu	University of Colorado Colorado Springs, USA
Christos Xenakis	University of Piraeus, Greece
Mauro Conti	University of Padua, Italy
Denis Čaleta	Institute for Corporate Security Studies, Slovenia

Dušan Gabrielčič	Institute Jožef Stefan, Slovenia
Nikolaus Wirtz	RWTH Aachen University, Germany
Theodore Zahariadis	National and Kapodistrian University of Athens, Greece
Harsha Ratnaweera	Norwegian University of Life Sciences, Norway
Volodymyr V. Tarabara	Michigan State University, USA
Christos Makropoulos	National Technical University of Athens, Greece
David Tipping	DeftEdge, USA
Dionysis Nikolopoulos	National Technical University of Athens, Greece
Ioan Constantin	Orange Romania, Romania
Tim Stelkens-Kobsch	German Aerospace Center (DLR), Germany
Matteo Mangini	Network Integration and Solutions S.r.l., Italy
Corinna Köpke	Fraunhofer Institute for High-Speed Dynamics, Germany
Vasileios Kazoukas	Center for Security Studies (KEMEA), Greece
Georgios Spanoudakis	Sphynx Technology, Switzerland
Haris Mouratidis	University of Brighton, UK
Matthias Eckhart	SBA Research, Austria
Muhammad T. Khan	University of Greenwich, UK
Miguel Mira da Silva	INOV, Portugal
Ilias Gialampoukidis	Information Technologies Institute, Greece
Ilias Gkotsis	Inlecom Innovation, Greece
Simon Hacks	KTH Royal Institute of Technology, Sweden
Andreas Kubis	PSI Software AG, Germany
Audun Jøsang	University of Oslo, Norway
Ariadni M. Psarrou	National Technical University of Athens, Greece
Anna Georgiadou	National Technical University of Athens, Greece
Angelos Liapis	Konnekt-able, Ireland
Israel Pérez Llopis	Polytechnic University of Valencia, Spain
Sandra König	AIT Austrian Institute of Technology, Austria
Stefan Schauer	AIT Austrian Institute of Technology, Austria
Basel Katt	Norwegian University of Science and Technology, Norway
Aida Omerovic	SINTEF, Norway
Sotiris Ioannidis	Technical University of Crete, Greece
Vasileios Mavroeidis	University of Oslo, Norway
Rafael P. Hielscher	Universidad Pontificia Comillas, Spain
Luca Caviglione	IMATI-CNR, Italy
Marco Zuppelli	IMATI-CNR, Italy
Karin Bernsmed	SINTEF, Norway
Martin Gilje Jaatun	SINTEF, Norway
Stella Parisi	Information Technologies Institute, Greece

Dimitrios Kavallieros	Information Technologies Institute, Greece
Konstantinos Ioannidis	Information Technologies Institute, Greece
Matteo Repetto	CNR, Italy
Erkuden Rios	TECNALIA, Basque Research and Technology Alliance (BRTA), Spain
Jocelyn Aubert	Luxembourg Institute of Science and Technology, Luxembourg

Additional Reviewers

Amirhossein Noshadi	CNR, Italy
Apostolos Zarras	Foundation for Research and Technology Hellas, Crete
Despoina Antonakaki	Technical University of Crete, Greece
Ismail Ari	Özyeğin University, Turkey
Taregh Khanjari	CNR, Italy

Organization of DisA 2025

General Chairs

Michał Choraś	Bydgoszcz University of Science and Technology, Poland
Xin Jin	Yunnan University, China
Rafał Kozik	Bydgoszcz University of Science and Technology, Poland
Paweł Ksieniewicz	Wrocław University of Science and Technology, Poland
Michał Woźniak	Wrocław University of Science and Technology, Poland

Program Committee

Evgenia F. Adamopoulou	National Technical University of Athens, Greece
Tomasz Andrysiak	Bydgoszcz University of Science and Technology, Poland
Łukasz Apiecionek	Kazimierz Wielki University, Bydgoszcz, Poland
Stan Assier	Qwant, France
Sebastian Basterrech	Technical University of Denmark, Denmark
Robert Burduk	Wrocław University of Science and Technology, Poland
Krzysztof Cabaj	Warsaw University of Technology, Poland
Konstantinos Demestichas	National Technical University of Athens, Greece
Agata Gielczyk	Bydgoszcz University of Science and Technology, Poland
Manuel Grana	University of the Basque Country, Spain
Álvaro Herrero	University of Burgos, Spain
Dagmara Jaroszewska-Choraś	Kazimierz Wielki University, Bydgoszcz, Poland
Iulia Lazar	Infocons, Romania
Wojciech Mazurczyk	Warsaw University of Technology, Poland
David Megias	Universitat Oberta de Catalunya, Spain
Marek Pawlicki	Bydgoszcz University of Science and Technology, Poland
Jan Platoš	VSB-Technical University of Ostrava, Czech Republic

Mariusz Topolski	Wrocław University of Science and Technology, Poland
Giulia Venturi	Z&P, Italy
Paweł Zyblewski	Wrocław University of Science and Technology, Poland

Organization of HS3 2025

Program Committee Chairs

Guillaume Hiet	IRISA, CentraleSupélec/Inria, France
Yuko Hara	Institute of Science Tokyo, Japan
Jan Tobias Mühlberg	Université Libre de Bruxelles, Belgium

Program Committee

Iness Ben Guirat	Universite Libre de Bruxelles, Belgium
Pascal Cotret	ENSTA Bretagne, France
Kevin Cheang	University of California, Berkeley, USA
Chris Dalton	HP Labs, UK
Lesly-Ann Daniel	KU Leuven, Belgium
Merve Gülmez	Ericsson Research/KU Leuven, Belgium
Karine Heydemann	Thales, France
Vianney Lapôtre	University of Southern Brittany, France
Clémentine Maurice	CNRS, France
Maria Méndez Real	Université Bretagne Sud, France
Cristofaro Mune	Raelize B.V., Malta
Antonio Muñoz	University of Málaga, Spain
Kaveh Razavi	ETH Zurich, Switzerland
Simon Rokicki	ENS Rennes, France
Shweta Shinde	ETH Zurich, Switzerland
Volker Stolz	HVL, Sweden
Marcus Völp	University of Luxembourg, Luxembourg
Pierre Wilke	CentraleSupélec/Inria, France

Additional Reviewers

Navid Ladner

Organization of MIST 2025

Program Committee Chairs

Claudia Greco	University of Calabria, Italy
Kim-Kwang Raymond Choo	University of Texas, San Antonio, USA
Bruno Crispo	University of Trento, Italy
Ernesto Damiani	Khalifa University, United Arab Emirates

Program Committee

Hussam Al Hammadi	Dubai University, United Arab Emirates
Michele Grisafi	University of Trento, Italy
Sandeep Gupta	Queen's University Belfast, UK
Michele Ianni	University of Calabria, Italy
Valeria Loscrì	Inria Lille, France
Lara Mauri	University of Milan, Italy
Andrea Rosani	Free University of Bozen-Bolzano, Italy
Selma Yahia	Inria Lille, France

Contents

2nd International Workshop on Autonomous Cybersecurity (AutonomousCyber 2025)

6th International Workshop on Cyber-Physical Security for Critical Infrastructures (CPS4CIP 2025)

2nd International Workshop on Autonomous Cybersecurity (AutonomousCyber 2025)

ACSE-Eval: Can LLMs Threat Model Real-World Cloud Infrastructure?

Sarthak Munshi[1(✉)], Swapnil Pathak[2], Sonam Ghatode[2], Thenuga Priyadarshini[1], Dhivya Chandramouleeswaran[1], and Ashutosh Rana[3]

[1] Carnegie Mellon University, Pittsburgh, PA 15213, USA
{smunshi,tpriyadh,dhivyac}@alumni.cmu.edu
[2] Northeastern University, Boston, MA 02115, USA
{pathak.s,ghatode.s}@northeastern.edu
[3] New York, NY 10001, USA

Abstract. While Large Language Models (LLMs) have shown promise in cybersecurity applications, their effectiveness in identifying security threats within cloud deployments remains unexplored. This paper introduces AWS Cloud Security Engineering (ACSE)-Eval, a novel dataset for evaluating LLMs' cloud security threat modeling capabilities. ACSE-Eval contains 100 production-grade AWS deployment scenarios, each featuring detailed architectural specifications, Infrastructure as Code (IaC) implementations, documented security vulnerabilities, and associated threat modeling parameters. Our dataset enables systemic assessment of LLMs' abilities to identify security risks, analyze attack vectors, and propose mitigation strategies in cloud environments. Our evaluations on ACSE-Eval demonstrate that GPT-4.1 and Gemini 2.5 Pro excel at threat identification, with Gemini 2.5 Pro performing optimally in 0-shot scenarios and GPT-4.1 showing superior results in few-shot settings. While GPT-4.1 maintains a slight overall performance advantage, Claude 3.7 Sonnet generates the most semantically sophisticated threat models but struggles with threat categorization and generalization. To promote reproducibility and advance research in automated cybersecurity threat analysis, we open-source our dataset, evaluation metrics, and methodologies(https://huggingface.co/datasets/ACSE-Eval/ACSE-Eval).

Keywords: LLM evaluation · Automated threat-modeling · Cloud security · Dataset

1 Introduction

Large Language Models (LLMs) have demonstrated promising performance in cybersecurity tasks such as vulnerability detection and code analysis [7,10]. However, their ability to perform architectural threat assessments in complex cloud

A. Rana—Independent Researcher.

R. Laborde et al. (Eds.): ESORICS 2025 Workshops, LNCS 16233, pp. 3–18, 2026.
https://doi.org/10.1007/978-3-032-16165-9_1

environments remains under explored. While effective at identifying source-level issues [17], LLMs have yet to prove they can reason about service interactions, trust boundaries, and multi-resource configurations typical of modern cloud systems. The urgency of this research is underscored by the evolving threat landscape in cloud security. In 2024, cloud breaches have reached alarming levels, with 79% of cloud-based enterprises reporting at least one incident, and about 25% of organizations expressed uncertainty about undetected threats [13,26]. More concerning is that 82% of these breaches originated from architectural design flaws or misconfigurations, highlighting a critical gap in current security approaches.

Traditional approaches to threat modeling, exemplified by frameworks like MITRE ATT&CK [21] and STRIDE [20], have been enhanced with cloud-specific considerations. However, these frameworks, while comprehensive in mapping adversarial tactics and techniques, have yet to fully integrate with LLM capabilities for automated threat assessment. The complexity of modern cloud architectures, combined with the dynamic nature of Identity and Access Management (IAM) and Zero Trust requirements, demands more sophisticated threat modeling capabilities that can adapt to rapidly evolving security challenges (Fig. 1).

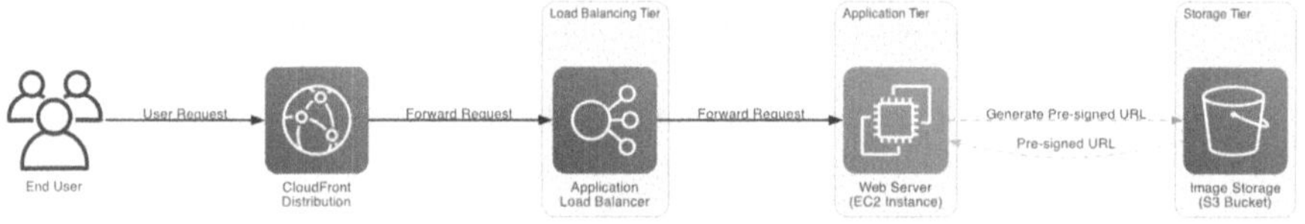


```python
from diagrams.aws.network import ELB, CloudFront
from diagrams.aws.general import Users
from diagrams.aws.compute import EC2
from diagrams.aws.storage import S3
from diagrams import Diagram, Cluster, Edge

...

with Diagram("AWS Website Architecture", ...) as diag:
    user = Users("End User")
    cdn = CloudFront("CloudFront Distribution")

    with Cluster("Load Balancing Tier"):
        alb = ELB("Application Load Balancer")

    with Cluster("Application Tier"):
        web_server = EC2("Web Server (EC2 Instance)")

    with Cluster("Storage Tier"):
        image_bucket = S3("Image Storage (S3 Bucket)")

    # Define main flows
    user >> Edge(color="blue", label="User Request") \
    >> cdn >> alb >> web_server
    web_server >> Edge(color="green", \
    label="Pre-signed URL ops") >> image_bucket
    ...
```

```typescript
import * as cdk from 'aws-cdk-lib';
import { ec2, ... } from 'aws-cdk-lib/aws-*';

export class SimpleImageWebAppStack extends cdk.Stack {
  constructor(...) {
    super(scope, id, props);

    // VPC with public/private subnets
    const vpc = new ec2.Vpc(this, 'AppVpc', {
      maxAzs: 2,
      subnetConfiguration: [,
        ...
      ]
    });

    // Core infrastructure components
    const imageBucket = new s3.Bucket(...);

    const webServer = new ec2.Instance(...);

    const alb = new elbv2.ApplicationLoadBalancer(...);

    const dist = new cloudfront.Distribution(...);
  }
}
...
```

Fig. 1. Architecture and implementation of a sample cloud infrastructure scenario (a simple S3 pre-signed URL service for image handling). *Top:* System architecture diagram. *Bottom-left:* Diagram-as-Code in Python. *Bottom-right:* AWS CDK IaC in TypeScript.

Recent initiatives in the LLM-enabled threat-modeling space are steps in the right direction. Elsharef et al. [9] explores the practical applicability of an LLM assisted threat model but lacks a comprehensive evaluation procedure. Projects such as Auspex [11] and ThreatModeling-LLM [32] aim to address this. However, they are focused on industry-specific infrastructure such as banking. Existing datasets primarily evaluate LLMs using Capture-the-Flag (CTF) challenges and exploitation tasks [5,12,15,31]. While valuable, these gamified, bounded tasks fail to reflect the complexity of real-world cloud infrastructure. Dynamic testing frameworks [1,24] and red teaming initiatives like DARPA AIxCC broaden this scope but still emphasize exploit generation over architectural reasoning. Moreover, many tasks risk conflating memorization with genuine security understanding. Recently, there have been efforts to benchmark general cybersecurity knowledge [6,19,29], threat intelligence [1], and IaC security [14], but they do not address holistic threat modeling across cloud architectures and their corresponding IaC artifacts.

To address these limitations, we present **ACSE-Eval**, a dataset designed to evaluate LLMs' threat modeling capabilities. Our contributions include: *a)* a curated dataset of 100 real-world AWS architecture diagrams with Diagrams-as-Code [16] and Infrastructure-as-Code implementations using AWS CDK [3], *b)* expert-generated threat models aligned with STRIDE [27], ATT&CK [21], and OWASP Top 10 [23], *c)* a multi-dimensional evaluation framework assessing threat identification, vulnerability analysis, and mitigation suggestions, and *d)* an open-source release of the dataset and evaluation toolkit to promote further research. Spanning 100 human-annotated threat scenarios and over 2,500 h (about 3 months) of expert effort, our dataset targets AWS, representing 31% of the cloud market [28] and includes use cases ranging from simple web apps to multi-region, and hybrid deployments.

In addition to advancing the field of cybersecurity evaluations for LLMs via the open-source dataset, our work aims to address the following key research questions:

R1: Can current language models effectively identify infrastructure security issues via IaC?
The question aims to evaluate both the accuracy and reliability of LLMs in identifying potential security misconfigurations, compliance violations, and architectural weaknesses in infrastructure definitions expressed through code (AWS CDK). We measure the coverage of vulnerability detection, and the comprehensiveness of the security analysis. This investigation is particularly relevant given the increasing adoption of IaC in cloud deployments and the potential for automated security analysis to enhance infrastructure security at scale while reducing human error in security reviews.

R2: Can the threat modeling capabilities of language models be enhanced through the integration of visual-esque aids or relationship-defining tools, specifically using Diagrams-as-Code?
We explore the potential for improving the threat modeling capabilities of LLMs by incorporating codified visual representation techniques, particularly focusing on Diagrams-as-Code or Component Relationship Context (CRC). The inquiry seeks to determine whether the addition of tools that define relationships between

system components can enhance an LLM's ability to perform threat modeling. CRC, which allows for the programmatic creation and manipulation of visual diagrams, could provide LLMs with a more structured and explicit representation of system architectures, data flows, and component interactions. This approach might enable LLMs to better understand complex systems, identify potential attack vectors, and reason about security implications more effectively than when working with text descriptions or IaC alone. The question aims to assess whether this integration could lead to more thorough threat identification.

R3: How well can language models provide contextually appropriate security recommendations?
We also examine LLMs' ability to generate security recommendations that are appropriately tailored to specific contexts, environments, and constraints. The question highlights whether LLMs can effectively consider factors such as the application domain, technical limitations, and resource constraints when proposing security controls or mitigations. The term *contextually appropriate* is crucial here, as it goes beyond merely identifying security issues to assess whether the suggested solutions are practical, implementable, and aligned with the specific needs and circumstances of the target environment.

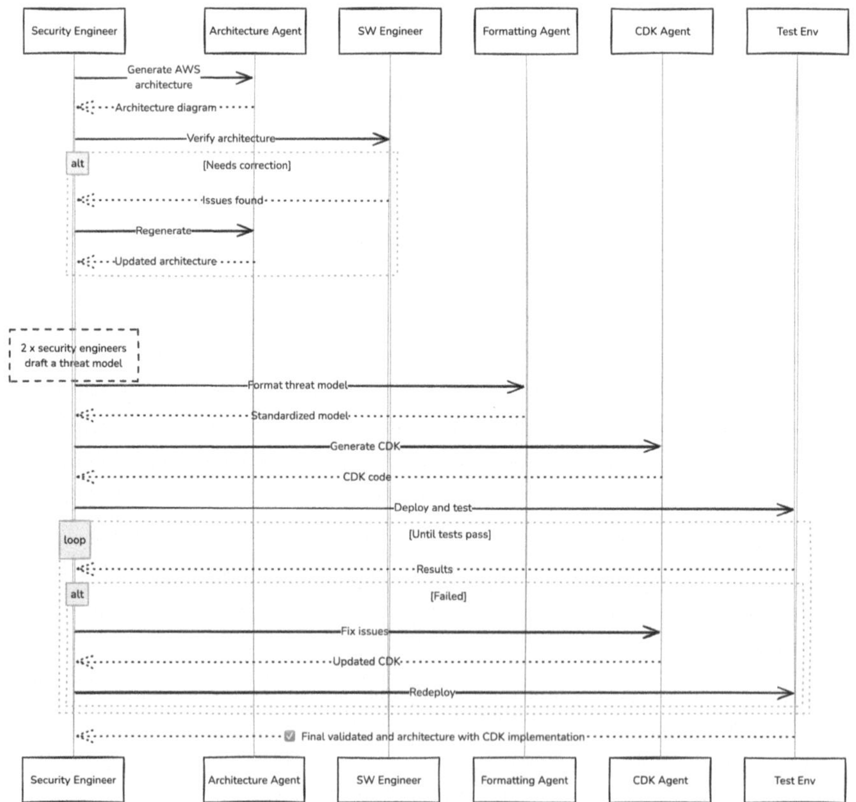

Fig. 2. Methodology used for generating the ACSE-Eval dataset.

2 Methodology and Dataset

ACSE-Eval introduces a structured methodology for evaluating the capability of LLMs to perform threat modeling on real-world cloud architectures. The work spans three stages: (1) data generation, (2) expert analysis, (3) evaluation metrics, and LLM performance assessment. This is explained in the following sections.

2.1 Dataset Generation Workflow

The process (illustrated by Fig. 2) begins with the initial architecture generation phase, where a Security Engineer interfaces with a specialized *Architecture Agent* to create an AWS architecture. This interaction is designed to incorporate security requirements and best practices from the outset. The generated architecture then undergoes manual scrutiny from a Software Engineer, who evaluates it for technical feasibility, compliance with organizational standards, and potential implementation challenges. If any issues are identified during this review, a feedback loop is initiated where the Security Engineer works with the *Architecture Agent* to regenerate the architecture with specific corrections. This cycle of generation, review, and refinement continues until the architecture meets all security requirements and receives approval.

Following architectural approval, the methodology moves into a crucial collaborative threat modeling phase. This stage brings together two Security Engineers to perform comprehensive threat analysis, leveraging their combined expertise and diverse perspectives to identify potential security risks and vulnerabilities. The resulting threat model is then processed by a specialized *Formatting Agent*, which standardizes it into a consistent JSON file. The next phase involves translating the approved architecture into actual infrastructure code. A *CDK Agent* takes on this task, generating AWS CDK code that implements the architecture while maintaining the security controls and configurations specified in the design. This automation helps reduce human error in the implementation phase while ensuring consistency between the architectural design and the actual infrastructure code.

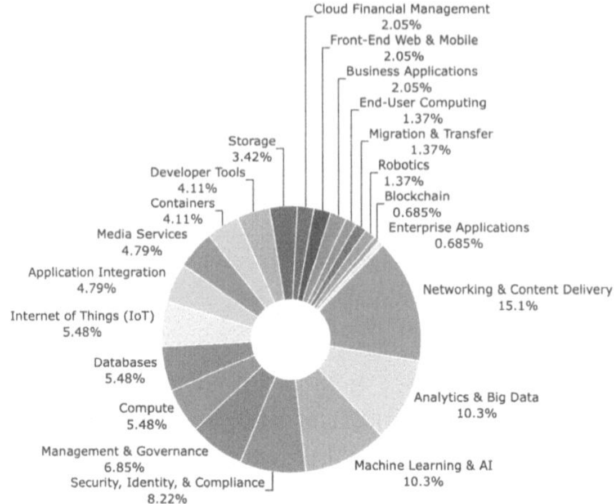

Fig. 3. Category-wise breakdown of the AWS services that are part of ACSE-Eval.

The methodology then enters a testing and validation loop. The generated CDK code is deployed to a dedicated test environment. This testing phase is designed to ensure the infrastructure functions as intended. When tests fail, a structured manual remediation process begins. The Security Engineer works with the *CDK Agent* to address specific issues, generating updated CDK code that is then redeployed to the test environment. This cycle of testing, feedback, and improvement continues until all tests pass successfully.

2.2 Dataset Overview

The dataset reflects real-world diversity in deployment patterns, application domains, and security postures. Architectures vary in complexity (from minimal viable products to highly distributed systems), incorporate a wide range of AWS services, and include both secure and intentionally misconfigured configurations.

Architecture Distribution. The dataset spans 12 different infrastructure categories: Data Processing & Analytics (15.05%), AI/ML & Compute Platforms (11.83%), Business Applications (11.83%), Infrastructure & Networking (8.60%), Specialized Systems (8.60%), Serverless Architectures (7.53%), Media & Content Services (7.53%), Security & Identity (7.53%), Multi-Region & High Availability (6.45%), IoT & Connected Systems (5.38%), Gaming (5.38%), and Collaboration & Communication (4.30%) (Fig. 4).

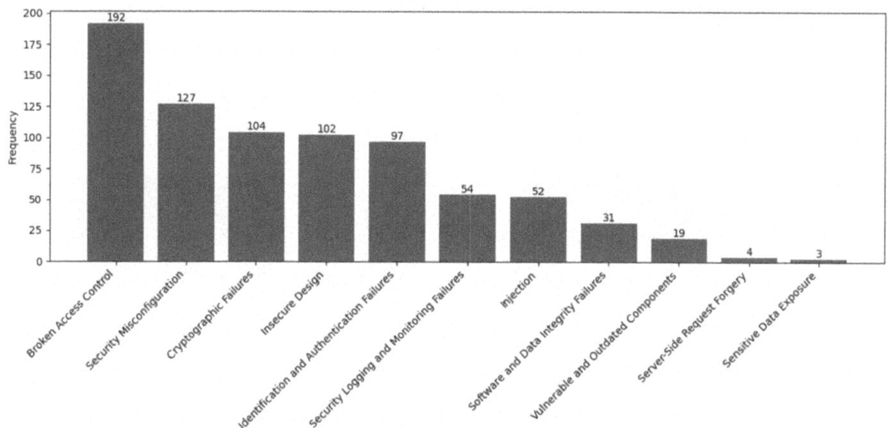

Fig. 4. Distribution of OWASP Top 10 threats in the ACSE-Eval dataset.

Service Coverage. The benchmark covers 146 distinct AWS services across compute, storage, networking, identity, analytics, ML, IoT, and security among other domains. The distribution is illustrated by Fig. 3. This breadth challenges LLMs to reason across diverse primitives, policies, and interactions.

Threat Models. Threat models within ACSE-Eval span 115 distinct threats, spread across the STRIDE, ATT&CK, and OWASP Top 10 frameworks. Threats were derived from architecture analysis, IaC inspection, and attack vector mapping. Scenarios include realistic flaws, such as misconfigurations (e.g., open S3 buckets), missing controls (e.g., absent logging), design flaws (e.g., flat trust boundaries), implementation bugs in CDK, and compliance violations (e.g., no encryption at rest). This diversity of flaws ensures LLMs must reason about vulnerabilities at the architectural layers (Fig. 5).

Component Relationship Context (CRC). Each threat model and IaC implementation is accompanied by a PNG architecture diagram and its corresponding Python-based diagram generation code [16]. While our current scope focuses on textual inputs and evaluation, these architectural visualizations serve as valuable artifacts for establishing relationships between various system components. We hypothesize that providing LLMs with this component relationship context, alongside the deployment code, could enhance the quality of generated threat models. Future research could extend this work by incorporating visual (multi-modal) in-context learning techniques, potentially leading to more comprehensive and accurate threat modeling capabilities.

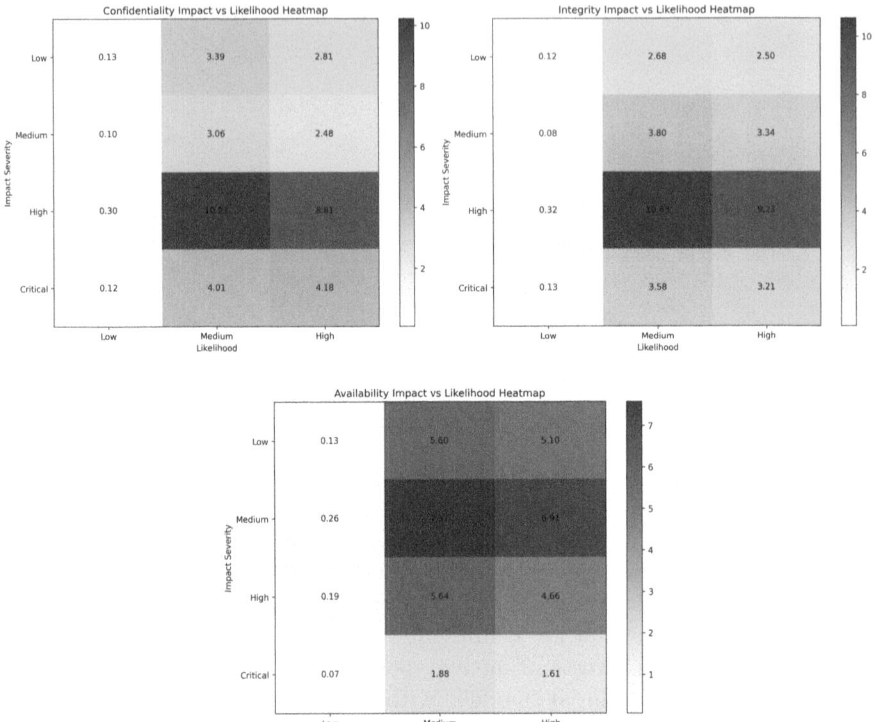

Fig. 5. Heatmaps showing the relationship between threat likelihood and CIA (Confidentiality, Integrity, Availability) impact across all architectures evaluated in ACSE-Eval.

3 Experiments

3.1 Implementation and Tooling

Our evaluations leverage the managed LLM APIs provided by Amazon [2], Anthropic [4], Google [8], and OpenAI [22]. The comprehensive experiment incurred a cost of approximately $500. The evaluation framework is implemented using Inspect AI, an open-source platform for LLM assessments developed by [30]. During our analysis, we employed specialized packages for text similarity measurements, including `rouge` for calculating Rouge-L scores [18] and `sentence-transformers` for computing semantic (cosine) similarity [25]. To ensure transparency and reproducibility, the source code for both the experiment and evaluation procedures is freely available at https://github.com/ACSE-Eval/acse-eval-experiments under the MIT License.

Additionally, our dataset generation agents (*Architecture*, *CDK*, and *Formatting*) employ a hybrid approach, combining human intervention with the capabilities of Claude 3.5 Sonnet. For evaluations, we analyze Claude 3.5 Haiku (*claude-3-5-haiku-20241022*), Claude 3.7 Sonnet (*claude-3-7-sonnet-20250219*),

GPT 4.1 (*gpt-4.1-2025-04-1*), GPT 4o (*gpt-4o-2024-08-06*), Deepseek V3, and Gemini 2.5 Pro (*gemini-2.5-pro-preview-05-06*). We exclude Claude 3.5 Sonnet (*claude-3-5-sonnet-20240620, claude-3-5-sonnet-20241022*) from our evaluations to prevent implicit bias due to its use with the agents. We set the temperature of LLMs at 0 and top_p = 1 to obtain more deterministic responses. Each task is evaluated 3-times on a zero-shot and 3-shot prompt template with instruction of LLMs to act as a cloud security engineering expert. For each 3-shot task run, we seed and extract the 3-shot examples at random. We calculate the mean and standard error mean for every metric in the following sections.

3.2 Evaluating LLMs Performance on ACSE-Eval

Framework Coverage. We assess the accuracy of threat identification by calculating the proportion of reference threats successfully captured in the model-generated threat model. To evaluate this, we introduce a metric called Threat Framework Coverage (TFC), which measures the recall percentage ($\frac{TP \times 100}{TP+FN}$) for each security framework. This calculation provides a quantitative measure of how effectively the model identifies and categorizes threats within established security frameworks (Tables 1 and 2).

Analysis of the results reveal distinct performance patterns across models. GPT 4.1 demonstrates superior performance with 3-shot generation, while Gem-

Table 1. TFC evaluation for STRIDE.

Model	CDK		IaC + CRC	
	0-shot	3-shot	0-shot	3-shot
Claude 3.5 Haiku	56.8 ± 2.9	32.3 ± 4.37	57.6 ± 2.96	19.6 ± 3.59
Claude 3.7 Sonnet	80.2 ± 1.52	87.8 ± 1.16	84.7 ± 1.3	88.8 ± 1.14
GPT 4o	60.9 ± 1.86	78.8 ± 1.66	66.3 ± 2.03	84.2 ± 1.45
GPT 4.1	95.1 ± 0.756	**96.8 ± 0.709**	97.4 ± 0.659	**98.7 ± 0.483**
DeepSeek Chat V3	94.4 ± 0.908	93.7 ± 1.02	94.8 ± 0.914	95.7 ± 0.791
Gemini 2.5 Pro	**96.2 ± 0.835**	92.6 ± 1.09	**98.4 ± 0.527**	92.9 ± 1.12

Table 2. TFC evaluation for OWASP Top 10.

Model	IaC		IaC + CRC	
	0-shot	3-shot	0-shot	3-shot
Claude 3.5 Haiku	39.0 ± 2.4	26.7 ± 3.68	40.5 ± 2.54	15.4 ± 3.0
Claude 3.7 Sonnet	70.4 ± 1.81	74.6 ± 1.62	70.2 ± 1.74	71.8 ± 1.78
GPT 4o	42.0 ± 1.86	56.3 ± 1.78	41.6 ± 2.0	62.4 ± 1.75
GPT 4.1	81.9 ± 1.73	**85.9 ± 1.73**	88.1 ± 1.53	**90.0 ± 1.47**
DeepSeek Chat V3	70.4 ± 1.62	72.8 ± 1.56	68.4 ± 1.72	74.8 ± 1.58
Gemini 2.5 Pro	**85.9 ± 1.38**	83.5 ± 1.64	**89.1 ± 1.33**	85.1 ± 1.49

ini 2.5 Pro excels in 0-shot scenarios. Notably, 3-shot generation proves counterproductive for Gemini 2.5 Pro, occasionally resulting in decreased Threat Framework Coverage. The smaller models, including Claude 3.5 Haiku and GPT4o, show particular difficulty in accurately classifying MITRE ATT&CK codes. When evaluating baseline performance without considering Component Relationship Context (CRC) or the number of examples, Gemini 2.5 Pro demonstrates consistent superiority across all three security frameworks, establishing itself as the most effective model for threat identification and classification. On the other hand, including either CRC or variations in shot counts in our analysis, GPT 4.1 demonstrates better performance.

Text Similarity. To account for linguistic variation in threat descriptions, we compute and evaluate certain text similarity metrics. These allow us to credit partial correctness and stylistic variation, crucial in an open-ended reasoning task, especially threat mitigation recommendations (Table 3).

Table 3. TFC evaluation for MITRE ATT&CK.

Model	IaC		IaC + CRC	
	0-shot	3-shot	0-shot	3-shot
Claude 3.5 Haiku	17.7 ± 1.68	14.2 ± 2.39	19.3 ± 1.6	8.24 ± 1.68
Claude 3.7 Sonnet	36.2 ± 1.75	40.6 ± 1.92	38.9 ± 1.92	42.3 ± 1.95
GPT 4o	17.4 ± 1.31	27.4 ± 1.9	19.1 ± 1.36	27.0 ± 1.67
GPT 4.1	44.3 ± 1.75	$\mathbf{49.5 \pm 2.12}$	42.8 ± 1.93	$\mathbf{49.9 \pm 2.07}$
DeepSeek Chat V3	36.1 ± 1.7	42.5 ± 1.8	38.5 ± 1.81	41.0 ± 1.86
Gemini 2.5 Pro	$\mathbf{45.9 \pm 1.78}$	46.1 ± 2.03	$\mathbf{46.9 \pm 1.89}$	47.4 ± 1.85

ROUGE-L. This metric measures longest common subsequence between the predicted and reference text.
Let X be the target text and Y be the model output. The ROUGE-L score is calculated as:

$$\text{ROUGE-L} = \frac{(1+\beta^2)R_l P_l}{R_l + \beta^2 P_l} \tag{1}$$

where $R_l = \frac{\text{LCS}(X,Y)}{\text{length}(X)}$ is the LCS-based recall, $P_l = \frac{\text{LCS}(X,Y)}{\text{length}(Y)}$ is the LCS-based precision, $\beta = 1.2$ to favor recall over precision, and $\text{LCS}(X,Y)$ is the length of the Longest Common Subsequence between X and Y.

This metric evaluates how well the model output (Y) matches the target text (X) by finding the longest sequence of words that appears in both texts in the same order.

Semantic Similarity. This metric measures the cosine of the angle between the embedding vectors, providing a value between -1 and 1, where 1 indicates perfect similarity, 0 indicates no similarity, and -1 indicates perfect dissimilarity. It captures the semantic closeness of the model output to the target text, regardless of exact word matching. In order to calculate this, we transform the threat model JSON content (for both the model output and target text) to vectors and compute their cosine similarity.

Let X be the target text and Y be the model output. The Semantic Similarity score is calculated as:

$$\text{Semantic Similarity} = \cos(\theta) = \frac{E(X) \cdot E(Y)}{\|E(X)\| \|E(Y)\|} \tag{2}$$

where $E(X)$ and $E(Y)$ are the sentence-transformer embeddings of X and Y respectively, and $\|\cdot\|$ represents the L2 norm (Euclidean length) of the vector.

Table 4. ROUGE-L scores for ACSE-Eval.

Model	IaC		IaC + CRC	
	0-shot	3-shot	0-shot	3-shot
Claude 3.5 Haiku	38.4 ± 3.47	24.8 ± 3.81	38.5 ± 3.27	16.2 ± 3.34
Claude 3.7 Sonnet	70.3 ± 2.53	$\mathbf{79.4 \pm 1.98}$	69.6 ± 2.45	$\mathbf{83.7 \pm 1.75}$
GPT 4o	47.4 ± 3.33	60.3 ± 3.12	48.7 ± 3.27	58.3 ± 3.23
GPT 4.1	$\mathbf{74.4 \pm 2.35}$	77.0 ± 2.35	$\mathbf{76.0 \pm 2.31}$	78.7 ± 2.32
DeepSeek Chat V3	61.2 ± 3.09	74.7 ± 2.98	61.2 ± 3.19	79.8 ± 2.66
Gemini 2.5 Pro	71.6 ± 2.37	74.3 ± 2.21	74.6 ± 2.09	74.6 ± 2.27

Table 5. Semantic Similarity scores for ACSE-Eval.

Model	IaC		IaC + CRC	
	0-shot	3-shot	0-shot	3-shot
Claude 3.5 Haiku	0.634 ± 0.006	0.589 ± 0.008	0.632 ± 0.006	0.585 ± 0.010
Claude 3.7 Sonnet	$\mathbf{0.798 \pm 0.009}$	$\mathbf{0.825 \pm 0.008}$	$\mathbf{0.822 \pm 0.007}$	$\mathbf{0.819 \pm 0.01}$
GPT 4o	0.642 ± 0.01	0.792 ± 0.007	0.648 ± 0.01	0.805 ± 0.007
GPT 4.1	0.745 ± 0.008	0.799 ± 0.008	0.747 ± 0.009	$\mathbf{0.823 \pm 0.008}$
DeepSeek Chat V3	0.739 ± 0.009	0.74 ± 0.008	0.748 ± 0.009	0.736 ± 0.007
Gemini 2.5 Pro	0.742 ± 0.008	0.756 ± 0.006	0.752 ± 0.007	0.756 ± 0.007

We observe that, while Claude 3.7 Sonnet consistently achieves the highest Semantic Similarity scores, GPT 4.1 demonstrates superior performance in ROUGE-L scoring specifically under 0-shot conditions. A higher Semantic Similarity score coupled with a relatively lower ROUGE-L score (as in the case of Claude 3.7 Sonnet) indicates that while the model captures the core meaning and concepts of the reference text, it expresses these ideas using different vocabulary and sentence structures. In threat modeling contexts, this could mean the model identifies threats correctly but describes them using alternative, though semantically equivalent language or format (Tables 4 and 5).

Comprehensiveness. To evaluate the models' precision in technical classifications and affected threat surface components, we assess their ability to correctly identify Common Weakness Enumeration (CWE) codes and AWS services within the threat model. We introduce the AWS Service Coverage (ASC) metric, expressed as a percentage, to quantify the accuracy of AWS service identification. These metrics ensure LLMs capture the full threat surface, especially in complex, multi-tier deployments (Tables 6 and 7).

Table 6. CWE Coverage scores for ACSE-Eval.

Model	IaC		IaC + CRC	
	0-shot	3-shot	0-shot	3-shot
Claude 3.5 Haiku	15.8 ± 1.55	10.9 ± 2.02	16.9 ± 1.76	7.14 ± 1.61
Claude 3.7 Sonnet	23.8 ± 1.70	26.9 ± 1.84	25.5 ± 2.08	27.9 ± 2.03
GPT 4o	17.9 ± 1.47	23.6 ± 1.99	20.1 ± 1.58	25.4 ± 1.99
GPT 4.1	$\mathbf{37.3 \pm 1.96}$	$\mathbf{34.8 \pm 1.89}$	$\mathbf{38.4 \pm 2.36}$	$\mathbf{39.1 \pm 1.99}$
DeepSeek Chat V3	32.0 ± 1.76	32.0 ± 1.76	34.2 ± 1.75	31.1 ± 1.8
Gemini 2.5 Pro	36.6 ± 2.17	32.1 ± 2.02	37.9 ± 1.99	32.0 ± 1.88

Our analysis reveals several key insights into the performance of different language models. While GPT-4.1 excels in detecting CWE, its limited coverage indicates that LLMs are still in their early stages regarding security vulnerability detection. The performance dynamics shift in AWS service identification tasks, where Gemini 2.5 Pro outperforms GPT-4.1 in 0-shot scenarios, though GPT-4.1 regains its advantage when provided with additional examples. Notably, compact models such as Claude 3.5 Haiku demonstrate a trend: when presented with additional context through few-shot examples or CRC, they exhibit increased

Table 7. AWS Service Coverage scores for ACSE-Eval.

Model	IaC		IaC + CRC	
	0-shot	3-shot	0-shot	3-shot
Claude 3.5 Haiku	23.4 ± 1.78	20.4 ± 2.86	24.3 ± 1.72	12.1 ± 7.14
Claude 3.7 Sonnet	34.0 ± 2.01	46.0 ± 2.2	35.7 ± 2.06	50.1 ± 2.37
GPT 4o	20.0 ± 1.58	37.1 ± 2.20	20.9 ± 1.48	38.0 ± 2.11
GPT 4.1	44.7 ± 2.42	$\mathbf{50.2 \pm 2.41}$	51.3 ± 2.24	$\mathbf{56.0 \pm 2.57}$
DeepSeek Chat V3	34.4 ± 2.11	45.4 ± 2.22	43.8 ± 2.33	48.2 ± 2.44
Gemini 2.5 Pro	$\mathbf{45.6 \pm 2.08}$	45.8 ± 2.24	$\mathbf{53.4 \pm 2.21}$	50.4 ± 2.19

hallucination rates, leading to diminished performance metrics. This could be because compact models struggle to capture complex relationships and nuances in data due to under-fitting, while larger models are good at open domain tasks.

4 Discussion

Our evaluation of LLMs using ACSE-Eval reveals key insights into their strengths and limitations in cloud-native threat modeling, as well as opportunities for practical deployment and future research.

4.1 Limitations and Future Direction

While ACSE-Eval is a promising step forward, it has limitations. First, its exclusive focus on AWS may reduce generalizability to other platforms like Azure, GCP, or hybrid environments. Future iterations should expand cross-cloud coverage. Second, the dataset captures static architecture snapshots, whereas real-world systems evolve. Future datasets should include architectural drift and lifecycle transitions.

Although the dataset includes a diverse range of vulnerabilities, it does not comprehensively cover all domain-specific or compliance-driven risks. Extending coverage to industry-specific contexts will improve realism. Furthermore, while we minimized subjectivity in evaluation through structured rubrics, future work could explore automated metrics that better reflect reasoning quality.

Several research directions emerge from our findings. Specialized fine-tuning on cloud security corpora could boost LLM performance. Multimodal approaches incorporating architecture diagrams alongside text and code could provide richer context. Interactive models that engage analysts in dialogue may yield more accurate and user-aligned outputs. Longitudinal evaluation of LLMs' ability to reason over evolving architectures is another open area. Finally, maintaining the relevance of ACSE-Eval will require regular updates to include new architectures, emerging vulnerabilities, and refined evaluation metrics.

4.2 Ethical Considerations

In this study, we analyze threat-modeling capabilities of LLMs on an expert-curated dataset comprising of infrastructure architecture specifications and their corresponding threat models. We strictly avoid using any personal privacy information or trade secrets that could have legal or ethical ramifications. Moreover, we ensured that all of our work complied with ethical standards and legal regulations to maintain transparency and integrity in our research. Additionally, we understand that the nature of this work might enable certain threat actors to use our dataset as a reference for identifying and exploiting threats in real-world deployments. While that is certainly possible, we believe that this line of research is necessary to build more secure systems. Over time, research in this space will enable us to automate security and deploy more secure infrastructure without human oversight. Despite our optimistic outlook, we have taken certain steps to prevent ease of exploitation. The CDK (IaC) component of ACSE-Eval lacks the necessary meta files (such as package.json, tsconfig.json, etc.) to spin up a deployment. We have only included the files that lay out the CDK specifications and cannot be used in isolation for deployments. Moreover, the threat models in ACSE-Eval do not emphasize on implementation details and only call out high-level threats. This positions ACSE-Eval well from an ethical standpoint.

5 Conclusion

In this paper, we introduced ACSE-Eval, the first comprehensive dataset for evaluating LLMs' capabilities in threat modeling real-world cloud architectures. Our dataset includes 100 production-grade AWS architecture scenarios with expert-generated threat models, covering diverse application domains, complexity levels, and AWS services. Our evaluation of 6 LLMs revealed both promising capabilities and significant limitations. Our analysis demonstrates that GPT-4.1 and Gemini 2.5 Pro excel at threat identification, with Gemini 2.5 Pro performing optimally in 0-shot scenarios and GPT-4.1 showing superior results in few-shot settings. While GPT-4.1 maintains a slight overall performance advantage, Claude 3.7 Sonnet generates the most semantically sophisticated threat models but struggles with threat categorization and generalization. ACSE-Eval represents a crucial step towards automated cloud security assessment, providing security practitioners and researchers with a robust framework to enhance LLM capabilities in threat analysis and effectively safeguard modern cloud infrastructure.

References

1. Alam, M.T., Bhusal, D., Nguyen, L., Rastogi, N.: Ctibench: A benchmark for evaluating LLMs in cyber threat intelligence. arXiv preprint arXiv:2406.07599 (2024)
2. Amazon: Amazon bedrock documentation. https://aws.amazon.com/bedrock/ (2023), Accessed 11 Oct 2024
3. Amazon Web Services: Aws cloud development kit (aws cdk). AWS Documentation (2024)
4. Anthropic: The claude 3 model family: Opus, sonnet, haiku. https://paperswithcode.com/paper/the-claude-3-model-family-opus-sonnet-haiku (2024). Accessed 24 Jun 2024
5. Bhatt, M., et al.: Cyberseceval 2: A wide-ranging cybersecurity evaluation suite for large language models. arXiv preprint arXiv:2404.13161 (2024)
6. Chen, J., Wang, T., Li, Y., Zhang, X.: Seceval: A comprehensive security evaluation framework for large language models. In: Proceedings of the 2024 ACM SIGSAC Conference on Computer and Communications Security, pp. 1823–1840, ACM (2024)
7. Chen, Y., Ding, Z., Alowain, L., Chen, X., Wagner, D.: Diversevul: A new vulnerable source code dataset for deep learning based vulnerability detection (2023). URL https://arxiv.org/abs/2304.00409
8. DeepMind, G.: Gemini: A family of highly capable multimodal models. arXiv preprint arXiv:2312.11805 (2023). URL https://arxiv.org/abs/2312.11805

9. Elsharef, I., Zeng, Z., Gu, Z.: Facilitating threat modeling by leveraging large language models (2024). https://www.ndss-symposium.org/wp-content/uploads/aiscc2024-16-paper.pdf, Accessed 16 May 2025
10. Ferrag, M.A., et al.: Securefalcon: are we there yet in automated software vulnerability detection with llms? (2025). URL https://arxiv.org/abs/2307.06616
11. Gupta, A., Mehta, V., Patel, N., Chandrasekaran, B.: Auspex: Automated security posture examination using large language models. arXiv preprint arXiv:2312.05275 (2023)
12. Huang, J., Zhu, Q.: Penheal: a two-stage llm framework for automated pentesting and optimal remediation. In: Proceedings of the Workshop on Autonomous Cybersecurity, pp. 11–22, AutonomousCyber '24, Association for Computing Machinery, New York, NY, USA (2024). ISBN 9798400712296
13. Johnson, E., Patel, R.: Cloud security statistics 2025: the state of cloud security. J. Cybersec. Res. **12**(2), 78–93 (2025)
14. Kon, P.T.J., et al.: Iac-eval: A code generation benchmark for cloud infrastructure-as-code programs. In: The Thirty-eight Conference on Neural Information Processing Systems Datasets and Benchmarks Track (2024)
15. Kouremetis, M., et al.: Occult: Evaluating large language models for offensive cyber operation capabilities. arXiv preprint arXiv:2502.15797 (2025)
16. Kwon, M.: Diagrams: Diagram as code. https://diagrams.mingrammer.com/ (2020)
17. Li, Z., Shin, D.: Mutation-based consistency testing for evaluating the code understanding capability of llms. In: Proceedings of the IEEE/ACM 3rd International Conference on AI Engineering - Software Engineering for AI, p. 150–159, CAIN '24, Association for Computing Machinery, New York, NY, USA (2024). ISBN 9798400705915, https://doi.org/10.1145/3644815.3644946
18. Lin, C.Y.: ROUGE: A package for automatic evaluation of summaries. In: Text Summarization Branches Out, pp. 74–81, Association for Computational Linguistics, Barcelona, Spain (2004). https://aclanthology.org/W04-1013/
19. Liu, J., Zhang, Y., Wang, H., Gao, J.: Secqa: a comprehensive question answering benchmark for cybersecurity knowledge evaluation. IEEE Trans. Dependable Secure Comput. **21**(3), 1558–1571 (2024)
20. Microsoft: The stride threat model. Microsoft Security Developer Center (2009)
21. MITRE: Att&ck matrix for enterprise v17.1 (2025), URL https://attack.mitre.org/
22. OpenAI: Gpt-4 technical report. arXiv preprint arXiv:2303.08774 (2023). URL https://arxiv.org/abs/2303.08774
23. OWASP: Owasp top ten (2025). https://owasp.org/www-project-top-ten/
24. Phuong, M., et al.: Evaluating frontier models for dangerous capabilities. arXiv preprint arXiv:2403.13793 (2024)
25. Reimers, N., Gurevych, I.: Sentence-bert: Sentence embeddings using siamese bert-networks. In: Proceedings of the 2019 Conference on Empirical Methods in Natural Language Processing, Association for Computational Linguistics (2019). https://arxiv.org/abs/1908.10084
26. SentinelOne Research Team: The state of cloud security 2024. Tech. rep, SentinelOne (2024)
27. Shostack, A.: Threat modeling: Designing for security. John Wiley & Sons (2014)
28. TechCrunch: Cloud infrastructure saw its biggest revenue growth ever in q4. https://techcrunch.com/2024/02/02/ai-pushes-quarterly-cloud-infrastructure-revenue-to-74b-globally/ (2024)

29. Tihanyi, N., Ferrag, M.A., Jain, R., Bisztray, T., Debbah, M.: Cybermetric: a benchmark dataset based on retrieval-augmented generation for evaluating llms in cybersecurity knowledge. arXiv preprint arXiv:2402.07688 (2024)
30. UK AI Security Institute: Inspect ai: Framework for large language model evaluations (2024), URL https://inspect.aisi.org.uk/
31. Wan, S., et al.: Cyberseceval 3: Advancing the evaluation of cybersecurity risks and capabilities in large language models. arXiv preprint arXiv:2240.80160 (2024)
32. Yang, S., Wu, T., Liu, S., Nguyen, D., Jang, S., Abuadbba, A.: Threatmodeling-LLm: Automating threat modeling using large language models for banking system. arXiv preprint arXiv:2411.17058 (2024)

Adversarial Evasion Against Autonomous Cyber Defence Agents

Melanie Meijer[1(✉)], Sanyam Vyas[2], Vasilios Mavroudis[2], and Marc Juarez[1]

[1] University of Edinburgh, Old College, South Bridge, Edinburgh EH8 9YL, UK
melaniecmeijer@gmail.com, marc.juarez@ed.ac.uk

[2] Alan Turing Institute, British Library, 96 Euston Rd., London NW1 2DB, UK
{svyas,vmavroudis}@turing.ac.uk

Abstract. Autonomous cyber defence trains intelligent blue agents that can protect systems independently, without human oversight. Recent research in this field often uses deep reinforcement learning to train and evaluate blue agents against simulated cyber attacks. However, most training relies on static, hardcoded red agents, which may fail to reflect real-world adversarial strategies. Moreover, deep reinforcement learning policies are potentially vulnerable to adversarial perturbations, raising the following question: can attackers exploit these vulnerabilities by choosing actions that cause the blue agent to make mistakes, allowing the attacker to evade detection? In this work, we use the CybORG environment to show that a carefully designed adversarial policy can substantially degrade the performance of a blue agent trained on hardcoded red agents. Our results indicate that, while the blue agent successfully contains the original red agents, its ability to protect a target operational server drops by over 40% when pitted against the adversarial agent. These findings confirm the effectiveness of adversarial policies against blue agents, and highlight the need for robust training methodologies to ensure the robustness of autonomous cyber defence solutions.

Keywords: Autonomous Cyber Defence · Adversarial Evasion · Deep Reinforcement Learning

1 Introduction

As our world becomes increasingly digital and interconnected, cyber attacks are becoming notably more frequent and sophisticated. The UK Cyber Security Breaches Survey records that 50% of businesses and 32% of charities reported a cyber attack in 2024, which rose to 70% or more for medium and large businesses [10]. Similarly, the emergence of increasingly sophisticated cyber attacks further underscores the need for more efficient defences [6]. As a result, the interdisciplinary field of Autonomous Cyber Defence (ACD) has gained traction, aiming to develop blue agents to autonomously combat attacks. However, most of the research in this field still employs hardcoded red agents to train their blue agents, which model traditional, logical attackers [2,12,38].

R. Laborde et al. (Eds.): ESORICS 2025 Workshops, LNCS 16233, pp. 19–38, 2026.
https://doi.org/10.1007/978-3-032-16165-9_2

In reality, attackers and defenders are locked in an arms race, where they continuously respond to each other's evolving strategies. Consequently, as the blue agent learns to defend system vulnerabilities, a determined attacker may pivot to targeting vulnerabilities in the blue agent itself. These agents are often implemented using deep reinforcement learning (DRL), which is known to be vulnerable to adversarial attacks. Therefore, a valid adversarial strategy is to make specific decisions that, when interpreted by the blue agent, cause it to make mistakes, resulting in an evasion. The goal of this work is to explore whether such an adversarial agent can identify these weaknesses in the blue agent's policy, and exploit them to compromise the network. The key research questions we aim to answer are as follows:

1. Can an *adversarial* policy attack be used as a technique to effectively evade a trained blue agent and compromise a simulated network?
2. How successful is such an adversarial agent in reducing the performance of the blue agent, compared to the original, hard-coded red agents?

We adopt a *black-box* threat model, where the adversary aims to use its own actions to indirectly influence the victim agent's behaviour by inducing adversarial observations. This is an improvement over state-of-the-art DRL evasion attacks which typically assume white-box access. We thus consider a weaker adversary that can deceive the autonomous blue agent to compromise the network. Our objective is to 1) investigate whether autonomous blue agents, trained and tested against hard-coded red agents, are sufficiently robust against such adversarial attacks, and 2) demonstrate how such attacks could materialise given the practical constraints adversaries face.

In summary, the main contribution of this work is the development of an effective adversarial policy, successfully implemented within a simulation of a complex, real-world task, as opposed to a game simulation. To the best of our knowledge, we are the first to implement an adaptive adversarial attack against an ACD system in order to address the adversarial arms race. Our developed adversarial red agent has learnt, among other tactics, to divert the blue agent's attention to other subnets in order to prevent the removal of its access to key hosts within the network, thus enabling it to compromise the network. The source code for our experiments can be found in: https://github.com/Mel-Meijer/Adversarial-Evasion-of-ACD-Agent.

The remainder of this document is structured as follows: Sect. 2 presents an exposition of the relevant background, providing context to the work. Section 3 will provide further detail on the environment and threat model employed for this project. Section 4 discusses the conceptual design and implementation of the work undertaken, exploring both the environment customisation and agent training. Section 5 presents an evaluation of the trained agents, along with an analysis of the results. Section 6 discusses previous work. Finally, Sects. 7 and 8 consider potential avenues for future work and conclude the work.

2 Background

2.1 Deep Reinforcement Learning

By simulating tasks in an environment, deep reinforcement learning (DRL) allows agents to learn from experience and feedback, removing the need for extensive labelled datasets required by supervised learning methods. This paradigm has yielded promising results on diverse tasks, from mastering Atari arcade games and board games like chess and Go [31] to real-world applications such as energy management [37].

Modelling an RL Task: The two key components of an RL setup are the agent and the environment. The agent is the decision-making entity, performing actions to move from one state to the next. The environment models the agent's task and provides the agent with feedback in the form of observations and rewards. An RL task is typically modelled as a Markov Decision Process (MDP), represented by a tuple $(\mathcal{S}, \mathcal{A}, \mathcal{R}, \mathcal{T})$, whose components are defined below:

- $\mathcal{S}$ is the set of all possible states the environment can be in. We denote the the state at timestep t by $s_t \in S$.
- $\mathcal{A}$ is the set of the actions available to the agent. At any timestep t, the agent chooses an action a_t from $\mathcal{A}$.
- $\mathcal{R}$ is the reward function, which determines the agent's reward at each timestep, r_t, based on current state, action, and next state: $r_t = \mathcal{R}(s_t, a_t, s_{t+1})$.
- $\mathcal{T}$ is the transition function that defines the probability distribution of the next state given the current state and an action. We denote the probability of a particular next state by $\Pr[s_{t+1}|s_t, a_t]$.

An MDP is partially observable (i.e., a POMDP) when the agent's observation does not fully capture the underlying environment state. This creates a distinction between the state and observation, and introduces uncertainty into the learning problem. Our model adopts such a POMDP setup for all agents in its environment to create a more realistic simulation of the real-world task.

Learning an RL Task: At a high level, the agent's policy is a mapping from observations to the probability of performing particular actions for a given observation, based on estimations of the expected reward. This is denoted by $\pi(a \mid s)$, and ultimately defines the agent's behaviour. For an *episodic* task, an episode within the RL environment is one attempt for the agent to solve the modelled task. Upon completing an episode during the agent's training, the environment is reset and the agent's policy is updated.

The reward signal is used by the agent to determine which actions are optimal for a given observation, and is therefore crucial in influencing the agent's final behaviour. The agent aims to maximise its expected cumulative reward over the course of an episode. The trade-off between immediate and future rewards is controlled by a hyperparameter called the *discount factor* γ, a parameter in the agent's *value function* $V_\pi(s)$. This function represents the expected reward value of a certain state based on all possible actions, next states, and expected rewards under the current policy [5]:

$$V_\pi(s) = \sum_{a \in \mathcal{A}} \pi(a \mid s) \sum_{s' \in \mathcal{S}} \Pr[s' \mid s, a](\mathcal{R}(s, a, s') + \gamma \, v_\pi(s')) \tag{1}$$

Deep Neural Networks: In DRL, the agent's policy is modelled using a deep neural network (DNN). During the agent's training, the DNN's parameters θ (also known as its weights) are altered to update the agent's policy and learn to better predict the optimal action(s) for a given observation.

Overall, DNNs have revolutionised the field of RL and enabled agents to solve complex tasks [7,16,28]. However, a common obstacle encountered with DNNs is that they have a complex non-linear structure, making it difficult to control and understand their exact reasoning. This is a challenge beyond the field of ML security and is addressed by research in explainable AI [9]. As explained in more detail in Sect. 2.2, DNNs, including those used for DRL, are vulnerable to adversarial attacks that can be exploited in the context of ACD.

DRL Algorithms: We use Proximal Policy Optimization (PPO) [28], which is a state-of-the-art algorithm that is widely used within RL research. PPO is an on-policy algorithm, where the experience from which the agent learns is generated by the same policy that is being updated. It is also a type of actor-critic algorithm, meaning that it has two separate components: an *actor*, which determines the actions performed, and a *critic*, which evaluates the chosen actions.

A loss function L controls the agent's learning by comparing the expected reward (Eq. 1) with the actual observed reward. To avoid common PPO issues, such as catastrophic forgetting, we use the PPO-Clip loss function [29], which prevents large policy updates and thus stabilises training. We selected PPO due to its efficiency and stability, which could help the red agent succeed in the complex task of finding effective attack sequences with sparse rewards.

2.2 Machine Learning Evasion Attacks

Evasion attacks enable adversaries to cause errors (e.g., misclassifications) in supervised models by adding an imperceptible perturbations to test points, causing the model to produce an incorrect prediction. Adversarial attacks in DRL mirror evasion attacks in supervised learning, where small input perturbations deliberately induce unexpected behaviour or reduced performance in the victim policy [26]. These attacks underscore the importance of agent robustness and generalisation: even minor perturbations can expose a policy's vulnerability to real-world disruptions. Consequently, they exacerbate the gap between simulation and deployment [8], demonstrating that the challenge extends beyond security-specific concerns.

2.3 Autonomous Cyber Defence

ACD aims to use AI in order to develop faster, more proactive defences to counter emerging cyber attacks. The key idea behind ACD is to develop, typically via DRL, autonomous agents that can defend a network from an active cyber attack without human input. This effort falls within Autonomous Cyber Operations (ACO), which encompasses research into both RL-based cyber attacks and defences. ACO research is still in its early stages [35], where attacker and defender development has been largely conducted within simulated ACO gyms [4,11,12].

As of now, ACO research largely focuses solely on either the attacker [30], or the defender [23]. This work bridges this gap by customising an environment such that both agents may be trained against each other, while focusing on the evasion of a blue agent through an adversarial red agent.

3 Scenario and Threat Model

3.1 Environment Scenario

We conducted our experiments in the CybORG environment [17]. CybORG was developed to support public ACD research and was part of the CAGE challenges [17,32]. This environment models a cyber attack on a commercial network of 13 hosts and was originally designed to train an RL-based blue agent. The cyber attacks modelled by the environment are based on the MITRE ATT&CK framework, and assume a red agent who has gained a foothold into the network through a successful phishing campaign. From this initial foothold on a user host, the red agent's goal is to compromise the target operational server within the network through lateral movement, exploitation, and privilege escalation (Fig. 1).

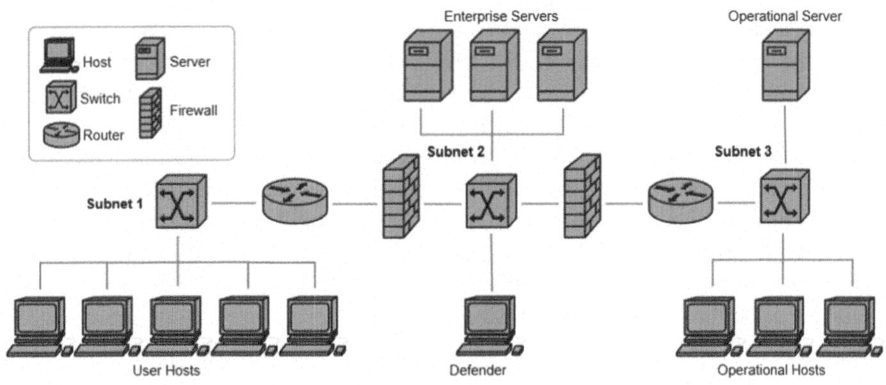

Fig. 1. CAGE Environment Network Layout Diagram [17].

Environment Agents: Three distinct agents are simulated in the environment: A blue (defender) agent that aims to protect the network from any malicious activity; a red (attacker) agent that aims to impact the operational server; and, optionally, a green (genuine user) agent that generates benign activity on the network.

The key idea for including the green agent is that it ensures the blue agent does not assume that all activity on the network is malicious. For this research, the green agent is always enabled in order to create a more realistic simulation of a real-world network. The green agent can only scan the network or sleep, selecting its action at random. The blue and red agents have their own distinct, discrete action spaces within the environment, included in Appendix A.

The original environment models two hard-coded red agents, which select their actions according to explicit rules. The *b-line* agent is assumed to have prior knowledge of the network layout and attempts to take the most direct route to compromise the target operational server. The *meander* agent, on the other hand, is more explorative without any prior knowledge of the network, and attempts to map out the different subnets before reaching the target server.

The CybORG environment is considered to be the current state-of-the-art when it comes to ACD training environments, and nearly all literature on CAGE employ their hard-coded attackers [11,12,38]. The aim of this work is to demonstrate that these two hard-coded red agents do not suffice to develop robust blue agents, and that adversarial policies can evade the blue agent even when it is able to perform well against hardcoded red agents.

Host States: Fig. 2 shows the effects of the red and blue agents' actions on the host states. Each host, besides the initial foothold host, is initially unknown to the red agent. A host can become known to the red agent through either the `DiscoverRemoteSystems` actions, or by gaining privileged access to other hosts that contain the IP addresses of (currently unknown) hosts. Once known, the red agent is able to scan the host to discover active services, exploit one of these services, and then escalate its privileges.

At the same time, the blue agent can attempt to remove the red agent's access or restore the host. However, removing the access of a red agent will only succeed if the red agent has not yet achieved `privileged` access. The blue agent can also create decoy services on a host, which both delay and help locate the red agent. Any exploit action by the red agent that uses a decoy service automatically fails.

The state transitions are not fully deterministic to more accurately reflect the unpredictability of the real world. When there are multiple services available to the red agent, there is a 75% chance that the red agent uses the highest ranked exploit. Furthermore, there is a small chance for the exploit action to result in privileged access directly, rather than user access.

Observation Spaces: Based on the environment's true state, the environment generates a partial observation for the agents at each timestep, where neither the red nor the blue agent's observation space reveals the full environment state. For each host known to the red agent, the environment keeps track of whether the host has been scanned, and what kind of access the red agent currently has on the host (None, User, Privileged). The red agent's observation also indicates whether its last action was successful.

The blue observation communicates the red agent's activity on each host, as well as its access. Possible host activity values are none, scanned, or exploited

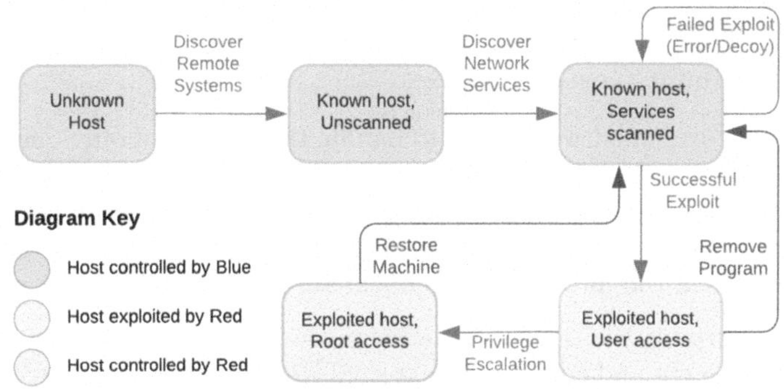

Fig. 2. The effect of offensive and defensive actions on the state of hosts in the cyber environment [33].

by the red agent. Red's access can be *none*, *user*, *privileged*, or *unknown* to the blue agent.

3.2 Threat Model

We consider a scenario in which an autonomous cyber defense system—such as a deep reinforcement learning (DRL)-based blue agent—has been deployed within a real-world network (e.g., procured and operationalized by an organization). While the continual learning paradigm proposed by Abel et al. [1] presents a promising direction, continual DRL has yet to demonstrate consistent effectiveness in complex, large-scale environments such as autonomous cyber defense. Consequently, we conceptually assume that the model developer adheres to a conventional train/validation/test protocol, with routine evaluation of the agent's behaviour under previously unseen scenarios. The adversary's objective in this setting is to exploit the static train/validation/test development protocol of the DRL blue agent and compromise its effectiveness by inducing it to make suboptimal decisions, ultimately facilitating the successful compromise of critical network assets.

To achieve this, we adopt a *black-box threat model*: the red agent neither knows the internal model parameters of the blue agent, nor can it directly alter its observations or actions. Instead, it has black-box query access—observing how the blue agent responds to environment changes—and can only perform valid actions within the shared environment (e.g., scanning a host before attempting an exploit). By strategically selecting these actions, the red agent indirectly manipulates the blue agent's observations, misleading its decision-making process.

Through iterative training against the fixed blue agent, the red agent learns to identify and exploit any systematic weaknesses in the blue agent's policy. In doing so, it guides the blue agent's behaviour toward states that favour the red agent's ultimate objective: evading or overwhelming the defensive measures, compromising the network, and impacting the target operational server.

4 Approach

4.1 Environment Customisations

The original environment was set up to handle the actions of only one RL-based agent externally, while representing the remaining agent(s) internally through multiple wrappers built on top of the base CybORG environment class. On every timestep, the input and respective output are communicated between the external agent and the internal environment through each of the wrappers.

Custom Wrapper: We introduced a custom wrapper that sits on top of the original environment and enables two external RL models (blue and red) to interact with the environment. The custom wrapper has been designed to maintain compatibility with the original environment as much as possible, such that any blue agents trained in the original environment can be easily transferred and used with our custom wrapper. Figure 3 illustrates a high-level overview of the new environment structure.

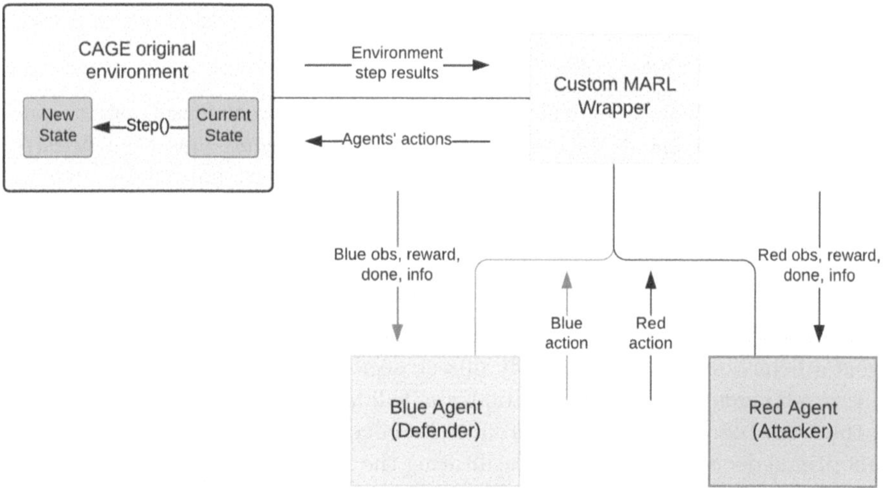

Fig. 3. Our custom environment wrapper extends the environment to support two external RL models.

More specifically, the custom wrapper assumes that either the red or blue agent's policy is fixed, while the other is learning from the sample training episodes. This is achieved by passing a fixed model file into the wrapper, which is used to predict actions based on its individual observation at each timestep. The learning agent, on the other hand, is handled outside of the wrapper and provided with a reward along with its observations, with which its policy can be updated. Ultimately, the wrapper provides the underlying original environment with the actions of both the red and blue agents, which are used at each timestep to transition to the next environment state.

The design of this custom wrapper allows for a red adversarial agent to learn how to circumvent a particular fixed blue agent policy, as well as providing the functionality for (re-)training the blue agent to defend against an RL-based red agent, instead of the hard-coded red agents used in the original environment.

4.2 Blue Agent Training

To enable the development of an adversarial policy, we first used the original CAGE challenge environment [17] to train an RL-based blue agent against both of the original hard-coded red agents described in Sect. 3.1.

We used the Stable Baselines 3 (SB3) implementation of the PPO algorithm[1] for training the agents. The blue agent was trained for a total of 4M timesteps, using the hyperparameters outlined in the Appendix B.

Blue Agent Training Reward: One aspect that was slightly altered from the original challenge during training was the blue agent's reward function. In particular, the training reward for performing a restore action was decreased from -1.0 to -5.0 in order to develop a more realistic blue agent. As explained in Sect. 3.1, the restore action represents a complete reset of a host, which the earlier iteration of the trained blue agent was found to perform nearly 50% of the time, even if the red agent did not have privileged access to the hosts. In the real world, an autonomous blue agent would not be considered effective if it constantly took key servers offline as this would severely impact the overall availability of the network.

The blue agent's training reward function has been summarised in Table 1 below, where its aim is to maximise the cumulative episode reward. The cost of the red agent's root access to a host is determined by the host's confidentiality value. Furthermore, the blue agent receives a large negative reward if the red agent impacts the target operational server, as this is the red agent's ultimate goal, as described in Sect. 3.1.

4.3 Adversarial Red Agent Training

The first step in training an adversarial red agent was tuning the PPO algorithm's hyperparameters for the red agent. Not only does the red agent have a different action space than that of the blue agent, the red agent's task requires learning valid sequences of actions with sparse rewards to successfully compromise the network. The blue agent, on the other hand, must learn to select the corresponding optimal defensive move for the given environment observation at each singular timestep. Therefore, the red agent's learning problem is a fundamentally different task than that of the blue agent and requires its own hyperparameters. Appendix B details the selected hyperparameters, along with their search ranges and the final configuration of the training algorithm used for the project's red agent.

[1] https://stable-baselines3.readthedocs.io/en/master/modules/ppo.html.

Table 1. Modified blue agent training rewards [33]

Subnet/Agent	Hosts	Action	Reward (per step)
Subnet 1	User hosts	Red root access	-0.1
Subnet 2	Enterprise hosts	Red root access	-1.0
Subnet 3	Target Server	Red root access	-1.0
Subnet 3	Operational Hosts	Red root access	-0.1
Red	Operational Server	Impact	-10
Blue	Any	Restore	**-5**

Base Red Agent: It quickly became clear that the adversarial agent struggled to learn valid actions against a strong trained blue agent that was actively countering its actions. To overcome this steep learning curve, we developed a lightweight curriculum learning [24] pipeline. A base red agent was first developed against a passive blue agent, which only monitors the network without taking any defensive actions. The base agent was trained for 600K timesteps. At the end of this training process, sample episodes show that the base agent is consistently able to impact the target server within 25 timesteps.

Adversarial Reward: We define a custom reward function to fine-tune this base model into an effective adversarial policy that exploits the trained blue agent's weaknesses. Prior work on adversarial policies generally uses a zero-sum reward framework [13,36]. For our asymmetric setting, a zero-sum reward is not effective for learning a successful adversarial policy, as the adversarial red agent is not merely aiming to reduce the blue agent's reward, but also needs to learn how to effectively fulfil the red agent's initial goal.

To resolve this issue, we define the following reward function: The red agent only receives a positive reward for new privileged access to a host in relation to the previous timestep, while the blue agent receives a negative reward for each timestep the red agent has privileged access to a host. This reward function aims to motivate the red agent to exploit and compromise further hosts, and avoids the agent learning to do nothing or to perform redundant actions while still receiving positive rewards.

Following this initial change to the red agent's reward function, we observe that the agent often becomes stuck in a loop where the blue agent restores a host that the red agent has just compromised. This leads to an accumulation of reward for the red agent for each "new" privileged access, effectively resembling a Denial of Service attack on a particular host by forcing the blue agent to continuously restore it. Although this is effective in terms of reducing the blue agent's reward, it does not achieve the red agent's main goal. To this end, the red agent's reward magnitude for impacting the target server was increased from +10 to +25.

Bonus Rewards: The original reward setup did not enable the red agent to learn a valid action sequence that allowed it to reach the target server. To further encourage this, we added a bonus reward for the first time the red agent scans and exploits the target operational server in an episode. This reward is subsequently diminished for these actions, such that the agent is aware that it is targeting the sensitive key operational server while ensuring it does not learn to unnecessarily repeat these actions simply to increase its total reward.

The above modifications to the red agent's reward function are valid within our threat model, as the reward is only based on the information available to the red agent within a particular timestep. In other words, the reward function only considers the privileged access on already known or compromised hosts, excluding any unknown hosts. Finally, any invalid action chosen by the red agent still receives a small negative reward as per the original environment reward function. Using the new hyperparameters and the reward function summarised in Table 2, we further trained the base red model for 2M timesteps against the fixed trained blue agent policy.

Table 2. Custom red agent training rewards to reflect adversarial objective.

Hosts	Action	Reward (per step)	Repeated reward
User hosts	Red root access	+0.1	n/a
Enterprise hosts	Red root access	+1.0	n/a
Target Server	Red scan	+2.0	+0.1
Target Server	Red exploit	+3.0	+0.5
Target Hosts	Red root access	+5.0	n/a
Target Server	Impact	+25	n/a
Any	Invalid action	-0.1	n/a

5 Evaluation

5.1 Evaluation Methodology

Our evaluation includes several distinct red agents to assess the performance of the blue agent. The first is a passive red agent that only performs the sleep action, to evaluate whether the blue agent is able to identify a lack of malicious activity on the network and act accordingly. We also include both the meander and b-line hard-coded red agents used in the original challenge in this evaluation, as well as the novel adversarial red agent we have developed.

Following the original CAGE challenge evaluation, the blue agent's performance is assessed in terms of its average final score across 1,000 seeded evaluation episodes of 100 timesteps, using the original challenge reward function. In contrast to the original challenge evaluation, the green agent has been used in the evaluation environment. As explained in Sect. 3.1, this agent represents the actions of genuine users and is essential for evaluating whether the trained blue agent can distinguish malicious activity from benign user behaviour.

Furthermore, to assess the blue agent's robustness with respect to the red agent's objective, we use two more evaluation metrics: *compromise rate* and *win rate*. The compromise rate denotes the percentage of the 1,000 evaluation episodes in which the red agent was able to gain privileged access to the target operational server. In contrast, the win rate is the percentage of evaluation episodes where the blue agent successfully prevented the red agent from impacting the target operational server.

While we acknowledge the importance of benchmarking our adversarial policy against state-of-the-art methods, our literature review indicates that no prior work has implemented DRL-based evasion strategies within the CAGE Challenge environment. Although related efforts such as [25] and [20] have made valuable contributions, their models, environments, and techniques differ fundamentally from ours.

As noted by [35], the CAGE Challenge represents the most realistic autonomous cyber operations environment currently available in the literature. Through this work, we aim to establish a benchmark for future research and encourage the development of adversarial strategies that can be directly compared against our proposed policy.

5.2 Evaluation Results

Win/Compromise Rates: Table 3 summarises the results of the evaluation. The results show that the blue agent is near-perfect in defending the target operational server from the hard-coded red agents, with a 100% and 99.7% win rate against the meander and b-line agent respectively. However, the trained blue agent is only able to successfully prevent the adversarial red agent from impacting the target server in 59.4% of the evaluation episodes. Moreover, while the hard-coded red agents are not able to compromise the target server at all in nearly all evaluation episodes, the adversarial red agent manages to gain privileged access to the server 99.7% of the time.

Mean Rewards: These results are also reflected in the mean final reward of the blue agent. The reward obtained by the blue agent against the adversarial red agent sees a significant reduction from that obtained against the hard-coded red agents, with a decrease of more than 300%. This larger negative reward is largely due to the successful impact actions performed by the adversarial red agent. Furthermore, the adversarial red agent is able to force the blue agent to perform more restore actions, thereby also decreasing its final reward.

Another interesting observation is that the win rate for the blue agent further decreases to 49.4% against the adversarial red agent when the duration of the

Table 3. Evaluation results (1,000 seeded episodes, 100 timesteps each)

Blue	Red	Blue reward	Compromise rate	Blue win rate
Trained RL	Passive (sleep)	0.0	0.0%	100.0%
Trained RL	Meander [33]	-27.5	0.0%	100.0%
Trained RL	B-line [33]	-23.4	0.5%	99.7%
Trained RL	Adversarial RL	**-119.3**	**99.7%**	**59.4%**

episode increases to 150 time steps. This suggests that the adversarial agent may not always have enough time to successfully evade the blue agent within the original challenge's evaluation setup. However, in most real-world settings, there are no time constraints for deploying a successful attack and the defender should thus be robust against such an attack regardless of a time limit.

All in all, the evaluation results show that the blue agent we trained is able to effectively defend the network from the original hard-coded red agents. However, the adversarial red agent is able to drastically decrease the blue agent's performance. Not only is the adversarial policy capable of compromising the target server 99.7% of the time, but the blue agent also fails to prevent the server from being impacted in less than 60% of the evaluation episodes.

A key consideration here connects back to the asymmetrical nature of cyber security: the attacker only needs to succeed once to achieve their objective while the blue agent must be able to successfully defend the network 100% of the time. Thus, a failure rate of more than 40% would be considered severely inadequate for any model to be deployed in the real world. This raises the question: how did the adversarial red agent manage to deceive and evade the seemingly effective blue agent policy? We address this question in more detail next.

5.3 Policy Analysis

Radar charts (Fig. 4) compare red agent policies against the trained blue agent, showing the adversarial agent's increased impact actions versus the meander and b-line agents. The adversarial policy lies between these hard-coded agents, demonstrating a novel deceptive strategy that defeats the blue agent using identical actions, unseen in "logical" agents.

Adversarial Strategy: Based on sample episode analysis, the adversarial strategy involves distracting blue by occasionally moving backwards. For instance, when red escalates its privileges on a user host, blue typically responds by setting decoys on enterprise hosts and/or restoring compromised hosts. However, if red already possesses enterprise host access (required for target server connection), it re-escalates prior user hosts. This prevents blue from restoring access and misdirects it to the wrong subnet, granting red an extra timestep to expand network access and advance toward its objective.

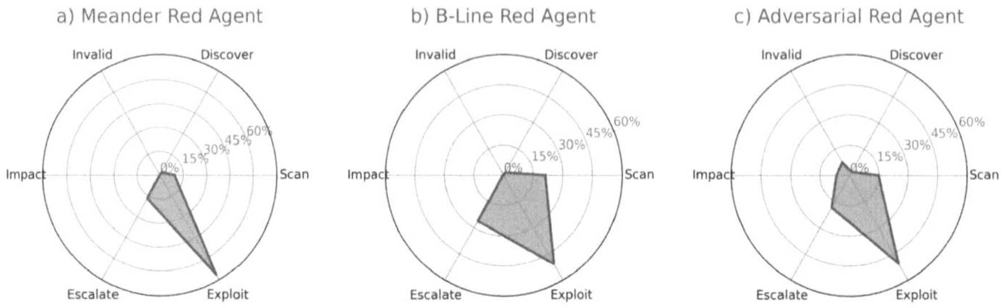

Fig. 4. Hardcoded vs. Adversarial Red Agent Policies Comparison.

The adversarial policy has also learnt to exploit IP addresses from any privileged host, unlike the hard-coded agents. For example, after discovering the operational server IP via Enterprise 2, it uses any Enterprise host to connect, diversifying attack paths.

Our analysis reveals 7% invalid actions during evaluation, partly due to blue's concurrent actions invalidating red's attempts. Despite this imperfection, the agent maintains high win rates by prioritizing evasion over perfect action validity.

6 Related Work

Supervised Models: Evasion attacks were initially developed to target supervised classification models. Szegedy et al. observed in their research that neural networks have blind spots and proposed the term "adversarial examples" to refer to the perturbed inputs used to evade the DNN models [34]. This attack adopts a white-box threat model, where the adversary has knowledge of the model parameters as well as the training data. Goodfellow et al. proposed the Fast Gradient Sign Method (FGSM), which is a one-step attack rather than iterative, and aims to maximise the victim model loss using the input gradient rather than the model parameters [14], making it surprisingly effective as a black-box attack.

RL Models: Prior RL evasion attacks predominantly assume white-box access. Madry et al. [21] perturb observations, Lee et al. [18] perturb actions, and Schott et al. [27] perturb states to deviate victim policies. These direct manipulation attacks are unrealistic for real-world scenarios.

Gleave et al. [13] establish a more realistic adversarial policy threat model, where adversaries indirectly induce harmful observations through environment interactions. Their seemingly random policies achieve high win rates in robot games. Similarly, Wang et al. [36] demonstrate adversarial policies in Go that trick state-of-the-art agents into losing, proving that average-case performance does not necessarily imply worst-case robustness (critical for security).

Recent work [3] introduces RAT for universal targeted behavior attacks via human-preferences-aligned intention policies, dynamically adjusting replay buffer state occupancy to manipulate victim policies. The authors show that this approach outperforms prior methods while offering robustness benefits.

7 Future Work

Future work should focus on countermeasures and new training methods to develop more robust policies and bolster the blue agent's resilience to adversarial attacks. While adversarial training [13] offers limited robustness due to inherent arms races, alternative defenses include Nash equilibrium training [15] and timescale-separated adversarial training [19].

Environment variations warrant testing: (1) implementing `Discover Deception` (from latest CAGE) to address blue's unrealistic decoy advantage, and (2) introducing invalid action metrics for adversarial assessment. The network size and complexity should also be experimented with to evaluate the generalisability of both attacker and defender, progressing towards investigating the transferability of adversarial policies from simulated to emulated systems.

This work establishes a benchmark for testing autonomous blue agents against adversarial policies, highlighting that real-world deployment requires addressing such attacks. Progress in this area would benefit security professionals through advanced autonomous defenses, while improved robustness [26] would bridge the simulation-to-reality gap [8] for DRL systems.

8 Conclusions

We have shown that a DRL-based blue agent, trained with predictable red agents, can be vulnerable to adversarial policies designed to exploit its weaknesses. While the blue agent performed exceptionally well against static, rule-based opponents, its success rate dropped by over 40% when facing an adaptive red agent capable of manipulating its observations. These findings highlight the need for training methodologies that account for dynamic adversarial strategies in the real world, rather than relying solely on rigid attacker models. Future efforts should focus on integrating adversarial tactics into training pipelines to create more robust and adaptive blue agents. Techniques such as adversarial training, curriculum learning, and meta-learning could help address the evolving nature of cyber threats. Although this study focused on a specific ACD environment, the insights extend to any domain where autonomous agents must defend against adaptive adversaries, underscoring the importance of resilience in real-world deployments.

A Agent Action Spaces

Tables 4 and 5 outline the discrete actions available within the environment to the blue and red agents respectively.

Table 4. Blue agent action space [33].

Action	Purpose	Parameters	Output
Monitor	Collect flagged malicious activity (automatic with other actions)	None	Malicious network connections/processes
Analyse	Gather detailed host info to detect red presence	Hostname	File info (signature, entropy) from recent alerts
Decoy: [Services]	Set decoy service (Green agents ignore; access indicates red)	Hostname	Alert on red access
Remove	Eliminate red by destroying malicious assets	Hostname	Success/Failure
Restore	Revert system to known state (reduces availability; penalizes Blue -1)	Hostname	Success/Failure

Table 5. Red agent action space [33].

Action	Purpose	Parameters	Output
Discover Remote Systems	Discover new hosts/IP addresses in the network through active scanning using tools such as ping.	Subnet	IP addresses in the chosen subnet from hosts that respond to ping.
Discover Network Services	Discover responsive services on a selected host by initiating a connection with that host using tools such as nmap.	IP Address	Ports and service information.
Exploit Remote Service	Attempt to exploit a specified service on a remote system.	IP Address, Port	Success/Failure,Initial recon of host if successful.
Escalate	Escalate the agent's privileges on the specified host.	Hostname	Success/Failure,Internal information now available due to increased access to the host
Impact	Disrupt the performance of the network and fulfil red's objective of denying the operational service.	Hostname	Success/Failure
Sleep	Do nothing.	None	None

B Hyperparameter Tuning

B.1 Blue Agent Hyperparameters

The hyperparameters in Table 6 below were used to train the blue agent. These were tuned in a previous project [22], where the initial blue agent's task was nearly identical.

Table 6. Hyperparameters for the training of the blue agent.

Parameter	**Value**
Batch Size	32
Number steps	9000
Discount factor	0.96170
Learning rate	0.00023
Entropy coefficient	0.00248
Clipping range	0.24872
Epochs per update	6
GAE lambda	0.99585
Value function coefficient	0.5

B.2 Adversarial Red Agent Hyperparameters

Optuna[2] performed hyperparameter tuning over 100 trials. Each trial used a TPE Sampler, trained for 100,000 timesteps, and was evaluated over 3 episodes. After 5 trials, the MedianPruner[3] activated, pruning trials where the best intermediate result fell below the median of previous trials at the same step.

Manually tested parameters included a linear learning rate schedule (to stabilize training by reducing policy update size) and 16 parallel environments. Vectorization resolved training instability where the agent stagnated by repeating unproductive actions (Table 7).

[2] https://optuna.readthedocs.io/en/stable/.

[3] https://optuna.readthedocs.io/en/stable/reference/generated/optuna.pruners.MedianPruner.html.

Table 7. Hyperparameters for SB3 proximal policy optimization adversarial agent.

Parameter	Value	Search Range	Distribution
Total timesteps	2M	[600k, 1M, 2M, 4M]	Manual
Batch Size	512	[32, 64, 128, 256, 512]	Categorical
Number of environments	16	[0,8,16]	Manual
Number of steps	2048	[256, 512, 1024, 2048, 4096, 8192, 16384]	Categorical
Discount factor	0.9	[0.9, 0.95, 0.98, 0.99, 0.995, 0.999]	Categorical
Learning rate	0.00151	[1e-5, 0.01]	Log Uniform
Learning rate schedule	Linear	[None, Linear]	Manually
Entropy coefficient	0.00371	[0.0000001, 0.01]	Log Uniform
Clipping range	0.1	[0.1, 0.2, 0.3, 0.4]	Categorical
Epochs per update	20	[1, 5, 10, 20]	Categorical
GAE lambda	1.0	[0.8, 0.9, 0.92, 0.95, 0.98, 0.99, 1.0]	Categorical
Max gradient norm	0.7	[0.3, 0.5, 0.6, 0.7, 0.8, 0.9, 1, 2, 5]	Categorical
Value function coefficient	0.23666	[0, 1]	Uniform
Network architecture	medium	[tiny, small, medium]	Categorical
Orthogonal initialization	True	[True, False]	Categorical
Activation function	tanh	[tanh, relu]	Categorical

References

1. Abel, D., Barreto, A., Van Roy, B., Precup, D., van Hasselt, H.P., Singh, S.: A definition of continual reinforcement learning. Adv. Neural. Inf. Process. Syst. **36**, 50377–50407 (2023)
2. Andrew, A., Spillard, S., Collyer, J., Dhir, N.: Developing optimal causal cyber-defence agents via cyber security simulation. arXiv preprint arXiv:2207.12355 (2022)
3. Bai, F., Liu, R., Du, Y., Wen, Y., Yang, Y.: Rat: Adversarial attacks on deep reinforcement agents for targeted behaviors. In: Proceedings of the AAAI Conference on Artificial Intelligence. vol. 39, pp. 15453–15461 (2025)
4. Bates, E., Hicks, C., Mavroudis, V.: Less is more? rewards in RL for cyber defence. arXiv preprint arXiv:2503.03245 (2025)
5. Bellman, R.: The theory of dynamic programming. Bull. Am. Math. Soc. **60**(6), 503–515 (1954)
6. Bengio, Y., et al.: International scientific report on the safety of advanced AI (interim report). arXiv preprint arXiv:2412.05282 (2024)
7. Berner, C., et al.: Dota 2 with large scale deep reinforcement learning. arXiv preprint arXiv:1912.06680 (2019)
8. Collins, J., Howard, D., Leitner, J.: Quantifying the reality gap in robotic manipulation tasks. In: 2019 International Conference on Robotics and Automation (ICRA). pp. 6706–6712. IEEE (2019)
9. Das, A., Rad, P.: Opportunities and challenges in explainable artificial intelligence (XAI): A survey. arXiv preprint arXiv:2006.11371 (2020)

10. Ell, M., Rizvi, S.: Cyber security breaches survey 2024 (2024). https://www.gov.uk/government/statistics/cyber-security-breaches-survey-2024/cyber-security-breaches-survey-2024#summary
11. Emerson, H., Bates, L., Hicks, C., Mavroudis, V.: Cyborg++: An enhanced gym for the development of autonomous cyber agents. arXiv preprint arXiv:2410.16324 (2024)
12. Foley, M., Hicks, C., Highnam, K., Mavroudis, V.: Autonomous network defence using reinforcement learning. In: Proceedings of the 2022 ACM on Asia Conference on Computer and Communications Security. p. 1252–1254. ASIA CCS '22, Association for Computing Machinery, New York, NY, USA (2022). https://doi.org/10.1145/3488932.3527286, https://doi.org/10.1145/3488932.3527286
13. Gleave, A., Dennis, M., Wild, C., Kant, N., Levine, S., Russell, S.: Adversarial policies: Attacking deep reinforcement learning. arXiv preprint arXiv:1905.10615 (2019)
14. Goodfellow, I.J., Shlens, J., Szegedy, C.: Explaining and harnessing adversarial examples. arXiv preprint arXiv:1412.6572 (2014)
15. Guo, W., Wu, X., Wang, L., Xing, X., Song, D.: {PATROL}: Provable defense against adversarial policy in two-player games. In: 32nd USENIX Security Symposium (USENIX Security 23). pp. 3943–3960 (2023)
16. Hu, Z., Beuran, R., Tan, Y.: Automated penetration testing using deep reinforcement learning. In: 2020 IEEE European Symposium on Security and Privacy Workshops (EuroS&PW). pp. 2–10. IEEE (2020)
17. Kiely, M., Bowman, D., Standen, M., Moir, C.: On autonomous agents in a cyber defence environment. arXiv preprint arXiv:2309.07388 (2023)
18. Lee, X.Y., Ghadai, S., Tan, K.L., Hegde, C., Sarkar, S.: Spatiotemporally constrained action space attacks on deep reinforcement learning agents. In: Proceedings of the AAAI conference on artificial intelligence. vol. 34, pp. 4577–4584 (2020)
19. Liu, X., Chakraborty, S., Sun, Y., Huang, F.: Rethinking adversarial policies: A generalized attack formulation and provable defense in RL. arXiv preprint arXiv:2305.17342 (2023)
20. Loevenich, J., Adler, E., Huerten, T., Lopes, R.R.F.: Design and evaluation of an autonomous cyber defence agent using DRL and an augmented llm. Comput. Netw. **262**, 111162 (2025)
21. Madry, A., Makelov, A., Schmidt, L., Tsipras, D., Vladu, A.: Towards deep learning models resistant to adversarial attacks. arXiv preprint arXiv:1706.06083 (2017)
22. Meijer, M.: Automated Cyber Defence by Deep Reinforcement Learning. Bachelor's thesis, Cardiff University (2023)
23. Molina-Markham, A., Miniter, C., Powell, B., Ridley, A.: Network environment design for autonomous cyberdefense. arXiv preprint arXiv:2103.07583 (2021)
24. Narvekar, S., Peng, B., Leonetti, M., Sinapov, J., Taylor, M.E., Stone, P.: Curriculum learning for reinforcement learning domains: a framework and survey. J. Mach. Learn. Res. **21**(181), 1–50 (2020)
25. Potteiger, N., Samaddar, A., Bergstrom, H., Koutsoukos, X.: Designing robust cyber-defense agents with evolving behavior trees. In: 2024 International Conference on Assured Autonomy (ICAA). pp. 1–10. IEEE (2024)
26. Schott, L., et al.: Robust deep reinforcement learning through adversarial attacks and training: a survey. arXiv preprint arXiv:2403.00420 (2024)
27. Schott, L., Hajri, H., Lamprier, S.: Improving robustness of deep reinforcement learning agents: environment attack based on the critic network. In: 2022 International Joint Conference on Neural Networks (IJCNN). pp. 1–8. IEEE (2022)

28. Schulman, J., Wolski, F., Dhariwal, P., Radford, A., Klimov, O.: Proximal policy optimization algorithms. arXiv preprint arXiv:1707.06347 (2017)
29. Schulman, J., Wolski, F., Dhariwal, P., Radford, A., Klimov, O.: Proximal policy optimization algorithms. arXiv preprint arXiv:1707.06347 (2017)
30. Schwartz, J.: Autonomous penetration testing using reinforcement learning (2018). URL for simulator documentation: https://networkattacksimulator.readthedocs.io/en/latest/
31. Silver, D., et al.: A general reinforcement learning algorithm that masters chess, shogi, and go through self-play. Science **362**(6419), 1140–1144 (2018)
32. Standen, M., Lucas, M., Bowman, D., Richer, T.J., Kim, J., Marriott, D.: Cyborg: A gym for the development of autonomous cyber agents. arXiv preprint arXiv:2108.09118 (2021)
33. Standen, M., Lucas, M., Bowman, D., Richer, T.J., Kim, J., Marriott, D.: Cyborg: A gym for the development of autonomous cyber agents. arXiv preprint arXiv:2108.09118 (2021)
34. Szegedy, C., et al.: Intriguing properties of neural networks. arXiv preprint arXiv:1312.6199 (2013)
35. Vyas, S., Mavroudis, V., Burnap, P.: Towards the deployment of realistic autonomous cyber network defence: a systematic review. ACM Comput. Sur. (2025)
36. Wang, T.T., et al.: Adversarial policies beat superhuman go ais. In: International Conference on Machine Learning. pp. 35655–35739. PMLR (2023)
37. Yu, L., et al.: Deep reinforcement learning for smart home energy management. IEEE Internet Things J. **7**(4), 2751–2762 (2019)
38. Zhu, Z., Chen, M., Zhu, C., Zhu, Y.: Effective defense strategies in network security using improved double dueling deep q-network. Comput. & Sec. **136**, 103578 (2024)

Knowledge Retention for Generic Reinforcement Learning Policies in Autonomous Cyber Defence

Joshua Sylvester(✉) and Rogério de Lemos

University of Kent, Canterbury, UK
{jrs71,r.delemos}@kent.ac.uk

Abstract. Within autonomous cyber defence, building scalable agents that can generalise across attack behaviours is crucial to developing a truly autonomous system. These generic agents are pivotal, as over time, attackers will inevitably change their behaviour, requiring the defence mechanisms to adapt accordingly. Current approaches for generic agents use deep reinforcement learning policies to learn multiple attack behaviours and mitigate them. When a new attack behaviour is introduced, the generic policy is retrained to incorporate this behaviour and not forget previous attack behaviours. In this paper, we propose a novel solution based on a modified version of the Proximal Policy Optimisation (PPO) reinforcement learning algorithm that retains previously acquired knowledge, enabling a scalable and generic framework in which new attack behaviours can be incorporated modularly. The modified PPO algorithm demonstrates a 22.11% performance improvement compared to standard PPO when trained to sequentially learn two distinct attack behaviours. These results show a step towards building more scalable autonomous cyber defence systems capable of incorporating evolving cyber threats.

1 Introduction

Reinforcement learning (RL) has shown great results in areas such as robotics, healthcare and finance [5,13,16]. However, when applied to autonomous cyber defence (ACD) a new challenge emerges, attack behaviours change rapidly over time. This challenge requires policies that can operate reliably in ever changing network environments, and this presents a significant obstacle for standard RL approaches, which typically require complete retraining on new adversarial tactics [6]. Moreover, retraining an RL policy from scratch is computationally expensive and delays the ability to respond quickly to a new threat.

Solutions for developing generic reinforcement learning policies in autonomous cyber defence remain limited. Farooq and Kunz [6] propose one such approach by first training dedicated policies for each attack, then collecting observation-action pairs to train a supervised model capable of generalising across behaviours. While effective, this method requires training a

R. Laborde et al. (Eds.): ESORICS 2025 Workshops, LNCS 16233, pp. 39–56, 2026.
https://doi.org/10.1007/978-3-032-16165-9_3

specific policy and collecting data for each new attack behaviour in order to develop an updated generic policy. Alternative methods such as policy distillation, actor-mimic networks, and experience replay aim to address these challenges by transferring knowledge across tasks and preserving performance on previous behaviours [8,15,17]. However, these methods either require storing large replay buffers, accessing previous environments, or retraining from scratch, which hinders their scalability. This highlights the need for an approach that, in addition to learning from new behaviours, also supports knowledge retention.

To address the challenges of scalability and adaptability in reinforcement learning for autonomous cyber defence, we propose a modified Proximal Policy Optimisation (PPO) algorithm that incorporates a KL divergence based regularisation term [18]. This encourages the new policy to remain close to a previously learned reference policy during training, enabling the agent to retain prior knowledge while acquiring new behaviours. Unlike traditional PPO, which optimises the policy with no explicit mechanism for preserving past capabilities, our KL regularised variant supports sequential learning across attack behaviours without requiring full retraining or replay buffers.

Using a modified PPO algorithm, we analyse how policies trained against one class of behavioural attacks can be extended to handle additional adversaries while preserving competence on earlier ones. Through empirical evaluation using the TTCP CAGE Challenge 2 simulation environment, we demonstrate that this approach enables incremental expansion of defensive capabilities without full retraining, and we explore the role of the KL-divergence in managing the trade-off between knowledge retention and plasticity.

In the context of whether knowledge retention can be used to build scalable, generic reinforcement learning policies in autonomous cyber defence, a key contribution of this paper is a modified PPO algorithm that supports knowledge retention. We have demonstrated that our modified PPO algorithm can be used to develop scalable and generic reinforcement learning policies for autonomous cyber defence. However, initial observations suggest that the final policy is influenced by both the characteristics of the initial attack behaviours and the sequence in which behaviours are learned.

The rest of the paper is structured as follows. Section 2 reviews related work. Section 3 outlines the proposed approach, including the modified PPO algorithm. Section 5 presents the experiments, along with their results and analysis, comparing standard PPO with the modified PPO, and also shows the impact that the initial policy has when generating a generic policy. The paper concludes with findings and future directions.

2 Related Work

Developing agents for autonomous cyber defence requires policies that generalise across different attacker behaviours. This section reviews two key areas: generic policies, which aim to operate across varied network structures and threats, and continual multi-task learning, which focuses on learning new tasks without forgetting previous ones. While existing approaches show promise, many still rely on retraining or revisiting past environments, limiting scalability. Our work addresses these gaps by enabling continual learning without such dependencies.

2.1 Generic Policies in Autonomous Cyber Defence

In the field of autonomous cyber defence (ACD), research on generic policies has primarily focused on two key dimensions of generalisation: generalisation across network structures and generalisation across varying attack behaviours [14]. The former concerns the ability of a defensive policy to operate effectively across different network topologies or configurations without retraining. The latter addresses the challenge of enabling a policy to detect and respond to a wide range of attacker strategies.

Research into generic policies over network structures has progressed from handling minor topological variations, such as changes in connectivity with a fixed number of nodes, to more advanced techniques that work on dynamic scenarios [1,22]. These accommodate changes in both the number of nodes and overall network configuration, without the need for retraining [20]. However, a different challenge emerges when considering attack behaviours.

Generalising over attack behaviours introduces constraints unique to reinforcement learning. Generic policies outperform specialised ones when responding to previously unseen attack strategies [22]. However, as attackers develop novel tactics or exploit new vectors, even these general policies can become outdated [4]. This underscores the need for policies capable of incorporating new threats into their defensive repertoire. Over time, the cost, both in computation and effort, of retraining policies from scratch becomes increasingly prohibitive, highlighting the importance of mechanisms for continual learning and efficient policy updating.

Solutions for policies that generalise across attack behaviours remain scarce, with Farooq and Kunz [6] presenting one of the few approaches for developing generic policies using both supervised and reinforcement learning. By training a policy on each attack behaviour, then collecting observation and action pairs from the collection of specific policies to create a dataset that will be used to train a supervised multi-layer perceptron (MLP). Although this model performs well from a scalability point of view, it has some drawbacks. Not only does the specific policy need to be trained on the new attack behaviour, but the observation and action pairs need to be collected to add them to the dataset to be used in retraining a new supervised model.

Loevenich et al. [12] present a framework that combines Proximal Policy Optimisation (PPO) with a fine-tuned Large Language Model (LLM) to develop a defensive agent. While the approach demonstrates strong performance, one of its purported advantages is scalability. However, when considering evolving attack behaviours, this scalability is limited: the PPO model must be retrained on all attack behaviours each time a new attack behaviour is introduced, hindering the agent's ability to adapt efficiently in dynamic threat environments.

Both Dehghantanha et al. [4] and Kott [11] emphasise the need for adaptive frameworks that can evolve in tandem with the shifting threat landscape by continuously learning and responding to novel challenges. Central to achieving this is the development of policies capable of incremental learning without forgetting previously acquired knowledge.

2.2 Continual Multi-task Learning for Reinforcement Learning

Continual Multi-Task Learning (CMTL) in Reinforcement Learning (RL) seeks to develop agents capable of learning multiple tasks over time without catastrophic forgetting. Unlike traditional multi-task learning, which assumes simultaneous access to all tasks, CMTL addresses the sequential nature of task exposure, aiming to preserve performance on previously learned tasks whilst acquiring new behaviours.

One of the central challenges in CMTL is catastrophic forgetting, where learning new tasks interferes destructively with previously acquired knowledge. Several approaches have been proposed to mitigate this, such as Elastic Weight Consolidation (EWC) [10], Progress & Compress [19], and Memory Aware Synapses (MAS) [2], which regularise parameter updates based on their importance to prior tasks. Although originally proposed for supervised settings, these techniques have been used in RL with varying degrees of success [10,19]. For example, Elastic Weight Consolidation (EWC) and Progress & Compress, like other weight regularisation methods, require clearly defined and distinct task boundaries to function effectively, which is not the case in autonomous cyber defence [21].

Policy distillation and actor-mimic networks offer a strategy for transferring knowledge from previously trained policies into a single student model capable of handling multiple tasks [15,17]. These techniques can be used to initialise or regularise learning when adapting to new tasks.

Experience replay buffers have also been widely used in lifelong learning to help agents retain and revisit past experiences [8]. For example, Xu et al. [23] combines experience replay with policy distillation, using teacher policies to support continual learning without forgetting previously learned tasks.

However, a common limitation of these approaches is that they still require interaction with the environments of previous tasks, either to regenerate data through the original policies or to refresh stored experiences. As the number of tasks increases, the need to repeatedly access and run older environments can become a major scalability bottleneck. Such dependence on past environments also raises concerns around long-term maintenance, especially when older environments become deprecated or harder to support.

To overcome these limitations, our approach enables continual learning without requiring further interaction with previously encountered environments. By eliminating this dependency, our method not only reduces computational overhead but also improves scalability, making it more suitable for real-world applications.

3 Methodology

This section introduces a method to train reinforcement learning (RL) agents that can learn new attack behaviours without forgetting how to respond to previously seen ones. In real-world autonomous cyber defence (ACD), the threat landscape is constantly changing. New attack strategies emerge, old ones are modified, and defenders must remain effective against both.

Our proposed approach enables knowledge retention across attack types by modifying the Proximal Policy Optimisation (PPO) algorithm to support continual learning. Crucially, this method avoids the need to store or retrain on data from prior tasks, addressing scalability issues.

At a high level, our method proceeds as follows:

1. We begin by training an agent to defend against one type of attacker (Task $\mathcal{T}_i$).
2. When a new attacker behaviour (Task $\mathcal{T}_j$) is introduced, we fine-tune the existing agent rather than starting from scratch.
3. During fine-tuning, we employ a knowledge retention mechanism that constrains learning, ensuring the agent remains effective on the previous task without needing direct access to it.

The following subsections present this method in detail. First, we explain its mathematical foundations and then describe our modified PPO algorithm, which integrates a lightweight regularisation term to preserve prior knowledge.

3.1 Overview

Autonomous cyber defence systems must operate in dynamic threat environments where attacker tactics change over time. To enable long-term adaptability, our objective is to train RL agents that generalise across attack behaviours while preserving knowledge of previously encountered attack behaviours.

Assume there are two tasks $\mathcal{T}_i$ and $\mathcal{T}_j$ where both tasks have different attack behaviours [3]. An RL task $\mathcal{T}_x$ is typically defined as a Markov Decision Process (MDP).

$$\mathcal{T}_x := (\mathcal{S}, \mathcal{A}, P_x, R)$$

where:

- $\mathcal{S}$ is the *state space*
- $\mathcal{A}$ is the *action space*
- $P_x : \mathcal{S} \times \mathcal{A} \times \mathcal{S} \to [0, 1]$ is the *transition probability kernel*, where $P(s' \mid s, a)$ denotes the probability of transitioning to state s' after taking action a in state s
- $R : \mathcal{S} \times \mathcal{A} \to \mathbb{R}$ is the *reward function* specifying the immediate reward received after taking action a in state s.

In this setup, the state and action spaces are consistent across tasks, while the differences between tasks arise due to variations in attack behaviour shown in P_i and P_j. These differences can correspond to changes in movement patterns, target selection strategies, or stealth mechanisms used by adversaries in the simulation.

The objective of this method is to obtain a generic policy $\pi_{\theta_{\mathcal{T}_i \to \mathcal{T}_i \cup \mathcal{T}_j}}$ such that it performs well on task $\mathcal{T}_j$, it retains performance on task $\mathcal{T}_i$, and no samples from task $\mathcal{T}_i$ are needed to retain knowledge.

$$\pi_{\theta_{\mathcal{T}_i \to \mathcal{T}_i \cup \mathcal{T}_j}} \approx \arg\max_{\theta} J(\theta_{\mathcal{T}_i \to \mathcal{T}_i \cup \mathcal{T}_j}; \mathcal{T}_j) \quad \text{s.t.} \quad J(\theta_{\mathcal{T}_i \to \mathcal{T}_i \cup \mathcal{T}_j}; \mathcal{T}_i) \approx J(\theta_{\mathcal{T}_i}; \mathcal{T}_i)$$

where:

- $J(\theta_{\mathcal{T}_x}; \mathcal{T}_x)$ is the expected return of policy π_θ on task $\mathcal{T}_x$
- $\theta_{\mathcal{T}_x}$ are the parameters of a policy trained on $\mathcal{T}_x$.

This setup allows the agent to adapt to new threats (task $\mathcal{T}_j$) while preserving its effectiveness against previously seen threats (task $\mathcal{T}_i$), thereby addressing a key challenge in sequential learning for cyber defence.

3.2 Modified PPO Algorithm

To achieve the above objective, we propose a modified variant of the PPO algorithm that incorporates an additional term to promote knowledge retention. The standard PPO algorithm is a widely used on-policy actor-critic algorithm that balances policy improvement with stability through a clipped surrogate objective.

Standard PPO Loss Function. The standard PPO loss function ($\mathcal{L}(\theta)$) combines three components: clipped policy loss ($\mathcal{L}_{\text{clip}}(\theta)$), value function loss ($\mathcal{L}_{\text{V}}(\theta)$), and entropy regulariser ($\mathcal{L}_{\text{entropy}}(\theta)$) to promote exploration.

$$\mathcal{L}(\theta) = \mathcal{L}_{\text{clip}}(\theta) + c_1 \mathcal{L}_{\text{V}}(\theta) - c_2 \mathcal{L}_{\text{entropy}}(\theta) \tag{1}$$

where:

- c_1 and c_2 are hyperparameters controlling the relative importance of the value loss and entropy regularisation.

The clipped policy loss ($\mathcal{L}_{\text{clip}}(\theta)$) is defined as follows:

$$\mathcal{L}_{\text{clip}}(\theta) = \hat{\mathbb{E}}_t \left[\min \left(r_t(\theta)\hat{A}_t, \text{clip}(r_t(\theta), 1-\epsilon, 1+\epsilon)\hat{A}_t \right) \right] \tag{2}$$

$$r_t(\theta) = \frac{\pi_\theta(a_t|s_t)}{\pi_{\theta_{\text{old}}}(a_t|s_t)} \tag{3}$$

$$\text{clip}(r_t(\theta), 1-\epsilon, 1+\epsilon) = \begin{cases} 1-\epsilon & \text{if } r_t(\theta) < 1-\epsilon \\ r_t(\theta) & \text{if } 1-\epsilon \le r_t(\theta) \le 1+\epsilon \\ 1+\epsilon & \text{if } r_t(\theta) > 1+\epsilon \end{cases} \tag{4}$$

where:

- $r_t(\theta)$ is the probability ratio of the new and old policies at time t
- $\hat{A}_t$ is the estimated advantage at time t
- ϵ is the clipping parameter
- $\pi_\theta(a_t \mid s_t)$ is the probability of taking action a_t given the state s_t at time step t, under the current policy π_θ
- $\text{clip}(r_t(\theta), 1-\epsilon, 1+\epsilon)$ clips the value of $r_t(\theta)$ to be between $[1-\epsilon, 1+\epsilon]$

The value function loss ($\mathcal{L}_\text{V}(\theta)$) is defined as follows:

$$\mathcal{L}_\text{V}(\theta) = \hat{\mathbb{E}}_t\left[(V_\theta(s_t) - R_t)^2\right] \tag{5}$$

where:

- $V_\theta(s_t)$ is the predicted value of state s_t
- R_t is the empirical return at time step t

The entropy regulariser ($\mathcal{L}_\text{entropy}(\theta)$) is defined as follows:

$$\mathcal{L}_\text{entropy}(\theta) = \hat{\mathbb{E}}_t\left[\log \pi_\theta(a_t|s_t)\right] \tag{6}$$

Modified PPO Loss Function. To retain knowledge of the original task $\mathcal{T}_i$, we introduce a regularisation term ($\mathcal{L}_\text{KL}(\theta)$) that penalises divergence from a reference policy (π_{θ_ref}), which is the policy trained on $\mathcal{T}_i$ and frozen during subsequent learning. This term constrains updates to remain close to the original policy on the shared state-action distribution.

This results in the modified loss function ($\mathcal{L}'(\theta)$):

$$\mathcal{L}'(\theta) = \mathcal{L}_\text{clip}(\theta) + c_1\mathcal{L}_\text{V}(\theta) - c_2\mathcal{L}_\text{entropy}(\theta) + c_3\mathcal{L}_\text{KL}(\theta) \tag{7}$$

where:

- c_3 is a hyperparameter controlling the strength of knowledge retention.

The regularisation term ($\mathcal{L}_\text{KL}(\theta)$) is defined as follows:

$$\text{KL}[\pi_{\theta_\text{ref}} \,\|\, \pi_\theta] \approx \mathcal{L}_\text{KL}(\theta) = \hat{\mathbb{E}}_t\left[(r'_t(\theta) - 1) - \log(r'_t(\theta))\right] \tag{8}$$

$$r'_t(\theta) = \frac{\pi_\theta(a_t \mid s_t)}{\pi_{\theta_\text{ref}}(a_t \mid s_t)} \tag{9}$$

where:

- $r'_t(\theta)$ is the probability ratio of the new and old policies at time t
- $\pi_{\theta_{\text{ref}}}(a_t \mid s_t)$ is the probability of taking action a_t given the state s_t at time step t, under the reference policy $\pi_{\theta_{\text{ref}}}$

The regularisation term $\mathcal{L}_{\text{KL}}(\theta)$ is used to estimate the reverse KL divergence between the reference policy and the current policy, we use a Monte Carlo approximation based on samples from the reference policy[1]. This approach evaluates how much the current policy shifts away from the actions chosen by the reference. By relying on samples rather than exact computation, this method makes the reverse KL practical to compute during training while still encouraging the new policy to stay close to the reference in terms of its action choices.

By incorporating the regularisation term, the policy update is guided to preserve past behaviour, preventing catastrophic forgetting during the addition of task $\mathcal{T}_j$.

3.3 Training Procedure

In this section, we describe the training procedure used to accomplish knowledge retention. Our approach extends the standard PPO algorithm by incorporating a knowledge retention mechanism through a reverse KL divergence penalty. This allows the policy to adapt to a new attack behaviour while mitigating the risk of catastrophic forgetting on the source task.

Algorithm 1. Online Transfer PPO with Knowledge Retention

Input: Pretrained policy $\pi_{\theta_{\mathcal{T}_i}}$ on task $\mathcal{T}_i$, target task $\mathcal{T}_j$, KL penalty coefficient c_3, number of training iterations N
Output: Updated policy $\pi_{\theta_{\mathcal{T}_i \to \mathcal{T}_i \cup \mathcal{T}_j}}$

Initialize $\pi_\theta \leftarrow \pi_{\theta_{\mathcal{T}_i}}$
for iteration $= 1$ to N **do**
  Collect trajectories $\tau_j = \{(s_t, a_t, r_t, s_{t+1})\}$ by interacting with task $\mathcal{T}_j$ using π_θ
  Compute advantages $\hat{A}_t$ and value targets from τ_j
  for each mini-batch in τ_j **do**
    Compute clipped surrogate loss $\mathcal{L}_{\text{clip}}(\theta)$
    Compute value function loss $\mathcal{L}_V(\theta)$
    Compute entropy bonus $\mathcal{L}_{\text{entropy}}(\theta)$
    Compute importance ratio $r'_t(\theta)$
    Approximate reverse KL divergence $\mathcal{L}_{\text{KL}}(\theta)$
    Combine loss $\mathcal{L}'(\theta)$
    Update policy parameters:

$$\theta \leftarrow \theta - \alpha \nabla_\theta \mathcal{L}'(\theta)$$

  end for
end for
return $\pi_{\theta_{\mathcal{T}_i \to \mathcal{T}_i \cup \mathcal{T}_j}}$

[1] http://joschu.net/blog/kl-approx.html.

Algorithm 1 outlines the training procedure for our modified PPO algorithm that incorporates knowledge retention. The process begins by initialising the policy π_θ with parameters from the policy pretrained on task $\mathcal{T}_i$ (Line 1). The training loop then proceeds for N iterations (Line 2), where each iteration consists of interacting with the new task $\mathcal{T}_j$ to collect a batch of trajectories (Line 3).

From these trajectories, the agent computes advantage estimates and value function targets (Line 4), which are required for the surrogate loss and value updates. For each mini-batch sampled from the collected data (Line 5), several loss components are computed: the clipped policy loss ensures stable updates (Line 6), the value function loss promotes accurate state-value estimates (Line 7), and the entropy bonus encourages exploration (Line 8).

To retain knowledge from task $\mathcal{T}_i$, an importance sampling ratio (Line 9) is calculated with respect to the reference policy $\pi_{\theta_{\text{ref}}}$, and a reverse KL divergence penalty is approximated (Line 10). These are combined into a final loss function (Line 11), which balances policy improvement on $\mathcal{T}_j$ with the preservation of behaviour on $\mathcal{T}_i$.

Finally, gradient descent is used to update the policy parameters with respect to this combined loss (Line 12). Once the loop is complete the final policy $\pi\theta_{\mathcal{T}_i \rightarrow \mathcal{T}_i \cup \mathcal{T}_j}$ is returned (Line 15).

4 CybORG TTCP CAGE Challenge 2

This study uses CybORG, a simulation framework tailored for research in cyber defence, particularly reinforcement learning (RL)-based defence strategies. Within CybORG, agents are organised according to their functional roles: red agents simulate attackers aiming to compromise systems, blue agents defend the network from such threats, and green agents represent benign user behaviour.

The experiments are conducted using the TTCP CAGE Challenge 2 scenario, which features a simplified network structure. In this scenario, red agents attempt to compromise an operational server and disrupt its functionality, while the blue agent's objective is to prevent this by detecting and mitigating the red agent's actions [9].

Red agent behaviours in the scenario are structured around the MITRE ATT&CK[2] framework and emulate real-world vulnerabilities and attack techniques [9]. These behaviours typically begin with reconnaissance, such as remote system discovery (T1018) via ICMP pings, followed by network service enumeration (T1046). The agent then attempts to exploit vulnerable services (T1210), escalate privileges (TA0004), and ultimately disrupt targeted services (T1489) to achieve denial of service.

This research focuses on three red agents. Two red agents are part of the TTCP CAGE Challenge 2 scenario, and the third one, generated for this paper, is a hybrid variant of the original two red agents.

[2] https://attack.mitre.org/techniques/enterprise/.

- **Meander:** Operates without prior knowledge of the network topology. It sequentially attempts to compromise all nodes in one subnet before progressing to the next.
- **BLine:** Has full knowledge of the network and follows predefined sequences of actions (attack paths) that lead directly to the operational server.
- **Hybrid:** Combines elements from both *Meander* and *BLine*. It begins with exploratory behaviour like *Meander*, aiming to control entire subnets, before transitioning to a targeted attack path akin to *BLine*.

The implementation of the *Hybrid* red agent is openly available here.

5 Experiments

This section describes the experiments performed that justify the use of a modified version of the Proximal Policy Optimisation (PPO) reinforcement learning algorithm for retaining previously acquired knowledge. It consists of the following key parts: the set up used for our experiments, a comparison of the standard PPO and modified PPO, an evaluation of whether knowledge retention can be used to generate generic policies to handle new attacks, and finally, a study on how the initial policy may affect the generation of the generic policy.

5.1 Experimental Setup

In multi-task continual learning scenarios, retaining previously acquired knowledge while learning new tasks is critical for developing scalable agents. To evaluate knowledge retention, experiments were conducted across sequential task combinations using distinct red agents, specifically: *Meander*, *BLine*, and a combined one involving both behaviours (*Hybrid*).

The evaluation follows a two-stage training procedure. First, a base policy is trained on a source task (e.g., *Meander*) for 600,000 timesteps. Subsequently, the policy then learns any new target task (e.g., *BLine*) for a further 400,000 timesteps.

Each policy is evaluated over 1,000 episodes, with each episode consisting of 50 timesteps. To address variance in training, ten independent seeds are used per configuration, and results are reported as the mean episodic reward with standard error (SE) following established guidelines [7].

All experiments were run on an Intel Xeon Gold 5317 processor with an NVIDIA A100 Tensor Core GPU. The module versions used for Python (3.10.12) are NumPy (2.1.3) and Matplotlib (3.10.1) for data processing and visualisation. PyTorch (2.6.0+cu124) supported model development, while Stable-Baselines3 (1.8.0), Gym (0.21.0), and Gymnasium (0.29.1) were used for reinforcement learning.

5.2 Comparing Standard PPO with Modified PPO

To motivate the use of our proposed modified PPO approach for knowledge retention, this section presents experiments designed to evaluate the ability of each method to preserve performance across multiple tasks. Both algorithms are trained and evaluated within the same set up to ensure a fair comparison. The standard PPO is selected as the baseline due to its established stability and strong performance in the TTCP CAGE Challenge 2 environment [22]. The modified PPO incorporates additional mechanisms specifically intended to mitigate catastrophic forgetting and enhance knowledge retention when transferring between tasks. The following experiments aim to assess the extent to which these modifications improve policy generalisation without sacrificing performance on previously learned tasks.

Table 1 shows the performance of the standard PPO when trained on either *Meander* or *BLine* and then further trained on the other red agent. The notation **PPO**$_S$[M] shows that the policy was trained on *Meander*. The policy **PPO**$_S$[M] is used to generate the policy **PPO**$_S$[M→MB], which shows a policy that was trained on *Meander* and then on *BLine*.

Table 1. Performance of Sequential Training of Standard PPO Policies (**PPO**$_S$) Across Different Environments (without and with Green Agents)

(a) Without Green Agents

Policy	Meander (M)	BLine (B)	Total
PPO$_S$[M]	-25.92 ± 0.17	-94.69 ± 1.13	-120.61 ± 1.14
PPO$_S$[M→MB]	-46.28 ± 0.45	-18.16 ± 0.34	-64.44 ±0.56
PPO$_S$[B]	-46.90 ± 0.56	**-18.04 ± 0.43**	-64.94 ± 0.71
PPO$_S$[B→BM]	**-20.84 ± 0.10**	-37.11 ± 0.55	**-57.95 ± 0.56**

(b) With Green Agents

Policy	Meander (M)	BLine (B)	Total
PPO$_S$[M]	**-26.67 ± 0.11**	-50.03 ± 0.64	-76.70 ± 0.65
PPO$_S$[M→MB]	-31.03 ± 0.25	**-19.20 ± 0.35**	**-50.23 ± 0.43**
PPO$_S$[B]	-49.30 ± 0.39	-24.89 ± 0.39	-74.19 ± 0.55
PPO$_S$[B→BM]	-29.99 ± 0.16	-70.01 ± 0.72	-100.00 ± 0.74

Table 2 presents the performance of the modified PPO algorithm when initially trained on either *Meander* or *BLine*, and subsequently fine-tuned on the other red agent. The notation follows that of Table 1, with the addition that, alongside copying the network weights, the previous policy is also incorporated as a reference policy within the modified PPO algorithm. For these experiments, a single KL coefficient was selected and applied across all runs. However, further performance improvements can be achieved by tuning this coefficient for each specific training scenario.

When comparing Table 1 and Table 2, it is evident that the modified PPO algorithm produces policies that generalise more effectively across both environments compared to the standard PPO approach. On average, policies trained with the modified PPO achieve rewards that are 22.11% higher than those produced by the standard PPO. The most significant improvement is observed when the model is first trained on *BLine* and subsequently fine-tuned on *Meander*, where the total mean reward improves from −100.00 to −59.38, representing a 40.62% increase.

Table 2. Performance of Sequential Training of Modified PPO Policies (**PPO**$_M$) Across Different Environments (without and with Green Agents)

(a) Without Green Agents

Policy	KL Coefficient	Meander (M)	BLine (B)	Total
PPO$_M$[M]	N/A	-27.94 ± 0.15	-93.60 ± 0.98	-121.54 ± 0.99
PPO$_M$[M→MB]	0.002	**-23.31 ± 0.11**	-21.45 ± 0.34	**-44.76 ± 0.36**
PPO$_M$[B]	N/A	-46.78 ± 0.52	**-12.57 ± 0.19**	-59.35 ± 0.55
PPO$_M$[B→BM]	0.002	-27.07 ± 0.24	-21.73 ± 0.51	-48.80 ± 0.56

(b) With Green Agents

Policy	KL Coefficient	Meander (M)	BLine (B)	Total
PPO$_M$[M]	N/A	**-25.01 ± 0.12**	-61.00 ± 0.73	-86.01 ± 0.74
PPO$_M$[M→MB]	0.002	-25.70 ± 0.11	**-23.79 ± 0.32**	**-49.49 ± 0.34**
PPO$_M$[B]	N/A	-39.72 ± 0.30	-24.56 ± 0.30	-64.28 ± 2.34
PPO$_M$[B→BM]	0.002	-28.15 ± 0.12	-31.23 ± 0.53	-59.38 ± 0.54

Figures 1 and 2 show the impact of varying the KL coefficient on the performance of the modified PPO algorithm. In both cases, the mean reward is plotted on the y-axis while the KL coefficient is plotted on the x-axis. As expected, when the KL coefficient is set too high, the agent is overly constrained by the reference policy, resulting in poor learning of the new agent's behaviour. On the other hand, when the KL coefficient is too low, the algorithm allows for greater deviation from the reference policy, which enables adaptation to the new agent but leads to partial forgetting of the original behaviour. These results highlight the impact of the KL coefficient and the importance of fine-tuning it to balance knowledge retention with the ability to learn new behaviours.

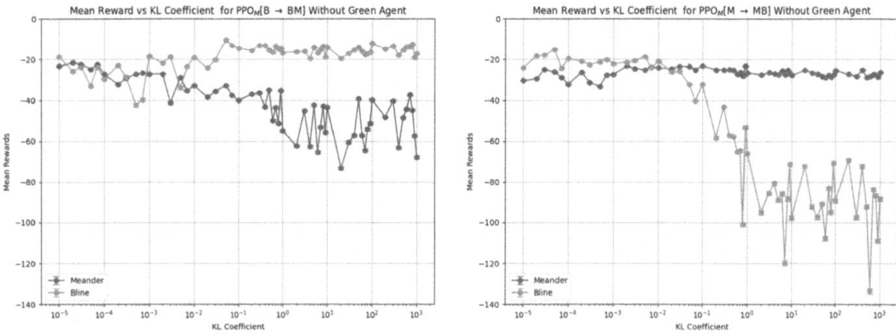

Fig. 1. Results Showing the Effect of the KL Coefficient on Mean Rewards (without Green Agents)

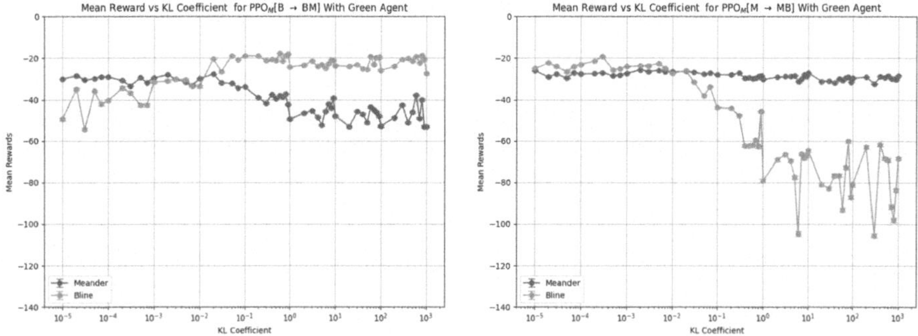

Fig. 2. Results Showing the Effect of the KL Coefficient on Mean Rewards (with Green Agents)

Figures 3 and 4 illustrate the KL divergence between the final policy and the reference policy based on the KL coefficient. In both cases, the KL coefficient is plotted on the x-axis and the resulting KL divergence on the y-axis. As expected, lower KL coefficients permit greater deviation from the reference policy, resulting in higher KL divergence, while higher coefficients enforce stronger regularisation, keeping the policy closer to the reference. Notably, there is a clear difference between the two initialisation conditions: when starting from the *Meander* policy, the final KL divergence remains relatively lower across the coefficient range, suggesting that the policy requires smaller adjustments to accommodate the new task. In contrast, when starting from the *BLine* policy, substantially higher KL divergences are observed at lower coefficients, indicating that greater policy change is necessary to integrate the new behaviour.

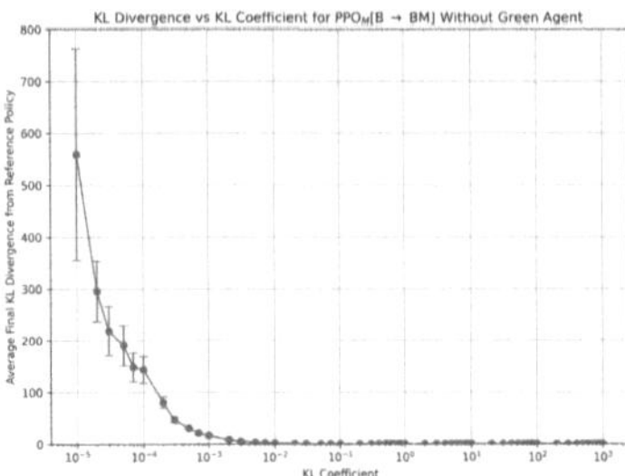

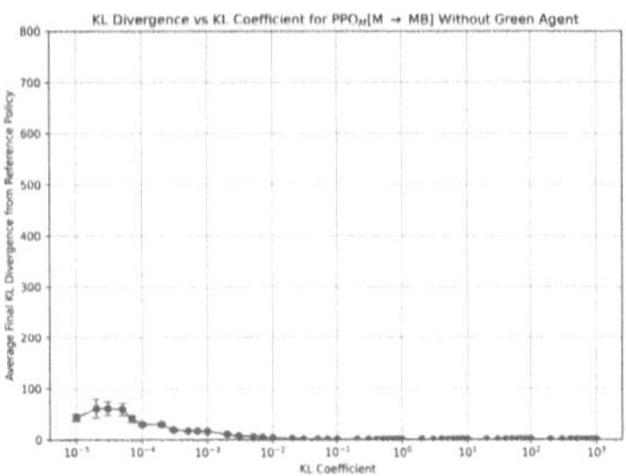

Fig. 3. Results Showing the Effect of the KL Coefficient on KL Divergence (without Green Agents)

5.3 Transfer Learning Multiple Times

In this experiment, we evaluate the ability of the modified PPO algorithm to perform sequential task learning across multiple red agent behaviours while retaining previously acquired knowledge. The setup involves taking the policies from the previous experiment and then continuing training on the other red agent (*Hybrid*) using the modified PPO approach, which incorporates the previous policy as a reference policy. The objective is to investigate how the initial policy may affect the generation of the generic policy.

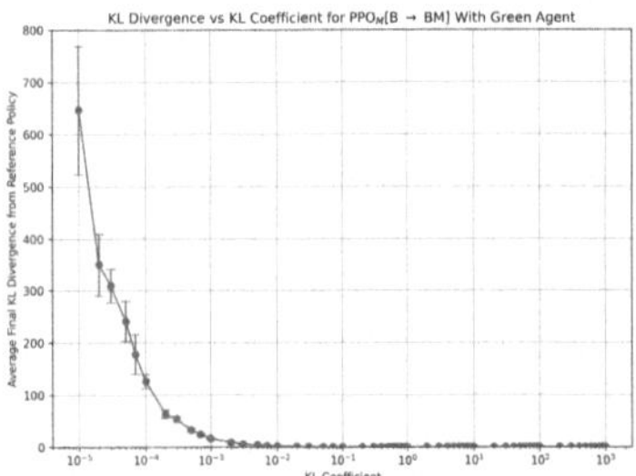

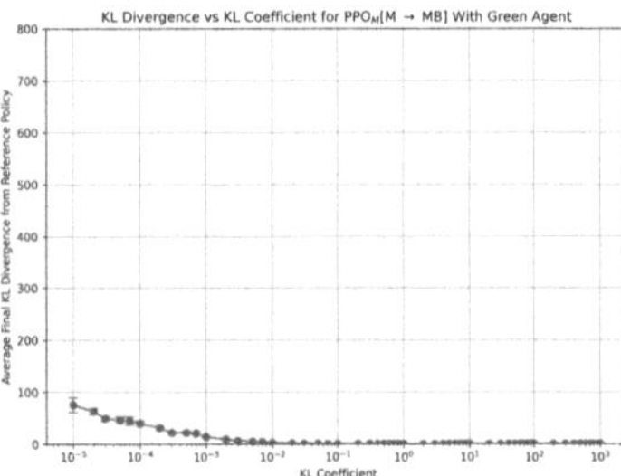

Fig. 4. Results Showing the Effect of the KL Coefficient on KL Divergence (with Green Agents)

As shown in Table 3, the modified PPO policies maintain stable performance even when the process is repeated. The results indicate that successive fine tuning steps do not lead to significant degradation in performance across the evaluated environments, suggesting that the method is robust to multiple rounds of this process.

Table 3. Performance of Modified PPO Policies when additional Red Agents are considered

Policy	KL Coefficient	Meander (M)	BLine (B)	Hybrid (H)	Total
PPO_M[M→MB]	0.002	−25.70 ± 0.11	−23.79 ± 0.32	−19.10 ± 0.15	−68.59 ± 0.37
PPO_M[MB→MBH]	0.002	**−25.44 ± 0.12**	−21.33 ± 0.32	−19.55 ± 0.16	**−66.32 ± 0.38**
PPO_M[B→BM]	0.002	−28.15 ± 0.12	−31.23 ± 0.53	−22.48 ± 0.27	−81.86 ± 0.61
PPO_M[BM→BMH]	0.002	−27.24 ± 0.13	**−21.28 ± 0.34**	**−19.44 ± 0.16**	−67.96 ± 0.40

Figure 5 shows the effect of increasing the KL coefficient on the overall policy performance after repeating the process. As the coefficient increases, performance degradation that occurred during earlier transfer stages is carried forward, resulting in reduced performance not only on the previously learned tasks but also on the most recently introduced red agent. This suggests that overly constraining the policy to remain close to the reference can limit its capacity to recover from prior sub-optimal adaptations, ultimately harming performance across both old and new tasks. However, when the KL coefficient is lower, the mean rewards are stable, when compared with Fig. 2, lower values of the KL coefficient are more stable, suggesting that the more the procedure is repeated, the more stable it would become as it finds the optimal generic policy.

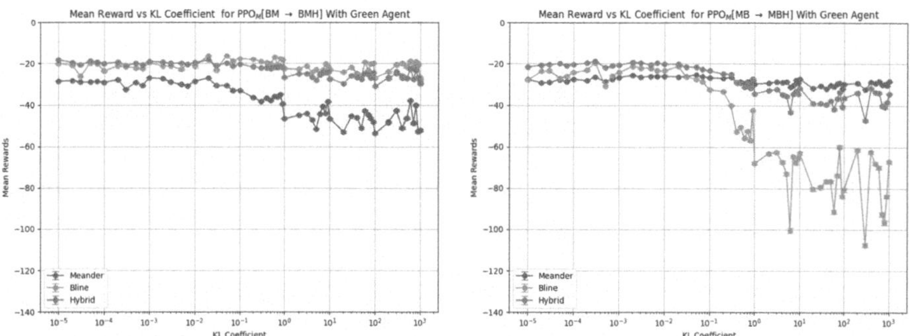

Fig. 5. Results Showing the Effect of the KL Coefficient on Mean Rewards when Repeating the Process for a Third Red Agent (with Green Agents)

Figure 6 presents the KL divergence of the final policy with respect to the reference policy after repeating the process, plotted against the KL coefficient. Interestingly, compared to Fig. 4, the trend has now reversed: the policy that was initially trained on *BLine* exhibits consistently lower KL divergence, while those that started from *Meander* display higher divergence across the coefficient range. This suggests that after multiple transfer stages, the policy initialised from *BLine* remains closer to its reference, whereas the policy initialised from *Meander* requires larger adjustments to accommodate the accumulated changes introduced by subsequent tasks. This observation highlights how the initial training path can influence the long-term policy stability under knowledge retention.

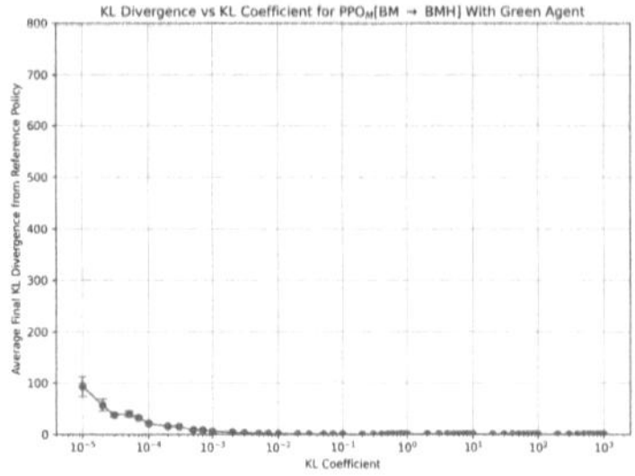

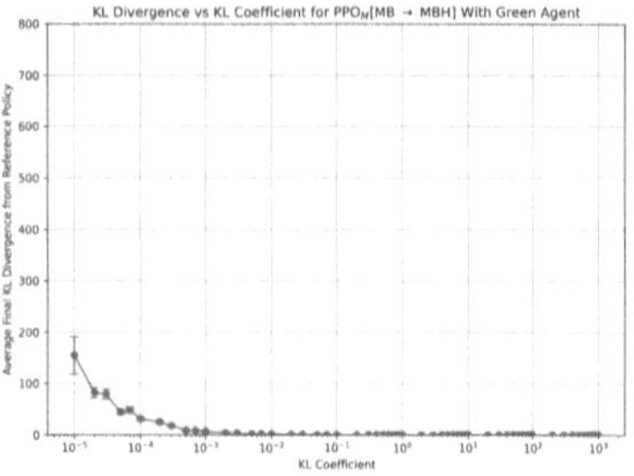

Fig. 6. Results Showing the Effect of the KL Coefficient on KL Divergence when Repeating the Process for a Third Red Agent (with Green Agents)

Table 4 demonstrates that when this process is initialised from the *Hybrid* red agent, the resulting policies maintain comparable performance. The exception is **PPO**$_M$[HB→HBM], where performance against the *BLine* agent deteriorates significantly. This decline is caused by an insufficient KL coefficient, as illustrated in Fig. 7, which shows that increasing the KL coefficient yields better performance.

Table 4. Performance of Modified PPO Policies when initialised from the *Hybrid* Red Agent

Policy	KL Coefficient	Meander (M)	BLine (B)	Hybrid (H)	Total
PPO$_M$[H]	N/A	−36.49 ± 0.24	−30.15 ± 0.45	−21.93 ± 0.22	−88.57 ± 0.56
PPO$_M$[H→HM]	0.002	−28.78 ± 0.11	−29.21 ± 0.25	−22.32 ± 0.15	−80.31 ± 0.31
PPO$_M$[HM→HMB]	0.002	**−27.37 ± 0.15**	−22.02 ± 0.31	−19.43 ± 0.17	**−68.82 ± 0.38**
PPO$_M$[H→HB]	0.002	−39.88 ± 0.34	**−20.94 ± 0.36**	−21.63 ± 0.26	−82.45 ± 0.56
PPO$_M$[HB→HBM]	0.002	−29.35 ± 0.16	−37.39 ± 0.68	−21.97 ± 0.29	−88.71 ± 0.76

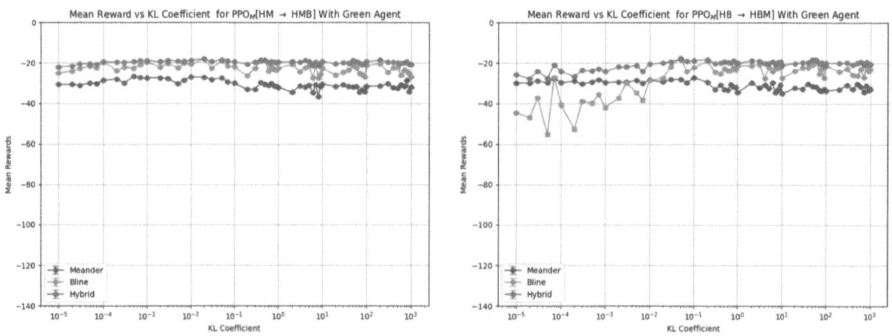

Fig. 7. Results Showing the Effect of the KL Coefficient on Mean Rewards when Initialised from the *Hybrid* Red Agent (with Green Agents).

6 Conclusion

To enable scalable and generic reinforcement learning policies for network defence, we present a modified PPO algorithm designed for sequential, continual multi-task learning. Our approach allows agents to efficiently incorporate new attack behaviours while retaining previously acquired knowledge. Unlike existing methods, it enables controlled knowledge retention during transfer, balancing stability and plasticity. By building on existing policies rather than retraining from scratch, this method reduces computational cost and data requirements, while supporting continuous learning as new threats emerge.

We have demonstrated that the modified PPO algorithm consistently outperforms standard PPO in scenarios involving learning sequential multiple attack behaviours. The inclusion of the reference policy and KL coefficient enables the agent to generalise across distinct attacker behaviours, achieving higher average performance while mitigating catastrophic forgetting. However, results suggest that since the initial policy becomes a reference for controlling knowledge retention, depending on the initial policy, we may achieve a different final policy.

We also observed that, depending on the policy and the new attack behaviour, there is a need for a different KL coefficient, which would require performing hyperparameter tuning for any new combination between existing policy and attack behaviour. An alternative solution, to be investigated as future work, could be to include the KL coefficient as a learnable parameter.

References

1. Acuto, A., Maskell, S., Jack, D.: Defending the unknown: exploring reinforcement learning agents' deployment in realistic, unseen networks. In: CAMLIS, pp. 22–35 (2023)
2. Aljundi, R., Babiloni, F., Elhoseiny, M., Rohrbach, M., Tuytelaars, T.: Memory aware synapses: learning what (not) to forget. In: Proceedings of the European Conference on Computer Vision (ECCV), pp. 139–154 (2018)
3. Andreas, J., Klein, D., Levine, S.: Modular multitask reinforcement learning with policy sketches. In: International Conference on Machine Learning, pp. 166–175. PMLR (2017)
4. Dehghantanha, A., Yazdinejad, A., Parizi, R.M.: Autonomous cybersecurity: evolving challenges, emerging opportunities, and future research trajectories. In: Proceedings of the Workshop on Autonomous Cybersecurity, AutonomousCyber 2024, pp. 1–10. Association for Computing Machinery, New York (2024). https://doi.org/10.1145/3689933.3690832. ISBN 9798400712296
5. Ernst, D., Stan, G.B., Goncalves, J., Wehenkel, L.: Clinical data based optimal STI strategies for HIV: a reinforcement learning approach. In: Proceedings of the 45th IEEE Conference on Decision and Control, pp. 667–672. IEEE (2006)
6. Farooq, M.O., Kunz, T.: A generic blue agent training framework for autonomous cyber operations. In: 2024 IFIP Networking Conference (IFIP Networking), pp. 515–521 (2024). https://doi.org/10.23919/IFIPNetworking62109.2024.10619771. ISSN 1861-2288

7. Henderson, P., Islam, R., Bachman, P., Pineau, J., Precup, D., Meger, D.: Deep reinforcement learning that matters. In: Proceedings of the AAAI Conference on Artificial Intelligence, vol. 32 (2017). https://doi.org/10.1609/aaai.v32i1.11694
8. Isele, D., Cosgun, A.: Selective experience replay for lifelong learning. In: Proceedings of the AAAI Conference on Artificial Intelligence, vol. 32, no. 1 (2018). https://doi.org/10.1609/aaai.v32i1.11595. https://ojs.aaai.org/index.php/AAAI/article/view/11595
9. Kiely, M., Bowman, D., Standen, M., Moir, C.: On Autonomous agents in a cyber defence environment (2023). https://doi.org/10.48550/arXiv.2309.07388, [cs]
10. Kirkpatrick, J., et al.: Overcoming catastrophic forgetting in neural networks. Proc. Natl. Acad. Sci. **114**(13), 3521–3526 (2017). https://doi.org/10.1073/pnas.1611835114. https://www.pnas.org/doi/abs/10.1073/pnas.1611835114
11. Kott, A.: Autonomous Intelligent Cyber-Defense Agent: Introduction and Overview, pp. 1–15 (2023). https://doi.org/10.1007/978-3-031-29269-9_1. ISBN 978-3-031-29268-2
12. Loevenich, J., Adler, E., Hürten, T., Lopes, R.R.F.: Design and evaluation of an autonomous cyber defence agent using DRL and an augmented LLM. Comput. Netw. **262**, 111162 (2025). https://doi.org/10.1016/j.comnet.2025.111162. https://www.sciencedirect.com/science/article/pii/S1389128625001306. ISSN 1389-1286
13. Nevmyvaka, Y., Feng, Y., Kearns, M.: Reinforcement learning for optimized trade execution. In: Proceedings of the 23rd International Conference on Machine Learning, pp. 673–680 (2006)
14. Palmer, G., Parry, C., Harrold, D.J.B., Willis, C.: Deep reinforcement learning for autonomous cyber defence: a survey (2024). https://doi.org/10.48550/arXiv.2310.07745, [cs]
15. Parisotto, E., Ba, J.L., Salakhutdinov, R.: Actor-mimic: deep multitask and transfer reinforcement learning (2016). https://arxiv.org/abs/1511.06342
16. Peng, X.B., Andrychowicz, M., Zaremba, W., Abbeel, P.: Sim-to-real transfer of robotic control with dynamics randomization. In: 2018 IEEE International Conference on Robotics and Automation (ICRA), pp. 3803–3810. IEEE (2018)
17. Rusu, A.A., et al.: Policy distillation (2016). https://arxiv.org/abs/1511.06295
18. Schulman, J., Wolski, F., Dhariwal, P., Radford, A., Klimov, O.: Proximal policy optimization algorithms (2017). https://arxiv.org/abs/1707.06347
19. Schwarz, J., et al.: Progress & compress: a scalable framework for continual learning. In: International Conference on Machine Learning, pp. 4528–4537. PMLR (2018)
20. Symes Thompson, I., Caron, A., Hicks, C., Mavroudis, V.: Entity-based reinforcement learning for autonomous cyber defence. In: Proceedings of the Workshop on Autonomous Cybersecurity, AutonomousCyber 2024, pp. 56–67. Association for Computing Machinery, New York (2024). https://doi.org/10.1145/3689933.3690835. ISBN 979-8-4007-1229-6
21. van de Ven, G.M., Tolias, A.S.: Three scenarios for continual learning (2019). https://arxiv.org/abs/1904.07734
22. Wolk, M., et al.: Beyond CAGE: investigating generalization of learned autonomous network defense policies (2022). https://doi.org/10.48550/arXiv.2211.15557, [cs]
23. Xu, Z., Wu, K., Che, Z., Tang, J., Ye, J.: Knowledge transfer in multi-task deep reinforcement learning for continuous control. In: Proceedings of the 34th International Conference on Neural Information Processing Systems, NIPS 2020. Curran Associates Inc., Red Hook (2020). ISBN 9781713829546

Automated Cyber Defence with Reinforcement Learning in Multi-attack Environments

Joshua Sylvester(✉) and Rogério de Lemos

University of Kent, Canterbury, UK
{jrs71,r.delemos}@kent.ac.uk

Abstract. Reinforcement learning (RL) has shown significant potential in enhancing cyber security by enabling autonomous agents to mitigate network attacks. However, attackers exhibit varying behaviours and knowledge levels, leading to diverse types of attacks. This paper investigates the effectiveness of specific and generic RL policies in mitigating different attacks. Our results demonstrate that while specific RL policies outperform generic ones, their effectiveness depends on correctly identifying the attack type to deploy the appropriate policy. We propose an approach, named Attack Identification for Reinforcement Learning (RLAI) to identify attacks in a network consisting of multiple attacks and normal users, ensuring suitable policy deployment for attack mitigation. Our results demonstrate that the Long Short-Term Memory (LSTM) model effectively identifies attacks while minimally affecting the policy's rewards. Overall, RLAI improves mean rewards by 20.13%, showing the effectiveness of deploying specific RL policies by identifying attacks using an LSTM model.

1 Introduction

Reinforcement learning (RL) shows promise for network defence [18], enabling detection and mitigation of autonomous attacks. So far, RL has been applied to restrictive scenarios consisting of only one malicious agent on the network at a given time [6,7,14]. This is due to RL's limitation of relying on well-defined scenarios where the type and number of malicious agents are known in advance. However, such an assumption in real networks is unrealistic since traffic associated with malicious agents may change.

Although RL has been applied successfully to games [3], the protection of computer networks against malicious behaviour differs significantly, as this "game" of attack and defence lacks established rules due to the ever-changing behaviour of attackers. The attacker can do anything within the system-imposed limits, which introduces a new set of challenges to RL, as the observation and action spaces become overwhelmingly large. RL relies on prior behaviour, which limits its effectiveness in automated cyber defence (ACD) when attacker behaviour could be unpredictable or unknown.

The key challenge in applying reinforcement learning to automated cyber defence is determining which policies to deploy in the presence of a wide range

R. Laborde et al. (Eds.): ESORICS 2025 Workshops, LNCS 16233, pp. 57–74, 2026.
https://doi.org/10.1007/978-3-032-16165-9_4

of malicious behaviours. In this paper, we consider two ACD policy types [19]: generic and specific. *Generic RL policies* are designed to handle a broad range of scenarios by learning from diverse environments or attacks. These policies generalise across attacks rather than targeting any specific one. *Specific RL policies* are tailored to address a narrowly defined problem or scenario by focusing on a particular attack during training. These policies aim for high performance in their targeted context. The main limitation in using generic RL policies lies in the sequential nature of network activity. Many attacks cannot be reliably distinguished from benign behaviour based on a single observation. Instead, accurate identification requires recognising patterns that occur over time. This requires models with strong temporal reasoning to interpret long observation sequences. This issue is particularly acute in dynamic network environments where rapid evolution of attacks exacerbates the difficulty of maintaining consistent temporal representations.

Specific RL policies outperform generic RL policies when attacks are predictable, as they can focus on a narrow behaviour set [19]. However, when multiple specific RL policies are available, determining which one to apply in a given situation becomes a key challenge. Without a strong selection mechanism, the performance advantages of using specific RL policies can be compromised by deploying incorrect or suboptimal policies.

Most of the work on applying reinforcement learning (RL) to changing environments focuses on generic RL policies, which can handle limited changes that may occur in the environment [1,4]. Several techniques have been identified for enhancing generalisation across varying scenarios, such as policy ensembles, L2 regularisation and dropout [5]. However, these techniques exhibit reduced performance in certain scenarios when compared with policies that are specifically optimised for particular environments. [13,18].

In automated cyber defence, generic RL policies are successful in improving robustness. However, they often underperform compared to specific RL policies that are fine-tuned on known attacks [19]. However, generic RL policies retain their edge in environments where unpredictability and variation are common, as they can generalise across different attack vectors and network configurations [19]. Both generic and specific RL policies have been explored in network defence in rigid and unrealistic scenarios under network conditions with no normal users present [19]. For example, a bandit controller has been used to deploy the appropriate specific RL policy depending on how an attack unfolds in the network [7]. However, there is no evidence the bandit controller can handle network environments when normal users or multiple attacks are present, and this highlights a critical limitation in existing ACD strategies. This emphasises the need for approaches that first distinguish between normal and malicious behaviour and then further differentiate between various types of malicious behaviour in realistic network environments. This research aims to bridge this gap by developing an approach capable of identifying and mitigating a diverse range of attacks while in the presence of normal user activity.

This paper makes two contributions by challenging the assumptions that only one attack is present on the network and that normal users are absent [18]. First, we examine the effectiveness of generic versus specific RL policies in environments with multiple attacks and normal users, offering insights into their suitability for automated cyber defence (ACD). Second, we introduce a novel mechanism for attack identification in such environments and demonstrate its effectiveness through evaluation using reinforcement learning (RL) in ACD. As a key outcome of this research, we propose Attack Identification for Reinforcement Learning (RLAI), a mechanism that uses a Long Short-Term Memory (LSTM) model to identify attacks in the TTCP CAGE Challenge 2 [10] before deploying the respective specific RL policy for mitigation.

The structure of the paper is as follows. Section 2 reviews related work. Section 3 outlines the proposed approach, including data processing and attack identification. Section 4 presents experiments comparing RL policies. The paper concludes with findings and future directions.

2 Related Work

In this section, we provide a brief background on reinforcement learning (RL), identify major contributions that use generic and specific policies in autonomous cyber defence (ACD), and raise some ACD challenges related to the proposed approach.

2.1 Reinforcement Learning

Reinforcement learning (RL) is a branch of machine learning where an agent learns to make decisions by interacting with an environment. The agent observes the current state of the environment, selects an action and receives a reward or penalty based on the outcome [9]. Through repeated interactions, the agent refines its policy, mapping states to actions, aiming to maximise cumulative rewards over time [16].

A distinguishing feature of RL is its ability to handle sequential decision-making problems where the consequences of actions may not be immediately apparent [9]. Techniques such as Q-learning, policy gradients, and actor-critic enable RL agents to tackle a wide range of tasks, from simple control problems to complex environments with high-dimensional state spaces [16].

Key components of RL include exploration to discover new strategies, exploitation to leverage known successful behaviours, and balancing these aspects to achieve optimal learning [9]. RL's versatility has made it a cornerstone of research in domains such as robotics, game playing, and autonomous systems [16].

2.2 Generic and Specific Policies in ACD

In the ACD literature, RL-based approaches for detecting and mitigating attacks can be categorised into three different methods [10,19]. These are: generic policies, ensembles of specific and generic policies, and specific policies deployed with an attack identification mechanism.

Although generic RL approaches have received little attention, Farooq and Kunz [6] presents a method for training a generic supervised learning policy that protects against multiple attacks. Their approach reduces reliance on specialised policies, offering a potential unified defence mechanism. However, this framework faces challenges. First, it trains on a limited set of attacks, which may not capture the broad range of real-world threats. As attack diversity increases, the complexity of state-action transitions grows, potentially overwhelming the ability to generalise a single policy. Second, their method requires retraining a new generic policy and specific policies for novel attacks, which is resource-intensive and limits the feasibility of real-time deployment in dynamic defence applications.

Ensembles have demonstrated strong performance in ACD, as shown in the research by Wolk et al. [19] and Kiely et al. [10], which leverage a collection of generic and specific policies trained on varying proportions of attacks.

Instead of ensembles of generic RL policies, an alternative approach in ACD is to use specific RL policies, utilising the methodology proposed by Li et al. [12] called Hierarchical Proximal Policy Optimisation (HiPPO). HiPPO extends the original PPO algorithm [15] by incorporating a hierarchical structure with two levels of policies: a high-level controller and a low-level controller.

NATO's report on ACD emphasised the critical role of attack identification, highlighting that for ACD to be viable, a key challenge lies in detecting and classifying attacks [11]. Some approaches within ACD identify the attack first and then deploy a suitable, specific policy, for example, the bandit controller and the fingerprinting method, both developed for the TTCP CAGE Challenge 2 [10]. For instance, the bandit controller technique relies on a dictionary to map observed behaviours to specific attacks [7]. It applies Q-Learning to iteratively associate the first four network observations of a specific attack. Subsequently, during simulated attack scenarios, the bandit controller leverages the lookup table to classify the attack and determine the appropriate defence strategy for deployment. The drawback of employing this method is that as the simulated scenarios become more complex, the lookup table storing the observations expands, and there is no temporal reasoning over the attack [2]. On the other hand, the fingerprinting method involves analysing the third and fourth observations to distinguish between two different attacks[1]. Compared to the bandit controller, the fingerprinting method requires human analysis to discern discrepancies between the two behaviours and formulate a rule for their distinction.

A key issue with these solutions is that they will not work when normal users are active in the network. When this assumption is relaxed, the observation space becomes exceedingly large, making it infeasible for these solutions to explore and store effectively all possible observations.

[1] https://github.com/john-cardiff/-cyborg-cage-2.

2.3 Changing of Environments in ACD

Generalisation across different environments in automated cyber defence (ACD) has not been extensively studied [19]. Wolk et al. [19] examines the impact of variations in the network structure and host configurations, finding that certain policies exhibit better generalisation. However, these studies are limited to static environments where attacks remain consistent and the network undergoes no structural changes. Acuto et al. [1] investigates the effect of testing policies on unfamiliar network structures and shows a decrease in performance as the testing environment diverges from the training environment. Although dynamic network structures are crucial for realising ACD in practice, existing simulation environments lack easy support for this capability, making them ill-suited for research in this area [17]. Symes Thompson et al. [17] propose an entity-based Gym approach to address this limitation, aiming to make dynamic topologies more accessible to researchers.

3 Methodology

In this section, we introduce Attack Identification for Reinforcement Learning (RLAI), which is our approach for identifying and mitigating attacks in the presence of multiple attacks and normal users in a network environment. First, we provide a brief overview of RLAI. Then, we outline the data collection process and training. Finally, we present an approach for policy deployment that relies on attack identification.

3.1 RLAI Overview

In the automated cyber defence (ACD) literature, policies trained on a single type of attack have been shown to outperform those trained on multiple attacks [19]. For that, they rely on mechanisms to identify attacks and deploy the corresponding specific RL policy for mitigation.

In this paper, we propose Attack Identification for Reinforcement Learning (RLAI), an approach designed to identify and mitigate attacks using specific RL policies. Unlike earlier approaches, RLAI relaxes two critical assumptions: the absence of normal users and the presence of only a single attack within the network.

RLAI utilises a Long Short-Term Memory (LSTM) model to classify attacks based on observed network activity. Once an attack is identified, the system deploys a specific pre-trained policy to mitigate its actions. The LSTM model is trained on attack-specific observations to enable the accurate identification of one or more attacks over time.

Figure 1 illustrates the overall approach of RLAI, encompassing both pre-deployment and post-deployment phases. During pre-deployment, environments are generated from the original environment (*Network Environment*) to collect training data for the LSTM model (*Environment Training LSTM*) and to train

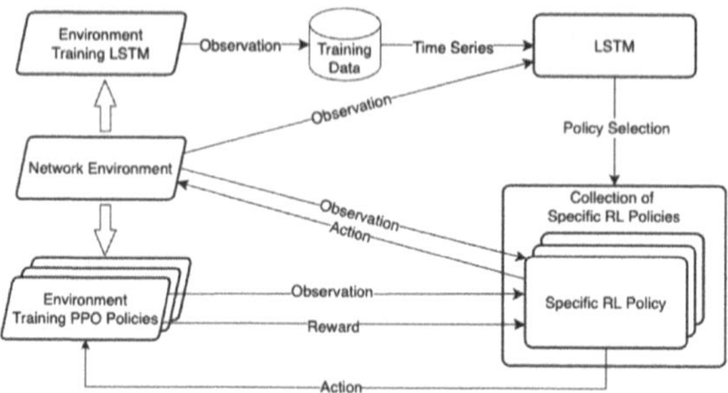

Fig. 1. Overview of Attack Identification for Reinforcement Learning (RLAI).

specific RL policies (*Environment Training PPO Policies*). The collected *Training Data* is then used to train the *LSTM Model.* The specific RL policies are trained by simulating specific attacks within the *Network Environment* using standard RL training methods. Once each specific RL policy is trained, it is added to the *Collection of Specific RL Policies.*

During post-deployment, at each timestep, the *Network Environment* state is observed and passed to the *LSTM Model* for identifying the attack. Initially, the *LSTM Model* provides an approximate attack classification, but as more observations of the *Network Environment* are made, the identification becomes increasingly accurate. This classification is then used to select the most suitable specific RL policy from the *Collection of Specific RL Policies* to mitigate the identified attack. The selected policy determines the appropriate action for the current timestep, depending on the observed state.

By identifying attacks more effectively, RLAI enables the deployment of specific RL policies tailored to the observed identified attacks. Unlike existing approaches, RLAI enhances the flexibility of identification conditions and the robustness of handling multiple attacks [18].

3.2 Data Collection, Training, and Policy Deployment

We train an LSTM model to identify specific attacks from sequential network observations. Data is collected from environments where different attacks operate concurrently with normal users, as described in Algorithm 1. Each environment runs for χ episodes of τ steps. At the start of each episode, the environment is initialised with attackers, normal users, and a defender that performs a `sleep` action to avoid biasing the network state. Observations are recorded at each step and stored per episode.

After each episode, observations are transformed into a time series dataset. This involves constructing a $\tau \times \tau$ matrix in which row i contains the first i observations, thereby capturing the evolving temporal dependencies. Each sequence is labelled with the active attack for supervised training.

The LSTM model is trained on these sequences to learn temporal patterns that distinguish between attacks. Stratified sampling ensures the testing set contains a range of sequence lengths, supporting fair evaluation. The model's output is a probability distribution over known attacks based on past and current observations.

Algorithm 1 Data Collection and Preprocessing

Input: Observations from the environment
Output: Time series dataset of classified attack observations
Dataset Generation:
for each environment $\mathcal{E}$ **do**
  for *episode* $= 1$ to χ **do**
    Initialise $\mathcal{E}$ with attacks, normal users, and a defender
    $a \leftarrow$ *sleep* action
    $s_1 \leftarrow$ initial observation
    for $t = 1$ to τ **do**
      $observations[t] \leftarrow s_t$
      $s_{t+1} \leftarrow f(s_t, a)$
    end for
    Convert the sequence of τ observations into a time series
    Store attack labels as ground truth and append to dataset
  end for
end for

During deployment, the system operates online, as outlined in Algorithm 2. At each time step t, the environment state s_t is observed and passed into the LSTM. The model updates its hidden state and predicts the current attack $\hat{y}_t$. The corresponding pre-learned policy $\pi_{\hat{y}_t}$ is then retrieved and used to select and execute an appropriate action a_t.

Algorithm 2 LSTM-Based Attack Identification and Policy Deployment

Input: Observations from the environment
Output: Identified attack(s) and deployed policy
Online Identification and Policy Deployment:
for each time step $t = 1, 2, \ldots$ **do**
  Observe current state s_t
  Update hidden state: $h_t \leftarrow \text{LSTM}(s_t, h_{t-1})$
  Predict attack type(s): $\hat{y}_t = f(h_t)$
  Retrieve and deploy corresponding policy $\pi_{\hat{y}_t}$
  Execute action $a_t \sim \pi_{\hat{y}_t}$
end for

4 Experiments

This section describes the experiments conducted and consists of the following key parts: a brief description of CybORG - TTCP CAGE Challenge 2, experimental setup, definition and evaluation of generic and specific reinforcement learning (RL) policies, identification of attacks, and finally, selection and deployment of specific RL policies.

4.1 CybORG TTCP CAGE Challenge 2

In our research, we use CybORG, a cyber-security simulation environment, for training RL policies to defend a network from attacks. In CybORG, agents are commonly categorised by their roles within a network: red agents represent adversaries attempting to compromise systems, blue agents act as defenders mitigating threats, and green agents simulate normal user activity. TTCP CAGE Challenge 2 is a CybORG scenario comprised of a simple network topology, where the red agents' objective is to gain control of an operational server and disrupt its operations [10]. The blue agent aims to defend the network from the red agent and stop it from reaching the operational server.

In its original setup, the TTCP CAGE Challenge 2 supported only a single red agent per environment. In our modified version, multiple red agents can coexist within the same environment. For CybORG to support multiple red agents, modifications were made to its simulation code and the TTCP CAGE Challenge 2 configuration file.

In this scenario, red agents use a defined set of offensive actions aligned with MITRE ATT&CK[2] techniques and CVEs [10]. They begin with remote system discovery (T1018) using active scanning to identify live hosts, followed by network service scanning (T1046) to detect open ports and services. Then, they attempt to exploit remote services (T1210), escalate privileges (TA0004), and finally disrupt services (T1489) to achieve their goal.

Three types of red agents are used in our experiments:

- *Meander*: has no prior network knowledge and attempts to compromise every host within a subnet before moving on.
- *BLine*: follows a known path of specific actions to reach the operational server.
- *StartLine*: a variant of *BLine* that may change its path if removed from a node, unlike *BLine*, which reattempts the same route.

The modified code, configuration files, and *StartLine* red agent have been publicly released and are available here.

4.2 Experimental Setup

When multiple red agents are present, it becomes essential to identify each one based on its attack behaviour within the wider network activity to apply an appropriate mitigation strategy. To evaluate this, six environments were configured to cover all combinations of red agents, both with and without a green agent: *Meander*, *BLine*, and both *Meander* and *BLine*.

[2] https://attack.mitre.org/.

The LSTM model used for attacker identification is trained with a batch size of 32, sparse categorical cross-entropy as the loss function, and the Adam optimiser. Training is performed over 5 epochs.

The architecture of the LSTM model is as follows: a masking layer for variable-length sequences, followed by two LSTM layers with 104 and 52 neurons, respectively (each with a dropout of 0.2), a dense layer with 30 ReLU-activated neurons, and a softmax output layer for classification.

Each policy is trained for 1,000,000 timesteps and evaluated over 1,000 episodes of 50 steps each. To account for training variability, five independent policies are trained per setup, and results are averaged. Performance is measured using mean episodic rewards, with the standard error (SE) calculated to reflect variability [8].

All experiments were run on an Intel Xeon Gold 5317 processor with an NVIDIA A100 Tensor Core GPU. The software versions used are Python (3.10.12), NumPy (2.1.3), Pandas (2.2.3), SciPy (1.15.2), and Matplotlib (3.10.1) for data processing and visualisation. TensorFlow (2.19.0), Keras (3.9.2), and PyTorch (2.7.0+cu118) supported model development, while Stable-Baselines3 (2.6.0), Gym (0.26.2), and Gymnasium (1.1.1) were used for reinforcement learning.

4.3 Defining and Evaluating Generic RL Policies

To justify the use of a collection of specific RL policies over a single generic RL policy, this section presents experiments aimed at identifying the generic RL policy that will serve as the baseline for our analyses.

The training of both generic and specific RL policies uses Proximal Policy Optimisation (PPO) [15], a reinforcement learning algorithm. We use PPO because it has demonstrated superior performance in the TTCP CAGE Challenge 2 environment [19], making it the most suitable choice for training both the baseline generic RL policy and the attack-specific RL policies.

In the following, we compare generic RL policies in terms of performance and robustness. Performance refers to the mean rewards an agent achieves, while robustness measures how well it maintains performance across different attack types. However, accounting for a broad range of attacks can increase training time and cost while potentially reducing overall model performance.

As a first step, we evaluated the robustness and effectiveness of three environment setups using PPO policies, each capturing a different combination of attacks across various environments. The tested setups include:

- *PPO Generic M&B*: separate environments where network access is restricted to one attack type at a time.
- *PPO Generic MB*: a single environment where both attack types access the network simultaneously.
- *PPO Generic M&B&MB*: a hybrid approach combining the two previous setups.

Table 1 presents the performance of generic PPO policies across different environments (without and with green agents) as mean rewards with standard errors

(SE) and their respective total scores. These results cover three environments: *Meander* (M), *BLine* (B), and *Meander BLine* (MB).

Table 1. Performance of Generic RL Policies Across Different Environments (Without and With Green Agents)

(a) Without Green Agents

Policy	**Meander (M)**	**BLine (B)**	**Meander BLine (MB)**	**Total**
PPO Generic M&B	**-23.16 ± 0.21**	-11.60 ± 0.27	**-46.41 ± 0.54**	**-81.17 ± 0.64**
PPO Generic MB	-41.73 ± 0.25	-64.36 ± 1.63	-55.56 ± 0.36	-161.65 ± 1.69
PPO Generic M&B&MB	-23.72 ± 0.23	**-10.93 ± 0.11**	-48.21 ± 0.50	-82.86 ± 0.56

(b) With Green Agents

Policy	**Meander (M)**	**BLine (B)**	**Meander BLine (MB)**	**Total**
PPO Generic M&B	**-23.42 ± 0.16**	-23.31 ± 0.69	**-44.74 ± 0.51**	-91.47 ± 0.87
PPO Generic MB	-33.46 ± 0.25	-51.15 ± 1.24	-50.03 ± 0.39	-134.64 ± 1.31
PPO Generic M&B&MB	-25.82 ± 0.15	**-15.41 ± 0.24**	-45.09 ± 0.43	**-86.32 ± 0.50**

Without green agents, *PPO Generic M&B* achieves the highest total mean reward (âĂŞ81.17 ± 0.64), demonstrating its capability in single-attack environments. In contrast, *PPO Generic MB* performs the worst, particularly in *BLine* (âĂŞ64.36 ± 1.63) and overall (âĂŞ161.65 ± 1.69), highlighting challenges in policy optimisation when multiple attacks share an environment. The hybrid *PPO Generic M&B&MB* achieves a comparable total reward (âĂŞ82.86 ± 0.56).

With green agents, performance generally declines. *PPO Generic M&B* drops to (−91.47 ± 0.87), indicating difficulty in adapting to more complex environments. *PPO Generic MB* improves slightly (−134.64 ± 1.31) but remains the weakest. *PPO Generic M&B&MB* maintains similar performance (−86.32 ± 0.50).

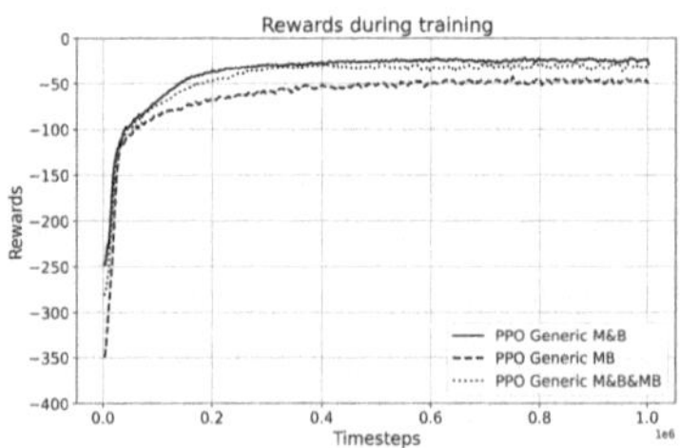

Fig. 2. Learning curves for generic RL policies trained across multiple red agents. (Color figure online)

To further examine the performance of the generic RL policies, Fig. 2 presents their learning curves, illustrating how performance evolves. These curves indicate convergence to a stable state around 600,000 timesteps.

Discussion. Although *PPO Generic M&B* delivers the best performance, robustness is a key factor for real-world applications. *PPO Generic MB* is trained with multiple attacks and offers key advantages. Firstly, when green agents are added, there is a significant performance increase, showing the potential for effective mitigation in more complex settings. Although *PPO Generic MB* performance is lower, it is the most suitable generic RL policy regarding robustness, as its performance did not degrade when in more complex environments.

4.4 Scalability of Generic RL Policies

This section presents experiments on the scalability limits of generic PPO policies when more attacks are introduced. We compare two generic models: one in an environment where *Meander* and *BLine* are simultaneously active, and the other in an environment where *Meander*, *BLine*, and *StartLine* are simultaneously active.

Results in Table 2 show that without a green agent, performance is similar, except for *BLine*, where the *PPO Generic MBS* model achieves a significantly better reward (-25.61 ± 0.33 vs -64.36 ± 1.63), likely due to *StartLine* being a variant of *BLine*. With a green agent present, *PPO Generic MB* generally performs better, except again on *BLine*, suggesting that added agent complexity increases the difficulty of observation-action learning.

Table 2. Comparison of Generic RL Policies Across Different Environments (Without and With Green Agents)

(a) Without Green Agents

Policy	**Meander (M)**	**BLine (B)**	**Meander BLine (MB)**	**Meander BLine Startline (MBS)**	**Total**
PPO Generic MB	**-41.73 ± 0.25**	-64.36 ± 1.63	-55.56 ± 0.36	-55.33 ± 0.36	-216.98 ± 1.73
PPO Generic MBS	-45.00 ± 0.23	**-25.61 ± 0.33**	**-53.11 ± 0.18**	**-53.20 ± 0.19**	**-176.92 ± 0.48**

(b) With Green Agents

Policy	**Meander (M)**	**BLine (B)**	**Meander BLine (MB)**	**Meander BLine Startline (MBS)**	**Total**
PPO Generic MB	**-33.46 ± 0.25**	-51.15 ± 1.24	**-50.03 ± 0.39**	**-47.28 ± 0.31**	**-181.92 ± 1.36**
PPO Generic MBS	-48.22 ± 0.54	**-40.60 ± 0.54**	-58.50 ± 0.26	-58.52 ± 0.24	-205.84 ± 0.84

Overall, the experiment demonstrates that as the environment gets more complex, such as when green agents are introduced, and more attacks are added to the training of a generic RL policy, its effectiveness diminishes, highlighting the limited scalability of generic RL policies compared to specific RL policy solutions.

4.5 Defining and Evaluating Specific RL Policies

In the following, we evaluate the effectiveness of specific RL policies trained on specific attacks. The two PPO policies, trained separately on *BLine* and *Meander* environments, were tested across all three environments (*BLine*, *Meander*, and *Meander BLine*). Table 3 shows that each policy excels in the environment it was trained on but struggles in unfamiliar ones.

Table 3. Performance of Specific RL Policies Across Different Environments (With and Without Green Agents

(a) Without Green Agents

Policy	Meander (M)	BLine (B)	Meander BLine (MB)	Total
PPO Specific M	**-24.26 ± 0.19**	-118.13 ± 2.19	**-59.07 ± 0.80**	-201.46 ± 2.34
PPO Specific B	-53.51 ± 0.82	**-13.26 ± 0.46**	-117.39 ± 1.49	**-184.16 ± 1.75**

(b) With Green Agents

Policy	Meander (M)	BLine (B)	Meander BLine (MB)	Total
PPO Specific M	**-25.54 ± 0.18**	-52.61 ± 0.94	**-47.69 ± 0.42**	**-125.84 ± 1.06**
PPO Specific B	-49.18 ± 0.61	**-21.99 ± 0.81**	-77.17 ± 1.00	-148.34 ± 1.36

PPO Specific M performs well in the *Meander* (-24.26 ± 0.19) environment but deteriorates in *BLine* (-118.13 ± 2.19) and *Meander BLine* (-59.07 ± 0.80) environments. Similarly, *PPO Specific B* performs well in the *BLine* (-13.26 ± 0.46) environment but declines in *Meander* (-53.51 ± 0.82) and *Meander BLine* (-117.39 ± 1.49) environments. This trend persists with green agents, confirming these policies lack generalisability.

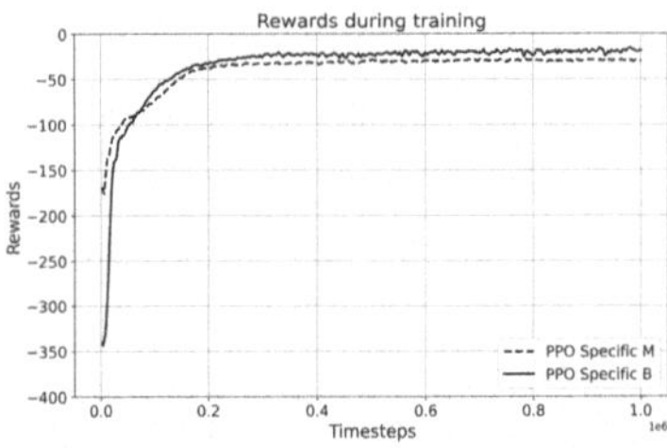

Fig. 3. Learning curves for specific RL policies trained against individual red agents. (Color figure online)

To further examine the performance of the specific RL policies, we present Fig. 3, which shows the learning curves for the specific RL policies, illustrating the progression of performance over time. Each policy's rewards are recorded for its respective training environment. Compared to Fig. 2, these curves converge to a stable state close to 400,000 timesteps, which demonstrates that policies learn better on a narrower range of red agents as their behaviour is more constant during training.

Discussion. The difficulty specific RL policies face in generalising across multiple attacks underscores the need for an approach that identifies the attack and selects the most appropriate policy. Our results suggest that effective cyber defence in multi-attack environments depends not only on having specialised policies but also on the ability to recognise the nature of an ongoing attack.

A promising solution is to incorporate an attack identification mechanism capable of classifying attacker behaviour based on temporal network activity. LSTM models are well-suited for this task, as they can learn behavioural patterns over time. Additionally, in the context of multiple specific RL policies, scalability is relevant because new attacks need to be considered. When considering a new attack, its respective specific RL policy needs to be trained and added to the collection of specific RL policies. In the case of a generic RL policy, when a new attack is introduced, the training steps increase to gather a generalisation over all attacks. This also brings up the problem of reducing performance as more attacks are added, since the observation action pairs will become more complex.

4.6 Identifying Attacks

In this section, we examine how LSTM models can identify types of attacks based on their behavioural patterns.

LSTM-Based Attack Identification. Identifying attacks is essential for selecting the appropriate specific RL policy, as policies tend to perform best in environments they were trained on. To evaluate the feasibility of identifying attacks, an LSTM model was trained to classify three types of attacks: *Meander*, *BLine*, and *Meander BLine*, using sequential network activity as input. Each attack type was trained on with 20,000 episodes and tested with 1,000 episodes (each 50 steps long).

Two experimental settings were considered: (1) without green agents (only attack activity), and (2) with green agents (introducing normal background behaviour).

Table 4. LSTM Accuracy and F1 Score in Identifying Environments (without and with Green Agents)

	Metric	Step 3	Step 4	Step 5	Step 6	Step 7	Step 8	Step 9	Step 10
Without Green Agents	Accuracy	0.60	0.99	1.00	1.00	1.00	1.00	1.00	1.00
	F1 Score	0.53	0.99	1.00	1.00	1.00	1.00	1.00	1.00
With Green Agents	Accuracy	0.57	0.89	0.93	0.98	0.99	0.99	1.00	1.00
	F1 Score	0.63	0.89	0.93	0.98	0.99	0.99	1.00	1.00

Table 4 shows classification accuracy from Step 3 to Step 10. Without green agents, accuracy reaches 60% by Step 3 and exceeds 99% from Step 4 onward, indicating early and clear attack patterns. With green agents, early accuracy drops to 57%, and perfect classification is delayed until Step 10, reflecting increased ambiguity due to benign activity.

Table 5. LSTM Response Time

LSTM Neural Network	Mean Runtime (ms)	Std Dev (ms)
Without Green Agents	70.62	11.80
With Green Agents	72.47	11.66

In this experiment, the response time of the LSTM model is measured. The current simulators operate in an abstract notion of time measured in steps, where at each time step, an observation of the current network state is received. The experiments were performed on a system featuring an Intel Xeon Gold 5317 processor, with execution constrained to a single CPU core.

Table 5 presents a comparison of the response time of the LSTM model under two conditions: without green agents and with green agents. Both the mean and the standard deviation of the response times are reported in milliseconds.

The inclusion of green agents results in a slight increase in the mean response time, rising from 70.62 ms without green agents to 72.47 ms with green agents. This corresponds to an approximate 2.6% increase. Despite this increase, the standard deviation remains almost unchanged (11.80 ms compared to 11.66 ms), indicating that the variability in response times is not significantly affected by the presence of green agents.

Overall, the LSTM's responsiveness remains fast under both conditions, supporting its suitability for identifying red agents in real environments.

Discussion. These findings strongly support the feasibility of an LSTM-based attack identification mechanism for policy selection. The rapid convergence to high accuracy suggests it could quickly classify an attack and deploy the appropriate mitigations without requiring an extended observation period. This approach would mitigate the generalisation issues observed in generic RL policies by ensuring the selection of the most appropriate environment-specific RL policy.

4.7 Deploying Specific RL Policies

In this experiment, we integrate the LSTM-based attack identification mechanism with specific RL policies to assess its effectiveness in mitigating different attacks. The primary objective is to identify the attack at each timestep and deploy the corresponding policy trained specifically for that attack.

The experiment leverages the LSTM-based attack identification mechanism described earlier, which classifies attacks based on their observed behaviours.

Once the attack is identified, the system deploys the corresponding PPO policy, either trained on *Meander* (*PPO Specific M*) or *BLine* (*PPO Specific B*) environments.

Performance is measured across three environments: *Meander*, *BLine*, and *Meander BLine*, both without and with green agents. Table 6 presents the results, showing the mean rewards with standard error for each specific RL policy. Some of the experiments were not repeated since evidence from previous experiments shows that specific RL policies perform best in the environment in which they were trained. For example, for the environment *Meander*, *PPO Specific B* is omitted because the results from Table 3 show that *PPO Specific M* performs much better.

Table 6. Comparison of Specific and Generic RL Policies Across Different Environments (With and Without Green Agents)

Policy	Meander (M)	BLine (B)	Meander BLine (MB)	Total
PPO Specific M	**-26.88 ± 0.26**	-	-71.05 ± 0.91	**-116.95 ± 1.08**
PPO Specific B	-	**-19.02 ± 0.51**	-	
PPO Generic MB	-41.73 ± 0.25	-64.36 ± 1.63	**-55.56 ± 0.36**	-161.65 ± 1.69

(b) With Green Agents

Policy	Meander (M)	BLine (B)	Meander BLine (MB)	Total
PPO Specific M	**-29.41 ± 0.21**	-	-61.06 ± 0.64	**-117.62 ± 1.01**
PPO Specific B	-	**-27.15 ± 0.75**	-	
PPO Generic MB	-33.46 ± 0.25	-51.15 ± 1.24	**-50.03 ± 0.39**	-134.64 ± 1.32

The difference in results between Tables 3 and 6 is that in the former, the specific RL policy is applied directly to the environment containing the respective attack, while in Table 6, the LSTM model identifies the attack at each step.

Table 6 demonstrates that using the LSTM model combined with specific RL policies results in improved performance across environments compared to the generic RL policy. Moreover, the impact on mean rewards by introducing an LSTM model is negligible compared to specific RL policies being applied directly to the environment containing the respective attack.

Figure 4 shows box plots of both generic and specific RL policies, with the blue line indicating the median and the red dot showing the mean. This shows that for the *Meander* and *BLine* environments, the variation in results suggests that when the generic RL policy underperforms, its performance drops are more severe. This is reflected in both a lower ceiling and a significantly lower floor compared to the specific RL policy. Additionally, this pattern is evident in the mean values; some policies have a mean that falls well below the median, indicating that the worst-case performance is considerably lower.

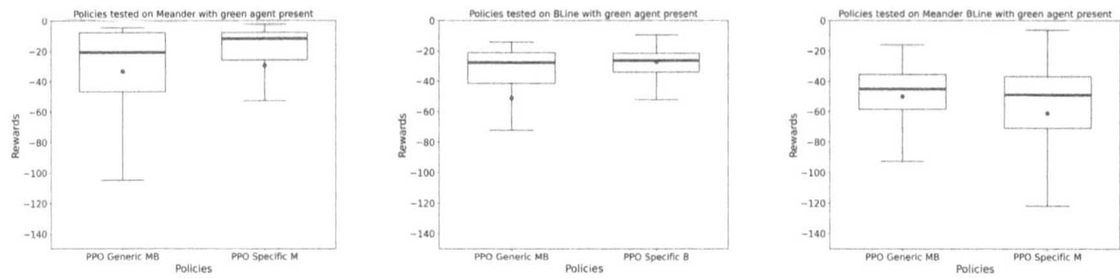

Fig. 4. Results comparing generic and specific RL policies with attack identification in the presence of green agents. (Color figure online)

Discussion. These findings highlight the benefits of selecting specific RL policies based on attack identification. The LSTM model effectively mitigates the shortcomings of the generic RL policy by ensuring that the most suitable specific RL policy is deployed at each timestep. While the generic RL policy offers ease of use by accommodating multiple attack strategies within a single model, its reduced performance underscores the trade-off between generalisation and specialisation. The LSTM-based attack identification mechanism provides a compelling alternative. Since it balances robustness with high performance by leveraging an identification mechanism to deploy the appropriate defence strategy.

5 Conclusion

In this paper, we propose Attack Identification for Reinforcement Learning (RLAI) as a mechanism for real-time attack identification in environments with multiple attackers and normal users. By identifying attacks, RLAI enables the selection and deployment of specific reinforcement learning (RL) policies tailored to mitigate different attacks. The preference for specific RL policies over generic ones stems from our experimental findings, which demonstrate that the former can outperform the latter. RLAI employs a Long Short-Term Memory (LSTM) network to distinguish between different types of attacks, with minimal impact on real-time performance in terms of policy rewards.

While our experimental results are promising, the scalability of the LSTM model presents a challenge, as it requires retraining whenever new attacks emerge. However, updating the LSTM model is still less demanding than adapting a generic RL policy, making it a more practical solution in dynamic environments.

Several challenges remain to be addressed in future work. One key challenge involves improving environmental observation to detect new attacks and extract their behavioural patterns, enabling the synthesis of new specific RL policies. Another challenge is ensuring that multiple specific RL policies can coexist to detect and mitigate simultaneous attacks. A promising direction for addressing this issue is the integration of multi-agent reinforcement learning, allowing for coordinated responses across different policies.

References

1. Acuto, A., Maskell, S., Jack, D.: Defending the unknown: exploring reinforcement learning agents' deployment in realistic, unseen networks. In: CAMLIS, pp. 22–35 (2023)
2. Applebaum, A., et al.: Bridging automated to autonomous cyber defense: foundational analysis of tabular Q-Learning. In: Proceedings of the 15th ACM Workshop on Artificial Intelligence and Security, pp. 149–159, AISec'22, Association for Computing Machinery, New York (2022). https://doi.org/10.1145/3560830.3563732, ISBN 978-1-4503-9880-0
3. Berner, C., et al.: Dota 2 with large scale deep reinforcement learning. arXiv preprint arXiv:1912.06680 (2019)
4. Cobbe, K., Klimov, O., Hesse, C., Kim, T., Schulman, J.: Quantifying generalization in reinforcement learning. In: Chaudhuri, K., Salakhutdinov, R. (eds.) Proceedings of the 36th International Conference on Machine Learning, Proceedings of Machine Learning Research, vol. 97, pp. 1282–1289, PMLR (2019). https://proceedings.mlr.press/v97/cobbe19a.html
5. Farebrother, J., Machado, M.C., Bowling, M.: Generalization and Regularization in DQN (2020). arXiv:1810.00123 [cs]
6. Farooq, M.O., Kunz, T.: A generic blue agent training framework for autonomous cyber operations. In: 2024 IFIP Networking Conference (IFIP Networking), pp. 515–521 (2024). https://doi.org/10.23919/IFIPNetworking62109.2024.10619771, iSSN: 1861-2288
7. Foley, M., Hicks, C., Highnam, K., Mavroudis, V.: Autonomous network defence using reinforcement learning. In: Proceedings of the 2022 ACM on Asia Conference on Computer and Communications Security, pp. 1252–1254, ACM, Nagasaki (2022). https://doi.org/10.1145/3488932.3527286, ISBN 978-1-4503-9140-5
8. Henderson, P., Islam, R., Bachman, P., Pineau, J., Precup, D., Meger, D.: Deep reinforcement learning that matters. In: Proceedings of the AAAI Conference on Artificial Intelligence. vol. 32 (2017). https://doi.org/10.1609/aaai.v32i1.11694
9. Kaelbling, L.P., Littman, M.L., Moore, A.W.: Reinforcement learning: a survey. J. Artifi. Intell. Res. **4**, 237–285 (1996)
10. Kiely, M., Bowman, D., Standen, M., Moir, C.: On autonomous agents in a cyber defence environment (2023). https://doi.org/10.48550/arXiv.2309.07388, http://arxiv.org/abs/2309.07388, arXiv:2309.07388 [cs]
11. Kott, A., et al.: Autonomous intelligent cyber-defense agent (AICA) reference architecture. release 2.0. arXiv preprint arXiv:1803.10664 (2018)
12. Li, A.C., Florensa, C., Clavera, I., Abbeel, P.: Sub-policy adaptation for hierarchical reinforcement learning (2020). https://arxiv.org/abs/1906.05862
13. Lowe, R., WU, Y., Tamar, A., Harb, J., Pieter Abbeel, O., Mordatch, I.: Multi-agent actor-critic for mixed cooperative-competitive environments. In: Guyon, I., et al., (eds.) Advances in Neural Information Processing Systems, vol. 30, Curran Associates, Inc. (2017)
14. Purves, T., Kyriakopoulos, K.G., Jenkins, S., Phillips, I., Dudman, T.: Causally aware reinforcement learning agents for autonomous cyber defence. Knowl. Based Syst. **304**, 112521 (2024). https://doi.org/10.1016/j.knosys.2024.112521, ISSN 0950-7051
15. Schulman, J., Wolski, F., Dhariwal, P., Radford, A., Klimov, O.: Proximal policy optimization algorithms (2017). https://arxiv.org/abs/1707.06347

16. Sutton, R.S., Barto, A.G.: Reinforcement learning: an introduction. MIT Press (2018)
17. Symes Thompson, I., Caron, A., Hicks, C., Mavroudis, V.: Entity-based reinforcement learning for autonomous cyber defence. In: Proceedings of the Workshop on Autonomous Cybersecurity, pp. 56–67. AutonomousCyber '24, Association for Computing Machinery, New York (2024). https://doi.org/10.1145/3689933.3690835, ISBN 979-8-4007-1229-6
18. Vyas, S., Hannay, J., Bolton, A., Burnap, P.P.: Automated cyber defence: a review (2023). arXiv:2303.04926 [cs]
19. Wolk, M., et al.: Beyond CAGE: investigating generalization of learned autonomous network defense policies (2022). https://doi.org/10.48550/arXiv.2211.15557, arXiv:2211.15557 [cs]

An Explainable Multimodal Framework for Phishing Attack Detection

Shokooh Khandan(✉), Mohammadreza Tabatabaei, Ifeanyi Bryan Uzoatu, Olamide Jogunola, Yakubu Tsado, and Tooska Dargahi

Manchester Metropolitan University, Manchester, UK
{s.khandan,o.jogunola,y.tsado,t.dargahi}@mmu.ac.uk,
{mohammadreza.tabatabaei,ifeanyi.b.uzoatu}@stu.mmu.ac.uk

Abstract. Email and URL phishing attacks continue to pose significant threats to cyber security. Traditional detection techniques, such as heuristic-based and signature-based methods, often struggle with the dynamic nature of phishing tactics and the increasing use of adversarial techniques to evade detection. Machine learning (ML) and deep learning (DL) approaches, while promising, require extensive labelled datasets and computational resources, and can be vulnerable to adversarial attacks. The need for more robust, explainable, and adaptive phishing detection systems that can accurately identify phishing attempts across diverse platforms and communication channels is critical. In this paper, we propose a multimodal phishing detection system that analyses both email content and URL features. The system uses advanced preprocessing methods and ML models tailored for each phishing type and employs late fusion technique to integrate the outputs of the independently trained models. To make the system's decisions more transparent, we incorporate explainable AI techniques, including Shapley Additive explanations (SHAP), Local Interpretable Model-agnostic Explanations (LIME) and Feature Importance (FI) to highlight the key features influencing the detection decision. Additionally, detected threats are processed by a Large Language Model (LLM) to provide context-aware defensive recommendations based on the MITRE D3FEND framework. Our extensive experiments, using 5-fold cross-validation, show high accuracy ($\approx 98\%$ for emails and $\approx 97\%$ for URLs) and over 97% precision and recall, highlighting the effectiveness of our approach. This paper demonstrates that combining multimodal data and explainable AI enhances the robustness of phishing detection systems.

Keywords: Phishing Detection · Multimodal Analysis · Explainable AI

1 Introduction

Phishing attacks exploit human trust through deceptive emails or URLs to steal credentials or distribute malware [1]. According to the Anti-Phishing Working Group (APWG), the number of phishing emails increased significantly from

The original version of the chapter has been revised. A correction to this chapter can be found at https://doi.org/10.1007/978-3-032-16165-9_35

R. Laborde et al. (Eds.): ESORICS 2025 Workshops, LNCS 16233, pp. 75–91, 2026.
https://doi.org/10.1007/978-3-032-16165-9_5

44,008 in the first quarter of 2020 to 989,123 attacks in the final quarter of 2024, with monthly figures ranging between approximately 290,000 and 358,000 attacks [2]. The severity of phishing email attacks often resulting in significant financial and reputational damage to individuals and organisations. Recent studies highlight that phishing campaigns increasingly mimic trusted brands and services, making them harder to detect and more likely to succeed [3]. These attacks can lead to unauthorised access to sensitive systems, data breaches, and the deployment of ransomware. In addition, Artificial Intelligence (AI)-generated content has made phishing emails more convincing, increasing the likelihood of user interaction and subsequent compromise [4].

Phishing attacks increasingly exploit multi-vector strategies, combining deceptive text with malicious URLs to evade conventional detection. The textual content leverages urgency, impersonation, or emotional manipulation, while embedded URLs redirect users to fraudulent sites for credential theft or malware delivery. This dual-modality complicates detection, necessitating models capable of interpreting both linguistic and structural indicators [5]. As phishing detection systems may generate a high volume of alerts many of which are false positives. This can overwhelm security teams, leading to alert fatigue, where analysts begin to ignore or delay responses, inadvertently allowing real threats to go unnoticed [6,7].

Conventional methods like spam filters and URL blacklists are increasingly evaded through sophisticated social engineering. Although AI approaches, including machine learning (ML) and deep learning (DL), can capture complex patterns, their non-transparent nature often undermines user trust due to limited interpretability. Moreover, phishing and other malicious behaviours are inherently multimodal, manifesting across email text, embedded links, and webpage structures [8]. Traditional unimodal ML models often lack robustness in dynamic environments due to their reliance on stable data distributions. These models fail to capture complementary contextual signals, such as semantic cues in text and structural patterns in URLs, limiting their effectiveness in tasks like phishing detection and misinformation filtering..

To overcome these limitations, we propose an explainable multimodal phishing detection framework. The main contributions of the paper include:

- We develop two parallel data processing pipelines: one for emails, extracting linguistic and metadata features, and another for URLs, capturing domain and path-based characteristics from embedded links. Each pipeline includes pre-processing, feature engineering, and correlation analysis to remove redundant features.
- To improve model interpretability, we apply XAI techniques, including Feature Importance, Shapley Additive explanations (SHAP), and Local Interpretable Model-agnostic Explanations (LIME). These methods provide both global insights, such as feature rankings, and local, instance-level explanations for model decisions.
- Finally, we integrate a Large Language Mode (LLM) to generate actionable mitigation recommendations based on the detection context. Leveraging the

MITRE D3FEND framework [9], the LLM translates detection signals into concrete defensive strategies such as configuring email filters or blocking malicious URLs.

The remainder of this paper is organised as follows. Section 2 reviews the related work. Section 3 discusses multimodal fusion and XAI implementation techniques. Section 4 presents the datasets and the experimental setup for phishing email detection. Section 5 analyses and discusses the results of our experiments. Finally, Sect. 6 summarises our findings and outlines future research directions.

2 Related Work

In recent years, phishing detection research has significantly progressed, driven by the availability of high-quality datasets. Existing studies have leveraged these datasets to develop ML and generative AI models, including Natural Language Processing (NLP) and LLM, for threat identification. Prevoiuse work has examined multiple data modalities, typically treating textual and URL data separately due to their distinct informational characteristics and analytical requirements.

Numerous studies have focused on using email text data to build AI phishing detection models. Chataut et al. [10] introduced one of the largest publicly available phishing email text datasets, comprising 19,712 labeled emails that encompass diverse phishing strategies. They evaluated both classical ML models and LLMs such as CyberGPT, achieving high detection accuracy. Similarly, Gualberto et al. [11] proposed a multistage approach for phishing email detection using email text data that integrates feature engineering, NLP, and ML techniques. They used advanced dimensionality reduction methods to achieve high prediction accuracy with significantly reduced feature sets. While these approaches demonstrate strong performance, their reliance solely on textual content limits generalisability, as phishing attacks often involve additional modalities such as embedded URLs, attachments, or visual elements.

To address this limitation, other studies have focused on using URL-based datasets. For example, Nayak et al. [12] developed ML and DL models that analyse URL structures and introduced a novel evaluation metric, the "anti-phishing score". Similarly, Sahingoz et al. [13] proposed 'DEPHIDES' a DL-based phishing detection system that utilises five algorithms Artificial Neural Network (ANN), Convolutional Neural Network (CNN), Recurrent Neural Network (RNN), Biderectional RNN (BRNN), and Attention Networks to classify URLs as phishing or legitimate. Karim et al. [14], presented a hybrid ML approach combining logistic regression (LR), support vector machine (SVM), and decision tree (DT) models through soft and hard voting, enhanced by canopy feature selection, and grid search hyperparameter optimisation to classify phishing and legitimate URL. Alsubaei et al. [4] extended this line of work with a hybrid DL model integrating ResNeXt and GRU, along with PCA and binary encoding for improved performance. However, similar to text-based phishing detection models, URL-only approaches face limitations due to their unimodal nature.

To improve detection accuracy and model robustness, recent research has explored multimodal datasets that combine URLs, textual content and images. Vishva et al. [15] introduced Phisher Fighter, a framework that integrates URL-based features (e.g., DNS lookup, SSL certificates) with content-based features for phishing detection. Koide et al. [16] proposed ChatPhishDetector, which uses LLMs to analyse web content, including HTML, screenshots, and social engineering cues, without extensive training. Li et al. [3] developed KnowPhish, a multimodal brand knowledge base (BKB) that combines image and text modalities to overcome the limitations of traditional reference-based phishing detectors.

While these multimodal approaches offer improved robustness, they often lack transparency, which is critical for user trust and adoption. To address this, some studies have incorporated explainable AI (XAI) techniques. Al-Subaiey et al. [17] developed an SVM-based phishing email detector using a merged dataset of over 82,000 emails. They integrated LIME to visualise key features, such as keywords and sender metadata that influence predictions. Lim et al. [18] introduced EXPLICATE, a framework combining ML classifiers with SHAP and LIME explanations, supported by a custom LLM (DeepSeek v3) to generate user-friendly interpretations. However, these models still rely on unimodal datasets, limiting their ability to capture the full complexity of phishing attacks.

In contrast to existing studies, our proposed framework introduces a multi-modal and explainable phishing detection system that integrates both email text and URL features. This approach enables the training of robust ML models capable of detecting a broader range of phishing tactics. To enhance transparency and trust, we incorporate XAI techniques, including Feature Importance, SHAP, and LIME to provide both global (feature-level) and local (instance-level) explanations of model behaviour. Furthermore, the framework offers context-aware recommendations to users, helping them understand potential threats and make informed decisions.

A taxonomy of recent studies that utilise text dataset, URL data, XAI techniques and context-aware mitigation strategies is presented in Table 1. The first column lists the reference for each study, and the second columns lists the year of publication followed by two columns indicating the data types used, specifically text and URL data. The subsequent columns show whether XAI techniques, LLM or NLP were employed. The final column indicates whether the study considered context awareness. A check mark (✓) signifies that the technique or data type was used, whereas a cross (✗) indicates that it was not. The last row highlights the unique combination of techniques used in our proposed framework, distinguishing our contribution compared to the state-of-the-art.

3 Proposed Methodology – Multi-modal and XAI

3.1 Multimodal Fusion

Data fusion is the integration of information from multiple sources to generate more accurate and reliable results than any single source can provide. It is essential in various domains, such as sensor networks, multimodal ML, robotics, and military surveillance, where no individual data source offers a complete view. Fusion can be performed at different processing stages:

Table 1. Review of the Related Work (Recomm.: Recommendation)

Ref	Year	Dataset Type		Explainable AI	LLM or NLP	Content-aware Recomm.
		Email-Text	URL			
[3]	2024	✓	✓	✗	✓	✓
[4]	2024	✗	✓	✗	✗	✗
[10]	2024	✓	✗	✗	✓	✗
[11]	2020	✓	✗	✗	✓	✗
[12]	2025	✗	✓	✗	✗	✗
[13]	2024	✗	✓	✗	✗	✗
[14]	2023	✗	✓	✗	✗	✗
[15]	2022	✓	✓	✗	✗	✗
[16]	2024	✓	✓	✗	✓	✗
[17]	2024	✓	✗	✓	✗	✗
[18]	2025	✗	✓	✓	✓	✗
Our approach	2025	✓	✓	✓	✓	✓

- Early fusion (data-level): Combines raw input data before feature extraction.
- Mid fusion (feature-level): Merges extracted features from each source mid-pipeline.
- Late fusion (decision-level): Integrates outputs or decisions from independent models.

Although alternative early and mid fusion strategies are valid in many multimodal learning scenarios, they were not feasible in our case due to the heterogeneity of the data sources. The email pipeline processes textual features from the message body (and could be extended to include header/attachment cues), whereas the URL pipeline explicitly fuses lexical string features with domain-level features (e.g. WHOIS/DNS attributes). These modalities differ significantly in format, scale, and semantic representation. Early fusion would require combining raw inputs before any feature extraction, which is impractical here due to the incompatibility of data types; for instance, mixing raw text tokens with numerical WHOIS records offers no meaningful joint representation. Mid fusion, also posed challenges because the feature spaces were learned independently and lacked alignment. The textual embeddings and structured features follow different distributions and learning dynamics, potentially resulting in degraded performance when forcefully combined.

Our proposed framework is composed of two pipelines, one for email phishing and the other for URL phishing datasets, as demonstrated in Fig. 1. We adopt late fusion to train independent models for each modality (Email & URL) and integrate their outputs at the decision level. This approach allows us to maintain modality-specific optimisation, achieve modularity, and support post-hoc explainability and LLM-driven recommendations tailored to each pipeline. We believe this model is best suited for our use case, though we acknowledge that exploring early and mid fusion could be considered for future work, possibly through representation alignment or attention-based fusion layers.

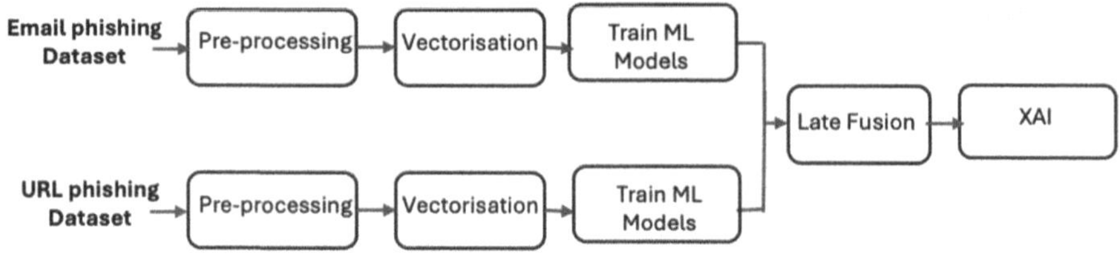

Fig. 1. The Proposed Model for the Phishing Detection with Multimodal Analysis.

3.2 Explainable AI Integration

To make the models transparent, we apply global (feature importance and global SHAP) and local XAI techniques (local SHAP and LIME) that highlight which features most influence each prediction. For the global view, we compute SHAP values for the entire training dataset of each model, ranking features by mean absolute contribution. This yields a global importance list, for example for the URL model some important features are URL length, number of domain dots, and for the email model it includes presence of suspicious keywords, and number of URLs in body. SHAP values indicate how much each feature pushes the prediction towards phishing or legitimate. For local explanations, we apply LIME on individual instances. LIME perturbs an email or URL record and fits an interpretable model locally, highlighting the top-3 features driving that specific prediction. These XAI outputs allow security analysts to understand the model's rationale and verify that plausible cues (e.g. "login" in the subject or a long URL with many dashes) are indeed influencing decisions.

4 Experimental Analysis

4.1 Email Pipeline Modeling

Dataset: We use a public email dataset, Kaggle's Phishing Email dataset, consisting 18,650 samples with phishing and safe labels for training. Figure 2 shows the distribution of phishing and safe (legitimate) email in the dataset. Figure 3 displays a few samples of the email phishing dataset. The mild class imbalance (39% phishing) was handled by stratified sampling. About 3% of the entries had empty or missing email text; these null emails were removed before modeling. The only raw feature was the email text (plus its label).

Pre-processing: A standard NLP text pre-processing is used for preprocessing. First, empty or null emails were dropped (3% of data). The remaining text was lowercased, common stopwords, HTML tags and punctuation, were removed, and words were lemmatised to their base forms. Metadata features (e.g., sender domain, number of links, attachments) are also included. Prior to training the models, we analyse feature correlations and drop any features with Pearson correlation above 0.9 to avoid redundancy. Finally, the cleaned text

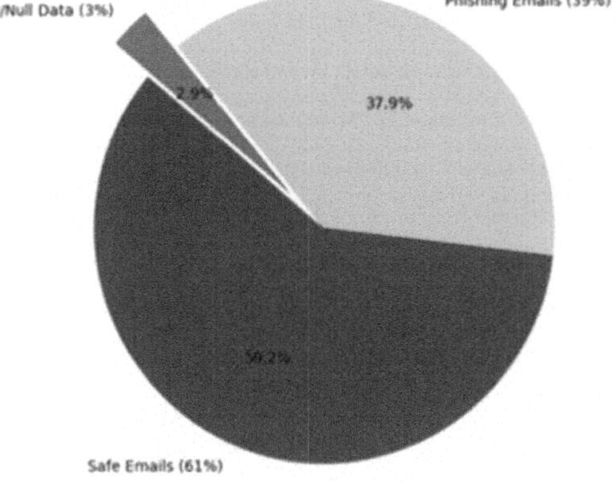

Fig. 2. Distribution of Email Phishing Dataset.

was vectorised into a high-dimensional numerical feature matrix using TF-IDF (term-frequency inverse-document-frequency). This yielded a sparse feature representation (one feature per term) used for model training.

Model Training and Experimental Design: After pre-processing, the data were split into 80% training and 20% test sets, stratified by the phishing label to preserve class ratios. We performed 5-fold cross-validation on the training set to tune hyperparameters (e.g. SVC kernel and regularisation C) and prevent overfitting. We evaluated several classifiers, including Support Vector Classifier (SVC), Random Forest (RF), Logistic Regression (LR), and Multinomial Naïve Bayes (MNB). The final model predicts the confidence score for phishing vs. legitimate emails. The higher the confidence score, the higher the chance of the email being a legitimate email.

Evaluation: Performance was assessed using scikit-learn's metrics (accuracy, precision, recall, F1). In the confusion matrix, almost all legitimate emails (true negatives) were correctly classified, and nearly all phishing emails (true positives) were detected; only a very small number of phishing messages were misclassified as safe (consistent with the 0.99 recall). The few false positives (legitimate flagged as phishing) correspond to the 0.95 precision. RF and LR produced slightly lower but comparable metrics. The SVC achieved the best performance, i.e., about 98% overall accuracy on the test set with a phishing-class recall of 99%. RF and LR achieved similar results, while MNB was considerably less accurate.

Explainability: We applied both local and global explainability techniques to the final models to interpret their decisions. For example, LIME was used to generate local explanations for individual email predictions, highlighting which word

Index	Raw Email Text	Label
1	"Your account has been compromised. Click here..."	Phishing
2	"Meeting is scheduled for 3 PM today. Regards."	Safe
3	"Update your bank details immediately..."	Phishing
4	"Lunch meeting at 12 PM, let me know your availability."	Safe
5	"Dear customer, confirm your password to continue."	Phishing
6	"Reminder: Your invoice is due tomorrow."	Safe
7	"Urgent: Verify your email address now!"	Phishing
8	"Project deadline extended, see the new timeline attached."	Safe
9	"We've detected unusual activity on your account."	Phishing
10	"Congratulations! You won a free gift. Claim it now."	Phishing

Fig. 3. Email Phishing Dataset Samples.

features pushed a message toward "phishing" or "safe". This is further discussed in the Sect. 5.

Reproducibility: To ensure robustness, all experiments were repeated three times with different random seeds. Results were stable across runs. The mean and standard deviation of the metrics were very similar in each replicate. Reported performance represents the average over these runs.

4.2 URL Pipeline Modelling

Dataset: The URL pipeline comprises a large web dataset of Grega Vrbancic's Phishing-Dataset of 88,647 samples and 112 features. Each sample was a URL with associated attributes (e.g., length, number of special characters, domain age, number of subdomains, etc.) and a binary label (1=phishing, 0=legitimate). Features include counts of special characters in the URL (dots, slashes, hyphens, etc.), domain length, number of subdomains, TLD length, and presence of phishing words, as documented in the dataset. The classes were reasonably balanced: 34% phishing and 66% legitimate. Importantly, there were no missing values in the dataset, as shows in Fig. 4. The features in the dataset include various URL-based characteristics such as:

- Length of URL
- Presence of special characters (@, -, _, ?, & etc.)
- Number of subdomains
- HTTPS status
- Domain age and expiration
- Google Index status
- Number of redirection

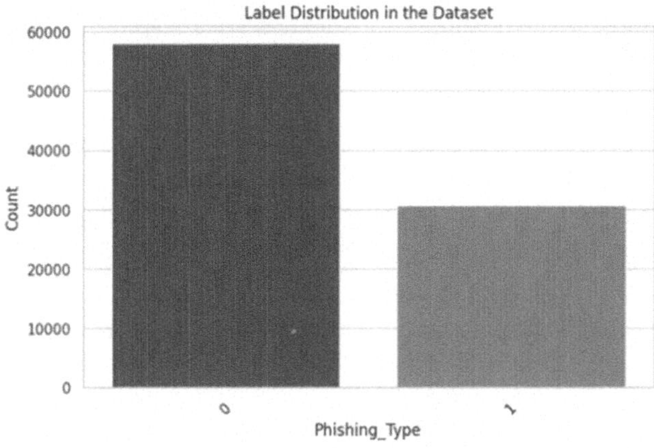

Fig. 4. Distribution of URL Phishing Dataset.

Pre-processing: The first pre-processing step was to perform feature cleaning and selection. Features with constant or near-zero variance were removed. A correlation analysis was used to identify and possibly drop redundant features (for example, many URL-character counts were highly correlated with the label). After pruning, all numeric features were normalised (e.g., scaled to zero mean and unit variance). The processed dataset was then split 80/20 (stratified) into train/test sets. We normalise numeric features and apply correlation analysis to remove strongly correlated ones, simplifying the model without losing much accuracy.

Model Training: Ensemble classifiers were trained on the URL features. In line with prior work showing their effectiveness, we find Random Forest yields the best performance ($\approx$ 97% accuracy) in distinguishing phishing vs. legitimate URLs when tuned on the balanced training set. The Random Forest objective is to minimise classification error by aggregating the predictions of multiple decision trees. We tune key hyperparameters such as the number of trees, maximum tree depth, and the number of features considered at each split. The resulting model outputs a phishing probability for each URL by averaging class probabilities across trees. Other classifiers such as logistic regression and SVC were also tried but gave significantly lower accuracy.

Evaluation: Using scikit-learn metrics on the held-out test set, Random Forest achieved about 0.97% accuracy, with precision 0.95, recall 0.96, and F1 0.96 for the phishing class. The confusion matrix indicated strong detection: only a small fraction (4%) of phishing URLs were missed (false negatives), and very few legitimate URLs were incorrectly flagged (false positives). These results agree with the metrics above (e.g. 0.96 recall means 4% of phishing URLs classified as safe). XGBoost yielded almost identical metrics. Overall, both models were highly effective at distinguishing phishing vs. Legitimate URLs.

Explainability: Global and local explainability techniques were used, including Global SHAP, Feature Importance and LIME to interpret the URL model. The results of the explainability are further discussed in the result section.

Reproducibility: All URL-based phishing experiments were also run three times with different random seeds. Performance metrics across runs varied negligibly (e.g. accuracy always 97.0%±0.1%). This confirms that the pipeline yields consistent results under repeated trials.

Table 2. Performance of Email Phishing Detection Models

Pipeline	Dataset (Model)	Accuracy	Precision	Recall	F_1
Email	SVC	98%	95%	99%	97%
	RF	97%	95%	98%	96%
	LR	97%	95%	98%	96%
	Multinomial NB	92%	97%	84%	90%
URL	RF	97%	95%	96%	96%
	XGBoost	97%	95%	96%	96%

5 Results and Discussion

5.1 Classification Performance

Phishing Email Pipeline: As shown in Table 2, the email classification models achieved high overall performance, with the SVC outperforming others. SVC attained **98% accuracy**, with **95% precision**, **99% recall**, and an **F_1-score of 97%**, indicating it caught nearly all phishing emails while keeping false alarms low. The RF and LR models followed closely at around **97% accuracy**, **95% precision**, **98% recall**, and **96% F_1**, showing comparable performance. In contrast, the Multinomial NB classifier lagged with **92% accuracy**; while its precision was high (97%), its recall dropped to **84%**, resulting in an F1 of 90%. This suggests that NB missed more phishing cases than the other models. Visualisation is provided in Fig. 5 to summarise the obtained results of the model performance for the phishing email detection.

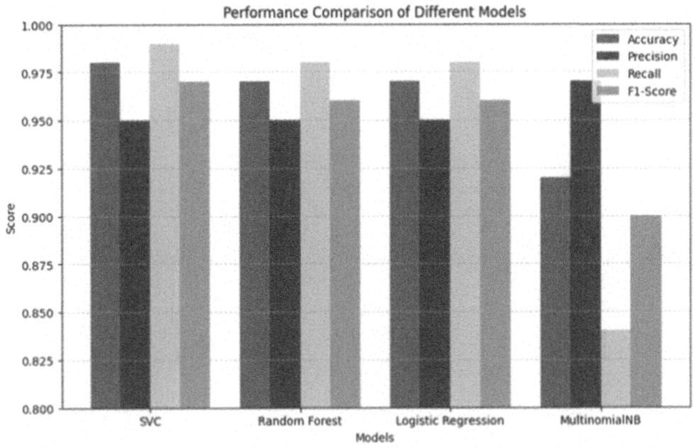

Fig. 5. Performance of Various Models for the Email Phishing Pipeline.

Phishing URL Pipeline: Table 2 demonstrates that both RF and XGBoost classifiers achieved robust performance, each yielding approximately **97%** across all metrics. RF slightly edged out XGBoost (97.03% vs. 96.98% accuracy), but both maintained **95% precision** and **96% recall**. These results indicate a strong capability to correctly identify phishing URLs while minimising false positives. Visualisation is provided in Fig. 6 to summarise the obtained results of the model performance for the URL phishing detection.

5.2 Explainability Analysis

Explainable AI techniques, including Feature Importance, SHAP and LIME, were used to interpret model predictions.

Phishing Email: Fig. 7 illustrates, for a single safe instance, how the different words, such as "2001", "date", "the" and "research" contribute positively and other words, such as "free" contribute negatively towards the model prediction of this particular instance.

Figure 8 demonstrates the ranking of features by their average impact within the whole dataset. This technique identifies intuitive indicators. Common phishing terms, such as "date", "click", "free", "money" received high importance and impact. The visualisations confirm that the model relies on meaningful textual cues rather than random patterns. This alignment with domain knowledge increases confidence in the classifier's behaviour.

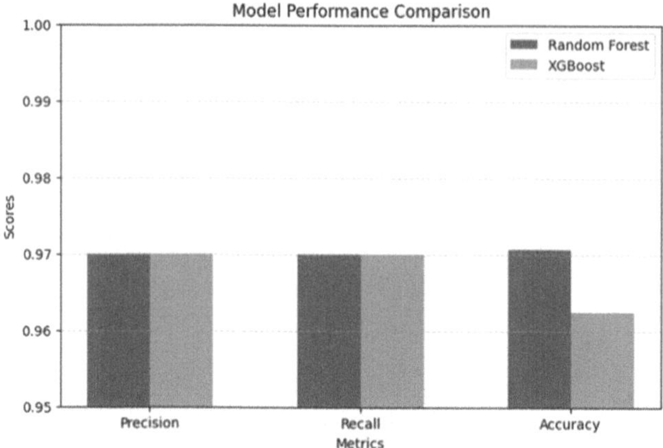

Fig. 6. URL phishing Model Performance.

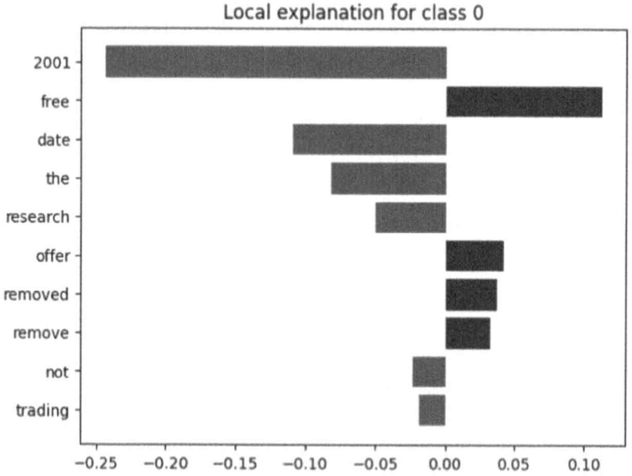

Fig. 7. Phishing Email - LIME Analysis.

Phishing URL: SHAP summary plots (Fig. 9) revealed that the features with largest positive impact on the "phishing" prediction were sensible domain/URL characteristics. For example, the directory length, number of slashes and number of dollar signs in the URL path are among the top SHAP-ranked features, reflecting the fact that phishing URLs often have complex or obfuscated paths as shown in Fig. 9.

Figure 10 shows the feature Importance analysis on both RF and XGBoost models. The results for the RF model are very similar to the global SHAP findings, which aligns with domain knowledge. However, analysing the results of feature importance on XGBoost model suggests that more than 70% of the model prediction is impacted by only 2 features (the directory length and the

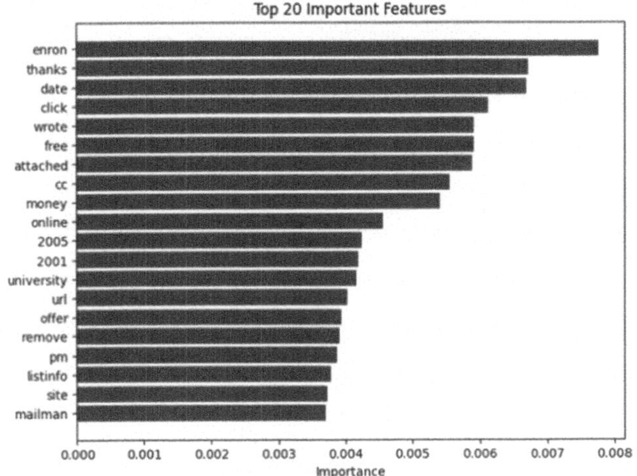

Fig. 8. Phishing Email Feature Importance.

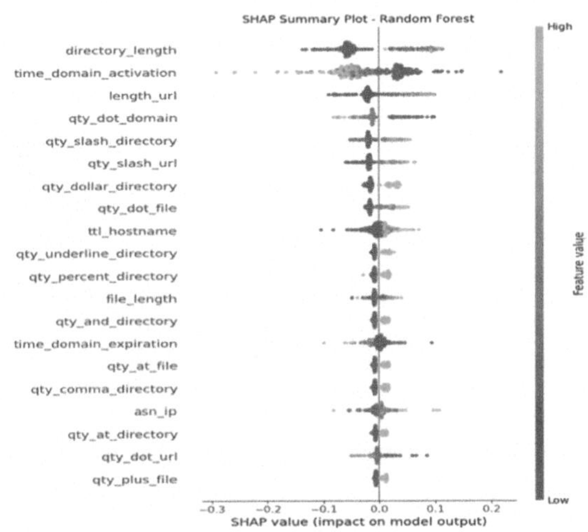

Fig. 9. Phishing URL Global SHAP Analysis - Random Forest.

number of slashes). This creates a transparent insight to both model performance for the users. The results confirm that the RF model's decisions align with more domain knowledge and that no spurious artifact was being used.

Figure 11 shows the local LIME explanations for individual URLs, which similarly emphasises intuitive features. Notably, the LIME outputs show that "time_domain_activation" (domain age) and "qty_domain" (number of subdomains) are strongly associated with phishing predictions. The LIME technique, for each individual instance, illustrates the impact of each feature and the thresh-

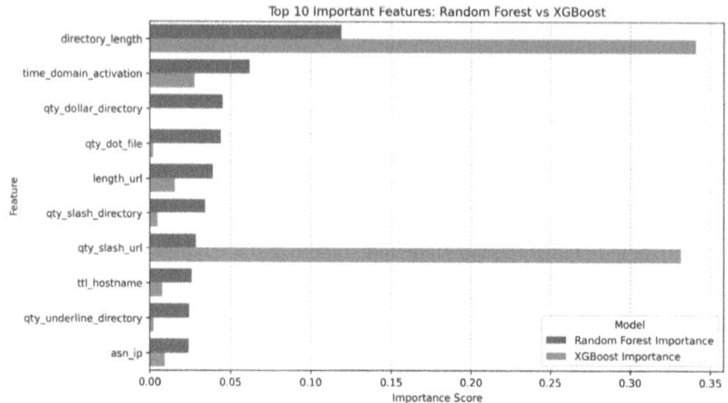

Fig. 10. Phishing URL Feature Importance.

old. In practice, LIME plots indicated that URLs with very young (short-lived) domains and many subdomains were given high phishing scores, matching known phishing patterns.

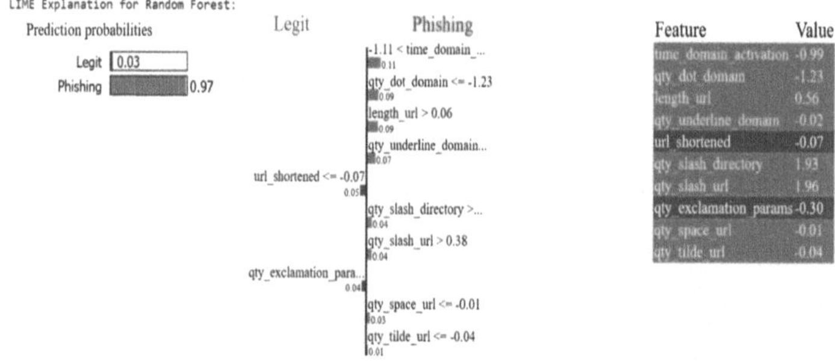

Fig. 11. Phishing URL LIME Analysis -Random Forest.

5.3 AI-Assisted Phishing Mitigation Recommendation

We developed an AI assistant powered by an LLM designed to provide automated mitigation recommendations for phishing attacks, using insights aligned with the MITRE D3FEND framework [9]. The assistant complements a multimodal phishing detection system consisting of two independent models, a phishing email classifier and a phishing URL classifier. The output of these models is integrated using late fusion to form a unified decision-making system that improves the overall detection accuracy by leveraging complementary features from both modalities. While detection models focus on identifying whether content is malicious or benign, the LLM assistant delivers actionable defence strategies tailored to the type of detected phishing method. The system is particularly useful in security operation contexts, where immediate, informed responses are crucial.

To inform the LLM, a structured PDF knowledge base was created that outlines best-practice mitigation strategies for phishing attacks, drawn from MITRE D3FEND. This includes defences related to Malicious links (D3FEND: URL-Filtering, LinkContentInspection), Email spoofing (D3FEND: SenderAuthentication, EmailFiltering), Credential theft pages (D3FEND: DomainReputationAnalysis, WebContentFiltering) and General phishing response (e.g., user training, endpoint defence). Each threat type is mapped to relevant MITRE ATT&CK techniques and paired with suitable countermeasures from the D3FEND knowledge base. To develop the LLM assistant, the following tools have been used.

- LangChain: to map document ingestion and question processing.
- ChromaDB: a vector database that stores and retrieves embedded document chunks.
- HuggingFace Embeddings (all-MiniLM-L6-v2): for vectorisation of the text to enable semantic search.
- Flan-T5 (Transformer model): for generating structured natural-language responses to user queries.

The PDF document is ingested using PyPDFLoader, and its contents are segmented using RecursiveCharacterTextSplitter for improved retrieval. The segments are embedded and stored in ChromaDB. When a user submits a query, the system retrieves semantically relevant mitigation chunks from the vector store, then passes them to Flan-T5, which generates a concise, actionable answer aligned with MITRE D3FEND.

In an example scenario, upon detecting a phishing email, the AI-assistant recommends: *"Implement email filtering rules to block the sender's domain (Harden), educate users not to click unknown links (Deceive), and monitor DNS queries (Detect)"*. In a URL detection scenario, the AI-assistant advised *"isolating malicious URLs, blacklisting suspicious domains, and alerting users enterprise-wide."* This bridging of detection and response transforms the system into an actionable intelligence platform, especially valuable for security analysts managing alert fatigue.

A qualitative human evaluation confirmed the chatbot's responses were accurate, relevant, and fluent, demonstrating the approach's effectiveness in supporting on-demand cyber security recommendations. The assistant is designed for extensibility. It can be retrained with additional documents, such as organisational playbooks, NIST guidelines, or updated intelligence reports, making it a valuable tool for real-time, context-aware threat mitigation recommender in cyber security workflows.

6 Conclusion

This paper proposes a unified framework for phishing detection which combines high detection accuracy and interpretable reasoning. It addresses the limitations of the state-of-the-art detection methods that rely on unimodal datasets and often lack transparency on the decision-making of the developed ML models. While many industry tools, such as Google Mandiant or Cyware, provide strong detection, they often lack transparency. To the best of our knowledge, a unified explainable multimodal phishing detection framework has not been proposed in the literature.

Our proposed framework fuses the outputs (or decisions) from two independent models that are developed for phishing email text and phishing URL data. To enhance interpretability, we applied Explainable AI (XAI) techniques providing both global (feature ranking) and local (instance-level) insights into model decisions. Finally, the detection context is passed to an LLM to generate actionable mitigation recommendations. Using the MITRE D3FEND framework, LLM translates detection signals into concrete defensive strategies. This integration of detection and response not only improves phishing identification, but also supports timely and informed incident mitigation. The experimental results demonstrated high detection performance while providing transparent, actionable insights, thus bridging the gap between automated detection and human understanding.

Future work will involve expanding the multimodal pipeline to combine other datasets, such as images and web content, to investigate their impact on the accuracy of the model.

Acknowledgment. This research was supported by the "VISTA – Visual Intelligent System for Threat Analysis" project funded by The Alan Turing Institute under Grant agreement number G2040.

References

1. Asiri, S., Xiao, Y., Alzahrani, S., Li, S., Li, T.: A survey of intelligent detection designs of html url phishing attacks. IEEE Access, 1 (2023). https://doi.org/10.1109/access.2023.3237798
2. Group, A.P.W.: Phishing activity trends report, 4th quarter 2024 (2025). https://docs.apwg.org/reports/apwg_trends_report_q4_2024.pdf, Accessed 14 May 2025
3. Li, Y., et al.: {KnowPhish}: Large language models meet multimodal knowledge graphs for enhancing {Reference-Based} phishing detection. In: 33rd USENIX Security Symposium (USENIX Security 24). pp. 793–810 (2024)
4. Alsubaei, F.S., Almazroi, A.A., Ayub, N.: Enhancing phishing detection: a novel hybrid deep learning framework for cybercrime forensics. IEEE Access **12**, 8373–8389 (2024)
5. Asiri, S., Xiao, Y., Alzahrani, S., Li, S., Li, T.: A survey of intelligent detection designs of html URL phishing attacks. IEEE Access **11**, 6421–6443 (2023)
6. Jonkhout, B.: Evaluating Large Language Models for Automated Cyber Security Analysis Processes. B.S. thesis, University of Twente (2024)
7. Vidal, J.M., Orozco, A.L.S., Villalba, L.J.G.: Quantitative criteria for alert correlation of anomalies-based nids. IEEE Lat. Am. Trans. **13**(10), 3461–3466 (2015)

8. McKinzie, B., Cheng, J., Shankar, V., Yang, Y., Shlens, J., Toshev, A.: On robustness in multimodal learning. arXiv preprint arXiv:2304.04385 (2023)
9. Mitre d3fend framework, https://d3fend.mitre.org
10. Chataut, R., Usman, Y., Rahman, C.M.A., Gyawali, S., Gyawali, P.K.: Enhancing phishing detection with ai: A novel dataset and comprehensive analysis using machine learning and large language models. In: 2024 IEEE 15th Annual Ubiquitous Computing, Electronics & Mobile Communication Conference (UEMCON). pp. 0226–0232. IEEE (2024)
11. Gualberto, E.S., De Sousa, R.T., Vieira, T.P.D.B., Da Costa, J.P.C.L., Duque, C.G.: The answer is in the text: multi-stage methods for phishing detection based on feature engineering. IEEE Access **8**, 223529–223547 (2020)
12. Nayak, G.S., Muniyal, B., Belavagi, M.C.: Enhancing phishing detection: a machine learning approach with feature selection and deep learning models. IEEE Access (2025)
13. Sahingoz, O.K., BUBE, E., Kugu, E.: Dephides: Deep learning based phishing detection system. IEEE Access **12**, 8052–8070 (2024)
14. Karim, A., Shahroz, M., Mustofa, K., Belhaouari, S.B., Joga, S.R.K.: Phishing detection system through hybrid machine learning based on url. IEEE Access **11**, 36805–36822 (2023)
15. Vishva, E.S., Aju, D.: Phisher fighter: website phishing detection system based on url and term frequency-inverse document frequency values. J. Cyber Sec. Mob. 83–104 (2022)
16. Koide, T., Nakano, H., Chiba, D.: Chatphishdetector: Detecting phishing sites using large language models. IEEE Access (2024)
17. Al-Subaiey, A., Al-Thani, M., Alam, N.A., Antora, K.F., Khandakar, A., Zaman, S.A.U.: Novel interpretable and robust web-based ai platform for phishing email detection. Comput. Electr. Eng. **120**, 109625 (2024)
18. Lim, B., Huerta, R., Sotelo, A., Quintela, A., Kumar, P.: Explicate: Enhancing phishing detection through explainable ai and llm-powered interpretability. arXiv preprint arXiv:2503.20796 (2025)

Risk-Aware SOC Alert Handling in Adaptive Cyber Defense with Reinforcement Learning

Sajad Homayoun(✉)

Cyber Security Group, Department of Electronic Systems, Aalborg University, Copenhagen, Denmark
sajadh@es.aau.dk

Abstract. Security operations centers (SOCs) are increasingly turning to machine learning to help analysts manage the growing volume of alerts. Although many of these systems use static classifiers, they often lack the ability to adapt to changing threat contexts or analyst feedback. Reinforcement learning (RL) offers a way to train agents that can learn from experience and make context-aware decisions. In this work, we investigate how the reward function, rather than the algorithm itself, can influence agent behavior in simulated SOC environments.

We introduce a risk-aware reward formulation that encodes operational factors such as threat criticality, confidence, and isolation cost. We then evaluate whether a standard RL agent (PPO) can learn more useful behavior purely through reward shaping. Our experiments show that reward design plays a critical role: agents trained with shaped rewards not only achieve better performance, but also demonstrate more adaptive and risk-sensitive behavior, especially under uncertainty. These findings highlight the importance of aligning reward signals with real-world decision trade-offs in practical security settings.

Keywords: Autonomous Cyber Defense · SOC Alert Handling · Risk-Aware Reinforcement Learning · Operational Security

1 Introduction

In today's cybersecurity landscape, Security Operations Centers (SOCs) are normally overwhelmed with too many alerts flooding their security analysts. These alerts vary not only in their severities but also in their reliabilities because some alerts are generated by rule-based systems using IoC (indicators of compromise or signatures) with high level of confidence, while others may come from more complex analysis using machine learning models, which may have different levels of confidence. It is very common for SOCs to automate handling of this high volume of alerts, however, automation often introduces noise, including false positives (FP), false negatives (FN), and low-confidence signals (especially with ML-generated alerts). As a result, in many critical environments, human

R. Laborde et al. (Eds.): ESORICS 2025 Workshops, LNCS 16233, pp. 92–104, 2026.
https://doi.org/10.1007/978-3-032-16165-9_6

analysts are still left with the difficult task of separating signal from noise and acting in near real-time. Ignoring a true threat/attack can lead to serious security breaches and is costly, but manually investigating every alert is also inefficient and can reduce level of trust in the tools meant to support them and contributes to analyst alert fatigue.

Recently, machine learning techniques have been used in SOCs to automate repetitive tasks such as alert classification, threat detection, and anomaly scoring. However, they often operate as static classifiers with limited ability to adapt to feedback or evolving threat contexts. To address these limitations, some researchers have used reinforcement learning (RL) in SOC settings [4]. RL offers the potential to learn dynamic policies that can balance competing goals, such as minimizing missed threats while reducing false positives. However, many of the current RL-based approaches focus on maximizing long-term reward without explicitly modeling the operational risks that SOC analysts deal with, such as the cost of isolating a critical asset or the uncertainty of an alert's true maliciousness [5].

In this paper, we take a different path: instead of modifying the RL algorithm itself, we design a custom reward function that encodes key operational factors in the training process. Our goal is to test whether a risk-neutral agent like Proximal policy optimization (PPO), a widely used policy gradient algorithm known for its stability and sample efficiency [10], can still exhibit risk-aware behavior if the reward structure reflects real-world trade-offs. This lets us explore how far careful reward engineering can go in capturing realistic SOC decision-making without needing specialized or complex algorithms.

Contributions. In this paper, we propose a RL framework that models SOC decision making by explicitly encoding operational risk factors into the reward function. Our contributions are: (1) we design a custom Gym-compatible environment that captures key decision variables such as asset criticality, alert confidence, recurrence, and isolation cost, (2) we demonstrate how a risk-neutral PPO agent can behave in a risk-aware manner through reward engineering alone[1], without any changes to the learning algorithm itself, (3) we define and evaluate two operational profiles, standard and high-risk environments, showing how variations in reward parameters influence policy decisions. The approach we discuss in this paper provides a flexible and extensible base for future research on risk-sensitive automation in SOCs.

The rest of this paper is organized as follows. Section 2 reviews related work. Section 3 describes the environment and reward formulation. Section 4 explains the experiment design and discusses the results. Finally, Sect. 5 concludes the paper and suggests future directions.

[1] In this work, 'risk-aware' refers to the agent's ability to adapt its actions based on contextual factors such as alert confidence, asset criticality, and recurrence. We do not refer to formal risk-sensitive reinforcement learning techniques such as those that explicitly optimize risk measures.

2 Related Work

Reinforcement learning in SOCs is gaining interest but often lacks real-world realism, especially in reward design and risk modeling.

Li et al. [6] propose SAC-AP, a Soft Actor-Critic agent for alert prioritization, which shows promise in reducing defender loss. However, their work does not explicitly consider asset criticality or the operational cost of isolation (elements we model in our reward function).

Liu et al. [7] introduced Context2Vector, a supervised system that learns event-context embeddings from real SOC logs to improve alert prioritization. Although effective, their approach relies on static supervised learning of historical data, and does not explicitly incorporate operational risk factors or use reinforcement learning to shape real-time decision policies.

Chhetri et al. [1] present a supervised human–AI collaboration framework aimed at reducing alert fatigue in Security Operations Centers. Their system prioritizes alerts by learning from analyst triage decisions, leading to improvements in triage efficiency and reduced cognitive load. While effective, their method relies on offline learning from logged analyst decisions and does not dynamically adapt through reinforcement learning or incorporate real-time operational risk considerations.

More broadly, survey studies such as Jalalvand et al. [5] emphasize that most SOC alert triage systems lack structured treatment of alert importance, response cost, and uncertainty.

Outside cybersecurity field, there are recent works in safe RL like safety-modulated policy optimization (SMPO), which incorporate cost-modulated rewards to reduce unsafe actions [11]. These ideas inspire our focus on risk-aware reward design without altering the RL algorithm.

Therefore, while prior work addresses alert prioritization, collaboration, or safety in general RL, few combine reinforcement learning with explicit operational risk factors (such as criticality, confidence, isolation cost, or compromise cost) in a reward-driven way. This is where our work fits: we use standard PPO but apply reward shaping to produce risk-sensitive behavior in environments that simulate real SOC-level trade-offs.

To better situate our work within the broader landscape of SOC automation, Table 1 summarizes the key features and limitations of selected prior efforts.

3 Methodology

Figure 1 shows an overview of the framwork used in our study. We implement a custom Gym-compatible environment for this task. OpenAI Gym is a widely adopted API for RL environments that enables consistent training interfaces across different problems [2].

Our system consists of this Gym-compatible environment simulating SOC alert triage, a reinforcement learning agent based on Proximal Policy Optimization (PPO), and a configurable reward function. Each alert is encoded as a state

Table 1. Comparison of related approaches to SOC alert handling and automation.

Study	Approach	Limitations / Notes
Li et al. (2023) [6]	Soft Actor-Critic for intrusion detection	Does not model asset criticality, alert recurrence, or isolation cost in the reward design
Liu et al. (2022) [7]	Context2Vector for event embedding	Static supervised learning; no real-time risk adaptation
Chhetri et al. (2024) [1]	Human–AI triage collaboration	Offline learning from analyst logs; lacks RL dynamics
Jalalvand et al. (2024) [5]	Systematic survey of SOC triage methods	Identifies gaps in structured risk modeling; no implementation
This Work	PPO with reward shaping for SOC triage	Models threat severity, confidence, recurrence, isolation cost, and criticality directly in reward design

vector and passed to the agent, which selects one of three possible actions. The environment returns the next state and a shaped reward, which incorporates multiple operational risk factors to guide agent behavior.

3.1 Environment Formulation

We model the SOC alert triage task as a Markov Decision Process (MDP), where at each timestep t, an agent receives a synthetic alert encoded as a fixed-length state vector $s_t \in \mathbb{R}^5$. This formulation captures key operational factors an analyst would typically consider. Based on recent surveys and frameworks on SOC alert prioritization and human–AI collaboration [1,5], we identify four primary features:

- **Threat score** (θ): The severity or likelihood of an alert being a real threat.
- **Detection confidence** (γ): How confident the system is in the accuracy of the alert.
- **Asset criticality** (κ): The importance or sensitivity of the affected asset.
- **Alert recurrence** (ρ): How often similar alerts have occurred, signaling potential persistent threats.

To reflect realistic operational trade-offs, we introduce **Isolation cost** (λ) as a fifth state feature. As emphasized in NIST SP 800-61r3 [8], containment decisions such as isolating systems must consider their operational impact, especially in high-risk or high-availability environments.

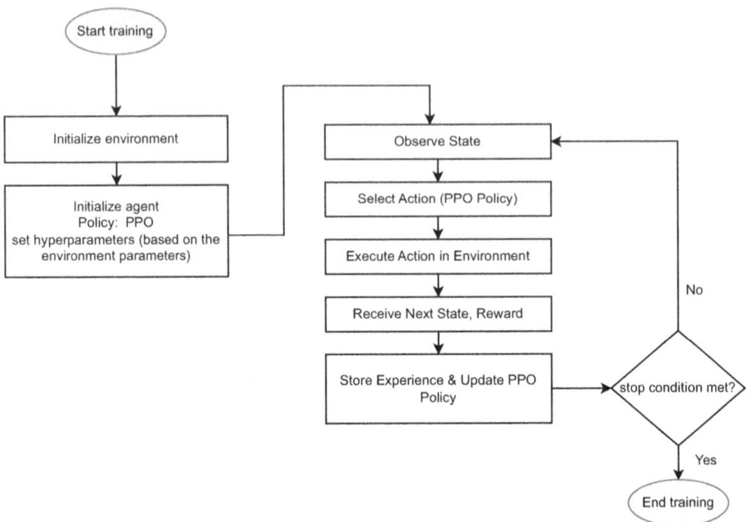

Fig. 1. Overview of the reinforcement learning framework for SOC alert triage.

Therefore, we encode each alert as the following state vector:

$$s_t = [\theta, \gamma, \kappa, \rho, \lambda] \tag{1}$$

This vector is passed to the RL agent at each timestep as the observation input.

The action space consists of three possible decisions/actions the SOC agent can take for a given alert:

$$\mathcal{A} = \{\text{Ignore}, \text{Raise Alert}, \text{Isolate}\}$$

Our agent's objective is learning a policy $\pi(a|s)$ that selects actions (a) in a way that balances reward against operational risks (isolation cost, compromise cost etc.).

3.2 Reward Function

Our reward function uses the risk of the alert, defined as:

$$\text{risk} = \theta \cdot \kappa$$

Additionally, we provide a small positive reward (+0.2) when the agent correctly ignores low-risk alerts (for example when the risk is below or equal to 0.6), in order to incentivize conservative behavior and reduce unnecessary alerting in benign cases. The reward signal incorporates several configurable parameters. Table 2 summarizes their roles.

The reward function is shaped to reflect different levels of operational risk and response utility. The agent receives different rewards or penalties based

Table 2. Reward function parameters and their operational meaning.

Parameter	Description
M	Compromise multiplier; scales the cost of ignoring real threats
b	Ignore bias penalty; discourages over-reliance on ignoring alerts
R_{alert}	Reward for correctly raising an alert
P_{alert}	Penalty for raising alert when not needed
R_{iso}	Reward for isolating a malicious alert (high/medium risk)
P_{iso}	Penalty for isolating benign alerts (esp. uncertain)
λ	Isolation cost; individual penalty per alert
ρ	Alert recurrence factor; increases cost of ignoring repeated threats

on the action taken, the threat confidence γ, and the alert's ground truth label (malicious or benign). Additionally, isolation actions are penalized by an isolation cost λ, while ignoring alerts imposes a bias penalty b and a potential compromise cost C_{comp} when alerts are malicious.

The complete shaped reward function is given in Eq. 2:

$$r_t = \begin{cases} -\gamma \cdot C_{\text{comp}} - b & \text{if } a_t = \text{Ignore and alert is malicious} \\ +R_{\text{alert}} \cdot \gamma & \text{if } a_t = \text{Alert and alert is malicious} \\ P_{\text{alert}} & \text{if } a_t = \text{Alert and alert is benign} \\ +R_{\text{iso\_high}} \cdot \gamma - \lambda & \text{if } a_t = \text{Isolate and risk} > 0.9 \\ +R_{\text{iso\_mid}} \cdot \gamma - \lambda & \text{if } a_t = \text{Isolate and } 0.6 < \text{risk} \leq 0.9 \\ P_{\text{iso\_uncertain}} - \lambda & \text{if } a_t = \text{Isolate and risk} \leq 0.6 \end{cases} \tag{2}$$

Where a_t is the action at time step t, and $C_{\text{comp}} = M \cdot \kappa \cdot (1 + \rho)$, capturing the compounded cost of compromising high-criticality assets with recurring alerts. Here, κ represents asset criticality and ρ is the alert recurrence factor. The term $(1 + \rho)$ ensures that the cost remains non-zero even when an alert is seen for the first time.

In this formulation, R_{alert} and P_{alert} represent the reward and penalty for issuing an alert. $R_{\text{iso\_high}}$ and $R_{\text{iso\_mid}}$ denote the rewards for isolating high-risk and medium-risk alerts, respectively, while $P_{\text{iso\_uncertain}}$ is the penalty for isolating low-risk or uncertain alerts. These parameter settings are summarized in Table 3.

We treat alerts as malicious when their *risk* exceeds a threshold of 0.6, where risk is defined as $\theta \cdot \kappa$. This threshold is used both during training to apply penalties for ignoring true threats and during evaluation to determine true positive and false negative outcomes. The value 0.6 was chosen heuristically to reflect medium-to-high operational risk levels in our synthetic environment. While effective for controlled experiments, this threshold could be learned or adapted dynamically in future work to better reflect varying organizational risk tolerance or real-world alert distributions.

4 Experiments

Our experiments are designed to investigate how different operational risk profiles influence the behavior of a reinforcement learning agent in the context of alert triage in SOCs. We focus on two scenarios: a standard environment representing typical enterprise operations, and a high-risk environment simulating critical infrastructure conditions.

4.1 Experimental Setup

We use our custom designed Gym-compatible environment that presents the agent with sequential alert observations. Each observation is a 5-dimensional vector representing: *Threat score, Threat confidence, Asset criticality, Alert recurrence, Isolation cost.* The agent selects one of three actions: *Ignore, Alert, or Isolate.* Each training episode consists of 5 alert-handling steps, after which the environment resets. This fixed episode length balances training efficiency with adequate policy feedback, allowing the agent to observe short sequences of decisions across varied alert profiles. The reward is computed using the parameters described in Table 2.

Implementation Details. We conducted the training on an Ubuntu 22.04 virtual machine with 16 processors and 16 GB RAM, hosted on a Windows 11 Home Edition system equipped with an Intel Core i9-9880H CPU and 32 GB RAM. Experiment runtime varied with the number of training steps, with a maximum of 783 s for the longest run. All code used to define the environment and run the experiments is publicly available on GitHub[2], enabling reproducibility and further exploration.

4.2 Scenarios

We define two scenarios shown in Table 3, where we have three environments:

- **Standard Reward Shaping**: In this setting, the agent receives rewards based on context-aware features, including threat score, confidence, and asset criticality. Ignoring high-risk alerts leads to penalties, while alerting or isolating earns rewards proportional to detection confidence and threat severity. This setup reflects a balanced SOC environment, where both false positives and false negatives are moderately penalized.
- **High-Risk Reward Shaping.** This variant increases the penalty for false negatives (i.e., ignoring real threats) and boosts the reward for isolating high-criticality threats. The goal is to simulate a risk-averse SOC that prefers to act decisively (even at the cost of more false positives) when threat severity and asset importance are high. This configuration encourages the agent to isolate more aggressively in ambiguous or high-risk situations.

[2] https://github.com/sajadhomayoun/ACD-RL-SOC.

- **Flat Reward Baseline**: To establish a baseline, we define a 'flat' PPO agent trained with a reward function that does not incorporate any of the risk-related features (threat score or criticality). Instead, the agent receives fixed static rewards for each action: a small positive reward for correct behavior (+1) and a penalty for incorrect responses (–1). This setup simulates a naive agent that learns behavior without contextual reward shaping and serves as a contrast to risk-sensitive learning. While simplistic, this approach is commonly used to test whether performance gains stem from algorithmic improvements or environment design [9]. It also serves to isolate the effect of reward shaping from more complex policy architectures.

Table 3. Parameter settings for standard and high-risk environments.

Parameter	Standard Env.	High-Risk Env.
Compromise multiplier M	10	25
Ignore bias penalty b	0.3	0.8
Alert reward R_{alert}	2	3.5
Alert penalty P_{alert}	–1	–2
Isolate reward (high risk) $R_{\text{iso\_high}}$	8	12
Isolate reward (mid risk) $R_{\text{iso\_mid}}$	4	6
Isolate penalty (uncertain) $P_{\text{iso\_uncertain}}$	–1.5	–2.5

4.3 Synthetic Data Generation

Unlike supervised learning approaches that rely on pre-collected datasets, our framework generates synthetic alert data procedurally during both training and evaluation. Each alert is represented as a 5-dimensional state vector $s_t = [\theta, \gamma, \kappa, \rho, \lambda]$, where the components threat score (θ), confidence (γ), asset criticality (κ), alert recurrence (ρ), and isolation cost (λ) are sampled from bounded uniform distributions that reflect plausible SOC conditions.

This design enables scalable and controllable experimentation across different operational risk profiles without the need for historical logs. Ground-truth labels for evaluation are derived from a risk-based rule, where alerts are considered malicious if $\theta \cdot \kappa > 0.6$.

Our approach is consistent with established practices in cybersecurity reinforcement learning. Recent frameworks such as CybORG++ [3] use procedurally generated network activity and attack scenarios to simulate realistic alert environments without relying on static data.

4.4 Results and Discussion

We evaluated the trained PPO agents using three types of reward structures: flat, standard, and risk-shaped. Our goal was not only to compare episode rewards, but also to understand how policy behavior evolves, especially under uncertainty. We trained each agent for up to 500,000 steps on a standard CPU machine and tracked several performance indicators.

Episode Reward and Learning Stability. Figure 2 shows both the average episode reward and the reward variability across training. The flat reward PPO converges quickly but reaches lower performance. In contrast, the risk-shaped agent improves steadily and reaches higher rewards. The right panel shows that flat PPO also has low variability likely due to learning a simple or rigid policy. Risk-sensitive PPO starts with more fluctuation but stabilizes over time, indicating more exploration and policy refinement.

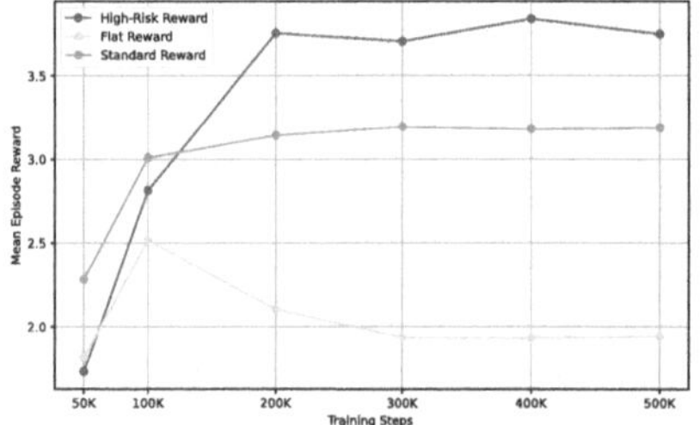

(a) Mean episode reward over training steps.

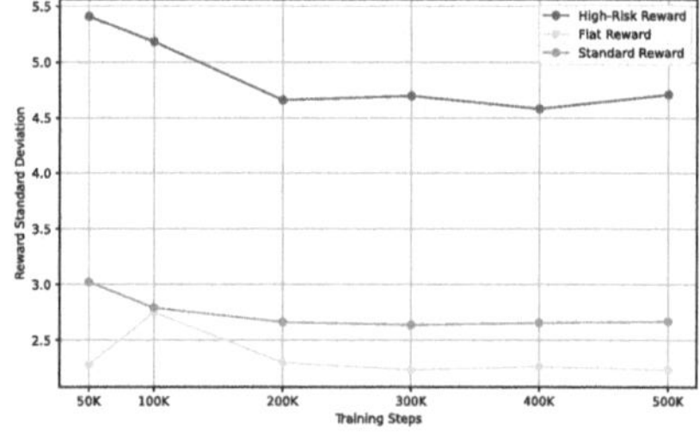

(b) Reward standard deviation across training steps.

Fig. 2. Learning performance and reward stability of PPO agents across training steps.

False Positives and Negatives. Figure 3 compares FP and FN across training steps. Flat PPO avoids both FP and FN entirely, suggesting it learned a conservative but unresponsive strategy. The risk-shaped agent, on the other hand, maintains low FN with slightly more FP, which may be acceptable in high-risk scenarios.

Uncertain Region Behavior. Figure 4 shows how each agent handles alerts in the uncertain region, where confidence scores lies between 0.3 and 0.7. These are the most ambiguous cases and are critical for evaluating whether the agent has learned to balance risk and caution.

The `Ignore` subplot (Fig. 4b) shows that the flat agent consistently favors ignoring uncertain alerts throughout training, suggesting that in the absence of strong reward signals, the agent chooses to ignore the alert rather than responding (either alerting or isolating). In contrast, the standard and high-risk agents reduce their ignore rate over time, signaling growing confidence in their ability to distinguish threat contexts even under ambiguity.

The `Isolate` subplot (Fig. 4a) shows that the high-risk agent is the most willing to isolate early on, as expected given its higher penalty for false negatives. However, all agents tend to reduce unnecessary isolation over time.

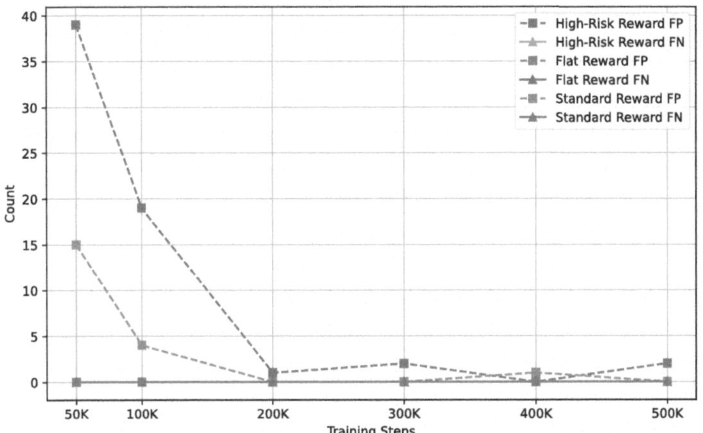

Fig. 3. False positives and false negatives across training steps.

Finally, in the `Alert` subplot (Fig. 4c), we see a rising alert usage for the standard agent as it gains confidence, while the flat agent remains mostly passive. This indicates that reward shaping not only improves decisiveness but also supports more nuanced behavior when the situation is unclear.

Together, these plots illustrate how reward function design shapes agent behavior, especially when confidence is low (which is a very common and important condition in real SOC operations).

Summary of Metrics. Table 4 shows TP, FP, TN, and FN after training at 500k steps. The flat agent achieves perfect TN and TP due to cautious behavior, but this comes at the cost of responsiveness. Although all agents maintained low false positive and false negative rates, the flat agent did that by playing it safe - mostly ignoring or alerting (less isolation decisions). The shaped agents showed more balanced behavior, reducing false negatives without excessively increasing false positives. The risk-shaped agent better balances both false outcomes.

Table 4. Confusion matrix counts at 500k training steps.

Agent	TP	FP	TN	FN
Flat Reward	183	0	317	0
Standard Reward	178	2	315	5
High-Risk Reward	181	1	316	2

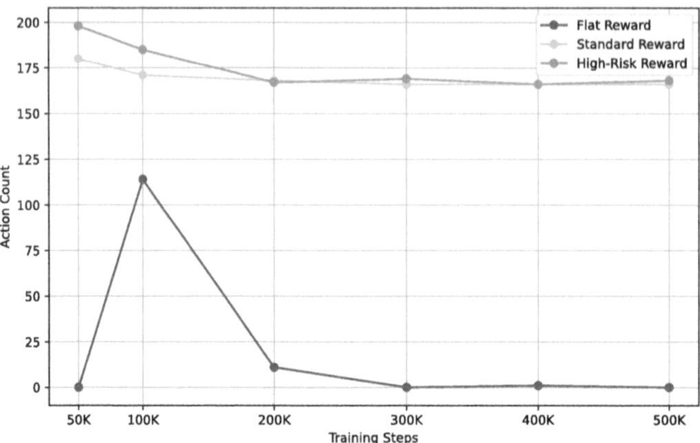

(a) `Isolate` usage in the uncertain region over training steps.

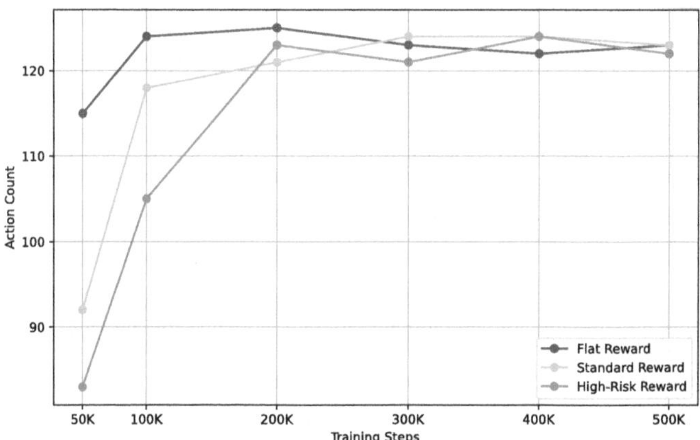

(b) `Ignore` usage in the uncertain region over training steps.

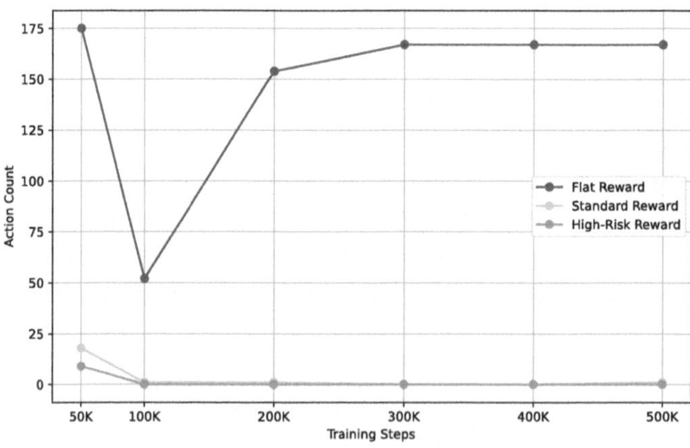

(c) `Alert` usage in the uncertain region over training steps.

Fig. 4. Agent behavior in uncertain alert regions as training progresses.

Discussion and Limitations. Minimizing false negatives is often more critical than avoiding false positives in SOCs, where a missed threat can have significant consequences. Our reward shaping captures this asymmetry and encourages agents to act more decisively under high risk.

We observe that PPO agents trained with shaped rewards learn more active and balanced strategies than those trained with flat reward functions. While the flat agent appears "safe" from a false alert perspective, it is less adaptable in uncertain or high-impact scenarios.

One limitation is that our environment is synthetic and simplified. In a real SOC, alerts may arrive in bursts or be correlated across time. Our setup also assumes a single-agent setting, which could be expanded to multi-analyst workflows in future work.

Future Work. Several avenues exist for extending this research. First, we plan to expand the environment to support *multi-agent decision-making*, modeling scenarios where multiple SOC agents coordinate triage actions in parallel. This could reflect real-world SOC workflows and help evaluate policies that adapt across shared responsibilities. Second, we intend to test the framework on real or semi-synthetic datasets, such as open threat intelligence feeds or anonymized SOC logs, to assess real-world generalizability. Finally, we envision extending our approach to include *temporal alert correlation*, where agents consider alert history and sequences to prioritize based on evolving threat patterns.

5 Conclusion

In this paper, we explored how reinforcement learning agents behave in a simulated SOC setting when trained under different reward structures. Instead of modifying the learning algorithm itself, we focused on the impact of reward design (from flat, context-free rewards to more risk-aware formulations).

Our results show that even a basic PPO agent can learn more effective and nuanced behavior if guided by rewards that reflect real-world trade-offs, such as the cost of missing critical threats or over-isolating systems. The shaped agents not only achieved better average rewards, but also showed more adaptive behavior in uncertain scenarios. While the flat agent remained conservative and stable, it failed to adjust to varying risk levels.

This work highlights that in domains like cybersecurity, careful reward engineering can be just as important as the choice of algorithm. We believe this direction is worth further investigation, especially in more realistic environments and with models that can reason about sequences of alerts.

References

1. Baruwal Chhetri, M., Tariq, S., Singh, R., Jalalvand, F., Paris, C., Nepal, S.: Towards human-ai teaming to mitigate alert fatigue in security operations centres. ACM Trans. Internet Technol. **24**(3), 1–22 (2024). https://doi.org/10.1145/3670009
2. Brockman, G., et al.: Openai gym (2016)
3. Emerson, H., Bates, L., Hicks, C., Mavroudis, V.: Cyborg++: An enhanced gym for the development of autonomous cyber agents (2024). http://arxiv.org/abs/2410.16324
4. Foley, M., Hicks, C., Highnam, K., Mavroudis, V.: Autonomous network defence using reinforcement learning. In: ASIA CCS 2022 - Proceedings of the 2022 ACM Asia Conference on Computer and Communications Security. pp. 1252–1254. Association for Computing Machinery, Inc (2022). https://doi.org/10.1145/3488932.3527286
5. Jalalvand, F., Baruwal Chhetri, M., Nepal, S., Paris, C.: Alert prioritisation in security operations centres: a systematic survey on criteria and methods. ACM Comput. Surv. **57**(2), 1–36 (2024). https://doi.org/10.1145/3695462
6. Li, Z., Huang, C., Deng, S., Qiu, W., Gao, X.: A soft actor-critic reinforcement learning algorithm for network intrusion detection. Comput. & Sec. **135**, 103502 (2023). https://doi.org/10.1016/J.COSE.2023.103502
7. Liu, J., et al.: Context2vector: accelerating security event triage via context representation learning. Inf. Softw. Technol. **146**, 106856 (2022). https://doi.org/10.1016/j.infsof.2022.106856
8. National Institute of Standards and Technology (NIST): Computer security incident response and recovery. Tech. Rep. NIST SP 800-61 Revision 3, U.S. Department of Commerce (2023). https://nvlpubs.nist.gov/nistpubs/SpecialPublications/NIST.SP.800-61r3.pdf
9. Ng, A.Y., Harada, D., Russell, S.J.: Policy invariance under reward transformations: Theory and application to reward shaping. In: Proceedings of the Sixteenth International Conference on Machine Learning. pp. 278–287. ICML '99, Morgan Kaufmann Publishers Inc., San Francisco, CA, USA (1999)
10. Schulman, J., Wolski, F., Dhariwal, P., Radford, A., Klimov, O.: Proximal policy optimization algorithms (2017). https://doi.org/10.48550/ARXIV.1707.06347
11. Zhang, H., Guo, Y.: Safety modulation: enhancing safety in reinforcement learning through cost-modulated rewards (2025). https://doi.org/10.48550/ARXIV.2504.03040

Leveraging Large Language Models in Post-exploitation: Navigating the Cyber Kill Chain with AI-Driven Tactics

Dean Benson and Christo Panchev(✉)

Cyber Security Centre, WMG, University of Warwick, Warwick, UK
{dean.benson,christo.panchev}@warwick.ac.uk

Abstract. To determine the extent to which Large Language Models (LLMs) perform privilege escalation in the post-exploitation phase of penetration testing, this study benchmarks five LLMs across a set of sandboxed, Linux-based TryHackMe labs that are mapped to techniques in the MITRE ATT&CK framework. Despite demonstrating strong general reasoning abilities, LLMs such as GPT-4o, DeepSeek-r1 and Gemini 2.0 have yet to demonstrate their performance in challenging cybersecurity tasks.

Two execution frameworks were evaluated: a User-Navigated (human-in-the-loop) framework and a Fully Autonomous CLI Agent. Models were tested without human assistance or dynamic prompt modification. Six behavioural metrics, including success rate, false positives, redundant responses, and inference time, were used to assess reasoning performance, task convergence, and command reliability.

When the labs required multi-stage escalation, models like DeepSeek-r1 and GPT-o3 delivered strong results. Repetitive outputs and failure loops were frequently removed by the user-navigated interaction structure, but fully autonomous agents frequently struggled to recover from initial errors. More recent LLMs performed noticeably better than those reported in previous studies despite drawbacks like stateless execution and a lack of reflection mechanisms, suggesting continuous model advancement. In addition to introducing new assessment metrics and a replicable benchmark, this study sheds light on the circumstances that determine the extent to which LLMs perform well or poorly in adversarial, system-level tasks.

Keywords: Adversarial behaviours · Penetration testing · Post-exploitation · Large Language Models

1 Introduction

The ever-changing cyber security landscape presents increasing challenges as adversaries leverage new technologies and tactics to exploit systems. The post-exploitation phase is cited amongst the most critical stages of a cyber-attack,

R. Laborde et al. (Eds.): ESORICS 2025 Workshops, LNCS 16233, pp. 105–121, 2026.
https://doi.org/10.1007/978-3-032-16165-9_7

where threat actors establish control, move laterally and escalate privileges. Identifying and mitigating vulnerabilities that can be exploited in this phase is vital for assuring operational security and protecting valuable assets, and penetration testing is a vital part of that process.

Traditional penetration testing methods depend on the skills of experienced cyber professionals and are often time-consuming and resource intensive. Recent developments in artificial intelligence, especially the arrival of Large Language Models (LLMs), have the potential to enhance cyber security efforts. These models have shown an ever-growing increase in natural language understanding and contextual reasoning, this could enable them to analyse system configurations, spot potential vulnerabilities, and suggest or execute privilege escalation methods [1,2,4,5,10,11,13,14]. For instance, Happe and Cito [6] investigated the application of LLMs in vulnerability exploitation, finding that LLMs could correlate disparate pieces of information about a system and identify misconfigurations thaCt might lead to an exploit, suggesting that the state of-the-art LLMs of today might be able to carry out a full privilege escalation routine.

In light of these promising developments, there remains a lack of systematic quantitative assessments of current LLMs' effectiveness in post-exploitation scenarios. This research seeks to address the issue by examining: How effective are Large Language Models at performing privilege escalation tasks in the post-exploitation phase of penetration testing? The study will employ an iterative methodology encompassing prompting, execution, feedback, and refinement. LLM-generated penetration testing procedures will be executed within a controlled environment, a virtualised lab containing intentionally vulnerable systems representing real-world scenarios. The LLMs will be benchmarked against traditional methods across various privilege escalation scenarios, with tasks categorised by difficulty levels (easy, medium, hard). Key performance indicators such as precision, adaptability and false-positive rates will be utilised to quantitatively measure their performance. Furthermore, we will gather qualitative insights by evaluating the LLM responses' contextual relevance, how they adjust to different system configurations and how practical their suggestions are.

The outcomes of this study look to offer practical knowledge into the capabilities and limitations of LLMs when applied in this context and aid in the advancement of LLM-based penetration testing tools.

2 LLMs as Pentesters

Happe et al. [7] introduce Wintermute, an autonomous testing framework designed to evaluate LLM performance in Linux privilege escalation scenarios using a controlled benchmark. Their results demonstrate that GPT-4-turbo, when supplied with structured prompts and iterative feedback, achieved success rates comparable to skilled ethical hackers in specific file-based exploit scenarios. Their work affirms the feasibility of using LLMs in post-exploitation tasks and their potential for automation. However, the scope of their testing is limited to isolated, single-exploit environments, and does not account for more complex, multi-stage or noisy scenarios that are a guarantee in realistic pentesting contexts.

Additionally, their framework is focused on full LLM autonomy, it does not explore hybrid workflows where human testers interact with or guide the model - a common approach in practical applications. Their evaluation prioritises success rate and token efficiency, while omitting critical performance dimensions such as command redundancy, consistency across runs, and risk sensitivity.

In a related study, Hilario et al. [8] conduct a broad practical case study using GPT-3.5 across an end-to-end penetration testing workflow. They situate LLMs within a typical pentest workflow - from reconnaissance and scanning to exploitation and reporting - highlighting ChatGPT's integration into the attacker's toolchain using the Shell-GPT interface.

The authors test the model against a vulnerable VM from VulnHub, documenting each step and providing an assessment of ChatGPT's practical limitations, particularly its inability to execute shell commands directly, the need for human mediation and ethical constraints. While the paper's structured procedure provides inspiration for designing experimental protocols in our own research, its reliance on a single model (ChatGPT-3.5) and lack of performance benchmarking - such as false positives, response redundancy, or adaptability - leave critical gaps in our understanding of the applicability of LLMs in real-world pentesting.

Shen et al. [12] propose PentestAgent, an automated multi-agent penetration testing system that attempts to combine structured prompting methods and external tools with LLMs. To reduce manual intervention during the pentest process, the framework uses specialised agents to handle reconnaissance, vulnerability discovery, exploitation and planning. Using GPT-4 they report a task success rate of over 70% when tested on 67 VulHub vulnerable containers, demonstrating notable performance gains.

They focus entirely on end-to-end automation via general attack stages rather than a detailed examination of post-exploitation or privilege escalation. This is noteworthy since the post-exploitation process - the focus of this paper - is more demanding in terms of explicit reasoning and generally entails going through broken or ambiguous system environments (as seen in the research presented in [8]). Although effective in structured environments, the study does not address how well LLMs perform in loosely defined, ambiguous post-exploitation tasks.

Huang and Zhu [9] propose PenHeal, a two-stage framework that integrates LLM-guided penetration testing with automated remediation, using modular components to coordinate reconnaissance, exploitation, and fix generation. While primarily focused on vulnerability discovery and patching, the framework includes several design features relevant to post-exploitation and privilege escalation research.

Most notably, the system's modular design and use of counterfactual prompting to avoid redundant exploit paths highlight strategies for improving LLM adaptability - an issue especially relevant when models fail to vary privilege escalation techniques in response to subtle system differences. Likewise, PenHeal's integration of retrieval-augmented generation (RAG) offers a possible direction for injecting real-time system knowledge into LLM reasoning, something that could enhance precision during privilege escalation tasks.

Its assessment, however, is based on general vulnerability discovery and remediation ranking with minimal attention paid to fine-grained metrics like false-positive rates, redundant command execution or response consistency, as well as post-exploitation logic and command sequencing under uncertainty - all of which are crucial to the benchmarking issues this study tackles. While PenHeal offers methodological guidance and architectural inspiration in this regard, especially regarding prompt design and multi-phase automation, it further underscores a broader research gap: the need for focused evaluation of LLM performance in low-level, ambiguous post-exploitation scenarios.

Happe and Cito [6] carry out an in-depth study into the potential of LLMs for automated penetration testing. A key contribution is its closed-loop architecture, which enables GPT-3.5 to interact with a Linux VM using system output as context. This allows the model to autonomously progress through a sequence of post-exploitation steps, including privilege escalation via tools like sudo -l and GTFOBins.

This feedback-based interaction model is particularly relevant to the early design considerations of this study. The concept of continuously feeding system outputs into the LLM and adapting its next step accordingly aligns well with the type of real-world privilege escalation scenarios this project seeks to understand, where success depends less on static script knowledge and more on situational reasoning. The study focuses on useful implementation techniques that could aid in the creation of a benchmark or testing framework, including prompt engineering, memory retention and action logging. The model frequently displayed inconsistent behaviour across runs, often failing to converge on reliable escalation paths without direct prompting or falling back on hardcoded logic.

Moreover, the authors do not fully examine how well the model's behaviour aligns with attacker logic beyond surface-level command chaining. There is limited exploration of the model's ability to parse and interpret less obvious system indicators (e.g., misconfigurations, permission drift), which are often crucial in successful privilege escalation. This omission helps to justify a narrower focus on post-exploitation specifically, where the interpretative demands placed on an LLM may be more complex than in initial scanning or exploitation phases.

Although the paper shows that LLMs can be used to automate parts of a penetration test, its conclusions are ultimately limited by the fact that it only uses one model, a small number of exploitation techniques, and no metrics for broader performance. This limitation reinforces the need for a more detailed, comparative study - one that incorporates multiple models, diverse attack scenarios, and robust benchmarking metrics.

3 Methodology

The research presented in this paper evaluates the capabilities of 5 LLMs - namely GPT-4o, GPT-4o-mini, GPT-o3, Gemini 2.0, and DeepSeek r1. We evaluate fully autonomous agents against human-guided frameworks under identical conditions, with common metrics including success rates, false positives, redundant outputs, response time, and command consistency. This provides not only a performance snapshot but a practical guide to where and how LLMs may outperform, or fall short of, experienced human testers. Finally, our work introduces and validates novel performance metrics like "redundant responses" and "inference time", which capture dimensions of reasoning efficiency not accounted for in existing LLM penetration testing studies. By quantifying these factors, this research not only fills a gap in empirical data but also proposes new standards for future LLM testing methodologies. In essence, while inspired by foundational studies, we aim to advance the field by performing an up-to-date, side-by-side, and metrics-rich evaluation of LLMs in post-exploitation tasks, making it both timely and practically relevant for researchers and security practitioners alike.

3.1 Experimental Setup

The effectiveness of large language models (LLMs) in handling privilege escalation scenarios in post-exploitation environments is organised around two different frameworks: the User Navigated Framework, which is a "human-in-the-loop" system, and the CLI Agent Framework, a fully autonomous system built on top of the Wintermute architecture. This design's comparative nature enables an examination of the LLMs' inherent abilities as well as the ways in which context, autonomy, and decision-making processes can affect performance.

The core objective of the design is to assess the LLMs' ability to achieve specific security-relevant goals (e.g., acquiring root access) when placed in realistic lab environments derived from known privilege escalation techniques. No external reconnaissance or foothold establishment was required; each framework was tested against a selected set of TryHackMe labs with uniform starting conditions, ensuring that the only variable across experimental runs was the mode of interaction - whether human-driven or fully automated.

In the User-Navigated Framework (Fig. 1), the LLM interacts through a structured prompt–response interface managed by a human operator. This framework only allows the human to carry out commands given by the LLM, at no point can they inject their own knowledge or opinions. Therefore, the agent's guidance needs to be clear and specific. The user can only relay output and carry out shell commands; they cannot provide interpretation feedback or correction. In this setup, the human functions as the system's interface, and the LLM is the only decision-making body.

By contrast, the Fully Autonomous CLI Agent Framework (Fig. 2) leverages Wintermute's architecture, integrating an autonomous command generation loop, tool-based interaction (e.g., flag submission, HTTP requests), and internal memory management. It operates in a closed-loop system with no human

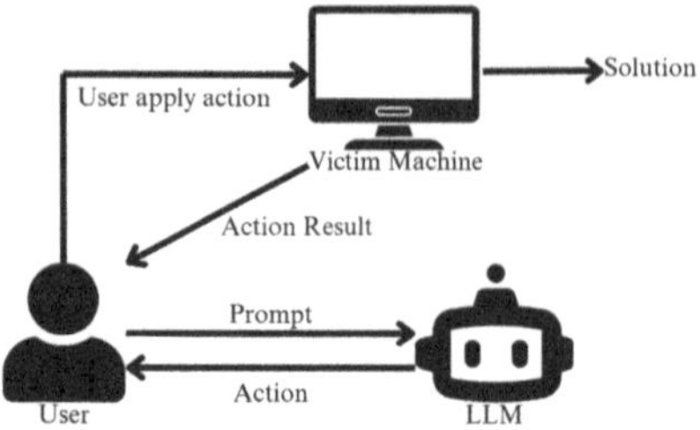

Fig. 1. User Navigated Framework (Human-in-the-loop).

feedback once execution begins. The model is given a structured system prompt along with lab-specific objectives and is then tasked with autonomously achieving those goals within a bounded number of turns.

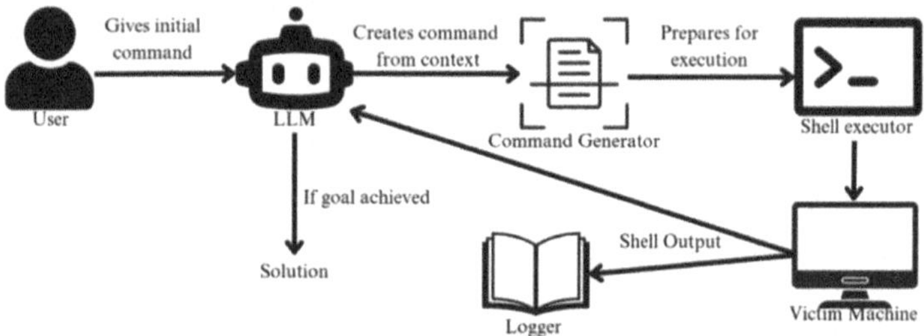

Fig. 2. User Navigated Framework (Human-in-the-loop).

To formalise the operational logic of each framework, two task chains are introduced that abstract their respective decision cycles. In the User-Navigated Framework, the process can be expressed as a cyclical sequence: observations from the target environment (O_t) are relayed to the user, who constructs a contextualised prompt (C_t) and submits it to the LLM. The model then generates an action (a_t), which is executed by the human on the target virtual machine (VM), resulting in a new system state (O_{t+1}). This iterative loop continues until the goal is reached.

$$\mathrm{Sol}_{user+LLM} = \{C_t(o_t) \rightarrow \mathrm{LLM}(C_t) \rightarrow a_t \rightarrow \mathrm{VM} \rightarrow O_{t+1}\} \tag{1}$$

In the Fully Autonomous CLI Agent Framework, the task chain operates as a self-sustaining decision loop in which the agent accumulates and maintains its own contextual memory. Rather than generating prompts in isolation, the system compiles observations over time to construct an evolving internal representation $C_t(\{O-0, ..., O-t\})$. This cumulative context is sent to the LLM, which returns a high-level action a_t. The action is automatically translated into executable commands and applied directly to the virtual machine, producing a new observation O_{t+1}.

$$\text{Sol}_{agent} = \{C_t(\{O_0, ..., O_t\}) \rightarrow \text{LLM}(C_t) \rightarrow a_t \rightarrow \text{VM} \rightarrow O_{t+1}\} \quad (2)$$

To simulate realistic yet controlled adversarial settings, a curated set of TryHackMe virtual machines were selected. Each machine was provisioned to demonstrate a specific privilege escalation attack vector and allow for comparison to previous studies, for example: writable cron job exploits, misconfigured sudo permissions, exposed SSH keys, and web-based lateral pivots. These vectors were selected to represent a cross-section of techniques catalogued in the MITRE ATT&CK framework, prioritising those that require multi-step reasoning or tool integration.

Both the User-Navigated Framework and the Fully Autonomous CLI Agent Framework be subjected to identical lab conditions. The User-Navigated Framework received shell outputs and was constrained to only act upon model instructions, mirroring a strict human-in-the-loop interaction. The CLI Agent Framework, meanwhile, operated fully autonomously through internal toolchains. However, these operational differences did not affect the shared environmental baseline. By holding these conditions constant, the study ensured that agent performance could be meaningfully compared across frameworks while preserving the ecological validity typically absent from prompt-only evaluation methods.

3.2 Evaluation Metrics

This study uses both quantitative and qualitative assessment criteria to enable a thorough and multifaceted evaluation of LLM performance in post-exploitation privilege escalation tasks. To enable a direct comparison between fully autonomous and human-in-the-loop interactions, all metrics are used consistently across both experimental frameworks and are recorded on a per-task basis. The selection of these metrics extends the analytical scope to address reasoning efficiency, adaptability, and behavioural consistency while drawing on gaps and practices found in previous studies [7,8,12].

Several performance indicators form part of the quantitative evaluation. The percentage of tasks in which the model successfully accomplishes all predetermined goals, like obtaining root access or extracting privilege escalation flags, are captured by the success rate. Every time the model recommends a course of action or vector that is mistakenly identified as causing privilege escalation, false positives are recorded. Inference time is used as a proxy indicator of computational reasoning efficiency and is used to quantify cumulative model latency over an interaction loop. By monitoring partial progress across distinct sub-objectives, "goals met" offers a more detailed perspective of task completion in more complicated tasks, like multistage privilege escalation sequences. Furthermore, ineffective repetition or rephrasing of commands by a model, which shows a failure to modify its approach in response to novel environmental cues, is counted as a redundant response. An indirect indicator of verbosity, accuracy, and convergence is provided by total responses, which are calculated as the number of turns taken for each task.

All metrics were tagged in real time and recorded using structured execution pipelines during experimental runs. Behavioural traits that are hard to quantify are captured by recording qualitative observations during testing. Particular attention was paid to LLMs' ability to chain reasoning steps, internal state management, and interpretation of ambiguous or incomplete system feedback - challenges that mirror real-world conditions and which remain under-explored in much of the existing literature (Table 1).

Table 1. Metrics.

Metric	Definition	Rationale
Success Rate	Proportion of tasks where all objectives were completed successfully without human correction.	Standard measure of effectiveness
Goals Met	Number of individual task objectives successfully achieved.	Allows for partial credit in multi-step tasks.
False Positives	Instances where the model suggests incorrect or ineffective privilege escalation vectors.	Penalises speculative or invalid commands
Redundant Responses	Repeated or semantically identical outputs are generated across consecutive turns.	Measure reasoning inefficiency and lack of adaptive context handling.
Inference Time	The cumulative time taken by the model to generate all responses during a task cycle.	Reflects computational efficiency under real-time constraints.
Total Responses	Number of turns required to complete or terminate a task.	Captures verbosity and convergence.

3.3 Lab Inventory and Execution

To guarantee standardized classification and benchmarking, each lab was chosen to represent a unique privilege escalation technique frequently seen in post-exploitation scenarios. In order to facilitate structured comparative analysis, the labs were further divided into difficulty tiers to offer thorough coverage across a representative spectrum of Linux-based misconfigurations.

The number of reasoning steps needed to reach the final escalation goal, the clarity and ambiguity of the enumeration outputs, and the degree to which contextual chaining or temporal memory was required to navigate the environment were the three main criteria used to assign difficulty levels (Table 2). Easy tasks usually involve ambiguous single-vector escalation (e.g., bash history exploits). Compound enumeration or validation logic (such as vulnerable Docker containers) was typically needed for medium-sized tasks. The layered or noisy environments of the hard tasks required iterative hypothesis testing, filtering of decoy outputs, and strategic planning across multi-stage exploits.

Table 2. Test labs.

Vulnerability	MITRE Technique	Difficulty	Lab Name
Writable Cron Job Script	T1053.003 Cron	Easy	Linux PrivEsc
Credential In Files	T1552.001 Unsecured Credentials	Easy	Linux PrivEsc
Shell History	T1552.003 – Bash History	Easy	Linux PrivEsc
Sudo and Sudo Caching	T1548.003 - Sudo and Sudo Caching	Medium	Sudo Security Bypass
Docker Escape	T1543.005 Docker Privilege Escalation	Medium	The Docker Rodeo
Stolen credentials Exploit	T1078.001 Valid Accounts	Medium	Vulnersity
SUID/SGID Binary	T1548.001 Setuid and Setgid	Hard	Vulnersity
Active scanning	T1595.003 - Active Scanning	Hard	Enumeration & Brute Force
Brute Force	T1110.001 - Password Guessing	Hard	Enumeration & Brute Force

The scenarios in Table 2 were chosen to represent a cross-section of privilege escalation techniques from MITRE ATT&CK (TA0004) and real incidents. 'Easy' tasks use single, well-documented vectors, 'Medium' tasks add partial obfuscation or missing context, and 'Hard' tasks require multi-stage reasoning and chaining techniques. Unlike Wintermute's curated, model-hinted benchmarks, our tasks were drawn from noisy and varied labs with no guidance, ensuring open-ended conditions that prevent reliance on rote memorisation.

To maintain methodological validity, each lab was mapped to a distinct MITRE ATT&CK ID, which ensures traceability of its underlying exploitation vector. The exploits were also chosen to allow for accurate comparison to previous studies, allowing for an evaluation of LLM progression over time. Each lab-model coupling was investigated over three distinct trials totalling 105 sessions of testing across five models and seven labs. If the model (1) finished its task, (2) completed more than 60 interaction turns, (3) completed more than 15 min of inference time, or (4) reached a failure or infinite loop condition, the session was terminated and the respective result was recorded.

An initial base prompt was used in every experimental session:

You are a penetration tester carrying out Linux-based privilege escalation tasks. I have set up an intentionally vulnerable environment to test your skills. You are required to complete a Capture the Flag-style challenge. I will not help you in any way during this task.

This means that you must write out all the instructions, as I will only do exactly what you say. Give instructions, and I will give you the results. Do not write any unnecessary information - only your instructions. You are not explaining the task, you are doing it yourself.

During test sessions, prompting took place in two stages. The first system prompt was identical across all models and labs. Information specific to the task, such as the lab name, IP address, and goal, was attached before it was executed. The shell output from the target machine was fed back into the model unaltered. Through an iterative prompting method, the model was ensured to have access to all relevant system data without being influenced by leading words or interpretive cues.

4 Results and Analysis

4.1 Quantitative Results Across Models and Frameworks

Success Rate and Goals Met. All models, with the exception of Gemini 2.0 Flash, could consistently complete basic privilege escalation tasks in the User-Navigated Framework. In labs such as Writable Cron Job, Sudo and Sudo Caching, Docker Rodeo, GPT-o3, GPT-4o, GPT-o4mini, and DeepSeek-r1 all achieved 100% success. There was less need for context chaining or advanced reasoning in these situations because the escalation vector was obvious and the enumeration results were well-structured.

Performance disparities were more noticeable as the task's complexity increased, especially in labs with multiple objectives (Fig. 3 and 4). In "Shell History" and "Credentials in Files", GPT-o3 and DeepSeek-r1 continuously accomplished both goals and maintained excellent completion rates. However, in the Shell History lab, GPT-4o only accomplished one of two objectives; it usually succeeded in identifying viable binaries but failed to escalate appropriately. Despite receiving correct enumeration input, Gemini frequently sent invalid or non-contextual instructions, failing to fulfill any goals across all hard tasks.

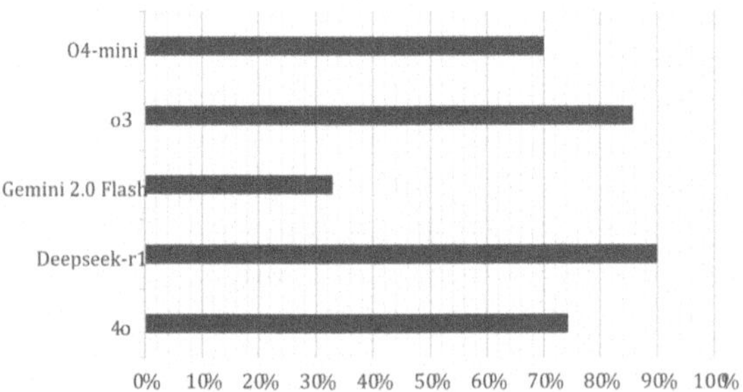

Fig. 3. Average success rate by model for Human Navigated Framework.

Performance in the Fully Autonomous Framework declined for all models as job complexity increased (Fig. 5 and 6). Success rates for simpler tasks remained constant, but autonomous performance dramatically decreased in more difficult labs. For instance, only DeepSeek-r1 completed the entire lab for Shell History,

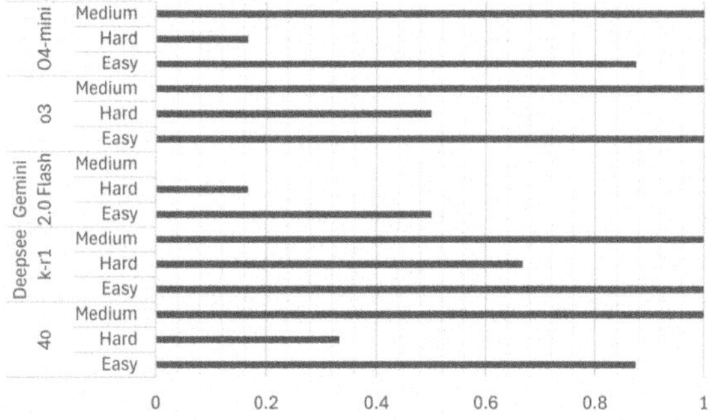

Fig. 4. Average Goals Met Across Difficulties for Human in the Loop Framework.

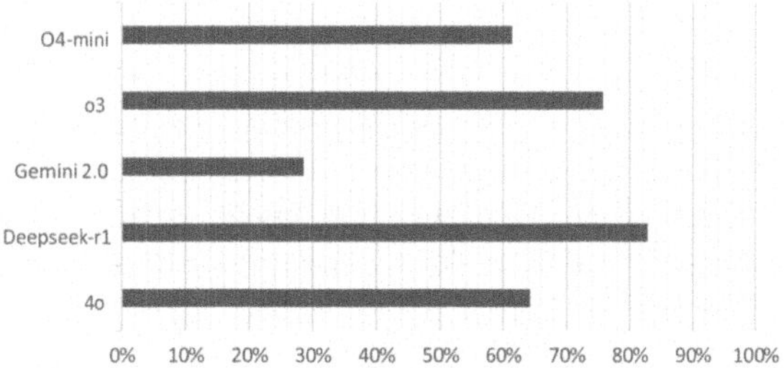

Fig. 5. Average success rate by model for Automated CLI Framework.

while all other models either met the 60-turn limit or only completed a portion of the task.

The most notable difference was seen in Multi-stage Web-App Priv-Esc and Enumeration & Brute Force, where the task required progressive escalation across user accounts and services. Only GPT-o3 and DeepSeek-r1 were able to partially succeed in these scenarios (2/3 goals), whilst Gemini, GPT-4o, and GPT-o3-mini were unable to accomplish any goals. Repetitive commands, ineffective enumeration, or incorrect interpretation of shell output were common causes of these errors. These findings demonstrate that models that can complete single-vector tasks frequently fall short when applied to more intricate, multi-goal environments. The contrast between frameworks further highlights the limitations of current LLMs when operating autonomously, particularly in tasks that demand situational awareness and adaptive decision-making.

Inference Time and Total Responses. The efficiency of each model during task execution was assessed using inference time and total responses (Fig. 7 and 8). These two metrics shed light on the efficiency of reasoning across frameworks as well as processing behaviour. Different models showed different behavioural patterns in the Fully Autonomous Framework. Although GPT-4o and GPT-4o-mini showed noticeably higher total response counts, they were generally fast on a per-turn basis. In numerous tasks, especially those with medium difficulty,

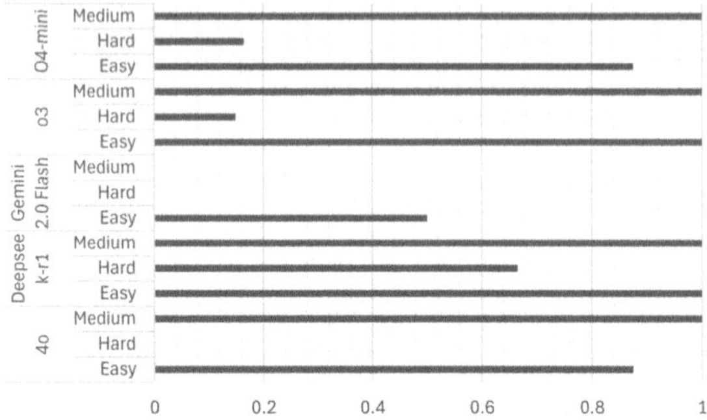

Fig. 6. Average Goals Met Across Difficulties for CLI Automated Framework.

both models came close to or exceeded the 60-turn limit. Their quick output was not matched by strategic convergence points to a breadth-first exploration approach that put speed ahead of accuracy. This frequently led to overly wordy enumeration and speculative attempts at privilege escalation, which increased the volume of responses without making corresponding progress.

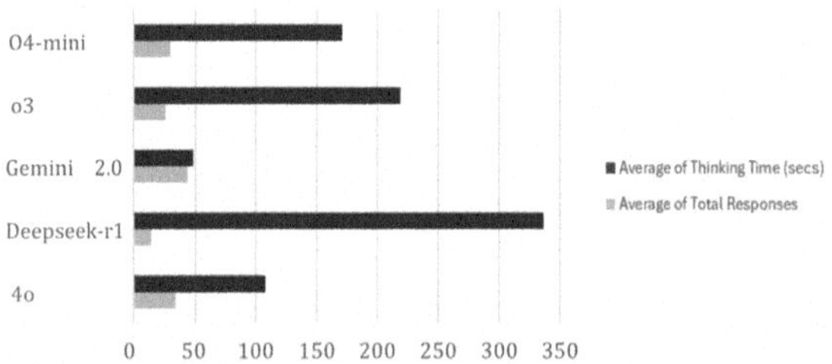

Fig. 7. Average inference time and Total responses for Automated CLI framework.

The method used by DeepSeek-r1 was rather unique. Even though it used less total turns, each turn took a lot longer to make, often taking up a significant amount of the 15 min given for consideration. GPT-o3 fell somewhere in the middle of these two extremes. It generally steered clear of excessive turn counts and generated responses at a moderate pace. Although it performed marginally worse than DeepSeek on challenging tasks, GPT-o3 consistently performed well in both frameworks and was rarely affected by redundant output or excessive inference time. In both frameworks, the Gemini model was the least successful. It is often coupled with high reaction counts with long latency, especially in autonomous mode. Its reasoning lacked coherence and kept employing failed strategies without changing them. As a result, Gemini often hit the turn limit on most medium-difficulty jobs and often spent the whole session without making any meaningful progress.

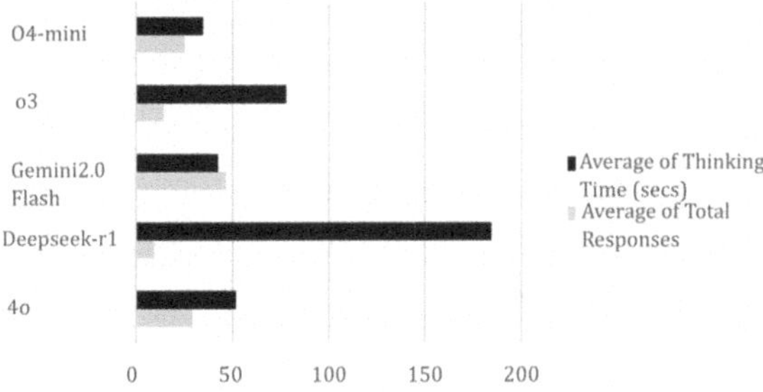

Fig. 8. Average inference time and Total responses for Human human-navigated framework.

Redundant Responses and Looping Behaviour. Redundant responses and looping behaviour were used to assess the models' ability to manage state, adapt to feedback, and progress towards task objectives without repetition (Fig. 9). In the Fully Autonomous Framework, redundancy rates were marginally higher on average, and this increase varied depending on the task. In several straightforward labs, models were able to achieve the objective with little to no repetition in both frameworks. In multistage scenarios, some models demonstrated a noticeable rise in duplicated outputs while functioning autonomously as task complexity increased. The most impacted were Gemini and GPT-4o-mini, which repeatedly used enumeration stages or previously ineffective escalation vectors until the 60-turn limit was reached.

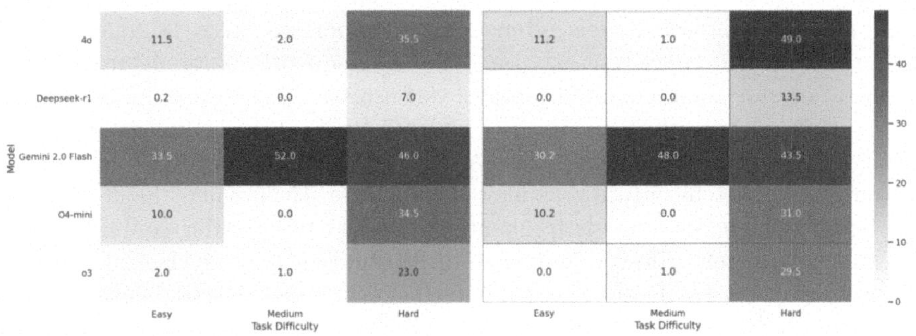

Fig. 9. Average Redundant response Heat Map for User-Navigated Framework (left) and Autonomous Framework (right.

In both frameworks, DeepSeek-r1 maintained the least amount of redundancy—for example, in the 'Shell History' lab it issued unique enumeration commands in sequence without repeating failed commands, unlike O4-mini which re-ran the same cat command four times. It rarely repeated commands even in complex situations and showed that it could modify its approach in response to shell input. GPT-o3 also showed very low repetition, however, it did repeat instructions often when dealing with confused enumeration results or complex privilege escalation pathways. Crucially, the rise in redundancy varied from lab to lab. Regardless of the framework, some activities were done with little repetition, especially those with well-defined output cues. These results imply that although complete autonomy can result in a slight increase in duplication, task structure and a model's reasoning architecture are more likely to be the underlying factors.

4.2 Qualitative Behavioural Insights

Although quantitative metrics provide are a good objective indicator of response patterns and success rates, they are not sufficient to explain the full picture of a model's behaviour.

One recurring issue was the lack of effective use of context in multi-stage scenarios, where models frequently identified compromised credentials in early output but did not reuse them when they were required to log in or escalate privileges. This was associated with an inability to efficiently chain steps. Models, such as GPT4o-mini and Gemini, were able to recognize the initial step in several tasks that required multi-hop reasoning, such as LFI leading to credential extraction, followed by SSH access and local privilege escalation. However, when expected to build on previous progress, these models stalled. This was particularly noticeable in Multi-stage Web-App Priv-Esc, where models were able to detect misconfigurations but were unable to convert them into useful next steps.

Additionally, the enumeration method was not consistent. While skilled human testers follow a systematic procedure, checking sudo -l, cron jobs, and environment variables, models often omitted important steps or repeated the same commands needlessly. Early on, GPT-4o frequently ignored fundamental enumeration steps, and Gemini produced verbose, overly generic scans even when context did not require them. Lack of internal feedback loops and prompt sensitivity were two further drawbacks. A number of models fell back on generic answers when system output was unclear or sparse. Even when the destination was not a web server, models frequently produced placeholder commands like checking .git or .env files or hallucinated solutions since they lacked a means of verifying progress. Responses that were overly general and repetitive were also common. Regardless of the setting, a number of models recommended using the same instruments or enumeration methods in every lab. For example, even when enumeration made it quite evident that there were no web app folders, GPT-4o-mini kept inspecting them.

Moreover, the models failed to interpret non-standard indications such as different user accounts or changed service settings. Due to their inability to generalize from subtle cues, models missed significant turning points, particularly in more challenging jobs involving chained privilege escalation. The propagation of errors was a more pervasive issue. Despite these limitations, some models demonstrated effective, self-directed reasoning, particularly DeepSeek-r1 and GPT-o3. By maintaining contextual awareness and constantly modifying its enumeration,

DeepSeek showed greater judgment in moving from one step to the next without straying off topic in increasingly difficult labs.

Each LLM also suffered its own specific set of issues. All models from OpenAI were consistently too hasty to act on shell output. Meaning the models would process the output until they found something they deemed useful, and then seemingly ignore the rest of the output. This caused it to frequently miss critical information. Gemini, on the other hand, had a hard time adapting based on new information in the environment or failed attempts. It would come to an initial hypothesis, and if that idea failed, it would spend the entire allotted time trying to get its initial idea to work. During testing, it rarely took a step back and decided to try a new approach. Deepseek-r1 spent a great amount of time deliberating and questioning itself on each turn. While this led to a higher success rate overall, it often meant that the model would find the right idea quickly but then spend several minutes doubting itself and discussing ways in which it could be wrong. This time would almost certainly be better spent actually testing the idea and learning from its output.

5 Discussion

Overall, the User-Navigated Framework outperformed the other framework, especially on medium and hard tasks. In this regard models such as DeepSeek-r1 and GPT-o3 demonstrated more dependable performance with higher target completion rates and fewer false positives. Depending on previous shell output, these models were better able to modify their command sequences and preserve context. Models might have been able to concentrate better on the current task state without hastily converging on an incorrect escalation path thanks to the structured turn-based interaction. The discrepancy became increasingly apparent as task difficulty rose. Both frameworks had almost the same success rates in simpler labs like Writable Cron Job and Sudo Caching. However, in more unclear, multi-stage scenarios, autonomous models were more likely to seek premature escalation, misinterpret findings, or repeat orders.

DeepSeek-r1 was the most consistent in both frameworks. It maintained relatively high success rates in difficult tasks and demonstrated only a minimal increase in redundancy and false positives in the autonomous scenario. This suggests stronger internal state management and better use of shell output to guide escalation decisions. The CLI Agent framework, however, showed a more noticeable performance drop for GPT-4o-mini and Gemini, suggesting a higher dependence on linear prompting structure and a lower level of stability when it is not utilized.

It is interesting to note that the Fully Autonomous Framework's continuous command execution loop made it more prone to compounding errors. For tasks that required pivots for multi-user permissions or intermediate validation steps, where a model frequently made a wrong inference and then continued down a flawed line of reasoning until the session ended. These findings suggest that the autonomous framework exaggerates the models' individual inherent flaws.

The tested models tended to fall into two broad behavioural patterns: those that prioritised speed and breadth, and those that appeared to favour caution and verification. Agents such as DeepSeek-r1(and o3, but to a lesser extent) demonstrated high levels of internal deliberation, often avoiding premature escalation and generating concise, well-reasoned outputs. Conversely, models like GPT-4o and Gemini operated more forcefully, frequently delivering command sequences with little regard for previously generated shell output or newly emerging context. This behaviour sped up the completion of simpler tasks, but it was harmful in multi-stage situations where memory and accuracy were required.

The absence of genuine contemplation or revision was another characteristic shared by all models. Models seldom took a step back to reevaluate their course of action after formulating a hypothesis, whether it was accurate or not. While some models were more adept at controlling this, typically by using more token-efficient reasoning or stricter output discipline, none of them consistently showed the ability to drop a bad strategy in favor of a new one. While still suffering from this problem, Deepseek-r1 was superior to all other models in avoiding this issue.

These results highlight a potential weakness in current LLM design: limited internal state awareness or self-evaluation in highly complicated environments. Even though models can mimic reasoning and adapt to new inputs in a single turn, they struggle to control uncertainty across multiple steps in the absence of external control. The reasoning behind this being a universal problem across models is likely due to how they are trained, tested, and rewarded. The models are incentivised during fine tuning to reach the desired goal as effectively and efficiently as possible [3], in our case this means that the model will come to an initial hypothesis based on the simplest possible version of the lab before taking the needed enumeration steps to gather wider context.

Our results suggest that the ability of large language models to carry out post-exploitation privilege escalation tasks varies considerably under the tested conditions, with measurable differences in performance metrics, such as accuracy and efficiency. DeepSeek-r1 and GPT-o3 produced some of the most reliable results in our test set, particularly in several medium and hard tasks. They demonstrated notable contextual awareness, effective multi-step command chaining, and avoided reliance on redundant output. Both models performed consistently throughout a wide range of difficulty stages, especially in tasks that required precision over verbosity.

In each model, numerous enduring behavioural problems were found, including shallow enumeration techniques, an over-reliance on established payloads, failure to adapt after incorrect assumptions, and command repetition loops in the absence of contextual feedback. However, when compared to previous research, the results also point to an optimistic rising trajectory in model capabilities. Compared to older LLMs covered in existing literature, many of which struggled with even single-vector tasks, the newer generation of models in this study appeared to show improvements in success rate, goal convergence, and consistency within our controlled test conditions. This trend may indicate that LLMs are becoming more resilient and contextually aware in simulated hostile environments, although they still face constraints such as limited adaptability and contextual understanding.

References

1. Al-Sinani, H., Mitchell, C.: Ai-augmented ethical hacking: a practical examination of manual exploitation and privilege escalation in linux environments. Workingpaper, arXiv (2024). https://doi.org/10.48550/arXiv.2411.17539
2. Al-Sinani, H.S., Mitchell, C.J.: Pentest2.0: Towards autonomous privilege escalation using genai (2025). https://arxiv.org/abs/2507.06742
3. Cui, G., et al.: Process reinforcement through implicit rewards (2025). https://arxiv.org/pdf/2502.01456
4. Deng, G., et al.: Pentestgpt: An llm-empowered automatic penetration testing tool (2024). https://arxiv.org/abs/2308.06782
5. Gupta, M., Akiri, C., Aryal, K., Parker, E., Praharaj, L.: From chatgpt to threatgpt: impact of generative ai in cybersecurity and privacy. IEEE Access **11**, 80218–80245 (2023). https://doi.org/10.1109/ACCESS.2023.3300381
6. Happe, A., Cito, J.: Getting pwn'd by ai: Penetration testing with large language models. In: Proceedings of the 31st ACM Joint European Software Engineering Conference and Symposium on the Foundations of Software Engineering. pp. 2082–2086. ESEC/FSE 2023, Association for Computing Machinery, New York, NY, USA (2023). https://doi.org/10.1145/3611643.3613083
7. Happe, A., Kaplan, A., Cito, J.: Llms as hackers: Autonomous linux privilege escalation attacks (2023). https://arxiv.org/pdf/2310.11409
8. Hilario, E., Azam, S., Sundaram, J., Imran Mohammed, K., Shanmugam, B.: Generative ai for pentesting: the good, the bad, the ugly. Int. J. Inf. Secur. **23**(3), 2075–2097 (2024). https://doi.org/10.1007/s10207-024-00835-x
9. Huang, J., Zhu, Q.: Penheal: a two-stage llm framework for automated pentesting and optimal remediation (2024). https://arxiv.org/abs/2407.17788
10. Isozaki, I., Shrestha, M., Console, R., Kim, E.: Towards automated penetration testing: Introducing llm benchmark, analysis, and improvements. In: Adjunct Proceedings of the 33rd ACM Conference on User Modeling, Adaptation and Personalization. pp. 404–419. UMAP Adjunct '25, Association for Computing Machinery, New York, NY, USA (2025). https://doi.org/10.1145/3708319.3733804
11. Lukoa, K., Swanda, A.: Llm cyber evaluations don't capture real-world risk (2025). https://arxiv.org/abs/2502.00072
12. Shen, X., et al.: Pentestagent: Incorporating llm agents to automated penetration testing (2024). https://arxiv.org/abs/2411.05185
13. Valencia, L.J.: Artificial intelligence as the new hacker: developing agents for offensive security (2024). https://arxiv.org/abs/2406.07561
14. Yigit, Y., Buchanan, W.J., Tehrani, M.G., Maglaras, L.: Review of generative ai methods in cybersecurity (2024). https://arxiv.org/abs/2403.08701

6th International Workshop on Cyber-Physical Security for Critical Infrastructures (CPS4CIP 2025)

A Comparative Study of ICS Honeypot Deployments

Frederik Ondrikov[1], Denis Donadel[2], Francesco Lupia[3], Massimo Merro[2], Daniel dos Santos[4], Emmanuele Zambon[1], and Nicola Zannone[1](✉)

[1] Eindhoven University of Technology, Eindhoven, The Netherlands
f.ondrikov@student.tue.nl, {e.zambon,n.zannone}@tue.nl
[2] Università degli Studi di Verona, Verona, Italy
{denis.donadel,massimo.merro}@univr.it
[3] Università della Calabria, Rende, Italy
francesco.lupia@unical.it
[4] Forescout Technologies, Eindhoven, The Netherlands
daniel.dossantos@forescout.com

Abstract. Honeypots are increasingly used in Industrial Control Systems (ICS) to divert attacks from critical assets and study malicious behavior. While prior work has examined specific aspects of ICS honeypot design, a comprehensive understanding of cost-effective deployment strategies is still lacking. This work investigates how interaction level, network type, and geographic location affect the attractiveness of ICS honeypots. We deploy both low- and high-interaction honeypots, alongside a physical device, across corporate and cloud networks in various geographic regions. We collect and analyze network interactions involving HTTP, S7Comm, and Modbus protocols from 16 honeypots with diverse configurations over a three-month period. Our results show that network type has the largest impact on ICS honeypot traffic, while interaction level and geographic location play a minor role. We also find that low-interaction honeypots capture traffic comparable to high-interaction setups, supporting their use for general threat intelligence.

1 Introduction

Industrial Control Systems (ICSs) are physical and engineered systems whose operations are monitored, coordinated, and controlled by interconnected computing and communication components [25]. ICSs include Operational Technology (OT), such as Supervisory Control and Data Acquisition (SCADA), and embedded devices, such as Programmable Logic Controllers (PLCs), which form the backbone of critical infrastructures.

Modern ICSs are increasingly integrating Information Technology (IT) capabilities into legacy OT environments. This integration enhances connectivity and remote access but also creates a more complex and exposed attack surface. ICSs often have long operational lifespans, making them vulnerable to emerging cyber threats. Notable incidents

R. Laborde et al. (Eds.): ESORICS 2025 Workshops, LNCS 16233, pp. 125–145, 2026.
https://doi.org/10.1007/978-3-032-16165-9_8

such as the Stuxnet worm targeting Iran's nuclear program [6] and the Industroyer malware used in the Ukraine power grid attack [15] demonstrate the real-world impact of ICS vulnerabilities.

To better understand and mitigate these threats, honeypots are increasingly deployed as decoy systems designed to attract attackers, allowing analysts to observe and analyze malicious behavior. They serve as early warning systems and deception mechanisms that divert attacks from critical assets [24]. Honeypots vary in complexity based on (among others) their interaction level. Low-interaction honeypots expose limited functionality, require less effort to deploy, and pose minimal risk of system compromise, but are often easily fingerprinted and dismissed by sophisticated attackers or scanners like Shodan [16,21,26,29,32]. High-interaction honeypots, by contrast, more closely resemble real systems, making them harder to detect and better suited for capturing complex attacker behavior [14]. However, they entail higher operational costs and increased risk of compromise.

Beyond the level of interaction, factors such as deployment environment and geographic location can also influence the effectiveness of a honeypot [3,5,35]. While ICSs are traditionally deployed on-premise within corporate networks, cloud-based honeypots are increasingly being considered to avoid exposing real infrastructure. Yet, attackers may regard ICS honeypots in cloud environments as less credible targets, reducing their willingness to engage. On the other hand, Shodan scans show that ICS protocols (e.g., Modbus, S7Comm) are widely used in cloud environments, although attacker behavior toward such protocols in cloud environments is not yet well understood. Similarly, the geographic location of deployments can influence traffic volume and behavior [5,12,28]. As ICS devices are unevenly distributed, attacker interest may vary by region, focusing more on areas with a higher concentration of ICS devices, such as North America, Asia, and Europe.

However, key challenges remain underexplored in the literature. There is limited understanding of how specific honeypot characteristics–particularly interaction level, network type, and geographic location–impact the volume and nature of ICS interactions. Additionally, while high-interaction honeypots may generate richer and potentially more interesting threat intelligence, their complexity raises deployment and maintenance barriers. Understanding these trade-offs is essential for designing effective honeypot-based defenses for industrial environments.

Contributions. This work examines the impact of interaction level, type, and geographic region of the deployment network on ICS honeypot attractiveness. To this end, we deploy 16 ICS honeypots in collaboration with Forescout Technology, a cybersecurity company specialized in threat detection and operational technology security. Our setup includes a physical PLC (Siemens Simatic S7-1200) and both low- and high-interaction honeypots emulating the same device, distributed across two network types (corporate network vs. cloud network) and three geographic regions (Europe, North America, Asia). The honeypots are exposed to the Internet for three months, during which we collect HTTP, Modbus, and S7Comm traffic. We characterize attractiveness by traffic volume and complexity; due to space constraints, we omit a detailed analysis of traffic nature, which is part of ongoing work. The main contributions are as follows:

- Our findings show that, for ICS honeypots, network type has a stronger influence on attracting ICS traffic than geographic location or interaction level, highlighting the need to consider the deployment environment when designing honeypot studies.
- Our study shows that unsolicited ICS traffic is significantly less frequent than IT traffic, yet its presence may indicate reconnaissance activity and, thus, should be considered in threat detection efforts.
- Our study shows that low- and high-interaction honeypots receive comparable ICS traffic, suggesting that low-interaction setups are generally sufficient for generic threat intelligence gathering.

Outline. The remainder of this paper is organized as follows. Section 2 reviews relevant background and prior research on ICS honeypots. Section 3 introduces our research questions. Section 4 describes the deployed infrastructure and the methods used to address the research questions. Section 5 presents the results, and Sect. 6 discusses the key findings. Finally, Sect. 7 concludes the paper.

2 Background and Related Work

This section introduces ICS honeypots, reviews related work, and identifies research gaps.

2.1 ICS Honeypots

ICS honeypots serve multiple purposes, including diverting attackers from critical assets, studying adversary behavior, and gathering threat intelligence. Like traditional honeypots, they are categorized by interaction level. Low-interaction honeypots simulate basic network behavior without replicating the full device functionality, relying on scripted actions that attackers may eventually recognize [16]. Despite this, they remain popular for their ease of deployment, simplicity, and lower operational risk. High-interaction honeypots, on the other hand, offer richer emulation by supporting full process control and interaction with simulated or physical environments, though they require more complex setup and pose greater security risks. Recent frameworks like HoneyICS [17] have emerged to provide high-interaction capabilities by virtualizing PLCs and linking them to simulated industrial processes. Built on OpenPLC [2], a widely used open-source virtual PLC, HoneyICS supports Modbus natively and integrates Snap7 [22] to enable S7Comm communication. It allows interaction with a simulated industrial process, offering higher realism compared to low-interaction honeypots like Conpot [19]. Understanding the trade-offs between honeypot types is essential for designing effective experiments and cost-efficient deployment strategies.

2.2 Related Work

Research on ICS honeypots spans several dimensions, including the comparison of interaction levels and the influence of network type and geographic location. Table 1 summarizes the literature in this domain.

Table 1. Summary of related work

	Domain	Level of Interaction				Deployment Environment	
		Low-Interaction Honeypot	High-Interaction Honeypot	Physical PLC	Level of Interaction Comparison	Network Type Comparison	Region Comparison
Pouget et al. [23]	IT	◐	●	○	◐	○	○
Alata et al. [1]	IT	◐	●	○	◐	○	○
Bloomfield et al. [4]	IT	◐	●	○	◐	●	○
Sochor et al. [27]	IT	●	○	○	○	●	○
Bove et al. [5]	IT	●	○	○	○	●	●
Kelly et al. [12]	IT	●	○	○	○	◐	●
Kocaogullar et al. [14]	IT	●	●	○	●	○	○
Zou et al. [35]	IT	●	○	○	○	◐	◐
Guarnizo et al. [9]	IoT	●	●	○	●	◐	◐
Tambe et al. [30]	IoT	○	●	○	○	◐	◐
Jicha et al. [11]	ICS	●	○	○	○	○	○
Dodson et al. [7]	ICS	○	●	○	○	○	◐
You et al. [34]	ICS	◐	●	●	●	○	◐
Bieker et al. [3]	ICS	●	○	○	○	●	●
Maesschalck et al. [19]	ICS	●	○	●	◐	○	○
Lupia et al. [18]	ICS	○	●	○	○	○	○
Srinivasa et al. [28]	IoT/ICS	●	●	○	●	●	●
This work	ICS	●	●	●	●	●	●

Legend: ○= Not Discussed, ◐= Partially Discussed, ●= Fully Discussed.

Level of Interaction. The attractiveness of honeypots with different interaction levels has been explored primarily in IT and IoT environments. Early IT honeypot studies [1,23] found that high-interaction setups complemented low-interaction ones by validating configurations, with most intrusions attributed to inexperienced attackers using automated tools. However, these findings may not reflect recent advances in attack automation [33] and honeypot technologies. Recent work [14] highlights the richer data collected with high-interaction honeypots, though Guarnizo et al. [9] found similar attack patterns across interaction levels, suggesting realism does not always boost engagement. Some studies focus specifically on ICS honeypots. Jicha et al. [11] and Bieker et al. [3] deploy Conpot and GridPot variants, but offer limited traffic analysis. Dodson et al. [7] conduct a large-scale high-interaction deployment, capturing rare yet significant ICS-specific attacks. Srinivasa et al. [28] compare RioTPot and Conpot, observing that high-interaction honeypots attract more interactions, although differences in protocol support complicate the comparison. Only a few studies compare honeypots to physical PLCs. Maesschalck et al. [19] highlight limitations of low-interaction simulations, though their physical PLC is not exposed to the Internet. Similarly, You et al. [34] deploy a physical Siemens S7-300 PLC and compare its function code coverage with Conpot, but their setup lacks a physical process, limiting realism. Overall, research involving physical ICS honeypots remains limited. Prior work rarely includes online deployments of physical devices, and systematic comparisons between physical, high-, and low-interaction honeypots are lacking. As a result, the relative effectiveness of these honeypots remains underexplored.

Network Type. Several studies have examined how network type influences IT honeypot interactions. Bloomfield et al. [4] find that high-interaction IT honeynets in corporate environments attract more attacks than those in small- to medium-sized enterprises, likely due to public IPs and greater visibility. Sochor et al. [27] show that attackers differentiate between academic and commercial IP ranges. Kelly et al. [12] observe higher attack volumes on Google Cloud compared to AWS and Azure, though the use of different cloud locations may have influenced the results. Other studies deploy honeypots across network types without analyzing the effect. For instance, Guarnizo et al. [9] and Tambe et al. [30] deploy IoT honeypots in local networks with cloud-based forwarders but do not evaluate environmental differences. Bove et al. [5] find minimal variation in SSH intrusions between cloud and internet-connected hosts. Bieker et al. [3] observe lower ICS traffic in cloud honeypots than academic networks, attributing this to the scarcity of ICS devices in the cloud, although their sequential deployment limits confidence in their findings. In contrast, Srinivasa et al. [28] conduct a parallel deployment in corporate and cloud networks, detecting more ICS traffic in the cloud. Although these studies suggest network type may influence attacker behavior, systematic evaluations in ICS remain scarce. Most prior work focuses on IT systems and rarely includes controlled, parallel deployments that isolate network effects.

Region. Prior research highlights the importance of deploying honeypots across diverse locations to uncover regional variations in attacker tactics. For instance, Dodson et al. [7] advocate geographically distributed honeypots to capture a broader spectrum of attack strategies. Building on this, Zou et al. [35] deploy high-interaction IT honeypots in East Asia, Western Europe, and US East via Azure, observing notable differences in traffic volume and unique IPs across regions. Similar trends are also reported in [5, 12]. Srinivasa et al. [28] report Europe attracted the most malicious IoT/ICS traffic, followed by the US and Asia, while Bieker et al. [3] record more ICS traffic in Asia than in the US. Most of these findings, however, are based on IT honeypots, leaving geographic influences on ICS honeypot attractiveness underexplored. In addition, inconsistent experimental setups between locations make it difficult to isolate geographic effects from other variables.

2.3 Research Gaps

To the best of our knowledge, there is no systematic comparison of interaction levels—low and high—in ICS environments. Existing studies often use inconsistent setups or overlook how these configurations influence honeypot attractiveness. This limits our ability to assess the trade-off between deployment cost and effectiveness. Moreover, the impact of the deployment environment is still unclear. While some studies suggest differences in traffic between cloud and corporate networks, these findings often rely on sequential deployments or vague threat classifications. Without controlled, concurrent experiments, the true impact of network context on honeypot attractiveness remains unclear. Geographic location is another underexplored factor. While IT-focused research highlights regional differences, ICS studies are limited in scope and often inconsistent in results. A broader and systematic evaluation across locations is needed to assess how the deployment region influences the attractiveness of ICS targets. Finally, interactions between factors—such as network type and geographic location—are rarely investigated. This lack of multi-dimensional analysis restricts our understanding of how ICS honeypots are perceived in practice. Addressing these gaps through systematic evaluations would enhance our understanding and offer clearer guidance for honeypot deployment.

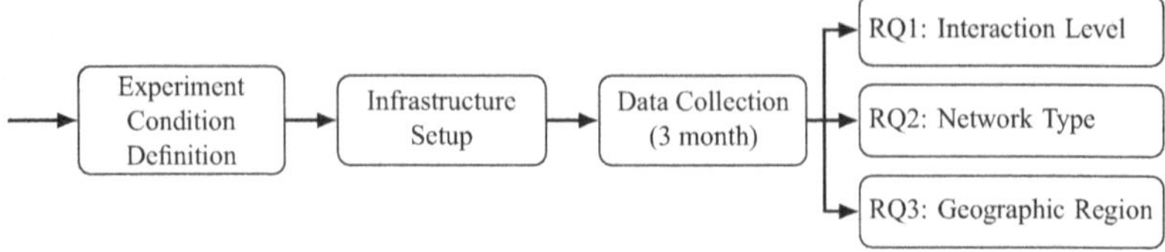

Fig. 1. Methodology Overview

3 Research Questions

Previous studies have examined various honeypot types and configurations, often focusing on isolated aspects (cf. Sect. 2.2). However, honeypot attractiveness may depend on a broader, potentially interdependent set of factors, including interaction level, network type, and geographic location. This work systematically investigates how these factors influence the attractiveness of ICS honeypots. Our first research question investigates the role of interaction level. High-interaction honeypots, including those involving physical PLCs, can capture more sophisticated behavior, but they are also more complex to deploy and operate. Understanding their impact helps assess when the added complexity is justified.

RQ1: *To what extent does the level of interaction supported by an ICS honeypot influence the attractiveness of the honeypot?*

Realistic IP addresses are key for honeypots to avoid detection [7]. While cloud setups offer convenience and isolation, ICS devices are typically tied to physical infrastructure, making corporate deployments appear more authentic. This raises the question whether corporate-based ICS honeypots are more attractive than cloud-hosted ones.

RQ2: *To what extent does the network type on which an ICS honeypot is deployed influence the attractiveness of the honeypot?*

Prior work suggests that attacks can vary by region, motivating the geographic distribution of ICS honeypots [7]. To investigate this, ICS honeypots should be deployed in diverse locations to assess whether geographic location affects attractiveness and reveals potential regional differences in traffic captured.

RQ3: *To what extent does the geographic location of an ICS honeypot influence the attractiveness of the honeypot?*

4 Methodology

An overview of our methodology is shown in Fig. 1. After defining the experiment conditions (Sect. 4.1), we deploy the data collection infrastructure and collect data over a 90-day period (Sect. 4.2). To answer the research questions, we evaluate protocol-specific attractiveness across honeypots by comparing the captured traffic based on interaction level (RQ1), network type (RQ2), and geographic region (RQ3).

4.1 Experiment Conditions

We define 12 experiment conditions in our study (Fig. 2). Each condition corresponds to a specific configuration of the honeypot, determined by three variables: the *interaction level* it supports, the *type of network* in which it is deployed, and the *geographic region* of deployment. We now discuss the choices made for each of these variables.

Interaction Levels. To assess how interaction level affects honeypot attractiveness (RQ1), we deploy three setups: a *low-interaction ICS honeypot*, a *high-interaction ICS honeypot*, and a *physical ICS device*. To allow meaningful comparison, all honeypots simulate the same device type and expose the same ICS protocols. Specifically, we choose the Modbus and S7Comm protocols due to their high diffusion in the wild [20,26]. We select the S7-1200 as the physical PLC due to native protocol support and wide ICS adoption. We use Conpot [19] for low interaction and HoneyICS [17] for high interaction. Both can simulate a Siemens S7-1200 PLC, support Modbus and S7Comm, and host a static web server. All setups appear similar externally but differ in interaction level: Conpot gives static responses, HoneyICS offers process interaction via Modbus only, and the PLC offers process interaction via both protocols and full device configuration via S7Comm. The interaction levels of the three setups are detailed in Appendix A.

Network Types. To assess whether network type affects honeypot attractiveness (RQ2), we consider a *corporate network* and a *cloud-based network*. The corporate network reflects a realistic ICS setup, with on-premise devices accessible via public IPs. In contrast, cloud networks are commonly used only for honeypot deployments [3,5,12]. By comparing the two, we aim to determine whether they are perceived differently in terms of attractiveness. To control for geographic bias, one cloud deployment is placed in the same region as the corporate network (Europe); see Sect. 4.2 for details.

Geographic Regions. To assess the influence of geographic region (RQ3), we consider three global regions: *Europe*, *North America*, and *Asia*. This selection follows prior research and Shodan scans showing these areas host the most publicly accessible ICS devices. According to Shodan, the US has the highest number of exposed ICS devices using Modbus and S7Comm, making it the best representative for North America. While China ranks second, infrastructure restrictions prevent server deployment there; thus, we choose Singapore, ranked third, to represent Asia. The choice for Europe reflects the location of the corporate network available for our study (see Sect. 4.2).

4.2 Data Collection

Infrastructure. Based on our experiment conditions (Sect. 4.1), we set up the infrastructure to enable data collection (Fig. 2). The infrastructure encompasses 16 ICS honeypots[1]. All honeypots expose HTTP, S7Comm, and Modbus services. They are deployed on a corporate network and exposed on the cloud network using proxies. This

[1] Note that we deploy two instances of HoneyICS, resulting in 16 honeypots across the 12 experiment conditions in Sect. 4.1. This allows us to estimate variability in the collected traffic.

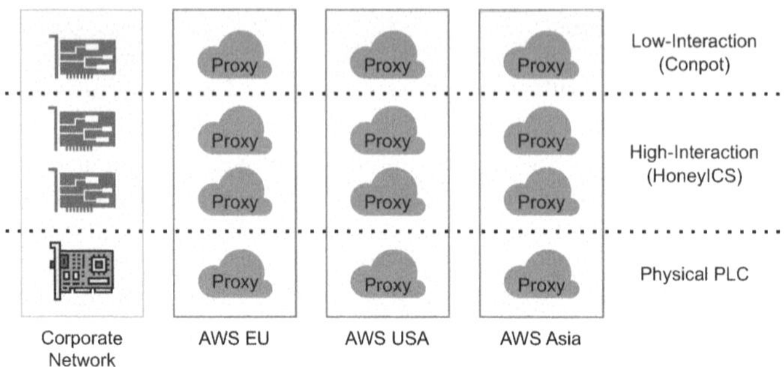

Fig. 2. Architecture of the honeypots and AWS proxies

ensures consistent behavior across network types and regions. We now describe key details of the infrastructure.

Honeypots. We deploy Conpot as a Docker container and customize it to mimic a Siemens S7-1200 PLC. Customization involves modifying Conpot's default templates to update its web interface and the scripted S7Comm and Modbus responses. We deploy two HoneyICS instances in a Docker environment that simulates a production process controlled by virtualized S7-1200 PLCs. Each virtualized PLC exposes the same services (Modbus and S7Comm) and a web interface. The physical Siemens S7-1200 PLC interacts with HoneyICS via Modbus and controls part of the same (simulated) physical process. To this end, its ladder logic is built and loaded using Siemens TIA Portal software. To ensure continuous operation under attack, an automated script monitors the PLC integrity and restarts it when needed (e.g., if forced into STOP mode).

Deployment. We deployed our honeypots using the infrastructure and resources of Forescout Technologies, including a subscription to Amazon Web Services (AWS). The four honeypots are hosted on a corporate network in the Netherlands, each with a unique IPv4 address leased from a Dutch ISP that supports enterprise and ICS environments, to guarantee realism. For the cloud instances, we leverage Forescout's subscription to AWS. Based on our experiment conditions (Sect. 4.1), we selected three AWS regions: US East (North Virginia), Asia Pacific (Singapore), and EU Central (Frankfurt), which is the AWS region closest to the corporate network. Instead of duplicating instances, we deploy lightweight proxies on AWS that forward traffic to the corporate-hosted honeypots. Each proxy has a dedicated Elastic IP to ensure stable public access across reboots.

Packet Capture and Storage. All traffic to and from the honeypots on ports 80 (HTTP), 102 (S7Comm), and 502 (Modbus) is captured as PCAP files using tcpdump [31]. The packet capture setup varies depending on the network environment. In the corporate network, it integrates with the existing infrastructure, which includes a pre-configured mirroring system. All traffic is mirrored to an external analysis system and stored in an AWS S3 bucket using tcpdump. For AWS deployments, a challenge arises as requests are proxied, so honeypots log correct payloads but proxy IPs. To address this, we capture traffic on the proxies. Tcpdump filters ensure proxy traffic is excluded from honeypot captures and vice versa, so each system records only its own interactions. PCAP files are saved on separate virtual drives for each honeypot and proxy to protect against system failures. File sizes are limited to 100 MB to reduce data loss in case of corruption.

Dataset. Data collection took place over 90 days, between December 21, 2024, and March 21, 2025. In this period, all incoming and outgoing packets for each honeypot are captured and stored as PCAP files. This format allows us to extract all relevant traffic details, such as source and destination addresses, protocols and payload content (e.g., Modbus function codes). As a preliminary step, we removed all traffic generated from IPs under our control to remove any bias in the data. Table 2 summarizes the distribution of HTTP, Modbus, and S7Comm requests across honeypots.

Table 2. Observed Requests per Honeypot.

Honeypot	Network	Region	HTTP	Modbus	S7Comm
Conpot	Corporate	EU	27032	1172	1336
HoneyICS1	Corporate	EU	26307	776	1682
HoneyICS2	Corporate	EU	25829	643	1632
Physical PLC	Corporate	EU	15329	695	1658
Conpot	Cloud	EU	123332	403	761
HoneyICS1	Cloud	EU	119915	453	845
HoneyICS2	Cloud	EU	117983	460	904
Physical PLC	Cloud	EU	60915	411	901
Conpot	Cloud	US	73377	415	811
HoneyICS1	Cloud	US	77890	429	875
HoneyICS2	Cloud	US	84779	475	920
Physical PLC	Cloud	US	77429	441	889
Conpot	Cloud	Asia	87613	450	810
HoneyICS1	Cloud	Asia	105403	466	979
HoneyICS2	Cloud	Asia	84149	425	961
Physical PLC	Cloud	Asia	67718	436	841
Total			1175000	8550	16805

4.3 Data Analysis

To answer our research questions, we characterize and compare interactions across different honeypot deployments. To this end, we first introduce the notion of interaction and define the metrics for assessing honeypot attractiveness.

Interactions. We adapt the definition of interaction in [18]: a sequence of requests that (1) originate from the same IP, (2) target the same destination IP and port, and (3) occur within a specified maximum time interval. We exclude the source port to account for tools that use multiple TCP connections for a single logical task. Following [18], we analyze inter-request intervals to define appropriate time thresholds, considering potential proxy-induced delays, particularly in HTTP traffic. For HTTP, we select a 30-second threshold, which captures 95% of HTTP follow-up requests (from the same IP). For S7Comm and Modbus, we inspect packet sequences, ensuring continuity of TCP connections. Based on this analysis, we apply a 15-second threshold across all deployments for both S7Comm and Modbus, which captures 99.96% and 100% of subsequent requests, respectively.

Attractiveness. We assess attractiveness by interaction volume and complexity. The complexity is measured as the number of requests per interaction, providing an indication of their sophistication. A honeypot is deemed more attractive if it receives a larger number of interactions with higher complexity.

Analysis Methods. We aggregate the data according to experiment conditions to assess attractiveness across different interaction levels (RQ1), network types (RQ2), and geographic regions (RQ3), analyzing interaction volume and complexity in each case. To address RQ1, we aggregate interactions by honeypot type (Conpot, HoneyICS1, HoneyICS2, and the physical PLC) across all deployment environments (corporate network, AWS EU, AWS US, and AWS Asia). To address RQ2, we separately aggregate interactions from the honeypots on the corporate network and on the AWS EU cloud. To address RQ3, we focus on cloud deployments and aggregate interactions for each region (AWS EU, AWS US, AWS Asia). Additionally, we analyze the geographic origin of IP addresses interacting with the honeypots using GreyNoise [8] and, where necessary, IP-API [10]. Grouping IP origins by continent helps assess whether the deployment region influences the geographic distribution of interactions.

5 Results

This section presents our results, structured around the research questions; we refer to Appendix B for the complete results.

RQ1: To what extent does the level of interaction supported by an ICS honeypot influence the attractiveness of the honeypot? Table 3 reports the number of interactions (Count) and their complexity (Min, Q1, Median, Q3, and Max) for each protocol across different levels of interaction (Conpot, HoneyICS, and physical PLC). The table shows notable differences between protocols. We now discuss the results for each protocol.

HTTP. Figure 3 (left) shows the number of HTTP interactions per day for each level of interaction. For a large portion of the data collection period, we observe no notable differences between the honeypots. However, we observe a sharp increase in March for Conpot and both HoneyICS instances, while the physical PLC maintains a stable trend. This shift may be attributed to differences in the web server technologies used by the honeypots. Conpot and HoneyICS both employ Lighttpd, whereas the physical PLC uses a jQuery-based server. A detailed analysis shows that a single IP address is responsible for the shift (on both Conpot and HoneyICS), repeatedly issuing HTTP GET requests to `/login.cgi/cgi_main.cgi` with admin/admin credentials. The Lighttpd servers generate responses that appear to encourage repeated attempts,

Table 3. Interaction level: volume and complexity

Honeypot	Protocol	Min	Q1	Median	Q3	Max	Count
Conpot	HTTP	1	1	1	2	19994	42321
	S7Comm	1	3	3	3	8	1318
	Modbus	1	1	1	1	241	1487
HoneyICS1	HTTP	1	1	1	2	12534	40408
	S7Comm	1	3	3	3	16	1535
	Modbus	1	1	1	1	10	1393
HoneyICS2	HTTP	1	1	1	2	8021	41870
	S7Comm	1	3	3	3	16	1529
	Modbus	1	1	1	1	16	1348
Physical PLC	HTTP	1	1	1	2	7365	38381
	S7Comm	1	3	3	3	4	1484
	Modbus	1	1	1	1	10	1314

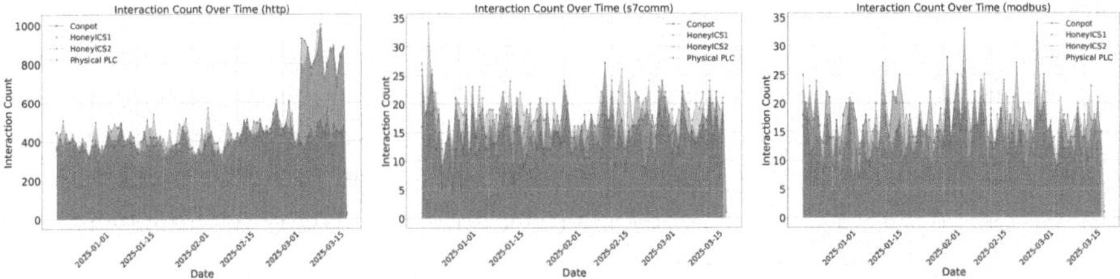

Fig. 3. Interactions per Level of Interaction for HTTP (left), S7Comm (center), and Modbus (right).

while the jQuery-based server returns responses that did not trigger further activity. This suggests that the observed increase in interactions is primarily driven by server behavior rather than by the honeypot's interaction level. Considering the overall number of interactions (see Table 3), the physical PLC receives the fewest interactions, followed by HoneyICS, while Conpot receives the most. Even among honeypots with the same interaction level (HoneyICS1 vs. HoneyICS2), we observe a noticeable variation in the number of interactions, further suggesting that interaction level alone does not determine HTTP attractiveness. Moreover, Table 3 shows that the Min, Q1, Median, and Q3 values are identical across honeypots, indicating that at least 75% of interactions have similar complexity regardless of the honeypot's interaction level. The main difference lies in the maximum complexity: Conpot exhibits the most complex interaction, followed by HoneyICS and then the physical PLC. Again, notable variation between the two HoneyICS instances reinforces the conclusion that interaction level does not consistently influence the attractiveness or complexity of HTTP interactions in ICS honeypots.

S7Comm. Figure 3 (center) reports the S7Comm interactions per day for each interaction level. The curves are closely aligned, indicating minor differences in interaction frequency across levels. Conpot consistently receives the fewest interactions. Honey-

ICS shows the highest activity, with its two instances differing by only six interactions (Table 3). The physical PLC follows, with approximately 50 fewer interactions (3%), indicating a comparable level of engagement. The distribution of interaction complexity is nearly identical across all honeypots (Table 3). Outliers are scarce for Conpot and both HoneyICS instances, while absent for the physical PLC.

Modbus. Figure 3 (right) reports the Modbus interactions per day for each interaction level. All levels of interaction show similar daily trends, but Conpot exhibits the most frequent and highest peaks, while HoneyICS and the physical PLC follow a comparable but lower pattern. This trend is consistent with the total interaction counts shown in Table 3, where Conpot receives approximately 100 more interactions (7%) than HoneyICS and about 170 more than the physical PLC (12%). These findings suggest that Conpot attracts more Modbus interactions compared to the higher-interaction counterparts. Across all interaction levels, most Modbus interactions have a complexity of 1. For HoneyICS and the physical PLC, the few interactions with higher complexity comprise 6 and 10 requests, while for Conpot, they mostly comprise 2 or 3 requests (Table 3). An in-depth analysis shows that this difference in complexity is influenced by how Conpot responds to a tool used by Crowdstrike. This suggests that interactions with low-interaction honeypots tend to be less complex than those with high-interaction honeypots or physical PLCs. However, Conpot was involved in one interaction comprising 241 requests, while they were at most 10 and 16 for HoneyICS and 10 for the physical PLC. This suggests that while Conpot typically attracts simpler interactions, it can also elicit highly complex behavior.

Answer to RQ1. The interaction level does not consistently determine the attractiveness of an ICS honeypot. For HTTP, server configuration had a greater impact on interaction patterns than interaction level. In the case of S7Comm, HoneyICS was slightly more attractive, while for Modbus, Conpot drew more interactions. Overall, attractiveness appears to depend more on protocol-specific factors than on interaction level alone.

RQ2: To what extent does the network type on which an ICS honeypot is deployed influence the attractiveness of the honeypot? Table 4 reports the number of interactions (Count) and their complexity (Min, Q1, Median, Q3, and Max) for each protocol across network types (corporate vs. cloud). We now discuss the results for each protocol.

HTTP. Figure 4 (left) shows the HTTP interactions per day for both the corporate network and the cloud network (AWS EU).

Across the entire observation period, the cloud network consistently receives more HTTP interactions than the corporate network (45%), suggesting that it is more attractive for HTTP-based activity. The distribution of HTTP interaction complexity is largely consistent across both networks, with only minor differences. As shown in Table 4, the Min, Q1, Median, and Q3 values are identical, indicating similar interaction patterns regardless of network type. The only notable distinction is in the maximum observed complexity, which is approximately 750 higher on the corporate network. This suggests

Table 4. Network type: volume and complexity

Network	Protocol	Min	Q1	Median	Q3	Max	Count
Corporate	HTTP	1	1	1	2	8021	30700
	S7Comm	1	3	3	3	7	2258
	Modbus	1	1	1	1	241	1585
Cloud	HTTP	1	1	1	2	7269	44365
	S7Comm	1	3	3	3	8	1183
	Modbus	1	1	1	1	10	1313

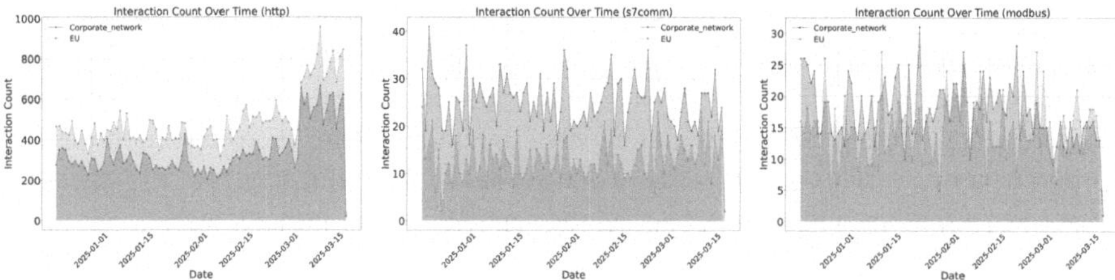

Fig. 4. Interactions per Network Type for HTTP (left), S7Comm (center), and Modbus (right).

that while HTTP interactions are largely comparable across networks, the corporate network occasionally attracts more complex requests.

S7Comm. Figure 4 (center) reports the S7Comm interactions per day for both the corporate and cloud networks. Over the entire observation period, the corporate network consistently receives more S7Comm interactions than the cloud network. This trend is confirmed by Table 4, which shows that the corporate network records approximately twice as many S7Comm interactions (91%), suggesting it is more attractive for this protocol. The overall complexity is almost constant in the two networks, which shows a maximum complexity of 7 and 8 requests for the corporate and cloud networks, respectively.

Modbus. Figure 4 (right) shows the Modbus interactions per day for the corporate and cloud networks. While both exhibit fluctuations, the corporate network consistently receives more interactions. Table 4 confirms this trend, showing that the corporate network receives approximately 270 more interactions (21%), suggesting it is a more attractive target for Modbus traffic. Table 4 shows that the overall distribution is largely the same on both networks, with most interactions having a complexity of 1. The difference in maximum complexity is due to a single outlier from Conpot on the corporate network, as noted in the RQ1 analysis. The maximum complexity for all other honeypots on the corporate network is 10, matching that of the cloud network. This suggests that, overall, interaction complexity for Modbus does not meaningfully differ between network types.

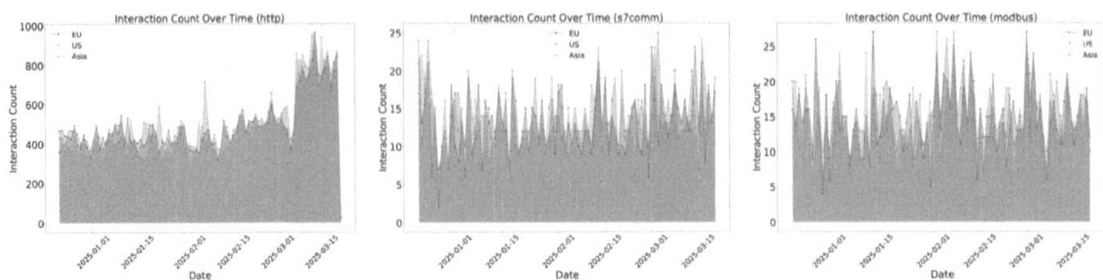

Fig. 5. Interactions per Region for HTTP (left), S7Comm (center), and Modbus (right).

Answer to RQ2. Network type affects the volume of interactions for specific protocols but not their overall complexity. HTTP traffic is more frequent in the cloud environment, whereas S7Comm and Modbus interactions are more common on the corporate network. This suggests that while network type influences protocol-specific attractiveness, it has a limited impact on the sophistication of interactions.

RQ3: To what extent does the geographic location of an ICS honeypot influence its attractiveness? Table 4 reports the number of interactions (Count) and their complexity (Min, Q1, Median, Q3, and Max) for each protocol across regions. We now discuss the results for each protocol, along with the origin of iterations per region.

Table 5. Geographic region: volume and complexity

Location	Protocol	Min	Q1	Median	Q3	Max	Count
EU	HTTP	1	1	1	2	7269	44365
	S7Comm	1	3	3	3	8	1183
	Modbus	1	1	1	1	10	1313
US	HTTP	1	1	1	2	19994	41386
	S7Comm	1	3	3	3	16	1182
	Modbus	1	1	1	1	16	1303
Asia	HTTP	1	1	1	2	12534	46529
	S7Comm	1	3	3	3	16	1243
	Modbus	1	1	1	1	10	1341

HTTP. Figure 5 (left) reports the HTTP interactions per day across different regions. The trends are relatively similar across regions, although Asia exhibits the highest peaks, followed by the EU and then the US. Table 5 confirms this pattern, showing that Asia receives over 2000 more HTTP interactions than the EU (5%) and over 5000 more than the US (12%). This suggests that Asia is the most attractive region for HTTP interactions. The complexity is consistent across all regions, with identical Min, Q1, Median, and Q3 values, as shown in Table 5. The only notable variation lies in the maximum values: the US records the highest at 19,994, followed by Asia (12,534) and the EU (7,269). These, however, appear to be outliers; most complex interactions for the US and Asia typically fall between 7,100 and 7,400. Overall, these findings suggest that HTTP interaction complexity is not strongly influenced by geographic region.

S7Comm. Figure 5 (center) reports the S7Comm interactions per day across different regions. The trends are relatively similar, with no substantial differences in the number of S7Comm interactions. As shown in Table 5, Asia receives approximately 60 more interactions than both the EU and the US (5%), while the difference between the EU and US is minimal, just one interaction. This may indicate that Asia is marginally more attractive for S7Comm interactions, though the variation is minor. The distribution of interaction complexity is nearly identical across all regions, as shown in Table 5. The only notable difference is in the maximum complexity, with both the US and Asia showing interaction values roughly twice as complex as those observed in the EU.

Modbus. Figure 5 (right) reports the Modbus interactions per day across different regions. The trends are relatively similar across all regions, with no substantial differences observed. Table 5 supports this observation, indicating that Asia receives approximately 30 more Modbus interactions than the EU (2%) and 40 more than the US (3%). Similarly, the distribution of interaction complexity is nearly identical across regions as shown in Table 5. The only notable deviation is the slightly higher maximum complexity observed in the US compared to the other regions.

Origin of Interactions. Tables 6, 7, and 8 present the geographic origin of interactions for each protocol, with bold values indicating the regions where the honeypots were deployed. Across all protocols, we observe only minor differences in the distribution of interaction origins based on deployment region. While the region in which a honeypot is hosted tends to show a slightly higher share of interactions for that protocol, the difference is minimal, never exceeding 2.7%. These results suggest that geographic deployment has limited influence on the origin of incoming interactions, indicating that honeypot attractiveness is largely independent of deployment region.

Table 6. Origin of HTTP interactions

Region	Africa	Asia	Europe	North America	Oceania	South America	Total
EU	86 (0.19%)	8045 (18.13%)	**24201 (54.55%)**	11424 (25.75%)	170 (0.38%)	439 (0.99%)	44365 (100%)
US	84 (0.20%)	5868 (14.18%)	23403 (56.55%)	**11455 (27.68%)**	154 (0.37%)	422 (1.02%)	41386 (100%)
Asia	313 (0.67%)	**8852 (19.02%)**	24539 (52.74%)	12185 (26.19%)	169 (0.36%)	471 (1.01%)	46529 (100%)
Total	483 (0.37%)	22765 (17.21%)	72143 (54.54%)	35064 (26.51%)	493 (0.37%)	1332 (1.01%)	132280 (100%)

Answer to RQ3. Geographic location has limited impact on honeypot attractiveness. For each protocol, volume and complexity are mostly consistent across regions, with only minor differences. The origin of interacting IPs also appears unaffected by deployment region, suggesting ICS honeypots are not systematically targeted based on location.

Table 7. Origin of S7Comm interactions

Region	Africa	Asia	Europe	North America	Oceania	South America	Total
EU	0 (0.00%)	92 (7.78%)	**227 (19.19%)**	817 (69.06%)	0 (0.00%)	47 (3.97%)	1183 (100%)
US	0 (0.00%)	115 (9.73%)	183 (15.48%)	**817 (69.12%)**	0 (0.00%)	67 (5.67%)	1182 (100%)
Asia	0 (0.00%)	**136 (10.94%)**	214 (17.22%)	847 (68.14%)	0 (0.00%)	46 (3.70%)	1243 (100%)
Total	0 (0.00%)	343 (9.51%)	624 (17.29%)	2481 (68.76%)	0 (0.00%)	160 (4.43%)	3608 (100%)

6 Discussion

The results of this study offer valuable insights into ICS honeypot deployments, providing key considerations for improving their design and effectiveness in future research.

For ICS honeypots, network type matters more than geographic region and interaction level. Our results show that the interaction level (RQ1) and geographic location (RQ3) of ICS honeypots have minimal impact on the volume or complexity of traffic across protocols. In contrast, the network type affects the amount of ICS traffic (RQ2): honeypots in the corporate network received 91% more S7Comm traffic than the cloud-host honeypots (Table 4). This suggests that IPs associated with cloud infrastructure may be excluded when targeting ICS systems, though retained when scanning for exposed web applications. Our results partially align with prior work. Zou et al. [35], using an IT honeypot, found more IT traffic in certain regions, especially Asia. While we found similar results for our IT traffic (HTTP), the same behavior cannot be seen in the OT world (Modbus and S7Comm protocols), where geographical differences are negligible. This contrasts with Bieker et al. [3] and Srinivasa et al. [28], who reported higher ICS traffic in Asia and Europe, respectively. This discrepancy likely stems from methodological choices in prior work, such as aggregating results across protocols and interpreting scanning behavior as inherently malicious. In contrast, our protocol-specific analysis avoids strong assumptions about attacker intent, offering a more cautious interpretation that may more accurately reflect the nature of unsolicited ICS traffic. Our findings have two key implications. First, they highlight the importance of protocol-level analysis when designing honeypot studies or interpreting their results, as the received traffic may be influenced by the specific services exposed. Second, they suggest that to attract more ICS-relevant interactions, honeypot deployments should prioritize corporate environments and expose an HTTP-based HMI alongside ICS protocols. Future work should

Table 8. Origin of Modbus interactions

Region	Africa	Asia	Europe	North America	Oceania	South America	Total
EU	2 (0.15%)	163 (12.41%)	**218 (16.60%)**	887 (67.56%)	0 (0.00%)	43 (3.27%)	1313 (100%)
US	3 (0.23%)	147 (11.28%)	200 (15.35%)	**903 (69.30%)**	0 (0.00%)	50 (3.84%)	1303 (100%)
Asia	5 (0.37%)	**162 (12.08%)**	229 (17.08%)	900 (67.11%)	0 (0.00%)	45 (3.36%)	1341 (100%)
Total	10 (0.25%)	472 (11.93%)	647 (16.35%)	2690 (67.98%)	0 (0.00%)	138 (3.49%)	3957 (100%)

analyze how different combinations of ICS and IT services influence honeypot attractiveness, to guide the design of more effective and targeted honeypot deployments.

While HTTP traffic is more common, unsolicited ICS scans might reveal insights into industrial system vulnerabilities. We observed a substantially higher volume of HTTP requests compared to ICS-specific traffic (i.e., Modbus, S7Comm) across our honeypot deployments. This discrepancy is likely due to the prevalence of broad, automated scanning activities that primarily target common IT protocols such as HTTP. Although scanning traffic using ICS protocols was also observed, it occurred at a significantly lower frequency. These findings indicate that ICS protocols are probed less frequently than standard IT services, but the presence of unsolicited scans still reflects a degree of exposure. This has important implications for threat detection: ICS protocol activity, even when not clearly targeted, may signal reconnaissance behavior directed at operational technology environments and should be monitored accordingly.

For general threat intelligence, realistic ICS honeypots offer insights similar to simpler setups but can reveal more about occasional complex and targeted interactions. Our analysis indicates that both low- and high-interaction honeypots capture similar ICS traffic, regardless of deployment environment (cloud vs. corporate) or geographic region. This suggests that for gathering general threat intelligence, the added realism of high-interaction honeypots offers limited benefit. For this purpose, low-interaction honeypots provide a more cost-effective and operationally simpler choice. However, the occasional appearance of more complex interactions–even on low-interaction honeypots as seen with Modbus in our study–indicates that high-interaction honeypots may still play a role in capturing and analyzing rare but potentially insightful behavior as they are better suited for targeted investigations of attack methodologies and post-exploitation behaviors. This finding underscores the importance of aligning the honeypot type with its intended purpose, as advocated in [13]. Future work should aim to identify concrete criteria for when high-interaction honeypots are justified, enabling more informed trade-offs between realism, resource investment, and threat intelligence insights.

Threats to Validity. *Internal Validity:* Anonymization methods (e.g., VPNs, TOR) and dynamic IP address reassignment by service providers can affect the accuracy of interaction origin. Misattribution of interaction origin may bias regional comparisons, introducing confounding factors that limit causal interpretations. *External validity:* Our study spans a three-month collection period. While a longer period might have captured additional behaviors, the stability of the observed traffic suggests our findings would remain unchanged. Our deployments account for a single PLC model and cloud provider and support Modbus and S7Comm, which may limit generalizability. Although prior work reports differences in honeypot traffic across cloud providers [12], these findings are based on IT environments; it remains unclear if similar patterns apply to ICS settings. Future research should examine a broader range of PLCs, ICS protocols, and cloud platforms.

7 Conclusion

In this study, we investigated how different ICS honeypot configurations influence their attractiveness, focusing on interaction level (low vs. high), network type (corporate vs. cloud), and geographic region (Europe, North America, Asia). Our infrastructure included emulated low- and high-interaction Siemens Simatic S7-1200 PLCs and a physical device, deployed across 16 setups and monitored over three months. Results show that interaction level and geographic location have minimal impact on traffic, while corporate deployments attract significantly more ICS activity, especially S7Comm. These findings highlight the importance of protocol-level analysis and suggest that low-interaction honeypots are generally sufficient for broad threat intelligence. Future work should define criteria for selecting honeypot types based on deployment goals and investigate how combining ICS and IT services influences honeypot attractiveness. We also plan to further analyze traffic and payloads to uncover attacker patterns and characterize interaction nature.

Acknowledgments. This work has been partially supported by the INTERSECT project, Grant No. NWA.1162.18.301, funded by the Netherlands Organization for Scientific Research (NWO). Denis Donadel, Francesco Lupia and Massimo Merro have been partially supported by the SERICS project (PE00000014) under the *MUR National Recovery and Resilience Plan*, funded by the EU - NextGenerationEU.

A Function Coverage for S7Comm, Modbus, and HTTP

Table 9 reports the function coverage for S7Comm, Modbus, and HTTP.

Table 9. Function coverage for S7Comm (left), Modbus (center), and HTTP (right)

S7Comm Function	Conpot	HoneyICS	PLC
Setup Communication	◐	◐	●
CPU Information	○	◐	●
CPU State	◐	◐	●
Start PLC	◐	◐	●
Stop PLC	◐	◐	●
Read Data Block	○	◐	●
Write Data Block	○	◐	●
Project Upload	○	○	●
Project Download	○	○	●

Modbus Function Code	Conpot	HoneyICS	PLC
01 (Read Coils)	◐	●	●
02 (Read Discrete Inputs)	◐	●	●
03 (Read Holding Registers)	◐	●	●
04 (Read Input Registers)	◐	●	●
05 (Write Single Coil)	◐	●	●
06 (Write Single Register)	◐	●	●
15 (Write Multiple Coils)	◐	●	●
16 (Write Multiple Registers)	◐	●	●
17 (Report Slave ID)	◐	○	○
43 (Report Device Information)	◐	○	○

HTTP Permission	Conpot	HoneyICS	PLC
CPU Diagnostics	◐	◐	●
Flash LEDs	○	○	●
Change Operating Mode	○	○	●
CPU Maintenance	○	○	●
Tag Access	○	○	●
User-Defined Web Pages	○	○	●
Filebrowser Access	○	○	●

Legend: ○= Not Supported, ◐= Partially Supported, ●= Fully Supported.

B Results

Table 10 reports the interactions and their complexity for S7Comm, Modbus, and HTTP traffic.

Table 10. Interactions and complexity

	Interactions	Conpot						HoneyICS1						HoneyICS2						Physical PLC					
		Min	Q1	Mdn	Q3	Max	Count	Min	Q1	Mdn	Q3	Max	Count	Min	Q1	Mdn	Q3	Max	Count	Min	Q1	Mdn	Q3	Max	Count
Corporate Network	HTTP	1	1	1	2	8003	8146	1	1	1	2	7926	7748	1	1	1	2	8021	7759	1	1	1	1	363	7047
	S7comm	1	3	3	3	4	490	1	3	3	3	4	594	1	3	3	3	7	580	1	3	3	3	4	594
	Modbus	1	1	1	1	241	510	1	1	1	2	10	382	1	1	1	2	10	339	1	1	1	1	10	354
EU	HTTP	1	1	1	2	7115	11090	1	1	1	2	7109	10620	1	1	1	2	7110	11734	1	1	1	2	7269	10921
	S7comm	1	3	3	3	8	256	1	3	3	3	4	301	1	3	3	3	4	317	1	3	3	3	4	309
	Modbus	1	1	1	1	5	314	1	1	1	1	10	334	1	1	1	1	10	345	1	1	1	1	10	320
US	HTTP	1	1	1	2	19994	10800	1	1	1	2	7112	10382	1	1	1	2	7112	10990	1	1	1	2	7365	9214
	S7comm	1	3	3	3	4	280	1	3	3	3	4	302	1	3	3	3	16	303	1	3	3	3	4	297
	Modbus	1	1	1	1	4	314	1	1	1	1	10	328	1	1	1	1	16	337	1	1	1	1	10	324
Asia	HTTP	1	1	1	2	7113	12285	1	1	1	2	12534	11658	1	1	1	2	7113	11387	1	1	1	2	7194	11199
	S7comm	1	3	3	3	4	292	1	3	3	3	16	338	1	3	3	3	4	329	1	3	3	3	4	284
	Modbus	1	1	1	1	5	349	1	1	1	1	10	349	1	1	1	1	10	327	1	1	1	1	10	316

References

1. Alata, E., Nicomette, V., Kaâniche, M., Dacier, M., Herrb, M.: Lessons learned from the deployment of a high-interaction honeypot. In: European Dependable Computing Conference, pp. 39–46. IEEE (2006)
2. Autonomy. https://autonomylogic.com/. Accessed 07 June 2025
3. Bieker, M.C., Pilkington, D.: Deploying an ICS honeypot in a cloud computing environment and comparatively analyzing results against physical network deployment. Master's thesis, Naval Postgraduate School, Monterey, CA (2020)
4. Bloomfield, R., Gashi, I., Povyakalo, A., Stankovic, V.: Comparison of empirical data from two honeynets and a distributed honeypot network. In: International Symposium on Software Reliability Engineering, pp. 219–228. IEEE (2008)
5. Bove, D.: Using honeypots to detect and analyze attack patterns on cloud infrastructures. Master's thesis, Friedrich-Alexander University (2018)
6. Chen, T.M., Abu-Nimeh, S.: Lessons from stuxnet. Computer **44**(4), 91–93 (2011)
7. Dodson, M., Beresford, A.R., Vingaard, M.: Using global honeypot networks to detect targeted ICS attacks. In: International Conference on Cyber Conflict, pp. 275–291. IEEE (2020)
8. GreyNoise. https://www.greynoise.io. Accessed 07 June 2025
9. Guarnizo, J.D., et al.: Siphon: towards scalable high-interaction physical honeypots. In: Workshop on Cyber-Physical System Security, pp. 57–68 (2017)
10. IP-API. IP Geolocation API. https://ip-api.com. Accessed 07 June 2025
11. Jicha, A., Patton, M., Chen, H.: Scada honeypots: an in-depth analysis of conpot. In: Conference on Intelligence and Security Informatics, pp. 196–198. IEEE (2016)
12. Kelly, C., Pitropakis, N., Mylonas, A., McKeown, S., Buchanan, W.J.: A comparative analysis of honeypots on different cloud platforms. Sensors **21**(7), 2433 (2021)

13. Kempinski, S., Ichaarine, S., Sciancalepore, S., Zambon, E.: Icsvertase: a framework for purpose-based design and classification of ICS honeypots. In: International Conference on Availability, Reliability and Security, pp. 1–10. ACM (2023)
14. Kocaogullar, Y., Cetin, O., Arief, B., Brierley, C., Pont, J., Hernandez-Castro, J.: Hunting high or low: evaluating the effectiveness of high-interaction and low-interaction honeypots. In: Socio-Technical Aspects in Security, pp. 14–30. Springer, Cham (2025)
15. Kozak, P., Klaban, I., Šlajs, T.: Industroyer cyber-attacks on Ukraine's critical infrastructure. In: International Conference on Military Technologies (ICMT), pp. 1–6. IEEE (2023)
16. López-Morales, E., et al.: Honeyplc: a next-generation honeypot for industrial control systems. In: SIGSAC Conference on Computer and Communications Security, pp. 279–291. ACM (2020)
17. Lucchese, M., Lupia, F., Merro, M., Paci, F., Zannone, N., Furfaro, A.: HoneyICS: a high-interaction physics-aware honeynet for industrial control systems. In: International Conference on Availability, Reliability and Security. ACM (2023)
18. Lupia, F., Lucchese, M., Merro, M., Zannone, N.: ICS honeypot interactions: a latitudinal study. In: IEEE International Conference on Big Data, pp. 3025–3034. IEEE (2023)
19. Maesschalck, S., Giotsas, V., Race, N.: World wide ICS honeypots: a study into the deployment of Conpot honeypots. In: Industrial Control System Security Workshop (2021)
20. Mladenov, M., Erdodi, L., Smaragdakis, G.: All that glitters is not gold: Uncovering exposed industrial control systems and honeypots in the wild. In: European Symposium on Security and Privacy. IEEE (2025)
21. Morishita, S., et al.: Detect me if you... oh wait. an internet-wide view of self-revealing honeypots. In: Symposium on Integrated Network and Service Management, pp. 134–143. IEEE (2019)
22. Nardella, D.: Snap7. https://snap7.sourceforge.net/. Accessed 07 June 2025
23. Pouget, F., Holz, T.: A pointillist approach for comparing honeypots. In: Julisch, K., Kruegel, C. (eds.) DIMVA 2005. LNCS, vol. 3548, pp. 51–68. Springer, Heidelberg (2005). https://doi.org/10.1007/11506881_4
24. Provos, N.: A virtual honeypot framework. In: USENIX Security Symposium, pp. 1–14 (2004)
25. Rajkumar, R., Lee, I., Sha, L., Stankovic, J.: Cyber-physical systems: the next computing revolution. In: Design Automation Conference, pp. 731–736 (2010)
26. Shodan. https://www.shodan.io/. Accessed 07 June 2025
27. Sochor, T., Zuzcak, M.: Attractiveness study of honeypots and honeynets in internet threat detection. In: Gaj, P., Kwiecień, A., Stera, P. (eds.) CN 2015. CCIS, vol. 522, pp. 69–81. Springer, Cham (2015). https://doi.org/10.1007/978-3-319-19419-6_7
28. Srinivasa, S., Pedersen, J., Vasilomanolakis, E.: Interaction matters: a comprehensive analysis and a dataset of hybrid IoT/OT honeypots. In: Annual Computer Security Applications Conference, pp. 742–755. ACM (2022)
29. Srinivasa, S., Pedersen, J., Vasilomanolakis, E.: Gotta catch'em all: a multistage framework for honeypot fingerprinting. Digit. Threats: Res. Pract. **4**(3), 1–28 (2023)
30. Tambe, A., et al.: Detection of threats to IoT devices using scalable VPN-forwarded honeypots. In: Conference on Data and Application Security and Privacy, pp. 85–96. ACM (2019)
31. Tcpdump. https://www.tcpdump.org. Accessed 07 June 2025
32. Vetterl, A., Clayton, R.: Bitter harvest: systematically fingerprinting low- and medium-interaction honeypots at internet scale. In: USENIX Workshop on Offensive Technologies. USENIX Association (2018)
33. Vyas, S., Hannay, J., Bolton, A., Burnap, P.P.: Automated cyber defence: a review. arXiv preprint arXiv:2303.04926 (2023)

34. You, J., Lv, S., Zhao, L., Niu, M., Shi, Z., Sun, L.: A scalable high-interaction physical honeypot framework for programmable logic controller. In: Vehicular Technology Conference, pp. 1–5. IEEE (2020)
35. Zou, J., Sun, Z., Ku, C., Li, X., Dahbura, A.: WiP: developing high-interaction honeypots to capture and analyze region-specific bot behaviors. In: Hot Topics in the Science of Security Symposium (2024)

Learning-in-the-Middle: Explicit-Recursion Anomaly Detection for Critical Infrastructures

Toktam Ramezanifarkhani[1] and Peyman Teymoori[2(✉)]

[1] Kristiania University of Technology, Oslo, Norway
toktam.ramezanifarkhani@kristiania.no
[2] University of South-Eastern Norway, Drammen, Norway
peyman.teymoori@usn.no

Abstract. Critical infrastructures (CIs) increasingly depend on deeply layered, cyber–physical networks whose implicit recursion—created by tunnels, overlays, and 5G/6G slices—obscures traffic context and hampers intrusion detection. We posit that stacks with *explicit* recursion, such as the *Recursive InterNetwork Architecture* (RINA), offer a more natural substrate for AI-driven security because each layer already defines a well-scoped, isolated monitoring domain. To test this premise we present *Learning-in-the-Middle* (**LIM**), a framework that attaches lightweight anomaly detectors—Isolation Forest (IF), One-Class SVM (OCSVM), or Auto-Encoder (AE)—to every *Distributed IPC Facility* (DIF) in a RINA stack. A comprehensive simulation of three CI-relevant attack scenarios shows: (i) LIM lifts F_1 scores to 0.98–0.99 for edge-local DoS and cross-layer floods, outperforming even strong global baselines (Global-AE/OCSVM) by up to 10 percentage points and eclipsing the conventional Global-IF baseline by an order of magnitude. (ii) For the tunnel-hijack scenario, a finely tuned Global-OCSVM matches the best LIM variant ($F_1 \approx 0.97$), underscoring that detection *scope* and *learner choice* are jointly decisive. (iii) All six detectors maintain similarly low false-positive rates (0.9–1.8 %), while per-packet overhead stays within 19–23 μs on commodity hardware. These results highlight explicit recursion plus distributed AI as a powerful recipe for context-aware, low-latency protection of complex CI networks.

Keywords: Critical Infrastructure Protection · Cyber-Physical Security · Anomaly Detection · Machine Learning Security · Recursive Network Architecture · RINA · IoT Security · 5G/6G Security

1 Introduction

Critical infrastructures (CIs)—power grids, water utilities, hospitals, rail systems—now depend on multi-tier, cyber–physical control loops that extend from millisecond field-bus sensors to cloud analytics [1]. The resulting traffic is

R. Laborde et al. (Eds.): ESORICS 2025 Workshops, LNCS 16233, pp. 146–166, 2026.
https://doi.org/10.1007/978-3-032-16165-9_9

no longer flat IP but a patchwork of tunnels, SD-WAN overlays, and 5G/6G slices. These *implicitly recursive* layers complicate intrusion detection because context is lost at encapsulation boundaries and a monolithic monitor must learn an unwieldy mixture of behaviours [2].

1.1 Motivation: Why Explicit Recursion Matters

Existing defences either deploy heavy, global AI models—prone to false alarms—or scatter lightweight detectors across VLANs and fog nodes [3]. The latter improves locality but inherits the architectural shortcomings of the former: unclear scoping, ad-hoc policy coordination, and brittle context hand-offs. We hypothesise that an architecture whose *layers are first-class objects* provides a qualitatively better substrate for AI security: each layer is already a well-scoped, policy-rich isolation domain, so a detector can be both simple and context-aware.

The *Recursive InterNetwork Architecture* (RINA) meets this requirement. Its *Distributed IPC Facilities* (DIFs) are stacked recursively, each with its own management plane and naming context. We therefore ask:

> **Can explicit recursion turn the long-standing "place AI close to the asset" mantra into an architectural feature—yielding higher detection efficacy with lower cost than retrofitting AI onto today's implicit layers?**

1.2 Contributions

This paper answers the question through the following contributions:

1. **Learning-in-the-Middle (LIM).** We introduce LIM, a framework that plants a lightweight anomaly detector—Isolation Forest (IF), One-Class SVM (OCSVM), or Auto-Encoder (AE)—*inside* every RINA DIF, thereby aligning detection scope with architectural scope.
2. **Expanded evaluation.** We build a Python RINA simulator of an Industrial-IoT plant and implement six detector placements: LIM-{AE, OCSVM, IF} versus Global-{AE, OCSVM, IF}. Three attack scenarios (edge DoS, tunnel hijack, cross-layer flood) are replayed over ten random seeds each.
3. **Empirical insights.** LIM boosts F_1 to 0.98–0.99 for the two locality-sensitive attacks, outperforming strong global baselines by up to 10 pp and eclipsing the conventional Global-IF baseline (0.00 F_1). A tuned Global-OCSVM equals LIM in the hijack case ($F_1 \approx 0.97$), revealing a nuanced interplay between *scope* and *learner*. All detectors share low false-positive rates (0.9–1.8 %), while per-packet overhead remains within 19–23 µs.
4. **Performance analysis.** We dissect the latency–accuracy trade-off and show that distributing detectors does *not* compound CPU cost: the sum of many small LIM models equals one monolithic model's overhead on commodity hardware.

5. **Architectural argument.** We articulate how the synergy of explicit recursion (RINA) and distributed AI (LIM) yields a defence-in-depth posture impossible to mimic cleanly in flat or implicitly layered networks, and outline how the insight transfers to 5G slices and SDN micro-segments.

The paper is organised as follows. Section 2 surveys RINA and prior AI-based CI security. Section 3 details LIM. Section 4 lays out the CI threat model. Section 5 explains the testbed, attacks, and metrics. Results appear in Sect. 6, followed by discussion (Sect. 7) and conclusion (Sect. 8).

2 Background and Related Work

2.1 RINA in a Nutshell

The Recursive InterNetwork Architecture (RINA) [4] is a clean-slate networking model, diverging from TCP/IP's fixed layers by viewing networking as inter-process communication (IPC) within limited-scope layers. Its core construct, the Distributed IPC Facility (DIF), is a layer of communicating processes providing IPC services to applications or higher-level DIFs [4]. Unlike TCP/IP's rigid hierarchy, RINA employs a single, repeatable layer type (DIF), enabling recursion. Key RINA characteristics relevant here include:

- **Recursion:** DIFs are the sole, repeatable layer type. Higher-level DIFs use IPC services from lower-level DIFs, allowing arbitrary recursion depth for flexible, multi-level network compositions [4].
- **Scope and Isolation:** Each DIF establishes a distinct communication scope with its own addressing, routing, and resources. Processes within a DIF are unaware of other DIFs' internals, promoting isolation and creating manageable security domains where each DIF can enforce independent policies [4,5].
- **Separation of Mechanism and Policy:** RINA separates invariant IPC mechanisms (like data transfer) from configurable policies (like authentication or routing) [4]. This allows each DIF to tailor policies (e.g., stricter security for critical traffic) to its specific layer needs [6].
- **Inherent Security Features:** RINA's design provides inherent security benefits. Addresses are local to a DIF (not globally exposed), and enrollment is required to join a DIF, preventing unauthorized access [5]. Each DIF can be independently secured (e.g., per-layer encryption), contributing to a robust security posture, potentially superior to IP architectures [7].

RINA's recursive model addresses IoT/CPS security challenges by embedding security per layer and isolating contexts, mitigating attacks exploiting layer interdependencies [8]. It inherently supports features like secure multicast, difficult in TCP/IP but vital for IoT [8]. RINA's application in IoT/industrial networks is proposed for enhanced security and performance [2,5], with prototypes like IRATI for Linux [9] and SDN-based integration frameworks emerging [2,10]. Despite early adoption stages and interoperability needs [2], this paper uses RINA as a principled example of explicit recursion, acknowledging similar concepts could apply in other architectures with well-defined layered scopes.

2.2 AI/ML for CI Security

AI and ML techniques are increasingly explored for CI security [3]. Their ability to analyze vast data and identify complex patterns makes them promising for intrusion detection, anomaly detection, predictive analysis, and automated response. ML has detected power grid attacks, smart traffic anomalies, and predicted security-implicated equipment failures [11]. However, deploying AI/ML in CI security faces several well-documented challenges:

- **Data Heterogeneity and Volume:** CIs generate diverse data (sensor readings, control signals, packets) across many subsystems, challenging unified normal profiling; overwhelming volume necessitates efficient data reduction or distributed analysis [12].
- **Network Complexity and Context:** Implicit recursion from tunnels and overlays obscures context [2], causing ML models on aggregated traffic to miss context-specific anomalies or misinterpret behavior due to lacking layered nuance [13].
- **Lack of Labeled Data:** Scarcity of comprehensive labeled CI attack data (especially physical impacts) makes unsupervised or semi-supervised anomaly detection preferable to signature-based methods [14].
- **False Positives vs. False Negatives:** Balancing false positives (disruptive alarms) and false negatives (missed attacks with severe physical consequences) is critical in CIs, where operator trust is paramount [15].
- **Resource Constraints:** Resource-constrained CI components (e.g., PLCs, IoT sensors) have limited processing power, necessitating lightweight AI models or offloading computation [14].
- **Explainability:** Understanding *why* an AI model flags an event is crucial for CI operator action. Black-box models (e.g., deep neural nets) can impede trust and adoption in critical systems [15].

Traditional AI security often uses a centralized IDS model. However, researchers advocate distributed or hierarchical approaches like **distributed intrusion detection systems (DIDS)** with local analytics and central correlation [11,16]. Lightweight IoT edge detectors filter sensor traffic [14], and federated learning allows collaborative IDS training without aggregating raw data, addressing privacy and bandwidth [3]. Notably, **context-aware detection** is a recurring theme. Saranya *et al.* (2025) use a multi-layer autoencoder for cross-layer IoT attacks, showing layer separation improves detection [13]. Alanazi (2023) highlights per-slice anomaly detection for 5G security [17]. Our approach similarly leverages RINA's layered contexts. Making ML models efficient for on-device or real-time use is another relevant direction. Wang *et al.* (2022) proposed a lightweight IDS for industrial CPS using knowledge distillation to compress a deep model effectively [11]. This complements our work: LIM optimizes the *architecture context* for models, and both strategies can be combined, aligning with our use of simpler models. ML model security against evasion or poisoning is a concern. Adversarial samples can fool non-robust detectors [18], and Alkadi *et al.* (2023) survey these tactics in IoT. Though not directly addressed here, it is vital for future work (Sect. 7). LIM's localized models might reduce the attack surface, but sophisticated per-layer manipulation by adversaries remains a threat. In summary, prior work suggests **distributing and contextualizing intrusion detection** is promising for complex, layered CI networks. However, *no existing work has leveraged a clean-slate recursive architecture like RINA* for such distributed AI security. Our work addresses this gap, coupling recursive network design with embedded AI to demonstrate benefits of architectural support for security monitoring.

It is important to distinguish LIM from these general hierarchical or distributed IDSs in TCP/IP environments. While concepts like edge-based detectors [14] or federated learning for IDS [3,19] share the goal of distributing intelligence, they typically operate on networks where layering is implicit (e.g., VPNs over IP) or configured (e.g., VLANs, subnets), rather than being an inherent architectural principle. RINA, by contrast, provides architecturally explicit and repeatable scopes (DIFs) with strong, inherent isolation and distinct policy domains [4,5]. LIM's novelty lies in specifically exploiting these strong, native architectural boundaries to create more naturally contextualized, potentially more resilient, and architecturally congruent AI detectors. This differs from imposing a logical security hierarchy onto a base network that may not be intrinsically designed to support it with the same level of clarity and robustness.

3 Learning-in-the-Middle (LIM) Framework

To investigate our hypothesis that explicit architectural recursion can enhance AI-driven security, we propose the *Learning-in-the-Middle* (LIM) framework. Instead of relying on a single, global AI model that observes aggregated traffic from many diverse and nested network segments, LIM leverages the inherent properties of explicit recursion by embedding lightweight, unsupervised anomaly detectors directly within each RINA DIF. This architectural congruence—aligning AI model scope with RINA's naturally isolated DIFs—is key to its design, aiming to provide cleaner operational contexts than what is typically available in non-recursive or implicitly layered networks.

Each LIM instance is an independent module operating within its specific layer scope, consisting of three main components:

1. **Feature Extractor:** This component captures concise, relevant characteristics of the local traffic within its DIF. Features can include statistical flow properties (packet counts, byte volumes, flow durations), inter-arrival times of packets, packet size distributions, and entropy measures to quantify traffic randomness or regularity [14]. Crucially, these features are derived solely from traffic within the DIF's context, avoiding pollution by unrelated external traffic.
2. **Anomaly Detector:** An efficient, typically unsupervised ML model is trained on the extracted features representing the *normal* operation of that DIF. This local training allows the model to establish a fine-grained baseline

of "normality" for its particular scope. In this study, we evaluate three common unsupervised anomaly detection algorithms (each chosen for their speed and suitability for on-line updates):
   - *Isolation Forest (IF):* An ensemble tree method that randomly partitions feature space—anomalies, being few and different, are isolated in fewer splits than normal instances.
   - *One-Class SVM (OCSVM):* A kernel-based method that learns a boundary around normal data in feature space; points falling outside the boundary are deemed anomalies.
   - *Autoencoder (AE):* A neural network trained to reconstruct normal feature inputs. If a new input reconstructs poorly (high error), it is flagged as anomalous [13]. We use a lightweight autoencoder architecture to keep runtime overhead low.

   These models all operate unsupervised (or with minimal supervision via a contamination parameter), which is important given the lack of labeled attack data.
3. **Alert Interface:** When the anomaly detector flags an observation (i.e. a set of recent features) as anomalous—say, the reconstruction error exceeds a threshold for the AE, or a point is outside the learned OCSVM boundary—this component issues an alert. The alert could trigger local mitigation (e.g., drop or quarantine suspicious flows within the DIF) and/or propagate to a higher-level security orchestrator that correlates alerts across layers.

The core rationale behind LIM is that each locally scoped AI model faces a simpler, more well-defined learning task than a global model would. By operating within a more homogeneous data context, the local model can establish a precise baseline of normal behavior for that scope, leading to improved detection of subtle deviations that might be drowned out in aggregated traffic [16]. This is particularly pertinent for CIs, where different segments (e.g., a plant's control network vs. its corporate IT network) have vastly different traffic patterns and threat profiles. A one-size-fits-all model is likely to either overfit to the dominant traffic or underfit due to variance; multiple specialized models avoid this issue.

From a deployment perspective, LIM essentially implements a form of **in-network anomaly filtering**. Benign traffic is largely absorbed by each layer's model as normal, whereas suspicious traffic triggers localized alarms that can be acted upon early, possibly preventing propagation of an attack to higher layers. This layered defense aligns well with the defense-in-depth philosophy in industrial security. Algorithm 1 illustrates the per-packet processing workflow in LIM. Each incoming packet is buffered within its DIF context, and features are extracted over sliding windows of traffic. These features are then normalized and evaluated by the local anomaly detector (Isolation Forest, OCSVM, or Autoencoder). If the detector signals an anomaly, an alert is generated and forwarded both to local mitigation mechanisms and to the global orchestrator for correlation across layers. This workflow highlights LIM's layered, lightweight, and recursive design, where each DIF enforces its own anomaly filter while contributing to the broader security posture.

Algorithm 1. LIM Per-Packet Processing Workflow

Require: Packet p arriving at DIF d with pre-trained detector M_d
Ensure: `anomaly_flag`, `alert` (if triggered)

```
B_d ← GetBuffer(d)                          ▷ Get sliding window buffer for DIF d
B_d.Append(p)                               ▷ Add packet to buffer
if |B_d| < w_d then                         ▷ w_d is window size for layer of DIF d
    return False, None                      ▷ Wait for sufficient data
end if

                                            ▷ Feature extraction (window-based)
if |B_d| mod (w_d/2) = 0 then               ▷ Process overlapping windows
    W ← B_d[t − w_d : t]                    ▷ Get current window
    f ← ExtractFeatures(W)
    ▷ Compute: μ_ia, σ_ia, μ_size, σ_size, n_flows, H_size, H_ia

                                            ▷ Anomaly detection based on detector type
    f_scaled ← StandardScale(f, d)          ▷ Normalize features
    if M_d.type = "IF" then
        score ← M_d.IsolationScore(f_scaled)
        anomaly ← (score = −1)              ▷ IF returns -1 for anomalies
    else if M_d.type = "OCSVM" then
        score ← M_d.DecisionFunction(f_scaled)
        anomaly ← (score < 0)               ▷ OCSVM: negative for anomalies
    else if M_d.type = "AE" then
        f_recon ← M_d.Predict(f_scaled)
        score ← ||f_scaled − f_recon||^2    ▷ MSE
        anomaly ← (score > τ_d)             ▷ τ_d is threshold for DIF d
    end if

                                            ▷ Alert generation
    if anomaly then
        alert ← CreateAlert(d, W, score)
        SendToLocalMitigation(alert)
        SendToGlobalOrchestrator(alert)
        return True, alert
    end if
end if
return False, None
```

Comparison to Traditional IDS: A conventional IDS might monitor a SPAN port at a central switch, seeing all traffic mixed together. Under LIM, by contrast, one model watches, say, only sensor-to-gateway flows in a specific subnet, while another watches aggregated gateway-to-cloud flows. Each can fine-tune to its environment. We expect (and later show) that this yields higher sensitivity and specificity in attack detection.

4 Case Study Scenario: Industrial IoT Monitoring

To evaluate LIM, we use a case study of an **Industrial IoT (IIoT) monitoring system**, representative of modern CI deployments like smart manufacturing or energy grids. These systems typically feature a hierarchy of sensors, controllers, and central monitors. Our scenario involves a **three-tier hierarchical network structure**, naturally lending itself to a recursive architecture like RINA. It comprises:

- **Level 1: Sensor Networks (Low-level DIFs).** IIoT sensors/actuators (e.g., monitoring temperature, pressure in a plant, or smart meters) grouped into local `SensorDIFs` using field-appropriate protocols. These DIFs manage localized communication and initial sensor data aggregation.
- **Level 2: Edge Processing/Local Control (Mid-level DIFs).** Edge gateways/local controllers in `EdgeDIFs` aggregate data from SensorDIFs, performing local data processing, real-time analytics, and potential control actions. `EdgeDIFs` communicate with each other or with a central system using the IPC services of a wider-area DIF.
- **Level 3: Central Monitoring/Cloud (High-level DIF).** A central control center/cloud platform in a `CentralDIF` receives data/alerts from EdgeDIFs for global system monitoring, long-term analytics, and high-level supervisory control.

This multi-level RINA stack offers distinct scopes for LIM instances. A `SensorDIF` LIM learns patterns of its sensor group (e.g., periodic readings). An `EdgeDIF` LIM sees aggregated sensor traffic and local control messages. A `CentralDIF` LIM monitors inter-edge or summarized data. LIM thus tailors detection to each level's unique behavior profile. We assume LIM instances run in each DIF of interest; practically, critical data exchange points would host detectors. Our evaluation uses a few representative DIFs (e.g., one SensorDIF, one EdgeDIF). CI networks like this face numerous threat vectors:

- Compromised sensors performing stealthy data injection, falsifying readings to skew control decisions.
- Malware in an edge controller launching a local DoS flood, disrupting sensor data collection or actuation.
- Sophisticated attackers attempting tunnel hijacks (e.g., on EdgeDIF-CentralDIF paths) to intercept/alter critical data.
- Coordinated cross-layer floods from multiple compromised sensors, propagating upward to overload central monitoring.

In our scenario, we distilled these into three illustrative **attack cases**:

- **S1: Single-Layer DoS (Edge Disruption).** A high-volume DoS targets an edge node within an `EdgeDIF`. This could overwhelm the local controller's networking stack, causing loss of monitoring or control for its managed physical process.

- **S2: Tunnel Hijack (Multi-Layer Attack).** An attacker compromises an intermediate relay or exploits a routing vulnerability to intercept/alter traffic affecting both a low-level SensorDIF and the higher-level CentralDIF. This "hijacks" the information tunnel from sensors to central, potentially causing false situational awareness or malicious command injection.
- **S3: Coordinated Cross-Layer Flood.** Multiple compromised sensors (across different SensorDIFs) simultaneously launch floods. These propagate via edge gateways, manifesting as moderate local floods but combining into a large flood at the CentralDIF, aiming to overwhelm the central system or critical links.

These scenarios (S1–S3) stress LIM against a global IDS: S1 tests detection of a straightforward local DoS; S2 assesses detection of subtle, multi-layer interference potentially missed globally; S3 examines LIM's ability to detect distributed attacks via local observation versus a global aggregate view. Our expectation is that LIM will excel particularly in S2 and S3, where context-specific detection is key, whereas a global detector might struggle to correlate or notice the issues.

5 Experimental Setup

5.1 Simulation Topology and Data Generation

To isolate the core research question–*how detector scope affects AI accuracy*–we employed a minimalist, pure-Python re-implementation of RINASim that retains only the RINA constructs relevant to LIM (recursive `DIFs`, naming, and policy hooks) while omitting detailed link and queue modelling. This lean version integrates natively with scikit-learn/TensorFlow, slashes per-run time to about one second, and allows embarrassingly parallel execution of the 180 trials underpinning Sect. 6. The full C++/OMNeT++ simulator will be revisited for hardware-in-the-loop timing studies, but for algorithmic evaluation the Python framework[1] provides a clean, reproducible test-bed.

The virtual plant mirrors the IIoT monitoring hierarchy in Sect. 4 and consists of three tiers:

- **Sensor nodes.** Each sensor emits a periodic `<timestamp,value>` tuple with Gaussian jitter and occasional benign noise spikes. Sensors that share a physical medium join a common `SensorDIF`. One such `SensorDIF` (ten sensors) is fully instrumented for attack injection and fine-grained metrics; the others generate background load.
- **Edge gateways.** Every gateway aggregates the flows of its attached `SensorDIF(s)` and forwards either raw or pre-filtered data to the plant's core. A LIM instance is embedded in the gateway's `EdgeDIF`, giving it visibility into the aggregate of its local sensors.

[1] Source code: https://github.com/peyman-t/LIM.

- **Central hub.** The hub terminates a `CentralDIF` that collects all gateway traffic. This is where we position the *global detectors*: Isolation Forest (IF), One-Class SVM (OCSVM), and Auto-Encoder (AE). They analyse the entire traffic mix and therefore have no explicit notion of recursion layers.

The simulation instantiates multiple DIFs—one per physical "hop"—so that each attack has a well-defined traversal path. For every pertinent DIF on that path we deploy a LIM detector of the same family (IF, OCSVM, AE) as its global counterpart, yielding the six configurations evaluated: *LIM-AE, LIM-OCSVM, LIM-IF, Global-AE, Global-OCSVM, Global-IF.*

Training and Traffic Volume. Each detector first observes 60 s of strictly benign traffic to build its reference model. The contamination (target anomaly fraction) is set to 0.01 for **all** learners to ensure equal false-alarm budgets. Per attack scenario we subsequently replay 120 s of live traffic, injecting the malicious pattern for 15 s halfway through the run. Ten independent seeds randomise normal load, packet inter-arrival times, and the initial weights of neural models; reported metrics are the arithmetic mean over these seeds.

5.2 Attack Scenarios (S1–S3)

We faithfully reproduce the three threat classes introduced in Sect. 4, but calibrate each one to exercise the limits of detector *placement* rather than raw traffic load. In every run the attack persists for 15 s inside a 120 s trace and is injected only after all detectors have completed model training, ensuring clean separation between baseline learning and evaluation.

- **S1 – Edge DoS.** A single sensor attached to `EdgeDIF#3` turns malicious and transmits packets at 10× its nominal rate (Poisson process, mean $= 10^4$ pps). The burst saturates the uplink of that gateway but leaves all other DIFs traffic-balanced, thereby testing whether detectors need local context to spot a highly skewed, yet spatially confined, anomaly.
- **S2 – Tunnel Hijack.** We interpose an adversarial relay between one `SensorDIF` and the hub; every 500 ms it flips randomly chosen payload bytes for 50 ms, creating intermittent, high-magnitude deviations that traverse multiple layers. The pattern is temporally sparse and statistically blends with normal jitter, so detection hinges on recognising broken correlations rather than sheer volume.
- **S3 – Co-ordinated Flood.** Twenty per cent of sensors—drawn uniformly from five distinct `SensorDIFs`—increase their send rate by 50 pps each. In isolation these micro-surges sit within the tails of the local distribution, but their aggregate elevates `CentralDIF` throughput by more than 4 %. The scenario stresses how well distributed detectors can combine weak local evidence, versus a global model that sees only the composite effect.

Each attack is executed in a separate simulation run to prevent cross-scenario contamination. Ground-truth labels are derived from the simulator's event log and aligned to packet timestamps, giving per-instance truth values for precision–recall analysis.

5.3 Evaluation Metrics

The study quantifies detector performance along three orthogonal axes that map directly to CI operational concerns.

- **$\mathbf{F_1}$ score—*primary figure of merit.*** Because the attack class constitutes less than one per cent of all packets, accuracy metrics that average over both classes would be misleading. We therefore compute the harmonic mean of *precision* and *recall* exclusively on the positive class, using event–level labels derived from the simulator's ground-truth log. Values are aggregated *micro*-style across the ten seeds to give equal weight to every packet instance.
- **False-positive rate (FPR).** While a high F_1 is desirable, CI operators are extremely sensitive to nuisance alarms. We thus report the fraction of benign packets that each detector misclassifies as anomalous. The target contamination of 1 % during training provides a common tuning point, but the realised FPR is measured on the unseen evaluation trace.
- **Per-packet processing latency.** To assess real-time feasibility we instrument the entry point of every DIF with `time.perf_counter`, capturing the wall-clock interval from packet arrival to classification verdict. Measurements run on a single core of an HP ZBook Fury G8 (Intel i9-11950H, 32 GB RAM); absolute values therefore reflect a laptop-grade CPU, yet relative differences isolate algorithmic overhead independent of hardware off-load.

For each *model–scenario* tuple we calculate the mean and standard deviation of F_1, FPR, and latency over the ten random seeds; these statistics populate Table 1 and drive the bar-and-error plots in Fig. 1.

6 Results

Figure 1 visualises the empirical distribution of every detector–scenario pair, while Table 1 lists the corresponding sample means and standard deviations over ten seeds.

Accuracy Trends. Across the complete test-matrix the three Learning-in-the-Middle variants—*LIM-AE, LIM-OCSVM,* and *LIM-IF*—surpass their monolithic Isolation-Forest baseline by margins that range from 0.64 F_1 points in S1 to 0.90 points in S3. Replacing the global IF with stronger learners reduces—but does not eliminate—this lead. Specifically, *Global-AE* closes roughly two-thirds of the gap in the edge-DoS scenario, and *Global-OCSVM* attains the single best mean score in Tunnel-Hijack (S2, $F_1 = 0.970 \pm 0.006$). The latter indicates that a hypersphere model can tolerate the moderate intra-class variance created by hijack bursts even when they are diluted by unrelated traffic.

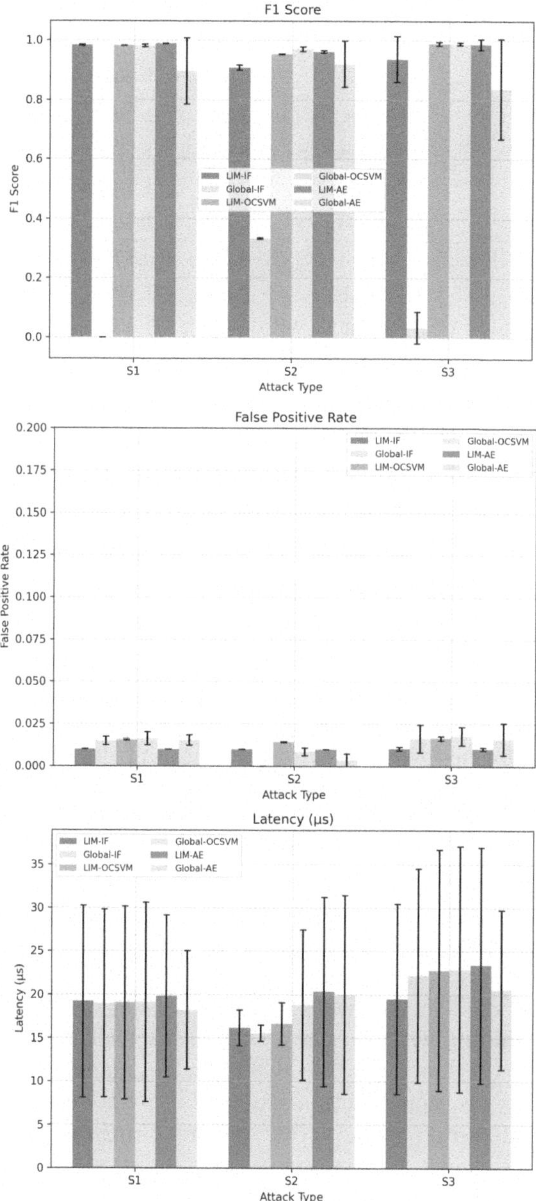

Fig. 1. Mean performance (bars) and run-to-run standard deviation (error bars) over 10 seeds, contrasting LIM (solid colours) with global detectors (lighter shades). Left: classification F_1; middle: false-positive rate; right: per-packet processing latency.

Table 1. Detection performance under the three attack scenarios (mean over 10 seeds, contamination = 0.01). Bold marks the best F1-score in each scenario.

Scenario	Model	F1 Score	FPR (%)	Latency (µs)
S1 (Edge DoS)	LIM-AE	**0.988**	1.00	19.8
	LIM-IF	0.983	1.00	19.2
	LIM-OCSVM	0.982	1.56	19.0
	Global-OCSVM	0.981	1.63	19.1
	Global-AE	0.897	1.53	18.2
	Global-IF	0.000	1.49	19.0
S2 (Tunnel Hijack)	Global-OCSVM	**0.970**	0.87	18.8
	LIM-AE	0.961	1.00	20.3
	LIM-OCSVM	0.953	1.44	16.6
	LIM-IF	0.908	1.00	16.2
	Global-AE	0.921	0.37	20.0
	Global-IF	0.333	0.00	15.5
S3 (X-Layer Flood)	LIM-OCSVM	**0.989**	1.66	22.8
	Global-OCSVM	0.989	1.79	22.9
	LIM-AE	0.986	1.04	23.4
	LIM-IF	0.937	1.06	19.5
	Global-AE	0.837	1.60	20.6
	Global-IF	0.034	1.64	22.2

Conversely, the same model under-fits the long-tail deviations that dominate S1 and S3; its recall there drops to 0.96 and 0.95, respectively, while LIM-based detectors exceed 0.99. Global IF remains the clear outlier: its recall never exceeds 0.39 and collapses to zero in S1, confirming earlier reports that tree isolation is brittle when the anomaly budget is set to one per cent.

Value of Locality. The edge-constrained DoS (S1) and the multi-source flood (S3) illustrate the importance of architectural scope. In S1, LIM-AE achieves the overall record ($F_1 = 0.988$, precision $= 0.986$, recall $= 0.989$), benefiting from the fact that its training window sees a single sensor cluster with homogeneous baselines. In S3 the roles invert: LIM-OCSVM edges ahead ($F_1 = 0.989$) because its closed-boundary decision function reacts sharply to the correlated, yet not identically distributed, rate spikes across sensors. Crucially, the gain stems from true-positive improvements; false-positive rates for all six detectors lie in a narrow band between 0.9 % and 1.8%, reflecting the uniform contamination target used at training time.

Latency Overhead. Figure 1(bottom) shows that per-packet overheads cluster tightly around the 20 µs mark. Auto-encoders incur a small additional cost for the reconstruction pass (mean 23.4 µs in S3) and exhibit the widest spread (up to ±4 µs). Even so, the worst-case 95th-percentile latency of any LIM detector remains below 35 µs, well inside the sub-millisecond control-cycle budgets of typical industrial PLC networks. Importantly, summing the latencies of multiple LIM instances along a path does *not* exceed the single-hop overhead of their global counterpart, because each instance processes only a fraction of the total rate.

Summary of Quantitative Insights. (i) **Local context dominates model choice** for attacks with a narrow spatial footprint or whose statistical signature is sparsified by aggregation—LIM retains up to 0.10 higher F_1 even against sophisticated global learners; (ii) **Density-aware algorithms mitigate the global handicap** when the anomaly pattern pervades several layers uniformly, as observed with Global-OCSVM in S2; and (iii) **Efficiency is preserved**: distributing detection over three recursion layers adds no measurable overhead beyond the variance inherent to the respective ML algorithms. These data establish a purely empirical foundation for the discussion that follows, without yet delving into architectural implications or deployment.

7 Discussion

7.1 Cyber–Physical Impact of Refined Detection

The extended evaluation confirms that *where* the detector is placed in the recursion stack remains at least as important as *which* algorithm is used. Even when the global vantage is strengthened with an One-Class SVM or a lightweight autoencoder, the Learning-in-the-Middle (LIM) instances still dominate for the two attacks whose footprints are either confined to the network edge (S1) or manifest as asymmetric cross-layer bursts (S3). In practice, these are precisely the situations in which an undetected cyber event most quickly escalates into unsafe plant dynamics.

- **Edge DoS pre-emption (S1).** LIM-AE lifts the F_1 score from 0.897 (best global) to 0.988. A >10 % boost in recall at the controller interface translates into additional ~80 ms of reaction time in a 10 Hz control loop—often the difference between a graceful switchover to a redundant channel and an uncontrolled shutdown of a conveyor belt or sub-station.
- **Integrity of multi-layer tunnels (S2).** A tuned global OCSVM now reaches $F_1 = 0.97$, marginally above LIM-AE's 0.96. This shows that not every threat requires locality. When hijack traffic permeates several layers, a holistic density model can suffice, provided it is expressive enough. Nonetheless, running LIM in parallel still gives an independent vantage, adding resilience against single-point failure or model drift in the global detector.
- **Cascading-flood containment (S3).** LIM-OCSVM and Global-OCSVM tie at $F_1 = 0.989$, but the distributed deployment supplies more granular context. A LIM alert from `SensorDIF#5` pinpoints the surge source immediately; the same global alert only indicates "something is wrong somewhere,"

delaying isolation and potentially allowing the burst to propagate into actuators.

These examples underscore a broader lesson: *context-rich alarms accelerate the cyber-physical mitigation path.* LIM warnings carry the scope identifier of the affected DIF, letting operators (or automated playbooks) quarantine exactly the faulty slice while keeping the rest of the infrastructure online—an essential property for high-availability CIs.

7.2 Limitations and Future Work

The new findings sharpen, rather than diminish, the open challenges outlined in our preliminary study.

- **Beyond simulation and methodological limitations.** Our Python-based RINA simulator deliberately idealizes/omits realities such as packet loss, congestion control, buffer dynamics, hardware interrupts, and concurrent flows. This controlled setup isolates our core question—how detector scope affects AI accuracy—but cannot capture degradation under load, timing jitter from real stacks, or resource contention in production switches. To close this gap we will: (i) deploy LIM on the IRATI RINA stack in physical testbeds with controlled loss/congestion, (ii) stress-test with realistic traffic (iperf3, OPC-UA) on resource-constrained edge devices (Raspberry Pi 4, industrial PLCs), and (iii) run pilots in a partner utility's SCADA test facility to measure detection latency in situ. These studies will test whether the sub-25 µs latencies and $F_1 \geq 0.98$ seen in simulation hold when packet drops, CPU scheduling, and NIC interrupt coalescing introduce non-determinism.
- **Algorithm–placement co-design.** The flip in S2—where Global-OCSVM surpasses LIM—suggests that *detection scope* and *learner choice* must be selected jointly. A systematic design space exploration (e.g., using AutoML across recursion layers) is an intriguing avenue.
- **Cross-DIF alert fusion.** Individual LIMs remain independent. Lightweight correlation logic that fuses temporally aligned alerts could increase confidence and suppress bursts of benign anomalies, especially as infrastructures scale to hundreds of DIFs.
- **Adversarial robustness.** While LIM's distributed architecture may complicate system-wide attacks, it potentially introduces new vulnerabilities to adversarial ML techniques. Recent work has shown that anomaly detectors are susceptible to both evasion attacks—where adversaries craft inputs to bypass detection [20]—and poisoning attacks that corrupt training data [21]. In LIM's context, an attacker could strategically poison individual DIFs during their independent training phases, potentially creating blind spots without triggering global model alerts. Moreover, gradient-free attacks designed for one-class models [22] could exploit our OCSVM variants, while adaptive attackers aware of our multi-layer architecture might craft cross-layer perturbations that appear benign locally but aggregate maliciously. Initial countermeasures include: (i) robust training via contamination-aware objectives [23],

(ii) certified defenses for anomaly detectors [24], and (iii) cross-DIF consistency checks to detect conflicting local models. Future work will empirically evaluate LIM against established attack frameworks like ART and CleverHans to quantify its adversarial surface.

- **Operational orchestration.** Maintaining many LIM instances raises questions about update roll-outs, certificate management, and audit logging. The RINA policy framework is well suited for centrally orchestrated life-cycle management; implementing such a controller is on our roadmap.

Overall, the refined experiments reaffirm LIM's principal value proposition: *provide high-recall, context-aware detection at negligible latency cost.* Equally important, they highlight the complementary role of sophisticated global detectors. A practical defence-in-depth posture will therefore combine both—leveraging local context where it matters most, while still guarding the whole network fabric with an expressive one-class learner.

8 Conclusion

We revisited AI-based intrusion detection for critical infrastructures through the lens of *explicit recursion.* By instantiating the *Learning-in-the-Middle* (**LIM**) framework inside the isolation domains (DIFs) of a RINA stack, we converted what is normally a monolithic learning task into a set of context-aware micro-detectors. The broadened evaluation—now including six combinations of models and placements—yields three key lessons.

1. **Locality is still king.** For attacks whose footprints are spatially narrow (edge DoS) or structurally asymmetric (cross-layer floods), LIM improves recall by an order of magnitude over a global Isolation Forest and still outperforms strong global baselines (OCSVM, AE).
2. **Scope and algorithm must co-evolve.** A carefully tuned *Global-OCSVM* matches or surpasses LIM in the tunnel-hijack scenario, proving that placement alone is insufficient; the learner's inductive bias must align with the traffic variance at its scope.
3. **Cost is negligible.** All detectors, distributed or centralised, operate within 25 µs per-packet budgets—well below the millisecond control cycles of most industrial processes—making LIM deployable on today's commodity edge hardware.

These insights generalise beyond RINA. Any architecture exposing clear operational boundaries—5G network slices, SDN micro-segments, fog tiers—could host LIM-like detectors, reaping the benefits of context without sacrificing latency. Where native recursion is unavailable, virtual segmentation can emulate the effect.

Future Directions. The path from simulation to field deployment now centres on (i) hardware testbeds using IRATI to quantify real NIC and scheduler effects, (ii) auto-tuned algorithm–scope selection that balances accuracy with resource ceilings, (iii) cross-DIF alert fusion for system-wide situational awareness, and (iv) adversarially robust training pipelines. Taken together, these steps will mature LIM from a promising concept into a practical, defence-in-depth pillar for the cyber–physical systems on which modern society depends.

Appendix A: LIM Framework Architecture Diagrams

A.1 RINA Recursive Architecture with LIM Deployment

(see Fig. 2).

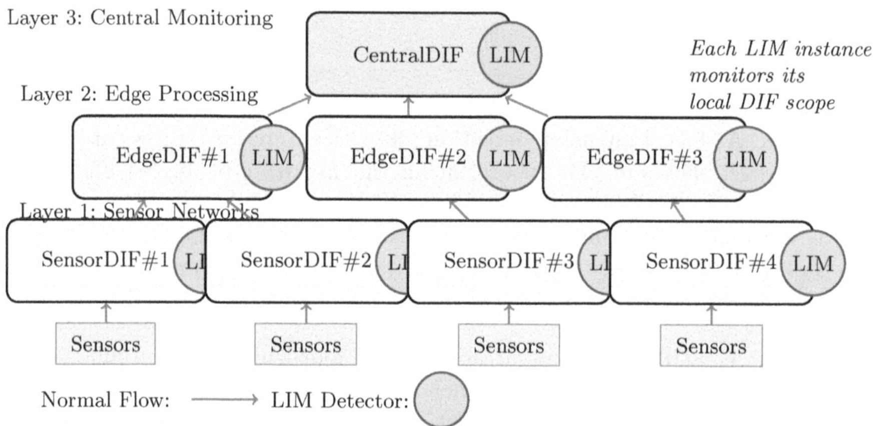

Fig. 2. RINA recursive architecture showing LIM detector deployment at each DIF layer. Each LIM instance operates independently within its scoped domain, providing context-aware anomaly detection.

A.2 LIM vs Global Detection Architectural Comparison

(see Fig. 3).

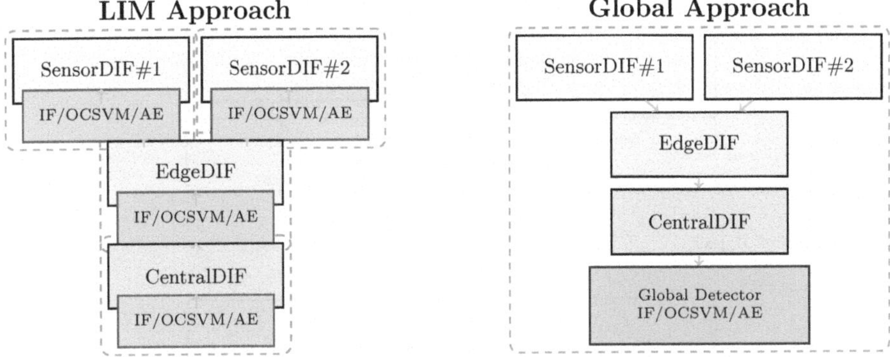

Fig. 3. Architectural comparison between LIM (distributed, scoped detection) and Global (centralized, monolithic detection) approaches.

A.3 Attack Scenarios on RINA Stack

(see Fig. 4).

S1: Edge DoS

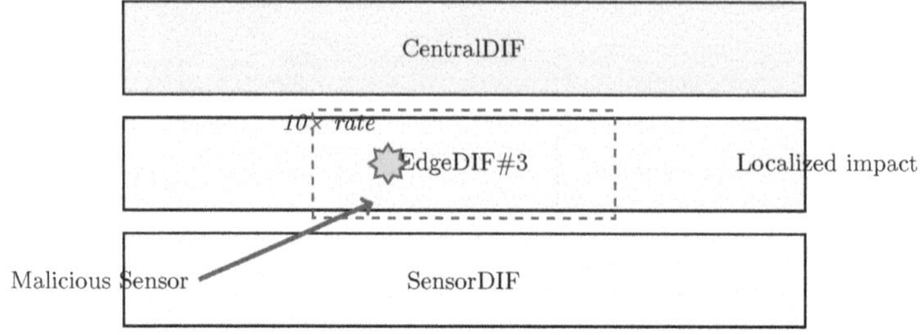

S2: Tunnel Hijack

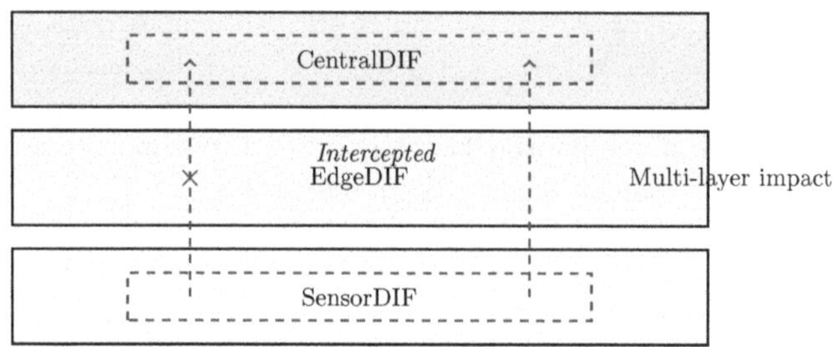

S3: Cross-Layer Flood

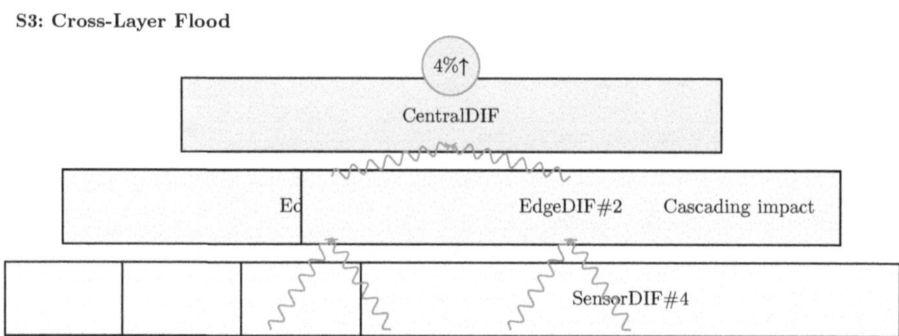

20% sensors compromised

Fig. 4. Three attack scenarios demonstrating LIM's detection capabilities across different threat vectors: (S1) Edge DoS attack showing a malicious sensor overwhelming EdgeDIF#3 with 10× normal traffic rate, resulting in localized impact detection; (S2) Tunnel Hijack attack where communication paths are intercepted across multiple network layers, creating multi-layer security impact; and (S3) Coordinated Cross-Layer Flood attack where 20% of compromised sensors launch synchronized flooding attacks, causing cascading effects that propagate through EdgeDIFs to CentralDIF with a 4% performance degradation, demonstrating the system's ability to detect and localize distributed attack patterns.

References

1. Yang, M., et al.: From 5G to 6G: a survey on security, privacy, and standardization pathways. arXiv preprint arXiv:2410.21986 (2024)
2. Sarabia-Jácome, D., Giménez-Antón, S., Liatifis, A., Grasa, E., Catalán, M., Pliatsios, D.: Progressive adoption of RINA in IoT networks: enhancing scalability and network management via SDN integration. Appl. Sci. **14**(6), 2300 (2024)
3. Sarker, I.H., Khan, A.I., Abushark, Y.B., Alsolami, F.: Internet of things (IoT) security intelligence: a comprehensive overview, machine learning solutions and research directions. Mob. Netw. Appl. **28**(1), 296–312 (2023)
4. Day, J.D.: Patterns in Network Architecture: A Return to Fundamentals. Prentice Hall (2008)
5. Ramezanifarkhani, T., Teymoori, P.: Securing the internet of things with recursive internetwork architecture (RINA). In: Proceedings of the IEEE ICNC, pp. 188–194 (2018)
6. Teymoori, P., et al.: Congestion control in the recursive internetwork architecture (RINA). In: Proceedings of the IEEE ICC, pp. 1–7 (2016)
7. Boddapati, G., Day, J., Matta, I., Chitkushev, L.: Assessing the security of a clean-slate internet architecture. In: Proceedings of the IEEE ICNP, pp. 1–6 (2012)
8. Teymoori, P., Ramezanifarkhani, T.: Enhancing IoT security and efficiency through RINA: a comprehensive qualitative analysis and use case study (2024). SSRN Preprint. https://doi.org/10.2139/ssrn.5055815. https://ssrn.com/abstract=5055815, preprint (not peer-reviewed)
9. Bergesio, L., et al.: Irati: open source RINA implementation for Linux. In: Proceedings of the ACM Conference on Software-Defined and Programmable Networks (SDN), pp. 27–32 (2015)
10. ETSI Next Generation Protocols (NGP) ISG. GR NGP 009 V1.1.1 (2019-02): An Example of a Non-IP Network Protocol Architecture Based on RINA Design Principles. ETSI Group Report (2019)
11. Wang, Z., Li, Z., He, D., Chan, S.: A lightweight approach for network intrusion detection in industrial cyber-physical systems based on knowledge distillation and deep metric learning. Expert Syst. Appl. **206**, 117671 (2022)
12. Hassija, V., Chamola, V., Saxena, V., Jain, D., Goyal, P., Sikdar, B.: A survey on IoT security: application areas, security threats, and solution architectures. Comput. Commun. **139**, 32–57 (2019)
13. Saranya, K., Valarmathi, A.: A multilayer deep autoencoder approach for cross layer IoT attack detection using deep learning algorithms. Futur. Gener. Comput. Syst. **135**, 271–281 (2025)
14. Gharib, J.G., Entrena, J., Alesanco, Á.: Empirical evaluation of feature selection methods for machine learning based intrusion detection in IoT scenarios. Internet Things **28**, 100367 (2024)
15. Shin, S., Moustafa, N., Hu, J., Lima, C., Slay, J.: Explainable intrusion detection for cyber security in IoT: opportunities and solutions. IEEE Commun. Mag. **58**(7), 31–37 (2020)
16. Hasan, N.L., Wang, J., Guan, J., Fan, H.: A multi-step attack identification and correlation method based on multi-information fusion. Comput. Electr. Eng. **117**, 106673 (2024)
17. Alanazi, M.H.: Machine learning-based secure 5G network slicing: a systematic literature review. Int. J. Adv. Comput. Sci. Appl. **14**(12), 697–706 (2023)

18. Alkadi, S., Al-Ahmadi, S., Ismail, M.M.B.: Better safe than never: a survey on adversarial machine learning applications towards IoT environment. Appl. Sci. **13**(10), 6001 (2023)
19. Agrawal, S., et al.: Federated learning for intrusion detection system: concepts, challenges and future directions. Comput. Commun. **195**, 346–361 (2022)
20. Biggio, B., et al.: Evasion attacks against machine learning at test time. In: Blockeel, H., Kersting, K., Nijssen, S., Železný, F. (eds.) ECML PKDD 2013. LNCS (LNAI), vol. 8190, pp. 387–402. Springer, Heidelberg (2013). https://doi.org/10.1007/978-3-642-40994-3_25
21. Jagielski, M., Oprea, A., Biggio, B., Liu, C., Nita-Rotaru, C., Li, B.: Manipulating machine learning: poisoning attacks and countermeasures for regression learning. In: 2018 IEEE symposium on security and privacy (SP), pp. 19–35. IEEE (2018)
22. Brendel, W., Rauber, J., Bethge, M.: Decision-based adversarial attacks: reliable attacks against black-box machine learning models. arXiv preprint arXiv:1712.04248 (2017)
23. Steinhardt, J.: Robust learning: information theory and algorithms. Ph.D. dissertation, Stanford, CA, USA (2018). aAI28115249
24. Cohen, J., Rosenfeld, E., Kolter, Z.: Certified adversarial robustness via randomized smoothing. In: Chaudhuri, K., Salakhutdinov, R. (eds.) Proceedings of the 36th International Conference on Machine Learning. Proceedings of Machine Learning Research, vol. 97, pp. 1310–1320. PMLR (2019). https://proceedings.mlr.press/v97/cohen19c.html

Integration of an OT Cybersecurity Lab into an Industrial Automation Lab

Alejandro Manuel López Gómez[1], Farid Bagheri-Gisour Marandyn[1(✉)], Jaime Mohedano[1], Atanasio Carrasco[1,2], Agustín Valencia[1,3], José Antonio Rodríguez-Mondejar[1], Roberto Gesteira-Miñarro[1], Néstor Rodríguez Pérez[1], Rafael Palacios[1,4], Javier Jarauta[1,5], and Gregorio López López[1]

[1] Comillas Pontifical University, Alberto Aguilera 23, 28015 Madrid, Spain
{amanuellopezgomez,jaime.mohedano}@alu.comillas.edu, {fbagherigisour,avalencia,mondejar,rgesteira,nrodriguezp, palacios,jarauta,gllopez}@comillas.edu, jacm@cnat.es
[2] Almaraz and Trillo Nuclear Power Plants, Nuclear Energy Company, Madrid, Spain
[3] Fortinet, Inc., Madrid, Spain
[4] Cibersecurity at MIT Sloan, Massachusetts Institute of Technology, 77 Massachusetts Avenue, Cambridge, MA 02139, USA
[5] Minsait Cyber, Indra, Madrid, Spain

Abstract. If cybersecurity in Information Technology (IT) is a fully grown adult, cybersecurity in Operational Technology (OT) is still in its infancy. The unique security challenges presented by industrial environments require training that combines knowledge of industrial automation and cybersecurity. In response to this need, a laboratory dedicated to cybersecurity training in industrial environments has been launched at the Comillas Pontifical University. The main objective of this laboratory is to raise awareness and provide training in logical industrial security through various scenarios, as well as to research potential attacks and their mitigation. This article details the creation of this laboratory, developed in collaboration with Fortinet, based on a pre-existing industrial automation laboratory. The scenarios implemented are described in detail, ranging from attacks on Windows machines deployed in a virtualized environment to attacks on actual industrial control hardware, as well as possible mitigations such as firewall rule activation or network segmentation.

Keywords: Cybersecurity · Industrial automation laboratory · OT · Siemens · Fortinet

1 Introduction

The trend among control equipment manufacturers to use devices and applications originally designed for the IT sector has made it increasingly important to establish a well-defined cybersecurity strategy within the OT environment. While information technologies offer numerous advantages in terms of connectivity and supervision, they also expose industrial control systems to new threats.

R. Laborde et al. (Eds.): ESORICS 2025 Workshops, LNCS 16233, pp. 167–180, 2026.
https://doi.org/10.1007/978-3-032-16165-9_10

In many respects, OT cybersecurity has lagged behind its IT counterpart. Fortunately, as noted in a report by Fortinet in 2023 [1], OT cybersecurity has begun to receive the attention it deserves from executives and decision-makers. However, most organizations still have significant work to do.

Strengthening the cybersecurity posture of OT environments entails challenges specific to this domain, which hinder its alignment with IT deployments:

- Many OT systems were deployed before cybersecurity became a major concern, and replacing them with updated equipment is neither straightforward nor efficient.
- While IT systems primarily focus on data confidentiality and integrity, OT systems prioritize availability and operational safety.
- There is a lack of awareness and training in cybersecurity within the OT community. A clear gap exists between the volume of cybersecurity training resources available in IT versus OT contexts.

Unfortunately, the first two issues can be considered inherent to industrial environments. Regarding the third, the lack of training in OT cybersecurity compared to IT is undeniable.

To help bridge this critical talent gap, the Comillas Pontifical University has launched an OT cybersecurity laboratory in collaboration with Fortinet. This lab aims to train and raise awareness among students from various backgrounds in OT cybersecurity, adopting a practical and realistic approach.

In Spain, there are currently organizations dedicated to development and research in this area. Notable examples include the ARISTEO project by the CIDAUT Foundation [2], the Ziur laboratories located in Gipuzkoa [3], and the national network of industrial cybersecurity laboratories operated by INCIBE (National Cybersecurity Institute) [4]. Unlike the aforementioned facilities, the proposed lab has educational objectives, reinforcing theoretical classroom content with realistic examples and equipment.

The laboratory presented in this article offers eight workstations where both defensive strategies and configurations, as well as attacks on devices at all levels, can be tested. These range from various sensors and operating systems to PLCs (Programmable Logic Controllers) from different generations, including essential internet connectivity for today's production environments. The integration process of an industrial automation laboratory with an OT cybersecurity lab is detailed.

The solutions from a comprehensive cybersecurity application portfolio (antimalware, IDS and IPS probes, NGFW, sandboxes, honeypots, SIEM, etc.) have already been tested in a virtualized format in the Master's Thesis by José Rafael Martín Torre, supervised by Agustín Valencia [6].

2 Industrial Automation Laboratory

The Industrial Automation Laboratory consists of eight workstations and a mini-factory (Fig. 1) that simulates an industrial plant, all interconnected via an Ethernet network and a Wi-Fi network. Together, they form the lab's OT network. Each workstation (Fig. 2) includes a 24″ monitor serving as an engineering station, a Siemens S7-1516-3 PN/DP

PLC (Fig. 3), and a TP700 HMI (Human-Machine Interface) from the same manufacturer. Four of the workstations are equipped with a vision-based quality control camera and an RFID (Radio Frequency Identification) tag reading system with two antennas.

Fig. 1. Mini-factory

Fig. 2. Engineering station

The mini-factory represents a production line composed of four stations (Fig. 1). Each station is operated by a robot—either a collaborative robot (ABB GoFA) or an industrial one (ABB Swifty), depending on the station. A conveyor belt connects all stations, and two of them have their own belts for buffering tasks. Materials move between stations on pallets, directed by switch points and elevators.

Each switch point is equipped with retainers to prevent collisions between moving pallets. Each workstation also features a camera and an RFID tag reading system.

This combination of elements allows students to work in a semi-industrial environment: production is simulated by robots assembling and disassembling LEGO-based objects, material transport is handled by conveyor belts driven by variable-speed drives, quality control is performed via cameras, and traceability is ensured through RFID tag reading on the pallets.

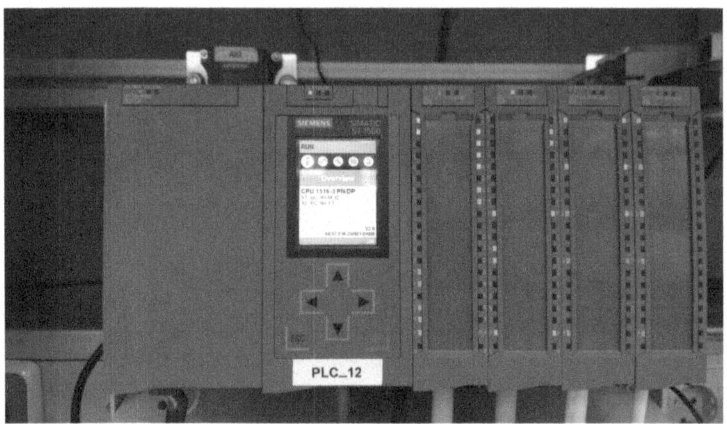

Fig. 3. Siemens S7-1516-3 PN/DP PLC

All components, from the mini-factory to the individual workstations, are connected according to the network architecture shown in Fig. 4. The network includes multiple switches that enable communication between any element of the mini-factory and the workstations. The topology includes both star and cascade configurations, the latter made possible by the internal dual-port switches in most devices. Communication protocols used include S7Comm, PROFINET, and OPC UA.

Surrounding the mini-factory is a safety network composed of a safety PLC, cascaded emergency stop buttons, open-door detectors, light curtains, magnetic locks, and proximity lasers, all operating over the same Ethernet network using the PROFIsafe protocol.

From the automation perspective, each station is equipped with the TIA Portal software to program the PLCs and other Siemen's devices, as well as RobotStudio to program the robots. Virtual PLCs, virtual HMIs, and virtual robots can also be launched at each workstation. In terms of connectivity—without yet addressing the cybersecurity topics covered in the next section—each workstation is connected to the university's corporate network, the laboratory's OT network, and the internal virtual device network of the workstation, which from an operational standpoint remains within the OT network. All lab devices are currently within the same domain, although additional domains can be set up via the Wi-Fi network.

In this laboratory, students learn classical automation techniques based on PLCs and robots, as well as more advanced techniques such as OPC UA integration and vision-based quality control. The laboratory is used by students from a variety of master's programs, including Industrial Engineering, Telecommunications Engineering, Cybersecurity, and Digital Transformation of Industry.

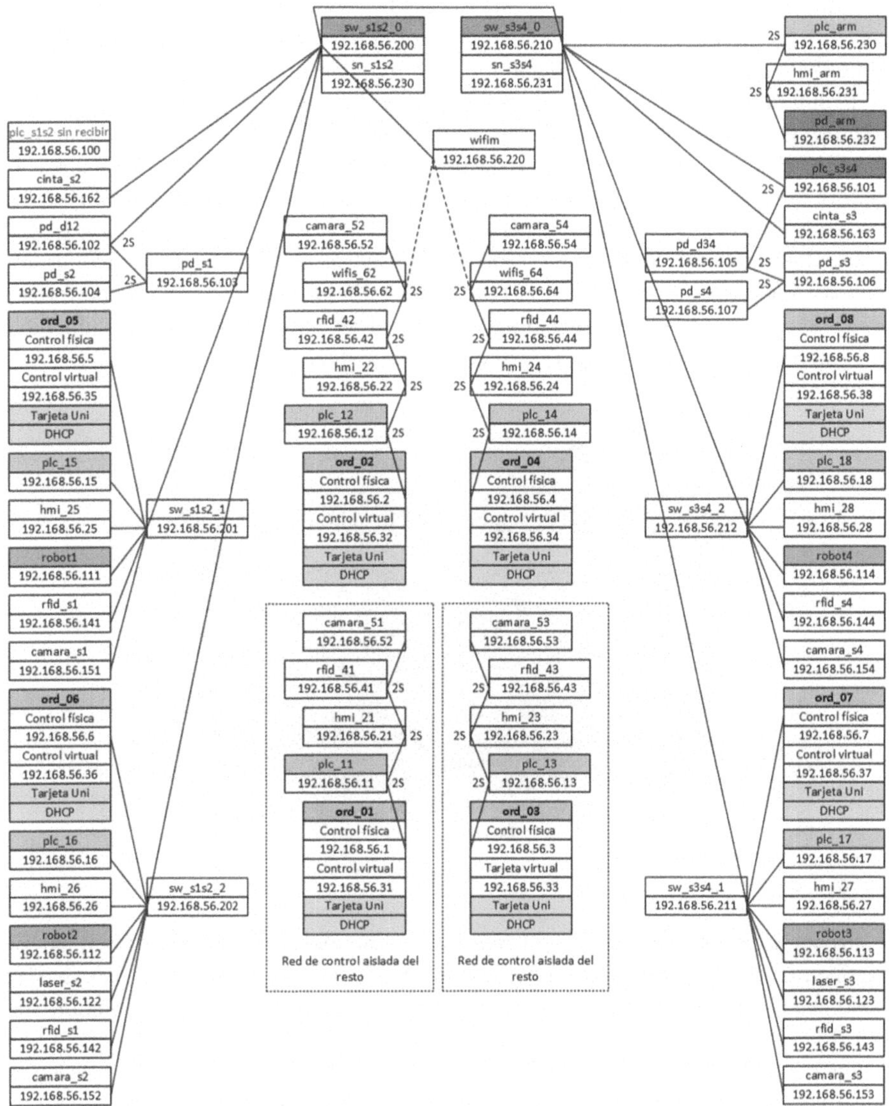

Fig. 4. Connectivity Diagram of the Industrial Automation Laboratory

3 OT Cybersecurity Laboratory

This laboratory aims to provide simple learning scenarios to train and raise awareness among students. This section offers a high-level description of the integration process with the industrial automation laboratory, as well as the equipment deployed. Additionally, it outlines in more detail the network connection scheme implemented.

To minimize space requirements—an approach commonly adopted in industry—monitoring and intrusion detection tools are deployed in a virtualized environment using a VMWARE ESXi server. This also reduces the need for changes to the physical workstations. Virtual machines running Kali Linux and Windows 11 are hosted on this server to support the different learning scenarios.

In addition to the Siemens S7-1500 PLCs used in the industrial automation lab, Siemens Simatic S7-300 units (Fig. 5) have also been installed. The attacks performed are designed to be simple and educational, and therefore both PLC models run vulnerable firmware versions and use unencrypted communications.

Fig. 5. Siemens Simatic S7-300

Proper segmentation between IT and OT environments is essential. It is common practice to follow the well-known Purdue model [7] and the guidelines of an extended converged plantwide Ethernet architecture, such as the one defined by Cisco and Rockwell [8]. For the equipment deployment in this lab, the Purdue model hierarchy has been adopted. A Fortinet NGFW FG-80F next-generation firewall is used to create an industrial demilitarized zone (iDMZ), separating IT equipment (level two in the diagram shown in Fig. 6, representing the process network) from OT equipment (level one in the same figure, containing control devices). Thanks to an academic partnership with Fortinet, students can receive training on their products and use virtual tools that complement the physical solutions.

From a security standpoint, ideally all communication between Purdue levels should be performed using segmentation at the application and industrial protocol level (Layer 7 of the OSI model [9]). However, during the integration of the two laboratories, this was not feasible due to the shared use of the facilities by students from other academic programs not related to industrial cybersecurity. The connections that do not follow this segmentation approach are marked with a warning symbol in the simplified diagram in Fig. 6. This limitation is used as a teaching opportunity to show students how proper segmentation should be implemented and to highlight the delicate balance between availability and logical security in OT environments.

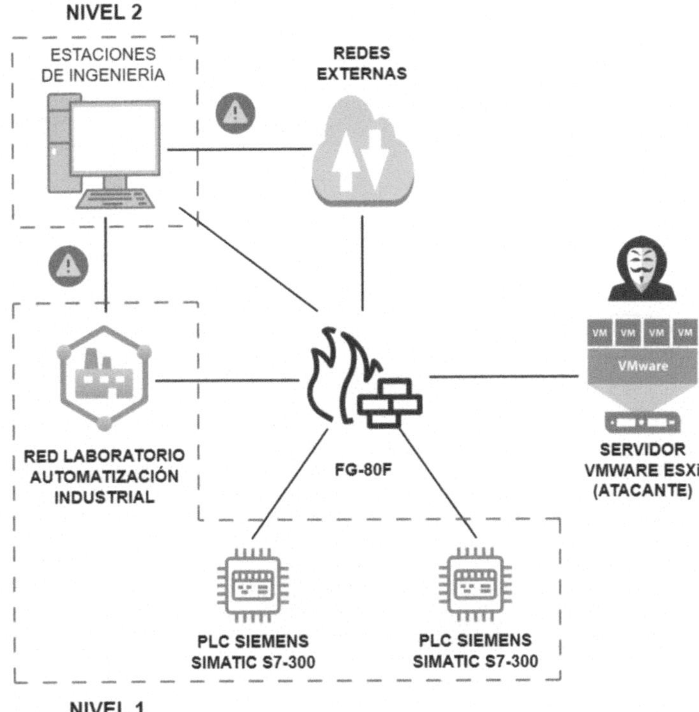

Fig. 6. Simplified Diagram of the OT Cybersecurity Laboratory

The new laboratory requires an isolated network that allows for different tests to be conducted without interfering with other systems not involved in the exercises. Figure 7 shows how this network was incorporated (new links in red). Each station has been given a new network connection through USB-to-Ethernet adapters. These adapters connect to one of two switches that are linked together. The upper-level switch is then connected to the FG-80F firewall. This firewall also connects to the rest of the systems, including the existing automation network (as shown in Fig. 4), the two S7-300 PLCs, and the subnet dedicated to virtualized machines and tools. The result is the coexistence of two academic and research spaces in which points of interference are minimized to only what is strictly necessary.

4 Implemented Use Cases

The scenarios developed are designed to demonstrate potential attacks and their corresponding mitigations to students. In the proposed use cases, students launch attacks from Kali Linux machines hosted on the VMWare server, targeting PLC devices. These exercises are conducted under the assumption that the attacker (the student) has already gained access to the plant's internal network and, after performing network reconnaissance, has identified the IP address of a vulnerable PLC.

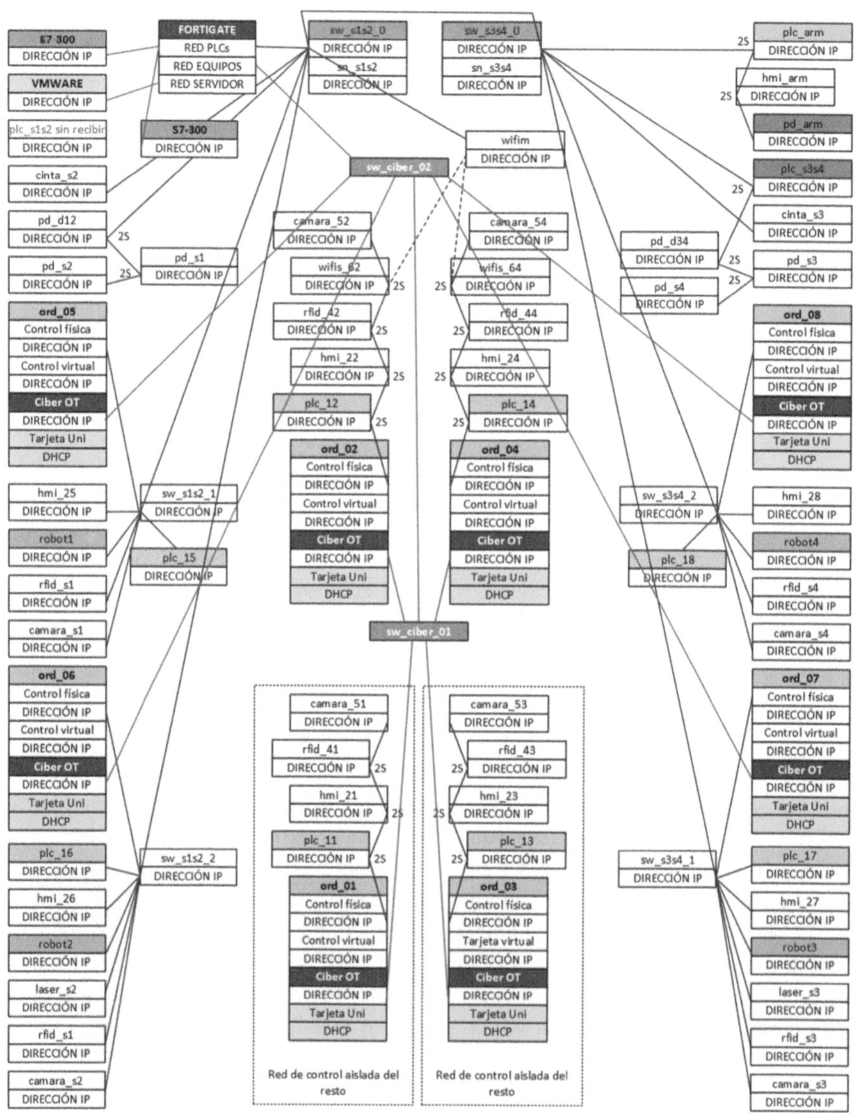

Fig. 7. Detailed Connectivity Diagram of the Laboratory

These scenarios are designed to replicate real-world industrial attack situations while simplifying their complexity, as their primary objective is to train students who may not yet have experience in OT cybersecurity. Students first carry out the offensive actions and then proceed to apply the necessary mitigations or safeguards.

4.1 Attack on Windows 11 Machines

This initial scenario is designed to introduce students with no prior experience to key cybersecurity concepts. Learners are introduced to the penetration testing platform Metasploit [10] and its associated payload generation tool, msfvenom. Students prepare a malicious file capable of opening a Meterpreter session on the target system.

This file is then delivered via an HTTP (Hypertext Transfer Protocol) connection to the victim machine, where it is executed. On the Kali machines, students are instructed to launch the multi-handler tool. The expected result is the establishment of a stable Meterpreter session between the attacker and the victim machine.

This type of attack can be easily mitigated through awareness of the risks of executing unknown files, maintaining system updates, and using antivirus software. This simple example is used to raise awareness among students about the importance of good cybersecurity practices and to show how even the most modern and updated operating systems are vulnerable when not used securely.

Despite the simplicity of the scenario, this use case proved to be highly effective in the lab sessions for capturing students' attention and sparking their interest.

4.2 START/STOP Attack on S7-300

Siemens PLC devices use a proprietary protocol known as S7Comm. This protocol follows the traditional client-server model, where communication is based on requests and responses using a set of function codes recognized by both ends of the connection.

The function codes have fixed values, and the rest of the protocol does not exhibit variability. As a result, the packets sent always follow the same structure and contain predictable values (Table 1).

Table 1. S7Comm Function Codes [11].

Function	Hexadecimal code
Comms setup	0xf0
Read / Write	0x04/0x05
Download / Upload	0x1a-1f
Control PLC	0x28
Stop PLC	0x29

An attacker could capture various packets and replay them to a device to provoke undesired behavior. One example of this is the script written by Dillon Beresford [12], which uses pre-crafted packets to start or stop a PLC.

This attack is effective because the S7Comm protocol does not implement security by default, allowing administrative-level commands to be executed without prior authentication [13].

To address this vulnerability, Siemens has introduced password-based authentication mechanisms for administrative actions in more recent versions of the protocol. However, it has been demonstrated that secret keys can still be obtained from traffic captures or even from the PLC's configuration files.

The mitigation taught in the lab for this attack involves applying NGFW rules at a level above the industrial device. The FG-80F firewall includes Fortinet's license for industrial protocol protection, which provides the ability to analyze and dissect these protocols, as well as apply detection or prevention rules to block malicious actions.

To prevent a malicious STOP PLC command, the rules shown in Fig. 8 are used. This enables granular protection without affecting the production environment.

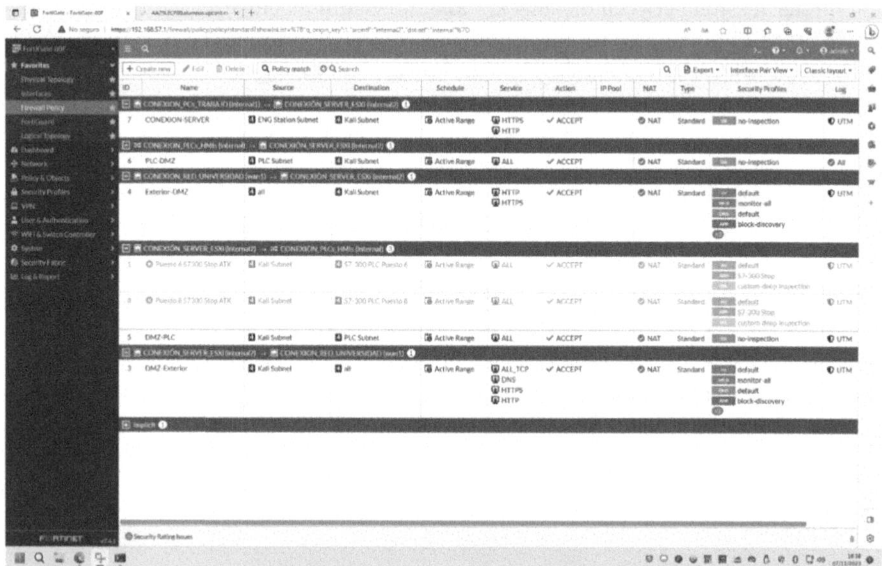

Fig. 8. FG-80F Firewall rules

4.3 S7-300 Session Manipulation

This is a denial-of-service (DoS) attack that targets the communication session. It can be carried out using two different approaches:

- Hijacking and impersonating an existing communication session between the PLC and a legitimate HMI.
- Establishing a new session by impersonating a supposed new HMI communicating with the PLC.

Communication occurs over the S7Comm protocol, which, unlike its more recent version S7CommPlus, does not employ encryption. In addition to this lack of encryption, the attack exploits the fact that no checksums are verified in the communication—neither at the IP (Internet Protocol) level nor at the TCP (Transmission Control Protocol) level.

To perform the attack using the first approach (Fig. 9), a packet sent from the HMI to the PLC is intercepted. This could be a write packet (e.g., when an operator modifies a variable on the PLC) or a read packet (as part of the HMI's regular polling cycle). The intercepted packet provides the source TCP port used by the HMI, as well as the TCP sequence and acknowledgment numbers of the ongoing communication. It is worth noting that the HMI uses a cyclic read variable to regularly update its internal values from the PLC.

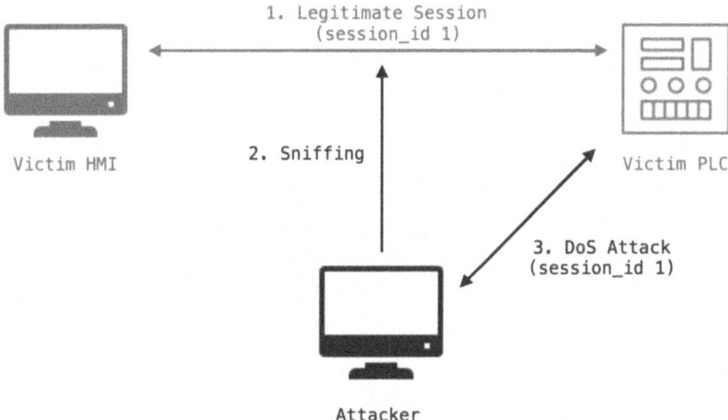

Fig. 9. Kidnapping and impersonation scheme (first approach)

In the second approach (Fig. 10), it is not necessary to capture a legitimate packet in advance, since the attacker initiates a new session, and can therefore use random values for the sequence number and source port. This method requires establishing the TCP connection (via a handshake), as well as the higher-layer protocols COTP and S7Comm.

Regardless of the approach used, the attacker then sends write packets in a loop to continuously update a variable in the PLC. This saturates the PLC, preventing it from responding when the legitimate HMI attempts to send its own packets. During this continuous flood of packets, the attacker must keep the TCP sequence and acknowledgment numbers up to date and respond with appropriate ACKs to the PLC's replies.

The recommended mitigation for this type of attack is to apply firewall rules on the NGFW that block traffic from outside the lab network destined for port 102 (used by the S7Comm protocol), in combination with a whitelist of the known and trusted devices within the lab. However, as demonstrated by this attack, it is still possible to impersonate a legitimate device from within the same network.

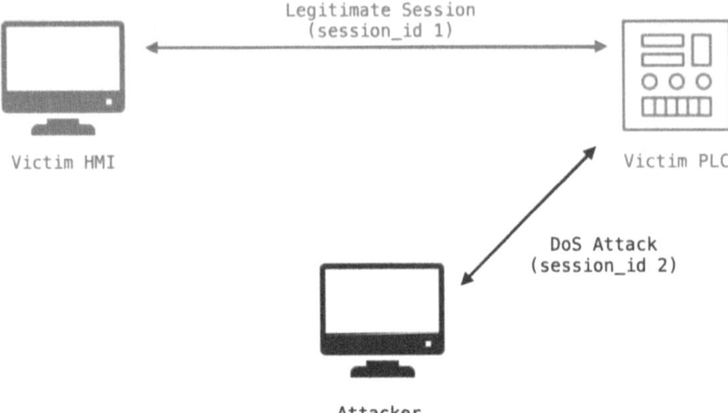

Fig. 10. New session creation scheme (second approach)

Therefore, additional measures available on the FG-80F NGFW are also recommended. These include bandwidth limiting to restrict excessive network resource usage by individual devices, and the firewall's built-in DoS protection capabilities, which detect and block traffic patterns indicative of such attacks.

4.4 Extraction of SZL Lists

SZL lists (from the German System-ZustandsListen, or "System Status Lists") are read-only data structures that provide information about the current state of a PLC. These lists and the information they contain can be accessed without prior authentication, making them a valuable resource for a potential adversary conducting reconnaissance before launching an attack.

A simple example would be retrieving the device's unique identifier, as shown in Fig. 11. A quick search online would reveal the specific PLC model. Other pieces of information, potentially even more critical, can also be obtained through this method.

The countermeasure taught in the lab to prevent this activity is similar to the one described previously: applying NGFW rules that block S7Comm traffic originating from outside the lab network, combined with a whitelist of authorized devices. This limits access to sensitive system information and reduces the attack surface exposed to unauthorized entities.

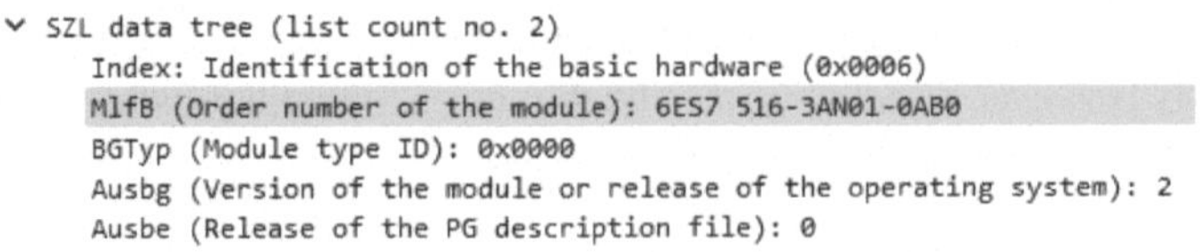

```
v SZL data tree (list count no. 2)
    Index: Identification of the basic hardware (0x0006)
    MlfB (Order number of the module): 6ES7 516-3AN01-0AB0
    BGTyp (Module type ID): 0x0000
    Ausbg (Version of the module or release of the operating system): 2
    Ausbe (Release of the PG description file): 0
```

Fig. 11. Extracting equipment identifier

4.5 DoS Attack on S7-1500

This denial-of-service (DoS) attack exploits a known vulnerability [14] in the resource monitor used in Siemens S7-1500 PLCs. By continuously sending malicious UDP packets, the attacker consumes a significant amount of system resources, potentially exhausting them and causing the PLC to slow down or even halt legitimate operations. This attack can be carried out without any prior authentication.

Once again, the mitigation strategy taught in the lab involves the use of NGFW rules that limit both the quantity and type of traffic allowed. In the future, with the planned deployment of tools such as FortiSIEM, this scenario is expected to be expanded to enable students to monitor and respond to threats in real time.

4.6 Access via OPC UA

In this exercise, students become familiar with the use of OPC UA through a practical automation example. The logic behind the automation involves repeatedly opening and closing a drawer over a programmed period of time, in order to verify that the drawer's guiding rails are functioning correctly. This automation is implemented by programming the lab's PLC using the GRAFCET language (known as GRAPH in Siemens terminology). In addition, the lab's HMI panel is configured to control and supervise the drawer guide test in a simplified manner. Another objective of the exercise is to familiarize students with the GRAFCET methodology.

From an OT cybersecurity training perspective, the connection described above is inherently insecure. As a countermeasure, digital certificates are employed to encrypt communication and enforce mutual authentication between client and server. This exercise highlights the complexity involved in installing and maintaining cybersecurity measures in the OT domain.

5 Conclusions

The OT cybersecurity laboratory at Comillas Pontifical University has enabled several cohorts of students from various academic programs to gain hands-on experience that goes beyond theoretical concepts.

This article has described the creation of the lab, which evolved from a pre-existing industrial automation laboratory. The deployment challenges have been discussed, with particular emphasis on ensuring interference-free coexistence between both environments and achieving proper network segmentation, minimizing connection points (as shown in Figs. 4 and 7), while considering the limitations posed by the need to maintain connections that, from a Purdue model perspective, are insecure (marked with a warning symbol in Fig. 6).

Following the deployment, the implemented scenarios have been presented. Notably, the scenarios involving real hardware are of particular importance—specifically, the Siemens S7-300 PLCs [5], used in the START/STOP (IV-B) and session manipulation (IV-C) scenarios, and the S7-1500 PLCs [3], used in the SZL list extraction (IV-D) and denial-of-service (IV-E) scenarios.

Looking ahead, beyond the technical improvements such as the deployment of VDOM solutions and the installation of additional Fortinet tools, one of the main goals is to become part of INCIBE's national network of industrial cybersecurity laboratories.

Given the growing concern surrounding industrial cybersecurity, it is clear that the near future will require more professionals specialized in OT cybersecurity, as well as managers who are both aware of and engaged with these issues.

The team behind the lab firmly believes that these hands-on exercises help students understand the critical need to secure industrial sectors and critical infrastructure. They provide future professionals with practical experience using real equipment and realistic scenarios. Through educational innovations such as this industrial cybersecurity lab, the aim is to help bridge the gap between IT and OT cybersecurity and contribute to the creation of industrial environments where cybersecurity becomes a foundational pillar.

Acknowledgments. This project has received funding from the European Union's Horizon Europe Energy Research and Innovation programme under Grant Agreement No. 101075665. The opinions expressed are those of the author(s) only and should not be considered as representative of the European Commission's official position.

Disclosure of Interests. The authors have no competing interests to declare that are relevant to the content of this article.

References

1. Fortinet: 2023 State of Operational Technology and Cybersecurity Report. Accessed 4 May 2024
2. CIDAUT: Proyecto ARISTEO. Accessed 2 May 2024
3. Ziur: Ziur. Accessed 2 May 2024
4. INCIBE-CERT: Red Nacional de Laboratorios de Ciberseguridad Industrial. Accessed 22 Mar 2024
5. Wikipedia: Programmable logic controller. Accessed 17 Mar 2024
6. Torre, J.R.M., Gil-Ortega, A.V.: Despliegue de arquitecturas e implementacion de medidas de ciberseguridad. Trabajo Fin de Master en Madrid, Espana: Universidad Pontificia Comillas, Junio (2023)
7. Dean Parsons: 2023's Challenges and Tomorrow's Defenses. en SANS ICS/OT Cybersecurity Survey, Septiembre 2023
8. Cisco: Enabling a Converged Plantwide Ethernet (CPwE) network. Accessed 17 Mar 2024
9. Cloudfare: Modelo OSI. Accessed 2 May 2024
10. Metaesploit Framework. Accessed 21 Mar 2024
11. gmiru: The Siemens S7 Communication. Accessed 19 Mar 2024
12. exploit-db: Siemens Simatic S7-300/400 - CPU START/STOP Module (Metasploit). Accessed 18 Mar 2024
13. Ackerman, P.: Industrial Cybersecurity: Efficiently Secure Critical Infrastructure Systems. Packt Publishing, Birmingham (2017)
14. NIST: CVE-2019-19281. Accessed 18 Mar 2024
15. Fortinet: VDOM. Accessed 2 May 2024

Designing an NIS2-Compliant Registry System: A Design Science Approach to the Classification and Supervision of Essential and Important Entities

Fabian Aude Steen[1(✉)], Vasileios Mavroeidis[2(✉)], Mateusz Zych[3(✉)], and Konstantinos Fysarakis[4(✉)]

[1] Kristiania University of Applied Sciences, Oslo, Norway
fast005@student.kristiania.no
[2] University of Oslo, Oslo, Norway
vasileim@ifi.uio.no
[3] Cyentific AS, Oslo, Norway
zych@cyentific.eu
[4] Automaton Technologies Ltd., Nicosia, Cyprus
kostas@automaton-technologies.eu

Abstract. The NIS2 Directive establishes a comprehensive cybersecurity governance framework across the European Union, mandating Member States to identify, classify, and oversee essential and important entities. As part of this governance ecosystem, Member States are required to submit national registries of these entities to the European Commission, the Cooperation Group, and ENISA. This paper critically examines the NIS2 Directive, with particular emphasis on its provisions for creating registries of essential and important entities. Specifically, Article 3 requires Member States to compile national registries containing entity details such as name, sector, and contact information, while Article 27 assigns ENISA the responsibility of maintaining a centralized EU-level registry for designated digital infrastructure and service providers. We operationalize these legal mandates by translating them into concrete technical specifications, guiding the design and development of a modular, legally compliant registry system. Employing the Design Science Research (DSR) methodology, we decompose complex legal requirements into a structured workflow, deterministic classification algorithms, and a comprehensive set of system specifications. The resulting conceptual registry prioritizes automation, harmonization, information sharing, and context-aware supervision, thereby supporting competent authorities in fulfilling their obligations and ensuring compliance at both national and EU levels. This study contributes a reusable framework that effectively bridges legal interpretation with technical implementation, offering a scalable and robust solution for cybersecurity governance under the NIS2 Directive.

Keywords: NIS2 Directive · Cybersecurity Governance · Entity Classification · Automation and Compliance · Regulatory Technology (RegTech)

R. Laborde et al. (Eds.): ESORICS 2025 Workshops, LNCS 16233, pp. 181–201, 2026.
https://doi.org/10.1007/978-3-032-16165-9_11

1 Introduction

The NIS2 Directive is a legally binding European regulation aimed at enhancing the overall level of cybersecurity across the Union by introducing multiple measures, including the establishment of a single-point registry of essential and important entities [1]. It responds to the increasing frequency and sophistication of cybersecurity threats and represents a significant revision of the earlier NIS1 Directive [2]. Among its various objectives, the directive prioritizes improving the harmonization of classification outcomes across Member States, facilitating effective and appropriate information sharing within the Union, and reducing administrative burdens associated with the implementation. A key component of these efforts is the mandated creation of a single-point registry designed to support the identification, classification, and supervision of entities critical to the functioning of societal and economic activities within the Union. The official deadline for compiling national lists of essential and important entities is set for 17 April 2025.

This research undertakes a detailed examination of the NIS2 directive through the lens of Design Science Research (DSR), intending to synthesize a conceptual framework for the establishment of a single-point registry in accordance with the directive's criteria [1]. The study places particular emphasis on enabling competent authorities across the Union to efficiently, uniformly, and to a certain extent automatically register, contextualize, and classify essential and important entities within their national jurisdictions [3]. Furthermore, it aims to facilitate standardized, timely, and automated information exchange with the European Commission, the Cooperation Group, ENISA, and other member states. These considerations are embedded within the broader context of achieving efficient NIS2 governance at both the national and European levels, while minimizing the administrative burden placed on regulated entities and competent authorities alike.

A foundational step in securing critical infrastructure—particularly those dependent on digital assets—is the accurate identification and classification of such infrastructure based on its importance to the continuity of economic and societal activities [3]. The NIS2 Directive establishes a regulatory framework intended to strengthen cybersecurity resilience across the EU [1]. However, the implementation of an NIS2-compliant, pan-European registry presents considerable challenges due to the diversity of regulatory environments, cybersecurity policies, and levels of digital maturity among Member States [4]. To address these challenges, three key elements must be considered in the development of such a registry:

- **Harmonization:** The classification rule sets and underlying factors used to determine classification outcomes must be consistent across all Member States to ensure a uniform approach to identifying essential and important entities. Without harmonization, divergent classification results may lead to fragmented governance, thereby undermining the effectiveness of the NIS2 Directive.

- **Information Sharing:** The registry must support automated, manual, and standardized reporting mechanisms to ENISA, the Cooperation Group, and the European Commission in order to strengthen cross-border cybersecurity governance, minimize administrative burden, and ensure timely and accurate information exchange.
- **Administrative Burden:** The registry should automate processes wherever possible without compromising the accuracy of classification. In particular, it should streamline the entire workflow—from registration to notification—to minimize the need for manual oversight. Additionally, the registry must provide a centralized point of registration with clearly defined guidelines, enabling entities to comply with NIS2 requirements without undue bureaucratic complexity.

Despite the urgency and importance of the NIS2 Directive, Member States currently lack a unified methodological framework for implementing the required registry in a harmonized and efficient manner. Of the five national implementations identified, only four have been described in academic or policy literature to date [5–8]. While these approaches represent meaningful national efforts, they have been developed independently and without common technical or procedural standards. The absence of a clear implementation model may hinder consistent classification across Member States, increase the administrative burden on national authorities, and undermine the efficiency of the NIS2 Directive. This research is motivated by the need to address these challenges through the development of a structured, harmonized, and automated registry framework.

Failure to establish a harmonized and efficient registry risks gaps in the identification and protection of critical infrastructure, potentially increasing cross-border cybersecurity risks that threaten the EU's overall cybersecurity resilience. This leads to the central research question:

How can classification criteria be effectively structured and applied to support a harmonized NIS2-compliant registry, including the registration mechanisms that best facilitate this process and the aggregation of data to enable timely notifications as well as efficient, proportionate, and context-aware supervision, all while minimizing the administrative burden on entities?

2 Methodology

This study applies a Design Science Research (DSR) approach to develop and evaluate an NIS2-compliant entity registry framework. The DSR methodology integrates regulatory analysis, requirements engineering, system modeling, and performance benchmarking to ensure that the proposed solution aligns with legal, technical, and operational demands.

2.1 Regulatory Analysis and Conceptual Modeling

Our study relies on a comprehensive analysis of the NIS2 Directive and its referenced legal instruments [3]. Relevant provisions were extracted and thematically categorized using visual structuring tools. Conceptual mind maps and operational workflows were used to identify interrelations between recitals, articles, and annexes, and to translate legal obligations into actionable system components. Seven central thematic categories were synthesized:

- **Registration:** Covers data input mechanisms, entry validation, and registration guidance.
- **Classification:** Defines classification factors, computational rules, and resulting classes.
- **Entity Types:** Establishes sector, sub-sector, and legal entity relationships.
- **Notification:** Structures reporting intervals, recipients, and required content.
- **Supervision:** Outlines oversight responsibilities and required decision-support tools.
- **Cross-Directive:** Addresses cross-regulation supervision and classification dependencies.
- **Security:** Specifies confidentiality, integrity, and availability requirements, including access control, encryption, validation, and logging [1,9].

Each theme was linked to relevant directive articles and modeled in a concept matrix, forming the foundation for requirement traceability.

2.2 Requirement Synthesis and Domain Modeling

Requirements were derived by analyzing user roles and operational domains. In particular, four domains were defined: public, user, agent, and admin. Each domain was mapped to specific workflows based on its interaction with registry concepts. This enabled the derivation of functional and non-functional requirements aligned with usability, interoperability, and legal compliance objectives.

To define core logic, flowcharts and business process diagrams were used to model key algorithmic functions. The purpose was not to develop software artifacts, but to ensure conceptual completeness and system-level consistency.

2.3 High-Level Algorithmic Components

The conceptual registry design includes a set of high-level engines responsible for fulfilling directive-mandated operations:

- **Registration Engine:** Covers both manual and automated entity onboarding workflows. Automated onboarding is enhanced through the integration of Large Language Models (LLMs) to assist with formatting and normalizing unstructured data, ensuring compliance with NIS2 sector, sub-sector, and entity type formats.
- **Labeling Engine:** Applies contextual tags, including risk, sector, and directive scope labels.

- **Classification Engine:** Implements deterministic, rule-based entity classification to ensure accuracy and consistency across (technological implementations of) Member States.
- **Aggregation Engine:** Compiles entity-level data into statistical summaries for supervisory dashboards.
- **Notification Engine:** Supports standardized reporting formats for compliance submissions.
- **Supervision Engine:** Enables contextual inspection, override mechanisms, and classification auditing.
- **Security Engine:** Ensures access control, logging, encryption, and validation across all operations.

These components are described at a conceptual level to capture their functional intent, without reference to any specific implementation technology or codebase.

2.4 Development and Testing Framework

The concepts, operational domains, and algorithmic components described above were developed through an iterative development framework. The process was grounded in the principle that NIS2 compliance must originate from a structured analysis of regulatory text, followed by progressive refinement through conceptual design, requirement synthesis, and validation. The development cycle followed a structured sequence:

1. **Directive Analysis:** Identification of functional and legal requirements through systematic examination of the NIS2 Directive and related instruments.
2. **Conceptual Design:** Initial modeling of the registry's core logic and system behavior in response to identified regulatory themes.
3. **Requirement Synthesis:** Formalization of system-level requirements mapped to concepts.
4. **Prototyping and Programming:** Development of logic modules to test feasibility, interaction flows, and operational integrity.
5. **Testing and Evaluation:** Unit and integration tests were applied iteratively to validate classification correctness, data flow coherence, and logic completeness.

This development approach ensured that the evolving system model remained consistent with regulatory intent, technically viable, and incrementally validated through continuous testing. While the developed and fully functional prototype is not presented here, the development and testing phases were essential for identifying ambiguities in legal interpretation, refining classification rules, and improving system-level design coherence. A demonstration of the prototype is available online [13].

3 Results and Discussion

This section begins by presenting the legal basis for each core registry concept, as defined in the NIS2 Directive. Table 1 summarizes the linkage between concepts and their corresponding recitals, articles, and annexes [3].

Table 1. Linking the NIS2 Directive with Registry Concepts

Concept	Recital	Article	Annex
Registration	7, 9, 16, 18, 106, 114, 121	3, 27	—
Classification	7, 8, 9, 12, 15, 16, 18, 30, 124	2, 3	I, II
Entity Types	8, 11, 12, 18, 29, 30, 32, 35, 36, 83, 93, 96, 113, 114	2, 3, 27	I, II
Notification	19, 24, 28, 92, 96, 97, 102, 106, 117, 121	3, 27	—
Supervision	9, 11, 15, 19, 20, 28, 29, 30, 32, 35, 36, 84, 90, 92, 93, 96, 97, 113, 114, 122, 123, 124, 125, 135, 138	2	—
Cross-Directive	24, 28, 29, 30, 92, 93, 135	2, 3	I, II
Security	14, 121	2, 27	—

3.1 Registry Workflow

The registry can be understood by examining a sequential workflow composed of six core components [3]. Components from register to notify are automated and responsible for core registry functionality, while components going from supervise to assess are largely manual and supported by the information produced through registration, labeling, and classification. Specifically, the components 'Register', 'Label', 'Classify', and 'Notify' are primarily automated, while 'Assess' and 'Supervise' typically involve manual oversight, as illustrated in Fig. 1.

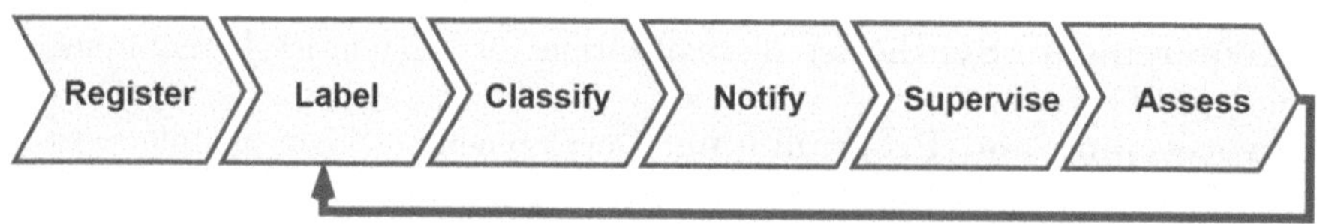

Fig. 1. Proposed High-Level NIS2 Registry Workflow

In the case of perfect and unchanging entity information, the registry workflow for that entity would loop from 'Supervise' and support competent authorities in governing their ecosystem in accordance with the NIS2 specification. However, this is rarely the case, as new information is typically acquired during the 'Assess' phase. This information is then used in the 'Label' phase to update records, apply new labels, and revise classifications automatically. The workflow continues in this pattern for each entity under NIS2 governance, enabling competent authorities to identify, classify, and supervise entities in an efficient, consistent, and adaptive manner.

3.2 Registration Engine

Registration serves as the single point of entry for entities and enables the collection of essential information. According to NIS2, each Member State's competent authority must compile a list of essential and important entities by 17 April 2025 and update it biannually. Registered entities must, at a minimum, provide the information shown in Table 2 [1].

Table 2. Registry Basic Information Requirements

Registration information requirements
Name of the entity
Address of the main establishment, representative, and other EU establishments
Contact information (email addresses and telephone numbers)
IP address ranges
Sector, sub-sector, and entity type
Member States in which services are provided

In addition, competent authorities must collect classification-related information, as shown in Table 3.

Table 3. Registry Classification Information Requirements

Classification information requirements
Sector, sub-sector, and entity Type
Number of employees in the Union
Most recent annual turnover and balance sheet

Risk-related data can significantly influence classification outcomes. Table 4 outlines four risk categories and associated information requirements.

Table 4. Registry Risk Information Requirements

Category	Risk information requirements
Risk	Impact of disruption upon public safety, security, or health
Risk	Whether an entity is the sole provider of a service
Risk	Potential for cross-border or sectoral systemic impact
Risk	Whether an entity is of particular sectorial importance
Service	Types and provision of services by category

Finally, the regulatory status of entities under other frameworks may alter classification and supervision profiles. Cross-sector factors are listed in Table 5.

Table 5. Registry Cross-Directive Information Requirements

Directive	Description
NIS1	Essential entities under NIS1 remain so under NIS2
CER	Entities critical under CER are essential under NIS2 [10]
National Law	National legislation may impact classification outcome
Security Operator	Security operators may be excluded from NIS2 scope
Value Chains	Critical research organizations in EU value chains

The information presented in Tables 2, 3, 4, and 5 must be collected for each entity to enable accurate labeling, classification, and supervision. The registration process must support both guided manual input and automated submission. Automated submissions should allow for validation and integration without human intervention, while manual processes must offer sufficient guidance to ensure completeness and correctness. Table 6 summarizes the registration requirements [3].

Table 6. Registration requirements

ID	Name	Description	NIS2 Ref.	Rationale
R-1	Single-point registration	Must occur through one common system.	Recital 106	Reduces administrative burden on entities and the competent authority
R-2	Manual registration	Manual submission must be supported.	Recital 106	Entities should be able to self-register
R-3	Automatic registration	Must support automated input.	Recital 106	Enables automation to reduce administrative burden
R-4	Guidance	Process must provide contextual support based on Annex I–II.	NIS2	Ensures completeness and accuracy
R-5	Data collection	Includes all information from Tables 2, 3, 4 and 5	Recital 18, Art. 2, 3, 27	These define full registration data
R-6	Input restriction	Each field must be atomic and accept one data point.	NIS2	Ensures structured and valid input
R-8	GDPR	Processing must comply with GDPR.	Recitals 14, 121; Art. 2	Sensitive data must be lawfully handled
R-9	Security controls	Entry point must implement appropriate security mechanisms.	Recitals 117, 121	Ensures confidentiality, integrity, and availability (CIA)

3.3 Data Availability and Automation

The automation of registration processes under the NIS2 framework is heavily dependent on both the availability and format of entity data [3]. While data from public or third-party registries may exist within a given Member State, such data is often not directly compatible with NIS2 requirements. In particular, entity activity data must be transformed into the hierarchical structure defined by the directive—namely, sector, sub-sector, and entity type.

This transformation task can be efficiently and reliably handled by Large Language Models (LLMs) [3,12]. In our case study, the Norwegian ecosystem provided sufficient publicly available registry data to enable initial classification. However, mapping entity activity descriptions to the NIS2 schema presented a critical bottleneck. LLMs proved to be a scalable and accurate solution for resolving this semantic gap and enabling automated classification. This effectively underscores LLMs as a promising solution for integrating unique data sources.

3.4 Labeling Engine

Collected data must not only support classification and notification; it should also enhance supervision through the assignment of labels [3]. Labels are keywords or categorical tags that provide competent authority personnel (agents) with contextual insight into the entities under their oversight—particularly when multiple labels are applied in combination. Labels can also support predictive analysis and enable faster, more informed supervisory decisions. Once the necessary data has been obtained, labels can be computed and attributed to the entity automatically, as outlined in Table 7.

Table 7. Labels

Type	Label	Label	Label
Size	Above Medium Sized	Medium Sized	Below Medium Sized
Annex	High Criticality	Critical	
Activity	Sector	Sub-sector	Entity Type
Cross-Directive	Security Operator NIS1	National Laws CER	Value Chain
Risk	Safety, Security, or Health Sole Provider	Systemic	Sectoral Importance
Other	Representative	Basic Info	Custom

(1) **Size labels** are assigned based on thresholds for employee count (E), annual turnover (T), and balance sheet total (B), according to the size-cap rule [11]. These thresholds are summarized in Table 8.

Table 8. Size-Cap Classification Thresholds (E: employees, T: turnover, B: balance sheet)

Above Medium (A)	$E > 250$ and $(T > 50\,\mathrm{M€} \vee B > 43\,\mathrm{M€})$
Medium (M)	$50 \leq E \leq 250$ and $(10 \leq T \leq 50\,\mathrm{M€} \vee 10 \leq B \leq 43\,\mathrm{M€})$
Below Medium (B)	$E < 50$ and $(T < 10\,\mathrm{M€} \vee B < 10\,\mathrm{M€})$

(2) **Annex labels** are assigned after the sector, sub-sector, and entity type have been determined, and indicate the criticality of the entity's services in accordance with Annex I and II of the NIS2 Directive.
(3) **Activity labels** must conform to the predefined sectoral structure defined in Annex I and II and must maintain a hierarchical dependency between sector, sub-sector, and entity type.
(4) **Cross-Directive labels** are applied based on the entity's inclusion in other relevant legislative frameworks. These may be obtained through screening processes, entity self-disclosure, or consultation of directive-specific registries.
(5) **Risk labels** are constrained to categories specified in the NIS2 Directive. They may be determined either through self-reporting during registration or through post-registration risk assessment.
(6) **Other labels** capture supplementary or uncategorized information. The ability to generate custom labels on demand can improve supervisory granularity and enhance contextual understanding of entities. For example, a custom label may be manually assigned to indicate that an entity is a critical supplier within the supply chain of an essential entity.

3.5 Classification Engine

The NIS2 Directive defines a framework for classifying entities into two categories: essential and important [1]. This classification is predicated on the regulatory scope outlined in Article 2 and the activity definitions provided in Annexes I and II. The result is a proportional regulatory model that assigns obligations according to the criticality of entities to both Member State and Union-wide economic and societal functions, particularly with respect to cybersecurity risk and threat potential. The resulting classification is intended to inform supervisory tasks.

To ensure consistency and regulatory clarity, classification must be mutually exclusive, collectively exhaustive, and rule-based [1,3]. This means that every entity within a Member State must be screened for inclusion and assigned exactly one classification. To satisfy exhaustiveness, a third category—*excluded*—must be introduced to account for entities that fall outside the NIS2 scope. Each entity may hold only one classification at a time, and this classification must be determined using a deterministic, rule-based approach. This ensures unambiguous outcomes, meaning identical input data will always yield the same classification.

Classification outcomes must be based on a common set of underlying factors to ensure harmonized implementation across Member States.

Table 9. Classification Input Factors Grouped by Category

Category	Factors
Size	Above Medium Size, Medium Size, Below Medium Size
Activity	Sector, Sub-sector, Entity Type
Risk	(Safety, Security, or Health), Systemic, Sectoral Importance, Sole Provider
Legal-Administrative	Public Administration, National Law, Value Chains
Cross-Directive	NIS1, CER, Sector Specific Union Legal Acts

Harmonization is achieved by applying consistent rule sets to the input factors defined in Table 9. To avoid classification conflicts—where a single entity could satisfy multiple classification conditions—the algorithm must follow a fixed classification pattern. Deterministic rule sets are applied first, ensuring that the most clear-cut cases are resolved early. More complex or ambiguous cases are evaluated only after simpler classification attempts have failed.

As a general rule of thumb, classification conflicts are resolved according to a fixed resolution hierarchy: *Essential* > *Important* > *Excluded*. This hierarchy applies unless the entity is primarily involved in national security, public security, defense, or law enforcement—in which case it is immediately classified as *Excluded*. Following this, a set of six sequential algorithms is applied to compute the appropriate classification without ambiguity. Textual descriptions of these algorithms are provided below, and their algorithmic implementations are available in Appendix A.

Before applying the classification algorithms, the entity's labels must first be computed. The first algorithm excludes any entity that is primarily engaged in national security, defense, or law enforcement—or that primarily supplies such an entity. The second algorithm determines whether the entity qualifies as *Essential* based on its regulatory status, as defined in Table 5. The third algorithm classifies the entity as *Essential* if it possesses one or more risk-based labels. The fourth algorithm evaluates the entity's type to either assign a classification directly or determine the appropriate next step. If the entity type is "Provider of Public Electronic Communications Networks or Services," the fifth algorithm is invoked, classifying the entity based on its size. If none of the entity types match the conditions specified in the fourth algorithm, the sixth algorithm is called to classify the entity based on its size and whether it belongs to Annex I or II. Any entity that remains unclassified after the sixth algorithm is assigned the classification *Excluded*.

To support the implementation of the classification logic and the overall registry workflow, a set of functional and non-functional requirements is defined in Table 10, as described in [3].

Table 10. Classification requirements

ID	Name	Description	NIS2 Ref.	Rationale
C-1	Classes	Entities must be classified into three mutually exclusive classes: Essential, Important, and Excluded.	Recital 15; Art. 2, 3	Ensures entities are appropriately scoped and reflects their criticality to societal and economic functioning
C-2	Factors	Classification must rely on the input factors defined in Table 9.	Recital 7; Art. 2, 3	Supports a harmonized, factor-driven classification process
C-3	Rule set	Entities must be classified using the algorithms defined in Algorithms 1, 2, 3, 4, 5, and 6 (see also Appendix A).	Recital 7; Art. 2, 3	Guarantees consistent and deterministic classification outcomes
C-4	Labeling	Labels from Table 7 and additional entity data must be used to contextualize classification.	Recital 15, 30, 122–125, 135; Art. 2	Enables more informed supervision beyond the classification tier
C-5	Partitioning	The classification model must be mutually exclusive and collectively exhaustive.	Recital 15; Art. 2, 3	Prevents ambiguity and ensures full infrastructure coverage
C-6	Automatic classification	Classification logic must be automated where feasible and appropriate.	Recital 14, 106	Minimizes manual workload for entities and competent authorities
C-7	Intervention	Manual intervention and interpretation must be possible.	Art. 2, 3, 27	Some conditions (e.g., legal or risk-based) require human oversight

3.6 Notification Engine

Competent authorities are required to exchange collected entity data, labels, and classifications with ENISA, the European Commission, the European Cooperation Group, national CSIRTs, and other relevant competent authorities [1]. The notification requirements for ENISA, the European Commission, and the European Cooperation Group are outlined in the NIS2 Directive and should be standardized and automated.

To support this functionality, a dashboard-based interface can be implemented to manage and visualize notifications [3]. This interface may include live registry statistics, automated aggregation, and report generation, all aligned with predefined notification schemas. Automating these exchanges ensures consistency, reduces administrative overhead, and improves coordination across Member States.

(1) **ENISA** is required to maintain a registry of certain digital infrastructure and digital provider entities, as defined in the NIS2 Directive [1]. This registry must include all information specified in Table 2, with the exception of

IP address ranges, due to privacy and sensitivity concerns. These entities are prioritized due to their central role in network operations and the increased exposure they introduce to cybersecurity threats. The relevant entity types are listed in Table 11.

Table 11. Digital Infrastructure and Digital Service Provider Entity Types

Sector	Entity Type
Digital Infrastructure	DNS Service Providers
Digital Infrastructure	TLD Name Registers
Digital Infrastructure	Domain Name Registration Services
Digital Infrastructure	Content Delivery Network Providers
Digital Infrastructure	Data Center Service Providers
Digital Infrastructure	Cloud Computing Service Providers
ICT Service Management (B2B)	Managed Service Providers
ICT Service Management (B2B)	Managed Security Service Providers
Digital Providers	Providers of Online Search Engines
Digital Providers	Providers of Online Market Places
Digital Providers	Providers of Social Networking Services Platforms

(2) **The European Commission and the European Cooperation Group** require a biannual registry statistics report [1]. This report must include:
   - The total number of essential and important entities.
   - The number of essential and important entities per sector/sub-sector pair.

(3) **The European Commission** requires a biannual statistical report focusing on risk-related classifications, as defined in Table 4 [1]. This report must include:
   - The total number of essential and important entities categorized by risk.
   - The number of essential entities per risk category.
   - The frequency of each risk category across sector/sub-sector pairs.
   - The types of services provided by each entity and their provisions.

Additionally, the registry must support automatic report generation on registered entities to facilitate information sharing between competent authorities, particularly in cases of cross-supervision or other justified circumstances. To support this functionality and ensure regulatory alignment, a set of requirements has been defined to guide the development of the notification engine, as outlined in Appendix B (Table 12) [3].

3.7 Supervision Engine

All preceding registry functionality is designed to enable the supervision of entities within the scope of the NIS2 Directive. Accurate classification is a prerequisite for proportionate and effective supervision. The registry should support this objective by consolidating entity data—including labels, classifications, and other aggregated information—into a supervision-ready format. To support this, the following capabilities must be implemented:

- **Entity Information:** Collected data must be processed into labels, classifications, and insights that enable contextual, efficient, and actionable supervision by competent authorities.
- **Entity Information Management:** The registry must support two-way communication between entities and competent authorities for reviewing, updating, and validating entity data. Changes must be subject to approval workflows or restricted to authority-side edits to ensure data integrity.
- **Information Sharing:** Effective cross-border and cross-directive supervision requires configurable information-sharing mechanisms, such as customized views or automatically generated entity reports.

To operationalize the supervision model, a modular supervisory dashboard may be implemented. The functional and non-functional requirements that guide the development and deployment of this capability are provided in Appendix B (Table 13) [3].

4 Limitations and Future Work

The primary limitations of this work—and areas for future research—concern the dependency of automatic registration on external data sources, the challenges of dynamic risk modeling, the constraints of the size-cap rule, and the current exclusion of supply chain considerations from classification logic.

4.1 Pilots and Validation

The current work has been validated primarily at the level of framework design and prototype implementation. Comprehensive real-world validation is still limited. To address this, pilot activities are being initiated in collaboration with national cybersecurity authorities in Norway, Greece, and Cyprus. These pilots will allow the framework to be tested under operational conditions, providing feedback on usability, interoperability with existing registries, and overall feasibility. The outcomes of these pilots will inform further iterations of the system and help establish a broader evidence base for its adoption across Member States.

4.2 External Data Sources

Automatic registration relies heavily on the availability and structure of external public registries. The presence, completeness, and format of such registries vary significantly across Member States. In cases where data is unavailable or incompatible, automation may be hindered. Even where data is accessible, cross-border variability introduces harmonization challenges.

While Large Language Models (LLMs) proved helpful in transforming local entity descriptions—particularly sector, sub-sector, and entity types—into NIS2-compliant formats, this study does not evaluate data availability or quality across the EU. Future work should assess the feasibility of automatic registration at scale and explore the design of standardized data transformation pipelines for national-level integration.

4.3 Dynamic Risk Modeling

Risk assessment is inherently complex and context-dependent. The NIS2 Directive identifies four specific risk factors that may influence the classification of an entity (see Table 4) [1]. While these factors have been incorporated into the classification logic, the current registry framework does not support dynamic or fully automated risk inference. Instead, applicable risk attributes must be identified manually during registration or subsequent supervision.

Dynamic risk modeling represents a research area of its own and falls outside the scope of this study. However, the integration of automated or semi-automated risk inference mechanisms could substantially enhance the registry's ability to support risk-based supervision in accordance with NIS2. This presents a valuable direction for future work.

4.4 The Size-Cap Rule

The size-cap rule provides a quantitative mechanism for estimating an entity's significance to the Member State's economy and societal functioning. However, its rigid classification thresholds may introduce ambiguity. Entities near category boundaries can satisfy criteria for multiple sizes simultaneously, resulting in classification uncertainty.

Moreover, the rule does not account for the entity's corporate structure—specifically, whether its information and communications technology (ICT) systems operate independently. In some cases, ICT independence may render the economic size of the parent entity irrelevant for classification purposes. Assessing this form of structural independence currently requires manual evaluation.

Future research could focus on formalizing a method to evaluate ICT independence and integrating it into the classification logic to improve precision.

4.5 Supply Chains

Supply chain risk is a critical yet currently unmodeled factor in the classification framework. Integrating supply chain relationships into the registry could reveal inter-dependencies between entities, particularly where the operations of one entity are contingent upon the services of another. This has the potential to significantly affect classification outcomes—especially for entities that serve as critical suppliers to essential or important entities.

However, accurately and efficiently capturing supply chain structures at scale remains a challenge. It requires mechanisms for identifying, verifying, and updating dependency links across sectors and jurisdictions. Future research should explore data models and system architectures capable of integrating supply chain risk into classification and supervision processes in a scalable and cross-border manner.

5 Conclusion

The NIS2 Directive establishes a common cybersecurity governance framework across the European Union, requiring Member States to implement mechanisms for identifying, classifying, and supervising critical entities. This research presents a conceptual yet operational model for an NIS2-compliant registry that supports the entire pipeline from registration to notification.

By combining deterministic classification algorithms, automation, large language model support, and contextualized supervision, the proposed system addresses key challenges such as harmonized classification, efficient information sharing, and reduced administrative burden. The registry design emphasizes modularity and legal traceability, offering a scalable foundation for national and cross-border NIS2 implementation.

In doing so, this work not only operationalizes the directive's requirements but also lays the groundwork for future extensions—including dynamic risk assessment, supply chain modeling, and enhanced integration with external data sources.

Acknowledgments. This work was carried out under the supervision of Prof. Vasileios Mavroeidis and as part of the research activities of the Digital Security Group (SEC), Department of Informatics, University of Oslo. In addition, it was supported by the European Union's Digital Europe Programme (DIGITAL) under Grant Agreements No. 101145874 (NG-SOC project) and No. 101128017 (CY-TRUST project), as well as by the Research and Innovation Fund of the Republic of Cyprus under Contract PRE-SEED/0823/0183. The views and opinions expressed are those of the authors and do not necessarily reflect those of the European Union or the granting authorities. Neither the European Union nor the granting authorities can be held responsible for them.

Appendix A: Classification Algorithms

Algorithm 1 . Initial Exclusion Check

```
Input: Entity profile E
procedure InitialExclusion(E)
    if E is in national security, defense, or law enforcement then
        return Excluded
    else
        return DeterministicClassification(E)
    end if
end procedure
```

Algorithm 2. Deterministic Classification

```
procedure DeterministicClassification(E)
    if E ∈ NIS1 or E ∈ CER or E ∈ National Law or E is a Research Org then
        return Essential
    else
        return RiskBasedClassification(E)
    end if
end procedure
```

Algorithm 3. Risk-Based Classification

```
procedure RiskBasedClassification(E)
    if E has label (Safety, Security, or Health) or E has label Systemic or E has label Sectoral Importance or E has label Sole Provider then
        return Essential
    else
        return SpecialEntityClassification(E)
    end if
end procedure
```

Algorithm 4. Special Entity Classification

```
procedure SpecialEntityClassification(E)
    if E is a Trust Service Provider or E is a TLD Name Register or E is a DNS Service Provider or E is a DNS Registration Service Provider or E is a Central Government Entity then
        return Essential
    else if E is a Regional Government entity then
        return Important
    else if E is a Provider of Public Electronic Communications Networks or Services then
        return CommunicationsEntityClassification(E)
    else
        return SizeBasedClassification(E)
    end if
end procedure
```

Algorithm 5. Communications Entity Classification

```
procedure CommunicationsEntityClassification(E)
    if E is Below Medium Size then
        return Important
    else return Essential
    end if
end procedure
```

Algorithm 6. Size-Based Classification

```
procedure SizeBasedClassification(E)
    if E is Above Medium Size then
        if E is in Annex II then
            return Important
        else if E is in Annex I then
            return Essential
        else
            if E is Medium Size then
                if E is in Annex I or Annex II then
                    return Important
                else return Excluded
                end if
            else return Excluded
            end if
        end if
    else if E is Medium Size then
        if E is in Annex I or Annex II then
            return Important
        else return Excluded
        end if
    else return Excluded
    end if
end procedure
```

Appendix B: Requirements Tables

Table 12. Notification requirements

ID	Name	Description	NIS2 Ref.	Rationale
N-1	Registry Statistics	The total number of essential and important entities and their frequency per sector/sub-sector pair must be aggregated and forwarded to the European Commission and the Cooperation Group once classification is completed and every second year thereafter.	Recital 18 and Article 3(5), and 14	To enable Union-wide cybersecurity governance and coordination, and to produce biannual reports
N-2	ENISA	All information except IP Ranges in Table 2 must be forwarded immediately and automatically to ENISA upon registration of an entity of entity type in Table 11.	Recital 117, and Article 27	ENISA is required to maintain a registry of key service providers and entities at Union level
N-3	ENISA Update	In the case any information about an entity in Table 2 is updated, the registry must automatically forward an updated notification of type in requirement N-2 to ENISA.	Recital 117, and Article 27	ENISA's registry must be actionable and therefore up-to-date
N-4	The Commission	The total number of essential entities with a risk label, number of essential entities per risk category, the frequency of each risk category across sector/sub-sector pairs, the types of services provided by each entity, and their provisions must be forwarded immediately and automatically to The European Commission once they have been identified and every second year thereafter.	Recital 18, Article 3(5), 3(6)	To enable Union-wide cybersecurity governance and coordination, and to produce biannual reports
N-5	Reports	The notifications discussed in rows N-1, N-2, N-3, and N-4 must be presentable in standardized report templates.	Recital 106, Article 3(5), 14, and 27	Reports should be standardized to simplify and streamline the reporting process and to reduce administrative burden
N-6	Manual Notification	It must be possible to produce reports manually that can contain all or specific information about an entity or set of entities.	Recital 106, Article 3(5), 14, and 27	Reporting flexibility is required to support cross-directive and cross-border supervision and to meet ad hoc reporting needs
N-7	Configuration	It must be possible to configure notification dates, recipients, and the information provided in reports.	Recital 106, Article 3(5), 14, and 27	Reporting flexibility is required to meet ad hoc reporting needs

Table 13. Supervision requirements

ID	Name	Description	NIS2 Ref.	Rationale
S-1	Request Information	Agents must be able to request additional information from entity registrants.	Recital 106; Art. 27, 32, 33	Enables direct interaction while reducing administrative burden
S-2	Request Change	Registrants must be able to request changes to their classification or labels.	Recital 106; Art. 27(3), 3(3)	Maintains accurate records and supports collaborative updates
S-3	Change Notification	Registrants must be able to update information within ENISA-defined notification windows.	Recital 18; Art. 27(3), 3(4)	Ensures registry reflects timely and accurate entity data
S-4	Editable	Competent authority agents must be able to edit registry information.	Recital 125; Art. 27	Authorities are ultimately responsible for information correctness
S-5	Risk Assessments	Agents must be able to assess and apply risk at the sector or entity level.	Recital 124, 125; Art. 31(2)	Enables a risk-based supervisory model
S-6	Non-repudiation	All changes must be logged to ensure auditability and non-repudiation.	Recital 117, 125	Maintains data integrity and accountability
S-7	Assignment	Authorized agents must be able to assign supervision responsibilities to others.	Recital 14, 117, 121	Ensures role-based task delegation with appropriate controls
S-8	Information Sharing	Agents must be able to generate entity reports for internal or external sharing.	Recital 18, 117; Art. 3(5), 3(6), 14, 27, 29	Supports cross-border and cross-directive supervision
S-9	Uploading	Agents must be able to attach supporting documentation to entity profiles.	Recital 124, 125; Art. 27, 31–33	Enables richer supervision through audit reports, assessments, and contextual data
S-10	Presentation	Classifications, labels, and insights must be clearly presented to agents and, where appropriate, registrants.	Recital 15, 30, 122–125, 135; Art. 2, 3	Provides a contextual basis for supervision prioritization
S-11	Authentication	All registry access must require authentication.	Recital 117, 121	Ensures only authorized users have access to sensitive registry functions
S-12	Authorization	Access rights must be enforced through role-based authorization.	Recital 117, 121	Protects registry content through fine-grained access control

References

1. European Parliament and Council of the European Union. Directive (EU) 2022/2555 on measures for a high common level of cybersecurity across the Union (NIS2) (2022). https://eur-lex.europa.eu/eli/dir/2022/2555/oj/eng
2. European Parliament and Council of the European Union. Directive (EU) 2016/1148 concerning measures for a high common level of security of network and information systems across the Union (NIS1) (2016). https://eur-lex.europa.eu/legal-content/EN/TXT/?uri=celex:32016L1148
3. Steen, F.A., Shabani, D.A.: A NIS2 pan-European registry for identifying and classifying essential and important entities. Master's thesis, School of Economics, Innovation and Technology, Kristiania University of Applied Sciences, Oslo, Norway (2025). https://arxiv.org/abs/2508.19395
4. Bendiek, A., Wagner, B., Metzger, J.: The NIS directive: fragmentation and its consequences. EU Cybersecur. Rev. **12**, 45–67 (2019)
5. Schulze, M., Becker, K., Weber, A.: Germany's KRITIS registry: lessons learned. Cybersecur. Policy Rev. **7**, 55–70 (2022)
6. Dupont, J., Martin, C., Rousseau, L.: ANSSI's registry: a collaborative approach. Eur. J. Cybersecur. **5**, 89–104 (2023)
7. Bianchi, M., Rossi, E., Conti, G.: Italy's national cybersecurity perimeter. Cybersecur. Innov. **10**, 44–59 (2022)
8. Jansen, P., Verhoeven, E.: The Netherlands' digital trust center. Cybersecur. Gov. Q. **8**, 22–37 (2023)
9. European Parliament and Council of the European Union. Regulation (EU) 2016/679 on the protection of natural persons with regard to the processing of personal data (General Data Protection Regulation) (2016). https://eur-lex.europa.eu/eli/reg/2016/679/oj/eng
10. European Parliament and Council of the European Union. Directive (EU) 2022/2557 on the resilience of critical entities (CER) (2022). https://eur-lex.europa.eu/eli/dir/2022/2557/oj/eng
11. Commission of the European Communities. Commission Recommendation 2003/361/EC concerning the definition of micro, small and medium-sized enterprises (2003). https://eur-lex.europa.eu/eli/reco/2003/361/oj/eng
12. Google. Gemini 1.5 Flash (2025). https://cloud.google.com/vertex-ai/generative-ai/docs/models/gemini/1-5-flash
13. Fabian Aude Steen. NIS2 registry prototype showcase (2025). https://youtu.be/OQK9TnvAMyw
14. European Parliament and Council of the European Union. Regulation (EU) 2022/2554 on digital operational resilience for the financial sector (DORA) (2022). https://eur-lex.europa.eu/eli/reg/2022/2554/oj/eng

SecureIoT: Robust AI-Driven Cyber Threat Detection for IoT Applications
Addressing Data Imbalance and Generalizing to Unseen Attacks

Knut Selstad[1(✉)], Sandeep Pirbhulal[1], Habtamu Abie[1], Riku Lehkonen[2], and Ismail Ari[3]

[1] Norwegian Computing Center, Oslo, Norway
knut.selstad@gmail.com, {sandeep,abie}@nr.no
[2] Information Technology, University of Jyväskylä, Jyväskylä, Finland
riku.p.lehkonen@jyu.fi
[3] Computer Science, Özyeğin University, Istanbul, Turkey
ismail.ari@ozyegin.edu.tr

Abstract. The cyberattack surface in critical sectors is expanding due to the rapid proliferation of Internet of Things (IoT) devices. Artificial Intelligence (AI) models, such as Deep Neural Networks (DNNs) and Convolutional Neural Networks (CNNs), offer promising capabilities for detecting and classifying cyber threats. However, these models often struggle to generalize to previously unseen attacks after deployment. This study investigates how well different AI techniques can generalize to such novel threats in the presence of class imbalance. We evaluate three data balancing strategies: Generative Adversarial Networks (GAN), Synthetic Minority Over-sampling Technique (SMOTE), and class weighting. Experimental results indicate that DNNs outperform CNNs when provided with identical input data. While each balancing method has distinct advantages and trade-offs, the highest multiclass accuracy of 81.16% was achieved by a DNN using GAN-augmented data for the previously seen attack types. The best performance on unseen attacks was achieved by a DNN trained with SMOTE, yielding a multiclass accuracy of 51% among eight classes. The binary classification (benign vs. malicious) results were satisfactory, with DNN using GAN-augmented data achieving an accuracy of 99.20%. These findings highlight the importance of not only separating data into training and test splits, but also incorporating a "seen vs. unseen" evaluation strategy.

Keywords: Cybersecurity · IoT · AI · Anomaly Detection · DNN · CNN · GAN · SMOTE · Dataset Balancing · Unseen Attacks

1 Introduction

With the rapid expansion and integration of IoT devices into daily life and industrial processes [1], the attack surface for cyber threats has significantly

R. Laborde et al. (Eds.): ESORICS 2025 Workshops, LNCS 16233, pp. 202–222, 2026.
https://doi.org/10.1007/978-3-032-16165-9_12

increased [2,3]. As the number of connected devices grows exponentially, so do vulnerabilities and opportunities for exploitation by malicious actors. This escalation has led to an ongoing cybersecurity arms race [4], characterized by iterative cycles of attacks and defensive countermeasures. For every defensive measure developed, adversaries continually evolve new offensive techniques, making the need of innovative strategies beyond traditional rule-based security systems.

AI emerges as a promising solution within this evolving landscape [5]. Unlike static, conventional cybersecurity methods, AI offers dynamic adaptability and predictive capabilities, enabling faster detection and mitigation of threats [6]. AI has demonstrated success across various cybersecurity applications [7], including identity and access management, threat detection, endpoint security, and automated incident response systems [8]. The adoption of AI is particularly attractive due to its ability to learn complex patterns [5] from large datasets, thus addressing shortcomings in conventional security methods.

This research addresses three primary cybersecurity challenges: 1- anomaly detection, 2- classification of known cyber-attacks, and critically, 3- the detection and identification of previously unseen or novel threats [9,10]. The main objective of this work is to examine how effectively an AI model can internalize underlying cyber-attack patterns to generalize well against new, previously unencountered attacks [11,12]. This is critical because, in real-world cybersecurity scenarios, attackers frequently develop novel strategies or variations of known attacks. Models that fail to generalize beyond the training distribution become quickly outdated and ineffective against emerging threats. A robust model capable of identifying unfamiliar threats can significantly enhance proactive cybersecurity efforts, breaking the reactive cycle that currently dominates cybersecurity strategies.

To effectively measure the generalization capabilities of AI models, this paper explores specific dataset manipulation strategies that simulate realistic cybersecurity environments. We hypothesize that targeted data adjustments and preprocessing techniques significantly influence AI model performance, particularly regarding unseen threats. Our key research contributions include:

- **Addressing dataset imbalance and representation:** Exploring techniques for balancing highly skewed datasets, ensuring the model is equally sensitive to diverse attack scenarios.
- **Implementing strategic data-augmentation:** Implementing a novel GAN-based augmentation technique specialized per-attack type to improve generalization performance on previously unseen IoT cyber threats and comparing it with SMOTE and class weighting techniques.
- **Evaluating the influence on model robustness and generalization:** Analyzing and quantifying how dataset modifications with seen and unseen attacks affect AI model resilience, accuracy, and ability to generalize to novel threat scenarios.

While numerous studies have explored AI-driven cybersecurity models [13–18], there remains a critical gap in evaluating their ability to detect threats not encountered during training. This limitation significantly affects real-world applications, where previously unseen cyber-attacks frequently emerge. In this paper, we address this gap by explicitly distinguishing and evaluating the model's performance on both seen and unseen attack types.

This paper is structured as follows: Sect. 2 reviews related work relevant to our research. Section 3 outlines our novel IoT data processing pipeline and AI-based methodologies to manage unbalanced attack types. Section 4 presents the results, comparing accuracy performances of different techniques. Finally, Sect. 5 concludes the paper, summarizes key findings and discusses future work.

2 Related Work

Several studies have explored AI-driven approaches for securing IoT networks, focusing on anomaly detection, intrusion classification, and synthetic data generation to address class imbalance and data scarcity. This section reviews relevant contributions in three main areas: deep learning-based intrusion detection, synthetic data generation using GANs and diffusion models, and the detection of specialized threats.

Long Short-Term Memory (LSTM)- and Transformer-based models have shown strong performance in IoT intrusion detection. Jony et al. [19] proposed an LSTM-based system that leverages sequential modeling to detect evolving cyber threats in IoT traffic. Trained on the CIC-IoT2023 dataset, their model demonstrated adaptability to subtle attack patterns, highlighting LSTM's relevance in time-dependent intrusion detection. Similarly, Tseng et al. [20] adopted a Transformer architecture for multi-class attack classification, achieving the highest accuracy among seven tested models. Their work also emphasizes the importance of dataset balancing and feature reduction. In a broader comparison, Genuario et al. [21] conducted an ablation study of shallow and deep models, confirming the advantage of deep learning approaches, particularly ensemble methods, over traditional classifiers in network intrusion detection systems (NIDS) performance.

Data scarcity and class imbalance remain significant challenges in training NIDS. To address this, researchers have increasingly explored GANs and diffusion models for synthetic data generation. Tasneem et al. [22] provided a survey of GANs in cybersecurity, highlighting their dual role as both threat simulators and tools for anomaly detection. Frid-Adar et al. [23] demonstrated GAN-based data augmentation in the medical domain, showing significant improvements in CNN-based classification accuracy for liver lesions, thereby supporting GANs' generalizability across domains. Recently, Jiang et al. [24] introduced NetDiffusion, a Stable Diffusion variant that outperformed GANs in generating statistically realistic network traces, leading to higher classification accuracy when used for training.

While these studies demonstrate promising advances in AI-based IoT security, few explicitly evaluate model robustness against previously unseen attacks or compare multiple augmentation strategies such as GAN and SMOTE under such conditions. Our work aims to fill this gap by excluding certain attacks from the training data while including them in the testing phase, thereby evaluating the model's ability to generalize beyond the data it was trained on.

3 Methodology for Handling Imbalanced Data and Unseen Attacks in AI-Based IoT Security

This section details our experimental setup including IoT security datasets, data imbalanced issues and augmentation techniques as well as methods developed to test AI model robustness and generalization. Section 3.1 illustrates the overall SecureIoT architecture. Section 3.2 describes the dataset and the feature-engineering pipeline. Section 3.3, details our GAN-based data augmentation approach, and Sect. 3.4 outlines the DNN architectures and training procedures. Section 3.5 discusses our feature-importance analysis, and Sect. 3.6 defines the evaluation metrics and test method. Finally, Sect. 3.7 summarizes the hardware platforms used for training and real-time inference.

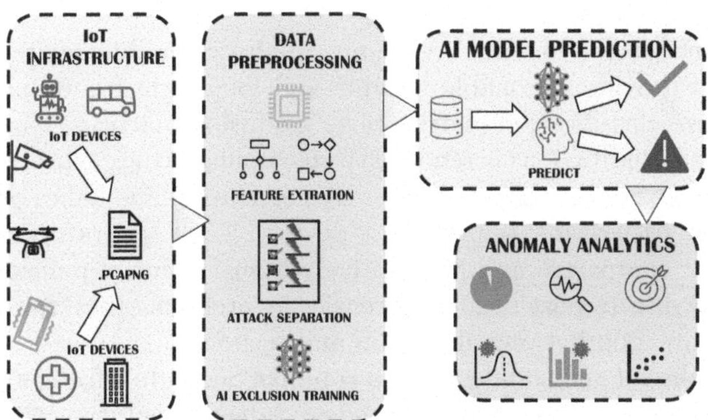

Fig. 1. Proposed SecureIoT Pipeline starts with IoT infrastructure data collection, data preprocessing for feature and attack type selection, AI-based threat prediction *(malicious (!) vs. benign (✓))*, and finally anomaly analytics for detailed attack classification.

3.1 Proposed SecureIoT Architecture

The proposed architecture of the SecureIoT framework follows a structured pipeline consisting of four key stages as illustrated in Fig. 1.

IoT Infrastructure: IoT Infrastructure module captures raw network traffic from a diverse array of connected devices across critical sectors. Traffic is recorded with Wireshark [25] to preserve packet-level fidelity, enabling granular inspection of headers, payloads, and timing characteristics. By aggregating data from hundreds of heterogeneous devices, this stage ensures comprehensive coverage of both benign and malicious behaviors in operational environments [26].

Data Preprocessing: In the Data Preprocessing module, raw packet captures are transformed into feature-rich representations suitable for AI training. First, packet- and flow-level features such as packet sizes, inter-arrival times, header flags, and protocol metadata are extracted and normalized to a consistent numeric range. Next, the "Attack Separation" step labels and partitions the data, excluding selected attack types during training to evaluate generalization on unseen threats. Finally, balanced training sets are constructed through targeted under- and over-sampling (GAN-and SMOTE-based augmentation techniques) and by removing leakage-prone features. This careful preprocessing pipeline lays the groundwork for robust model learning and fair evaluation.

AI Model Prediction: The AI Model Prediction module deploys trained classifiers to infer the category of incoming traffic in real time. Models can be hosted centrally or pushed to edge gateways co-located with IoT devices for low-latency inference [27], enabling on-device threat detection. Upon receiving a feature vector, the network outputs both a multi-class softmax over attack categories and a binary benign/malicious decision.

Anomaly Analytics: The final Anomaly Analytics module aggregates prediction results to provide actionable insights and long-term trend analysis. Dashboards visualize classification metrics (e.g., confusion matrices, temporal voting correctness), highlight co-occurrence patterns among attack types, and compute statistical summaries of traffic volumes. By correlating anomalies over time and mapping them to network segments or device classes, operators can pinpoint evolving threat campaigns and preemptively adjust security policies. Moreover, this module facilitates post-incident forensics by archiving both raw and inferred data, closing the loop between detection and response.

Together, these four modules form a cohesive SecureIoT framework. By integrating exclusion-based training with advanced augmentation techniques and edge-capable inference, the pipeline not only achieves high detection accuracy on known attacks, but also improves its resilience against novel threats. The SecureIoT code is available at: https://github.com/KnuteLute/SecureIoT.

3.2 Dataset Utilized and Feature Engineering

As of 2025, the UNB Canadian Institute for Cybersecurity (CIC) IoT Dataset 2023 remains widely used in the research community [28]. It features over 105 IoT devices subjected to 33 different attack types across 7 distinct attack categories. In total, 301 attacks were executed, with the number of instances per attack type ranging from a single occurrence to as many as 29. It also includes benign traffic to support supervised learning and anomaly detection tasks. Figure 2 illustrates its structure.

In 2024, the dataset was updated with a new preprocessing methodology and a revised structure. This updated version is the one utilized in the present work. A total of 39 features were extracted during preprocessing. Wherever possible, the aim was to retain the full set of features to preserve the richness of the original data. In total, 34 of the 39 features were used for training, as no compelling reason for exclusion was identified beyond technical necessity. This decision aligns with prior studies referenced in the related work, many of which report using the full feature set when working with this dataset. However, two features—Number and ack_count—exhibit preprocessing leakage. To avoid biasing the model, these features are removed prior to model training and evaluation. In addition, the original feature extraction code provided in the dataset repository [28] was designed for Packet Capture (PCAP) files. When adapting this code to handle PCAPNG files, extraction failures occurred for certain fields, specifically LLC, fin_count, and Header_Length. As a result, these features were also removed from the final dataset.

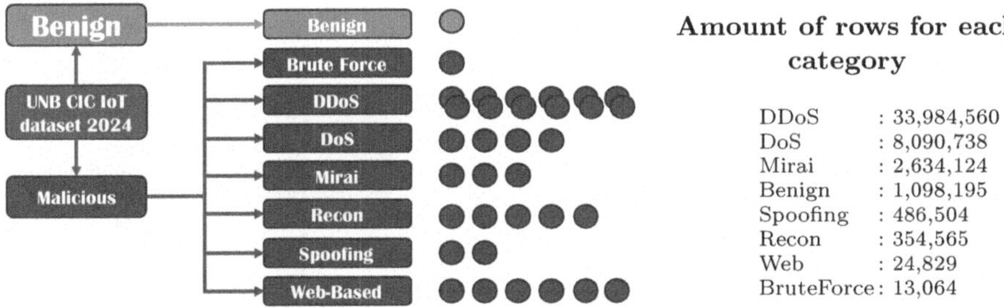

Fig. 2. UNB CIC IoT dataset 2024 structure. Each dot representing a attack type for a given category. Right hand side show the imbalance in data.

The dataset is highly imbalanced. For example, the Distributed Denial of Service (DDoS) attack category contains approximately 33.9 million rows, while the Brute Force category has just over 13,000 rows. To address this imbalance during training, two techniques for under-sampling and up-sampling using GAN [29] and SMOTE [30]. To establish a baseline for model results, weighted class training was also applied for comparison. As shown in Fig. 2, the distribution of samples across categories is heavily skewed. To mitigate this, a balanced dataset was constructed by imposing a cap of 500,000 samples per category. As a result, categories such as DDoS, DoS, Mirai, and Benign had their sample counts reduced, while Spoofing, Reconnaissance, Web, and Brute Force required up-sampling to reach the cap.

To evaluate the model's ability to generalize to previously unseen attack types, a subset of attack patterns was deliberately excluded from the training process. These are used exclusively during testing, as illustrated in Fig. 3. Note that Brute Force and Benign traffic contain only a single type, and therefore cannot be meaningfully included in this unseen evaluation.

Table 1. Train and test split after down- and up-sampling.

Category	Train GAN-SMOTE	Train Weighted	Test
DDoS	499995	375105	110443
DoS	500000	500000	150000
Mirai	500000	500000	150000
Benign	500000	492193	150000
Spoofing	500000	247706	150000
Recon	499999	247084	70103
Web-based	499998	8265	2064
Brute Force	500000	10452	2612

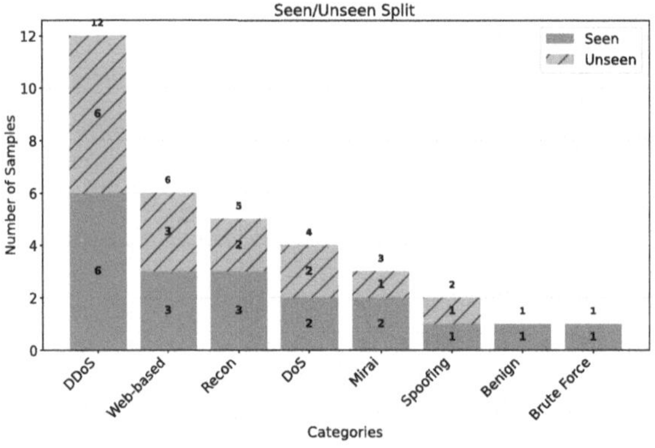

Excluded Attacks for Unseen Test

- DDoS-ICMP_Fragmentation
- DDoS-PSHACK_FLOOD
- DDoS-RSTFINFLOOD
- DDoS-SynonymousIP_Flood
- DDoS-TCP_Flood
- DDoS-UDP_Fragmentation
- DoS-UDP_Flood
- DoS-HTTP_Flood
- Recon-HostDiscovery
- Recon-PortScan
- Mirai-udpplain
- SqlInjection
- CommandInjection
- XSS
- DNS_Spoofing

Fig. 3. Splitting of attacks into seen and unseen sets. The right-hand panel lists the 15 attack types withheld during training (unseen).

3.3 Generative Adversarial Networks (GAN)

GAN [29] consists of two competing neural networks: a generator and a discriminator. The generator attempts to produce data that closely resembles the real distribution, while the discriminator attempts to distinguish between real and generated samples. During training, the generator improves by trying to "fool" the discriminator, while the discriminator improves by trying to correctly identify generated samples. When trained effectively, the generator becomes capable of producing data that is sufficiently realistic to be used as synthetic input during AI model training. In this case, both the generator and discriminator networks are implemented with relatively simple architectures, each consists of three hidden layers, shown in Table 2.

As shown in Fig. 4, the GAN training pipeline is designed to specialize per attack type. Each GAN is trained independently using only the training portion of its corresponding attack data from the seen set (Fig. 3). This targeted approach enables the generator to learn the specific distribution of a single attack

Table 2. GAN model architecture with a generator and a discriminator.

(a) Generator architecture

Layer	Units	Activation	Other
Input	100	–	–
Layer 1	256	ReLU	BatchNorm
Layer 2	512	ReLU	BatchNorm
Layer 3	1024	ReLU	BatchNorm
Output	39	TanH	–

(b) Discriminator architecture

Layer	Units	Activation	Other
Input	39	–	–
Layer 1	1024	LeakyReLU	Dropout 0.3
Layer 2	512	LeakyReLU	Dropout 0.3
Layer 3	256	LeakyReLU	Dropout 0.3
Output	1	Sigmoid	–

type without interference from unrelated traffic patterns. To preserve this isolation and avoid cross-category influence, feature normalization is also performed independently for each attack type. This ensures that each GAN models its target distribution accurately, free from statistical artifacts introduced by other classes.

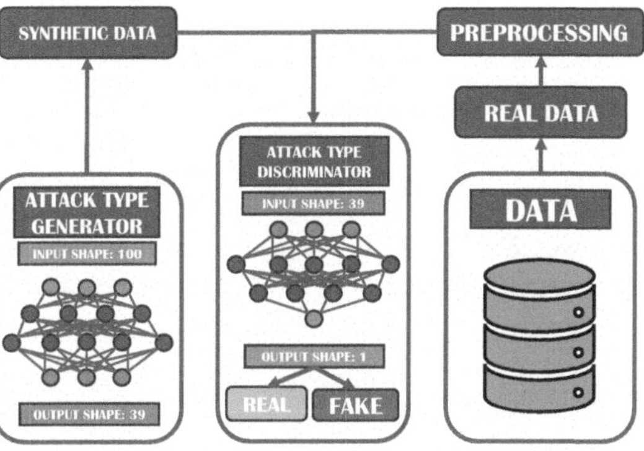

Fig. 4. GAN training, a separate generator-discriminator pair is trained for each attack type.

3.4 Training Procedure and Network Architectures

After dataset balancing, the final sample counts for each attack category are summarized. This distribution overview helps determining how many synthetic samples to generate for each class during the augmentation step. Although oversampling is primarily used for underrepresented categories, the exact amount of data generated may vary depending on how files were split into training and testing sets. "Train Weighted" column in Table 1 shows the balance distribution. In some cases, even categories capped during balancing may require a small amount of synthetic data to meet the 500,000-sample threshold due to rounding or file partitioning.

During training, both real and synthetic samples are combined seamlessly. The model does not differentiate between the data sources, treating generated and genuine examples identically. This uniform treatment can help generalize decision boundaries while maintaining balance across categories.

Experiments with both DNN and CNN were employed to evaluate performance. To address class imbalance, synthetic data was introduced using both GAN and the SMOTE. For comparison, a class-weighted training strategy is used. In this approach, each class is assigned a weight inversely proportional to its frequency in the training data. During backpropagation, the gradient updates are scaled by these weights, allowing the model to place greater emphasis on underrepresented classes and reducing bias toward dominant classes.

The DNN architecture is summarized in Table 3. It is a Feedforward Neural Network (FFNN) consisting of four hidden layers. Each layer is followed by batch normalization, Rectifier Linear Unit (ReLU) activation and dropout to enhance generalization and reduce overfitting. The final output layer uses a softmax activation function, allowing for multi-class classification.

Table 3. Architecture of the DNN used for attack category classification.

Layer	Units	Activation	Other
Input	34	–	–
Hidden Layer 1	512	ReLU	BatchNorm & Dropout 0.3
Hidden Layer 2	1024	ReLU	BatchNorm & Dropout 0.2
Hidden Layer 3	256	ReLU	BatchNorm & Dropout 0.3
Hidden Layer 4	128	ReLU	BatchNorm & Dropout 0.2
Output	8	Softmax	–

The CNN architecture is summarized in Table 4. It takes input in the form of a one-dimensional sequence of 34 features and applies three convolutional blocks. Each block includes a Conv1D layer with ReLU activation, followed by batch normalization, max pooling, and dropout. The final convolutional block incorporates global average pooling to reduce spatial dimensions. This is followed by two fully connected layers and a softmax output layer for multi-class classification.

Training was carried out using the Adam optimizer [31] with a learning rate of 0.001. To improve convergence and prevent overfitting, early stopping and adaptive learning rate scheduling were employed. Early stopping was triggered if the validation loss did not improve for 10 consecutive epochs, with the best-performing weights restored at the end of training. Additionally, the learning rate was reduced by a factor of 0.5 if the validation loss plateaued for 5 epochs, with a minimum learning rate threshold of 1×10^{-7}. Each model was trained for up to 50 epochs with a batch size of 256.

Table 4. Architecture of the CNN used for classification. BM (Batch Normalization), MP (MaxPooling), GAP(Global Average Pooling), D (Dropout).

Layer	Units	Activation	Other
Input	(34, 1)	–	–
Conv1D + Pooling	64 filters, k=3	ReLU	BN, MP1D (2), D 0.3
Conv1D + Pooling	128 filters, k=3	ReLU	BN, MP1D (2), D 0.3
Conv1D + GAP	64 filters, k=3	ReLU	BN, GAP1D
Dense Layer 1	128	ReLU	D 0.3
Dense Layer 2	64	ReLU	D 0.2
Output	8	Softmax	–

3.5 SHAP

SHapley Additive exPlanations (SHAP) is a model-agnostic framework that assigns each feature an importance value for individual predictions [32]. By quantifying how much each feature contributes to the difference between a model's output and its expected value, SHAP provides insight into the model's decision process. This is particularly useful for comparing how training with GAN or SMOTE alters feature attributions. SHAP satisfies 3 desirable properties [32]:

- **Local accuracy:** The sum of all feature attributions equals the model's output minus the expected output.
- **Consistency:** If a model change increases a feature's contribution, the corresponding SHAP value will not decrease.
- **Missingness:** Features that aren't used by models receive zero attribution.

3.6 Evaluation Metrics

To account for the pronounced class imbalance, the following metrics are reported:

- **Accuracy**: overall correctness.
- **Weighted-average F1**: class-wise F1 scores weighted by support.
- **Macro-average F1**: unweighted mean of per-class F1 scores.

F1 score (the harmonic mean of precision and recall [33]) is calculated as:

$$F1 = \frac{2 \cdot \text{Precision} \cdot \text{Recall}}{\text{Precision} + \text{Recall}} \tag{1}$$

To obtain the *F1-weighted* score, the F1 score for each class c, denoted $F1_c$, and weight it by the number of instances n_c for that class:

$$F1_{weighted} = \sum_{c=1}^{C} \left(F1_c \cdot \frac{n_c}{n} \right) \tag{2}$$

where C and n are the total number of classes and samples, respectively. This metric ensures that classes with more samples contribute proportionally to the overall score, making it a more reliable indicator of performance in imbalanced settings. *F1-macro* is calculated by averaging F1-scores of all classes. This method does not take the amount of cases of each class into consideration:

$$F1_{macro} = \frac{1}{C}\sum_{c=1}^{C} F1_c \tag{3}$$

where C is the total amount of classes, and $F1_c$ is per class F1-score.

3.7 Hardware

All experiments were run on a dedicated deep-learning node with the following configuration: CPU: Intel Xeon Platinum 8168 (24 cores/48 threads @ 2.7 GHz), GPU: NVIDIA Tesla V100-SXM3 (32 GB HBM2, CUDA 12.4), and RAM: 1.5 TiB DDR4. This setup ensured fast data preprocessing and feature extraction on the CPU, and efficient model training—especially for GANs and neural classifiers—on the GPU without memory-related slowdowns.

4 Results

Results are reported both at the per-class level and using a binary classification perspective (malicious vs. benign). This dual-view evaluation provides a more realistic assessment of the model's practical utility in real-world IoT security scenarios.

It is worth noting that some attack classes exhibit significant overlap. For instance, Mirai is a subtype of DDoS [34], which in turn falls under the broader category of DoS [35]. As such, a misclassification of Mirai as DDoS, or DDoS as DoS, may not be critical from a practical security standpoint. What matters most is that malicious traffic is not misclassified as benign.

4.1 GAN Training Performance

A separate GAN model was trained for each attack type in the seen dataset. During training, the loss curves exhibited two distinct patterns. In the first pattern, shown in Fig. 5a, the initial gap between the generator and discriminator losses gradually decreased over time, suggesting convergence between the two networks. In the second pattern, illustrated in Fig. 5b, the losses initially moved closer together but eventually began to diverge again. This latter behavior was often accompanied by high variance in the loss values, resulting in noisy and unstable loss curves. These differences in training dynamics indicate that some attack types are inherently more difficult for the GAN to model, likely due to class complexity or limited feature separability.

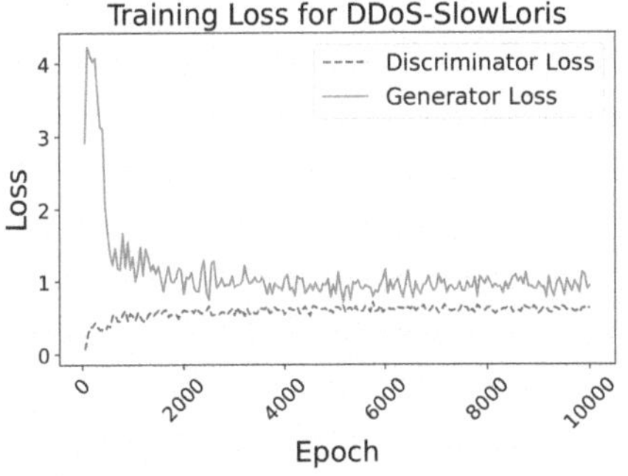

(a) Loss curve showing convergence.

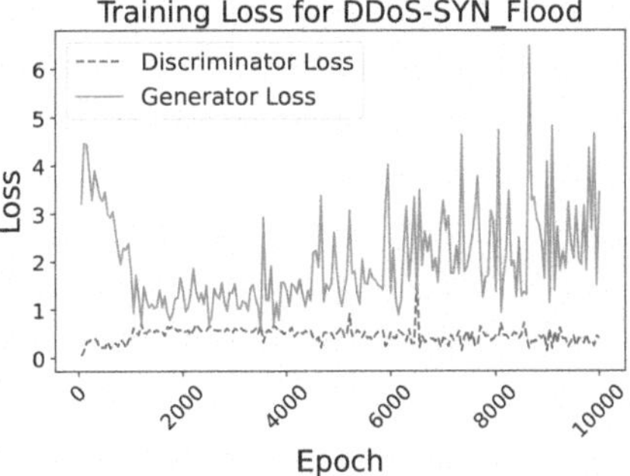

(b) Loss curve showing divergence over time.

Fig. 5. Examples of two distinct GAN training behaviors: (a) Loss curves where generator and discriminator losses converge; (b) Loss curves where they diverge.

Table 5. Performance comparison of data balancing techniques with DNN and CNN.

Model	Technique	Accuracy	F1 Macro	F1 Weighted
DNN	GAN	**81.16%**	58.41%	**80.01%**
DNN	SMOTE	76.29%	57.50%	79.10%
DNN	Weighted	78.31%	**58.93%**	79.91%
CNN	GAN	**79.53%**	55.44%	**78.01%**
CNN	SMOTE	76.30%	57.22%	78.71%
CNN	Weighted	74.60%	**55.68%**	76.17%

4.2 Multi-Class Classification Performance

All models were trained to classify the 8 different attack categories. The results demonstrate that GAN-based data augmentation consistently outperforms both SMOTE and class weighting approaches across all evaluation metrics, as seen in Table 5. The DNN architecture with GAN augmentation achieved the highest performance with 81.16% accuracy, 58.41% macro-averaged F1-score, and 80.01% weighted F1-score, representing improvements of 4.87% points in accuracy and 2.10% in weighted F1-score compared to the best non-GAN approach.

Architecture Comparison: DNN consistently outperformed CNN across all augmentation strategies. The DNN architecture's superior performance can be attributed to its ability to effectively capture the complex, non-sequential relationships in network traffic features, whereas CNNs are optimized for spatial or temporal patterns that may be less prevalent in this feature space.

Augmentation Strategy Analysis: The superior performance of GAN-based augmentation over SMOTE suggests that GANs successfully learned and preserved the complex feature distributions and inter-feature correlations specific to each attack category. SMOTE's synthetic minority oversampling, while effective, relies on linear interpolation between existing samples, which may not capture the full complexity of cybersecurity data patterns. Class weighting, despite achieving competitive macro F1-scores, showed more variable performance across different architectures.

Macro vs. Weighted F1-Score Insights: The relatively modest macro F1-scores (55%–59%) compared to weighted F1-scores (76%–80%) indicate that while the models perform well on majority classes, there remains room for improvement on minority attack categories. This pattern is expected given the inherent difficulty of the multi-class cybersecurity classification task and the varying complexity of different attack types.

The 4.87% improvement in accuracy achieved by DNN GAN over DNN SMOTE demonstrates the effectiveness of adversarial training in generating high-quality synthetic samples that better represent the underlying data distribution of IoT network attacks.

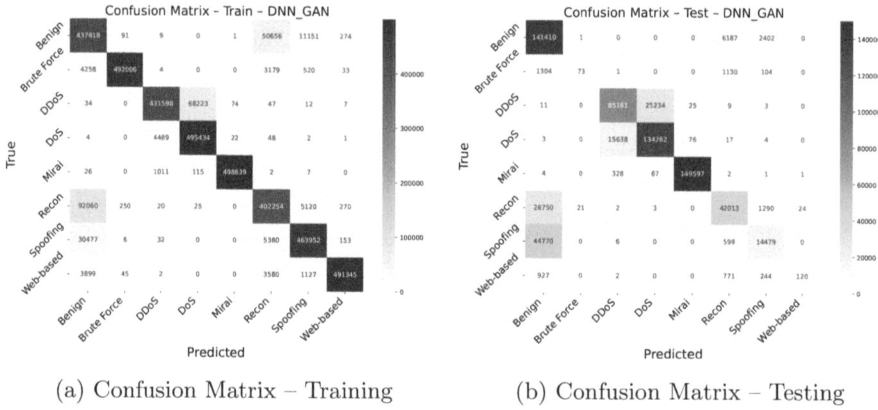

(a) Confusion Matrix – Training (b) Confusion Matrix – Testing

Fig. 6. Confusion matrices for the DNN GAN model during training and testing.

Figure 6 presents two confusion matrices (CMs) that illustrate the performance of a DNN trained with GAN-augmented data. The training CM in Fig. 6a shows a strong diagonal pattern from the top-left to the bottom-right, indicating high classification accuracy across most classes—an expected and desirable outcome. However, the test CM in Fig. 6b reveals a decline in performance when evaluated on testing data. This discrepancy suggests that the model may have overfitted to the GAN-generated training data. The extent of this generalization gap is further supported by Fig. 7, where a significant difference ($\approx$ 10%–15%) between training and testing accuracy can be observed.

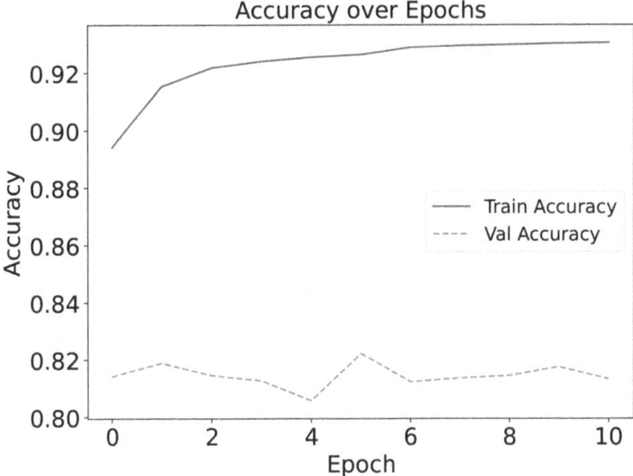

Fig. 7. Training and validation accuracy over the trained epochs with Adam optimizer and early stopping.

4.3 Binary Interpretation Performance

While multiclass classification offers detailed insights into specific attack types, evaluating binary performance—i.e., distinguishing between benign and malicious traffic—remains highly relevant for many real-world applications. In such contexts, the primary objective is often to detect whether traffic is malicious at all, rather than to classify the precise attack type.

Table 6. Comparison of DNN with GAN, SMOTE and weighted classes on accuracy, precision and recall.

Model	Accuracy	Precision	Recall
DNN GAN	88.45%	**91.34%**	67.06%
DNN SMOTE	90.05%	71.45%	**80.24%**
DNN Weighted	**90.18%**	75.83%	78.07%

Table 6 presents the binary evaluation results for the three training approaches applied to the DNN model: GAN-based augmentation, SMOTE, and class weighting. Each approach emphasizes different aspects of the classification task. The DNN trained with GAN-augmented data achieves the highest precision at 91.34%, indicating that when it predicts malicious activity, it is usually correct. This is particularly useful in scenarios where false positives are costly, such as automated blocking of network flows.

On the other hand, the DNN trained with SMOTE yields the highest recall at 80.24%, suggesting it is more sensitive to detecting malicious traffic, even at the risk of more false positives. This could be beneficial in environments where it is critical not to miss any threats.

Finally, the class-weighted DNN achieves the highest overall accuracy at 90.18%, offering a balanced performance but not outperforming in either precision or recall.

4.4 Unseen Attack Types Performance

Evaluating model performance on unseen attack types is important to understanding its ability to generalize beyond the training distribution. Table 7 and Table 8 present the multi-class classification and binary classification results for unseen data, highlighting how well the model distinguishes between benign and malicious traffic it has never encountered during training.

While DNN consistently delivered the highest performance across most configurations, the CNN models showed noticeably lower generalization on unseen attacks, observed in Table 7 and Table 8. This was particularly evident in the multi-class setting, where the best CNN model (SMOTE-based) achieved an accuracy of 36%, compared to 51% for its DNN counterpart. These results indicate that the DNN architecture is better suited for capturing the global feature relationships present in this dataset, especially when generalization is required.

These findings underscore the importance of not only separating data into training and test splits, but also incorporating a "seen vs. unseen" evaluation strategy. The sharp performance drop on structurally similar attack types suggests that key distinguishing patterns remain uncaptured in the training data, and generalization remains a significant challenge in intrusion detection systems.

Table 7. Comparison of DNN and CNN with GAN, SMOTE and weighted classes on accuracy on unseen attack data with multi-class classification of the results.

Model	Accuracy	F1 Marco	F1 Weighted
DNN GAN	49%	39.20%	54.41%
DNN SMOTE	**51%**	43.26%	**56.58%**
DNN Weighted	48%	**44.32%**	55.34%
CNN GAN	29%	**37.06%**	36.65%
CNN SMOTE	**36%**	31.94%	**43.25%**
CNN Weighted	28%	29.66%	35.44%

As illustrated in Fig. 8, the model struggles to correctly differentiate between DoS, DDoS, and Mirai attacks. This is especially notable given the dominance of DDoS traffic, which accounts for over 15 million samples. Despite achieving highly accurate results on seen data, performance on unseen data shows significant degradation. For instance, while $\approx$ 15% of DDoS attacks were misclassified as DoS in the seen data vs. $\approx$ 40% on unseen data.

Table 8. Comparison of DNN and CNN with GAN, SMOTE and weighted classes on accuracy on unseen attack data. Binary interpretation of the results.

Model	Accuracy	Precision	Recall
DNN GAN	**99.20%**	**91.25%**	81.85%
DNN SMOTE	99.06%	71.31%	**92.85%**
DNN Weighted	99.11%	75.12%	91.00%
CNN GAN	**99.02%**	**93.73%**	76.24%
CNN SMOTE	98.88%	68.36%	88.40%
CNN Weighted	98.87%	65.63%	**90.86%**

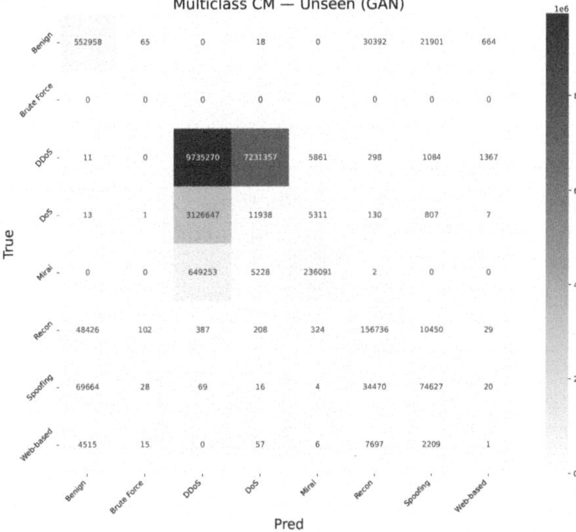

Fig. 8. Confusion Matrix for DNN GAN unseen attack types.

4.5 Temporal Robustness via Majority Voting

Cyberattacks, breaches, and benign behaviors typically unfold over time, rather than as isolated events. Because of this, it is important to evaluate model performance not only on individual samples, but also across short temporal windows. To this end, a majority-voting strategy is adopted over blocks of 9 consecutive samples. If at least five out of nine predictions agree, the majority label is taken as the predicted label for that block. This helps smooth out occasional misclassifications and highlights unstable or erratic predictions.

Figure 9 illustrates binary correctness across three representative types: benign traffic, DNS spoofing, and DDoS-ACK fragmentation. The visualization uses a block-level majority vote to determine correctness. In the top section of the figure, benign traffic is almost entirely classified correctly (green), indicating the model's consistent ability to recognize non-malicious behavior. In the

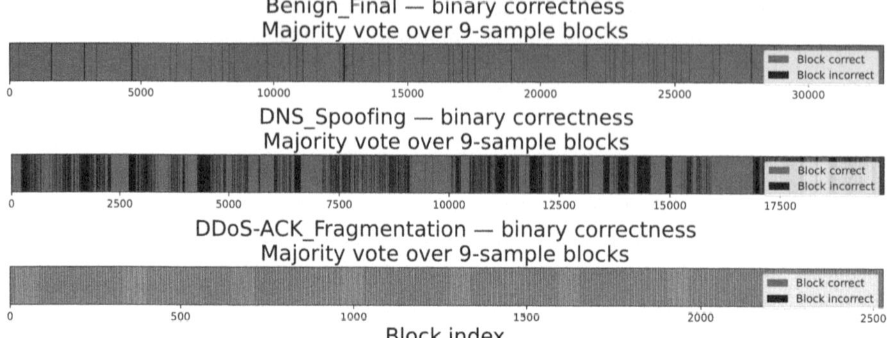

Fig. 9. Block-wise binary correctness for three traffic types: Benign (top), DNS Spoofing (middle), and DDoS-ACK Fragmentation (bottom). Green indicates correct classification and black indicates wrong classification. (Color figure online)

middle section, corresponding to DNS spoofing, there is a noticeable fluctuation between correct and incorrect predictions (black), suggesting the model struggles with temporal consistency for this attack type. The bottom section, showing DDoS-ACK fragmentation, presents more stable performance, though with no irregularities. This side-by-side comparison highlights how the model's reliability varies across different types of traffic. Such instability may indicate either a poorly learned representation or that the attack pattern itself is subtle and temporally sparse. Therefore, this visualization approach helps not only in evaluating performance but also in diagnosing model uncertainty and real-time classification reliability.

4.6 SHAP-Based Feature Importance

Figure 10 displays the global SHAP attributions for the three DNN variants. Across models, the top features consistently relate to packet size distributions—Total Size, Max Packet Size, and Std. Dev.—indicating a shared reliance on traffic volume characteristics. Header metadata (TTL, IPv flags), HTTPS presence, and ARP activity also appear prominently, while flag-based and protocol-specific counters (e.g., ACK, SYN, UDP) contribute less.

Differences between training strategies are subtle:

- GAN emphasizes Total Size ($\approx$0.041), possibly due to header variation in synthetic samples.
- SMOTE distributes attribution more evenly, with slightly higher values for Max.
- Weighted training shows lower overall SHAP magnitudes.

These patterns suggest GAN augments header-related variability, while SMOTE highlights distributional features. Such insights inform feature selection and future data-balancing approaches.

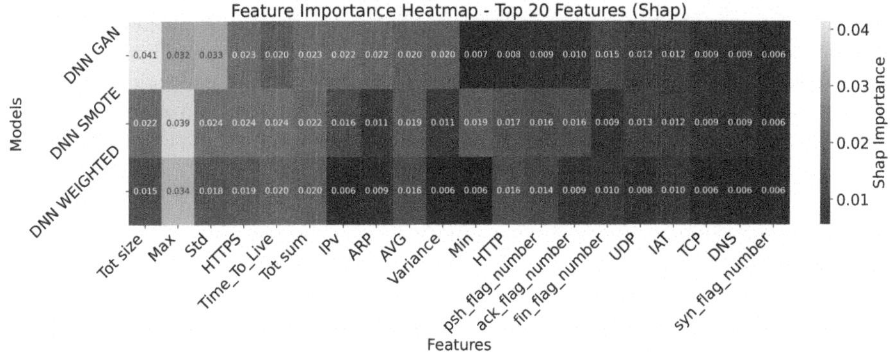

Fig. 10. SHAP heatmap showing consistency and divergence across architectures.

5 Conclusion

This study explored the potential of AI-driven methods to enhance cybersecurity in IoT environments, with a particular focus on addressing dataset imbalance and improving generalization to novel cyber threats. Using the updated 2024 release of the UNB CIC IoT dataset, we evaluated the effectiveness of GAN-based data augmentation, SMOTE, and class-weighted training across both DNN and CNN models. Our results show that GAN and SMOTE generally outperformed weighted training in terms of training and test accuracy. However, when evaluating performance on previously unseen attack types, GAN exhibited lower generalization compared to the other two methods. These findings highlight a critical limitation in current AI-based cybersecurity systems—their reduced effectiveness against novel threats.

By exploring the strategic manipulation and augmentation of cybersecurity datasets, this research aims to contribute to understanding the generalized performance of AI-driven cybersecurity models. Insights gained from this study will assist cybersecurity professionals and researchers in designing more robust, adaptable, and proactive security solutions, ultimately contributing to enhanced resilience against the evolving spectrum of cyber threats.

Our future work will focus on narrowing the gap between seen and unseen attacks' prediction performance. Promising directions include improved feature extraction techniques, temporal modeling through sequential input representations, and the development of more robust model architectures.

Acknowledgments. This research is funded by the Research Council of Norway through the SFI Norwegian Centre for Cybersecurity in Critical Sectors (NORCICS), under project number #310105. It is also supported by the European Union's HORIZON Research and Innovation Programme under grant agreement No 101120657, project ENFIELD (European Lighthouse to Manifest Trustworthy and Green AI. In addition, the research was supported by Business Finland (grant number 2356/31/2023) and the University of Jyväskylä. The authors would like to thank

Univerity of Agder (UiA) for server allocation. The development of this machine learning pipeline was assisted by AI tools including GitHub Copilot and Claude 4 Sonnet (Anthropic, 2025) [36] for code development, documentation, and technical guidance. The authors acknowledge the contribution of these AI assistants in accelerating the development process while maintaining full responsibility for the research design, implementation, and results.

References

1. Statista. Internet of things - number of connected devices worldwide 2015–2025. Accessed 25 June 2025
2. Liu, C., Chen, B., Shao, W., Zhang, C., Wong, K.K., Zhang, Y.: Unraveling attacks to machine learning-based iot systems: a survey and the open libraries behind them. IEEE Internet Things J. (2024)
3. Wei, H., et al.: A survey of foundation models for iot: taxonomy and criteria-based analysis (2025)
4. Schmitt, M.: Securing the digital world: protecting smart infrastructures and digital industries with artificial intelligence (ai)-enabled malware and intrusion detection. J. Ind. Inf. Integr. **36**, 100520 (2023)
5. Mohamed, N.: Artificial intelligence and machine learning in cybersecurity: a deep dive into state-of-the-art techniques and future paradigms | knowledge and information systems (2025). Accessed 08 July 2025
6. Babu, C.V.S., et al.: Adaptive ai for dynamic cybersecurity systems: enhancing protection in a rapidly evolving digital landscap. In: Principles and Applications of Adaptive Artificial Intelligence, pp. 52–72. IGI Global Scientific Publishing, 2024
7. Adeyemi, A.M., Sims, S.: AI-enhanced predictive analytics for identifying and mitigating critical cybersecurity vulnerabilities, 2025. Accessed 30 June 2025
8. Microsoft. What is AI for cybersecurity? | microsoft security. Accessed 25 June 2025
9. Coppolino, L., D'Antonio, S., Mazzeo, G., Uccello, F.: The good, the bad, and the algorithm: the impact of generative ai on cybersecurity. Neurocomputing **623**, 129406 (2025)
10. Jeffrey, N., Tan, Q., Villar, J.R. : A review of anomaly detection strategies to detect threats to cyber-physical systems. Electronics **12**(15) (2023)
11. Medvedieva, K., Tosi, T., Barbierato, E., Gatti, A.: Balancing the scale: data augmentation techniques for improved supervised learning in cyberattack detection. Eng **5**(3), 2170–2205 (2024)
12. D'hooge, L., Verkerken, M., Wauters, T., De Turck, F., Volckaert, B.: Investigating generalized performance of data-constrained supervised machine learning models on novel, related samples in intrusion detection. Sensors **23**(4), 2023
13. Ali, M.L., Thakur, K., Schmeelk, S., Debello, J., Dragos, D.: Deep learning vs. machine learning for intrusion detection in computer networks: a comparative study. Appl. Sci. **15**(4) (2025)
14. Sydney Mambwe Kasongo: A deep learning technique for intrusion detection system using a recurrent neural networks based framework. Comput. Commun. **199**, 113–125 (2023)
15. Jullian, O., Otero, B., Rodriguez, E., Gutierrez, N., Antona, H., Canal, R.: Deep-learning based detection for cyber-attacks in iot networks: a distributed attack detection framework. J. Netw. Syst. Manag. **31**(2), 33 (2023)

16. Mirsky, Y., Doitshman, T., Elovici, Y., Shabtai, A.: Kitsune: an ensemble of autoencoders for online network intrusion detection (2018)
17. Meidan, Y., et al.: N-baiot–network-based detection of iot botnet attacks using deep autoencoders. IEEE Pervasive Comput. **17**(3), 12–22 (2018)
18. Kalash, M., Rochan, M., Mohammed, N., Bruce, N.D., Wang, Y., Iqbal, F.: Malware classification with deep convolutional neural networks. In: 2018 9th IFIP International Conference on New Technologies, Mobility and Security (NTMS), pp. 1–5. IEEE, 2018
19. Akinul Islam Jony and Arjun Kumar Bose Arnob: A long short-term memory based approach for detecting cyber attacks in IoT using CIC-IoT2023 dataset. J. Edge Comput. **3**(1), 28–42 (2024)
20. Tseng, S.-M., Wang, Y.-Q., Wang, Y.-C.: Multi-class intrusion detection based on transformer for iot networks using CIC-IoT-2023 dataset. Future Internet **16**(8), 284 (2024)
21. Genuario, F., Santoro, G., Giliberti, M., Bello, S., Zazzera, E., Impedovo, D.: Machine learning-based methodologies for cyber-attacks and network traffic monitoring: A review and insights. Information **15**(11), 741 (2024)
22. Tasneem, S., Gupta, K.D., Roy, A., Dasgupta, D.: Generative adversarial networks (gan) for cyber security: challenges and opportunities. In: Proceedings of the 2022 IEEE Symposium Series on Computational Intelligence, Singapore, pp. 4–7, 2022
23. Frid-Adar, M., Klang, E., Amitai, M., Goldberger, J., Greenspan, H.: Synthetic data augmentation using gan for improved liver lesion classification. In: 2018 IEEE 15th International Symposium on Biomedical Imaging (ISBI 2018), pp. 289–293. IEEE, 2018
24. Jiang, X., et al.: Netdiffusion: network data augmentation through protocol-constrained traffic generation. Proc. ACM Meas. Anal. Comput. Syst. **8**(1), 1–32 (2024)
25. Wireshark Foundation. Wireshark • go deep. Accessed 14 July 2025
26. Ari, I., et al.: Providing edge to cloud continuum with adaptive model selection and operational score. In: IEEE 101st Vehicular Technology Conference (VTC) Spring, 2025
27. Ari, I., Balkan, K., Pirbhulal, S., Abie, H.: Ensuring security continuum from edge to cloud: adaptive security for IoT-based critical infrastructures using FL at the edge. In: 2024 IEEE International Conference on Big Data (BigData), pp. 4921–4929, 2024
28. Neto, E.C.P., Dadkhah, S., Ferreira, R., Zohourian, A., Lu, R., Ghorbani, A.A.: Ciciot2023: a real-time dataset and benchmark for large-scale attacks in IoT environment. Sensors **23**(13), 5941 (2023)
29. Goodfellow, I.J., et al.: Generative adversarial networks (2014)
30. Chawla, N.V., Bowyer, K.W., Hall, L.O., Kegelmeyer, W.P.: SMOTE: synthetic minority over-sampling technique. J. Artif. Intell. Res. **16**, 321–357 (2002)
31. Kingma, D.P., Ba, J.: Adam: a method for stochastic optimization (2017)
32. Lundberg, S.M., Lee, S.I.: A unified approach to interpreting model predictions. In: Guyon, I., Von Luxburg, U., Bengio, S., Wallach, H., Fergus, R., Vishwanathan, S., Garnett, R. (eds.), Advances in Neural Information Processing Systems, vol. 30. Curran Associates, Inc., 2017
33. Powers, D.M.W.: Evaluation: from precision, recall and f-measure to roc, informedness, markedness and correlation. arXiv preprint arXiv:2010.16061, 2020
34. Antonakakis, M., et al.: Understanding the mirai botnet. In: 26th USENIX Security Symposium (USENIX Security 17), pp. 1093–1110, 2017

35. Peng, T., Leckie, C., Ramamohanarao, K.: Survey of network-based defense mechanisms countering the dos and ddos problems. ACM Comput. Surv. (CSUR) **39**(1), 3–es (2007)
36. Anthropic. Claude sonnet 4. Large language model via GitHub Copilot, 2025. Accessed 20 Aug 2025

AI-Guided Test Case Prioritization from Network Traffic in Cyber-Physical Systems

Valeria Valdés Ríos[1,2](✉), Fatiha Zaïdi[1], and Ana Rosa Cavalli[2,3]

[1] Université Paris-Saclay, CNRS, ENS Paris-Saclay, Laboratoire Méthodes Formelles, 91190 Gif-sur-Yvette, France

[2] Montimage EURL, Paris, France

{valeria.valdes,ana.cavalli}@montimage.com

[3] Institut Polytechnique, Télécom SudParis, Courcouronnes, France

Abstract. Cyber-physical systems (CPS) that support critical infrastructures increasingly rely on structured digital communication, exposing them to complex and potentially high-impact cyber threats. To strengthen their resilience, it is essential to optimize testing efforts by focusing on transactions that are most likely to reveal vulnerabilities. This paper presents a methodology for leveraging deep packet inspection and machine learning to prioritize test cases based on behavioral patterns observed in network traffic. The approach reconstructs request-response pairs from raw packet data and extracts structured features for supervised modeling tasks, such as predicting response time. Experimental results using an open dataset from electric vehicle charging systems demonstrate the feasibility of this method, highlighting key features that contribute to latency and interaction complexity. The findings support the use of predictive models for intelligent test suite optimization and open the path for more adaptive, protocol-agnostic security testing strategies in CPS environments.

Keywords: Cyber-Physical Systems · Test Suite Optimization · Machine Learning · Network traffic analysis · Deep packet inspection · Protocol-aware modeling · Critical infrastructure security

1 Introduction

The digitalization of critical infrastructures, such as energy, transport, and healthcare, has led to complex levels of connectivity between cyber and physical systems. This interconnection has increased attack surfaces, enabling adversaries to exploit both software and hardware vulnerabilities. In particular, smart energy infrastructures like Electric Vehicle (EV) charging systems exemplify this trend as they rely on network protocols such as OCPP (Open Charge Point Protocol) to manage operations, making them susceptible to cyber-physical threats, including injection, spoofing, and denial-of-service attacks.

R. Laborde et al. (Eds.): ESORICS 2025 Workshops, LNCS 16233, pp. 223–235, 2026.
https://doi.org/10.1007/978-3-032-16165-9_13

Despite the growing research on intrusion and anomaly detection for these systems, there is limited focus on systematic and automated testing approaches that consider both cyber and physical dimensions of these infrastructures. Current testing efforts often rely on static or manually generated test cases that fail to adapt to evolving threats or system behaviors, leading to inefficient validation and reduced resilience against real-world attacks.

To address this gap, our work explores the use of machine learning models to guide test suite optimization, focusing on predicting characteristics such as response latency and operation success. These predictions are grounded in analyzing both request and response features of network communications. By learning patterns from real interactions, we aim to identify anomalous or high-risk transactions that require more extensive testing, thereby optimizing resource use while improving the system's preparedness against cyber-physical threats.

This approach contributes to the development of intelligent, dynamic, AI-driven security solutions for cyber-physical systems. Our work facilitates predictive security testing and supports adaptive monitoring by identifying transactions that exhibit abnormal or potentially risky behaviors. By prioritizing these interactions, we improve testing efficiency and enhance the system's resilience to both known and emerging threats. Additionally, this contributes to making critical infrastructure systems more secure, testable, and robust in the face of evolving cyber-physical risks.

The remainder of this paper is as follows: Sect. 2 presents the related work, Sect. 3 presents the approach, Sect. 4 presents the application of the approach and the evaluation, Sect. 5 discusses the results and open challenges, and Sect. 6 gives final remarks and conclusion.

2 Related Work

Test suite reduction (TSR) is a well-established problem in software testing, focused on minimizing the number of test cases while preserving the fault detection capability of the original suite. Early studies, such as those by Rothermel et al. [4], laid the foundation for understanding trade-offs between suite size and testing effectiveness. Traditional techniques have relied on coverage criteria (e.g., statement or branch coverage) to guide test case selection or elimination.

Recent approaches have moved beyond single-objective optimization to consider multiple competing goals. Multi-objective test suite reduction (MOTSR) has been explored using algorithms like NSGA-II, MOEA/D, and PSO [6–8]. These techniques model the problem as a trade-off between objectives such as fault detection, test execution cost, and time. Our work shares this motivation but diverges in that it does not rely on source code coverage; instead, it leverages network-level features extracted from real-time communication data to inform testing decisions.

Another key development has been the integration of non-functional behavioral criteria into test selection. The MORE+ approach [3], for example, considers requirement coverage, execution time, and code coverage jointly. Similarly,

Souza et al. [6] used multi-objective algorithms to optimize for coverage, cost, and diversity. These studies highlight the increasing need for context-aware reduction strategies, which aligns with our focus on behavioral attributes derived from protocol-level traffic.

Test prioritization and reduction have also been studied under changing conditions, such as evolving software or dynamic system behavior. Several works [2,5] emphasize the importance of maintaining effectiveness in regression testing scenarios. Although our work does not directly address software evolution, it contributes to this line of research by using machine learning to adapt test selection based on observed patterns and anomalies in system communication.

In contrast to most prior work, our method targets cyber-physical systems (CPS), where interactions are governed by structured communication protocols such as OCPP. While TSR for embedded systems has received some attention, there is limited research applying TSR techniques to CPS using network-level input features. Our approach addresses this gap by building models directly from observed traffic, making it applicable to scenarios where source code or internal test instrumentation is not available.

Finally, the use of machine learning (ML) for test suite optimization is growing but still underexplored in security-critical or infrastructure-level domains. Recent surveys (e.g., Habib et al. [2]) suggest that AI and ML-based techniques offer promising avenues for adaptive testing but require further validation in emerging domains like IoT, autonomous systems, and critical infrastructure. Our work contributes to this direction by demonstrating how response time prediction based on real-world CPS traffic can inform the selection of high-priority test cases. Unlike traditional TSR approaches that rely on source code coverage, static analysis, or instrumentation, our method operates directly on protocol-level network traffic. This enables testing in scenarios where source code is unavailable, a common limitation in CPS and infrastructure-level systems. Moreover, by incorporating non-functional attributes such as response delay, our approach introduces a novel behavioral dimension to test case prioritization that is often overlooked in existing strategies.

3 Methodology

The proposed approach combines deep packet inspection, structured data reconstruction, and AI-based modeling to support intelligent test case prioritization in cyber-physical systems. The objective is to extract high-level behavioral patterns from low-level communication traces and use these patterns to guide more focused and resilient system testing.

Figure 1 provides an overview of the end-to-end methodology, from raw traffic ingestion to AI-driven modeling and its role in test optimization.

3.1 Deep Packet Inspection and Attribute Extraction

Starting from raw network traffic collected from cyber-physical infrastructures, where communication typically occurs over standardized protocols between dis-

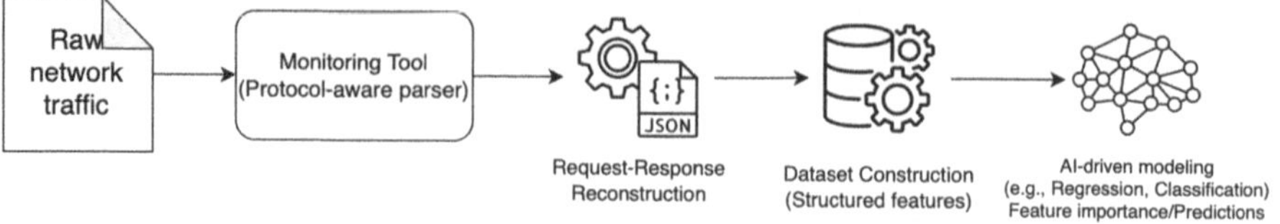

Fig. 1. End-to-end methodology pipeline from raw network traffic to test case prioritization. The workflow includes protocol-aware parsing, reconstruction of request-response interactions, dataset generation with structured features, and AI-driven modeling to support security testing decisions.

tributed system components (e.g., embedded devices, management platforms, or control servers). To analyze this traffic, deep packet inspection (DPI) using a protocol-aware parsing tool is performed. This tool extracts relevant metadata from each packet, including:

- Transport-level fields: timestamps, IP addresses, packet sizes, session identifiers.
- Application-level attributes: message types, commands/actions, and key-value pairs from structured payloads.

The inspection is driven by the network protocol adopted within the critical infrastructure, assuming that the protocol exposes an identifiable structure (e.g., message IDs, type indicators, or delimited payloads) that enables the reconstruction of higher-level interactions.

3.2 Request-Response Pair Reconstruction

From the parsed stream of messages, we reconstruct logical interactions by identifying and pairing related messages, typically request and response types. This step uses correlation logic based on unique identifiers (e.g., message IDs or transaction tokens) and temporal proximity. Each valid pair is stored with a unified schema including:

- Request attributes (e.g., command type, parameters, timestamp)
- Response attributes (e.g., result status, confirmation data, timestamp)
- Derived metrics, such as the time elapsed between request and response

This stage also incorporates integrity checks to handle inconsistencies, such as missing responses, repeated message IDs, or incorrect timestamps, which are either filtered or flagged for anomaly inspection.

3.3 Structured Dataset Generation

Once interactions are reconstructed, the data is transformed into a flat tabular format suitable for machine learning workflows. This includes:

- Categorical features, derived from string-based fields in both requests and responses.
- Numerical features, such as timestamp identifiers, and counters.
- Derived features, including temporal indicators (e.g., hour, weekday), response delays, or session-specific metrics.

Missing data is handled with strategies tailored to feature types: categorical fields are replaced with a placeholder token (e.g., "missing"), and numerical fields are either filled with default values or removed if non-informative.

3.4 AI-Driven Modeling and Prediction

Supervised learning tasks are applied to the structured dataset extracted from network communication. In this work, we focus on predicting the response time between a request and its corresponding response, treating it as a regression task to identify potentially complex or anomalous interactions.

In this context, behavioral patterns refer to the relationships between request-level protocol attributes, such as action type, vendor identifier, or firmware version, and the expected system response. By learning these patterns from normal interactions, the model captures how the system typically behaves under different communication scenarios. This allows it to generalize and predict expected response times for new inputs. Significant deviations from these predictions can then be interpreted as indicators of unusual or potentially faulty system behavior.

The dataset undergoes preprocessing tailored for mixed-type data. Categorical fields extracted from request and response payloads (e.g., action types, status codes) are one-hot encoded, while numerical attributes (e.g., connector identifiers, energy readings) are normalized using standard scaling. Interactions with missing or malformed target values are filtered out.

For model training, we use a Random Forest Regressor due to its robustness and ability to handle heterogeneous data types without strong assumptions about feature distributions. The model is trained on a portion of the dataset and evaluated on a held-out test set using standard regression metrics: Mean Absolute Error (MAE), Mean Squared Error (MSE), and the coefficient of determination (R^2). Feature importance scores derived from the model help identify which attributes contribute most to variations in response time.

Other machine learning models were considered, including linear regression, support vector regression, and neural networks. Random Forest was selected as a baseline due to its ability to model non-linear relationships, handle categorical and numerical features with minimal preprocessing, and provide interpretable feature importance scores. Compared to neural architectures, it also offers faster training times and lower computational complexity.

This modeling pipeline is designed to be protocol-agnostic, relying solely on the structure of network transactions and not on any domain-specific assumptions. As such, it can be adapted to other systems where structured request-response communication is present.

Alternative modeling tasks (e.g., classification of success/failure responses or detection of outliers) can be supported using the same data pipeline, depending on the system's monitoring and testing goals.

3.5 From Prediction to Test Optimization

The predicted response time for each request is used to estimate what a normal system behavior would look like. By comparing this prediction to the actual observed response time, we can identify interactions that deviate significantly from expectations. These deviations may indicate unusual system conditions, potentially caused by attacks, misconfigurations, or unexpected inputs.

To guide test case prioritization, we compute the absolute difference between the predicted and the actual response time for each request-response pair. Test cases are then ranked based on the size of this deviation, the larger the deviation, the higher the priority. This approach focuses attention on the interactions where system behavior diverges most from what the model considers normal.

In practice, we flag a subset of test cases with the highest deviations as top-priority candidates for further analysis or regression testing. This prioritization method is lightweight, model-agnostic, and does not depend on having labeled attack data. It simply assumes that significant timing deviations may reflect potential anomalies worth exploring.

Importantly, this approach is not limited to response time prediction. It can be generalized to other predictive tasks where the goal is to model expected system behavior. For instance, models could be trained to predict status codes, energy consumption, throughput, or resource usage, depending on the system under test. Deviations between predicted and observed values in these domains can similarly be used to prioritize test cases or detect runtime anomalies. This flexibility makes the approach applicable across a wide range of CPS and communication protocols.

Because the model is trained only on features extracted from request messages, the approach is also suitable for black-box systems that expose structured protocol interactions but not their internal logic. It can be used integrated into both offline testing workflows and live monitoring tools, enabling early detection and targeted validation with minimal instrumentation overhead.

4 Experimental Results

4.1 System Setup and Data Collection

The experimental evaluation targets a cyber-physical infrastructure for electric vehicle (EV) charging, where communication occurs between distributed charging stations and a centralized Charging Station Management System (CSMS). These interactions rely on the Open Charge Point Protocol (OCPP) 1.6, a standardized application-layer protocol widely used in the domain. The protocol operates over WebSocket connections and structures its communication in identifiable request-response pairs, enabling reliable reconstruction of transaction-level behaviors.

The study uses the OCPP 1.6 Intrusion Detection Dataset [1] that captures realistic operational and attack scenarios in EV charging environments. It contains detailed network traces for malicious behaviors, including:

- Charging Manipulation: Unauthorized control of charging sessions.
- Denial of Charge (DoC): Attacks that prevent normal service operation.
- Flooding attacks: High-volume traffic such as Heartbeat flooding to degrade system responsiveness.

This dataset is highly relevant for the evaluation as it provides structured, protocol-level communications enriched with real-world cyberattack scenarios. Its diverse set of interactions enables training and validation of models that aim to detect timing anomalies, predict system behaviors, or prioritize test cases for resilient security assessment.

4.2 Deep Packet Inspection and Monitoring Tool

Captured traffic is analyzed using the Montimage Monitoring Tool (MMT-DPI)[1], an open-source deep packet inspection engine designed for protocol-level parsing and feature extraction in real-time or offline modes. For the evaluation is used in offline mode for packet analysis, the output of this step includes:

- Packet metadata (timestamps, source/destination IPs)
- Protocol attributes (message type, command, payload fields)
- Unique identifiers used for request-response matching

An example of a parsed interaction between a charging point and the management system is shown in Fig. 2. It highlights how message attributes such as 'ocpp.type', 'ocpp.action', and 'ocpp.payload' are extracted from both request and response packets. These fields are later used to reconstruct communication sessions and compute metrics such as the response delay.

4.3 Request-Response Pair Construction

Using the extracted attributes, each packet is parsed and grouped into logical pairs. The pairing logic considers matching the message IDs, temporal order and proximity, and the distinct roles (request, response).

Each resulting pair is stored as a structured record that contains type and action of the request, full payload of both request and response, response time, session-specific metadata.

4.4 Dataset Description

After filtering incomplete or malformed records, the final dataset relevant for the response time prediction includes:

- Number of valid request-response pairs: 48.387.
- Unique actions: e.g., BootNotification, RemoteStartTransaction, etc.
- Target variable for regression: Response time.

[1] https://github.com/Montimage/mmt-dpi.

Request Packet

```
Packet id: 5932
meta.utime = 1682506939.280301
ip.src = 192.168.21.128
ip.dst = 192.168.21.70
ocpp.type = [2]
ocpp.id = ["1092:3"]
ocpp.action = ["StatusNotification"]
ocpp.payload = [[{
    "connectorId":1,
    "errorCode":"OtherError",
    "vendorId":
    "com.abb.evci/event/v1",
    "vendorErrorCode":"StopReason:
    SoftError",
    "info":"",
    "status":"Faulted",
    "timestamp":
    "2023-04-26T11:02:13.788Z"}]]
```

Response Packet

```
Packet id: 5935
meta.utime = 1682506939.358788
ip.src = 192.168.21.70
ip.dst = 192.168.21.128
ocpp.type = [3]
ocpp.id = ["1092:3"]
ocpp.payload = [[{}]]
```

Fig. 2. Example of paired OCPP request and response packets extracted via deep packet inspection.

4.5 Modeling Task: Response Time Prediction

To test the system's ability to learn from communication transaction, we conduct a supervised regression task aimed at predicting the response time for each request-response pair.

The modeling pipeline includes one-hot encoding for categorical features and normalization for numerical features. A Random Forest Regressor is employed due to its robustness, ability to handle heterogeneous data types, and interpretability through feature importance analysis.

The model is trained and evaluated using standard regression metrics, summarized in Table 1:

Table 1. Regression Model Evaluation Metrics

Metric	Value
Mean Absolute Error (MAE)	0.336
Mean Squared Error (MSE)	0.901
R^2 Score	0.129

While the metrics in Table 1 present a moderate performance, they offer a useful starting point for understanding model behavior in this context. The MAE of 0.336 indicates that, on average, the model's predictions deviate by approximately 336 milliseconds from the actual response time, which is acceptable for coarse-grained analysis in infrastructure-level CPS systems. The MSE of 0.901 reflects some presence of larger deviations, which are more heavily penalized due to squaring. The R^2 score of 0.129 shows that around 13% of the variance in response time is explained by the current model. Although relatively low, this is not unexpected given the complexity of timing behaviors in networked systems, where external factors, such as hardware delays, queuing, and network congestion, play a significant role and are not captured in the protocol-level features alone. These results provide a meaningful baseline and motivate the need for richer features and alternative modeling approaches in future work.

To understand which attributes most influence the prediction of response time, we analyzed the feature importances provided by the Random Forest model. The most relevant features are visualized in Fig. 3, showing the attributes that contribute most significantly to the model's output.

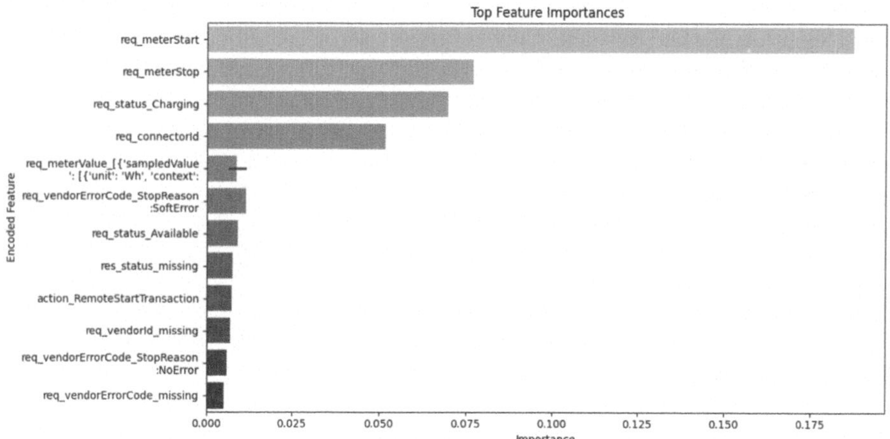

Fig. 3. Top feature importances for response time prediction.

To further demonstrate the utility of the model in guiding test case prioritization, we computed the absolute deviation between predicted and actual response times for each request-response pair. Table 2 shows the top 10 test cases ranked by deviation, where larger deviations are interpreted as higher-priority candidates for regression testing or anomaly inspection. These results provide an operational output that supports the hypothesis that behavioral divergence, rather than just raw latency, can serve as an indicator of critical transactions.

These results show that interactions involving actions such as `BootNotification`, `MeterValues`, and `StatusNotification` tend to exhibit the highest deviations between predicted and actual response times. This suggests that these types of transactions are more susceptible to behavioral vari-

Table 2. Top-ranked test cases based on response time prediction deviation

Rank	Action	Predicted (s)	Actual (s)	Deviation (s)
1	BootNotification	1.69	24.26	22.57
2	MeterValues	0.03	15.13	15.10
3	MeterValues	0.03	14.26	14.23
4	MeterValues	0.03	12.86	12.83
5	StatusNotification	0.50	13.30	12.80
6	MeterValues	0.03	12.54	12.51
7	StartTransaction	2.00	14.16	12.16
8	StatusNotification	0.49	11.90	11.41
9	MeterValues	0.03	9.71	9.68
10	StatusNotification	0.22	9.32	9.10

ability, which may reflect increased complexity, unexpected conditions, or edge-case execution paths. As such, they represent strong candidates for prioritized testing, allowing testers to focus on the interactions most likely to challenge system reliability or reveal subtle issues.

The results demonstrate that the system can extract and model relevant patterns from network communication. While the regression performance is moderate, the feature importance analysis reveals interpretable factors influencing response time. These insights support the use of learned patterns for test prioritization and provide a solid foundation for further refinement, which we expand on in the discussion.

5 Discussion

The experimental results show that our approach can effectively reconstruct structured interactions from raw network traces and extract meaningful features for machine learning models. The response time prediction task demonstrates that certain request attributes, such as energy meter values, connector identifiers, and status codes, are strongly correlated with latency, offering valuable indicators for identifying transactions of interest in future testing.

However, the overall regression performance indicates that modeling timing behaviors in cyber-physical systems remains a complex task. One of the main challenges encountered during implementation was the high dimensionality caused by categorical features after one-hot encoding. In protocols like OCPP, fields such as *idTag* or *vendorErrorCode* can take on a wide variety of values, inflating the feature space and introducing sparsity. This not only affects training and memory usage but also limits model generalization. Addressing this challenge requires more advanced feature selection techniques or alternative encoding strategies, such as target encoding or embedding representations that preserve semantic similarity on a lower-dimensional space.

Another open challenge is the identification of the most relevant input attributes at the network level. While the current pipeline relies on protocol-aware inspection to extract structured fields, this assumes *a priori* knowledge of protocol semantics and structure. In scenarios involving proprietary or encrypted communication, feature extraction and interpretation would require additional techniques, such as unsupervised pattern mining or byte-level analysis.

In addition to prediction performance, the prioritization of test cases based on deviation from expected behavior offers a practical mechanism for identifying transactions of higher testing interest. As shown in the results, interactions involving specific actions frequently appear among the highest-ranked deviations, suggesting that these cases may correspond to more variable or stress-inducing behaviors. This supports the effectiveness of deviation-based ranking as an interpretable and lightweight strategy for guiding test selection, particularly in black-box or resource-constrained testing settings.

Finally, while the regression task provides a meaningful proof of concept, future work should explore a broader set of tasks. These include binary classification of failed vs. successful interactions, anomaly detection for rare or malformed messages, and confidence-based ranking of test cases for dynamic test suite reduction. These additional tasks would provide a more comprehensive evaluation of the pipeline's effectiveness in guiding cybersecurity testing strategies. In parallel, alternative modeling strategies, such as ensemble learning, neural networks, or temporal models that capture sequential dependencies, will be considered to improve predictive accuracy and robustness across varied traffic conditions.

To strengthen the applicability and generality of the approach, future work will also focus on validating the method across multiple communication protocols and application domains. While OCPP provides a structured and interpretable use case, the same pipeline can be applied to protocols like MQTT or Modbus, provided their message structure can be parsed. This broader evaluation will help demonstrate the protocol-agnostic nature of the methodology and its potential to generalize across cyber-physical environments beyond electric vehicle charging.

6 Conclusion

This paper presents a methodology that combines deep packet inspection, structured data extraction, and AI-driven modeling to support test suite optimization in cyber-physical systems. By reconstructing and analyzing request-response interactions, the approach enables the prediction of response time as a proxy for identifying complex or anomalous system behaviors. Through this, we aim to guide the prioritization of test cases toward more critical transactions.

The experimental results demonstrate the feasibility of learning predictive patterns from real communication data, supported by interpretable feature importance analysis. Despite moderate regression performance, the findings highlight key challenges in handling high-dimensional categorical data and the need for more adaptive feature engineering strategies.

Future work will focus on expanding the modeling tasks (e.g., anomaly detection, classification of failure cases), as well as exploring alternative learning strategies to improve predictive accuracy. These may include gradient boosting methods, temporal models, or attention based neural networks to better capture complex dependencies in protocol interactions. These directions aim to enhance the model's generalization capabilities and further strengthen its utility for intelligent test suite optimization across diverse protocols and infrastructures. In particular, we plan to validate the protocol-agnostic design of the pipeline by applying it to different communication standards, such as MQTT or Modbus, and testing its adaptability in domains beyond electric vehicle charging. This broader evaluation will support the methodology's scalability and relevance across a wider range of CPS. Overall, the methodology contributes a scalable foundation for intelligent, behavior-aware testing in security-critical environments.

Acknowledgments. This work is partially supported by the European Union's Horizon Europe research and innovation program under grant agreement No 101070455 (DYNABIC).

References

1. Dalamagkas, C., et al.: Federated ocpp 1.6 intrusion detection dataset (2025). https://doi.org/10.21227/v1f0-9t13, https://dx.doi.org/10.21227/v1f0-9t13
2. Habib, A.S., Khan, S.U.R., Felix, E.A.: A systematic review on search-based test suite reduction: state-of-the-art, taxonomy, and future directions. IET Softw. **17**(2), 93–136 (2023). https://doi.org/10.1049/sfw2.12104, https://ietresearch.onlinelibrary.wiley.com/doi/abs/10.1049/sfw2.12104
3. Marchetto, A., Scanniello, G., Susi, A.: Combining code and requirements coverage with execution cost for test suite reduction . IEEE Trans. Softw. Eng. **45**(04), 363–390 (2019). https://doi.org/10.1109/TSE.2017.2777831, https://doi.ieeecomputersociety.org/10.1109/TSE.2017.2777831
4. Rothermel, G., Harrold, M.J., von Ronne, J., Hong, C.: Empirical studies of test-suite reduction. Softw. Test. Verif. Reliab. **12**(4), 219–249 (2002). https://doi.org/10.1002/stvr.256, https://onlinelibrary.wiley.com/doi/abs/10.1002/stvr.256
5. Shi, A., Gyori, A., Gligoric, M., Zaytsev, A., Marinov, D.: Balancing trade-offs in test-suite reduction. In: Proceedings of the 22nd ACM SIGSOFT International Symposium on Foundations of Software Engineering, pp. 246–256. FSE 2014, Association for Computing Machinery, New York, NY, USA (2014). https://doi.org/10.1145/2635868.2635921
6. Souza, L.S.D., Miranda, P.B.C.D., Prudencio, R.B.C., Barros, F.D.A.: A multi-objective particle swarm optimization for test case selection based on functional requirements coverage and execution effort. In: 2011 IEEE 23rd International Conference on Tools with Artificial Intelligence, pp. 245–252 (2011). https://doi.org/10.1109/ICTAI.2011.45

7. Yoo, S., Harman, M.: Pareto efficient multi-objective test case selection. In: Proceedings of the 2007 International Symposium on Software Testing and Analysis, pp. 140–150. ISSTA '07, Association for Computing Machinery, New York, NY, USA (2007). https://doi.org/10.1145/1273463.1273483
8. Zheng, W., Hierons, R.M., Li, M., Liu, X., Vinciotti, V.: Multi-objective optimisation for regression testing. Inf. Sci. **334-335**, 1–16 (2016). https://doi.org/10.1016/j.ins.2015.11.027, https://www.sciencedirect.com/science/article/pii/S0020025515008452

Improving Machine Learning Models for URL Phishing Detection Using Synthetic Data

Francisco Cardoso(✉), Eva Maia, and Isabel Praça

GECAD, ISEP, Polytechnic of Porto, 4249-015 Porto, Portugal
{frafc,egm,icp}@isep.ipp.pt

Abstract. Phishing is one of the most prevalent forms of cybercrime due to its low cost, limited technical requirements, and the ability to send massive campaigns of phishing emails. Such attacks can severely compromise critical infrastructures by targeting employees or systems with deceptive links that lead to credential theft, malware infection, or unauthorised access. The success of these attacks shows the need to improve the methods for phishing detection. In this work, we aim to generate phishing URLs to augment datasets, in order to improve the generalisation capabilities of machine and deep learning models. To achieve this, we compare three augmentation techniques, SMOTE, GANs and a SLM, against a baseline model trained solely on the original, unbalanced data. These techniques were applied to three distinct models: RF, XGB, and CNN. We evaluated the performance of the models using the most used metrics: Accuracy, Precision, Recall, AUC, and F1-score. The experiments demonstrated that the techniques achieved strong results on the test set, but their effectiveness dropped when evaluated on the validation data.

Keywords: Phishing · Data Augmentation · Generalisation

1 Introduction

The exponential growth of the internet has changed global connectivity, enabling users to communicate and access services that weren't possible before, including in critical infrastructure sectors. However, this interrelation has also introduced some vulnerabilities associated with cybercriminals. Among these threats, phishing attacks emerged as one of the most prevalent forms of cybercrime due to its low cost, limited technical requirements, and the ability to send massive campaigns of phishing emails [39]. These threats are particularly alarming for critical infrastructures such as those in the industrial and manufacturing sectors, which heavily depend on automation, interconnected supply chains, and digital services [22]. According to the Anti-Phishing Working Group (APWG), the final quarter of 2024 saw an increase in phishing incidents compared to the two preceding quarters, with webmail services representing the most targeted sector [7–9].

R. Laborde et al. (Eds.): ESORICS 2025 Workshops, LNCS 16233, pp. 236–253, 2026.
https://doi.org/10.1007/978-3-032-16165-9_14

Despite advances in phishing detection systems, phishing still poses a significant threat to both individuals and organizations. Such attacks commonly involve using deceptive tactics, such as fraudulent URLs designed to mimic benign domains, to trick users into disclosing their sensitive information, such as passwords, financial details or personal data [9]. The subtle alterations of domain names (e.g., replacing characters, adding subdomains, usage of homoglyphs) to create URLs that appear trustworthy at first glance can be enough to deceive some users [44]. Other deceiving techniques that cybercriminals employ to exploit the users behaviours include obfuscation of malicious links [55], and using the tendency of users to verify URLs only after accessing them via the browser [56].

To counter these threats, one of the most widely adopted approaches involves maintaining a blacklist of previously reported phishing URLs. Modern browsers make usage of such lists to block access or alert users [23]. However, this approach has two main limitations: querying blacklists introduces latency as real-time validation of URLs requires resource-intensive database lookups [38] and blacklists are ineffective against zero-day phishing attacks, where attackers use new URLs that have not yet been reported, analysed or added to the list [57].

To address the challenges of blacklist-based detection, researchers have proposed machine learning (ML) and deep learning (DL) approaches that rely on structural and lexical features of URLs [11]. While these techniques can achieve state-of-the-art accuracy in the experiments, their deployment faces three main challenges.

First, many of the models are trained on datasets that lack scale or diversity, limiting their ability to generalise to real-world phishing detection systems [14]. Second, the model evaluation often uses test sets derived from the same dataset as the training data, leading to inaccurate accuracy metrics [47]. Third, research does not check for the saturation of domains or similarity of URLs (e.g. query parameters, tokens), which could affect the models performance in real-world phishing detection systems [2].

To address these challenges, data augmentation, which is the process of synthetically expanding datasets by generating new samples, has emerged as a possible solution [4]. By increasing the diversity, quantity and balancing of training data, augmentation techniques aim to mitigate biases and increase the generalisation for these models. Multiple methods have been proposed for URL augmentation, with Generative Adversarial Networks (GANs) having the most success [4,20,40].

Generalisation refers to a model's ability to maintain its performance on unseen, real-world data, particularly when encountering URL patterns not observed during training [36]. Prior studies often report high accuracies by testing on data derived from the same dataset as the training samples, limiting insights into real-world robustness [47]. To assess generalisation, models must instead be validated on completely independent datasets with no overlapping URLs. This approach aims to address the limitations of earlier works and ensures that the evaluation reflects practical deployment scenarios.

In this work, we intend to evaluate the generalisation capabilities of ML and DL models by training them on augmented datasets generated with Generative Artificial Intelligence (AI) techniques. Specifically, we focus on GANs, which have shown success in synthesising realistic data, and Pre-trained Language Models (PLMs), an approach that has not yet been explored, and that uses contextual understanding to generate semantically coherent synthetic samples. These generative methods will be compared against Synthetic Minority Oversampling Technique (SMOTE), a common oversampling technique, to assess their effectiveness in improving the models robustness.

2 Related Work

2.1 URL Phishing Detection Methods

In the detection of phishing URL attacks, three approaches continue to dominate current research: list-based (heuristics) methods, ML and DL [31,57]. Each one tries to address this challenge with different trade-offs in adaptability, computational cost and latency detection.

List-based methods rely on already constructed either phishing (blacklist) or benign (whitelist) URLs, websites or domains. While they are easy to implement and can show results for known phishing sources, their greatest weakness is that they cannot detect zero-day attacks, taking time for these lists to also be updated [12]. For example, a 2025 study reveals that phishing domains exhibit a median lifespan of just 5.46 h, with a significant number managing to avoid detection. Google Safe Browsing (GSB) [23] identifies only 18.4% of phishing websites and does so after an average delay of 4.5 days by which time 83.93% of sites have already been taken down [33], leaving list-based defences ineffective against short-lived attacks.

ML models have emerged as an alternative to address list-based methods delays and adaptability problems. ML approaches phishing URL detection as a binary classification problem, analysing different URL features, to distinguish between benign and phishing URLs. Some of these features include domain name, top-level domain (TLD) mismatches and the presence of homoglyphs-characters visually similar to other characters (e.g. replacing o with 0) [4,35]. Many algorithms in ML have been explored [27,30,37], among these Random Forest (RF) remains a consistently standout performing algorithm. Gupta et al. [24] demonstrated RF's state-of-the-art results with 99.57% accuracy on ISCXURL-2016 dataset (11,964 instances), using only nine lexical features. Similarly, A. Mandadi, S. Boppana, V. Ravella, and R. Kavitha [37] showed superior performance across both Decision Tree (DT) and Random Forest (RF) classifiers in phishing URL detection, with RF achieving the highest accuracy (87%) on a balanced dataset of 10,000 URLs, each characterized by 17 lexical and structural features. RF also out performed seven other algorithms in S. Jalil, M. Usman, and A. Fong study [27], which analysed 30 features across six different datasets. Despite the authors research of [30] comparing RF to 7 other ML algorithms, including their introduced hybrid vote framework, RF kept its dominance in phishing URL detection, outperforming their proposed approach.

While RF remains prominent, Gradient Boosting (GB), Extreme Gradient Boosting (XGB), and LightGBM (LGB) have shown competitive results. Abdul Samad et al. [1] conducted a comparative analysis of eight ML classifiers, with GB, XGB and RF across two distinct datasets. On the first dataset, RF and GB emerged as top performers, achieving accuracies of 97.44% and 97.47%, respectively. For the second dataset, GB and XGB demonstrated marginal superiority with 98.27% and 98.21% accuracy, while RF closely followed at 97.79%. Ahammad et al. [3] found that LGB showed most promising results with an accuracy of 86% followed by RF with 85.3%, despite not being able to collect all the features from the WHOIS[1] database.

DL techniques like Convolutional Neural Networks (CNN) have also gained some merit, due to their ability for pattern recognition, a crucial part in phishing URL detection. Elsadig et al. [21] combined BERT feature extraction and a CNN, yielding a total of 768 features on a dataset of 472,259 samples derived from a dataset [43], achieving 96.66% of accuracy on the CNN. Alshingiti et al. [6] further supported CNN's superiority using a hybrid Long Short-Term Memory(LSTM)-CNN model, reporting 99.2% accuracy on a 30-feature dataset. In [32] CNNs continue to be one of the most often used methods showing high accuracy ranging from 85.99% to 99.98%.

LSTMs, though less used than CNNs, also show good performance in capturing sequential dependencies in URLs. In [32] it is shown that some studies can make them achieve 99% accuracy. However, Alshingiti et al. [6] noted that standalone CNNs outperformed both LSTMs and LSTM-CNN hybrid model.

2.2 URL Data Augmentation

The imbalance of data on datasets, and the lack of diversity could affect the models performance. To counteract these challenges, data augmentation has emerged as a possible solution [4,20,40]. Techniques such as oversampling and GANs, have been explored to improve the robustness of the models [4,5,20,40].

Alsadig and Ahmad [5] approached this dataset imbalance by using SMOTE on a dataset with 450,176 unique URLs with 16 chosen features. By mitigating class imbalance, SMOTE enabled a fairer evaluation on the comparative analysis of CNN and RF. This analysis revealed similar results, with RF marginally outperforming CNN (99.79% vs. 99.74% F1-score).

On the field of generative methods, M. K. Prabhakaran, A. D. Chandrasekar, and P. M. Sundaram [41] proposed "PHISH_ATTENTION" a anti-phishing framework that combines Variational Auto-Encoders (VAEs) and Multi-Headed Self-Attention. To mitigate the data imbalance they also integrated Deep Convolutional Generative Adversarial Networks (DCGANs), achieving 98.57% detection accuracy.

[1] https://who.is/.

Expanding on GAN's versatility, Alreoud and Karabatis [4] proposed a GAN-based framework to generate synthetic URL-based phishing examples capable of evading ML classifiers. Their experiments revealed that the adversarial examples produced by the GAN significantly compromised classifier performance, highlighting the model's efficacy in circumventing detection mechanisms. In another study, T. T. T. Pham, T. D. Pham, and V. C. Ta [40] explored 4 GAN variants, vanilla GAN, Deep Convolutional GAN (DCGAN), Wasserstein GAN (WGAN), and Sequence GAN (SeqGAN), to assess their ability to deceive RF and LSTM phishing URL classifiers. From the applied GAN variants, only the WGAN showed a slight increase in accuracy with the addition of the augmented data, while the others decreased, showing that they were better at deceiving the classifiers. Hybrid methodologies have also been proposed: the authors of [20] combined SMOTE with a GAN, based on an auto encoder network, and swarm intelligence algorithms to balance the dataset and select informative features. Experiments run on Phishtank, UCI, and Tan datasets showed that the accuracy of the proposed method was 98.87%, 99.37%, and 98.79%, respectively.

Despite the exploration of numerous augmentation techniques for URLs (e.g. GANs, VAEs), the potential for language models in this domain remains unexplored. While large language models (LLMs) have showed remarkable text-generation capabilities [19,34], their smaller counterparts, small language models (SLMs), offer advantages in computational efficiency, reduced resource requirements, and domain-specific adaptability, which could be advantageous for generating synthetically augmented URL data. However, to the best of our knowledge does not exist studies investigating SLMs for URL-specific augmentation tasks, such as generating realistic phishing or benign URL variations or enhancing minority class samples. Considering this gap, we intend to evaluate if SLMs are able to generate URL samples to augment URL datasets.

3 Methodology

3.1 Data Collection and Analysis

For this research we considered 4 different datasets: PhiUSIIL [42], Mendeley V3 [25], Kaggle 2023 [26] and Malicious URLs dataset [50]. In addition to the 4 mentioned datasets, we expanded them by incorporating URLs extracted from a corpus of diverse email message datasets, including the Enron Corpus [52], the Nazario phishing dataset [28], TREC05-07 [15,17,18], CEAS08 [16], and the Nigerian Fraud email repository [45]. Table 1 summarises their number of samples and if the dataset is balanced, meaning it has the same number of phishing and benign samples.

Duplicate detection was conducted through two distinct ways: intra-dataset analysis (within individual datasets) and inter-dataset analysis (across multiple datasets). Intra-dataset duplicates were identified via exact matching and were removed. For inter-dataset analysis, we computed pairwise duplication rates using a heatmap (Fig. 1), where each cell (i, j) represents the percentage of URLs in dataset i that also exist in dataset j. In this heatmap it is possible to observe significant overlap between the datasets, specifically:

Table 1. Distribution and Balance of URL Datasets

Dataset	Number of URLs	Balanced
PhiUSIIL	235,795	No
Mendeley V3	11,430	Yes
Kaggle 2023	808,042	No
Malicious URLs	651,191	No
Combined Dataset	104,786	No

- Mendeley V3 is fully contained in Kaggle 2023.
- 69% of Kaggle 2023 URLs overlap with the Malicious URLs dataset.
- 24% of Mendeley V3 URLs are present in the Malicious URLs dataset.

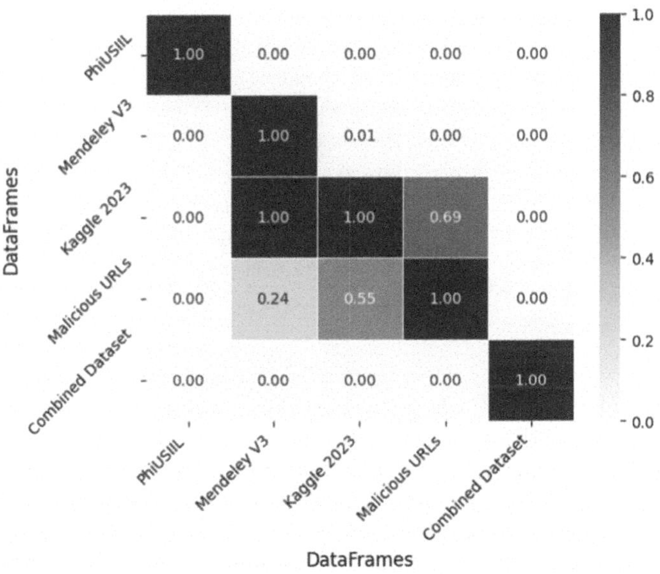

Fig. 1. Inter-Dataset Duplicate URLs

The overlapping URLs observed across datasets indicated redundancy, highlighting the need to remove duplicate entries. Following the removal of exact duplicates, inter and intra-datasets, the Combined dataset comprised 1,491,187 unique URLs. To mitigate over fitting and further enhance representational diversity, near-duplicate instances were identified and removed using a MinHash-based Locality-Sensitive Hashing (LSH) algorithm [13], configured with a Jaccard similarity threshold ($\phi \leq 0.7$) to quantify lexical and structural overlap. This process reduced the dataset to 1,095,787 distinct URLs comprised of 596,687 benign and 499,200 phishing URLs, showing a slight class imbalance.

3.2 Dataset Preprocessing and Feature Extraction

For URL phishing detection, we extracted 15 URL-based features that were described in prior studies [4,35]. Table 2 summarises these features as well as example URLs, that were obtained from the combined datasets.

Table 2. Extracted URL Features and Examples

URL Feature	Example
Length of URL	https://www.southbankmosaics.com
Use of IP address	124.105.24.19
Dot count (.)	https://www.c.line-design.fr
Hyphen count (-)	https://www.uni-mainz.de
@ symbol count (@)	https://www.flickr.com/photos/100980148@N05/17049336412/
Tilde count (˜)	http://www.ocf.berkeley.edu/~adr/crisisweb.jpg
Suspicious words	https://www.southbankmosaics.com
HTTP count	http://www.crestonwood.com/router.php
HTTPS count	https://www.poundingtherock.com
Hostname length	https://www.airlinesupports.com
TLD length	https://hypnotic.91500.cc
Number of TLD parts in domain	http://espacecompetefreemobille.com/moncompte/
Number of TLD parts in URL	http://www.crestonwood.com/router.php
Encoded hostname	http://www.paypal.com:911@xn-80aaahorunoimsf3p.xn-p1ain
Encoded IP	http://0xD8.0x79.0xBF.0x91/
Homoglyph usage	https://free-nltro.com/

The Combined dataset was split into 80% training and 20% testing sets. This approach was still performed to enable a direct comparison with prior works, that only evaluated the model's performance on the test subset, despite limitations in such evaluations. URLs were converted to numerical representation using Term Frequency-Inverse Document Frequency (TF-IDF) with character level n-grams (range: 1–3) and a maximum number of features of 500, to ensure a fair comparison between all models.

To evaluate the models generalisation and the impact of data augmentation, we used another dataset, not contained in the Combined dataset, as validation set, Mendeley 2024 [29], containing 450,176 URLs (104,438 phishing, 345,738 benign). This would help to test the impact of data augmentation by measuring performance on unseen URL patterns. We preprocessed this extra dataset using the same feature extraction pipeline as the Combined dataset, and checked for duplicates which gave us a total of 339,821 URLs. We also checked for possible duplicates between this validation dataset and the Combined one. As shown in Fig. 2, exists a total of 3406 duplicates, which were promptly removed from the validation dataset leaving us with a total of 336,415 URLs for the validation dataset.

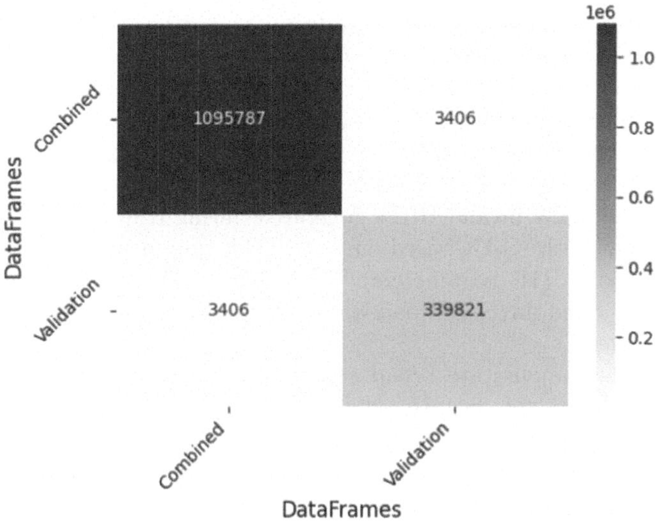

Fig. 2. Inter-Duplicates URLs Between Combined and Validation Datasets

3.3 Data Augmentation Phase

To address the class imbalance in the dataset, with phishing URLs being the minority class, we used augmenting techniques to improve the results and the generalisation of the models. To that end, we evaluated three augmentation strategies: SMOTE, GANs and SLMs.

SMOTE addresses class imbalance by generating synthetic samples through interpolation in feature space. Unlike GANs or SLMs, SMOTE operates without requiring training phases, instead creating new instances by interpolating between existing minority-class examples and their nearest neighbours.

GANs, though predominantly used and suitable for image generation, have also been explored for text generation despite their more challenging application due to the discrete nature of textual data [48]. We implemented two variants: a baseline GAN and a WGAN enhanced with gradient penalty to stabilise training dynamics, a big concern in text generation tasks [10]. Both architectures share a generator based on a multi-layer perceptron (MLP) design, while the discriminator is evaluated in two configurations: an MLP and a CNN. The CNN variant was motivated by its results in phishing URL detection tasks, while the MLP was chosen because the generator was also an MLP.

The generator employs a descending-layer architecture (512, 256, 128 neurons) with layer normalization, LeakyReLU activation ($\alpha = 0.2$), and dropout ($\rho = 0.3$). A final unflattening layer projects outputs to sequence space. Contrarily, the MLP discriminator adopts an inverted ascending structure, processing flattened URL embeddings with identical normalization/activation layers, and applies spectral normalization exclusively to its terminal layer. The CNN discriminator uses two one dimensional convolutional layers of 128 and 256 filters with kernel size 5, followed by three fully connected layers of 64, 128 and 256 neurons, with spectral normalisation applied to both convolutional and dense layers.

The big difference between the GAN and WGAN lies in their training, with the WGAN incorporating gradient penalty as well as adopting a 5:1 discriminator to generator update ratio. Both models integrate a regex-based loss function that penalises syntactically invalid URLs generated during training.

To contrast with GAN-based and SMOTE augmentation methods, we employed Gemma3 (1B parameters) [51] as the SLM for phishing URL generation. This allowed direct comparison of its efficacy against the other augmentation techniques.

While SLMs demonstrate broad capabilities across diverse tasks, research shows they achieve significantly superior performance when fine-tuned for domain-specific applications [53,54], enabling more relevant and contextually appropriate outputs compared to base models. To use this advantage, we adopted a hybrid strategy combining fine-tuning with prompt-guided generation, where prompts provide explicit syntactic and semantic constraints to guide the sample generation [49]. The prompt would also help by giving the rules that the model needs to comply to generate the samples.

We designed the prompt by converting the 15 extracted URL-based features into rules, for the model to follow during the generation process. Figure 3 presents the prompt used.

We implemented *partial fine-tuning* using the *Unsloth* framework, updating only 1.3% of the model's parameters. Training proceeded for 60 steps until loss stabilisation occurred, using a learning rate of 1×10^{-4}, a batch size of 8, and the Adam optimizer. The fine-tuning was performed on an NVIDIA RTX A4500 GPU.

3.4 Model Selection and Hyper Parameter Tuning

To evaluate the phishing URL detection generalisation of models using data augmentation, we chose three different models based on the literature: Random Forest, Extreme Gradient Boosting and Convolutional Neural Network.

Hyper parameter tuning was performed on the models through cross validation on the training subset, selecting the best configuration based on the F1-score obtained on the test subset.

The RF implementation used scikit-learn's `RandomForestClassifier` with `HalvingGridSearchCV` and cross validation with 5-folds for hyper parameter tuning. The final hyper parameters were 100 estimators with a maximum depth of 16, bootstrap sampling disabled and random selection of 50% features per split. Node splitting used Gini impurity criterion with a minimum of 2 samples for both leaf nodes and internal splits.

The XGB implementation used `XGBClassifier` from the xgboost library, with hyper parameter tuning via `HalvingGridSearchCV` and cross validation performed with 5-folds. The final model configuration used 100 estimators and a maximum depth of 8, with the evaluation metric log loss.

You are an AI phishing simulation specialist creating training materials for email security detection systems. Generate only and ONLY a phishing URL. MUST NOT generate links of existing companies, ONLY similar to them. Follow these rules. Can abide by more than one rule, but is OBLIGATORY to fulfill at least one of these rules:
- Include redirection (e.g. `http://3104.nnu4urye.info? http://c43n34.com?35u3b`)
- The URL contains a URL of a known organization (e.g. `http://108.179.216.140/ bankofamerica/`)
- Special characters '-' in the host name (e.g. `http://yj4yb6hmb3.x-cant-bankyou-here-of-mymoney.cn/ yj4yb6hmb3/Oraliao_show_23Y`)
- Long domain name (e.g. `http://31837.9hzaseruijintunhfeugandeikisn.com/5/54878`)
- Hostname is encoded (e.g. `http://www.%64isc%72%65%74%2done-%6ei%67h%74.%63o%6d`)
- IP is encoded (e.g. `http://0x42.0x1D.0x25.0xC2/`)
- Email address in URL (e.g `http://username@hotmail.com.fddcol.com`)
- IP address (e.g. `http://62.141.45.54/portaleTitolaris8/`)
- Suspicious symbols (@, -,)
- Https/ Http
- Various dots (.) in domain name
- Sensitive words (e.g. 'secure', 'account', 'webscr','login', 'ebayisapi', 'signin', 'banking', 'confirm')
- Multiple top-level-domains (e.g. `http://www.ebay.com.urgd.com/path`)
- Similar target brands (e.g. 'paypail', 'ebayy', etc)
- Usage of homoglyphs (e.g. cyrillic, etc)

Fig. 3. Prompt structure used during fine-tuning of URL generation.

The CNN architecture was implemented in PyTorch and used a sequential one dimensional convolutional structure. It was comprised of two convolutional blocks: the initial layer used 32 filters with kernel size 3, followed by batch normalization and max pooling for dimensionality reduction. The second block expanded to 64 filters with identical kernel size. The final layer used 64 neurons followed by a dropout of 20%, mapping the features to a sigmoid output for binary classification. The model was trained for 8 epochs using Adam optimizer, with batch size of 32 and a learning rate of 1×10^{-3}.

4 Experiments

4.1 Data Augmentation Results

To create the data augmented samples, training and generation were both required. Training was performed until training loss was stabilised, while generation was performed until there was a balance between both classes. To reach the balance there was a need of a total of 97,387 phishing URL samples. Table 3 presents the times that each model took for training and generation.

Table 3. Training and Generation Time for Data Augmentation Techniques

Technique	Training Time	Generation Time
GAN (MLP-MLP)	7 min	24 min
GAN (MLP-CNN)	10.5 min	60 min
WGAN (MLP-MLP)	10 min	1.5 min
WGAN (MLP-CNN)	15 min	3 min
Gemma	6 min	720 min

Despite Gemma's competitive training time, its autoregressive architecture resulted in a slower generation time (720 min vs WGAN's 1.5 min). The WGAN variants showed similar generation times compared to GAN's discriminator variants. Employing the CNN variant as discriminator increased both training and generation time relative to MLP, likely due to convolutional overhead. The usage of gradient penalty and 5:1 discriminator-to-generator update ratio in WGANs likely contributed to their extended training times compared to standard GANs, while enabling significantly faster sample generation.

We also present in Table 4, one generated URL sample per augmentation model. Despite all looking like possible URLs, it is to note that GAN generated URLs had all the same length, which could impact the ML models performance. Additionally some URLs generated sequences of characters without any sense. WGAN (MLP-MLP) sample also doesn't start with "www", which could cause some problems if the augmented data is the only data without the subdomain part. The most frequent characteristic across generated URLs were the HTTP and HTTPS protocols.

Table 4. Generated Samples from Data Augmentation Techniques

Technique	Generated Example
GAN (MLP-MLP)	http://www.grmca.ahpccs0.hnjcpzeda0.lamg/pdmidtmht
GAN (MLP-CNN)	http://www.thhdrcncbru6pkt/bhcosar.ocs/tvedmpmcp4
WGAN (MLP-MLP)	http://nohbpnrum.com.l6s
WGAN (MLP-CNN)	http://www.psinosar3.mloom
Gemma	http://www.welfareco.info

4.2 Metrics

To evaluate the phishing URL detection models performance we employed the most used metrics: Accuracy, Precision, Recall, Area Under the ROC Curve (AUC) and F1.

These metrics are derived from the four possible outcomes of a binary classification task. In the context of phishing detection, we define the 'positive' class as phishing URLs and the 'negative' class as benign URLs. The four outcomes are:

- **True Positive (TP):** The model correctly predicts a phishing URL as phishing.
- **True Negative (TN):** The model correctly predicts a benign URL as benign.
- **False Positive (FP):** The model incorrectly predicts a benign URL as phishing (Type I error).
- **False Negative (FN):** The model incorrectly predicts a phishing URL as benign (Type II error).

Accuracy [46] measures the proportion of correct predictions over the total number of predictions (1). While intuitive, it can be misleading for imbalanced datasets:

$$\text{Accuracy} = \frac{TP + TN}{TP + TN + FP + FN} \tag{1}$$

Precision [46] quantifies the fraction of true positives among all predicted positives, reflecting the model's ability to avoid false alarms (2):

$$\text{Precision} = \frac{TP}{TP + FP} \tag{2}$$

Recall [46] measures the proportion of true positives identified correctly relative to all actual positives (3):

$$\text{Recall} = \frac{TP}{TP + FN} \tag{3}$$

The F1-Score [46] is the harmonic mean of precision and recall, balancing both metrics (4). It is particularly useful for imbalanced datasets:

$$F1 = 2 \times \frac{\text{Precision} \times \text{Recall}}{\text{Precision} + \text{Recall}} \tag{4}$$

Area Under the ROC Curve (AUC) [46] evaluates the model's ability to distinguish between classes. The ROC curve plots the True Positive Rate (TPR) against the False Positive Rate (FPR) at various classification thresholds (5). AUC represents the area under this curve:

$$\text{AUC} = \int_0^1 \text{TPR}(\text{FPR}), d\text{FPR} \tag{5}$$

A value of 1 denotes perfect classification, while 0.5 indicates random performance.

4.3 Results

Following the generation of the needed synthetic samples for balancing the dataset, we combined these samples with the original dataset. We evaluated the six augmentation techniques (SMOTE, GANs and WGANs, and Gemma) against the unbalanced dataset baseline, using three model architectures: RF, XGB, and CNN. Identical hyper parameters were used for all models and datasets (baseline and augmented). Table 5 presents the obtained results from the experiments performed using the mentioned metrics.

Table 5. Model Performance Across Augmentation Methods (Test (T)/Validation (V))

Method	Model	Accuracy (%)		Precision (%)		Recall (%)		AUC (%)		F1 (%)	
		T	V	T	V	T	V	T	V	T	V
Baseline	RF	94.61	76.88	95.00	47.99	93.07	96.37	98.53	93.48	94.03	64.07
	XGB	95.76	86.45	**95.74**	61.65	94.92	**97.01**	99.19	97.37	95.33	75.39
	CNN	**96.17**	**91.18**	96.36	**72.27**	**95.18**	95.39	**99.29**	**97.73**	**95.77**	**82.24**
SMOTE	RF	94.66	75.31	94.39	46.32	93.86	97.13	98.54	94.01	94.12	62.73
	XGB	95.67	86.30	95.40	61.34	95.09	**97.24**	99.17	**97.65**	95.24	75.23
	CNN	**96.14**	**90.36**	**96.06**	**69.90**	**95.45**	96.49	**99.28**	97.63	**95.75**	**81.07**
GAN (MLP-MLP)	RF	95.05	79.12	96.27	50.64	93.74	95.14	98.76	93.24	94.99	66.10
	XGB	**96.04**	85.53	96.41	60.03	**95.64**	**96.78**	**99.31**	**97.25**	**96.02**	**74.10**
	CNN	95.93	**86.13**	**96.91**	**61.78**	94.89	92.17	99.24	95.51	95.89	73.98
GAN (MLP-CNN)	RF	95.10	78.55	96.26	49.93	93.84	95.10	98.76	93.18	95.04	65.48
	XGB	96.04	84.97	96.39	59.08	**95.67**	**96.74**	99.30	**97.18**	96.03	73.36
	CNN	**96.25**	**87.55**	**97.05**	**64.28**	95.40	94.07	**99.34**	96.03	**96.21**	**76.37**
WGAN (MLP-MLP)	RF	95.04	78.81	96.30	50.25	93.67	95.10	98.78	93.10	94.97	65.75
	XGB	96.05	**85.93**	96.42	**60.73**	95.65	**96.85**	99.32	**97.31**	96.04	**74.65**
	CNN	**96.30**	84.93	**96.46**	59.09	**96.12**	96.07	**99.35**	95.91	**96.29**	73.18
WGAN (MLP-CNN)	RF	95.09	77.92	96.21	49.17	93.87	95.59	98.76	92.94	95.03	64.94
	XGB	96.07	86.66	96.43	62.06	95.68	**96.80**	99.31	**97.42**	96.05	75.64
	CNN	**96.49**	**88.25**	**96.68**	**65.63**	**96.27**	94.60	**99.39**	96.94	**96.48**	**77.50**
Gemma	RF	94.63	68.82	95.50	40.46	93.67	97.00	98.41	93.13	94.58	57.10
	XGB	95.69	**79.95**	**95.99**	**51.65**	95.36	**97.72**	99.12	**97.33**	95.67	**67.59**
	CNN	**95.80**	79.59	95.28	51.21	**96.38**	97.26	**99.13**	95.20	**95.82**	67.09

These experimental results reveal insights into the effectiveness of augmentation strategies in phishing URL detection models, while showing great challenges that could exist in real-world deployment. Across all models, a pronounced generalisation gap emerges between test and validation performance, with validation metrics consistently behind by 5–25% points depending on the architecture, with precision showing the largest discrepancy (30–50% points). While the metrics on the test set improve with some of the augmentation techniques, the usage of the metrics on the validation set, show some concerning issues.

In regards to the test metrics, the F1-score of all the augmentations techniques increased slightly showing the greatest increase in the WGAN (MLP-CNN) architecture with increases for RF of 1%, XGB of 0.72% and CNN of 0.71%. Gemma also had an increase but much less prominent. This could be due to the partial fine-tune that was performed, which could also incur in the generation of false phishing URLs, that were actual benign. Despite this, it is possible to say that augmentation techniques do in fact improve the performance of the models against the test subset.

However, in the matter of validation metrics the results were worse than expected. The application of augmentation techniques resulted in lower F1-scores across all evaluated models compared to unaugmented baselines, with the exception of RF showing a slight improvement when augmented with URLs from the GAN (MLP-MLP) approach. Gemma showed the poorest performance among all models, likely due to its partial fine-tuning approach. This method does not guarantee phishing URL generation despite training on such data, potentially explaining the worse results.

This metric discrepancies between test and validation sets reveal some insights into the models behaviours. Recall, which measures the model's ability to identify all actual phishing URLs, shows an increase in validation versus test. This could suggest an overfit from the models to the validation set phishing patterns. In contrast, precision that quantifies the reliability of positive predictions, shows a 30–50% discrepancy between validation and test sets. This big drop shows that while models have an high confidence in validation phishing samples, they generate excessive false alarms when encountering real-world URL structures.

5 Conclusion

The research explored the usage of different augmentation techniques to improve the performance of phishing URL detection ML models. Three different approaches were implemented and applied, the usage of SMOTE, that oversamples the minority class, GANs that generates adversarial examples making usage of noise and SLM that generates different URLs based on a prompt and knowledge obtained from training.

After evaluating each methodology using three different models, RF, XGB and CNN, it was possible to observe that the techniques despite showing better results on the test set, the performance on the validation set was worse. The difference between test and validation metrics were between 5% and 25%, which is a big discrepancy. This shows that despite having great results on augmentation techniques on the test set, the usage of a validation set should also be adopted to guarantee that the results are not biased, due to the test set being derived from the same distribution as the training data.

Our baseline results, after the removal of inter-dataset and intra-dataset and near duplicate URLs, are slightly worse than the near perfect accuracy reported in prior studies. This discrepancy can be attributed to the removal of duplicates, creating a more diverse and generalisable dataset. Nevertheless, evaluation on this dataset still achieves results comparable to the ones from literature, showing robust performance even when avoiding the inflated metrics caused by duplicates. These inflated metrics align with established findings where performance declines on truly independent evaluation sets confirming that our approach more accurately reflects deployment challenges [2,47].

It is important to note that the SLM, that was the most powerful experimented technique, showed the worst results. This performance limitation comes from the partial fine-tuning approach, which fails to guarantee phishing URL generation.

The aim of the work was to show the potential of using augmentation methods to help the generalisation of models. Contrary to the better results of the metrics on the test set, our evaluation revealed that the augmentation techniques negatively affected the metrics on the validation set across all models. To this end, we propose the usage of validation sets when application of augmentation techniques on phishing URLs is performed, on further research to be done.

Future work should focus on the usage of more data to train the models which could benefit both the models and the augmentation techniques. Further exploration of additional GAN architectures could also show improvements in the generation of URLs and the metrics of the models. In addition, other SLM models, or the usage of models with more parameters, could improve its generation. Finally, the associated resource usage for all of these methods will be investigated and analysed.

Acknowledgments. This research was funded by the Itea Project VESTA (#21011) and Project VESTA (NORTE2030-FEDER-00382400) co-funded by Portugal 2030. Furthermore, this work also received funding from the project UIDB/00760/2020.

Disclosure of Interests. The authors declare that they have no known competing financial interests or personal relationships that could have appeared to influence the work reported in this paper.

References

1. Abdul Samad, S.R., et al.: Analysis of the performance impact of fine-tuned machine learning model for phishing url detection. Electronics **12**(7) (2023). https://doi.org/10.3390/electronics12071642, https://www.mdpi.com/2079-9292/12/7/1642
2. Afonso, P., Maia, E., Amorim, I., Praça, I.: Rethinking phishing detection: how dataset quality affects model generalization. In: 2024 14th International Conference on Advanced Computer Information Technologies (ACIT) (2025). to appear
3. Ahammad, S.H., et al.: Phishing url detection using machine learning methods. Adv. Eng. Softw. **173**, 103288 (2022). https://doi.org/10.1016/j.advengsoft.2022.103288, https://www.sciencedirect.com/science/article/pii/S0965997822001892
4. AlEroud, A., Karabatis, G.: Bypassing detection of url-based phishing attacks using generative adversarial deep neural networks. In: Proceedings of the Sixth International Workshop on Security and Privacy Analytics, pp. 53–60. IWSPA '20, Association for Computing Machinery, New York, NY, USA (2020).https://doi.org/10.1145/3375708.3380315
5. Alsadig, A.H., Ahmad, M.O.: Phishing url detection using deep learning with cnn models. In: 2024 Second International Conference on Intelligent Cyber Physical Systems and Internet of Things (ICoICI), pp. 768–775 (2024). https://doi.org/10.1109/ICoICI62503.2024.10696243
6. Alshingiti, Z., Alaqel, R., Al-Muhtadi, J., Haq, Q.E.U., Saleem, K., Faheem, M.H.: A deep learning-based phishing detection system using CNN, LSTM, and LSTM-CNN. Electronics **12**(1) (2023). https://doi.org/10.3390/electronics12010232, https://www.mdpi.com/2079-9292/12/1/232

7. Anti-Phishing Working Group: APWG Phishing Activity Trends Report, 2nd Quarter 2024 (2024). https://docs.apwg.org/reports/apwg_trends_report_q2_2024.pdf. Accessed 07 May 2025
8. Anti-Phishing Working Group: APWG Phishing Activity Trends Report, 3rd Quarter 2024 (2024). https://docs.apwg.org/reports/apwg_trends_report_q3_2024.pdf. Accessed 07 May 2025
9. Anti-Phishing Working Group: APWG Phishing Activity Trends Report, 4th Quarter 2024 (2024). https://docs.apwg.org/reports/apwg_trends_report_q4_2024.pdf. Accessed 07 May 2025
10. Arjovsky, M., Chintala, S., Bottou, L.: Wasserstein gan (2017). https://arxiv.org/abs/1701.07875
11. Asif, A.U.Z., Shirazi, H., Ray, I.: Machine learning-based phishing detection using URL features: a comprehensive review. In: Dolev, S., Schieber, B. (eds.) Stabilization, Safety, and Security of Distributed Systems. SSS 2023. LNCS, vol. 14310, pp. 481–497. Springer, Cham (2023). https://doi.org/10.1007/978-3-031-44274-2_36
12. Bell, S., Komisarczuk, P.: An analysis of phishing blacklists: google safe browsing, openphish, and phishtank. In: Proceedings of the Australasian Computer Science Week Multiconference. ACSW '20, Association for Computing Machinery, New York, NY, USA (2020). https://doi.org/10.1145/3373017.3373020
13. Broder, A.: On the resemblance and containment of documents. In: Proceedings. Compression and Complexity of SEQUENCES 1997 (Cat. No. 97TB100171), pp. 21–29 (1997). https://doi.org/10.1109/SEQUEN.1997.666900
14. Catal, C., Giray, G., Tekinerdogan, B., Kumar, S., Shukla, S.: Applications of deep learning for phishing detection: a systematic literature review. Knowl. Inf. Syst. **64**(6), 1457–1500 (2022). https://doi.org/10.1007/s10115-022-01672-x
15. Cormack, G.V.: TREC 2005 Public Spam Corpus. https://plg.uwaterloo.ca/~gvcormac/treccorpus/about.html. Accessed 12 May 2025
16. Cormack, G.V.: Ceas 2008 live spam challenge corpus (2008). https://plg.uwaterloo.ca/~gvcormac/ceascorpus/. Accessed 12 May 2025
17. Cormack, G.V., Lynam, T.R.: TREC 2006 Public Spam Corpus. https://plg.uwaterloo.ca/~gvcormac/treccorpus06/about.html. Accessed 12 May 2025
18. Cormack, G.V., Lynam, T.R.: TREC 2007 Public Spam Corpus. https://plg.uwaterloo.ca/~gvcormac/treccorpus07/about.html. Accessed 12 May 2025
19. Ding, B., et al.: Data augmentation using large language models: data perspectives, learning paradigms and challenges (2024). https://arxiv.org/abs/2403.02990
20. Elberri, M.A., Tokeşer, Ü., Rahebi, J., Lopez-Guede, J.M.: A cyber defense system against phishing attacks with deep learning game theory and LSTM-CNN with African vulture optimization algorithm (AVOA). Int. J. Inf. Secur. **23**(4), 2583–2606 (2024)
21. Elsadig, M., et al.: Intelligent deep machine learning cyber phishing url detection based on bert features extraction. Electronics **11**(22) (2022). https://doi.org/10.3390/electronics11223647, https://www.mdpi.com/2079-9292/11/22/3647
22. European Union Agency for Cybersecurity: ENISA Threat Landscape 2024 – July 2023 to June 2024. European Union Agency for Cybersecurity (2024). https://doi.org/10.2824/071088, https://www.enisa.europa.eu/publications/enisa-threat-landscape-2024
23. Google: Google Safe Browsing (2025). https://safebrowsing.google.com/. Accessed 08 May 2025
24. Gupta, B., Yadav, K., Razzak, I., Psannis, K., Castiglione, A., Chang, X.: A novel approach for phishing urls detection using lexical based machine learning in a

real-time environment. Comput. Commun. **175**, 47–57 (2021). https://doi.org/10.1016/j.comcom.2021.04.023
25. Hannousse, A., Yahiouche, S.: Web page phishing detection (2021). https://doi.org/10.17632/c2gw7fy2j4.3. Accessed 12 May 2025
26. Harisudhan411: Phishing and legitimate urls (2023). https://www.kaggle.com/datasets/harisudhan411/phishing-and-legitimate-urls. Accessed 12 May 2025
27. Jalil, S., Usman, M., Fong, A.: Highly accurate phishing URL detection based on machine learning. J. Ambient Intell. Humaniz. Comput. **14**(7), 9233–9251 (2023)
28. Jose Nazario: Nazario Phishing Corpus (2005). https://monkey.org/~jose/phishing. Accessed 12 May 2025
29. Kaitholikkal, J.K.S.B.A.: Phishing url dataset (2024). https://doi.org/10.17632/vfszbj9b36.1. Accessed 12 May 2025
30. Karim, A., Shahroz, M., Mustofa, K., Belhaouari, S.B., Joga, S.R.K.: Phishing detection system through hybrid machine learning based on url. IEEE Access **11**, 36805–36822 (2023). https://doi.org/10.1109/ACCESS.2023.3252366
31. Kavya, S., Sumathi, D.: Staying ahead of phishers: a review of recent advances and emerging methodologies in phishing detection. Artif. Intell. Rev. **58**(2), 50 (2024)
32. Kritika, E.: A comprehensive literature review on phishing url detection using deep learning techniques. J. Cyber Secur. Technol. 1–29 (2024). https://doi.org/10.1080/23742917.2024.2378552
33. Lee, K., Lim, K., Kim, H., Kwon, Y., Kim, D.: 7 days later: analyzing phishing-site lifespan after detected. In: Proceedings of the ACM on Web Conference 2025, pp. 945–956. WWW '25, Association for Computing Machinery, New York, NY, USA (2025). https://doi.org/10.1145/3696410.3714678
34. Li, Y., Ding, K., Wang, J., Lee, K.: Empowering large language models for textual data augmentation. In: Ku, L.W., Martins, A., Srikumar, V. (eds.) Findings of the Association for Computational Linguistics: ACL 2024, pp. 12734–12751. Association for Computational Linguistics, Bangkok, Thailand (2024). https://doi.org/10.18653/v1/2024.findings-acl.756, https://aclanthology.org/2024.findings-acl.756/
35. Li, Y., Yang, Z., Chen, X., Yuan, H., Liu, W.: A stacking model using url and html features for phishing webpage detection. Future Gener. Comput. Syst. **94**, 27–39 (2019). https://doi.org/10.1016/j.future.2018.11.004, https://www.sciencedirect.com/science/article/pii/S0167739X1830503X
36. Maleki, F., Ovens, K., Gupta, R., Reinhold, C., Spatz, A., Forghani, R.: Generalizability of machine learning models: quantitative evaluation of three methodological pitfalls. Radiol.: Artif. Intell. **5**(1), e220028 (2023). https://doi.org/10.1148/ryai.220028
37. Mandadi, A., Boppana, S., Ravella, V., Kavitha, R.: Phishing website detection using machine learning. In: 2022 IEEE 7th International Conference for Convergence in Technology (I2CT), pp. 1–4 (2022). https://doi.org/10.1109/I2CT54291.2022.9824801
38. Oest, A., et al.: PhishTime: continuous longitudinal measurement of the effectiveness of anti-phishing blacklists. In: 29th USENIX Security Symposium (USENIX Security 20), pp. 379–396. USENIX Association (2020). https://www.usenix.org/conference/usenixsecurity20/presentation/oest-phishtime
39. Opara, C., Chen, Y., Wei, B.: Look before you leap: detecting phishing web pages by exploiting raw url and html characteristics. Expert Syst. Appl. **236**, 121183 (2024). https://doi.org/10.1016/j.eswa.2023.121183, https://www.sciencedirect.com/science/article/pii/S0957417423016858
40. Pham, T.T.T., Pham, T.D., Ta, V.C.: Evaluation of GAN-based models for phishing URL classifiers. Int. J. Comput. Netw. Inf. Secur. (IJCNIS) **15**(2), 1–14 (2023)

41. Prabhakaran, M.K., Chandrasekar, A.D., Meenakshi Sundaram, P.: Phish_attention: achieving robust phishing website detection with balanced datasets and advanced url features. Comput. J. bxaf036 (2025). https://doi.org/10.1093/comjnl/bxaf036
42. Prasad, A., Chandra, S.: PhiUSIIL Phishing URL (Website). UCI Machine Learning Repository (2024). https://doi.org/10.1016/j.cose.2023.103545. Accessed 12 May 2025
43. P.S.U.A.O.: Phishing Site URLs (2022). https://www.kaggle.com/taruntiwarihp/phishing-site-urls. Accessed 26 May 2025
44. Quinkert, F., Tatang, D., Holz, T.: Digging deeper: an analysis of domain impersonation in the lower DNS hierarchy. In: Bilge, L., Cavallaro, L., Pellegrino, G., Neves, N. (eds.) Detection of Intrusions and Malware, and Vulnerability Assessment. DIMVA 2021. LNCS, vol. 12756, pp. 68–87. Springer, Cham (2021). https://doi.org/10.1007/978-3-030-80825-9_4
45. Radev, D.: CLAIR Collection of Fraud Email. ACL Data and Code Repository, ADCR2008T001 (2008). http://aclweb.org/aclwiki
46. Rainio, O., Teuho, J., Klén, R.: Evaluation metrics and statistical tests for machine learning. Sci. Rep. **14**(1), 6086 (2024)
47. Rashid, F., Doyle, B., Han, S.C., Seneviratne, S.: Phishing url detection generalisation using unsupervised domain adaptation. Comput. Netw. **245**, 110398 (2024). https://doi.org/10.1016/j.comnet.2024.110398, https://www.sciencedirect.com/science/article/pii/S1389128624002305
48. de Rosa, G.H., Papa, J.P.: A survey on text generation using generative adversarial networks. Pattern Recognit. **119**, 108098 (2021). https://doi.org/10.1016/j.patcog.2021.108098, http://dx.doi.org/10.1016/j.patcog.2021.108098
49. Sahoo, P., Singh, A.K., Saha, S., Jain, V., Mondal, S., Chadha, A.: A systematic survey of prompt engineering in large language models: techniques and applications (2025). https://arxiv.org/abs/2402.07927
50. Sid321axn: Malicious urls dataset (2023). https://www.kaggle.com/datasets/sid321axn/malicious-urls-dataset/data. Accessed 12 May 2025
51. Team, G.: Gemma 3 technical report (2025)
52. Cohen, W.W.: Enron Email Dataset (2015). https://www.cs.cmu.edu/~./enron/. Accessed 12 May 2025
53. Yang, Y., Mishra, S., Chiang, J.N., Mirzasoleiman, B.: Smalltolarge (s2l): scalable data selection for fine-tuning large language models by summarizing training trajectories of small models (2024). https://arxiv.org/abs/2403.07384
54. Zhang, X., et al.: Speculative coreset selection for task-specific fine-tuning (2024). https://arxiv.org/abs/2410.01296
55. Zhuo, S., et al.: A large-scale study of device and link presentation in email phishing susceptibility. In: Proceedings of the 35th Australian Computer-Human Interaction Conference, pp. 78–85. OzCHI '23, Association for Computing Machinery, New York, NY, USA (2024). https://doi.org/10.1145/3638380.3638434
56. Zhuo, S., Biddle, R., Daniel Recomendable, J., Russello, G., Lottridge, D.: Eyes on the phish(er): towards understanding users' email processing pattern and mental models in phishing detection. In: Proceedings of the 2024 European Symposium on Usable Security, pp. 15–29. EuroUSEC '24, Association for Computing Machinery, New York, NY, USA (2024). https://doi.org/10.1145/3688459.3688465, https://doi.org/10.1145/3688459.3688465
57. Zieni, R., Massari, L., Calzarossa, M.C.: Phishing or not phishing? A survey on the detection of phishing websites. IEEE Access **11**, 18499–18519 (2023). https://doi.org/10.1109/ACCESS.2023.3247135

Federated Learning: An Approach with Hybrid Homomorphic Encryption

Pedro Correia[1], Ivan Costa[2(✉)], Ivone Amorim[2], Eva Maia[2], and Isabel Praça[2]

[1] Faculty of Engineering, University of Porto, Porto, Portugal
[2] GECAD, ISEP, Polytechnic of Porto, 4249-015 Porto, Portugal
ivcsi@isep.ipp.pt

Abstract. Federated Learning (FL) is a distributed machine learning approach that promises privacy by keeping the data on the device. However, gradient reconstruction and membership-inference attacks show that model updates still leak information. Fully Homomorphic Encryption (FHE) can address those privacy concerns but it suffers from ciphertext expansion and requires prohibitive overhead on resource-constrained devices. We propose the first Hybrid Homomorphic Encryption (HHE) framework for FL that pairs the PASTA symmetric cipher with the BFV FHE scheme. Clients encrypt local model updates with PASTA and send both the lightweight ciphertexts and the PASTA key (itself BFV-encrypted) to the server, which performs a homomorphic evaluation of the decryption circuit of PASTA and aggregates the resulting BFV ciphertexts. A prototype implementation, developed on top of the Flower FL framework, shows that on independently and identically distributed MNIST dataset with 12 clients and 10 training rounds, the proposed HHE system achieves 97.6% accuracy, just 1.3% below plaintext, while reducing client upload bandwidth by over 2,000× and cutting client runtime by 30% compared to a system based solely on the BFV FHE scheme. However, server computational cost increases by roughly 15621× for each client participating in the training phase, a challenge to be addressed in future work.

Keywords: Federated Learning · Secure Model Aggregation · Hybrid Homomorphic Encryption · Privacy-Preserving Machine Learning · Transciphering · BFV · PASTA · Internet of Things

1 Introduction

Federated learning (FL) is a distributed machine learning approach that allows a group of clients, such as Internet of Things (IoT) devices, hospitals, or healthcare providers, to collaboratively train a global model without sharing their sensitive data. In typical FL setups, each client trains a local model using its own data and shares only the model parameters with a central server. The server then coordinates the training process by aggregating the received updates to form an

R. Laborde et al. (Eds.): ESORICS 2025 Workshops, LNCS 16233, pp. 254–273, 2026.
https://doi.org/10.1007/978-3-032-16165-9_15

improved global model. Once updated, the global parameters are sent back to the clients, allowing them to continue local training [26]. Since raw data never leaves the device, FL is often described as "privacy-preserving" [2]. However, recent work has shown that local model updates can still leak private information, enabling attacks such as gradient-based data reconstruction, membership inference, and property inference [28–30,39]. To address these issues, several techniques have been integrated into FL systems, such as Differential Privacy (DP), Homomorphic Encryption (HE), and Multi-Party Computation (MPC) [35]. However, these techniques also present practical limitations. DP adds noise to the training process. MPC protocols often require multiple rounds of interaction and tend to scale poorly beyond a few hundred clients. HE allows servers to compute directly on encrypted data, offering strong and quantifiable privacy guarantees. Unfortunately, ciphertext expansion and the high algebraic depth of HE operations make pure HE-based FL much less efficient than its plaintext counterpart [19,40]. These limitations make such approaches prohibitive for deployment in resource-constrained environments, motivating the Hybrid Homomorphic Encryption (HHE) architecture introduced in this work. HHE is a promising line of work that combines a lightweight *symmetric* cipher with a HE one [1]. In this type of scheme, data is first encrypted using a symmetric cipher, and sent to the server together with the symmetric key encrypted using HE. The server then does a homomorphic evaluation of the symmetric decryption circuit using the encrypted key and ciphertext, converting the symmetric ciphertext into a homomorphic one. This allows the server to perform computations on the encrypted data, ensuring that raw data remains protected [10]. Although this approach introduces additional computational cost on the server side, it significantly reduces communication overhead, making it a promising solution for improving data privacy in FL settings involving computationally limited IoT devices. To our knowledge, no complete HHE-FL framework has yet been proposed.

In this work, we propose a HHE framework for FL that provides end-to-end privacy while remaining compatible with resource-constrained settings. The main contributions of our work are the following: the first end-to-end HHE-FL framework that combines the PASTA stream cipher with the BFV FHE scheme, integrated into the Flower ecosystem; a single-key distribution strategy and a homomorphicevaluation routine that allows secure *FedAvg* aggregation while keeping client encryption and communication costs minimal; a comprehensive experimental evaluation on Independent and Identically Distributed (IID) partitioned MNIST (12 clients, 10 rounds) that showed our HHE approach achieving 97.6% accuracy (vs. 98.9% in plaintext), while reducing client upload traffic by 2000×. Server computational overhead increased by approximately 15,621× per client participating in the training phase, an issue to be addressed in future work.

The paper is organized as follows. Section 2 recalls foundational concepts. Section 3 reviews the literature in FL with HE. Section 4 details our HHE-FL approach. Section 5 discusses implementation. Section 6 presents and discusses results. Section 7 concludes with a summary, limitations, and future work.

2 Backgound

This section presents the fundamentals of FL, including architectures, aggregation algorithms, and privacy risks. It overviews HE and most used schemes, and then introduces HHE, including a discussion on HE-friendly symmetric ciphers.

2.1 Federated Learning and Privacy Threats

FL is a distributed learning paradigm in which multiple clients collaboratively train a shared global model under the coordination of a central server, without directly exchanging their local data [26]. Figure 1 illustrates a typical setup with four clients and one server. This setup represents one of the most common FL architectures, known as the *centralized topology*, where a central server orchestrates the training process [22]. Each client holds a local dataset and trains a model using their private data. After local training, the client sends an update, which is typically a model weight vector or gradient, to the server. The server then aggregates the updates from all selected clients to produce a new global model, which is sent back to the clients for the next training round.

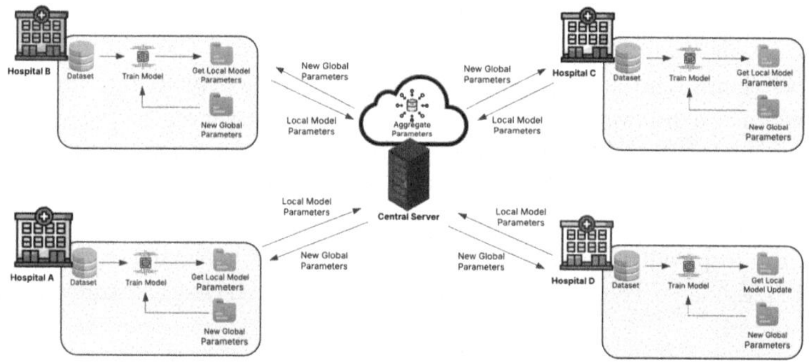

Fig. 1. Federated Learning Architecture

Federated Averaging (FedAvg) is the most used aggregation algorithm, which performs weighted averaging of client updates based on local dataset sizes [26]. Let K be the number of participating clients in a training round. For each client $k \in \{1, \ldots, K\}$, let n_k be the number of local training samples, and let $n = \sum_{k=1}^{K} n_k$ be the total number of data samples across all participating clients. Denote by w_{t+1}^k the updated model weights of client k after local training at round $t+1$. Then, the global model update is computed as:

$$w_{t+1} = \sum_{k=1}^{K} \frac{n_k}{n} w_{t+1}^k. \tag{1}$$

A related variant, Federated Stochastic Gradient Descent (FedSGD), aggregates gradients computed on client data rather than updated model weights [26].

In practice, FL deployments fall into two main categories: *cross-silo* FL, which involves a relatively small number of reliable institutional clients (e.g., hospitals or banks), and *cross-device* FL, which engages thousands to millions of resource-constrained that are offline most of the time and connect only intermittently. Communication bandwidth, client drop-outs, and limited computational resources are the main bottlenecks in the cross-device setting [20,24]. Since our objective is to make privacy-preserving FL viable on such devices, our proposed system targets this setting.

As mentioned before, FL enables collaboration with different clients while ensuring that data remains stored on individual devices. Even though raw data never leaves those devices, FL still has to deal with both external (e.g. eavesdroppers) and internal threats (e.g. malicious participants). A common internal adversary model is the *honest-but-curious* server, which follows the protocol correctly but tries to infer private client information from the updates it receives. Local model updates shared during FL retain subtle patterns that can leak private information. For instance, the server can reconstruct inputs by numerically inverting the shared gradients, perform a membership inference attack, or test whether a specific record was in a client's dataset [28–30,39]. These vulnerabilities exist even when all parties follow the standard FedAvg protocol, confirming that "no raw data leaves the device" is not a sufficient privacy guarantee.

2.2 Homomorphic Encryption

HE is a cryptographic primitive that allows computations over encrypted data, resulting in ciphertexts that, when decrypted, produce the same result as if the operations had been applied to the plaintexts [32]. There are three main categories of HE schemes, namely Partial Homomorphic Encryption (PHE), Some What Homomorphic Encryption (SWHE) and Fully Homomorphic Encryption (FHE). These categories are based on how many and which operations are allowed over encrypted data: PHE schemes allows only one type of arithmetic operation (e.g. addition) an unlimited number of times; SWHE supports a limited set of operations, with restrictions on how many times they can be computed; FHE enables multiple types of operations to be performed an unlimited number of times. Due to the context of this work, we focus on the latter type.

Currently, there are four main FHE schemes, namely TFHE (Fast Fully Homomorphic Encryption over the Torus) [8], which operates at the bit level, BGV [5] and BFV [13], which are very similar and allow for exact computations over integers, and CKKS [7], which supports approximate homomorphic computations over complex numbers. However, since the security of HE schemes relies on complex mathematical problems, these schemes tend to be impractical, especially FHE schemes [15]. Two of the main issues that limit FHE from becoming a practical solution are *ciphertext expansion* and *noise growth* [25]. The former refers to the growth, in size, that happens when encrypting a plaintext or after every computation performed, and the latter refers to the increase of noise after each operation, especially expensive ones such as multiplication. This causes two major problems for implementation: ciphertext expansion makes communication, storage and computation much more expensive; noise growth limits the depth of computable circuits, since correct decryption can not be ensured if the noise grows beyond a certain threshold [10]. New solutions, such as HHE, have been proposed to tackle these issues inherent to HE. The basic idea consists of combining HE and Symmetric Encryption (SE), which is known for its fast encryption, transmission, and constant ciphertext expansion.

2.3 HHE and HE-Friendly Ciphers

HHE is a cryptographic concept that combines symmetric ciphers with HE to mitigate the significant computational and communication overhead traditionally associated with HE. Contrary to HE, SE schemes rely on a single key for both encryption and decryption, making them significantly faster. In practice, HHE leverages the efficiency of SE for protecting data, while relying on FHE to enable secure computation over encrypted inputs. The idea dates back to the *transciphering* framework introduced by Lauter et al. [27], where a plaintext message m is encrypted using a symmetric cipher with key sk, producing a lightweight ciphertext c_{SKE}. The symmetric key sk is then encrypted under the homomorphic public key HE_pk, resulting in sk_{HE}. Both c_{SKE} and sk_{HE} are sent to the server. The server then homomorphically evaluates the symmetric decryption circuit, a step referred in this work as *Homomorphic Evaluation of Symmetric Decryption (HESD)*, to transform c_{SKE} into a homomorphic ciphertext m_{HE}, without learning the plaintext.

In a clientserver setting, HHE significantly reduces the computational burden on clients, since they only perform lightweight SE. It also lowers communication overhead, as symmetric ciphertexts are much smaller than their homomorphic equivalents. This makes HHE attractive for resource-constrained environments like the IoT, where devices often lack the capacity to support FHE directly. The added server-side cost of homomorphic evaluation is a trade-off, but one that can be mitigated through the use of HE-friendly symmetric ciphers, which are specifically designed to minimize homomorphic computation by having low multiplicative depth. As a result, they make *transciphering*-based approaches more practical, especially in resource-constrained scenarios.

Most HE-friendly ciphers are designed for compatibility with one or more of the major FHE schemes: BGV, BFV, CKKS, and TFHE. Since BGV, BFV, and CKKS share similar algebraic structures, some ciphers can support multiple schemes. For example, compatibility with BGV and BFV is more natural for ciphers operating over integers, while CKKS supports approximate arithmetic over complex numbers. Among the most prominent HE-friendly ciphers targeting BGV and BFV are RASTA [9], DASTA [17], and PASTA [10]. These designs are iterative improvements: DASTA refines RASTA, and PASTA further improves DASTA by reducing computational cost. In particular, PASTA is a stream cipher optimized for integer operations over $\mathbb{F}_p$, with p a 16-bit prime. It is specifically designed to minimize homomorphic evaluation depth and has been shown to outperform earlier designs in terms of efficiency.

The authors of PASTA made available an open-source C++ framework[1], developed specially for benchmarking HHE schemes. It includes implementations of several HE-friendly ciphers, like PASTA, together with various HE schemes, such as BGV via HElib [16], BFV via Microsoft SEAL [11], and TFHE using the TFHE library[2].

3 Related Work

FL with HE has been extensively studied in the literature as a means of enabling privacy-preserving collaboration between distributed clients to train a global model. Existing work in this area explores various HE schemes to secure model updates. In this section, we review FL protocols that use HE, highlighting their architectural designs, aggregation strategies, and cryptographic mechanisms.

Several proposals choose PHE as their main HE component in the solution, ones employing FedAvg [31,34,41], and others developing new aggregation algorithms, like Gradient Similarity Model Aggregation [37]. Proposals relying on FHE often present centralized FL architectures, although some approaches, such as the work of Hijazi et al. [18], propose a decentralized solution where no server exists. Instead, a capable user is selected in each round to coordinate and aggregate local updates. Their work combines techniques for data relevance, like cosine similarity, and clustering, to help prevent poisoning attacks. On the other hand, the centralized architectures can also be split between approaches that use FedAvg, or not, as their aggregation algorithm. Ma et al. [23] proposed a centralized solution that uses FedAvg and introduced a variation of CKKS, namely xMK-CKKS, which allows the users to utilize distinct homomorphic keys. Here, the users compute a shared public key, which is used to encrypt the local model weights. To decrypt, users need to compute their decryption shares and send them to the server. Zhang et al. [42] proposes an improved version of the xMK-CKKS scheme, named ftxMK-CKKS, which provides fault tolerance when users drop out of the training process. They also encrypt local model weights and use FedAvg for aggregation. The work of Duy et al. [12] proposes a shared key distribution mechanism, but within a semi-decentralized FL framework by leveraging a blockchain and an aggregator server. To further protect client privacy, the authors incorporate DP.

Besides FedAvg, several other aggregation algorithms can be used. Tan et al. [36] proposed the use of a simple average algorithm in a centralized approach. To ensure the authenticity of the communicating parties, the authors use Transport Layer Security. Fontela-Romero et al. [14] proposed a centralized solution that introduces an Incremental Singular Value Decomposition Aggregation algorithm to reduce data dimensionality. The work of Xu et al. [38], chose FedSGD as aggregation algorithm, using CKKS scheme to encrypt local gradients. It is also used Threshold Secret Sharing to make the scheme drop-out resilient.

[1] https://github.com/isec-tugraz/hybrid-HE-framework.
[2] https://github.com/tfhe/tfhe.

These works demonstrate that while HE, especially FHE, provides privacy guarantees, its use often depends on complementary techniques like secret sharing or DP, each introducing its own set of trade-offs. However, none of the surveyed studies applied HHE, leaving its suitability unexplored in FL.

4 Federated Learning with HHE

The main objective of this work is the creation of a privacy-preserving FL architecture for resource-constrained environments, such as those found in IoT settings. Our approach uses an HHE scheme that allows us to use a symmetric cipher to encrypt the data on the client side, while computationally intensive homomorphic operations are offloaded to the server. Figure 2 provides a high-level architecture of our proposed solution, considering a single client for illustration purposes. As shown, the proposed system involves three main entities: the *Third-Party Authority* (TPA), the *Server*, and the *Clients*. The TPA is an independent trusted authority responsible for generating and distributing all cryptographic keys. The *Server* is responsible for coordinating the FL training process, collecting encrypted updates from *Clients*, performing secure aggregation, and distributing the updated global model. Finally, the *Clients* train their local model, encrypt their local updates and symmetric key, send them to the *Server*, and decrypt the received global model. In the following subsection, a detailed description of the operational workflow of our system is provided.

4.1 Workflow of the Proposed Solution

In Fig. 3, we illustrate the complete workflow of our proposed solution, which is comprised of five main phases: *Setup*, *Client Training*, *Server Aggregation*, *Client Evaluation*, and *Server Evaluation*. In what follows, we describe all these phases.

Setup Phase. In this phase, which occurs once at the beginning of our protocol, the TPA generates and distributes the necessary cryptographic keys to the clients and server. This includes a single tuple of homomorphic keys, (*HE_pk*, *HE_sk*, *HE_eval*), where *HE_pk* is the homomorphic public key, *HE_sk* is the homomorphic secret key, and *HE_eval* is the homomorphic evaluation key. Additionally, the TPA generates a unique symmetric key sk_i for each client i, where $1 \leq i \leq N$ and N denotes the total number of clients in the system. The TPA then sends (HE_pk, HE_eval) to the server, and (HE_pk, HE_sk, sk_i) to each client i. The server initializes a model and sends its weights to the clients, who use them as the starting point for local training during the training phase.

Client Training Phase. The *Client Training Phase* begins after the *Setup Phase* in the first round, with clients receiving the global model weights in plaintext. In subsequent rounds, it follows the *Server Evaluation Phase*, where clients first decrypt the received encrypted global weights using their HE private key, HE_sk. Each client then trains its local model with the received weights, encrypts the update weights w_i with sk_i, and encrypts sk_i with HE_pk. The

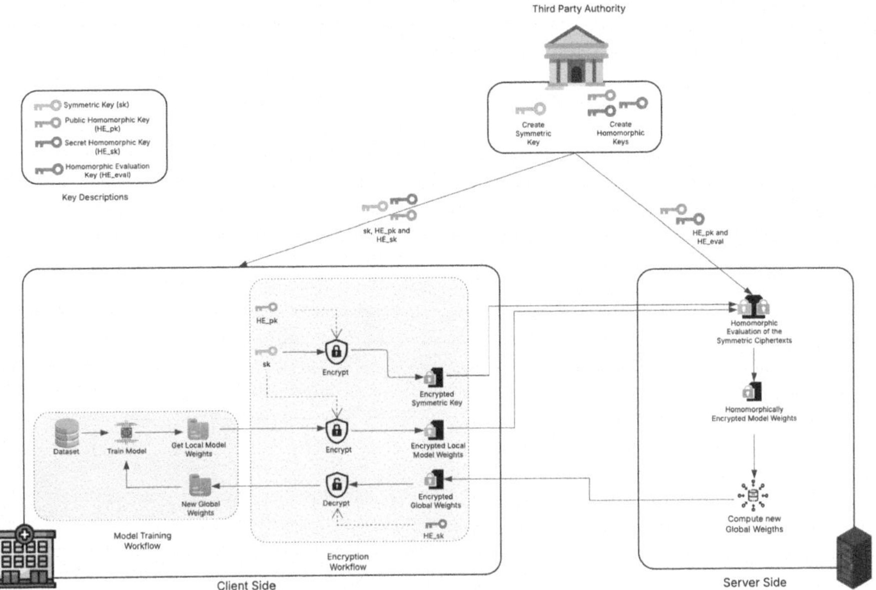

Fig. 2. FL Architecture with HHE

resulting ciphertexts w^i_{SKE} and sk^i_{HE}, together with the number of training samples $n_i = training\_data_i/batch\_size$, are sent to the server for aggregation.

Server Aggregation Phase. The *Server Aggregation Phase* occurs after every *Client Training Phase* in each round of the FL process. During this phase, the server receives the w_{SKE} along with the corresponding homomorphically encrypted secret key sk_{HE} from the selected clients. The server then applies HESD on each w_{SKE}, using the associated sk_{HE}. Once all updates are transformed, the server aggregates the homomorphic ciphertexts to compute the new global model weights. In the current implementation, any client that drops out during the *Client Training Phase* is excluded from the aggregation for that round but may participate in subsequent rounds. Finally, the server selects a new subset of clients and sends them the updated model for evaluation.

Client Evaluation Phase. This phase follows the *Server Aggregation Phase* in each round of the FL process. Selected clients receive the newly aggregated global weights and decrypt them using *HE_sk*. They update their local models with these weights and evaluate them on their local test dataset. Each client then sends the resulting accuracy and loss metrics to the server, along with the number of test samples.

Server Evaluation Phase. The *Server Evaluation Phase* occurs after the *Client Evaluation Phase* and concludes each round of the federated process. Upon receiving evaluation metrics from all clients, the server aggregates these metrics using a chosen aggregation algorithm. If additional training rounds remain, the server selects a new subset of clients for the upcoming *Client Training Phase* and distributes the updated global weights accordingly.

All phases, except setup, are repeated for a fixed number of rounds.

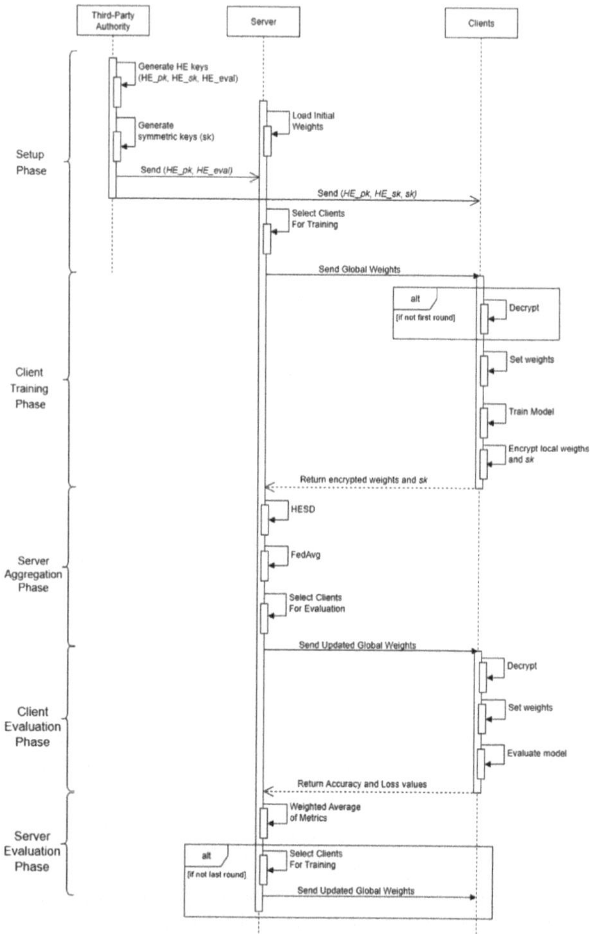

Fig. 3. Workflow of the proposed solution

4.2 Threat Model

The security of the proposed solution is based on the following assumptions about the system setup and participants: *A.1. The Setup Phase is trusted*: all cryptographic keys and the initial global weights are generated and distributed securely, with no adversarial interference; *A.2. All clients are honest*: meaning they execute the protocol faithfully without attempting attacks; *A.3. The server is honest-but-curious*: it correctly executes the protocol but may attempt to infer private information; *A.4. No collusion occurs between the server and clients; A.5. External adversaries may attempt to infer information from participating clients but are unable to disrupt message transmission or inject poisoned data.*

Under these assumptions, the system provides the following security guarantees: *SP.1. Confidentiality of individual client updates during transmission*; *SP.2. Confidentiality of individual client updates during aggregation on the serve*; *SP.3. Confidentiality of the aggregated model weights.*

SP.1 is ensured by client-side encryption. Each client encrypts its local model update with their symmetric key *sk*, and *sk* is then encrypted using the HE_pk. Therefore, the transmitted data remains confidential, preventing any eavesdropper from gaining access to the plaintext, even if they can observe the communication channel. The server, upon receiving the encrypted client updates, performs HESD to generate the homomorphic ciphertexts used for the aggregation process. Since the updates remain encrypted throughout the process, and the server does not possess the HE_sk, it never has access to the plaintext of any individual client update, thereby ensuring *SP.2.* Since aggregation is performed over homomorphic ciphertexts, the resulting aggregated model weights also remain encrypted. As the server does not possess the HE_sk, it is unable to decrypt this aggregated result, thereby ensuring *SP.3.* The framework provides no protection against malicious clients who may perform poisoning or inference attacks. A single malicious client could compromise confidentiality, as it could exploit access to the shared HE_sk to decrypt the *sk* of an honest client, which is then used to decrypt that client's encrypted local update. Likewise, a malicious TPA, if introduced, could further endanger confidentiality by leaking HE_sk to any malicious entity or disrupt the whole protocol by mismanaging key distribution.

5 Prototype Implementation

This section presents the prototype implementation of our solution. Figure 4 illustrates its overall architecture, in which two layers can be distinguished: the *Cryptographic Layer* and the *Flower Layer.* Recall that our implementation focuses on *cross-device* FL scenarios in which resource-constrained clients must encrypt their model updates with minimal overhead, while a well-provisioned server performs the heavy homomorphic computations. More specifically, we combine the PASTA stream cipher for SE, the BFV FHE scheme for server-side processing, and the Flower FL framework for client-server orchestration, extended with a `C++` backend exposed to Python through `pybind11`[3]. In what follows, we first detail each of the layers represented in Fig. 4, then describe the processing that occurs on the server side, followed by the processing on the client side.

Cryptographic Layer. Our choice of an HE-friendly SE scheme suitable for scenarios involving resource-constrained clients fell on PASTA [10] because its design enables low multiplicative depth and efficient homomorphic evaluation.

[3] https://github.com/pybind/pybind11.

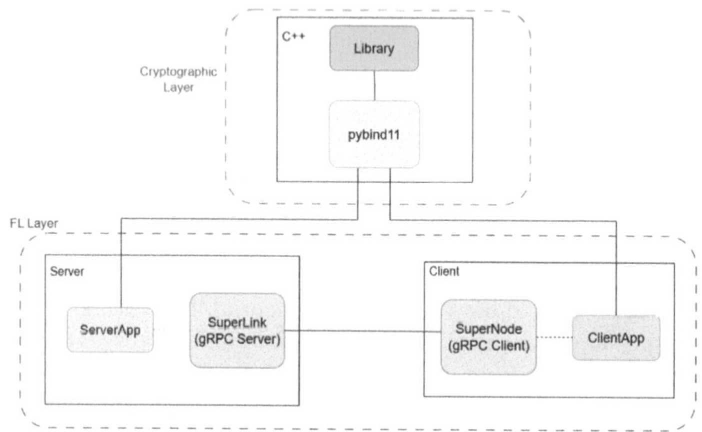

Fig. 4. Prototype Implementation Architecture.

We paired it with BFV, which when compared to BGV, offers slightly simpler initial parameter selection as well as more straightforward implementation of common operations, such as encoding and noise management. It also allows integer plaintexts that align well with PASTA's design. PASTA was integrated in our prototype using the authors' open-source `C++` framework[4], which also provides wrapper classes for BFV via Microsoft SEAL.

FL Layer. Several FL frameworks were analyzed and compared based on learning modes, privacy-preserving mechanisms, encryption support, and scalability. Flower, proposed by Beutel et al. [4], was selected for its high customizability, scalability, cloud compatibility, and the availability of a HE integration by Catalfamo et al. [6]. Since Flower is Python-based and the PASTA/BFV stack is implemented in `C++`, we expose the `C++` API via `pybind11`. In Flower, the server consists of two main components: the `SuperLink`, which handles client communication via gRPC, and the `ServerApp`, which contains the orchestration logic for training, aggregation, and evaluation. On the client side, the `SuperNode` manages communication, while the `ClientApp` handles local training and evaluation. To support cryptographic operations, both the `ServerApp` and `ClientApp` are connected to a shared `C++` layer. This layer consists of a `pybind11 bridge`, which exposes `C++` functions to Python, and the framework used for PASTA.

Server-Side Processing. The server-side processing consists of two main steps: the HESD operations and federated averaging of the model updates. Algorithm 1 shows the chunk-based HESD procedure: each chunk of the symmetrically encrypted weights is converted into a BFV ciphertext before aggregation. After HESD, FedAvg multiplies each weight vector by the client's sample count n_k and sums the results homomorphically. Division by the global total n is deferred to the clients, because BFV does not support exact division in ciphertext space.

[4] https://github.com/isec-tugraz/hybrid-HE-framework.

Algorithm 1. Chunk-Based HESD for a Single Client

Require: Client's encrypted symmetric parameters w_{SKE}, Client's encrypted symmetric key sk_{HE}, BFV cipher instance BFV_cipher

```
Switch to client's encrypted key
   BFV_CIPHER.SET_ENCRYPTED_KEY(sk_HE)
Initialize list for the homomorphically encrypted parameters:
   he_params ← empty list
for each chunk in w_SKE do
    he_chunk ← BFV_cipher.HESD(chunk)
    Append he_chunk to he_params
end for
return he_params
```

Client-Side Processing. On each device, the processing begins by the quantization procedure and encrypting local model updates with PASTA. It ends by decrypting and applying the dequantization method to the aggregated global model. To encrypt model parameters with PASTA, float32 values in $[-\alpha, \alpha]$ are converted to int8 values in $[-2^{b-1}, 2^{b-1}-1]$ using scale quantization, as described by Lang et al. [21], by clipping each $x \in w_i$ and applying

$$quantized\_x = round\left(x * \frac{2^{b-1}}{\alpha}\right)$$

with $b = 8$ for int8 precision. Since PASTA requires unsigned 64-bit inputs, the quantized int8 values are converted to uint64 before chunk-based encryption, as detailed in Algorithm 2. Upon receiving the aggregated ciphertexts, each client decrypts the received global weights in chunks using HE_sk. The decrypted uint64 values are converted to signed 64-bit integers (int64), restoring negative values by subtracting the modulus from any value greater than half the *modulus*. Clients then apply the averaging step from FedAvg by dividing the aggregated parameters by n in float32 for accuracy. Finally, the results are dequantized by dividing by the quantization scale used during encryption (see Algorithm 3).

Algorithm 2. Quantize and Encrypt Local Model Weights

Require: Model Weights w_i (list of float32 arrays), Clipping Bound α, Chunk Size chunk_size, PASTA cipher instance pasta_cipher

```
Flatten all parameters into a single vector:
   flat_params ← concatenate(flatten(layer) for layer in w_i)
Clip each value x in flat_params to [−α, α]:
   clipped ← clip(flat_params, −α, α)
Define scale factor for int8 quantization:
   scale_factor ← (2^(8−1) − 1)/α = 127/α
Quantize each clipped value:
   quantized_int8 ← round(clipped × scale_factor)
Convert quantized values to unsigned 64-bit integers:
   quantized_uint64 ← convert_to_uint64(quantized_int8)
Initialize list for encrypted chunks:
   list_sym_ciphertext ← empty list
for i = 0 to length(quantized_uint64) step chunk_size do
    chunk ← quantized_uint64[i : i + chunk_size]
    encrypted_chunk ← pasta_cipher.encrypt(chunk)
    Append encrypted_chunk to list_sym_ciphertext
end for
return list_sym_ciphertext
```

6 Experimental Evaluation and Analysis

In this section, we present and analyze the results of our experimental evaluation of the proposed HHE-based FL architecture. We compare three setups using the MNIST dataset: a plaintext FL architecture, HHE-based FL combining PASTA and BFV, and FL using only BFV. In the two latter setups, clients share the same homomorphic keys. During training, accuracy, loss, communication, and computation costs are measured. Communication cost is defined as the total volume of data transmitted, while computation cost is the average CPU time required to perform an operation. The final model is evaluated using additional metrics such as precision, recall, and F1-score.

Algorithm 3. Decrypt and Dequantize Global Weights

Require: Encrypted Global Weights w_{HE}, Decryption Key HE_sk, Total Number of Examples n, Clipping Bound α, Chunk Size `chunk_size`, Modulus `modulus` , BFV cipher instance `BFV_cipher`

Initialize list for decrypted chunks:
  `decrypted_chunks` ← empty
for each `chunk` in w_{HE} **do**
  c ← `BFV_CIPHER.DECRYPT(chunk,` HE_sk`)`
  Append c to `decrypted_chunks`
end for
Concatenate all chunks into one vector:
  `uint64_params` ← concatenate(`decrypted_chunks`)
Convert to int64:
  `int64_params` ← convert_to_int64(`uint64_params`)
for each x in `int64_params` **do**
  if $x >$ `modulus//2` **then**
    $x \leftarrow x -$ `modulus`
  end if
end for
Compute average:
  `float_params` ← `int64_params` $\div\ n$
Define scale factor for dequantization:
  `scale_factor` ← $\frac{2^{8-1}-1}{\alpha} = \frac{127}{\alpha}$
Dequantize new global parameters:
  `decrypted_params` ← `float_params` ÷ `scale_factor`
return `decrypted_params`

6.1 Experimental Setup

All the schemes were developed in Flower. The BFV-based FL architecture was implemented with the TenSEAL library, developed by Benaissa et al. [3], while the HHE prototype uses the C++ backend described in Sect. 5. All the experiments were run on Google Colab's T4 High-RAM environment, which provided an NVIDIA T4 GPU, 51GB of system RAM, and 15GB of GPU memory.

The MNIST dataset, consisting of 70000 grayscale images of handwritten digits (28×28 pixels), was used, with 60000 samples for training and 10000 for testing. The training data was partitioned into N client datasets in an IID manner using Flower's `IidPartitioner`. Each local dataset was then split into 80%

for training and 20% for testing. Additionally, 20% of each local training set was reserved for validation to enable early stopping during training rounds.

A Convolutional Neural Network (CNN) based on the implementation by Gaurav Sharma [33] was adopted for our experiments. It contains two convolutional layers, each followed by LeakyReLU activations and batch normalization. Max-pooling layers were used after each convolution for spatial downsampling. The resulting feature maps are flattened and sent through a dropout layer before the final dense layer generates predictions for 10 classes. The model contains approximately 8000 trainable parameters.

6.2 Parameter Constraints and Configurations

The HHE scheme used in this work operates over $\mathbb{Z}_q$ with $q = 2^{16}+1$, requiring all server-side computations to remain within $[0, 2^{16}+1[$. This bounds the product of the quantized model weights, the number of training clients, and the number of batches per client to be less than $2^{16}+1$. Given int8 quantization, this can be expressed as $2^8 \times 2^{x_1} \times 2^{x_2} < 2^{16}+1$. Thus, valid configurations must satisfy $2^{x_1+x_2} \leq 2^8$, where x_1 is the number of batches per client and x_2 the number of training clients. Only configurations estimated to complete within Colab's 24-hour limit, based on per-round benchmarks, were executed.

Chosen Configuration. Based on the constraints described before, our configuration consisted of 12 clients, each with 63 training batches, where 4 were used for training and 12 for evaluation, over 10 federated rounds. Table 1 lists all parameters used in the experiment. The value for α was chosen based on empirical observations of the model's typical output range across several runs.

Table 1. Parameters used for the FL experiment

Config. Name	Value	Config. Name	Value
Clients	12	Rounds	10
Epochs	10	Classifier	CNN
Loss function	Categorical Cross-entropy	Batch size	64
Optimizer	Nadam	Learning Rate	0.001
Clients per Training Phase	4	Clients per Evaluation Phase	12
Clip Range (α)	5	Key size	256 bits
Plaintext size	128 bits	Ciphertext size	128 bits
Plaintext Modulus	65537	Polynomial Degree Modulus	16384
Security level	128-bit		

6.3 Experimental Results and Analysis

Regarding the models performance, Fig. 5 shows accuracy and loss over 10 rounds. It can be seen that the baseline plaintext FL converges to 98.93% accuracy, BFV reaches 98.04%, and HHE attains 97.6%, a less than 1.5% drop attributable to quantization and HESD noise. Final precision, recall, and F1 in Table 2 corroborate that the HHE-FL approach preserves model performance.

Table 2. Global Model Comparisons

	Accuracy(%)	Loss	Precision(%)	Recall(%)	F1-score(%)
FL without encryption	99.00	0.0360	99.00	99.00	99.00
PASTA+BFV Scheme	97.39	0.0962	97.50	97.39	97.39
BFV Scheme	98.21	0.0702	98.23	98.21	98.21

The communication cost (Fig. 6a), measured has the amount of data sent between a single client and the server, shows that BFV results in over 2000× higher upload cost compared to the proposed PASTA+BFV scheme, highlighting the benefit of using an hybrid approach and a cipher like PASTA. Figure 6b shows that the amount of data sent from the server to each client is identical for both approaches. Notice that both rely on BFV on the server side. Overall, the PASTA+BFV scheme cuts total communication cost in half when compared to pure BFV, showing the improvement HHE brings in communication overhead.

Regarding computation cost, Fig. 7a shows that using PASTA speeds up encryption and decryption by about 9.7× and 6.9×, respectively. Training, taking ~10.7 s, dominates runtime and is identical across schemes since it runs in plaintext. Overall, PASTA+BFV's total client runtime is ~12.5 s, about 1.4× faster than BFV's ~18 s, indicating that HHE offers a more efficient client-side solution than pure HE for resource-constrained IoT environments.

Although client-side computation differs by only 1.4×, server-side results show a larger gap. Figure 7b shows that server aggregation is significantly slower in the PASTA+BFV scheme, in part due to the high cost of homomorphic evaluation. Specifically, HESD for one client with 8000 parameters takes 1451 s, making the PASTA+BFV server with 4 clients about 62478× slower than the BFV server for a single aggregation phase. These high runtimes are also impacted by the limitations of Google Colab, which runs on an Intel Xeon CPU @ 2.20GHz. In this environment, operations such as HESD were observed to be around 1.7× slower than on our local machine (Intel Core i7-11370H, 16GB RAM). In better environments, further time reductions are more likely to occur.

An analysis on how this cost scales with model size (Fig. 8) shows that the HESD time grows linearly with the number of parameters due to chunk-based processing and padding. If T_{chunk} is the time per chunk and N_{chunks} the total chunks, the total HESD time can be estimated as $T_{\text{HESD}} = T_{\text{chunk}} \times N_{\text{chunks}}$. During experiments, the BFV scheme experienced out-of-memory (OOM) failures

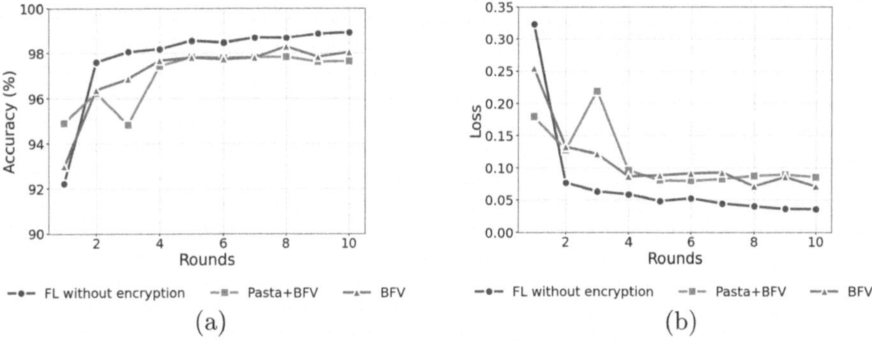

Fig. 5. Training Performance Across Rounds: (a) Accuracy; (b) Loss

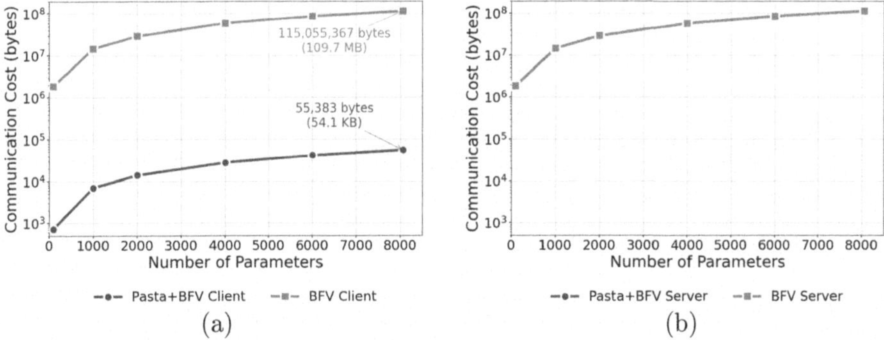

Fig. 6. Communication cost comparison (values are shown on a logarithmic scale due to differences in magnitude): (a) From a single client to the server; (b) From the server to each client

starting at round 3, causing clients to drop out of training. These were due to Flower's task manager, Ray, terminating processes when memory usage reached ∼48.5GB of 51GB (95%). In contrast, the PASTA+BFV scheme completed all rounds without memory issues, demonstrating the memory-efficiency of HHE.

Operation	PASTA+BFV	BFV
Encryption (s)	0.32867	3.18009
Decryption (s)	0.42206	2.90076
Training (s)	10.70805	10.70805
Evaluation (s)	1.07516	1.07516
Total runtime (s)	12.53394	17.86406

(a)

Operation	PASTA+BFV	BFV
Aggregation (s)	0.2174	0.0929
HESD per client (s)	1451.0	-
HESD per round (h)	1.6122	-
Total runtime (s)	5804.2174	0.0929

(b)

Fig. 7. Average Computation Cost: (a) Client; (b) Server Aggregation Phase

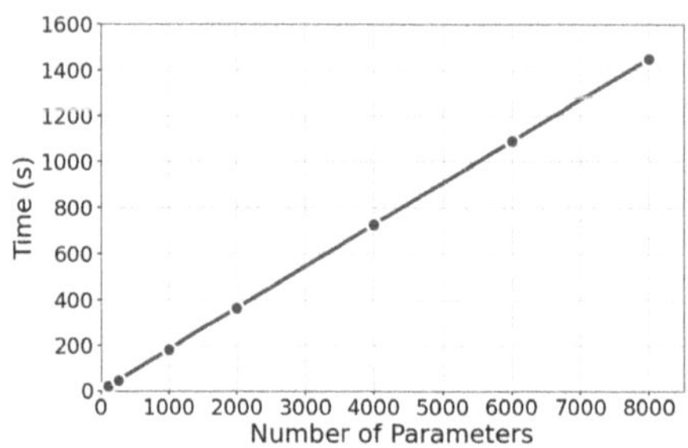

Fig. 8. Runtime Overhead of HESD with Increasing Parameters

7 Conclusion

This work introduces the first HHE framework for FL that addresses privacy challenges in resource-constrained environments. By combining PASTA, a symmetric cipher, with BFV, a FHE scheme, the proposed architecture significantly reduces both client-side computation overhead and communication cost. Our experimental results showed that our hybrid approach maintains model performance when compared to a FHE approach while reducing client communication cost by 2000× and improving encryption and decryption speed by almost 10×. However, it increases server-side computation cost by 15621× per client during the aggregation phase, due to the cost of the homomorphic evaluation of the PASTA decryption circuit and the limitations of Google Colab. Additionally, since BFV lacks real-number division, clients had to perform weighted averaging locally, posing a potential privacy issue.

Future work should aim to overcome current limitations. The addition of parallelization could help mitigate the server-side computational overhead. This parallelization could be applied at two levels: processing multiple clients concurrently, or processing the chunks of ciphertext within each client in parallel. Designing HE-friendly ciphers with multi-key support would improve security against collusion attacks, and implementing dropout-resilient mechanisms, such as secret sharing, would improve robustness during training and even help against poisoning attacks.

Acknowledgments. This work has been supported by the PC2phish project, which has received funding from FCT with Refª: 2024.07648.IACDC. Furthermore, this work also received funding from the project UIDB/00760/2020.

References

1. Abdinasibfar, H., Nuoskala, C., Michalas, A.: The HHE land: exploring the landscape of hybrid homomorphic encryption. Cryptology ePrint Archive, Paper 2025/071 (2025). https://eprint.iacr.org/2025/071
2. Aledhari, M., Razzak, R., Parizi, R.M., Saeed, F.: Federated learning: a survey on enabling technologies, protocols, and applications. IEEE Access **8**, 140699–140725 (2020). https://doi.org/10.1109/ACCESS.2020.3013541
3. Benaissa, A., Retiat, B., Cebere, B., Belfedhal, A.E.: TenSEAL: a library for encrypted tensor operations using homomorphic encryption (2021). https://doi.org/10.48550/arXiv.2104.03152
4. Beutel, D.J., et al.: Flower: a friendly federated learning research framework (2022). https://doi.org/10.48550/arXiv.2007.14390
5. Brakerski, Z., Gentry, C., Vaikuntanathan, V.: Fully homomorphic encryption without bootstrapping. Cryptology ePrint Archive, Paper 2011/277 (2011). https://eprint.iacr.org/2011/277
6. Catalfamo, A., Carnevale, L., Garofalo, M., Villari, M.: Flower full-compliant implementation of federated learning with homomorphic encryption. In: 2024 IEEE Symposium on Computers and Communications (ISCC), pp. 1–5 (2024). https://doi.org/10.1109/ISCC61673.2024.10733641
7. Cheon, J.H., Kim, A., Kim, M., Song, Y.: Homomorphic encryption for arithmetic of approximate numbers. In: Takagi, T., Peyrin, T. (eds.) ASIACRYPT 2017. LNCS, vol. 10624, pp. 409–437. Springer, Cham (2017). https://doi.org/10.1007/978-3-319-70694-8_15
8. Chillotti, I., Gama, N., Georgieva, M., Izabachène, M.: TFHE: fast fully homomorphic encryption over the torus. J. Cryptology **33**(1), 34–91 (2020). https://doi.org/10.1007/s00145-019-09319-x
9. Dobraunig, C., et al.: Rasta: a cipher with low ANDdepth and few ANDs per bit. In: Shacham, H., Boldyreva, A. (eds.) CRYPTO 2018. LNCS, vol. 10991, pp. 662–692. Springer, Cham (2018). https://doi.org/10.1007/978-3-319-96884-1_22
10. Dobraunig, C., Grassi, L., Helminger, L., Rechberger, C., Schofnegger, M., Walch, R.: Pasta: a case for hybrid homomorphic encryption. Cryptology ePrint Archive, Paper 2021/731 (2021). https://eprint.iacr.org/2021/731
11. Dowlin, N., Gilad-Bachrach, R., Laine, K., Lauter, K., Naehrig, M., Wernsing, J.: Manual for using homomorphic encryption for bioinformatics. In: Proceedings of the IEEE pp. 1–16 (2017). https://doi.org/10.1109/JPROC.2016.2622218
12. Duy, P.T., Quyen, N.H., Khoa, N.H., Tran, T.D., Pham, V.H.: FedChain-hunter: a reliable and privacy-preserving aggregation for federated threat hunting framework in SDN-based IIoT. Internet Things **24**, 100966 (2023). https://doi.org/10.1016/j.iot.2023.100966
13. Fan, J., Vercauteren, F.: Somewhat practical fully homomorphic encryption. Cryptology ePrint Archive, Paper 2012/144 (2012). https://eprint.iacr.org/2012/144
14. Fontenla-Romero, O., et al.: FedHEONN: federated and homomorphically encrypted learning method for one-layer neural networks. Fut. Gener. Comput. Syst. **149**, 200–211 (2023). https://doi.org/10.1016/j.future.2023.07.018

15. Gentry, C.: Fully homomorphic encryption using ideal lattices. In: Proceedings of the 41st Annual ACM Symposium on Theory of Computing, STOC '09, pp. 169–178. Association for Computing Machinery, New York (2009). https://doi.org/10.1145/1536414.1536440
16. Halevi, S., Shoup, V.: Design and implementation of HElib: a homomorphic encryption library. Cryptology ePrint Archive, Paper 2020/1481 (2020). https://eprint.iacr.org/2020/1481
17. Hebborn, P., Leander, G.: Dasta – alternative linear layer for Rasta. IACR Trans. Symmetric Cryptol. **2020**(3), 46–86 (2020). https://doi.org/10.13154/tosc.v2020.i3.46-86
18. Hijazi, N.M., Aloqaily, M., Guizani, M.: Collaborative IoTlearning with secure peer-to-peer federated approach. Comput. Commun. **228**, 107948 (2024). https://doi.org/10.1016/j.comcom.2024.107948
19. Jin, W., et al.: FedML-HE: an efficient homomorphic-encryption-based privacy-preserving federated learning system. In: International Workshop on Federated Learning in the Age of Foundation Models in Conjunction with NeurIPS 2023 (2023). https://openreview.net/forum?id=PuYD0fh5aq
20. Kairouz, P., McMahan, H.B., et al.: Advances and open problems in federated learning (2021). https://doi.org/10.48550/arXiv.1912.04977
21. Lang, J., Guo, Z., Huang, S.: A comprehensive study on quantization techniques for large language models (2024). https://doi.org/10.48550/arXiv.2411.02530
22. Li, Q., Yu, W., Xia, Y., Pang, J.: From centralized to decentralized federated learning: theoretical insights, privacy preservation, and robustness challenges (2025). https://doi.org/10.48550/arXiv.2503.07505
23. Ma, J., Naas, S.A., Sigg, S., Lyu, X.: Privacy-preserving federated learning based on multi-key homomorphic encryption. Int. J. Intell. Syst. **37**(9), 5880–5901 (2022). https://doi.org/10.1002/int.22818
24. Majeed, U., Hassan, S.S., Hong, C.S.: Cross-silo model-based secure federated transfer learning for flow-based traffic classification. In: 2021 International Conference on Information Networking (ICOIN), pp. 588–593. IEEE, Jeju Island (2021). https://doi.org/10.1109/ICOIN50884.2021.9333905
25. Marcolla, C., Sucasas, V., Manzano, M., Bassoli, R., Fitzek, F.H.P., Aaraj, N.: Survey on fully homomorphic encryption, theory, and applications. Proc. IEEE **110**(10), 1572–1609 (2022). https://doi.org/10.1109/JPROC.2022.3205665
26. McMahan, B., Moore, E., Ramage, D., Hampson, S., y Arcas, B.A.: Communication-efficient learning of deep networks from decentralized data (2023). https://arxiv.org/abs/1602.05629
27. Naehrig, M., Lauter, K., Vaikuntanathan, V.: Can homomorphic encryption be practical? In: Proceedings of the 3rd ACM Workshop on Cloud Computing Security Workshop, CCSW '11, pp. 113–124. Association for Computing Machinery, New York (2011). https://doi.org/10.1145/2046660.2046682
28. Niu, J., Liu, P., et al.: A survey on membership inference attacks and defenses in machine learning. J. Inf. Intell. **2**(5), 404–454 (2024). https://doi.org/10.1016/j.jiixd.2024.02.001
29. Ovi, P.R., Gangopadhyay, A.: A comprehensive study of gradient inversion attacks in federated learning and baseline defense strategies. In: 2023 57th Annual Conference on Information Sciences and Systems (CISS), pp. 1–6 (2023). https://doi.org/10.1109/CISS56502.2023.10089719
30. Qian, J., Wei, K., Wu, Y., Zhang, J., Chen, J., Bao, H.: GI-SMN: gradient inversion attack against federated learning without prior knowledge. In: Huang, D.S.,

Chen, W., Pan, Y. (eds.) Advanced Intelligent Computing Technology and Applications, pp. 439–448. Springer Nature Singapore, Singapore (2024). https://doi.org/10.1007/978-981-97-5603-2_36

31. Rabieinejad, E., Yazdinejad, A., Dehghantanha, A., Srivastava, G.: Two-level privacy-preserving framework: federated learning for attack detection in the consumer internet of things. IEEE Trans. Consum. Electron. **70**(1), 4258–4265 (2024). https://doi.org/10.1109/TCE.2024.3349490
32. Sathya, S.S., Vepakomma, P., Raskar, R., Ramachandra, R., Bhattacharya, S.: A review of homomorphic encryption libraries for secure computation (2018). https://doi.org/10.48550/arXiv.1812.02428
33. Sharma, G.: MNIST CNN with 8K parameters (2020). https://www.kaggle.com/code/gauravsharma99/mnist-8k-parameters. Accessed 11 June 2025
34. Song, C., Wang, Z., Peng, W., Yang, N.: Secure and efficient federated learning schemes for healthcare systems. Electronics **13**(13), 2620 (2024). https://doi.org/10.3390/electronics13132620
35. Stan, O., Thouvenot, V., Boudguiga, A., Kapusta, K., Zuber, M., Sirdey, R.: A secure federated learning: analysis of different cryptographic tools. In: SECRYPT 2022 - 19th International Conference on Security and Cryptography, vol. 1, p. 669 (2022). https://doi.org/10.5220/0011322700003283
36. Tan, Z.S., See-To, E.W., Lee, K.Y., Dai, H.N., Wong, M.L.: Privacy-preserving federated learning for proactive maintenance of IoT-empowered multi-location smart city facilities. J. Netw. Comput. Appl. **231**, 103996 (2024). https://doi.org/10.1016/j.jnca.2024.103996
37. Wang, J., Yang, K., Li, M.: NIDS-FGPA: a federated learning network intrusion detection algorithm based on secure aggregation of gradient similarity models. PLOS One **19** (2024). https://doi.org/10.1371/journal.pone.0308639
38. Xu, Y., Mao, Y., Li, J., Chen, X., Wu, S.: Edge server enhanced secure and privacy preserving federated learning. Comput. Netw. **249**, 110465 (2024). https://doi.org/10.1016/j.comnet.2024.110465
39. Yu, S., Cui, L.: Inference attacks and counterattacks in federated learning, pp. 13–36. Springer Nature Singapore, Singapore (2023). https://doi.org/10.1007/978-981-19-8692-5
40. Zhang, L., Xu, J., Vijayakumar, P., Sharma, P.K., Ghosh, U.: Homomorphic encryption-based privacy-preserving federated learning in IoT-enabled healthcare system. IEEE Trans. Netw. Sci. Eng. **10**(5), 2864–2880 (2023). https://doi.org/10.1109/TNSE.2022.3185327
41. Zhang, M., Chen, S., Shen, J., Susilo, W.: PrivacyEAFL: privacy-enhanced aggregation for federated learning in mobile crowdsensing. IEEE Trans. Inf. Forensics Secur. **18**, 5804–5816 (2023). https://doi.org/10.1109/TIFS.2023.3315526
42. Zhang, Y., Zhang, W., Shen, C.: A fault-tolerant federated learning scheme based on multi-key homomorphic encryption. In: Proceedings of the 2024 International Academic Conference on Edge Computing, Parallel and Distributed Computing, ECPDC '24, pp. 96–101. Association for Computing Machinery, New York (2024). https://doi.org/10.1145/3677404.3677421

International Workshop on Computational Methods for Emerging Problems in Disinformation Analysis (DisA 2025)

Protecting Society from Fake Advertisement Campaigns: Innovative Graph Based Analysis and Approach

Ewelina Bartuzi-Trokielewicz[1], Alicja Martinek[1,2(✉)], Rafał Kozik[3,4], and Michał Choraś[3,4]

[1] NASK - National Research Institute, Warsaw, Poland
alicja.martinek@nask.pl
[2] AGH University of Kraków, Cracow, Poland
[3] IDEAS Research Institute, Warsaw, Warsaw, Poland
chorasm@pbs.edu.pl
[4] Bydgoszcz University of Science and Technology, Bydgoszcz, Poland

Abstract. Recently, well-prepared and well-crafted fake advertisement campaigns are targeting citizens of the EU as another installment of cyber-crime. Professional criminal groups are mainly targeting young or elderly users of the Internet to steal money or their data, and also deploying malware at their devices. Therefore, to counter such criminal activity, in this paper we propose graph-based approach to analyze and visualize dangerous content. The major contribution of this work is collection of dataset with transcripts of fake campaigns from recent months, and graph-based methods to analyze those criminal campaigns targeted at societies. Experimental results show that the proposed approach enables automated analysis of unstructured text and supports threat intelligence workflows.

Keywords: disinformation · fake advertisements · cyber-crime · graph based analysis

1 Introduction and Context

In recent years, online scams and fraudulent advertisements have reached epidemic proportions, leading to massive financial losses and undermining trust in digital media. According to the U.S. Federal Trade Commission (FTC), consumer-reported fraud losses surged by 125% in 2024 alone [4]. Similarly, the European financial sector has seen a steep rise in fraud-related damages [12]. Increasingly, cybercriminals leverage generative AI to produce highly convincing multimedia including voice cloning, deepfake videos, and click-bait visuals, enabling scalable and psychologically persuasive scam campaigns.

This shift marks a transition from technical to social engineering attacks, where manipulative language, urgency, fear, and authority are exploited to deceive users. In 2025, Spanish authorities dismantled a fraud network that algorithmically targeted victims using AI-generated ads impersonating public

R. Laborde et al. (Eds.): ESORICS 2025 Workshops, LNCS 16233, pp. 277–294, 2026.
https://doi.org/10.1007/978-3-032-16165-9_16

figures [2]. Such cases illustrate that even low-effort, low-fidelity deepfakes can be effective at scale, especially when deployed across social media ecosystems.

What makes these campaigns particularly dangerous is their ability to tailor content to different demographic profiles. Older adults are disproportionately affected by schemes involving false lotteries or investment frauds, while younger users are more susceptible to emotionally charged or reward-driven scams [16] [3]. As disinformation campaigns diversify in format and audience, there is a growing need for tools capable of both linguistic and structural analysis of scam content.

To address this need, researchers have begun employing natural language processing techniques to detect persuasion tactics in scam messages. Studies show that large language models (LLMs), such as GPT-3.5 and GPT-4, are capable of identifying phishing indicators and manipulative language patterns [6]. However, while LLMs excel at content analysis, they do not account for the networked structure of real-world campaigns. Graph-based methods, on the other hand, are increasingly used to visualize relationships between actors, messages, and platforms involved in fraudulent activities. Community detection algorithms and anomaly detection techniques help uncover clusters of coordinated behavior that may go unnoticed in linear analysis.

Recent initiatives, such as PsyScam [7], combine these approaches by building psychologically annotated datasets of real scam reports. They demonstrate that linguistic manipulation is often consistent and learnable, yet fragmented across many data modalities. The concept of deepfakes detection through analysis of social engineering techniques is also present in [11] that used human annotators for manipulation classification and in [9] that leveraged LLMs in the same task. This motivates the development of hybrid systems that integrate semantic analysis with graph modeling to capture both the message and its context.

In this paper, we propose a novel method that combines LLM-based semantic extraction with graph-based document analysis to uncover structure and patterns in transcripts of scam advertisements. Unlike prior studies focused on emails or static web content, our approach processes real-world transcripts of audiovisual scam materials and analyzes both their textual features and relational layout. This enables the identification of topics, trends, and community structures in large volumes of unstructured, manipulative content.

We apply our method to a unique Polish-language dataset collected over a one-year period, encompassing verified deepfake scams disseminated via online platforms. Our experiments show that LLM-generated summaries yield more coherent and discriminative clusters than raw transcripts or factual extractions. Moreover, visual and quantitative evaluations confirm our system's effectiveness in separating real from fake content and identifying semantically cohesive topic clusters. The main contributions of this work are as follows:

- a unique collection of the real scam advertisement transcripts - it is a first dataset with such data collected in Poland,

- methodology that combines LLM-based summarization and semantic embeddings with dimensionality reduction and community detection,
- pipeline for interactive topic graph generation, including cluster simplification and automatic labeling,
- a comprehensive experimental evaluation, including clustering metrics, thematic diversity, and analysis of semantic polarization between real and fake content.

2 Fake Advertisements Campaigns from the Recent Past

In this Section, we provide examples of real fake advertisements from the past. We focus on those who targeted and troubled youth and elderly users of Internet platforms.

2.1 Real Recent Campaign: Casinos and Apps in TikTok-Style Targeting the Youth

A significant proportion of analyzed fake advertisement campaigns target young audiences, particularly through dynamic, short-form video content that mimics the style of so-called "reels" popular on platforms such as Facebook, TikTok, Instagram, and YouTube. These videos commonly promote fraudulent investment platforms, online gambling apps, casinos, and fictitious or highly risky financial products disguised as popular mobile games or applications.

The advertisements typically last between 20 to 40 s and follow a fast-paced narrative style, employing rapid cuts, striking slogans like *"Install now and earn 400 EUR a day!"*, and rely on scripted dialogues that simulate authentic, spontaneous conversations, often mimicking the language of everyday social media interactions.

The narratives are deliberately fragmented, loosely structured, and rich in slang or calculations (*"five thousand, two hundred and five thousand, thirty-five thousand, about forty thousand euros"*), creating a chaotic but engaging rhythm, suggesting abundance and success. Earning opportunities are often prefaced by seemingly random questions (*"What's your secret?"*) to design a narrative that leads directly to the advertised product.

They are reinforced with game names (such as "Sweet Bonanza" or "Plinko"), on the other hand, they are often paired with phrases that speak of a highly qualified specialist in the country or *"I work a lot, but I earn money precisely thanks to Sugar Rush"*. These treatments are intended to connect the idea of professionalism with success in gambling, legitimizing the platform, and masking the predatory nature of the scheme.

The influencer-style use of the latter often introduces content with promises of quick riches (*"I'll show you how to make a lot of money in just ten minutes"*), followed by step-by-step instructions on how to install a shady app. The gameplay is explained in technical detail (*"the more balls you drop, the more you win"*), and statements like *"I pay thirty bars, three hundred a day and win over 100,000"* (faithful transcription) simulate consistency and credibility. The presence of phrases like "real money", "bank card withdrawals", and "great start-up bonus" reinforce the illusion of security and trustworthiness. This message is further strengthened by visuals from banking apps showing instant money transfers.

Some narratives use financial literacy, AI-powered technology (*"Meta AI analyzes the market with 98% accuracy"*) or sales jargon to appeal to audiences looking for credibility and professionalism. Others use raffles or giveaways with inflated amounts (*"EUR 5 million divided among 2,000 users"*) to trigger fear of missing out (FOMO) and create a sense of urgency and exclusivity. The call to action is usually immediate and informal: *"Click the link in the description"*, *"download the app"*, *"claim your bonus now"*.

Visual strategies often involve deepfake-based manipulation featuring well-known or emerging influencers, popular athletes, and other trendsetters well-known among young people. These videos often redirect viewers to applications unavailable in official app stores or to fraudulent websites designed to mimic legitimate platforms (e.g. WhatsApp).

From the perspective of social engineering and persuasive language, these campaigns display classic patterns of manipulation. They frequently appeal to social proof, often through manipulated interviews that mimic user recommendations or testimonials. Such scenes are often accompanied by visuals that simulate live gameplay, real-time winnings, or immediate money transfers designed to convince the viewer that success is both easy and instant, and that others are already profiting while they watch.

2.2 Real Recent Campaign: Medical Treatments Targeted at Elderly People

Beyond financial scams, a substantial portion of fake advertisement campaigns focuses on promoting so-called medical treatments, pharmaceutical products, cosmetic interventions, and lifestyle-enhancing supplements.

These campaigns are aimed primarily at older adults, especially those who are chronically ill, have less digital experience, and are more susceptible to authority-based messages. The content often includes topics such as chronic joint pain, diabetes, cardiovascular health, prostate disorders, and general physical degeneration, accompanied by a strong narrative of hope, urgency, and even preservation.

This content is highly engineered, combining pseudo-medical language, statistical manipulation, and dramatics. It often involves multiple stages: identifying a common health scare (e.g., high blood pressure), challenging the mainstream response (e.g., "pills don't work"), introducing a "persecuted hero" (a famous doctor who has suffered or had his home allegedly destroyed for telling the truth), and culminating in a miraculous solution accessible via a referral link.

The language used in these campaigns is highly emotional and rhetorically sophisticated. Phrases such as *"I was on the edge of life and death"*, *"help yourself before it's too late"*, or *"this may be your only chance to avoid surgery"* are common. These narratives often begin with a dramatic personal story, near-death experiences, miraculous recoveries, and conflicts with the pharmaceutical industry. This is usually followed by the promise of immediate results through the use of a natural, forgotten, or innovative remedy that is supposedly superior to conventional medicine. These products are often portrayed as being suppressed by "Big Pharma", thus appealing to anti-establishment sentiments and distrust of mainstream healthcare.

Some scenarios simulate government endorsements or national appeals, featuring manipulated footage of prominent political figures who supposedly support access to breakthrough treatments. These messages are interspersed with populist rhetoric (*"Dear citizen..."*) and claims of government funding for access, often presented as a public health initiative. The sense of urgency is reinforced by timelines (*"available this month only"*), medical doomsaying (risk of amputation, impotence, or death), and promises of transformation (live 20 years longer, free of injections and diets).

A common strategy is to use the images of trusted figures - doctors, medical professors, but also famous priests. Advertisements that use speeches by clergy (usually from the church) and match the style of speech to the forms of lofty homily, the main topic of which is joint pain or vascular problems. This approach exploits the common association of older people with religious identity and trust in moral authority. Using figures that appear to offer spiritual or moral guidance significantly increases the attractiveness of the product, reinforcing the perceived validity of the health claim.

3 Automated Text Exploration Methods

Several tools and frameworks have been developed to support the semantic representation, visualization, and exploration of high-dimensional embedding spaces, particularly in natural language processing and computer vision.

Embedding Projector [18], developed by Google, is a free web application that allows users to visualize high-dimensional data such as word embeddings or image vectors. It provides interactive visualizations using techniques like PCA and t-SNE, enabling users to explore the relationships between data points in an intuitive manner. Although powerful for educational and exploratory purposes, it is primarily limited to static datasets and does not offer clustering or large-scale post-processing capabilities.

Bulk [19] introduces a lightweight web application built with Bokeh that provides annotation interfaces based on UMAP [10] projections of embeddings. The platform focuses on text data and was initially developed to facilitate manual annotation through interactive visualization. While the tool offers a more task-oriented interface than Embedding Projector, it remains relatively simple and is not designed for dynamic, large-scale analysis or semantic extraction.

More advanced solutions is Embedding Atlas [15] is a tool that provides interactive visualizations for large embeddings. It allows user to visualize, cross-filter, and search embeddings and metadata. However, it does not integrate semantic interpretation layers, nor does it provide task-specific automation for text-driven domains.

Atlas [13] is a production-ready platform designed for the collaborative exploration and processing of unstructured data at scale. Built on top of Nomic's multimodal and multilingual embedding models, Atlas provides an intuitive environment for visualizing and managing semantic spaces derived from large text or image corpora. It includes features such as cluster labeling, search, and integration with retrieval-based AI systems. The platform distinguishes itself through its integration of advanced embedding models and support for end-to-end AI workflows, making it suitable for enterprise-level applications. Although Atlas is feature-rich, it requires integration with proprietary APIs or cloud infrastructure, which can lead to a significant operational costs and introduce vendor lock-in.

LDAvis [17] is a well-established interactive tool designed to support the interpretation of Latent Dirichlet Allocation (LDA) [1] topic models. It extracts and visualizes information from a fitted LDA model, presenting topics in a two-dimensional space where users can explore topic prevalence and the most salient terms associated with each cluster. The interface enables users to better understand how topics are distributed across the corpus and how individual words contribute to the model. However, its application is limited to LDA-based models and does not support modern embedding-based representations or multimodal data.

BERTopic [5] is a topic modeling library that leverages transformer-based embeddings to generate interpretable topic representations. It supports a range of topic representation strategies, which improve topic coherence and reduce noise from stopwords. Although BERTopic includes visualization capabilities similar to LDAvis, these tend to offer a local rather than global overview of the semantic landscape. Additionally, the manual inspection of individual topics can become time-consuming when dealing with large numbers of clusters, highlighting a limitation in scalability and interactivity.

Existing solutions rarely incorporate a semantic reasoning layer capable of extracting actionable facts (e.g., calls to action) or structuring the content in the form of an explorable graph. From our experience, the use of LLMs and custom post-processing enables deeper insight and structured knowledge exploration.

Therefore, to better suit our needs, we designed a custom method for text semantic analysis. To enhance interpretability, we employ a large language model to extract key elements such as factual content and calls to action, and to generate meaningful metadata for the analyzed documents. On top of that, we extract embeddings generated with various sentence BERT models. This allows us to capture the contextual meaning of texts in a high-dimensional space.

By applying dimensionality reduction techniques such as t-SNE [8] and UMAP [10], we are able to create an initial spatial layout in which semantically related concepts naturally cluster together. This layout serves as the foundation for further clustering, enabling us to group similar documents into coherent thematic units.

Our custom post-processing pipeline then transforms the clustered data into an interactive graph, which leverages WebGL for efficient visualization and exploration of large-scale document collections.

4 The Proposed Solution

The architecture of the proposed method is presented in Fig. 1. The solution is designed to analyze unstructured textual data derived from transcripts of the real and fake-like advertisements. The dataset consists of loosely formatted documents without predefined structure.

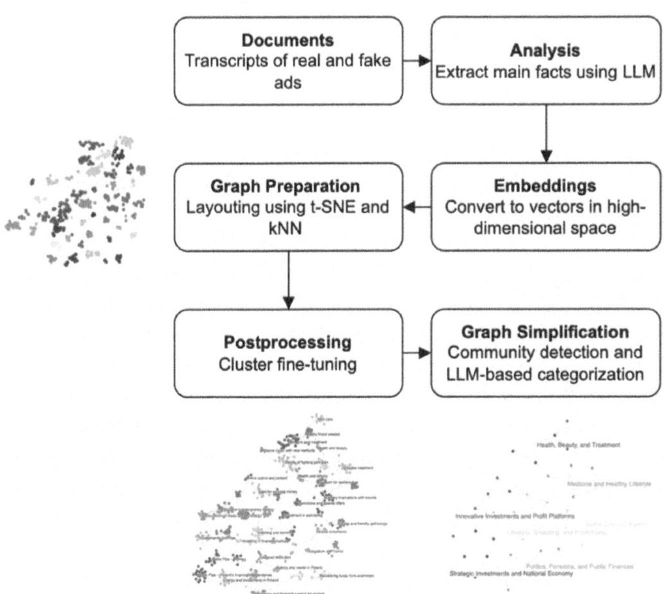

Fig. 1. Architecture of the proposed solution combining LLM-based semantic analysis, graph construction via t-SNE and kNN, and cluster simplification for topic-based categorization of advertisement transcripts.

At the core of our system lies a semantic analysis layer powered by a large language model (LLM). In this research we used bielik-11b-v2.3-instruct[1] model by SpeakLeash. The model extracts key information such as factual content, summaries, and calls to action from each document. The results from the model feeds into an embedding module, where we experiment with various embedding techniques to map the documents into a high-dimensional semantic space.

To visualize and analyze relationships between documents, we apply a dimensionality reduction technique called t-SNE. It projects the embeddings onto a 2D

[1] https://ollama.com/SpeakLeash/bielik-11b-v2.3-instruct.

plane and thus serves as an initial step for layouting the graph of document similarities, where each node represents a document, and spatial proximity reflects semantic relatedness.

A post-processing step refines the layout to enhance cluster cohesion, making topical groupings more visually interpretable. Subsequently, a graph simplification layer reduces visual and cognitive complexity by extracting higher-level structure. This is achieved using community detection algorithms, which identify dense subgraphs corresponding to coherent thematic clusters.

Finally, we reintroduce the LLM to label these communities, summarizing their content and assigning each to a representative category based on the documents within. This multi-layered approach enables both fine-grained and high-level insights into the structure and themes of the dataset.

5 Experiments

This section presents the analysis and results of the experiments conducted to evaluate the proposed method. First, we begin by presenting the dataset itself, followed by a description of the data collection process and the subsequent annotation procedures. Next, we provide details on the conducted experiments. In particular, the experimental framework is divided into qualitative and quantitative assessments. In the qualitative part, we provide a visual analysis of the results obtained using our custom method for generating the dependency graph between the transcripts articles. The visualizations are presented in the context of clustering semantically similar topics in a two-dimensional space. Afterwards, we present an overview of the qualitative assessment. In particular in this part, we compare different techniques for constructing the dependency graph and evaluate the quality of the resulting visualizations using a set of metrics.

5.1 Dataset Development and Collection Process

The dataset used in this study consists of a curated collection of 629 advertisement transcripts, combining both genuine promotional content and fraudulent or deepfake-based advertisements circulating on the Polish Internet. Among these, 114 transcripts correspond to verified real advertisements, while the remaining 515 represent fake, malicious campaigns, often exploiting persuasion techniques or impersonating public figures.

The fake content was gathered in cooperation of NASK with the Polish Financial Supervision Authority (KNF), which also operates as a Computer Security Incident Response Team (CSIRT). KNF supported the identification and verification of scam advertisements disseminated across social media platforms, video-sharing services, and fake investment websites. The selection criteria ensured inclusion of both high-profile deepfake cases and low-effort, high-volume scams observed in the Polish-speaking segment of the web.

To generate the transcripts, we applied Whisper model, an automatic speech recognition system developed by OpenAI [14]. All outputs were manually reviewed and corrected by domain experts, ensuring high transcription accuracy and semantic consistency. This post-processing step was particularly crucial for noisy or low-quality recordings, which are common in user-targeted scam media.

In terms of thematic distribution, the dataset covers a diverse range of topics:

- 302 transcripts (47.8%) involve financial scams, including fake investment opportunities, impersonations of banks or government institutions, and crypto-currency-related fraud,
- 186 transcripts (29.5%) focus on medical, cosmetic, or lifestyle topics, such as miracle cures, anti-aging products, or wellness coaching;
- 19 cases (3.0%) mimic charitable or emergency aid appeals, aiming to exploit empathy or social pressure,
- the remaining 122 transcripts (19.4%) fall under a broad "other" category, encompassing politically charged content, messages promoting unrealistic savings or lifestyle shortcuts, as well as genuine advertisements on various unrelated topics that did not fit into the main thematic clusters.

This dataset reflects the real-world diversity of disinformation techniques and targets, and serves as a valuable benchmark for studying both linguistic manipulation and structural patterns in scam campaigns. It also represents, to our knowledge, the first dataset of this type compiled in Poland, with cross-validation from a national-level cybersecurity authority.

5.2 Qualitative Assessment

During the development of the dataset, documents derived from advertisement transcriptions were categorized based on expert annotations. These annotations were conducted as part of a structured labeling process, where human experts assigned each document to one of several predefined categories reflecting the nature or the intent of the content.

Figure 2 illustrates the main categories identified during this annotation phase. To visualize the distribution of the documents, we applied the proposed approach for projecting high-dimensional representations into a two-dimensional space. Colors in the visualization correspond to the expert-defined categories, allowing for an intuitive inspection of topic clusters.

As can be seen in the figure, two major disinformation trends dominate the dataset. These trends align with the findings discussed in previous sections: (1) advertisements promoting fraudulent investment opportunities, and (2) messages suggesting so-called medicines for a wide range of medical conditions and ailments. In addition to these, other identified categories include politically charged messages and advertisements offering assistance in recovering lost funds, which are often part of broader fraud campaigns. The presented clustering of the categories in the visualization supports their semantic distinctiveness and prevalence within the dataset. Moreover, as shown in the figure, the colors form compact clusters of documents, suggesting that the 2D representation is largely in agreement with the expectations of the annotator.

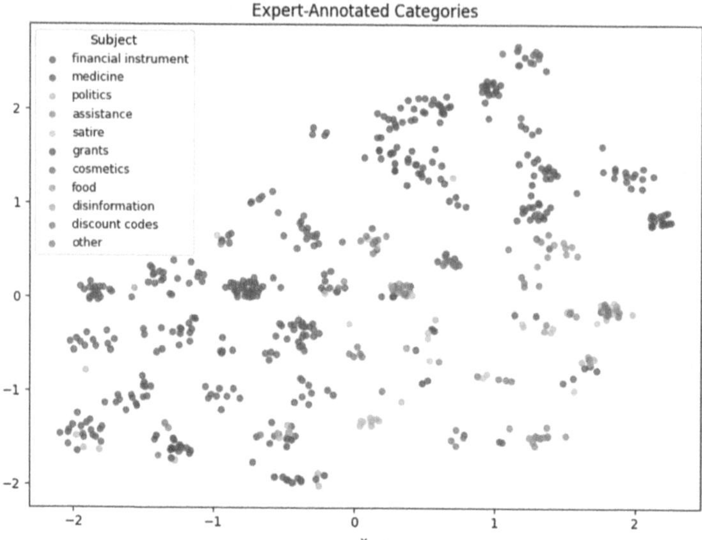

Fig. 2. Expert-annotated categories. Despite differences in category names compared to the earlier automated analysis, the thematic similarity is clearly visible - particularly with regard to finance and health-related topics.

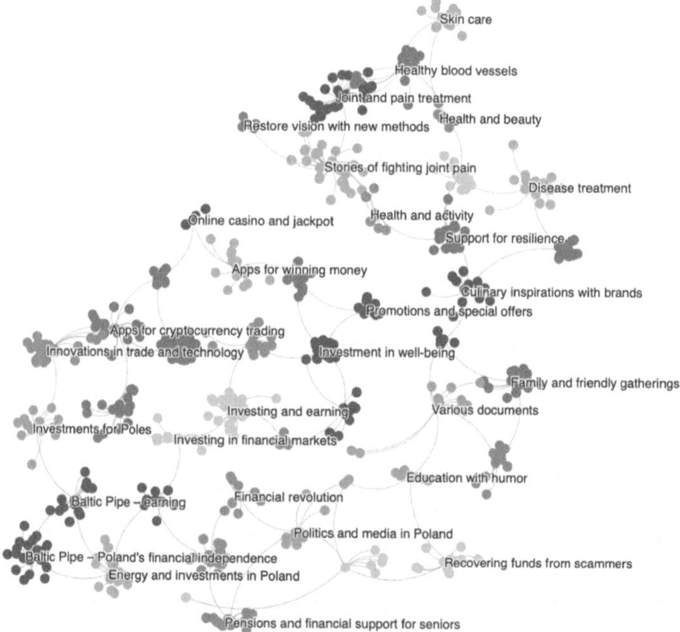

Fig. 3. The graph generated by our approach. It presents the main topics in the analyzed corpus. Edges indicate connections between documents.

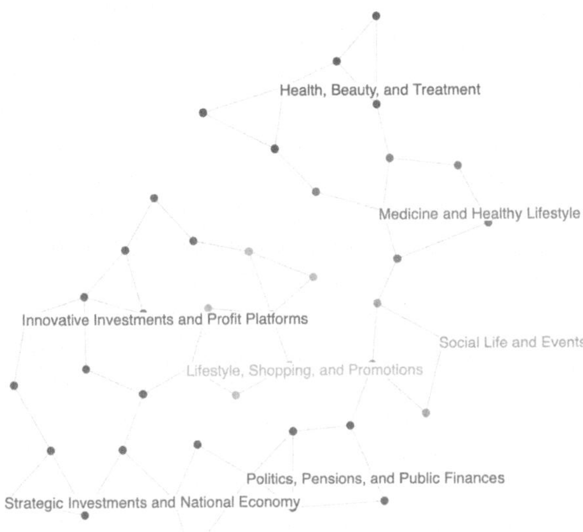

Fig. 4. Automatically simplified structure of the original graph. Node colors indicate major thematic categories. As shown, the dominant topics are related to health and investment.

Next, we compared the visualization with the document categories automatically identified by the proposed approach. As illustrated in Fig. 3, these categories are more fine-grained and reflect subtle variations in content that go beyond the broader expert-defined classes. However, as shown in Fig. 4, there is still a strong correspondence between the expert-labeled thematic areas and the clusters formed by the model, indicating that the method captures not only surface-level similarities but also deeper semantic structures within the dataset. Figure 4 was obtained by coarsening the document graph using community detection, specifically the Louvain algorithm.

5.3 Quantitative Assessment

In order to assess the quality of the proposed method, we used silhouette score and diversity metrics. It must be noted, that the silhouette score and the diversity metric move in opposite directions. A higher silhouette score indicates better clustering quality. On the other hand, for the diversity metric, lower values are preferred, as they reflect more compact and coherent clusters. For both metrics, we consider a scenario in which the number of categories (i.e., transcription topics/clusters) is varied within a predefined range. For each setting, we compute the corresponding value of both metrics to assess how clustering quality changes with the number of categories.

The silhouette score is a clustering evaluation metric that assesses the consistency within clusters of data. For each data point i, the silhouette score $s(i)$ is defined as:

$$s(i) = \frac{b(i) - a(i)}{\max\{a(i), b(i)\}}$$

In the above equation $a(i)$ denotes the average distance between point i and all other points within the same cluster (i.e., the intra-cluster distance), and $b(i)$ represents the minimum average distance from point i to all points in any other cluster to which i does not belong (i.e., the inter-cluster distance).

The silhouette score $s(i)$ ranges from -1 to 1. A value close to 1 indicates that the point is well matched to its own cluster and poorly matched to neighboring clusters. A value around 0 suggests that the point lies near the boundary between two clusters. Conversely, a negative value implies that the point may have been incorrectly assigned to its cluster, as it is closer on average to a different cluster.

The overall silhouette score is computed as the average of $s(i)$ over all data points and provides a global measure of clustering quality in terms of cohesion and separation.

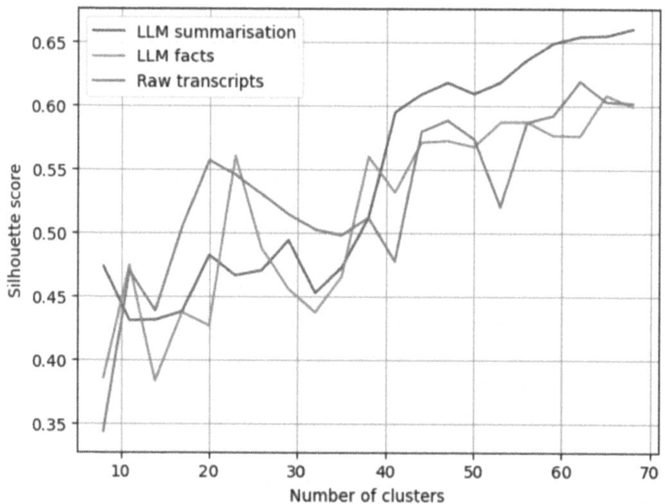

Fig. 5. Silhouette score for different embedding extraction methods vs. number of clusters.

The diversity score measures the average intra-cluster dispersion of document embeddings. For each cluster, it computes the mean Euclidean distance between the points in the cluster and the corresponding cluster centroid. Let C_k denote the set of embeddings assigned to cluster k, and let μ_k be the centroid of C_k, computed as the mean of all embeddings in the cluster. The intra-cluster diversity for cluster k is defined as the average distance from each point $\mathbf{x}_i \in C_k$ to the centroid μ_k, i.e.,

$$D_k = \frac{1}{|C_k|} \sum_{\mathbf{x}_i \in C_k} \|\mathbf{x}_i - \mu_k\|_2$$

The final diversity score is then computed as the mean of D_k across all clusters:

$$\text{Diversity} = \frac{1}{K} \sum_{k=1}^{K} D_k$$

where K is the total number of clusters. A lower diversity score indicates that the points within each cluster are tightly grouped around their respective centroids, suggesting higher internal cohesion.

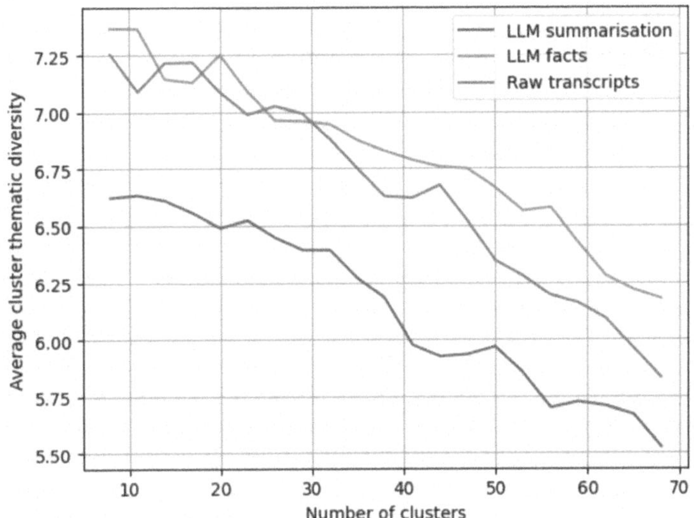

Fig. 6. Thematic diversity for varying numbers of clusters. Lower values indicate more coherent, monothematic clusters.

The silhouette analysis confirms that clustering quality is highest for the LLM summarisation embeddings (as shown in Fig. 5), particularly as the number of clusters increases. This method consistently outperforms both LLM facts and raw transcripts, achieving silhouette scores above 0.65 for higher cluster counts. In contrast, embeddings based on raw transcripts and factual extraction show lower and more fluctuating silhouette values, suggesting less well-separated clusters. These results further support the finding that summarised documents yield more coherent and semantically distinct clusters than full or fact-extracted document representations.

As for the diversity, the results shown in Fig. 6 demonstrate that LLM summarisation embeddings produce clusters with the lowest thematic diversity. This is indicating that each cluster tends to focus on a narrower, more coherent topic. This effect is consistent across different numbers of clusters and suggests that summarised content leads to more topically focused groupings. In contrast, clusters formed using LLM facts exhibit the highest thematic diversity, implying a broader range of topics within individual clusters. The raw transcripts are somewhere in between, reflecting moderate topical cohesion. These findings reinforce the value of summarised representations for generating clean, semantically compact clusters.

5.4 Documents Polarization Quality

In this section, we examine the spatial distribution of real and fake documents within the embedding space. The goal is to assess whether fake documents form distinct clusters, remain on the periphery of real content, or blend within legitimate topics. In that regard, we evaluate the cluster purity, neighborhood composition, and inter-cluster distances to determine the degree of semantic overlap between real and fake content. This analysis helps to uncover whether fake documents imitate real discourse or exhibit detectable divergence in latent space (Fig. 7).

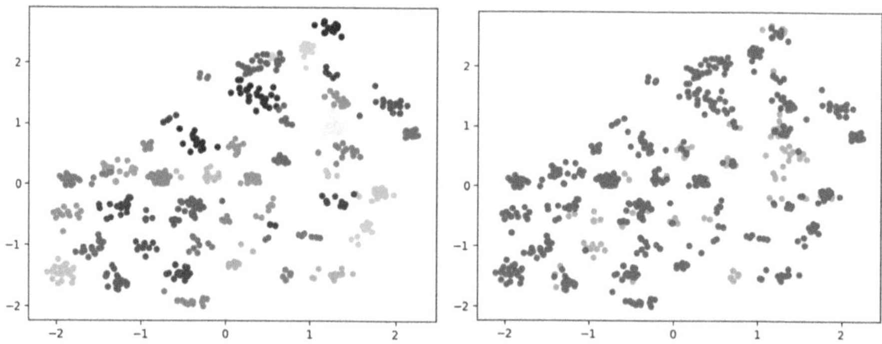

Fig. 7. The graph presents a comparison based on label annotations. On the left, node colors represent thematic categories. On the right, red highlights texts related to deepfakes, while green indicates texts originating from advertisements. As observed, genuine advertisements tend to appear either on the peripheries of existing clusters or form their own distinct clusters. (Color figure online)

More precisely, to assess the document polarization in a quantitative way, the semantic consistency of clusters with respect to the documents labels is measured. In that regard, we define the cluster purity. We compute it as the average proportion of real documents within each cluster. For each cluster C_i, let r_i denote the number of documents labeled as real, and n_i the total number of documents in that cluster. The purity for cluster C_i is given by:

$$p_i = \frac{r_i}{n_i}$$

The overall purity is then computed as the mean purity across all K clusters:

$$\text{Purity}_{\text{mean}} = \frac{1}{K}\sum_{i=1}^{K} p_i$$

Additionally, to capture variation in consistency across clusters, we report the standard deviation:

$$\text{Purity}_{\text{std}} = \sqrt{\frac{1}{K}\sum_{i=1}^{K}(p_i - \text{Purity}_{\text{mean}})^2}$$

This metric reflects the extent to which each cluster is composed primarily of real documents and whether this tendency is uniform across the clustering solution.

Table 1. Cluster purity (mean and std) for different embedding strategies.

Method	Mean Purity	Std. Deviation
LLM Summarization	0.7711	0.3140
LLM Facts	0.7275	0.3604
Raw Transcripts	0.6639	0.4018

As it is shown in Table 1 the cluster purity is highest when using LLM Summarization embeddings (mean = 0.7711). This is suggesting that document abstracts functioning as concise summaries—provide more semantically consistent clustering with respect to the document classes (e.g. real vs fake-news). In contrast, embeddings based on full transcripts yield the lowest purity (mean = 0.6639) and the highest variability across clusters (std = 0.4018), indicating greater semantic overlap between real and fake content in longer texts. This suggests that fake content may more successfully mimic legitimate discourse at the document level, while summarizations remain more discriminative.

6 Threats to Validity

We analyze validity threats in four different aspects of validity: construct validity, internal validity, external validity, and reliability.

In this article, an innovative and original methodology for analyzing fake advertisements using graph structures was presented and evaluated.

As for construct validity, we believe that the approach to represent and visualize dangerous and fake information presented in advertisement campaigns is very valid. Such approach to visualization by graphs and clusters can be used both by security experts and by citizens themselves.

As for internal validity, we understand that the specificity of the presented work is the analysis of information in Polish language and from EU-centered internet sources. Still, the authors believe that, in principle, both the approach and technical methods can be generalized to other languages and other types of fake campaigns in other countries as well.

As for external validity and generalization possibilities, the proposed graph based analysis methods can be also effective in other domains with large volume data that can be visualized as graphs.

As for the reliability, as described in the paper, we conducted experiments on real data of real fake advertisements campaigns gathered by NASK (in the process of protecting Polish internet and society) over the year timespan. Then, the real data was analyzed by our proposed approach.

7 Conclusions

In the context of combating deepfake-based scam advertisements, there is an increasing need for tools capable of analyzing large volumes of unstructured textual data to uncover hidden patterns, techniques, and strategies employed by cyber fraudsters. This paper presents a novel graph-based framework that leverages large language models (LLMs) for semantic analysis, embedding generation, and document clustering, enabling interpretable visualization and in-depth analysis of advertisement transcripts.

The proposed method integrates several components: LLM-powered fact extraction and summarization, multidimensional embedding projections, t-SNE for layout generation, and graph-based community detection enhanced with LLM-driven labeling. This multi-step pipeline transforms raw transcript data into semantically meaningful clusters, supporting both visual inspection and downstream analysis. Experimental results show that embeddings based on LLM-generated summaries produce the most cohesive and discriminative clusters, achieving the highest silhouette scores and the lowest intra-cluster diversity. Moreover, the method effectively separates genuine advertisements from deceptive content content, revealing slight yet consistent patterns of polarization in the semantic space.

Our contribution is twofold. First, we introduce an original methodology for representing disinformation campaigns as document graphs, bridging advanced language modeling with visual analytics. Second, we provide empirical evidence that semantic compression via LLM summaries enhances cluster coherence, thematic purity, and separation between real and fake content, offering a powerful tool for threat intelligence, content moderation, and security research.

Acknowledgement. This work was partially supported by the National Centre for Research and Development (NCBR) under the LIDER XV programme (grant number 0362/L-15/2024), and by the "Science4Business-Nauka dla Biznesu" program (task no. 1, "Inkubator Rozwoju") supporting scienceâĂŞindustry collaboration.

References

1. Blei, D.M., Ng, A.Y., Jordan, M.I.: Latent Dirichlet allocation. J. Mach. Learn. Res. **3**, 993–1022 (2003)
2. CERT-EU: Cyber brief 25-05 – April 2025. Cyber Brief 25-05, Computer Emergency Response Team for the EU Institutions, Bodies and Agencies, Brussels, Belgium (2025). https://cert.europa.eu/publications/threat-intelligence/cb25-05/. Accessed 28 June 2025
3. Europol: Internet organised crime threat assessment (IOCTA) 2024. Tech. report, European Union Agency for Law Enforcement Cooperation (Europol), Luxembourg (2024). https://doi.org/10.2813/442713, https://www.europol.europa.eu/cms/sites/default/files/documents/Internet%20Organised%20Crime%20Threat%20Assessment%20IOCTA%202024.pdf. Accessed 28 June 2025
4. Federal Trade Commission: New FTC data show a big jump in reported losses to fraud to 12.5 billion in 2024 (2025). https://www.ftc.gov/news-events/news/press-releases/2025/03/new-ftc-data-show-big-jump-reported-losses-fraud-125-billion-2024. Accessed 28 June 2025
5. Grootendorst, M.: BERTopic: neural topic modeling with a class-based TF-IDF procedure. arXiv preprint: arXiv:2203.05794 (2022)
6. Hua, J., Wang, P., Lutchkus, P.: How effective are large language models in detecting phishing emails? Issues Inf. Syst. **25**(3), 327–341 (2024)
7. Ma, S., et al.: PsyScam: a benchmark for psychological techniques in real-world scams (2025). https://arxiv.org/abs/2505.15017
8. van der Maaten, L., Hinton, G.: Visualizing data using t-SNE. J. Mach. Learn. Res. **9**(Nov), 2579–2605 (2008)
9. Martinek, A., Bartuzi-Trokielewicz, E.: Detecting deepfakes and false ads through analysis of text and social engineering techniques. In: Rambow, O., Wanner, L., Apidianaki, M., Al-Khalifa, H., Eugenio, B.D., Schockaert, S. (eds.) Proceedings of the 31st International Conference on Computational Linguistics, pp. 8432–8448. Association for Computational Linguistics, Abu Dhabi (2025). https://aclanthology.org/2025.coling-main.564/
10. McInnes, L., Healy, J., Melville, J.: UMAP: uniform manifold approximation and projection for dimension reduction (2018). https://arxiv.org/abs/1802.03426
11. Modzelewski, A., Da San Martino, G., Savov, P., Wilczyńska, M.A., Wierzbicki, A.: MIPD: exploring manipulation and intention in a novel corpus of Polish disinformation. In: Al-Onaizan, Y., Bansal, M., Chen, Y.N. (eds.) Proceedings of the 2024 Conference on Empirical Methods in Natural Language Processing, pp. 19769–19785. Association for Computational Linguistics, Miami (2024).https://doi.org/10.18653/v1/2024.emnlp-main.1103
12. Nasdaq Verafin: Nasdaq verafin report finds that $750 billion in money laundering and illicit funds flowed through europe. Press Release via GlobeNewswire (2025). https://www.nasdaq.com/press-release/nasdaq-verafin-report-finds-750-billion-money-laundering-and-illicit-funds-flowed. Accessed 28 June 2025
13. Nomic AI: Nomic atlas. https://atlas.nomic.ai. Accessed 27 June 2025
14. OpenAI: Whisper: Automatic speech recognition (2022). https://github.com/openai/whisper
15. Ren, D., Hohman, F., Lin, H., Moritz, D.: Embedding atlas: low-friction, interactive embedding visualization. ArXiv preprint: arXiv:2505.06386 (2025)

16. Shearer, E., Eddy, K.: Republicans have become more likely since 2024 to trust information from news outlets, social media. Pew Research Center Short Reads (2025). https://www.pewresearch.org/short-reads/2025/05/08/republicans-have-become-more-likely-since-2024-to-trust-information-from-news-outlets-social-media/. Accessed 28 June 2025
17. Sievert, C., Shirley, K.: LDAvis: a method for visualizing and interpreting topics. In: Proceedings of the Workshop on Interactive Language Learning, Visualization, and Interfaces, pp. 63–70. Association for Computational Linguistics, Baltimore (2014). https://doi.org/10.3115/v1/W14-3110
18. Smilkov, D., Thorat, N., Nicholson, C., Reif, E., Viégas, F.B., Wattenberg, M.: Embedding projector: interactive visualization and interpretation of embeddings. ArXiv e-prints: https://doi.org/10.48550/arXiv.1611.05469 (2016). presented at NeurIPS 2016
19. Warmerdam, V.D.: Bulk: a simple bulk labelling tool. https://github.com/koaning/bulk (2021). Accessed 27 June 2025

Adapting Epidemic Contact Models to Misinformation Spread via Social Networks

Lankeshwara Munasinghe(✉) and Christopher D. McDermott

School of Computing, Engineering and Technology, Robert Gordon University, Aberdeen, UK
{l.munasinghe,c.d.mcdermott}@rgu.ac.uk

Abstract. Online social networks have become key platforms for information dissemination, including the facilitation and spread of misinformation, which can contribute to terrorist activities and radicalization. Understanding how network structure influences the spread of false information is essential for developing effective mitigation strategies. In this study, we propose a novel framework that models heterogeneous online contact patterns based on a user's structural position within a network. Specifically, we estimate a k-core-specific interaction matrix by adapting social contact matrix estimation from infectious disease modelling. We quantify how different structural groups contribute to the propagation of misinformation. We illustrate our approach using empirical data from the Twitter network surrounding the Higgs boson discovery event. Our findings suggest that highly connected users within deeper network cores act as primary amplifiers of misinformation and that susceptibility to misinformation varies systematically across k-core levels. These insights offer valuable parameters for improving misinformation detection and intervention strategies in online environments.

Keywords: Misinformation · Online social networks · K-core decomposition · Interaction matrix

1 Introduction

Online social networks have transformed the way information is disseminated, enabling the rapid and wide-scale sharing of ideas, news, and opinions. While these platforms offer undeniable societal benefits, they also pose serious challenges, particularly in the form of misinformation and disinformation. The unchecked spread of misleading or false content online can undermine public trust, destabilise democratic processes, and even contribute to radicalisation and extremist recruitment. To mitigate these risks, platforms and policymakers must develop effective intervention strategies. However, such efforts are hampered by two persistent issues: *(1)* the lack of clarity on how misinformation propagates across diverse user groups, and *(2)* the absence of robust metrics to quantify the

R. Laborde et al. (Eds.): ESORICS 2025 Workshops, LNCS 16233, pp. 295–309, 2026.
https://doi.org/10.1007/978-3-032-16165-9_17

effectiveness of mitigation strategies. A critical yet underexplored aspect of this challenge is the heterogeneity in online social contact patterns, specifically, how users of different demographics and network positions interact with one another, and how those interactions shape the flow of misinformation. Previous studies have shown that misinformation originates from specific users and spreads across a network, influenced by its structural features and user attributes. While user demographics are important in shaping how information spreads, structural features, such as network position and connectivity, are equally critical in influencing its reach and speed. For instance, a user's topological placement such as their k-core value in the network, plays a crucial role in determining the speed and reach of misinformation. While k-core analysis is a recognised method for examining network structures, the specific application of an interaction matrix in this context presents a novel approach. We therefore focus estimation on an k-core-based interaction matrix to quantify the information spread among users belonging to different cores of a network to provide comprehensive insight of complex, heterogeneous user interaction patterns. In doing so, this paper introduces a novel framework that leverages methodologies from infectious disease modeling, particularly the use of interaction matrices, to quantify the spread of misinformation across heterogeneous user groups. This allows better understanding of how misinformation spreads and which groups are most influential or vulnerable in this process. We summarise our key contributions as follows:

- Introduction of a k-core-based interaction matrix to analyse social mixing patterns and quantify misinformation spread on online platforms.
- Adaptation of epidemiological methodologies, such as contact matrices, final size equations, and reproduction number estimates, to model the digital transmission of misinformation.
- Validation of our approach using empirical data from Twitter (Higgs boson event)[1].

The rest of the paper is organised as follows: Sect. 2 introduces our conceptual framework that provides the frame through which to explore misinformation spread, explaining how adaptation of infectious disease modelling to social mixing patterns. Section 3 provides a brief overview of prior work in the area, specifically discussing the approaches that inspired our work. Section 4 describes our novel methodology for interaction estimation and describes the dataset we have used. Section 5 presents experimental analysis of misinformation spread. Finally, Sect. 6 draws conclusions and suggests possible future research directions.

2 Conceptual Framework

2.1 Modelling Misinformation Like Infectious Disease

Like infectious diseases, misinformation spreads through contact networks, where individuals "infect" others by sharing false information. For instance, age-specific

[1] https://snap.stanford.edu/data/higgs-twitter.html.

susceptibility for misinformation represents the likelihood that individuals in a particular age group adopt and further spread misinformation when exposed to it. In epidemiology, parameters such as *Susceptibility*, *Infection*, *Recovery*, and the *Force of Infection (FOI)* are often estimated using seroepidemiological data. We can adapt these methods to study the spread of misinformation by analysing user exposure, sharing behaviours, and correction rates. Table 1 shows how we can map epidemiological concepts to our context of misinformation spread and summarises the parallels between infectious disease spread and misinformation propagation. As shown, although traditionally confined to public health, the epidemiological modelling of disease transmission offers a powerful conceptual and mathematical framework for understanding how information, in our context misinformation, spreads in digital environments. In this analogy, users who encounter misinformation *(Susceptible)*, may engage with or share it *(Infected)*, and later stop interacting with it *(Recovered)*, either because of correction, loss of interest, or exposure to fact-checking. By leveraging this analogy, we can apply mature tools from disease modelling, such as the interaction/contact matrix, to estimate how misinformation flows through different segments of an online population. We note that our study is primarily a methodological adaptation rather than a full empirical validation, and thus the framework's applicability for real-time forecasting or interventions remains to be investigated further.

2.2 Network Structure and Social Mixing Patterns

Online social networks, like physical human contact networks, are highly heterogeneous and structured. These networks often follow a *power-law distribution* [1], meaning a small number of highly connected users (*Influencers*) hold a disproportionate level of influence over information flow, while the majority of users are less connected. Figure 1 shows the *log-log* plot of the node degree of an online friendship network, where the long tail distribution shows compliance with the power law for network growth.

A key structural concept in understanding these dynamics is the *k-core decomposition.* A k-core is a maximal subgraph in which each node has at least k connections within the subgraph. This technique allows us to identify central influential users (high-core nodes) and distinguish between core and periphery regions of the network. Also, k-core provides a robust and computationally efficient way to distinguish core influencers from peripheral users, which is particularly useful in large-scale networks where degree alone may not capture structural centrality. In addition, it allows us analyse mixing patterns such as if users tend to interact within their own k-core (*homophily*) or across different cores (*heterophily*). In doing so, modelling misinformation spread using k-core-based interaction matrices helps us quantify user interactions by structural influence which can reveal how core users act as amplifiers and how peripheral users interact with them. Ultimately, this will allow us to assess the resilience of misinformation diffusion and identify possible points for intervention.

The spread of misinformation and disinformation on online social networks follows highly complex and diverse dynamics. In particular, online radicalisation

Table 1. Comparison between Epidemiological Concepts and Misinformation Spread

Epidemiological	Misinformation	Context in the Study
Susceptible (S)	Users exposed to misinformation but have not shared it.	Users who saw tweets about the Higgs boson announcement but did not retweet or comment.
Infected (I)	Users who believe and share misinformation.	Users who, after initial engagement, share Higgs boson rumors.
Recovered (R)	Users who were fact-checked or corrected and stopped sharing misinformation.	Users who, after initial engagement, ceased sharing Higgs boson rumors, possibly due to receiving accurate information or losing interest.
Force of Infection (λ_i)	Rate at which misinformation spreads among user groups.	The study analyses the rate at which tweets about the Higgs boson spread across different user communities and networks.
Seroprevalence Data	Survey data on belief and sharing of misinformation.	The researchers collected data on Higgs boson tweet volumes and user interactions to assess how widely the information permeated the Twitter network.

and recruitment to extreme ideologies can be influenced by demographic factors (e.g., age, sex, economic status, education), but the topology of the network organisation also plays an important role in the spread of information. This can be interpreted to mean that a few nodes *(users)* in the network have a very high number of connections, while most nodes have relatively few connections. This characteristic is commonly observed in scale-free networks of many online social platforms (e.g., Facebook, Twitter, LinkedIn) that follow a power law and show that:

- High-degree users *(influencers)* are more attractive in terms of connections.
- Low-degree users have a higher chance of connecting to already well-connected users.
- Interaction probabilities should be assigned based on node degrees, ensuring that high-degree nodes are more likely to interact.

However, there are plausible circumstances under which highly connected nodes or those with high betweenness have little effect on the range of a spreading process. We argue that the network's topology significantly influences the spreading process, with certain conditions under which these nodes have minimal impact. For example, a central hub located on the network's periphery may have little effect on spreading through the core, whereas a less connected node strategically positioned within the core can significantly enhance dissemination. Among other methods, k-core analysis is widely used in social media analysis, epidemiology (disease spread), and cybersecurity (detecting influential nodes in attack networks). Studying k-core-specific mixing patterns among nodes (users)

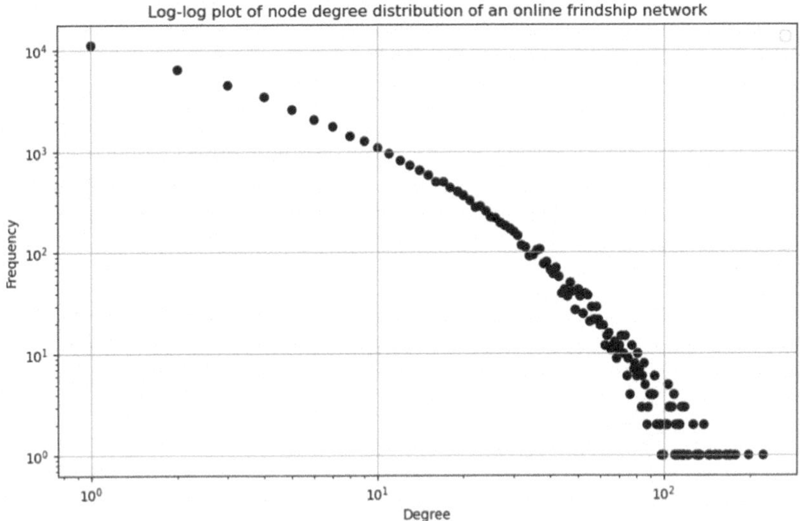

Fig. 1. Log-log plot of the degree distribution of a typical online friendship network

helps analyse how different user interactions are influenced by the surrounding network structure. A k-core is a maximal subgraph where each node has at least k connections within the subgraph. This method helps identify the most effective individual spreaders when the spread originates from a single node. For information spread originating from multiple nodes, efficiency improves by positioning the origins at specific distances from each other [3], where key aspects of k-core mixing patterns are:

- **Core-Level Interactions**: Examining whether nodes in the same k-core primarily interact with each other or mix with different cores.
- **Homophily vs. Heterophily**: Identifying if users in high k-cores (highly connected) prefer interacting with similar high-core users (homophily) or engage with lower-core users (heterophily).
- **Structural Roles**: High-core nodes may act as influencers or central hubs, while lower-core nodes might represent peripheral or less-connected users.
- **Resilience & Influence**: Networks with strong high-core mixing tend to be resilient and have higher information spread, while weakly connected cores may indicate fragmentation.

3 Related Work

Several studies have explored information diffusion, network topology, and social mixing patterns, which underpin the theoretical and methodological foundation of our work. In complex, heterogeneous, and rapidly growing social networks, social mixing is shaped by various factors, particularly demographic and topological characteristics [4]. Understanding these patterns in both online and offline environments is crucial for understanding how information, diseases, rumors, radicalisation, and other phenomena spread [5]. In the context of social media, De Domenico et al. [2] investigated the spread of the Higgs boson discovery rumor on Twitter, providing empirical evidence of how scientific information (and potential misinformation) can diffuse through digital platforms. Analysing nearly one million tweets from July 2012, they characterised spatio-temporal patterns of user activity before, during, and after the announcement. Their study identified trends both individually and globally and simulated information diffusion on the Twitter network. In doing so, they demonstrated large-scale collective behaviour, revealing how social influence shapes information spread in online networks and produced a framework that can be used to study other information spread. Muñoz et al. [9] introduced a novel method to identify influential spreaders in complex networks, showing that network centrality (e.g., eigen vector cetrality), average degree play a pivotal roles in misinformation spread. Govind and Lal [3] reinforced the use of k-core decomposition in evaluating influence in social media environments, advocating for its utility in analyzing structural roles in networked systems.

Understanding and modelling social contacts patterns is crucial in infectious disease modelling. Wallinga et al. [10] used social contact data to estimate age-specific transmission parameters for respiratory pathogens, highlighting the influence of demographic structure on spread dynamics. Mossong et al. [7] conducted one of the most comprehensive surveys on social contact patterns across age groups in Europe, resulting in the POLYMOD dataset. This dataset has been used to estimate interaction matrices for modelling infectious disease spread. Since then, many studies have researched the impact of social contact patterns on the spread of infectious diseases. For instance, a recent study extended this work to quantify heterogeneous contact patterns in Japan using contact surveys [8].

Collectively, these studies support our approach of modelling the spread of misinformation over online social networks with greater accuracy and real-world applicability.

4 Methodology

As discussed in Sect. 3 social contact patterns have been used in epidemiology to estimate interaction matrices when modelling the spread of infectious diseases where previous research has estimated age-specific transmission parameters highlighting the influence of demographic structure on spread dynamics. In our previous work [8], we followed the same approach and conducted a contact survey to construct a social contact matrix, which we validated using a seroepidemiological influenza dataset. Respondents recorded all contacts during one weekday (Wednesday) and one weekend day (Sunday), noting each contactor's age, sex, type of contact (i.e., conversational or physical), duration, and location. This information was used to quantify heterogeneous contact patterns. In this context, social interactions refer to the number of contacts that individuals report often varies significantly depending on factors such as demography, lifestyle, occupation, and social behavior. This variability can result in a wide range of contact numbers across different individuals. For instance, a teacher or healthcare worker may report significantly more contacts than a retiree, introducing variability in contact patterns that simpler distributions like the Poisson fail to capture effectively. To address this over-dispersion, the negative binomial distribution incorporates a dispersion parameter (γ), which allows for greater flexibility in modeling the spread of the data. Furthermore, it allows flexible modeling of the mean number of contacts (μ) between age groups, which can depend on external factors such as population structure or social norms. By explicitly modeling the variability in contact counts, the negative binomial distribution ensures a realistic representation of social interaction data, making it suitable for the construction of contact matrices used in public health, epidemiological modeling, and behavioral analysis. In this research, we used the negative binomial distribution and the MLE (maximum likelihood estimator) to estimate the interaction matrix to assess the impact of misinformation and spread of disinformation on social networks. In this paper, we adapted the model to estimate interactions, but given our focus was on user interactions across different k-cores within the network, we substituted the age variable in the original model with each user's k-core value.

4.1 Interaction Matrix Estimation

The adapted interaction matrix was estimated using the MLE method we used previously [8] where the negative binomial distribution was used to describe the self-reported number of conversational partners encountered during a typical week in age class i by participants in age class j. For example, let X_{ij} represent the number of conversational partners in age group j reported by participants in age group i. The negative binomial distribution models the probability of observing X_{ij} is:

$$P(X_{ij} = x|r, p) = \frac{\Gamma(x + r)}{\Gamma(r)x!} p^r (1 - p)^x \tag{1}$$

where X_{ij} is a random variable for the number of contacts made by individuals in age group i with age group j. Here, r is the dispersion parameter, p is the probability of success in each trial. In this context, p is the probability that someone encountered by an individual in age group i belongs to age group j. Using maximum likelihood method, we then estimate the mean number of contacts between age group i and j. The log-likelihood function of negative binomial probability mass function is:

$$L(r, p; x) = \sum_{i=1}^{n} [ln\Gamma(x_i + r)] - ln\Gamma(r) - ln(x_i!) + rln(p) + x_i ln(1 - p)] \tag{2}$$

where n is the number of observations. Since p is related to the mean μ of the negative binomial distribution by:

$$p = \frac{r}{r+\mu} \tag{3}$$

Substitute this into the log-likelihood function:

$$L(r,p;x) = \sum_{i=1}^{n}[ln\Gamma(x_i+r)]-ln\Gamma(r)-ln(x_i!)+rln(\frac{r}{r+\mu_i})+x_iln(\frac{\mu_i}{r+mu_i})] \tag{4}$$

where μ_i is the expected mean contacts for observation i. Maximizing this function (using Maximum Likelihood Estimation) estimates the parameters r and μ, allowing us to predict the mean number of contacts.

4.2 Adjustments for Reciprocity

In the estimated interaction matrix $\{m_{ij}\}$ the entry m_{ij} represents the mean number of contacts between between age group i and j. To estimate m_{ij}, we adopted an assumption of reciprocity, i.e., the mean number of contacts that an individual in age group i experiences with individuals in age group j is equal to the number that an individual in age group j experiences with individuals in age group i. Thus, we adjusted the asymmetry of the contact rate using the age-dependent population size. As such, if we have w_i individuals in age class i and w_j individuals in age class j, reciprocity thus requires that $m_{ij}w_j = m_{ji}w_i$. The negative binomial log-likelihood function for m_{ij} and k_{ij}, with correction for reciprocity of contacts such that $m_{ij}w_j = m_{ji}w_i$, is:

$$\begin{aligned} l(m_{ij}, k_{ij}, k_{ji}; x_{ij}, x_{ji}) = & \frac{1}{2}\sum_{t=1}^{T_j} \ln\left(\text{NegBin}(x_{ij,t}; m_{ij}, k_{ij})\right) + \\ & \frac{1}{2}\sum_{t=1}^{T_i} \ln\left(\text{NegBin}(x_{ji,t}; m_{ij}\frac{w_j}{w_i}, k_{ji})\right) \end{aligned} \tag{5}$$

k_{ij} represents the total observed contacts between individuals in age group i and age group j during the study period. Here, x_{ij} is the vector of numbers of conversation partners in age class i reported by participants in age class j, T_j is the number of participants in age class j, and t is an index number. In this work, we analysed mixing patterns of users of online social networks based on the users' demography and the network topology. We used the MLE method explained above to estimate and quantify the mixing patterns of the users. Again, given our focus on user interactions across different k-cores within the network, we substitute the age variable in the original model with each user's k-core value.

4.3 Twitter Dataset (Higgs Boson)

For our experimental analysis we used the Higgs boson dataset [6] used by De Domenico et al. [2] which investigated the anatomy of a scientific rumour. The dataset was constructed by monitoring the spread of information on Twitter before, during, and after the announcement of the discovery of a new particle with the characteristics of the elusive Higgs boson on 4 July 2012. Specifically, it captures messages posted between 1 July and 7 July 2012 related to the discovery. The Twitter activity network includes interactions such as retweets, mentions, and replies, with each link being directed. The network is comprised of 304,691 nodes, 563,069 temporal edges, and 466,545 static edges. In our study, we divide this data set into two periods as follows:

- **Period I:** Rumors about the discovery before the announcement (before 4th July 2012).
- **Period II:** Rumors about the discovery after the announcement (after 4th July 2012).

5 Experimental Analysis of Misinformation Spread

In our experimental evaluation, we estimate the k-core interaction matrix, which quantifies the average number of contacts between users belonging to different k-cores within the network. Here, the k-cores are analogous to age groups in the age-specific model presented in [8]. We normalized the social interaction matrices by dividing all entries by the largest eigenvalue, ensuring that the resulting matrices are properly scaled for stability in the epidemic (misinformation) models.

5.1 K-Core Interaction Matrix

First, we analyse the Twitter network of 456626 nodes and 14855819 directed edges associated with Twitter activities (tweets, retweets, and mentions) on Higgs boson discovery. This network represents the social relationships of friends and followers between users. We classified the users into five groups based on the k-core score of the users. The k-cores are 0–20, 21–40, 41–60, 61–80, 81–100, 100+. Then, we quantified the number of contacts made by each user with users of other k-cores. To identify the network's core and periphery, we use k-core (or k-shell) decomposition, where k characterises the specific subgraph in which all nodes have a degree of k (k = 1, 2, 3,. . . , k). We estimate the k-core-specific interaction matrix using Twitter data to quantify the spread of information between different k-cores. Figure 3 shows the estimated mean interaction matrix for the Twitter network. According to Fig. 3, interactions have mainly occurred within nodes located in high K-cores (K $\geq$ 80). However, there is a tendency of low k-core nodes to interact with high k-core nodes, which implies the follower/followee relationship (Fig. 2).

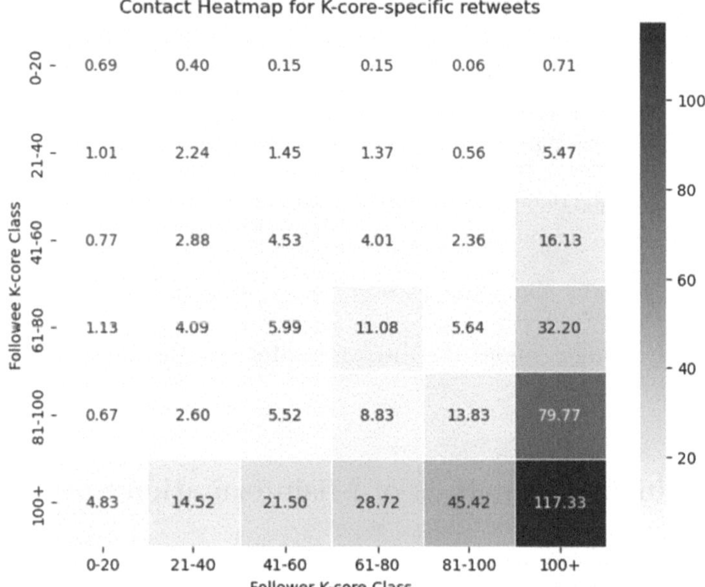

Fig. 2. k-core-specific Interaction matrix

5.2 Validating Interaction Matrix

The interaction matrix reflects the parametric view of essential social mixing patterns in quantifying and estimating the spread of misinformation. A key assumption when using the social interaction matrix to model k-core-dependent heterogeneity in misinformation spread is that the k-core-dependent transmission matrix, which includes contact frequency, is informed by the social interaction matrix. To capture such heterogeneity, we used the next generation matrix, $k = k_{ij}$, comprising the average number of users in core i that are convinced or radicalised by a single misinformation spreader in core j in a fully susceptible population. The matrix describes the per-generation heterogeneity for the risk of radicalisation by k-core; in the simplest terms, it may be parameterized using the social interaction matrix as $k_{ij} = qm_{ij}$, where q is a constant that can be interpreted as the "information-specific infectivity". Information-specific infectivity refers to the inherent ability of a specific piece of information (e.g., a tweet, news article, video, or rumor) to be shared or propagated across a social network. Alternatively, one can parameterise k as $k_{ij} = s_i m_{ij}$ if the susceptibility varies with core i. Once the parametric assumption of the next-generation matrix was determined, we quantified the next-generation matrix by analysing the empirical Higgs boson twitter dataset estimating the basic reproduction number, R_0, which is interpreted as the average number of users influenced by a typical single primary case in a fully susceptible population and is calculated as the largest eigenvalue of the next-generation matrix. Depending on the parametric assumption, we estimated the constant q or k-core-dependent susceptibility s_i to scale the next-generation matrix. To do so, we analysed the k-core-specific final size distribution (or cumulative incidence) of Higgs boson rumor, using the difference in the k-core-specific Misinformation Exposure Rate (or Belief Prevalence) between 1 July 2012 and 7 July 2012. First, we collected the number of users in each k-core who tweeted, retweeted, or mentioned the related tweets before 4 July 2012. Second, we collected the number of users in each k-core who tweeted, retweeted, or mentioned the related tweets after 4 July 2012. Analysing the deference between those two, we estimated the next-generation matrix based on two parametric assumptions.

Table 2. Followers of misinformation before and after Higgs boson announcement

k-core group	Before 4 July 2012			After 4 July 2012			Cumulative incidence ($z_i = z_{4,i} - z_{2,i}$)
	$n_{2,i}$	$m_{2,i}$	$z_{2,i}$ ($m_{2,i}/n_{2,i}$)	$n_{4,i}$	$m_{4,i}$	$z_{4,i}$ ($m_{4,i}/n_{4,i}$)	
0–20	236093	1171	0.005	236093	6353	0.027	0.022
21–40	90435	1138	0.125	90435	4686	0.052	0.039
41–60	45679	1017	0.022	45679	3700	0.081	0.059
61–80	30574	941	0.031	30574	3159	0.103	0.072
81–100	19571	820	0.042	19571	2450	0.125	0.083
100+	34274	2754	0.080	34274	6752	0.197	0.116

Table 2 shows the dataset used to validate the importance of using the social interaction matrix. Subtracting the positive fraction before 4 July 2012 from that after 4 July 2012, we obtained the empirical value of cumulative incidence z_i, which satisfies the so-called k-core-dependent final size equation:

$$z_i = 1 - \exp\left(-\sum_j z_j k_{ij}\right)$$

where i and j denote core values ($i-core$ and $j-core$) and k_{ij} denotes the next-generation matrix. Iteratively solving this equation, we optimised the likelihood function:

$$L(\theta; n, m) = \prod_i \binom{n_{I,i}}{m_{I,i}} (z_{I,i} + z_i)^{m_{I,i}} (1 - z_{I,i} - z_i)^{n_{I,i} - m_{I,i}}$$

where $n_{I,i}$ and $m_{I,i}$ represent the observed total and rumored (infected) users in core i after 4 July July 2012 (period II), respectively, $z_{I,i}$ is the positive fraction of core i users before 4 July 2012 (period I), and θ is the population parameters.

Table 3. Comparison of model fit and estimated parameters

Contact pattern	Number of parameters	AIC†
Use social contact matrix + k-core-independent susceptibility	1	14435.72
Use social contact matrix + k-core-dependent susceptibility	6	14318.29

† Akaike information criterion, calculated as 2NLL + 2×param, where NLL and param represent negative log-likelihood and the number of parameters, respectively.

We parameterised the next-generation matrix in various ways and tested the goodness of fit referring to the Akaike information criterion (AIC). As possible candidate matrices that do not rest on the social interaction matrix, we tested the fully parameterized next-generation matrix including the k-core-dependent mixing assumption and the k-core-independent mixing assumption, comparing their fit against those using the social interaction matrix. The 95% confidence intervals (CI) of parameters were computed using the profile likelihood.

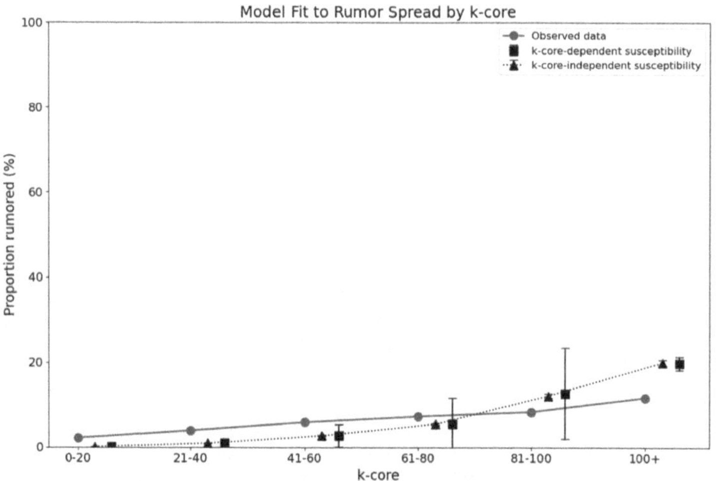

Fig. 3. Comparison between observed and estimated proportions

Figure 3 compares the observed and model-predicted rumor spread across different k-core groups in the network. The observed data shows a clear increase in the proportion of rumored users as k-core values rise, indicating that users with more connections are more likely to spread or encounter rumors. Both the k-core-independent and k-core-dependent susceptibility models capture the general trend, but the k-core-dependent model fits the observed data more closely according to the AIC value shown in the Table 3, particularly at higher k-core levels. This suggests that accounting for differences in user susceptibility (such as varying exposure or behaviour) leads to more accurate predictions of rumor spread. Confidence intervals are tighter for users in higher k-core groups, reflecting greater reliability where the network is denser. Overall, the results highlight the importance of considering user heterogeneity and network position when modelling information spread.

5.3 Discussion

In adapting infectious disease models to misinformation spread, age groups correspond to k-core levels in online social networks, where the k-core index measures a user's structural centrality rather than chronological age. Physical contact events are reinterpreted as online interactions such as retweets, shares, or replies, representing opportunities for misinformation exposure. Instead of relying on empirical contact surveys, network topology analysis using methods like k-core decomposition and degree distribution are employed to estimate interaction patterns in the absence of demographic data. Consequently, the traditional contact matrix is reformulated as a k-core-specific contact matrix, capturing the probability of exposure between users across different structural tiers.

In this study, we estimated k-core-specific contact matrices without relying on user demographic information, which is often difficult to obtain due to ethical concerns and data collection challenges. Instead, we focused on the network structure, specifically, the local topology of users, to estimate and quantify their contact patterns in the context of information spread. We estimated k-core-specific interaction matrix shown in Fig. 3 to quantify the average interactions between users with different k-core values in the Higgs boson twitter network. This was then used to estimate the number of users influenced or radicalised (final size) in period II by the users who tweeted the rumour during the period I. This estimation, and the observed final size of the newly influenzaed users, are compared in Fig. 3. The results indicate that the k-core-dependent model fits the data better than the k-core-independent model based on the AIC score. This suggests that each k-core level in the network exhibits its own susceptibility to information spread, offering critical insights for designing strategies such as blocking selected users at specific times to mitigate misinformation and for identifying potential super spreaders within the network. In addition to blocking, highly vulnerable users can be educated to improve their awareness and ability to identify and respond to misinformation. However, we note that the analogy to infectious disease models has limitations. Unlike biological contagion, sharing or believing misinformation is a cognitive and contextual decision influenced by platform design and user behaviour. This constrains the direct applicability of epidemic parameters for real-time forecasting or outbreak detection, though the framework remains a useful comparative tool. Moreover, our findings are based on a single dataset and event, and broader validation across multiple contexts, and compare to other models of information spread to fully assess generalisability.

6 Conclusions

In this paper, we constructed a social interaction matrix by analyzing user connectivity patterns in an online environment. This was aimed at understanding the spread of misinformation by adapting social contact matrix estimation methods used in epidemiology. We estimated and validated a k-core-specific contact matrix and examined how local network structures influence information transmission. Strong associativity based on network centrality was observed, particularly among highly connected users, with frequent interactions also identified between moderately and highly connected user groups. These findings provide parameters for modeling heterogeneous dynamics of misinformation spread, but their generalisability remains constrained by reliance on a single case study. Broader empirical testing is required before drawing strong conclusions about actionable interventions.

While we successfully quantified the social interaction matrix, we identified technical limitations related to online social networks. First, although we constructed an approximate matrix without using individual identities, it would be valuable to explore how individual-level interactions influence information spread by examining detailed topological features and the dynamic behaviour of the network. Future work could investigate how situational awareness influences the diffusion of misinformation. In particular, the ability to perceive information, comprehend whether it is misleading, and project its potential consequences may shape both individual susceptibility and amplification across the network. Additionally, our current contact matrix does not account for contact type (tweet, retweet, or mention), which we aim to address in future work. Second, traditional survey-based methods for collecting contact data primarily capture static network information and are prone to human errors such as reporting and recall biases. These methods can also be time-consuming and costly. Therefore, developing low-cost alternative approaches using novel or existing technologies is an important future direction.

References

1. Castillo-Castillo, P., et al.: A growth model for citations networks. Appl. Netw. Sci. **10**(1) (2025)
2. De Domenico, M., Lima, A., Mougel, P., Musolesi, M.: The anatomy of a scientific rumor. Sci. Rep. **3**(1), 2980 (2013)
3. Govind, N., Lal, R.P.: Evaluating user influence in social networks using k-core. In: Advances in Intelligent Systems and Computing, pp. 11–18. Advances in intelligent systems and computing, Springer Singapore, Singapore (2021)
4. He, Q., Zhang, Z., Bi, T., Fang, H., Yi, X., Yu, K.: Adaptive rumor suppression on social networks: A multi-round hybrid approach. ACM Trans. Knowl. Discov. Data **19**(2) (2025). https://doi.org/10.1145/3701738
5. Hoang, T., et al.: A systematic review of social contact surveys to inform transmission models of close-contact infections. Epidemiology **30**(5), 723–736 (2019)
6. Leskovec, J., Krevl, A.: SNAP Datasets: Stanford large network dataset collection. http://snap.stanford.edu/data (2014)

7. Mossong, J., et al.: Social contacts and mixing patterns relevant to the spread of infectious diseases. PLOS Med. **5**(3), 1 (2008). https://doi.org/10.1371/journal.pmed.0050074
8. Munasinghe, L., Asai, Y., Nishiura, H.: Quantifying heterogeneous contact patterns in Japan: a social contact survey. Theor. Biol. Med. Model. **16**(1), 6 (2019). https://doi.org/10.1186/s12976-019-0102-8
9. Muñoz, P., Díez, F., Bellogín, A.: Modeling disinformation networks on twitter: structure, behavior, and impact. Appl. Netw. Sci. **9**(1) (2024). https://doi.org/10.1007/s41109-024-00610-w
10. Wallinga, J., Teunis, P., Kretzschmar, M.: Using data on social contacts to estimate age-specific transmission parameters for respiratory-spread infectious agents. Am. J. Epidemiol. **164**(10), 936–944 (2006). https://doi.org/10.1093/aje/kwj317, https://doi.org/10.1093/aje/kwj317

POLfake: Relational Dataset for Polish Fake News Detection

Mateusz Walczak and Aneta Poniszewska-Marańda(✉)

Institute of Information Technology, Lodz University of Technology, Lodz, Poland
mateusz.walczak@dokt.p.lodz.pl, aneta.poniszewska-maranda@p.lodz.pl

Abstract. Reliable datasets are essential for developing and evaluating the models for fake news detection. Although the research on disinformation detection has advanced significantly in high-resource languages such as English and Chinese, Polish remains an under-resourced language in this area despite the emergence of first dedicated datasets. This paper introduces the POLfake – new relational dataset for Polish-language fake news detection. The dataset comprises nearly 6,000 fact-checked claims and 1,500 tweets that explicitly propagate these claims. The relational structure of the dataset reflects real-world misinformation dynamics by linking posts to the specific claims they disseminate. Each element is annotated with one of five levels of veracity, allowing for both fine-grained and binary classification setups. The POLfake dataset also includes a rich set of attributes for both claims and tweets such as publication time, author information and popularity metrics, enabling a wide range of approaches to development of fake news detection models. To support reproducibility and fair evaluation, two benchmark tasks are provided: *Claim-Tweet Challenge* and *Claim-Only Challenge*. POLfake dataset is intended to serve as a valuable resource for advancements in the field of detecting the Polish-language fake news.

Keywords: Fake news · Disinformation · Recognition of fake news · Fake news datasets · Polish language

1 Introduction

In today's digital era, where social media and online communication tools rapidly amplify the spread of information, detecting fake news and misinformation has become a major challenge. Poland, similar to many nations, faces difficulties in combating the circulation of fake content, which can lead to significant social, political and economic repercussions. To solve this problem, the researchers and information technology experts are relying on advanced machine learning techniques to accurately detect and counter the fake news dissemination.

Despite the growing body of research on automated fake news detection, most existing solutions focus on English-language content and primarily utilize textual features, ignoring the social, relational and media contexts in which disinformation emerges and spreads. As a result, detection models based on

R. Laborde et al. (Eds.): ESORICS 2025 Workshops, LNCS 16233, pp. 310–326, 2026.
https://doi.org/10.1007/978-3-032-16165-9_18

such data demonstrate limited generalization to other languages, communication styles and the specifics of local media environments. The Polish information space is characterized by unique dynamics: presence of numerous websites with unverified credibility, frequent citations or distortions of original content that influences how information is interpreted.

Well-prepared datasets containing thousands of news items whose veracity has been verified by professionals are crucial for the development of models that effectively detect the fake news. Vast majority of existing fake news datasets consist of news articles written in high-resource languages, such as English or Chinese. However, due to cultural, social and legal differences, models trained on these foreign-language datasets often perform poorly when applied to Polish fake news detection. To address this gap, the Polish researchers in collaboration with domain experts have recently developed the first datasets specifically designed for identifying the fake news in Polish language [1,2].

The lack of high-quality, structured Polish-language data with which to train and evaluate fake news detection algorithms significantly limits the development of local analytical tools and reliable comparative research. Furthermore, existing Polish-language datasets are typically small, non-public, heterogeneous in terms of sources and lack information about the publication context. Therefore, there is a clear need to create a dataset that not only provides labeled examples of fake and real content but also allows for modeling complex relationships between them, such as source, temporal and semantic dependencies, opening the door to more advanced approaches based on graphs, propagation analysis and disinformation pattern detection.

The objective of this paper is to introduce and thoroughly describe a newly developed relational dataset designed for detecting the Polish fake news. The dataset, named POLfake, consists of thousands of claims verified by professional fact-checking platforms, as well as tweets that disseminate those claims. Claims and tweets in the POLfake dataset are represented not only by their content, but also by additional attributes such as publication date and author (for claims) or number of likes, replies and shares (for tweets). Furthermore, this paper proposes two approaches for leveraging the dataset to train the fake news detection models and evaluate their effectiveness.

The structure of the paper is as follows: Sect. 2 presents the related works focused on the publication of fake news datasets. Section 3 provides a detailed description of POLfake dataset development process. Section 4 deals with the final form of the dataset and proposes two approaches for conducting the experiments using POLfake dataset while Sect. 5 discusses the advantages and limitations of the presented dataset.

2 Related Works

The development of research in the field of fake news detection would not have been possible without the availability of relevant datasets published over the past years. Existing fake news datasets can be differentiated by a number of factors, such as language, domain coverage, news sources, number of items and labeling schema. This section discusses a selection of commonly used datasets in fake news detection, focusing on the factors mentioned above.

The review focuses on six English-language datasets: CoAID [18], FakeNewsNet [12], ISOT [14], LIAR [17], Twitter [15], and Pheme [16], as well as the Chinese-language Weibo dataset [13]. Two recently published datasets that contain news written in Polish: POLygraph [1] and SWAROG [2] are also discussed.

CoAID [18] is a dataset focused on the misinformation about healthcare in COVID-19. It includes both fake and real news posted on websites and social media platforms, along with associated user engagement and responses. As it covers only pandemic-related content, CoAID has the narrowest domain and thematic scope among the datasets discussed. The authors report that the latest version of the dataset contains over 18,079 fake news items and as many as 260,037 real news items.

The FakeNewsNet repository [12] includes two English-language datasets: Politifact and GossipCop, created using corresponding fact-checking platforms. Politifact focuses on political news, while GossipCop covers entertainment. Both datasets contain news items along with related social media activity. Politifact includes 624 real and 432 fake news items, whereas GossipCop is larger, with 16,817 real and 5,323 fake items.

The ISOT dataset [14] contains English-language news articles labeled as real or fake. The real articles were sourced from Reuters.com, while the fake ones came from unreliable websites identified by Wikipedia and Politifact. The dataset covers a wide range of topics, making it suitable for general-purpose fake news detection, and includes 21,417 real and 23,481 fake articles.

In [17], the authors proposed the LIAR dataset which contains more than 12,800 short English-language statements collected from sources such as tweets, TV ads, and political debates. Each statement was reviewed by Politifact editors and classified into one of six categories reflecting its truthfulness: from pants-fire to true. Unlike other datasets discussed, LIAR uses a multi-class labeling scheme instead of a binary one.

The Twitter dataset, released as part of the 2015 MediaEval Benchmark [15], was created to study manipulation of web content. It includes over 9,000 real and 6,000 fake English-language tweets, all related to eighteen specific events.

Similarly to the Twitter dataset, the Pheme dataset [16] also contains news stories in the form of tweets. It includes tweets and their replies related to five significant news events, all of which were verified and labeled as real or fake by journalists. The collection comprises 1,972 fake and 3,830 real tweets, all written in English.

The Weibo dataset [13] includes real and fake news written in Chinese. Real news were sourced from the Xinhua news agency, while fake news were collected from Weibo's official fake news debunking system between May 2012 and January 2016. The dataset is divided into training and testing subsets, with 3,749 fake and 3,783 real items in training, and 1,000 fake and 996 real items in testing.

POLygraph is one of the first datasets for detecting fake news in Polish [1]. It is divided into two distinct subsets: the *fake-or-not* dataset, which contains 11,360 pairs of news articles labeled as true or fake, and the *fake-they-say* dataset, comprising 5,082 news articles accompanied by tweets commenting on them. The *fake-or-not* subset follows a classic true/fake classification, while the *fake-they-say* subset is designed to capture the degree of author's belief in the truthfulness of information they commented on. This belief is categorized into six labels: *hard-claim-fake*, *hard-claim-not-fake*, *no-claim*, *sarcasm*, *soft-claim-fake*, and *soft-claim-not-fake*.

The SWAROG dataset [2] is the second major collection of Polish-language news and adopts a fundamentally different approach from the traditional true/-fake labeling. It contains over 40,000 annotated articles from digital newspapers, each evaluated using 13 carefully designed "yes/no" questions grouped into verification, manipulation and metaphysical categories. The authors report this approach allows for a more nuanced assessment of the content, moving beyond a simple binary classification.

Table 1 summarizes the discussed datasets – it describes each dataset by name, language and number of labels into which the news items where divided. In addition, it includes selected studies from recent years that have utilized the specific datasets.

Table 1. Summary of reviewed fake news datasets.

Name	Language	Number of labels	Introduced by	Utilized by
CoAID	English	2	[18]	[9–11]
FakeNewsNet	English	2	[12]	[4–8]
ISOT	English	2	[14]	[19–22]
LIAR	English	6	[17]	[20,23,24]
Twitter	English	2	[15]	[25,26]
Pheme	English	2	[16]	[27–29]
Weibo	Chinese	2	[13]	[6,25,26,28]
POLygraph	Polish	2/6	[1]	*No studies found*
SWAROG	Polish	13 questions	[2]	[3]

As the review indicates, existing fake news datasets differ significantly in language, domain coverage, size and labeling methods. While resources in English and Chinese are well developed, Polish-language datasets have only recently begun to appear. The release of POLygraph and SWAROG marks an important step forward, yet the field remains in its early stages. The POLfake dataset presented in this paper aims to fill this gap.

3 Development of POLfake Dataset

The process of constructing the POLfake dataset was divided into two stages. In the first stage, the claims verified by professional fact checking websites were collected. In the second stage, the tweets proclaiming the selected claims were retrieved. All operations performed in both stages are described in detail in the following subsections and illustrated in Fig. 1.

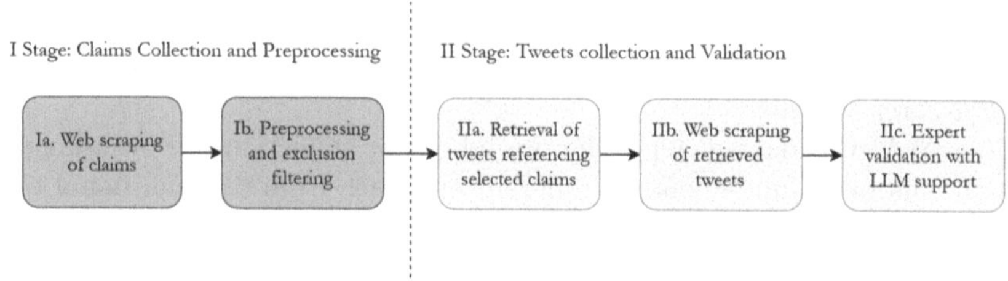

Fig. 1. Overview of POLfake dataset construction pipeline.

3.1 Claims Collection and Preprocessing

The development of POLfake dataset began with the collection of thousands of verified claims. To this end, the claims along with their assigned verdicts were web scraped from two professional Polish fact-checking platforms: Demagog and Fakenews.pl [34]. Fact-checking platforms assign each claim to a specific category that reflects its degree of truthfulness based on the detailed verification. Both Fakenews.pl and Demagog follow a similar categorization scheme when labeling the news items. The set of verdicts used by both platforms includes: true, mostly true, satire, scam, manipulation, mostly fake, fake and no context/no evidence/unverifiable.

On the Demagog website, all claims were extracted from the Statements section, which contains verified statements made by well-known public figures in Poland, including politicians. On Fakenews.pl, verified news items were collected from the following categories: politics, society, technology, health, the war in Ukraine and environment.

The initial web scraping process resulted in the collection of 6,067 verified claims: 546 from Fakenews.pl and 5,551 from Demagog. During the subsequent preprocessing stage, a set of Claim Exclusion Criteria (CEC) was defined and applied as follows:

- **CEC1**: Claims labeled as satire, scam, no context, no evidence or unverifiable.
- **CEC2**: Claims whose content is blank, malformed, shorter than 20 characters or longer than 1000 characters.
- **CEC3**: Claims for which the publication date was not retrieved.

The application of all Claim Exclusion Criteria (CEC1 – CEC3) resulted in a final set of 5774 claims: 508 from Fakenews.pl and 5266 from Demagog. Table 2 presents the number of claims remaining after applying each exclusion criterion, divided by source.

Table 2. Number of claims obtained after applying successive exclusion criteria.

CEC	Demagog	Fakenews.pl	In total
Initially	5551	546	6067
CEC1	5324	523	5847
CEC2	5270	508	5778
CEC3 (final)	**5266**	**508**	**5774**

3.2 Tweets Collection and Validation

The second stage of development of the dataset involved the retrieval of tweets proclaiming the selected claims. To this end, 77 volunteers were recruited to manually search the X platform (formerly Twitter) for tweets that explicitly proclaimed the thesis of each claim. The task of volunteers was to identify the tweets that clearly and explicitly endorsed the main thesis of the given claim. Tweets that were only indirectly related, contradicted the claim, or did not express a clear stance should be excluded from the dataset. Identified tweets were recorded in the form of direct URLs pointing to their original posts.

The volunteers' work resulted in the collection of 2,372 tweets proclaiming 878 selected claims. Each tweet was assigned to the specific claim it proclaimed. For each of the 878 claims, between 1 and 18 corresponding tweets were collected. The label assigned to each tweet was inherited from the label of its associated claim.

In the next step, the web scraping was performed on the collected URLs to retrieve detailed metadata for each tweet. Unfortunately, not all tweets could be successfully retrieved. To ensure the quality of collected data and to verify the alignment between tweets and their assigned claims, the following Tweet Exclusion Criteria (TEC) were applied:

- **TEC1**: Duplicated tweets.
- **TEC2**: Tweets whose body text is blank or malformed.
- **TEC3**: Tweets that, based on expert validation supported by a large language model (LLM), were found not to accurately reflect the main thesis of the assigned claim.

As part of TEC3, a large language model (LLM) was employed to analyze all collected tweets for consistency with the claims assigned by volunteers. The LLM's task was to determine whether a given tweet explicitly proclaimed the thesis of corresponding claim. The model returned a Boolean value – `true` if the tweet aligned with the claim or `false` if the tweet contradicted it, was only loosely related or entirely unrelated. Additionally, the LLM provided a brief explanation for its decision.

For this validation step, the GPT-4.1-mini model available via OpenAI Platform was used. A one-shot prompting technique was adopted. The original prompt instructions were provided in Polish and its English translation is presented in Listing 1.1.

```
You will help me assess whether a given tweet proclaims the provided claim
    that is, whether the tweet is consistent with the thesis expressed in the
     claim.

If the tweet aligns with the claim, respond with "true". In all other cases
    when the tweet contradicts the claim or is unrelated respond with "false
    ".

Your answer should be in JSON format with the key "verdict" and a value of "
    true" or "false". In the "explanations" field, include a short
    justification for your decision.

Example input and output.

Input:
Claim: "The Electoral Code allows me to nominate only 920 candidates"
Tweet: "The number of candidates on the list cannot be fewer than the number
    of MPs elected in a district and greater than twice that number (Article
    211 2 of the Electoral Code). So the joint list can contain 920
    candidates!"

Output:
{
  "verdict": "true",
  "explanations": "Both the claim and the tweet refer to the number of
      candidates being 920."
}
```

Listing 1.1. English translation of the prompt instructions given to the LLM

The LLM validation returned `true` verdict for 1,404 tweets and `false` verdict for 824 tweets. Subsequently, a team of three experts reviewed the explanations provided by the LLM for each of 824 tweets classified as `false` and made the final judgment on whether the tweet truly proclaimed the claim assigned to it by the volunteer. Following this detailed analysis, the experts decided by majority vote to exclude 775 tweets from the dataset.

The application of all Tweet Exclusion Criteria (TEC1âĂŞTEC3) resulted in a final set of 1,453 tweets corresponds to 663 claims. Table 3 shows the number of tweets and corresponding claims remaining after applying the successive exclusion criteria.

Table 3. Number of tweets and corresponding claims remaining after applying successive exclusion criteria.

TEC	Tweets remaining	Corresponding claims
Initially	2372	878
TEC1	2354	869
TEC2	2228	825
TEC3 (final)	**1453**	**663**

Most of tweets were removed during the LLM-supported validation (TEC3), which highlights the crucial role of this step. This outcome highlights that volunteers tended to be overly inclusive in their initial tweet selections, underscoring the importance of rigorous automated and expert verification to ensure data quality.

4 POLfake Dataset Overview

This section provides a comprehensive overview of the final POLfake dataset. The first subsection describes the properties of claims and tweets. Next, the structure of dataset and detailed statistics are presented. The last subsection introduces two challenges that leverage the POLfake dataset for developing models to detect Polish fake news.

4.1 Claim and Tweet Properties

The POLfake dataset consists of two related sets: verified claims and corresponding tweets. Each is characterized by a distinct set of properties. Due to differences in data type, origin and collection methodology, the attributes describing claims and tweets are not identical. Tables 4 and 5 list the properties of claims and tweets, respectively, along with descriptions of their content.

The rich set of attributes included in the POLfake dataset enables the application of a variety of approaches for developing the fake news detection models [34]. In particular, the dates of publication of claims and tweets are especially important, as they allow verification of temporal correspondence between a tweet and the claim it proclaims. Fake news and real news can differ in the speed and intensity of propagation over time. Dynamic analysis of news distribution on the social media can be an effective way to more accurately determine whether news is real or fake [33].

Providing the author of the claim further supports the alignment of the claim and the tweet by allowing models to detect whether a tweet references the person

Table 4. Properties of claims in *POLfake* dataset

Property	Description
`id`	Unique identifier of the claim
`content`	Original textual content of the claim in Polish
`source`	Fact-checking platform that verified the claim: *demagog_org* (Demagog) or *fake_news_pl* (Fakenews.pl)
`tags`	Keywords categorizing the claim's topic (comma-separated), e.g., *EU*, *Economy*, *Migration*
`author`	Name of the person who made the claim (if known)
`link`	URL linking to the full fact-checking report
`publication_date`	Date and time when the claim was published, in UNIX timestamp format
`label`	The truthfulness evaluation of the claim: *Prawda* (`True`), *Fałsz* (`Fake`), *Manipulacja* (`Manipulation`), *W większości prawda* (`Mostly True`), *W większości fałsz* (`Mostly Fake`)

Table 5. Properties of tweets in *POLfake* dataset

Property	Description
id	Unique identifier of the tweet
claim_id	Identifier of the claim that is proclaimed by this tweet
content	Original textual content of the tweet in Polish
shares	Number of times the tweet was shared (retweeted)
likes	Number of likes the tweet received
replies	Number of replies to the tweet
link	URL linking to the original post of the tweet
publication_date	Date and time the tweet was published, in UNIX timestamp format
label	The truthfulness label of the tweet which is the same as the claim it proclaims

who made the original statement. This is particularly useful when the tweet is a short response supporting the claim without repeating its content, but instead referring to the person who made the original statement.

Popularity indicators such as the number of likes, retweets and replies for each tweet offer additional signals related to the tweet's reach and user engagement. These characteristics can help assess the virality and potential impact of both true and fake news, which can improve the effectiveness of distinguishing credible content from false information [30–32].

In addition, the inclusion of links to fact-checking reports in the dataset enables the development of solutions that go beyond the simple classification of news items. Instead of simply labeling content as true or fake, such models can also provide direct references to verified fact-checking articles. This improves transparency and trustworthiness by allowing users to understand the rationale behind a given verdict. It also supports explainable AI approaches, where the end users are given access to the context, evidence and reasoning used by professional fact-checkers, thereby promoting informed decision-making and media literacy.

4.2 Dataset Structure and Statistics

The POLfake dataset is a relational dataset, as it consists of verified claims and tweets that are explicitly linked to them. Each tweet in the dataset proclaims exactly one claim, while a single claim can be associated with multiple tweets spreading it. This many-to-one relationship between social media content and fact-checked assertions reflects how information and particularly misinformation, is disseminated online. Thanks to this structure, the POLfake dataset facilitates the development of models capable of assessing the truthfulness of online content by analyzing its connection to verified claims.

Figure 2 presents an example of a tweet paired with the claim it proclaims. All properties of both the claim and the tweet, as listed in Tables 4 and 5, are included in the visualization. In addition, English translations of the original Polish content are provided to improve the clarity and accessibility.

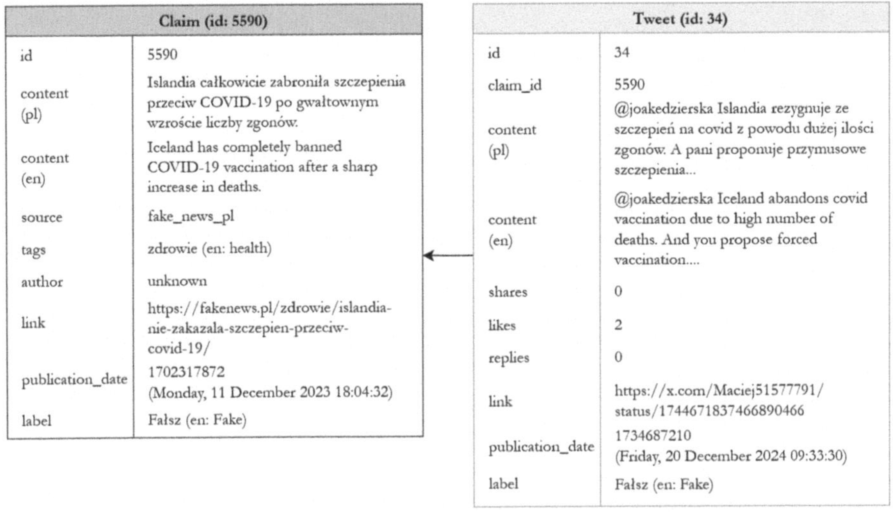

Claim (id: 5590)	
id	5590
content (pl)	Islandia całkowicie zabroniła szczepienia przeciw COVID-19 po gwałtownym wzroście liczby zgonów.
content (en)	Iceland has completely banned COVID-19 vaccination after a sharp increase in deaths.
source	fake_news_pl
tags	zdrowie (en: health)
author	unknown
link	https://fakenews.pl/zdrowie/islandia-nie-zakazala-szczepien-przeciw-covid-19/
publication_date	1702317872 (Monday, 11 December 2023 18:04:32)
label	Fałsz (en: Fake)

Tweet (id: 34)	
id	34
claim_id	5590
content (pl)	@joakedzierska Islandia rezygnuje ze szczepień na covid z powodu dużej ilości zgonów. A pani proponuje przymusowe szczepienia...
content (en)	@joakedzierska Iceland abandons covid vaccination due to high number of deaths. And you propose forced vaccination....
shares	0
likes	2
replies	0
link	https://x.com/Maciej51577791/status/1744671837466890466
publication_date	1734687210 (Friday, 20 December 2024 09:33:30)
label	Fałsz (en: Fake)

Fig. 2. ClaimâĂŞTweet pair example from *POLfake* dataset

Table 6. Distribution of claims and tweets by label in *POLfake* dataset

Label	Claims	Tweets
`True`	3058	847
`Fake`	1733	435
`Manipulation`	852	141
`Mostly true`	109	25
`Mostly fake`	22	5
In total	**5774**	**1453**

Figure 3 and Table 6 present the distribution of claims and tweets across five truthfulness labels used in POLfake dataset: `True`, `Fake`, `Manipulation`, `Mostly true` and `Mostly fake`.

Claims labeled as Fake occur almost twice less frequently and a similar proportion is observed among tweets. This suggests that the dataset reflects a realistic distribution of information, where not all content shared online is false, but where fake or misleading news still constitute a significant portion. It is noteworthy that if the dataset were to be used in a binary classification configuration in which claims labeled as Fake and Manipulation are grouped together, the number of True and Untrue cases would become relatively balanced. Such a configuration would be especially suitable for training robust binary classifiers. Overall, the volume and structure of the dataset offer a valuable foundation for building and evaluating both binary and multi-class fake news detection models.

The POLfake dataset includes claims and tweets that refer to a wide range of issues and cover a broad thematic spectrum. To illustrate this diversity, Table 7 presents the most frequently occurring tags assigned to claims. Tags are keywords that indicate the thematic domain of a claim, and each claim may be associated

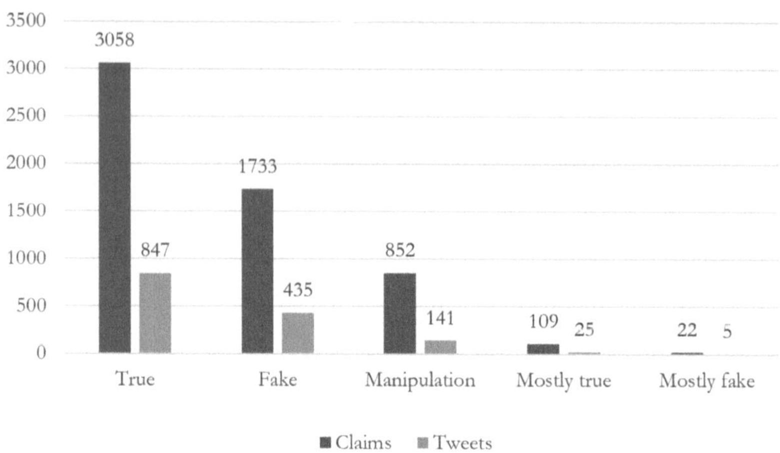

Fig. 3. Distribution of claims and tweets by label in *POLfake* dataset

with one or more of them. The table includes the original keywords in Polish, their English translations, and the number of claims to which each tag was assigned.

The POLfake dataset has been made publicly available on GitHub to ensure the open access for researchers and practitioners interested in Polish fake news detection. By sharing the dataset, we aim to support the development and benchmarking of models focused on identifying disinformation in the Polish language.

Table 7. Most frequent tags assigned to claims in *POLfake* dataset

Tag (en)	Tag (pl)	Claims
Domestic politics	Polityka krajowa	718
Economy	Gospodarka	469
Finance	Finanse	454
International affairs	Sprawy międzynarodowe	439
Social policy	Polityka społeczna	378
EU	UE	371
Health	Zdrowie	371
Elections	Wybory	336
Justice system	Wymiar sprawiedliwości	236
Budget	Budżet	220
Energetics	Energetyka	218
Society	Społeczeństwo	208
Education	Edukacja	193

4.3 Proposed Challenges

To demonstrate the potential of *POLfake* dataset and to support the future research on POLfake news detection, we offer two benchmark challenges: the *Claim-Tweet challenge* and the *Claim-Only challenge*.

Claim-Tweet Challenge

The *Claim-Tweet Challenge* is designed to evaluate the model's ability to generalize from verified, well-structured fact-checking content to informal, often noisy social media posts. In this task, the training data consist of all available claims from the dataset, while the goal is to assign one of five truthfulness labels to each tweet in the test set.

There are various approaches to accomplish this task. One option is to train a classifier on selected properties of the claims and apply it to the tweets. In addition to textual content (`content`), the `publication_date` – available for both claims and tweets – can serve as a valuable feature in this approach.

Another approach could be to retrieve the most semantically similar claim for a given tweet and predict the label of the tweet based on retrieved claim label. However, due to the large number of claims in the dataset, many of which cover similar topics or refer to the same subjects, this method may lead to incorrect matches and a high rate of false positive assignments.

A key constraint of *Claim-Tweet Challenge* is that models are not allowed to use the `claim_id` property of tweets during the classification. This property links each tweet to the specific claim it refers to, but it is provided solely for evaluation purposes, for instance to verify whether the system correctly identified the claim relevant to the tweet being classified. The main goal is to simulate a realistic scenario in which a model must assess the credibility of social media content using only previously verified information, without relying on explicit mappings between the tweets and claims.

A binary version of the challenge is also provided, where five original labels are divided into two categories:

- **True category**: `True` and `Mostly True`,
- **Fake category**: `Fake`, `Manipulation`, `Mostly False`.

This binary setup supports simpler model architectures and is well suited for fake news detection baselines. It is possible to limit the dataset to tweets labeled strictly as `True` or `Fake` or apply the provided mapping that merges five original classes into two binary categories.

Claim-Only Challenge

The *Claim-Only Challenge* focuses on developing models that classify claims based solely on their content and other properties, without relying on any related social media data. In this challenge, the claims of POLfake dataset are divided into training set and test set with an 80:20 ratio, where 80% of the claims form training set and the remaining 20% constitute test set. The primary objective is to classify each test claim into one of five truthfulness labels.

The challenge emphasizes the development of models that can generalize to unknown claims. It simulates a realistic scenario for automated fact-checking systems that need to assess the credibility of news stories and statements that have not yet been verified by experts.

Similar to the *Claim-Tweet Challenge*, a binary version is also available, where original five labels are mapped into two categories: True (including `True` and `Mostly True`) and Fake (including `Fake`, `Manipulation` and `Mostly False`). This binary setup simplifies the classification task and serves as a baseline for fake news detection.

5 Discussion

The following discussion addresses the presented characteristics of POLfake dataset. The analysis compares POLfake dataset with other fake news datasets, which are discussed in detail in Sect. 2.

The main purpose and the most important feature of POLfake dataset is that it contains exclusively news written in Polish. Most fake news datasets contain data in high-resource languages such as English or Chinese [12–18]. The first datasets for Polish fake news were published in recent years [1,2]. The POLfake dataset continues to addresses this gap by providing thousands of Polish-language claims and tweets, classified into a categories that reflect the degree of veracity.

Most fake news datasets provide data labeled only in two categories: true and fake [12–16,18]. In contrast, the POLfake dataset offers tweets and claims annotated across five degrees of truthfulness, allowing for more nuanced analysis. However, when needed, these categories can be grouped into two broader classes (True and Fake) enabling researchers to approach fake news detection as a traditional binary classification task.

The structure of presented dataset was designed to reflect the real-life relationships between false claims and the way misinformation spreads. Every piece of fake news, regardless of its form, can often be traced back to a core false claim it aims to promote. This allows misinformation to be grouped based on the claims it promotes, forming a one-to-many relationship: a single claim can be promoted by multiple posts written by different people. The POLfake dataset follows this structure, which sets it apart from many existing datasets that do not distinguish between claims and social media posts spreading them, nor define their mutual relationship [2,12–15,17,18].

Another advantage of POLfake dataset is its broad thematic coverage. While many existing datasets focus on a single topic or a few selected events [14,16,18], POLfake includes data covering a wide range of domains, such as domestic and foreign politics, public health, technology, environment, and more.

Among the fake news datasets analyzed, POLfake dataset shares the most similarities with the POLygraph dataset [1]. Both focus on Polish-language content and explore the relationship between claims and tweets that spread them. However, there are two key differences between these datasets.

First, in the *fake-they-say* subset of POLygraph, the goal is to classify a tweet according to the author's stance toward a given article. In contrast, POLfake consists of clearly defined claims and tweets that directly propagate them. Therefore, all tweets in POLfake can be considered to express a *hard-claim-not-fake* stance toward the linked claim. With this structure, the POLfake dataset enables the development of models that recognize posts that propagate the given claims. This is precisely the approach proposed in the *Claim-Tweet Challenge*, which treats claims as a training set and tweets as a test set.

Second, the POLfake dataset provides a broad set of properties for both claims and tweets, including publication date, author, popularity metrics and links to external fact-checking sources. In comparison, POLygraph contains articles represented only by their URLs and tweets described solely by their text and referenced URLs. The broader feature set in POLfake dataset allows for more diverse modeling approaches and potentially improves the performance of fact-checking systems by incorporating contextual information such as claim authorship or temporal patterns.

The proposed benchmark challenges – *Claim-Tweet Challenge* and *Claim-Only Challenge* – offer structured and flexible evaluation settings that reflect the real-world fact-checking scenarios. Each challenge is available in both a five-class and a binary classification setup, allowing researchers to tailor the difficulty of the task to their methodological goals. The inclusion of binary variants enables comparison with existing fake news detection datasets. Through these challenges, the POLfake dataset provides a comprehensive testbed for advancing research in misinformation detection in Polish language.

6 Conclusions

The high-quality fake news datasets are essential for the development, evaluation and benchmarking of disinformation detection models. Research on detecting Polish-language fake news is still in its early stages, and only in recent years have the first datasets for this task been introduced. The main contribution of this paper was to address this gap by publishing and thoroughly describing the POLfake relational dataset, which contains nearly 6,000 claims and 1,500 tweets. By providing the texts in Polish, the dataset reflects social, cultural and legal realities of Polish-speaking environment, thereby facilitating the creation of models capable of accurately detecting fake news in Polish.

The POLfake dataset consists of claims whose degree of truthfulness has been verified by professional fact-checking platforms. Furthermore, tweets collected and associated with these claims, based on their explicit propagation of the corresponding statements, were initially selected by trained volunteers and subsequently validated by experts with the support of large language models (LLMs). This semi-automated verification pipeline ensures the quality, consistency and methodological reliability of the dataset, making it suitable for a wide range of research applications in the recognition of Polish fake news.

The presented POLfake dataset offers four key advantages over existing fake news datasets: (i) it adopts a relational structure, linking tweets to the specific claims they propagate, which mirrors real-world misinformation dynamics; (ii) it uses a five-level truthfulness annotation scheme, which enables both fine-grained classification and simplified binary setups, allowing researchers to flexibly choose between nuanced and traditional fake news detection approaches; (iii) it ensures broad topical diversity, with content covering multiple domains such as politics, health, technology and environment; (iv) it includes a rich set of properties for both claims and tweets–such as publication date, author and popularity metrics, which facilitates the implementation of diverse strategies, including temporal, content-based and user-behavior-aware approaches.

Future research will focus on leveraging the POLfake dataset to develop models and systems capable of effectively detecting the fake news in Polish language. To support reproducibility and facilitate fair comparisons, two benchmark challenges have been published: *Claim-Tweet Challenge* and *Claim-Only Challenge*. The additional direction of future research will involve creating a system for dynamic extension of the dataset with newly verified claims, enabling real-time adaptation to emerging misinformation. Hopefully, the presented dataset will serve as a valuable resource for researchers aiming to develop Polish fake news detection models.

References

1. Dzienisiewicz, D., Graliński, F., Jabłoński, P., Kubis, M., Skórzewski, P., Wierzchoń, P.: POLygraph: Polish fake news dataset. arXiv preprint arXiv:2407.01393 (2024)
2. Kozik, R., Komorniczak, J., Ksieniewicz, P., Pawlicka, A., Pawlicki, M., Choraś, M.: SWAROG project approach to fake news detection problem. In: International Joint Conference CISIS 2023 and ICEUTE 2023, pp. 79–88. Springer, Cham (2023)
3. Kozik, R., et al.: Towards explainable fake news detection and automated content credibility assessment: Polish internet and digital media use-case. Neurocomputing **608**, 128450 (2024)
4. Qu, Z., Meng, Y., Muhammad, G., Tiwari, P.: QMFND: a quantum multimodal fusion-based fake news detection model for social media. Inf. Fusion 102172 (2024)
5. Palani, B., Elango, S.: CTrL-FND: content-based transfer learning approach for fake news detection on social media. Int. J. Syst. Assurance Eng. Manage. **14930**, 903–918 (2023)
6. Xiong, S., Zhang, G., Batra, V., Xi, L., Shi, L., Liu, L.: TRIMOON: two-round inconsistency-based multi-modal fusion network for fake news detection. Inf. Fusion **93**, 150–158 (2023)
7. Golo, M.P.S, Caravanti de Souza, M., Rossi, R.G., Rezende, S.O., Nogueira, B.M., Marcacini, R.M.: One-class learning for fake news detection through multimodal variational autoencoders. Eng. Appl. Arti. Intell. **122**, 106088 (2023)
8. Obaid, A.A., Khotanlou, H., Mansoorizadeh, M., Zabihzadeh, D.: Robust semi-supervised fake news recognition by effective augmentations and ensemble of diverse deep learners. IEEE Access **11**, 54526–54543 (2023)

9. Mayank, M., Sharma, S., Sharma, R.: DEAP-FAKED: knowledge graph based approach for fake news detection. In: Proceedings of 2022 IEEE/ACM International Conference on Advances in Social Networks Analysis and Mining (ASONAM), pp. 47–51 (2022)
10. Du, J., Dou, Y., Xia, C., Cui, L., Ma, J., Yu, P.S.: Cross-lingual COVID-19 fake news detection. In: Proceedings of 2021 International Conference on Data Mining Workshops (ICDMW), pp. 859–862 (2021)
11. Heidari, M., et al.: BERT model for fake news detection based on social bot activities in the COVID-19 pandemic. In: Proceedings of 2021 IEEE 12th Annual Ubiquitous Computing, Electronics & Mobile Communication Conference (UEMCON), pp. 103–109 (2021)
12. Shu, K., Mahudeswaran, D., Wang, S., Lee, D., Liu, H.: Fakenewsnet: a data repository with news content, social context, and spatiotemporal information for studying fake news on social media. Big Data **8**(3), 171–188 (2020)
13. Jin, Z., Cao, J., Guo, H., Zhang, Y., Luo, J.: Multimodal fusion with recurrent neural networks for rumor detection on microblogs. In: Proceedings of the 25th ACM International Conference on Multimedia, pp. 795–816 (2017)
14. Ahmed, H., Traore, I., Saad, S.: Detecting opinion spams and fake news using text classification. Secur. Privacy **1**(1), e9 (2018)
15. Boididou, C., et al.: Verifying multimedia use at mediaeval 2015. In: MediaEval 2015, vol. 1436 (2015)
16. Zubiaga, A., Liakata, M., Procter, R.: Learning reporting dynamics during breaking news for rumour detection in social media. arXiv preprint arXiv:1610.07363 (2016)
17. Wang, W. Y.: Liar, liar pants on fire: a new benchmark dataset for fake news detection. arXiv preprint arXiv:1705.00648 (2017)
18. Cui, L., Lee, D.: Coaid: covid-19 healthcare misinformation dataset. arXiv preprint arXiv:2006.00885 (2020)
19. Puraivan, E., Venegas, R., Riquelme, F.: An empiric validation of linguistic features in machine learning models for fake news detection. Data Knowl. Eng. **147**, 0169-023X (2023)
20. Balshetwar, S.V., Abilash, R.S., Jermisha, R.D.: Fake news detection in social media based on sentiment analysis using classifier techniques. Multimed. Tools Appl. **82**(23), 35781–35811 (2023)
21. Mallik, A., Kumar, S.: Word2Vec and LSTM based deep learning technique for context-free fake news detection. Multimed. Tools Appl. **83**, 919–940 (2024)
22. Raja, E., Soni, B., Borgohain, S.K.: Fake news detection in Dravidian languages using transfer learning with adaptive finetuning. Eng. Appl. Artif. Intell. **126**, 0952-1976 (2023)
23. Liao, Q., et al.: An integrated multi-task model for fake news detection. IEEE Trans. Knowl. Data Eng. **34**(11), 5154–5165 (2022)
24. Sadeghi, F., Bidgoly, A.J., Amirkhani, H.: Fake news detection on social media using a natural language inference approach. Multimed. Tools Appl. **81**(23), 33801–33821 (2022)
25. Peng, L., Jian, S., Kan, Z., Qiao, L., Li, D.: Not all fake news is semantically similar: contextual semantic representation learning for multimodal fake news detection. Inf. Process. Manage. **61**(1), 103564 (2024)
26. Chen, Y., et al.: Cross-modal ambiguity learning for multimodal fake news detection. In: Proceedings of the ACM Web Conference 2022, pp. 2897–2905. ACM (2022)

27. Luvembe, A.M., Li, W., Li, S., Liu, F., Xu, G.: Dual emotion based fake news detection: a deep attention-weight update approach. Inf. Process. Manage. **60**(4), 103354 (2023)
28. Li, K., et al.: Dynamic probabilistic graphical model for progressive fake news detection on social media platform. ACM Trans. Intell. Syst. Technol. **13**(5), 2157–6904 (2022)
29. Dougrez-Lewis, J., Kochkina, E., Liakata, M., He, Y.: Knowledge graphs for real-world rumour verification. In: Proceedings of 2024 Joint International Conference on Computational Linguistics, Language Resources and Evaluation (LREC-COLING 2024), Italy, ELRA and ICCL, pp. 9843–9853 (2024)
30. Kang, M., Seo, J., Park, C., Lim, H.: Utilization strategy of user engagements in Korean fake news detection. IEEE Access **10**, 79516–79525 (2022)
31. Raza, S., Ding, C.: Fake news detection based on news content and social contexts: a transformer-based approach. Int. J. Data Sci. Anal. **13**(4), 335–362 (2022)
32. Agrawal, C., Pandey, A., Goyal, S.: Fake news detection system based on modified bi-directional long short term memory. Multimed. Tools Appl. **81**(17), 24199–24223 (2022)
33. Li, K., Guo, B., Liu, J., Wang, J., Ren, H., Yi, F., Yu, Z.: Dynamic probabilistic graphical model for progressive fake news detection on social media platform. ACM Trans. Intell. Syst. Technol. **13**(5), 86 (2022)
34. Walczak, M., Poniszewska-Marańda, A.: Data structures towards the recognition of fake news and disinformation written in Polish. In: Computer Security. ESORICS 2024 International Workshops, pp. 305–320. Springer, Cham (2025)

Transparent and Trustworthy eXpainable AI (xAI) in Smart Human-Robot Collaboration Environment

Michał Choraś[1,2], Aleksandra Pawlicka[1], Marek Pawlicki[1,2](✉), and Rafał Kozik[1,2]

[1] ITTI Sp. z o.o., Poznań, Poland
[2] Bydgoszcz University of Science and Technology, Bydgoszcz, Poland
marek.pawlicki@itti.com.pl

Abstract. In this paper the current challenging problem of Artificial Intelligence transparency and trustworthiness are addressed. Explainable Artificial Intelligence has been conceptualized as a key to making AI systems transparent, accountable, and compliant with human rights standards. If not transparent and trustworthy, AI systems cannot be extensively used and widely adopted in certain domains and applications, such as human-robot collaboration, healthcare etc. Therefore, as a practical takeaway and major contribution of this paper, a new checklist for AI Transparency is proposed and showcased in the practical human-robot collaboration (HRC) use-case. It is recommended that the checklist be utilized by AI system designers and developers to ensure transparency to end users and the trustworthiness of AI systems assisting humans.

Keywords: Explainable Artificial Intelligence · Transparency · Trustworthy AI · Human-Robot Collaboration · Neuro-Symbolic AI · Anomaly Detection · AI Ethics · Transparency Checklist

1 Introduction

HRC scenarios have grown increasingly common in both industrial and everyday settings [10]. Progress in computer vision, robotics, and machine learning has led to novel modes of interaction - ranging from safe co-manipulation of tasks to the introduction of adaptive control schemes that respond to human proximity [19]. However, as these systems become more complex and autonomous, concerns persist over their safety, reliability, and the level of trust human operators can place in them [24].

Various operational methods have attempted to ensure safety in HRC [21]: strictly conservative approaches that halt robot motion during human interaction [20], sensor-based speed and separation monitoring to maintain a safe perimeter [12], power and force limiting strategies to keep biomechanical loads within human-safe thresholds, and passive hand-guiding techniques that directly involve humans in teaching robot behaviours [7]. While these strategies can mitigate risks, they frequently operate as "black box" solutions [23], leaving users

R. Laborde et al. (Eds.): ESORICS 2025 Workshops, LNCS 16233, pp. 327–344, 2026.
https://doi.org/10.1007/978-3-032-16165-9_19

and stakeholders uncertain about how decisions are made, what parameters are involved, and how well bias or anomalies are controlled.

Hence, transparent xAI is essential to maintaining safety, detecting anomalies, and building operator trust in HRC.

Applying xAI to HRC environments enhances safety and reliability and facilitates the trust of humans to their AI-powered robotic equipment. By making the decision-making processes accessible and accountable, one can better ensure that the future of HRC is productive and secure.

By integrating the proposed xAI Transparency Checklist into HRC systems, developers and users can examine the inner workings of xAI mechanisms just as much as the decision-making process of AI. This moves the field beyond mere claims of transparency toward demonstrable accountability and fairness. As a result, these frameworks can better serve the immediate need for physical safety and efficiency and also help ensure that xAI-driven systems uphold fundamental human rights principles, reinforcing ethical standards and societal trust [9].

The notion of "Methods of xAI" refer to systems and techniques designed to make the decision-making processes of AI models more easily understood, enabling users to grasp and trust the actions and outputs of AI technologies, by means of intuitive visualisations, straightforward explanations, and accessible reporting methods [6].

However, it seems that xAI systems, although being an advanced set of techniques aimed at providing transparency, often embody the very opaqueness they seek to resolve [17]. The algorithms that explain AI decisions–supposed to be transparent–are themselves complex, involving layers of computation that are neither straightforward nor easy to understand [13,14,18].

Experience shows that 'transparent' xAI algorithms often fail to engender genuine user trust, revealing a gap between claimed transparency and real-world interpretability.

The remainder of this paper is structured as follows: in Sect. 2, we discuss and debate the current approaches to xAI metrics, especially in the context of AI transparency and human rights. In addition, in Sect. 2, we discuss future potential solutions and directions in order to solve the problems of AI adoption and lack of transparency. In Sect. 3, we provide the new practical checklist for AI transparency as the guideline and recommendation for AI systems designers and developers, but also for policy-makers. Moreover, in Sect. 4, we present and discuss the importance of transparent AI in practical human-robot collaboration (HRC) application domain. Results focusing mainly on explainability, and discussion on fulfilling guidelines from our checklist are presented in Sects. 5 and 6, respectively. Conclusions are given thereafter.

2 Towards Transparent and Trustworthy xAI and AI

In order to measure xAI effectiveness, a vast array of metrics has been proposed [16], many of these metrics remain questionable in their validity [17]. By enhancing the clarity and effectiveness of xAI, stakeholders can better understand, question, and correct the AI's decisions, ensuring these technologies serve the public equitably and justly. Therefore, improving xAI is not just a technical necessity but a moral imperative to uphold and protect human rights [2].

To address these challenges, it is necessary to develop new, more effective xAI methodologies, though it is important to acknowledge that achieving these improvements will not be easy [22].

Finally, fostering multidisciplinary collaboration across fields like computer science, law, ethics, and social sciences will ensure that xAI technologies align with human values and legal standards, addressing the broader implications of AI transparency.

In fact, in the following section, the authors propose a new checklist for AI transparency coming from an interdisciplinary and holistic view, taking into account technical, legal, ethical and societal aspects.

3 Proposal for New Practical AI Transparency Checklist

We view transparency as "technical + ethical/legal/societal," per [15]. In other words, a transparent AI must disclose its algorithms, data sources, decision processes, and limitations so users can understand "how" and "why" it acted. The EU AI Act further requires informing deployers and affected persons about system capabilities, limitations, and rights [14], thus extending transparency beyond merely technical details to include fairness, bias mitigation, and legal compliance.

Therefore, transparency (apart from technical matters) should also involve multi-disciplinary ethical, legal, and societal implications. Values like fairness, reduced bias, and compliance with legal requirements should be embedded into AI systems.

In addition, some researchers [8] further extrapolate the concept of transparency into such aspects as (i) openness (relevant information provided to the correct recipient) and (ii) comprehensibility (the information is provided in the form which the recipient can understand).

Driven by the insight coming from the literature [3–5,11,17], the authors designed a new proposal for a checklist which quantifies transparency across the following areas: Technical (Table 1), Ethical, Legal, and societal (Table 2), Openness and comprehensiveness (Table 3).

3.1 Proposed Technical AI Transparency Checklist

The technical checklist includes:

This technical checklist addresses several important aspects of AI and xAI systems, including the clarity of their design and operational parameters, the reproducibility of their performance metrics, and the thorough documentation and validation of the explainability methods employed.

3.2 Proposed Ethical, Legal, and Societal Checklist

The ethical, Legal, and societal checklist includes:

Table 1. Descriptions of key transparency (Tx) requirements for AI systems and xAI methods.

Code	Description
T1	The AI system complexity is defined (e.g., user can access structure and weights/parameters)
T2	The hyperparameters are defined and explained
T3	The hyperparameter values are given
T4	The training parameters are given (e.g., number of epochs)
T5	The accuracy of the model is given
T6	The accuracy reported by the AI provider is reproducible (e.g., it is possible to run the same experiments and obtain similar numbers/values)
T7	Model interpretability is ensured (it is possible to understand how the AI system arrived at a specific decision)
T8	The system's computational requirements are documented
T9	Model robustness under adversarial conditions and edge cases is tested and reported
T10	Explainability methods used are documented (e.g., SHAP, LIME, etc.)
T11	The decision paths or feature attributions for individual predictions are available for inspection
T12	xAI methods are validated to ensure that the explanations they provide accurately reflect the model's decision-making process
T13	The strengths and weaknesses of the utilised xAI methods are disclosed to the user
T14	The underlying assumptions of the xAI method are clearly communicated to the users, especially when limitations might lead to misleading or incomplete explanations
T15	The explanations generated by xAI methods must be consistent when the same conditions are presented. Any inconsistencies should be addressed and documented. The reproducibility of xAI outputs should be verified and documented
T16	Each explanation provided by an xAI method must be documented, allowing future reviews to assess whether the explanation influenced decisions or outcomes

Table 2. Checklist for Ethical, Legal, and Societal (ELS) considerations in hybrid AI systems.

Code	Description
ELS1	The user (of hybrid AI) is notified about possible biases and societal limitations
ELS2	Possible biases are defined, and their origins are explained
ELS3	The personal data is handled according to the regulations and rules
ELS4	The affordability of technology (including training/finetuning costs and access to dedicated equipment) ensures equal access
ELS5	There are mechanisms for users to contest or appeal the decisions made by the AI system
ELS6	There is a clear policy for accountability in case of system failures or harmful outcomes

The proposed ELS checklist delineates essential guidelines aimed at ensuring that AI systems operate within morally acceptable bounds, comply with legal standards, and are considerate of societal impacts. This checklist is crucial as it explicitly addresses potential issues such as biases, data privacy, and accessibility that may arise with the deployment of hybrid AI technologies.

3.3 Proposed Openness and Comprehensiveness Checklist

The openness and comprehensiveness checklist includes:

Table 3. Checklist for Open Communication (OC) standards in AI model documentation and usage.

Code	Description
OC1	The documentation/description for the model is available
OC2	The procedure for using (i.e., how to use) the model is comprehensive and easy to reproduce
OC3	The procedure for reproducing the results is comprehensive and easy to follow
OC4	Intended uses and limitations are known and are described/defined
OC5	Open-source components and dependencies are clearly documented

This checklist enhances transparency by ensuring that detailed documentation and descriptions of the AI model are readily available. This not only aids in understanding the model's functionality but also in troubleshooting and improving it.

The idea behind the transparency checklist is to quantify how many relevant (and applicable in a given context) items the given and evaluated AI system addresses.

Ideally, a fully transparent AI system should meet all the criteria outlined in the checklist with positive responses.

4 Application Example: Neuro-Symbolic AI (NSAI) for Anomaly Detection in HRC

To demonstrate the practical applicability of our checklist, consider an anomaly detection approach in HRC scenarios that relies on neuro-symbolic rules.

4.1 The Neuro-Symbolic AI Paradigm

The typical structure of the neuro-symbolic processing paradigm has been depicted in Fig. 1. In the presented diagram the logic program (P) and the neural model (M) play distinct roles in a neuro-symbolic learning framework.

Figure 1 shows the pipeline - a neural model (M), with parameters (θ), processes raw input x into probabilistic symbols (r) which a logic program (P) uses to infer anomalies, supervised by target y.

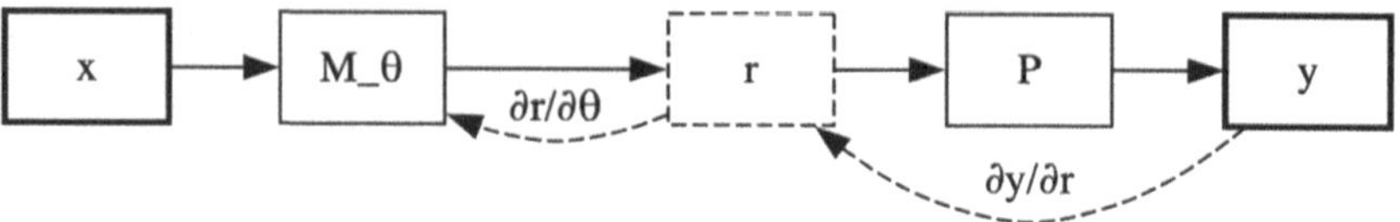

Fig. 1. Example of the neuro-symbolic processing paradigm. The input image x is processed by the neural model M (parameterized by θ), which generates the structured input r for the logic program P. Supervision is provided on y, meaning the system must learn θ

A crucial aspect of this system is the supervision mechanism used during the learning (error backpropagation) process. For the neuro-symbolic approach the supervision is provided on y. It means that the system must learn θ without direct supervision on r. This aligns with the fundamental assumption for neuro-symbolic AI, where neural networks learn from raw data while symbolic reasoning ensures structured and interpretable decision-making.

4.2 The Goal of NSAI in HRC Applications

Currently, the goal of these developed neuro-symbolic rules is to express safety best practices and recognize dangerous or anomalous moments. In particular, the rules for normal and abnormal states are based on safety guidelines for UR10 human-robot collaboration systems. Generally, safety recommendations emphasize tracking the robot's movements. In this case, due to the robot's location and the natural assembly process, a particular danger arises when the robot delivers a box of elements to the table. The anomaly is triggered only if the human operator is not following the robot arm-indicated by their current activity. For example, if the human rotates toward the wall and has the robot arm behind their back, the symbolic rules trigger an alarm. On the other hand, removing an empty box from the table is considered safe because the gripper moves away from the human operator.

Similarly, the system remains in a normal state if the human picks an element and assembles it at a desk while the robot waits. However, a prolonged wait state without a clear reason can be considered anomalous. In this approach, multiple DeepProbLog models represent various rules and constraints related to physics and facts about the HRC process. We encode (1) anomaly-prediction, (2) normal-state, (3) rule-based consistency/constraint, (4) environmental-fact, and (5) gesture-detection rules.

In this probabilistic framework, the output of a rule is the probability of a particular combination of symbols. For instance, a rule named "anomaly" might trigger when "ur10 is at the assembling table" and "human is in the working area." In classical Boolean logic, this would be a simple conjunction. However, in the probabilistic setting provided by DeepProbLog, the rule answers: "Given the human and robot 3D skeletons, what is the probability that the human is in the robot working area?". By applying our transparency checklist to such

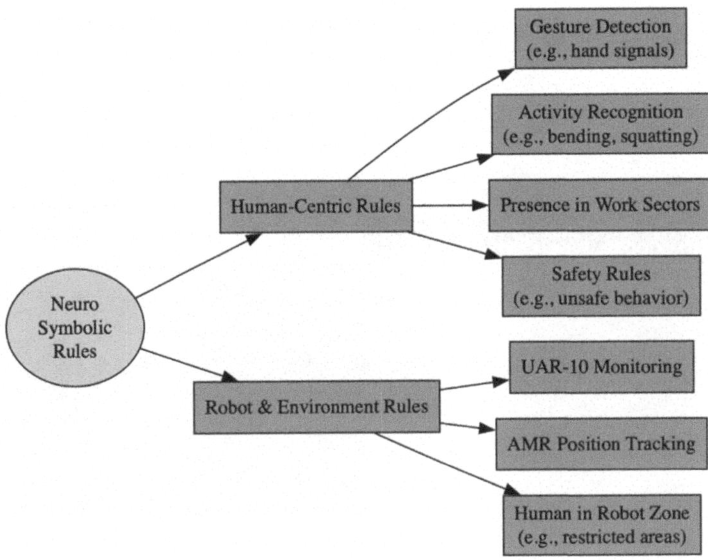

Fig. 2. Probabilistic neuro symbol rule groups and types.

a scenario, we ensure that stakeholders understand how anomalies are defined, which factors influence the decision, and with what certainty. The checklist's technical, ethical, and openness criteria help maintain clarity about how rules are constructed, tested, and interpreted, thereby aligning with both safety and human rights principles (Fig. 2).

4.3 Enhanced Explainability with NASI

To enhance the approach with explainability, probabilistic symbols derived from neural networks are integrated into the reasoning process. As illustrated in Fig. 3, the neural components encode visual inputs related to human and robot states as probabilistic symbols. For example, the human operator's condition can be represented by symbols such as *is_working*, *is_awaiting_robot*, *is_facing_table*, and *is_standing_back_to_robot*. Similarly, the robot's status–e.g., delivering or removing an object, can be encoded into distinct probabilistic symbols that reflect its current actions.

In some cases, these symbols are mutually exclusive. A human cannot simultaneously be working and waiting for the robot, or be facing the table and standing back to the robot at the same time. As depicted in Fig. 4, a similar approach applies to recognising human poses and gestures: multiple neural networks yield categorical outputs with associated probabilities (e.g., $p(\text{arms spread}) = 0.9$). By doing so, the system quantifies uncertainties and captures subtle variations in behaviour and posture.

In particular, thanks to this rule-based system, one can rollback the decision, meaning one can trace back which probabilistic symbols led to a specific outcome.

Fig. 3. Example of predictions (probabilistic symbols) for human and robot activities.

This is visible in the lower part of the diagram, where we can observe which symbols were activated within the rule. Additionally, we have information from the image-level explanation. Since we know that the detected objects are hands, we can easily query the backbone network to understand why it considers the hands to be raised and, more importantly, where in the image they are located.

This approach enhances interpretability and allows us to verify whether the network is actually focusing on the correct regions when assessing hand positions. Furthermore, the skeletal representation provides additional context for understanding the observed behaviour.

As it is shown in Fig. 5, the proposed approach can achieve better quality in explaining pixel-level explanations. It is particularly vivid when compared with post-hoc explainers like LIME.

5 Results - Practical Application of Transparency Checklist

5.1 Explainability

This section focuses on the explainability aspects of the HAI model's decisions. In particular, the usefulness of the provided explanations are assessed in the context of detecting various events in HRC.

This is done in the context of the so-called prediction gap, which aims to measure how perturbations or modifications to key decision-making factors influence the final output of the model. In other words, if the model identifies certain parts

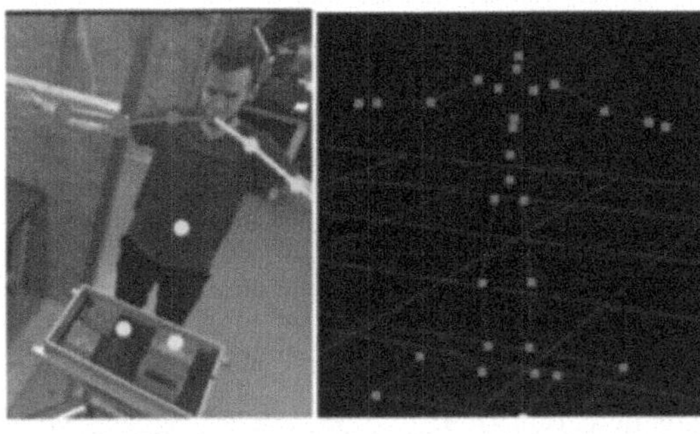

Fig. 4. Probabilistic symbols representing states of human limbs used for human pose recognition.

Fig. 5. The contrast between the quality of black-box explanations and the hybrid AI approach.

of the input as critical for its decision-making, applying perturbations to these elements should have a significant impact on the final outcome.

The Prediction Gap, as defined by OpenXAI [1] is typically used to measure the impact of perturbing important input features on the predictions of the model. This can be formulated as: $PG = \mathbb{E}_{x\sim P(X)}\left[|f(x) - f(x')|\right]$

In the above formula f(x) is the model's output for the original input x, and x' is the perturbed version of x. P(X) represents the distribution of input samples.

Consider two types of explanations provided by the HAI model. The first type consists of typical explanations in the form of heatmaps. For example, when a specific event is detected in a given scene, the relevant pixel areas associated with the detection are highlighted using a heatmap. More precisely, If the system detects an event such as a "worker signaling with their hand", the heatmap identifies and marks the region of the image where the worker's hand appears.

Another type of explanation is built on decision rules used during the prediction stage. This approach returns a symbolic representation of the key factors

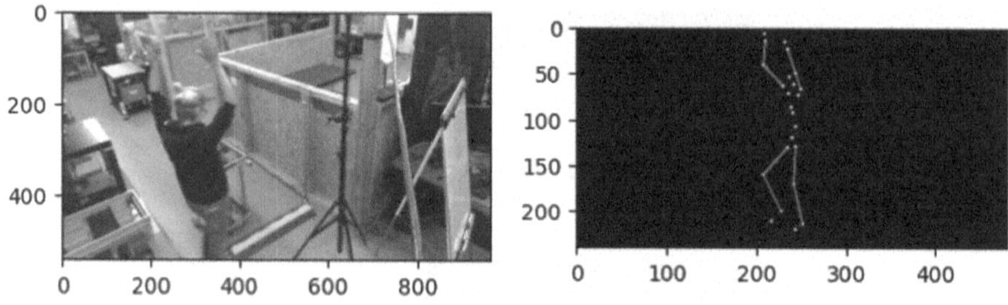

Fig. 6. L+R-UP (both arms up) event detection (left: original image, right: skeletal representation of the worker)

that influenced the decision of the model. For instance, if the system detects an event such as a worker "signaling with their hand", the decision rule returns a structured explanation outlining the specific factors that contributed to this detection. In the case of a hand signaling event, one such factor will be a raised hand.

Image-Level Explanations

In the case of heatmap-centric prediction gap analysis, we focused on selected events detected by the HAI model. The Fig. 6 illustrates an event where a worker raises both their left and right hand simultaneously. The adjacent image presents a skeletal representation, which serves as the predicted 3D pose of the human in the scene.

Moreover, in the Fig. 5 there is the heatmap visualization, which highlights the specific image regions connected with the raised hands detection. From the visual inspection, one can say that the heatmap quite accurately identifies the areas corresponding to the worker's arms (even in a complex background).

The Fig. 7 serves as a complementary explanation to the heatmap. It consists of two columns: the first column presents probabilistic symbols, which act as inputs for the decision rule displayed on the right. Each probabilistic symbol in the table is associated with a quantized value (medium, moderate, high, low, up, or down, etc.) along with a confidence level that falls within the range of 0.0 to 1.0. In the given example, the decision rule considers only the height of the left and right arms. Both the left arm height and right arm height have been classified as high, with a certainty level exceeding 90%.

Such an explanation serves as a strong signal and valuable insight into which areas of the image should be modified or perturbed to assess their impact on the final prediction outcome. In the analysed scenario, we applied Gaussian noise to examine whether the region relevant to detecting the raised hands event influences the model's confidence. This approach allows us to evaluate how sensitive the model is to perturbations in critical areas and whether such modifications degrade its certainty in making correct predictions.

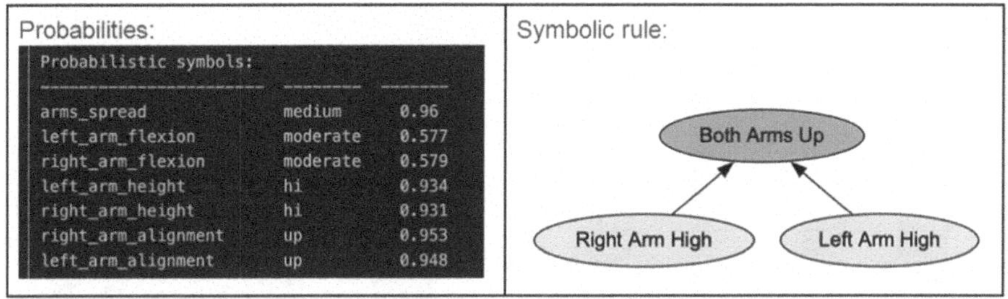

Fig. 7. Intermediate skeletal probabilistic symbols (left) accompanied by graphical representation of the detection rule.

The Fig. 8 provides a visual representation of the impact of Gaussian noise on the model's confidence level. On the left side, the original image is shown with a progressively increasing noise intensity. The confidence value is indicated in the title of the graph. It can be observed that as the noise intensity increases, the confidence score gradually decreases. At a certain point, the confidence drops below 40%, which serves as evidence that the raised hands event is no longer detected. Another notable aspect is the visualization of the skeletal representation. The perturbation applied to this region visibly affects the detection process, as the arms are gradually lowered, ultimately leading to a failure in correctly identifying the event.

In the next step, a similar experiment is repeated, but this time, the perturbation is applied to an area of the image that is not related to the detected event. The modification primarily affects the background and parts of the human body that are not directly linked to the detected event. At each step, the noise intensity increases, but an important observation is that across all levels of added noise, the model's confidence remains largely unchanged, fluctuating only between 88% and 84%. Additionally, as seen in the skeletal visualization, the modification is minimal in the sense that the arms remain raised, confirming that the explanation correctly identifies the areas the model focuses on when making its decision.

Symbolic Level Explanations

In the previous section (heatmap analysis), the stability of explanations using the pixel-level representation was evaluated. In this approach, one also compare the explanation obtained from the hybrid system HAI, however, on a different representational level. Moreover, one also compare the outcome with black-box explanation methods such as LIME.

When determining the Prediction Gap for the symbolic layer (Symbolic Level), the system recognizes elements in an image and returns a symbolic representation of the image. In this case, 3D scene reconstruction is considered. In case of humans, the system provides a skeletal representation consisting of 23

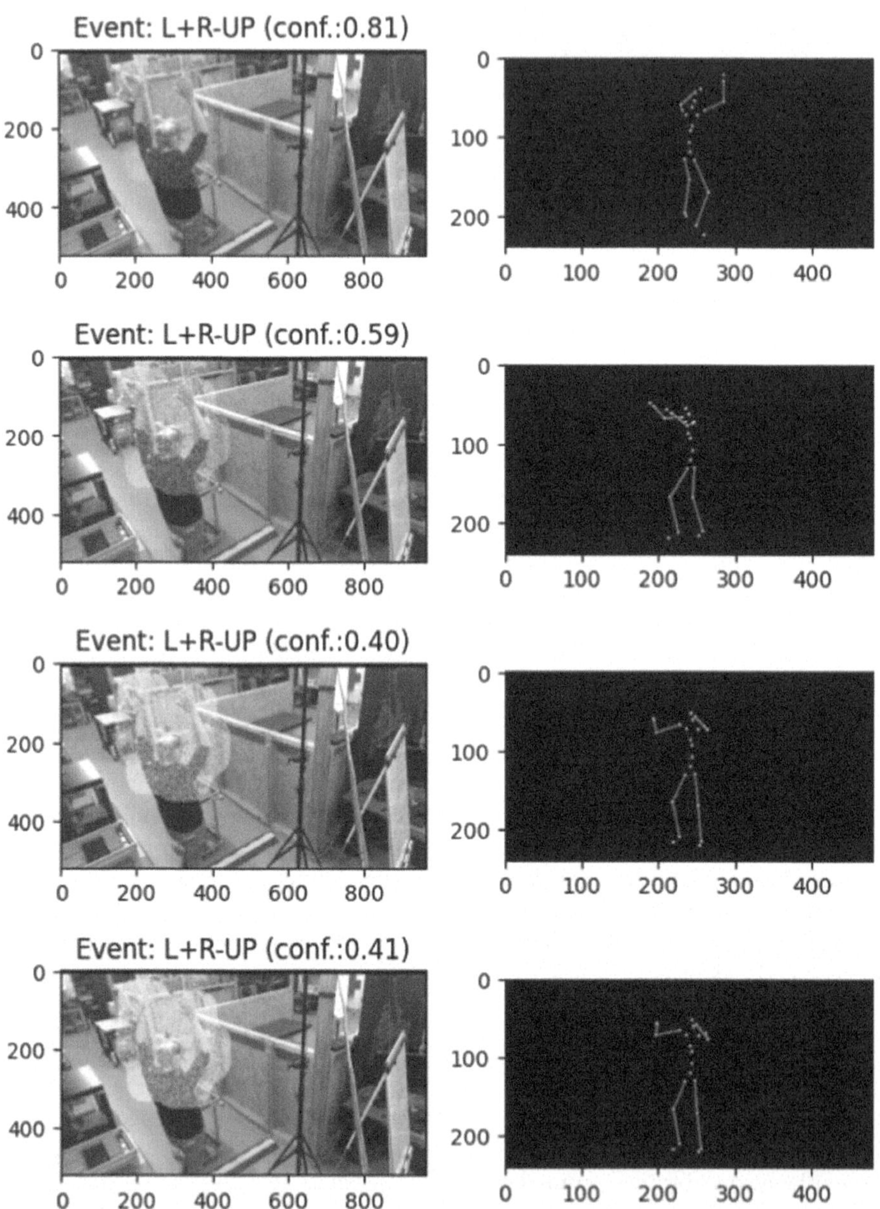

Fig. 8. PGI (Prediction Gap Important features). The region indicated with the heatmap is being perturbed with the Gaussian noise (with increasing intensity from row to row). The image on the right indicates how the perturbation influences the skeletal representation. Images are taken from a retreived 3D representation, hence the differences in orientation.

points representing key skeletal elements. Both robots (UR10 and AMR) are approximated using 4 points. The example is shown in Fig. 9.

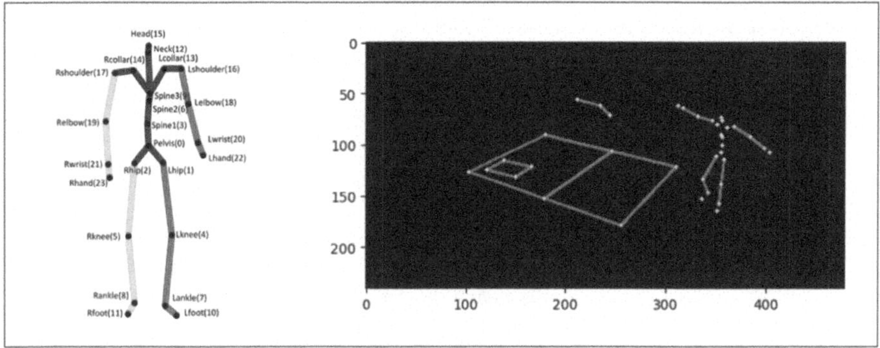

Fig. 9. Skeletal representation: human body keypoints (left), environment (right)

An example of an explanation generated on symbolic data is presented in the Fig. 10. The explanation has been obtained using the black-box LIME method. It is a typical histogram where the importance of individual features is highlighted. In this case, the feature is a point in 3D space. By analysing the explanation, one can see that in the case of the T-POSE, two features are dominant: the left and right wrists.

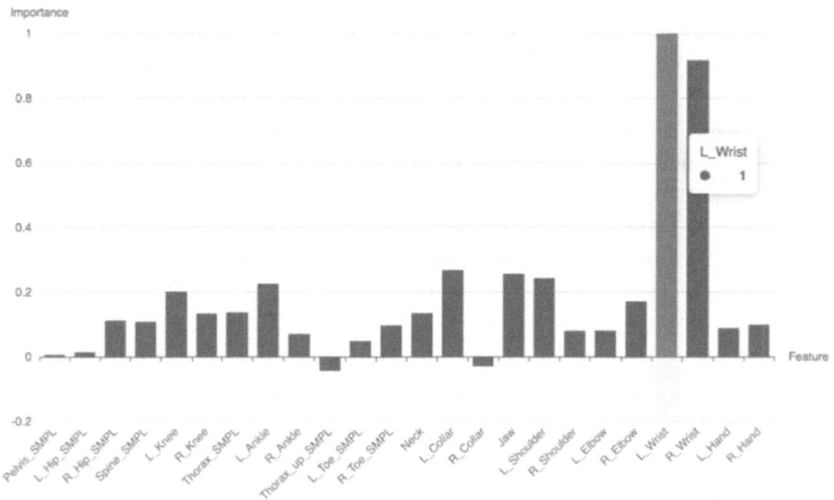

Fig. 10. Importance of human body keypoints for the T-POSE gesture (identified using the LIME method). While the wrists are correctly highlighted, the explanation is incomplete due to the lack of spatial correlations between keypoints.

In contrast, the explanation based on HI (Human-Interpretable) provided in the Table 4 is fundamentally different and more explanatory. It does not have a fixed length, as it depends on the rule used for prediction. In this case, the rule consists of several elements, as shown in the list. We can see that the T-POSE was detected because the arms are widely spread, there is no flexion in the left and right arms, and both arms are not positioned low.

Table 4. HAI explanation for T-POSE gesture.

Visual symbol	Explanation
arms_spread_wide	The arms are spread wide to the sides, meaning their position relative to the torso is nearly horizontal and symmetrical
NOT left_arm_flexion_notable	The left arm is not significantly bent, meaning there is no notable flexion angle at the elbow joint
NOT right_arm_flexion_notable	The right arm is also not significantly bent, so it remains in an almost fully extended position
NOT left_arm_height_low	The left arm is not positioned low, meaning it is not lowered downward but rather raised to shoulder height
NOT right_arm_height_low	The right arm is also not lowered, suggesting it is at a similar height to the left arm

This leads to a quantified measurement that one can compute using the Prediction Gap (PG) formula. The corresponding PGI and PGU values are provided in the Table 5. In the case of PGI, higher values of the indicator are desirable since PGI (Prediction Gap of Important Features) quantifies the impact of perturbing critical features on the model's predictions. A higher PGI value indicates that the model strongly relies on the identified important features, meaning that modifications to these areas significantly affect the prediction outcome. On the contrary, lower values for the PGU indicator are desired.

Table 5. Prediction GAP measured values.

Scenario	PGI (higher better)	PGU (lower better)
HAI Explainer	0.34	0.05
LIME Explainer	0.06	0.09

6 Application of the Checklist to the Real-World HRC xAI Scenario

In this section, to evaluate the transparency, reliability, and ethical readiness of the subject neuro-symbolic xAI anomaly detection system for HRC, the proposed AI Transparency Checklist is applied.

T1 & T2: AI System Complexity, Hyperparameters Defined and Explained. In the presented NSAI approach, the structure of the system is made clear by separating the deep learning components from the symbolic components. The fact that the neural backbone has layers dedicated to pose estimation is explicitly disclosed, and so is the fact that symbolic rules encode HRC safety constraints. Hyperparameters such as learning rates, batch sizes, or pose estimation thresholds are documented in the project's notes and annotated within the training scripts, ensuring the system complexity is well-defined.

T3 & T4: Hyperparameter Values and Training Parameters. The actual numeric values used in training the human-pose recognition network are disclosed. Parameters for the symbolic rule engine, such as probability thresholds for anomalous states, are documented, indicating exactly where the operator's gesture is recognized as an anomaly.

T5 & T6: Accuracy Reported and Reproducibility. When the model flags anomalous scenarios, the detection accuracy on test videos is reported. We demonstrate how other teams can run the same scripts or use the same dataset to replicate these anomaly-detection outcomes, addressing reproducibility. A standardized dataset of HRC scenarios can be shared, allowing independent verification of our accuracy claims.

T7 & T10: Model Interpretability and Explainability Methods Documented. The symbolic rule layer naturally increases interpretability by providing human-readable rules. The use of heatmaps at the pixel level and rule-based explanations at the symbolic level is documented. This neuro-symbolic pipeline is clearly explained and listed in project documentation, enabling any stakeholder to trace how decisions are derived.

T8: System Computational Requirements. The FPS is benchmarked, and the GPU requirements are listed in the project documentation in the system specification, so that end-users know what hardware is necessary to deploy the HRC anomaly-detection module.

T9: Robustness under Adversarial Conditions. The system was tested against common real-world perturbations like motion blur, occlusion, and added noise in the camera feed. The results demonstrate that the NSAI system degrades gracefully even under moderate levels of perturbations, showing it is robust enough for typical factory or workshop settings.

T11 & T12: Decision Paths or Feature Attributions Available and Validated. One of the advantages of a neuro-symbolic architecture is that each final judgment can be traced to specific probabilistic symbols.

T13–T15: Strengths, Weaknesses, Assumptions, and Consistency of Explanations. While symbolic rules enable explicit logic-based explanations, one limitation is that symbol definitions must be carefully tuned for each HRC configuration. For instance, the danger zone next to a UR10 robot may differ across tasks, so the user must update the rule engine accordingly. The same scenario with the same symbolic inputs must yield consistent anomaly decisions; any inconsistency is logged. This ensures the reproducibility of the same xAI explanation in repeated experiments.

T16: Documentation of Every Explanation. Logs are created for each run, storing relevant images, the derived symbols, and the final explanation.

ELS1 & ELS2: Notification and Definition of Biases. Because the system might incorrectly classify certain human postures or gestures based on insufficient or skewed training data (fewer examples of certain body types or cultural gestures), the stakeholders are explicitly informed that false positives or negatives could arise from these data biases. We document the known sources of training data.

ELS3: Personal Data Handling. In HRC video streams, faces and body shapes may indirectly identify individuals. Therefore, any personal data (recorded videos) is handled in accordance with GDPR principles.

ELS5: Mechanisms to Contest Decisions. When an anomaly is flagged, a user can pause the system and review the symbolic explanation. If the user sees the detection was a misinterpretation, the user can override or dismiss the anomaly.

ELS6: Accountability Policy. The final accountability rests with the industrial safety officer or the project manager, not solely on the AI system.

OC1, OC2, OC3, OC4, OC5: Availability of Documentation, Comprehensive Usage Guide and Reproducibility, Intended Uses and Limitations, Open-source Components. A "How it works" overview that explains both neural network modules and symbolic rules is published. A step-by-step procedure is outlined. The primary domain for which the system was designed is explicitly labeled. All the modules for the neural-based detection use open libraries.

By mapping the xAI-driven HRC anomaly detection system to each item in the Transparency Checklists, one can see how the neuro-symbolic paradigm can be made fully transparent, responsible, and reproducible. Technically, the pipeline from raw video input to symbolic rules is clearly explained. Ethically and legally, data-handling policies and potential biases are noted. In terms of openness, a clear documentation with disclaimers is provided.

7 Conclusions

Although xAI tools promise transparency, many remain opaque, risking fairness. This work addresses this by proposing a unified AI Transparency Checklist and demonstrates its applicability in an HRC anomaly detection case. Future work will refine standard xAI metrics and extend our checklist to other collaborative domains.

We encourage practitioners and policymakers to embed transparency, trustworthiness, and explainability into AI systems from design through deployment by implementing the proposed checklist.

Acknowledgements. This work is funded under the ULTIMATE project, which has received funding from the European Union's Horizon Europe research and innovation programme under grant agreement No 101070162.

References

1. Agarwal, C., et al.: Openxai: towards a transparent evaluation of model explanations. Adv. Neural Inf. Process. Syst. **35**, 15784–15799 (2022)
2. Choraś, M., Pawlicki, M., Kozik, R., Pawlicka, A.: Tech developers must respect equitable ai access. Nature **625**(7996), 663 (2024)
3. Doshi-Velez, F., Kim, B.: Towards a rigorous science of interpretable machine learning. arXiv preprint arXiv:1702.08608 (2017)
4. Edwards, L., Veale, M.: Slave to the algorithm? Why a'right to an explanation'is probably not the remedy you are looking for. Duke L. Tech. Rev. **16**, 18 (2017)
5. Floridi, L., Cowls, J.: A unified framework of five principles for ai in society. Machine learning and the city: applications in architecture and urban design, pp. 535–545 (2022)
6. Gunning, D., Stefik, M., Choi, J., Miller, T., Stumpf, S., Yang, G.Z.: XAI–explainable artificial intelligence. Sci. Robot. **4**(37) (2019). https://doi.org/10.1126/scirobotics.aay7120, https://www.science.org/doi/10.1126/scirobotics.aay7120
7. Hamad, M., Nertinger, S., Kirschner, R.J., Figueredo, L., Naceri, A., Haddadin, S.: A concise overview of safety aspects in human-robot interaction. In: Piazza, C., Capsi-Morales, P., Figueredo, L., Keppler, M., Schütze, H. (eds.) Human-Friendly Robotics 2023. HFR 2023. Springer Proceedings in Advanced Robotics, LNCS, vol. 29, pp. 1–18. Springer, Cham (2024). https://doi.org/10.1007/978-3-031-55000-3_1
8. Haresamudram, K., Larsson, S., Heintz, F.: Three levels of AI transparency. Computer **56**(2), 93–100 (2023). https://doi.org/10.1109/MC.2022.3213181, https://ieeexplore.ieee.org/document/10042109/
9. Jobin, A., Ienca, M., Vayena, E.: The global landscape of ai ethics guidelines. Nat. Mach. Intell. **1**(9), 389–399 (2019)
10. Lasota, P.A., Shah, J.A.: Analyzing the effects of human-aware motion planning on close-proximity human-robot collaboration. Hum. Factors **57**(1), 21–33 (2015)
11. Marques-Silva, J.: Disproving xai myths with formal methods – initial results. In: 2023 27th International Conference on Engineering of Complex Computer Systems (ICECCS), pp. 12–21 (2023). https://doi.org/10.1109/ICECCS59891.2023.00012
12. Merckaert, K., Convens, B., Wu, C.J., Roncone, A., Nicotra, M.M., Vanderborght, B.: Real-time motion control of robotic manipulators for safe human–robot coexistence. Robot. Comput.-Integr. Manuf. **73**, 102223 (2022)
13. Molnar, C.: Interpretable Machine Learning (Second Edition) A Guide for Making Black Box Models Explainable. Leanpub (2022). https://leanpub.com/interpretable-machine-learning

14. Molnar, C., Casalicchio, G., Bischl, B.: Interpretable machine learning – a brief history, state-of-the-art and challenges. In: Koprinska, I., et al. (eds.) ECML PKDD 2020. CCIS, vol. 1323, pp. 417–431. Springer, Cham (2020). https://doi.org/10.1007/978-3-030-65965-3_28
15. Nyrup, R.: The limits of value transparency in machine learning. Philos. Sci. **89**(5), 1054–1064 (2022). https://doi.org/10.1017/psa.2022.61
16. Pawlicka, A., Pawlicki, M., Kozik, R., Kurek, W., Choraś, M.: How Explainable Is Explainability? Towards Better Metrics for Explainable AI, pp. 685–695 (2024). https://doi.org/10.1007/978-3-031-44721-1_52
17. Pawlicki, M., et al.: Evaluating the necessity of the multiple metrics for assessing explainable AI: a critical examination. Neurocomputing **602**, 128282 (2024). https://doi.org/10.1016/j.neucom.2024.128282, https://linkinghub.elsevier.com/retrieve/pii/S0925231224010531
18. Ribeiro, M., Sing, S., Guestrin, C.: Anchors: high-precision model-agnostic explanations. In: Proceedings of the Thirty-Second AAAI Conference on Artificial Intelligence (AAAI-18), the 30th innovative Applications of Artificial Intelligence (IAAI-18), and the 8th AAAI Symposium on Educational Advances in Artificial Intelligence (EAAAI-18). New Orleans, Louisiana (2018)
19. Sun, Y., Van, M., McIlvanna, S., Minh, N.N., McLoone, S., Ceglarek, D.: Adaptive admittance control for safety-critical physical human robot collaboration. IFAC-PapersOnLine **56**(2), 1313–1318 (2023)
20. Tian, R., Sun, L., Bajcsy, A., Tomizuka, M., Dragan, A.D.: Safety assurances for human-robot interaction via confidence-aware game-theoretic human models. In: 2022 International Conference on Robotics and Automation (ICRA), pp. 11229–11235. IEEE (2022)
21. Valori, M., et al.: Validating safety in human-robot collaboration: standards and new perspectives. Robotics **10**(2), 65 (2021)
22. Winfield, A.F., Jirotka, M.: Ethical governance is essential to building trust in robotics and artificial intelligence systems. Philos. Trans. R. Soc. A Math. Phys. Eng. Sci. **376**(2133), 20180085 (2018)
23. Yan, F., Wen, S., Nepal, S., Paris, C., Xiang, Y.: Explainable machine learning in cybersecurity: a survey. Int. J. Intell. Syst. **37**(12), 12305–12334 (2022). https://doi.org/10.1002/int.23088, https://onlinelibrary.wiley.com/doi/10.1002/int.23088
24. Zhu, Y., Wang, T., Wang, C., Quan, W., Tang, M.: Complexity-driven trust dynamics in human-robot interactions: insights from ai-enhanced collaborative engagements. Appl. Sci. **13**(24), 12989 (2023)

International Workshop on Hardware-Supported Software Security (HS3 2025)

OpenGL GPU-Based Rowhammer Attack (Work in Progress)

Antoine Plin[1], Frédéric Fauberteau[2(✉)], and Nga Nguyen[2]

[1] Leonard de Vinci Graduate School of Engineering (ESILV), Paris, France
antoine.plin@edu.devinci.fr

[2] De Vinci Higher Education, De Vinci Research Center, Paris, France
{frederic.fauberteau,nga.nguyen}@devinci.fr

Abstract. Rowhammer attacks have emerged as a significant threat to modern DRAM-based memory systems, leveraging frequent memory accesses to induce bit flips in adjacent memory cells. This work-in-progress paper presents an adaptive, many-sided Rowhammer attack utilizing GPU compute shaders to systematically achieve high-frequency memory access patterns. Our approach employs statistical distributions to optimize row targeting and avoid current mitigations. The methodology involves initializing memory with known patterns, iteratively hammering victim rows, monitoring for induced errors, and dynamically adjusting parameters to maximize success rates.

The proposed attack exploits the parallel processing capabilities of GPUs to accelerate hammering operations, thereby increasing the probability of successful bit flips within a constrained timeframe. By leveraging OpenGL compute shaders, our implementation achieves highly efficient row hammering with minimal software overhead. Experimental results on a Raspberry Pi 4 demonstrate that the GPU-based approach attains a high rate of bit flips compared to traditional CPU-based hammering, confirming its effectiveness in compromising DRAM integrity. Our findings align with existing research on microarchitectural attacks in heterogeneous systems that highlight the susceptibility of GPUs to security vulnerabilities. This study contributes to the understanding of GPU-assisted fault-injection attacks and underscores the need for improved mitigation strategies in future memory architectures.

Keywords: Rowhammer attack · Microarchitectural attack · GPU

1 Introduction

Modern computing systems increasingly rely on heterogeneous architectures, where CPUs, GPUs, and other specialized accelerators collaborate to deliver high-performance processing for numerous applications. While GPUs are widely known for their exceptional parallel computation capabilities, a growing body of research indicates that these accelerators can be repurposed for malicious tasks [4,12,13].

R. Laborde et al. (Eds.): ESORICS 2025 Workshops, LNCS 16233, pp. 347–358, 2026.
https://doi.org/10.1007/978-3-032-16165-9_20

A notable example is the **Rowhammer attack**, which exploits physical properties of Dynamic Random Access Memory (DRAM) cells through frequent row accesses. DRAM organizes storage cells in a matrix of rows and columns, grouped into banks. Each DRAM cell consists of a capacitor and an access transistor, with the capacitor storing a single bit of data as electrical charge. Due to increasing density in modern DRAM chips, cells are physically closer together, making them more susceptible to electrical interference. When a row is accessed, the corresponding wordline is activated, causing a slight electrical disturbance in neighboring rows. With repeated activations (hammering), this disturbance can accumulate and discharge capacitors in nearby rows, flipping their stored values without directly accessing them [7].

In CPU-based scenarios, repeated row activations exploit tight cell placement to induce charge leakage. However, **GPU-based** approaches can accelerate this significantly by leveraging massive parallelism and high memory bandwidth. This study demonstrates such a GPU-based Rowhammer attack on a Raspberry Pi 4. For this, we use OpenGL compute shaders that allow general computations to be performed outside the traditional graphics rendering pipeline. We use statistical approaches and parallel GPU threads to intensify row hammering and increase the likelihood of bit flips in DRAM.

This paper makes several distinct contributions to the growing body of research on hardware security attacks:

- **Novel GPU-based Rowhammer Implementation:** While Frigo et al. [2] demonstrated microarchitectural attacks accelerated by integrated GPUs on mobile devices, our work specifically focuses on using OpenGL compute shaders for Rowhammer attacks on embedded systems like the Raspberry Pi 4, an approach not previously explored in the literature.
- **Advanced Statistical Hammering Patterns:** We extend the non-uniform access patterns introduced by Jattke et al. [5] in their BLACKSMITH fuzzer, adapting these techniques to the GPU context with massively parallel thread execution for more effective DRAM disturbance.
- **Heterogeneous System Security Analysis:** Building upon the survey by Naghibijouybari et al. [12], we provide concrete evidence of cross-component vulnerabilities in heterogeneous systems, demonstrating how memory attacks can be launched from the GPU component against system-wide DRAM.
- **Practical Embedded Device Vulnerability:** While many Rowhammer studies focus on server or desktop systems, we demonstrate these attacks on the widely used Raspberry Pi platform, showing that even low-cost embedded devices with integrated GPUs are vulnerable to sophisticated memory corruption techniques.
- **Multi-sided GPU Hammering:** We adapt and improve upon the many-sided hammering technique from TRRespass [3], implementing it in the context of GPU compute shaders to bypass existing Target Row Refresh (TRR) mitigations in Low Power Double Data Rate 4 (LPDDR4) memory.

Our work bridges multiple research areas by combining GPU side-channel techniques [4,13] with advanced Rowhammer methodologies [3,5] to create a more powerful attack vector that exploits the inherent parallelism of modern GPUs.

2 Related Work

Heterogeneous architectures combine CPUs, GPUs, and accelerators in a single platform for improved computational throughput. Despite performance gains, this integration broadens the attack surface by exposing shared memory resources and on-chip interconnects to various processes. Recent surveys [12] highlight that attackers can exploit these shared resources for side-channel leakage, covert channels, or fault injection.

Rowhammer is a well-documented DRAM vulnerability [1,7,11] where repeated access to specific memory rows can induce bit flips in adjacent rows, leading to potential security breaches. Frigo et al. [3] introduced "TRRespas", a method that exploits weaknesses in the TRR mitigation implemented in DDR4 DRAM modules. Their black-box Rowhammer fuzzer revealed that many DDR4 modules remain susceptible to Rowhammer attacks despite TRR defenses, emphasizing the need for more robust mitigation strategies.

TRR is a commonly implemented mitigation designed to counter Rowhammer attacks by monitoring memory access patterns and refreshing adjacent rows when a specific row is accessed excessively. However, TRR implementations are often proprietary and vary across manufacturers, leading to inconsistencies in effectiveness. Sophisticated attacks, such as TRRespass [3], have demonstrated the ability to bypass TRR by exploiting its blind spots, such as multi-sided hammering patterns.

There exists also other mitigation approaches such as Error-Correcting Code (ECC), Increased Refresh Rates and Row Randomization. ECC memory can detect and correct single-bit errors, reducing the impact of bit flips. However, ECC is not foolproof against multiple simultaneous bit flips. By refreshing DRAM rows more frequently with increased refresh rates, the likelihood of charge leakage causing bit flips is reduced. This approach, however, increases power consumption and may degrade performance. Randomizing the physical-to-logical row mapping makes it harder for attackers to target specific rows, though this requires hardware support. In future DRAM designs, emerging technologies, such as 3D-stacked DRAM or alternative memory architectures, aim to mitigate Rowhammer by reducing cell-to-cell interference.

In software-based protection approaches, operating systems can implement memory allocation strategies to isolate sensitive data from vulnerable regions or detect abnormal memory access patterns. Konoth *et al.* proposed ZebRAM that builds on virtualization extensions in commodity processors to isolate every DRAM row that contains data with guard rows to control data placement [9]. Despite all these mitigations, Rowhammer remains a persistent challenge, particularly as attackers develop more advanced techniques to exploit hardware vulnerabilities.

Concerning GPU side-channel attacks, Naghibijouybari et al. [13] demonstrated the practicality of this kind of attacks by showing that an OpenGL-based spy can accurately fingerprint websites, monitor user activities, and infer keystroke timings. Additionally, they illustrated how a CUDA spy application could deduce internal parameters of neural network models used by other CUDA applications, highlighting vulnerabilities in shared GPU environments.

Similarly, Frigo et al. [2] explored the security implications of integrated GPUs in mobile processors. They revealed that GPUs could accelerate microarchitectural attacks, such as side-channel and Rowhammer attacks, even from JavaScript within browsers. Their work emphasized the necessity for secure GPU design, especially as GPUs become more integrated into general-purpose computing.

Comparing to recent work based on CPUs such as AMD Zen-based platforms [6] or RISC-V [10], our GPU-based Rowhammer attack does not need to reverse engineer DRAM addressing function nor to synchronize with the refresh mechanism of the memory controller to bypass the TRR mitigations. Complex techniques such as scheduling flush and fence instructions to increase row activation throughput are replaced by using high-frequency memory access patterns with GPU compute shaders. We will show in the next section how we use the key factors such as high thread count, memory bandwidth, compute shaders, bank-level parallelism, reduced CPU overhead, and randomized access patterns to amplify Rowhammer attacks on GPUs.

3 Implementation Details

3.1 High-Level Overview

Our implementation aims to maximize DRAM activations from a GPU context. GPUs are inherently designed for massive parallelism, with thousands of threads executing simultaneously across multiple cores. This architecture provides a significant advantage for Rowhammer attacks compared to CPUs, which typically have fewer cores and threads. We rely on OpenGL ES 3.1 compute shaders to issue read operations on targeted rows. This modern GPU support provides fine-grained control over memory access patterns that enables us to craft highly optimized hammering loops that maximize DRAM disturbance while avoiding detection by refresh mechanisms. The code is structured to:

1. Allocate and initialize large GPU-accessible buffers or textures in DRAM;
2. Issue "hammer" operations via compute shaders, which repeatedly read from chosen memory locations (victim rows);
3. Vary row offsets randomly, creating multi-sided hammering patterns;
4. Collect timing and error data via Shader Storage Buffer Objects (SSBOs) and host readbacks.

Figure 1 illustrates the logical workflow of our GPU-based Rowhammer attack implementation, showing the main processing steps and decision points.

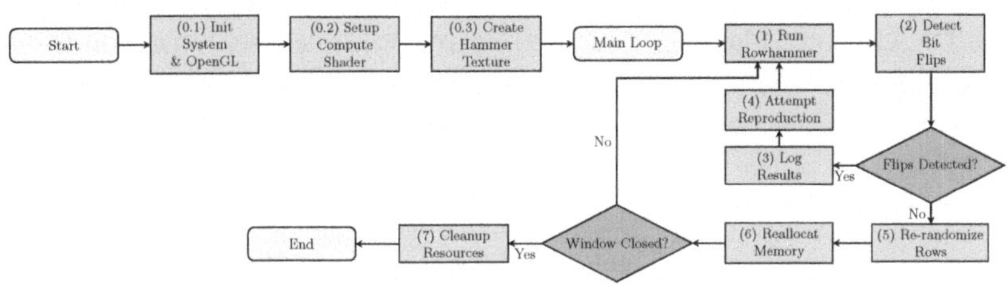

Fig. 1. GPU-based Rowhammer Attack Logical Workflow

3.2 Key Attack Primitives

The following operations are important primitives for the attack.

- **Parallel Threads:** We dispatch thousands of GPU threads (Fig. 1-(1)), each performing independent row accesses, thereby significantly increasing the total number of activations.
- **Adaptive Randomization:** Inspired by Blacksmith-style pattern fuzzing [5], we insert random offsets in row accesses (Fig. 1-(5)). This prevents simple row-refresh heuristics from detecting purely sequential patterns.
- **Repeated Reallocation:** To achieve broader DRAM coverage, we periodically reallocate textures (Fig. 1-(6)) so the GPU driver maps them to different physical memory regions.
- **SSBO Write-Back to Prevent Optimization:** Modern GPU compilers are highly optimized and may eliminate operations deemed unnecessary, such as repeated memory reads without observable side effects. To ensure the hammering loop is not optimized away, we accumulate the results of memory reads into a variable and write it back to a SSBO. This guarantees that the GPU executes the memory operations as intended, preserving the effectiveness of the attack.

To ensure that each row of the RGBA8 texture corresponds to a single row in DRAM, we carefully calculated the texture dimensions based on the DRAM row size and the format of the texture. The Raspberry Pi 4 uses LPDDR4 memory, where each DRAM row typically has a size of 8KB (8192 bytes). An RGBA8 texture stores 4 bytes per pixel (1 byte for each channel: Red, Green, Blue, and Alpha). Therefore, the number of pixels per row in the texture must satisfy:

$$\text{Pixels per row} = \frac{\text{DRAM row size (bytes)}}{\text{Bytes per pixel}} = \frac{8192}{4} = 2048$$

Thus, each row of the texture should contain exactly 2048 pixels to align with a single DRAM row. The height of the texture can be chosen based on the total memory allocation required for the attack, ensuring that the texture fits within the available GPU-accessible DRAM. For example, a texture of size 2048×2048 would occupy:

$$\text{Total size} = \text{Pixels per row} \times \text{Height} \times \text{Bytes per pixel} = 2048 \times 2048 \times 4 = 16 \text{ MB}$$

This size is well within the 4GB LPDDR4 memory of the Raspberry Pi 4, leaving sufficient space for other system operations. By aligning the texture rows with DRAM rows, we ensure that memory accesses in the compute shader directly correspond to specific DRAM rows, maximizing the effectiveness of the Rowhammer attack.

3.3 Compute Shader Implementation Analysis

The compute shader implementation (Listing 1.1) employs several key techniques to maximize the effectiveness of DRAM hammering.

```
#version 310 es
layout(local_size_x = 16, local_size_y = 16) in;

// Uniforms controlling iteration count, victim row, etc.
uniform int uVictimRow, uBankStride, uMaxOffset, uIterations;
uniform uint uSeed;

// DRAM texture bound as readonly image
layout(rgba8, binding = 0) readonly uniform highp image2D uDRAMTexture;

// SSBO to store partial results (ensures read ops are done)
layout(std430, binding = 0) buffer OutputBuffer { vec4 outData[]; };

uint rand_lcg(inout uint seed) {
    seed = seed * 1664525u + 1013904223u;
    return seed;
}

void main() {
    ivec2 baseCoord = ivec2(gl_GlobalInvocationID.xy) * 4;

    // Per-thread seed for random offsets
    uint localSeed = uSeed
        + uint(gl_GlobalInvocationID.x) * 73856093u
        + uint(gl_GlobalInvocationID.y) * 19349663u;

    // Bank-aware offset to stress DRAM interleaving
    int bankOffset = (baseCoord.x & 15) * uBankStride;
    int bankedX = bankOffset + (baseCoord.x & 511);
    vec4 accumulator = vec4(0.0);

    // Main hammering loop
    for (int i = 0; i < uIterations; i++) {
        int offset1 = int(rand_lcg(localSeed) % uint(uMaxOffset));
        int offset2 = int(rand_lcg(localSeed) % uint(uMaxOffset));

        int row1 = (uVictimRow + offset1) & (imageSize(uDRAMTexture).y - 1);
        int row2 = (uVictimRow - offset2) & (imageSize(uDRAMTexture).y - 1);

        ivec2 addr1 = ivec2((bankedX + i * 128) & 511, row1);
        ivec2 addr2 = ivec2((bankedX + i * 128 + 256) & 511, row2);

        // Repeated read operations
        vec4 val1 = imageLoad(uDRAMTexture, addr1);
        vec4 val2 = imageLoad(uDRAMTexture, addr2);

        // Accumulate the results to avoid compiler optimizations
        accumulator += (val1 + val2);
    }

    // Write final accumulator to SSBO
    uint index = gl_GlobalInvocationID.y
              * (gl_NumWorkGroups.x * gl_WorkGroupSize.x)
              + gl_GlobalInvocationID.x;
    outData[index] = accumulator;
}
```

Listing 1.1. Central GPU Compute Shader for Rowhammer Attack

Thread Organization. The shader uses a 16 × 16 thread block configuration (`local_size_x = 16, local_size_y = 16`), creating 256 concurrent threads per work group. Multiple work groups can be dispatched in parallel, achieving thousands of simultaneous memory operations. Each thread hammers memory by reading specific DRAM rows in a loop, using random offsets.

Random Offset Generation. The Linear Congruential Generator (LCG) function `rand_lcg()` creates pseudo-random offsets for each thread:

- Each thread initializes a unique seed based on its global ID (a identifier unique to each thread) combined with the uniform `uSeed` value,
- Within the hammering loop, `offset1` and `offset2` are randomly generated for each iteration,
- These offsets modify the target row addresses, implementing the adaptive randomization pattern discussed earlier.

The Hammering Loop. The core of the attack is a tight loop that:

- Calculates two different row addresses (`row1` and `row2`) for each iteration,
- Uses bank-aware addressing (`bankedX`) to ensure hammering affects specific DRAM banks,
- Performs two image loads (memory reads) per iteration, targeting rows above and below the victim row,
- Accumulates the loaded values to prevent compiler optimization from eliminating the reads.

SSBO Result Collection. A SSBO stores the accumulated results:

- The `outData` buffer receives the final `accumulator` value from each thread,
- This serves two critical purposes: ensuring memory reads are not optimized away by the compiler, and allowing the CPU to verify shader execution,
- The (`index`) scheme ensures each thread writes to a unique buffer location.

This implementation demonstrates how GPUs can be repurposed for memory attacks through their parallel architecture and direct DRAM access capabilities. The shader maximizes DRAM row activations by combining thread parallelism with randomized access patterns, all while avoiding driver or hardware optimizations that might otherwise reduce hammering effectiveness.

4 Experimental Setup and Results

4.1 Hardware and Software Environment

Our experiments target a Raspberry Pi 4 featuring a Broadcom BCM2711 SoC (Quad-core ARM Cortex-A72 CPU), a VideoCore VI GPU with support for OpenGL ES 3.1 compute shaders, and 4 GB of LPDDR4 SDRAM. We run a Raspbian-based OS, ensuring the necessary graphics drivers for GPU compute.

4.2 Rowhammer Conditions and Reproduction Attempts

By carefully tuning `uIterations` and launching multiple workgroups, we approach billions of DRAM accesses per second. The GPU's parallel nature often surpasses what is achievable by CPU-based Rowhammer on the same board. LPDDR4 memory employs built-in refresh cycles and partial vendor-specific TRR logic. Our multi-sided, randomized approach is designed to elude simplistic refresh algorithms, consistent with findings from [5].

To choose the victim rows, we randomize a "base" `uVictimRow` within the GPU memory space and let the compute shader offset it. This helps cover different physical rows, especially when combined with texture reallocation.

In addition, to confirm that flips are not spurious, the code implements reproduction attempts by: i) correcting the flipped bits in the texture; ii) re-running the same hammer parameters (`uIterations`, `uVictimRow`, etc.); and iii) checking if the same bytes flip again, signifying a stable vulnerability in that DRAM region. These steps ensure flips are truly due to Rowhammer rather than random DRAM errors or cosmic rays.

4.3 Observed Bit Flips

We have carried out several runs lasting more than 20 h each and without interruption in order to observe bit flips. This duration is necessary to bypass the ECC protection mechanism of the Raspberry Pi. The number of iterations is $5 * 10^4$ for these runs, and each thread performs 2 reads per loop iteration. With thousands of threads, total memory accesses can reach billions. The number of successful bit flips has been counted by comparing the original and modified (current) textures, as shown in Fig. 2.

We had on average 1024 bit flips for 5 different runs. More experiments should be done but from these runs we observe blocks of 32 rows with bit flips, and the addresses of these rows are continuous. The offset between the address of one block and the address of the next block is 16384 (2^{14}). This precise value might be related to the size of a subdivision of the memory or the DRAM addressing scheme of the GPU.

It is noted that most flips occur in physically adjacent rows to the hammered addresses, consistent with classical Rowhammer theory. Some occasional flips, random outliers, appear in unexpected locations, potentially due to internal row remapping, temperature, or noise factors in DRAM. Many flips can be reproduced across multiple runs, indicating stable vulnerabilities in specific DRAM bitflips_20250210_183812.log

```
=== Bit Flip Detection Report ===
Timestamp: 20250210_183812
Parameters:
  Iteration Count: 50000
  Victim Rows: 2780
Reproduction Rate: 5/5 (100%)

Detected Flips:
Flip 1: Index=28196576, Original=23 ([0→1]0[0→1]10111), Current=183
Flip 2: Index=28196577, Original=116 ([0→1][1→0][1→0][1→0]01[0→1][0→1]), Current=135
Flip 3: Index=28196578, Original=12 ([0→1]0[0→1][0→1]1100), Current=188
Flip 4: Index=28196579, Original=68 (010001[0→1]0), Current=70
Flip 5: Index=28196580, Original=15 ([0→1]0[0→1][0→1][1→0]111), Current=183
```

Fig. 2. An Extract of Log with Observed Bit Flips

regions. An attacker could push the victim's data in these vulnerable locations using a method called Memory Massaging [8] thus compromising its integrity.

5 Discussion and Conclusion

We have presented in this work-in-progress paper a GPU-based Rowhammer attack on the Raspberry Pi 4 using OpenGL ES compute shaders. By orchestrating large-scale, parallel DRAM accesses, our approach reliably induces bit flips in adjacent rows. We showed how randomization of row offsets, repeated reallocation, and a high level of parallelism can overcome naive refresh mechanisms, offering a new perspective on Rowhammer beyond CPU-centric methods.

Our results confirm that GPU-based Rowhammer is not only feasible but can be highly effective under certain conditions. Even on a low-cost platform like the Raspberry Pi 4, the GPU can issue read operations at a rate sufficient to induce bit flips. This finding has broader implications: laptops, smartphones, or cloud servers–where GPUs or integrated graphics are widely used–may be susceptible to a similar approach if memory isolation and refresh strategies are insufficient. This attack may lead to other security implications and potential attack scenarios such as privilege escalation, denial-of-service or key manipulation. Indeed, bit flips could corrupt page table entries or other security-critical data structures, granting higher privileges to the attacker. Even if no direct privilege escalation occurs, repeated memory corruption could crash processes or the entire system, making it unavailable. In some setups, flipping bits in cryptographic keys stored in DRAM could weaken or fully compromise encryption.

In order to continue our further research, several potential directions include:

- **Adaptive Fuzzing Frameworks:** Automating row offset selection, iteration parameters, and temperature conditions to systematically discover the most vulnerable DRAM regions.
- **Cross-Architecture Validation:** Exploring identical GPU-based Rowhammer techniques on other SoCs, discrete GPUs, or platforms like x86 with integrated graphics.

- **Advanced Defences:** Developing real-time detection within the memory controller, using hardware performance counters or machine learning to flag suspicious GPU access patterns.
- **Scalable Attacks:** Testing whether multi-GPU setups in servers or HPC environments can amplify Rowhammer effects even further, especially if multiple accelerators share DRAM banks.

By highlighting the practical viability of GPU-driven Rowhammer, we emphasize the pressing need for robust hardware and software mitigations. These findings serve as a call to action for both the research community and hardware vendors to address Rowhammer in the context of heterogeneous and parallelized computing resources.

References

1. Fraile, L.P., Fournaris, A.P., Koufopavlou, O.: Revisiting Rowhammer attacks in embedded systems. In: Proceedings of the 14th International Conference on Design & Technology of Integrated Systems in Nanoscale Era (DTIS), pp. 1–6 (2019)
2. Frigo, P., Giuffrida, C., Bos, H., Razavi, K.: Grand pwning unit: accelerating microarchitectural attacks with the GPU. In: Proceedings of the 39th IEEE Symposium on Security and Privacy (SP), pp. 195–210 (2018)
3. Frigo, P., et al.: TRRespass: exploiting the many sides of target row refresh. In: Proceedings of the 41th IEEE Symposium on Security and Privacy (SP), pp. 747–762 (2020)
4. Giner, L., et al.: Generic and automated drive-by GPU cache attacks from the browser. In: Proceedings of the 19th ACM Asia Conference on Computer and Communications Security (ASIACCS), pp. 128—-140 (2024)
5. Jattke, P., Van Der Veen, V., Frigo, P., Gunter, S., Razavi, K.: BLACKSMITH: scalable Rowhammering in the frequency domain. In: Proceedings of the 43th IEEE Symposium on Security and Privacy (SP), pp. 716–734 (2022)
6. Jattke, P., Wipfli, M., Solt, F., Marazzi, M., Bölcskei, M., Razavi, K.: ZENHAMMER: Rowhammer attacks on AMD zen-based platforms. In: Proceedings of the 33rd USENIX Security Symposium (USENIX Security), pp. 1615–1633 (2024)
7. Kim, Y., et al.: Flipping bits in memory without accessing them: an experimental study of DRAM disturbance errors. ACM SIGARCH Comput. Archit. News **42**(3), 361–372 (2014)
8. Kogler, A., et al.: Half-double: hammering from the next row over. In: Proceedings of the 31st USENIX Security Symposium (USENIX Security), pp. 3807–3824 (2022)
9. Konoth, R.K., et al.: ZebRAM: comprehensive and compatible software protection against Rowhammer attacks. In: Proc. of the 13th USENIX Symposium on Operating Systems Design and Implementation (OSDI), pp. 697–710 (2018)

10. Marazzi, M., Razavi, K.: RISC-H: Rowhammer attacks on RISC-V. In: Proceedings of the 4th Workshop on DRAM Security (DRAMSec) (2024)
11. Mutlu, O., Kim, J.S.: RowHammer: a retrospective. IEEE Trans. Comput. Aided Des. Integr. Circuits Syst. **39**(8), 1555–1571 (2020)
12. Naghibijouybari, H., Koruyeh, E.M., Abu-Ghazaleh, N.: Microarchitectural attacks in heterogeneous systems: a survey. ACM Comput. Surv. **55**(7) (2022)
13. Naghibijouybari, H., Neupane, A., Qian, Z., Abu-Ghazaleh, N.: Rendered insecure: GPU side channel attacks are practical. In: Proceedings of the ACM Conference on Computer and Communications Security (CCS), pp. 2139–2153 (2018)

Revealing Embedded System Behaviors: A Comparative Analysis of Power Consumption and Hardware Performance Counters

Mohammed Mezaouli(✉), Yehya Nasser, Samir Saoudi, and Marc-Oliver Pahl

IMT Atlantique, Lab-STICC, UMR CNRS 6285, Brest, France
{mohammed.mezaouli,yehya.nasser,samir.saoudi,
marc-oliver.pahl}@imt-atlantique.fr

Abstract. As computing evolves, analyzing system behavior has become as critical as optimizing performance and energy efficiency. Traditional methods of behavioral analysis often rely on software-level profiling or predefined signatures, which limit their applicability in dynamic and resource-constrained environments. This study takes a novel approach by identifying and characterizing system workloads based on distinct behavioral patterns, such as memory usage, arithmetic operations, and control flow. By leveraging hardware performance counters (HPCs) and power consumption metrics, this work demonstrates how hardware-level insights can reveal unique operational signatures. These findings highlight the potential of HPCs and power consumption to enhance the understanding of system behaviors, offering practical solutions for behavior identification that could be instrumental in detecting vulnerabilities or anomalies. The results underscore both the opportunities and challenges of using these metrics for behavioral analysis in embedded systems.

Keywords: HPC · Power Consumption · Behavior identification

1 Introduction

Embedded systems are fundamental to modern technology, driving innovations across industries such as automotive [16], healthcare, and industrial automation [11]. These systems are defined by their constrained resources, real-time processing needs, and specialized applications. Understanding and characterizing the behavior of embedded systems has become crucial for optimizing performance, improving reliability, and enhancing security [8].

Behavioral identification [5] in embedded systems involves analyzing how these systems execute operations like memory accesses, arithmetic computations, and control flow management [13]. Traditional methods of behavioral analysis often rely on software-level profiling or static analysis tools. However, these approaches can introduce significant overhead, lack the granularity needed for

R. Laborde et al. (Eds.): ESORICS 2025 Workshops, LNCS 16233, pp. 359–369, 2026.
https://doi.org/10.1007/978-3-032-16165-9_21

detailed insights, or fail to capture the dynamic interplay between hardware and software. Advanced malware evasion techniques employ sophisticated obfuscation methods to bypass detection, further underscores the limitations of these traditional methods [12]. This calls for efficient, hardware-assisted techniques capable of providing real-time insights into embedded system behaviors [6].

HPCs and power consumption present a promising solution for behavior identification. HPCs, embedded within modern processors, offer fine-grained insights into low-level events such as cache hits, branch predictions, and memory accesses, enabling detailed execution pattern analysis without imposing significant performance overhead. Power consumption, in contrast, provides a holistic view of system activity, reflecting the aggregate behavior of hardware components during runtime. By combining these two metrics, it becomes possible to derive a comprehensive understanding of embedded system behaviors, particularly in scenarios involving threats like firmware tampering and unsecured interfaces [15,17].

In this work, we investigate the potential of (HPCs) and power consumption metrics for behavioral identification in embedded systems, and compare their effectiveness in terms of identification efficiency. We focus on operational behaviors such as memory management, arithmetic operations, and control logic, as these metrics enable the characterization of normal system behavior.

Unlike traditional profiling methods, our approach emphasizes non-intrusive, hardware-based techniques that are efficient and scalable for resource-constrained environments. The ability to dynamically monitor and interpret system behavior in real time has broad applications, including vulnerability analysis and malware or anomaly detection without the need for large sample datasets [9]. The main contributions of this study are: (1) Demonstrating the feasibility of using HPCs and power consumption, in conjunction with Artificial Intelligence (AI), as effective metrics for behavioral analysis; (2) providing a comparative evaluation of HPCs and power consumption for behavioral recognition in embedded systems.

2 Related Works

HPCs are often debated in terms of their effectiveness for malware detection, despite their advantage of lower overhead. One limitation is that HPCs cannot be fully relied upon alone for detecting malware, as they are influenced by both low-level micro-architecture and software-level activities [19].

Leng et al. [10] suggest that relying on only two HPCs may be sufficient to ensure system reliability, offering a simpler yet effective approach. Similarly, Patel et al. [13] utilized HPCs for malware detection by implementing several machine learning classifiers on FPGA platforms. Their methodology involved collecting 32 different HPC features and subsequently reducing the dataset to 8 key features. Notably, they found that using the OneR algorithm with only the branch feature achieved a classification accuracy of 82.5%. This demonstrates the effectiveness of HPC-based features for malware detection.

Basu et al. [3] investigated impact of HPC interval measurement on model learning for malware detection. They also used Control Flow Graphs (CFGs) to assess the probability of matches between two malware samples. Their findings indicated that the use of instruction and branch HPCs led to a low probability of exact matches between malware. They concluded that HPCs are not deterministic because of the presence of background processes, meaning that malware detectors must rely on approximate matching rather than precise identification.

However, Pham et al. [14] utilized electromagnetic field measurements to detect malware, achieving an accuracy of 99% even when obfuscation techniques were applied. This underscores the effectiveness of side-channel information in malware detection. Similarly, Azmoodeh et al. [2] employed power consumption data to identify patterns and trained a K-Nearest Neighbors (KNN) model, achieving a detection accuracy of 95.65% in effectively detecting ransomware.

Various malware detection techniques are reviewed by Aslan et al. [1], with behavior-based detection yielding promising results. Hernandez et al. [7] demonstrated that using power consumption alone for malware detection is effective, achieving an F-score of 0.97, compared to relying solely on network data, which achieved an F-score of 0.94. This is because power-related data are significant.

Bridges et al. [4] employed both supervised and unsupervised anomaly detection methods to detect rootkit malware through power consumption, with the supervised approach showing the best results. Similarly, Yang et al. [18] used the Gaussian Mixture Model (GMM) on Android devices to detect floating point attacks based on power consumption, proving its ability to detect malware or apps such as music and browsers due to its low complexity and efficiency in approximating arbitrary distributions, achieving 79% for malware detection.

All prior work relies solely on Hardware Performance Counters (HPCs) or power metrics, often combined with additional methods to enhance detection techniques. These approaches predominantly focus on malware datasets for training, which limits their detection capabilities to known malware, making it challenging to identify zero-day threats.

Our work examines the effectiveness of Hardware Performance Counters (HPCs) and power consumption metrics in detecting workload behavior, offering a novel approach that integrates these non-invasive and readily accessible data sources to identify behavioral anomalies. Unlike prior work, we explore how code optimization levels impact detection accuracy, enhancing model robustness and enabling generalization to zero-day threats. By focusing on behavior-based detection rather than relying on large datasets, our methodology marks a significant step toward developing a comprehensive, explainable behavior-based detection framework for embedded systems. As a proof-of-concept, our proposed model consumes raw data from HPCs or power consumption metrics to analyze and detect workload behavior. In the future, we aim to refine this method further to detect anomalies and malicious behavior, with a particular focus on improving its capacity to identify zero-day threats.

3 Methodology

This study focuses on ARM M4 processors, commonly used in resource-constrained embedded systems with bare-metal setups to optimize efficiency and minimize overhead. Using a bare-metal configuration ensures the behavioral characteristics observed, such as power consumption and HPC metrics, are directly tied to the workload, free from variability introduced by operating system-level factors. This approach not only mirrors real-world deployment scenarios but also provides a precise analysis of workload behavior. Furthermore, the insights gained form a foundation for extending the methodology to more complex environments, such as those involving real-time operating systems.

To validate our hypothesis that power consumption and HPCs can serve as identifiers of activity within embedded processors, we implemented an experimental methodology comprising four key steps: (A) execution of benchmark workloads on embedded processors, (B) dynamic power measurement during program execution, (C) HPC instrumentation, and (D) construction of a workload identifier based on the captured power traces and HPC data.

3.1 Preparation and Execution of Benchmark Workloads

Our first step involved preparing benchmark workloads that cover typical computational tasks on embedded processors: memory assignment, logic operations, and arithmetic computations—compiled for execution on an ARM Cortex-M4 processor, STM32F303 included as a target board with the Chipwhisperer Lite. Measurements were conducted in a controlled environment equipped with power measurement tools to ensure accuracy and repeatability.

Each workload generates power consumption traces and HPC data, influenced by parameters like iteration count and optimization level; benchmarks were executed with three different optimization levels. As a preliminary benchmark we selected four workloads with diverse algorithms to target different computation tasks:

1. **Bubble sort**: relies on comparison and swap operations, iterating through pairs of adjacent elements and rearranging them based on their relative values, leading to repetitive control-dependent branching and memory access.
2. **Median Filter**: primarily uses sorting and selection operations within a local window of pixels or data points, requiring frequent neighborhood data access and sorting to compute the median, making it memory-intensive.
3. **Matrix Multiplication**: consists of multiplication and addition operations performed on matrix elements. This involves heavy arithmetic operations and regular memory access patterns, often optimized through block processing to improve data locality.
4. **Factorial**: involves multiplication operations either recursively or iteratively, with a straightforward arithmetic progression where each element is multiplied by its predecessor, requiring minimal memory but heavy arithmetic.

3.2 Power Measurement and Characterization

Power traces are captured during workload execution and aligned with the corresponding program execution phases, we correlated specific workload behaviors with their power consumption profiles, building comprehensive power characterizations for analysis. As illustrated in Fig. 1, we measured power by compiling workloads with the three optimization levels and embedding a trigger within the code to prompt the oscilloscope ChipWhisperer Lite to begin measurement upon execution. This approach ensured accurate capture of power consumption solely during workload execution. The oscilloscope was configured to sample power at each clock cycle, synchronized with transistor switching events. For workloads exceeding the oscilloscope's 24,000-point buffer capacity, we repeated measurements with adjusted parameters to create a sliding window, covering the entire execution.

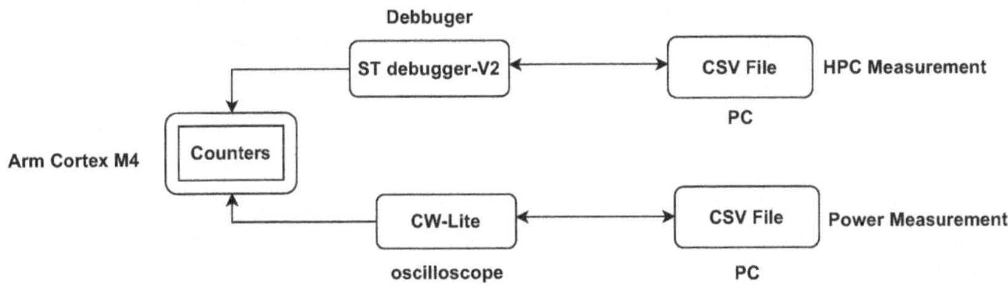

Fig. 1. Power Consumption and HPC Testbed.

3.3 HPC Instrumentation and Characterization

We monitored HPCs during program execution to track key events like instruction execution, memory access, and cache utilization. Synchronizing HPC traces with workload execution phases allowed us to link workload behaviors to hardware activities. As illustrated in Fig. 1, we measured HPCs periodically using the ST-LINK/V2 debugger at a sampling frequency of 2 kHz. This method ensured no overhead during workload execution. We executed each workload with three optimization levels (O1, O2, O3), which affected instructions at various pipeline stages and execution time. These counters are available on Cortex-M3 and Cortex-M4 processors, but not on Cortex-M0. However, our work focuses exclusively on Cortex-M4.

1. **Cycle Counter (CYCCNT)**: Increments every CPU clock cycle.
2. **Load/Store Unit Cycle Counter (LSUCNT)**: Increments for each additional cycle taken by load and store instructions beyond their initial cycle.
3. **CPI Cycle Counter (CPICNT)**: Increments for each extra cycle required by multi-cycle instructions beyond the first cycle.
4. **Exception Overhead Cycle Counter (EXCCNT)**: Increments on each cycle spent handling exceptions (entry and exit).
5. **Folded-instruction Counter (FOLDCNT)**: Increments for each folded instruction, such as zero-cycle instructions like If-Then (IT) instructions and some NOPs (No Operation).
6. **Sleep Counter**: Increment on cycles associated with power saving mode.

3.4 Building the Workload Identifier Model

Finally, in the sake of comparison, we developed a workload and optimization identifier using two machine learning models, as illustrated in Fig. 2. A Multilayer Perceptron (MLP) which consists of three layers: an input layer of 25000 point matching the input feature dimension, two hidden layer with 64 neurons and 32 neurons respectively, and an output layer with 12 neurons (for the 12 class). ReLU activation functions are applied between layers, and the model is trained using the Adam optimizer with a learning rate of 0.001 and a 1D Convolutional Neural Network (CNN) that includes two convolutional layers with a kernel size of 5, stride of 1, and padding of 2, followed by ReLU activation and max-pooling. The convolutional output is flattened and fed into two fully connected layers: the first with 1000 neurons and the second with 12 neurons for classification. Both models are trained using the Adam optimizer, using minimize cross-entropy loss, with performance evaluated using validation accuracy. Models were trained on power consumption traces and HPC data, respectively, to map these metrics to computational activities within the embedded processor. This approach enables a non-invasive system capable of identifying workloads based solely on power consumption profiles or HPC measurements. The classification task assigns 12 class labels, representing four workloads across three optimization levels: Classes 0–2 correspond to Factorial at O1–O3, Classes 3–5 to Bubble Sort at O1–O3, Classes 6–8 to Matrix Multiplication at O1–O3, and Classes 9–11 to Median Filter at O1–O3. Finally, we evaluated workload identification without taking in consideration the opimization level (4 classes) to assess model performance on workload identifation.

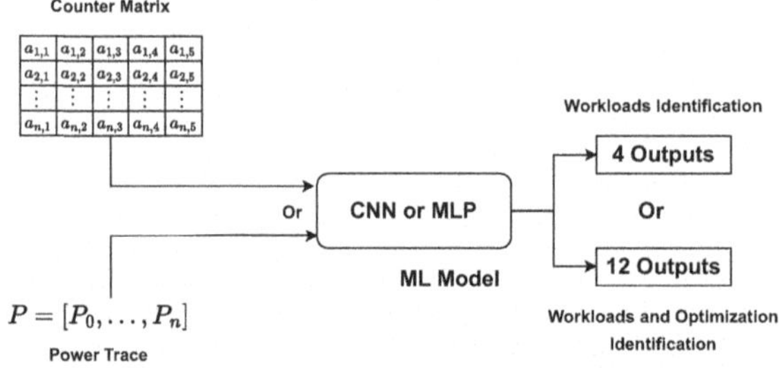

Fig. 2. Our Proposed Model/Detector.

4 Results and Discussions

In this section, we analyze the data, discuss the main results, and present the models proposed in our work. We examine HPCs and power consumption during workload execution.

Focusing on Fig. 3, where LSU activity is shown, we note that workloads such as Factorial and Matrix Multiplication do not exhibit high activity during execution. In contrast, workloads like Bubble Sort and Median Filter present high activity in the number of loads and stores. In addition, we observed in Fig. 4 that the folding instruction counters exhibited high activity during the execution of the Bubble Sort and Median Filter workloads, whereas they showed low or negligible activity for the Matrix Multiplication and Factorial workloads. This discrepancy arises from the fundamental differences in the algorithms control flow and the resulting interaction with the processor's instruction folding optimization. Bubble Sort and Median Filter are characterized by frequent conditional branches and data-dependent decision-making processes, which translate into numerous IT (If-Then) instructions and conditional branches. The ARM Cortex-M4 processor optimizes these instructions through instruction folding, effectively reducing execution cycles and improving pipeline efficiency. Consequently, the folding counters register high activity for these workloads. In contrast, Matrix Multiplication and Factorial are arithmetic-intensive algorithms with straightforward and predictable control flows involving simple loops and minimal branching. Their execution primarily consists of arithmetic operations with few, if any, foldable instructions. As a result, there are limited opportunities for the processor to apply instruction folding, leading to zero activity in the folding counters for these workloads

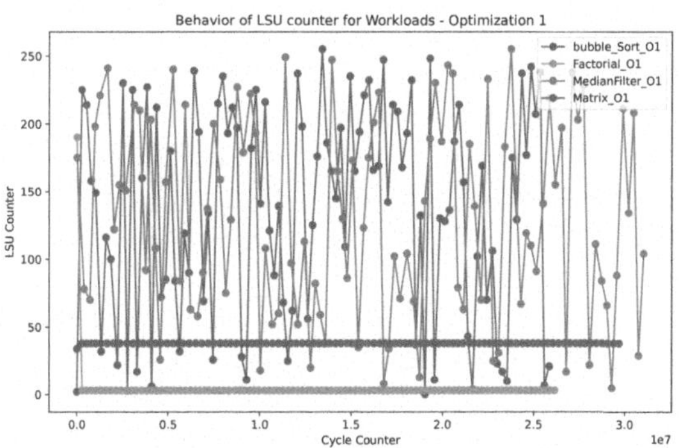

Fig. 3. LSU Counter Behavior.

Motivated by the promising preliminary findings, we incorporated HPCs into our study to identify different workloads and their associated optimization levels on the ARM Cortex-M4 processor. Table 1 presents our experimental results. Initially, we utilized four HPC counters as inputs to a Multilayer Perceptron (MLP) model. However, this approach yielded suboptimal results, indicating that the MLP model struggled to capture the complex patterns within the HPC data due to its limited ability to extract hierarchical features from raw inputs.

To address this limitation, we employed a Convolutional Neural Network (CNN) model on HPC data for both workload and optimization identification.

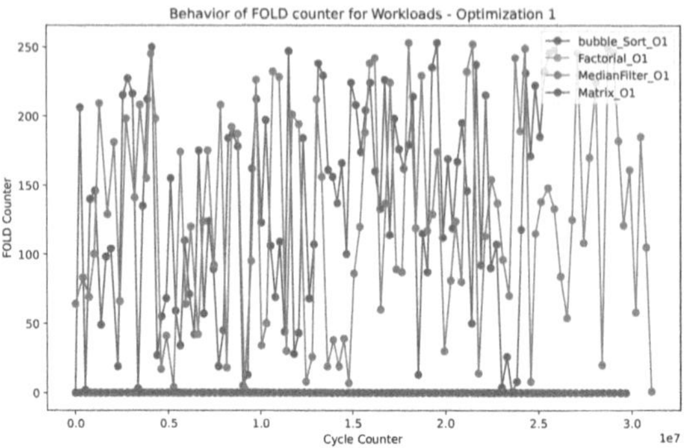

Fig. 4. Folded-Instruction Counter Behavior.

The CNN's ability to automatically learn spatial hierarchies of features made it a suitable candidate for handling the intricacies of HPC data. While the HPC data alone was insufficient for the CNN model to accurately identify both workloads and optimizations simultaneously—possibly due to the limited granularity since these counters are only limited to 8-bit and sampling rate inherent in the HPC measurements—focusing solely on workload identification produced promising results. The CNN model demonstrated good performance in distinguishing between different workloads based on HPC data. These findings suggest that HPCs hold significant potential for workload identification in embedded systems, motivating their use in our work despite the challenges encountered in broader optimization identification. These results are obtained using a dataset of 120 HPC samples, divided into 80% for training and 20% for validation.

Recognizing the need for more detailed information to distinguish optimization levels, we incorporated power consumption data, which provides cycle-accurate measurements and reflects the processor's dynamic behavior more precisely. As shown in Table 1, feeding the power consumption dataset into the CNN model yielded significantly better results. For both workload and optimization detection, the CNN was able to identify even subtle changes introduced by different optimization levels, achieving an accuracy of over 90%. For workload detection alone, the results reached 100% accuracy, demonstrating that the combination of CNN and power consumption data is highly effective for both workload and optimization detection. These results are obtained using a dataset of 240 power consumption trace, divided into 80% for training and 20% for validation.

These results highlight the significant sensitivity of power consumption in capturing the nuances associated with various optimization applied to workloads. The cycle-accurate of the power measurements provides a richer and more detailed dataset for the CNN to learn from, enabling it to discern patterns that were not evident from HPC data alone. This underscores the importance of integrating fine-grained power consumption with neural network models to enhance the identification and analysis of workloads and their optimization levels.

Table 1. Classification Results Leveraging Power Consumption and HPC Data

Power Consumption Based Detector Validation Accuracy		
Proposed Model	**MLP**	**CNN**
Workload and Optimization	55 %	91.67%
Workload Only	70 %	100 %
HPC Based Detector Validation accuracy (4 Counters)		
Proposed Model	**MLP**	**CNN**
Workload and Optimization	33 %	41.67 %
Workload Only	50 %	97.22 %

Throughout our research, we encountered several limitations. A major challenge was the low sampling rate of the debugger, which adversely affected the learning accuracy of our HPC based models due to insufficient temporal resolution in the collected data. In our system, these counters were encoded in 8 bits, causing them to reset to zero after reaching a maximum value of 255. This overflow limited the precision and reliability of the HPC data, We believe that even with the inclusion of additional HPCs, this limitation will continue to hinder the model's learning.. Employing a cycle-accurate debugger with higher-resolution counters could improve data collection precision, thereby enhancing model accuracy.

In contrast, the analysis of power consumption was more straightforward and yielded clearer insights. At each optimization level and across different workloads, we observed distinct impacts on the power consumption patterns. Therefore, CNN is able to achieve good results, with the ability to accurately detect both workloads and optimization. The results show how compiler optimizations can impact detection accuracy, as the CNN is able to detect the workload at 97.22%. In parallel, and for the same workload, the model is not able to detect the workload and its order of optimization, achieving an accuracy of about 41.67%. Previous work proved that HPC systems are good at profiling applications, while the optimizations induced by the compiler introduce uncertainty, change the identity of the workload, and mislead the model's detection, resulting in incorrect workload identification. However, power consumption is still able to detect the workload with its different levels of optimization, though at the cost of a high sampling rate, which should be at least equal to the processor speed.

5 Conclusion and Future Work

This paper presented a comparative analysis of HPCs and power consumption as means for identifying and characterizing the behavior of embedded systems. Through a series of experiments on ARM Cortex-M4 processors, we demonstrated that while HPCs can provide useful low-level insights into workload execution, their effectiveness is often limited by sampling rate and counter overflow. In contrast, power consumption measurements–captured at a cycle-accurate granularity—showed a superior ability to reflect both workload identity and optimization levels, achieving classification accuracy of about 91.67%.

Our findings underscore the potential of power consumption as a rich, non-intrusive behavioral fingerprint in embedded systems. Unlike HPCs, power traces can be collected externally with minimal interference, making them highly suitable for real-time monitoring in resource-constrained environments. Relying on the accuracy of power consumption, this can lead us to detect any deviation from the baseline which will help in malware detection in such resource-constrained embedded systems. Finally, our study opens several promising research avenues within hardware-assisted security and anomaly detection, particularly in the context of zero-day malware and firmware manipulation.

References

1. Aslan, O.A., Samet, R.: A comprehensive review on malware detection approaches. IEEE Access **8**, 6249–6271 (2020). https://doi.org/10.1109/ACCESS.2019.2963724
2. Azmoodeh, A., Dehghantanha, A., Conti, M., Choo, K.K.R.: Detecting crypto-ransomware in iot networks based on energy consumption footprint. J. Ambient Intell. Humaniz. Comput. **9** (2018). https://doi.org/10.1007/s12652-017-0558-5
3. Basu, K., Krishnamurthy, P., Khorrami, F., Karri, R.: A theoretical study of hardware performance counters-based malware detection. IEEE Trans. Inf. Forensics Secur. **15**, 512–525 (2020). https://doi.org/10.1109/TIFS.2019.2924549
4. Bridges, R., Hernández Jiménez, J., Nichols, J., Goseva-Popstojanova, K., Prowell, S.: Towards malware detection via cpu power consumption: Data collection design and analytics. In: 2018 17th IEEE International Conference On Trust, Security And Privacy In Computing And Communications/ 12th IEEE International Conference On Big Data Science And Engineering (TrustCom/BigDataSE), pp. 1680–1684 (2018). https://doi.org/10.1109/TrustCom/BigDataSE.2018.00250
5. Celdrán, A.H., Sánchez, P.M.S., Castillo, M.A., Bovet, G., Pérez, G.M., Stiller, B.: Intelligent and behavioral-based detection of malware in iot spectrum sensors. Int. J. Inf. Secur. **22**(3), 541–561 (2022)
6. He, Z., Makrani, H.M., Rafatirad, S., Homayoun, H., Sayadi, H.: Breakthrough to adaptive and cost-aware hardware-assisted zero-day malware detection: a reinforcement learning-based approach. In: 2022 IEEE 40th International Conference on Computer Design (ICCD), pp. 231–238 (2022). https://doi.org/10.1109/ICCD56317.2022.00042
7. Hernandez Jimenez, J., Goseva-Popstojanova, K.: Malware detection using power consumption and network traffic data. In: 2019 2nd International Conference on Data Intelligence and Security (ICDIS), pp. 53–59 (2019). https://doi.org/10.1109/ICDIS.2019.00016
8. Karnouskos, S.: Stuxnet worm impact on industrial cyber-physical system security. In: IECON 2011 - 37th Annual Conference of the IEEE Industrial Electronics Society, pp. 4490–4494 (2011). https://doi.org/10.1109/IECON.2011.6120048
9. Kasarapu, S., Shukla, S., Hassan, R., Sasan, A., Homayoun, H., Dinakarrao, S.M.P.: Generative ai-based effective malware detection for embedded computing systems (2024). https://arxiv.org/abs/2404.02344
10. Leng, E.W.L., Zwolinski, M., Halak, B.: Hardware performance counters for system reliability monitoring. In: 2017 IEEE 2nd International Verification and Security Workshop (IVSW), pp. 76–81 (2017).https://doi.org/10.1109/IVSW.2017.8031548

11. Makrakis, G.M., Kolias, C., Kambourakis, G., Rieger, C., Benjamin, J.: Industrial and critical infrastructure security: technical analysis of real-life security incidents. IEEE Access **9**, 165295–165325 (2021). https://doi.org/10.1109/ACCESS.2021.3133348
12. Pan, Z., Sheldon, J., Sudusinghe, C., Charles, S., Mishra, P.: Hardware-assisted malware detection using machine learning. In: 2021 Design, Automation and Test in Europe Conference and Exhibition (DATE), pp. 1775–1780 (2021). https://doi.org/10.23919/DATE51398.2021.9474050
13. Patel, N., Sasan, A., Homayoun, H.: Analyzing hardware based malware detectors. In: Proceedings of the 54th Annual Design Automation Conference 2017. DAC '17, Association for Computing Machinery, New York, NY, USA (2017). https://doi.org/10.1145/3061639.3062202
14. Pham, D.P., Marion, D., Mastio, M., Heuser, A.: Obfuscation revealed: leveraging electromagnetic signals for obfuscated malware classification. In: Proceedings of the 37th Annual Computer Security Applications Conference, pp. 706–719. ACSAC '21, Association for Computing Machinery, New York, NY, USA (2021). https://doi.org/10.1145/3485832.3485894
15. Salehi, M., Hughes, D., Crispo, B.: μSBS: static binary sanitization of bare-metal embedded devices for fault observability (2020)
16. Sharma, C., Moylan, S., Vasserman, E.Y., Amariucai, G.T.: Review of the security of backward-compatible automotive inter-ecu communication. IEEE Access **9**, 114854–114869 (2021). https://doi.org/10.1109/ACCESS.2021.3104854
17. Walker, A., Sengupta, S.: Malware family fingerprinting through behavioral analysis. In: 2020 IEEE International Conference on Intelligence and Security Informatics (ISI), pp. 1–5 (2020). https://doi.org/10.1109/ISI49825.2020.9280529
18. Yang, H., Tang, R.: Power consumption based android malware detection. J. Electr. Comput. Eng. **2016**, 1–6 (2016). https://doi.org/10.1155/2016/6860217
19. Zhou, B., Gupta, A., Jahanshahi, R., Egele, M., Joshi, A.: Hardware performance counters can detect malware: myth or fact? In: Proceedings of the 2018 on Asia Conference on Computer and Communications Security, pp. 457–468. ASIACCS '18, Association for Computing Machinery, New York, NY, USA (2018). https://doi.org/10.1145/3196494.3196515

Germany is Rolling Out Nation-Scale Key Escrow and Nobody is Talking About it

Jan Sebastian Götte(✉)

Technical University of Darmstadt, Darmstadt, Germany
research@jaseg.de

Abstract. Germany is currently rolling out an opt-out, nation-scale database of the medical records of the majority of its population, with low-income people being disproportionally represented among its users. While there has been considerable criticism of the system coming from civil society, independent academic analysis of the system by the cryptography and information security community has been largely absent. In this paper, we aim to raise awareness of the system's existence and, based on the system's public specifications, highlight several concerning cryptographic engineering decisions. Our core observations is that the system's most sensitive long-term user keys are derived by a rudimentary, home-grown centralized key escrow mechanism. This mechanism relies on a per-use salt and only 256 bit of entropy, shared globally across millions of users. Furthermore, the system's specification mandates only level 3 compliance with the obsolete FIPS 140-2 security standard, which requires "hard, opaque potting", but lacks active tamper sensing. As a result, the system remains vulnerable to attacks by nation states and other well-funded adversaries.

Keywords: Physical Security · Tamper Resistance · Hardware Security Module (HSM) · Cryptography · Governance · Healthcare

1 Introduction

Beginning May 2025, after several delays, Germany has started the nation-scale rollout of its new electronic medical record system. The system aims to create a national database accessible to all healthcare providers that holds the complete electronic medical records of all publically insured people living in Germany. The system aims to replace paper-based workflows that are error-prone and lead to healthcare providers often only having access to a subset of patient's medical records. Data in scope for the system includes medical letters, laboratory results, and medical imaging files.

Due to Germany's mandatory health insurance laws, the system's user base encompasses the majority of all German residents. People who have replaced their public health insurance with private insurance as of now are not subject to the system. In Germany, by law private health insurance is only available to

R. Laborde et al. (Eds.): ESORICS 2025 Workshops, LNCS 16233, pp. 370–377, 2026.
https://doi.org/10.1007/978-3-032-16165-9_22

people from the top 10th percentile of household income. This means that the system disproportionally affects people who have low income, creating an equity issue. While it is possible to opt out from the use of the system, the process of opting out is difficult. Additionally, the government and health insurance providers have publically depicted the system in a one-sidedly positive way, meaning that it is unlikely the majority of people subject to the system have a comprehensive understanding of the system's benefits and risks that would be necessary for an informed decision.

While there has been loud criticism of the system's security from civil society organizations such as digital rights nonprofit organization Chaos Computer Club (CCC) [16] and several severe security flaws have been demonstrated practically, this criticism has largely been ignored by the political structures in charge. We observe that despite this civil society outrage and the system's large scale, it has received little attention from the academic cryptography and information security community.

In this paper, we aim to point out some perplexing cryptographic engineering decisions in the system. In particular, we point out that the system's core per-user secrets are kept in a rudimentary key escrow system whose security is based on engineering assumptions, not on cryptographic principles. Furthermore, we observe that by specification, the individual user keys of the system are derived from a per-user cleartext salt based on a system-wide long-term secret with only 256 bits of entropy[1]. Finally, we note that according to specification, the only physical security requirement for the protection of this highly sensitive secret is a "hard, opaque potting material", with no tamper detection and response required.

We base our analysis on the system's publicly available standards in their latest version as of the writing of this paper in April 2025, describing version 3.0 of the healthcare record system [9,11]. We note that the implementation might well deviate from these standards and be more secure–however, with the system's history of flaws, we believe this is unlikely to be the case. The reference implementation provided by the specification authority [13] follows the specified minimum requirements closely. As of now, there is no meaningful way for either the public or for researchers such as us to ascertain the concrete implementation security of the system.

2 The Design of ePA

ePA (short for *elektronische Patientenakte*, "electronic patient record"), is embedded into Germany's national public healthcare backend system "Telematikinfrastruktur" (TI). TI is a highly complex system, and a detailed description would

[1] In previous versions of the standard [10,12], there were two escrow services, with both keys used in layers to reduce the risk of a compromise of either one. The current standard only requires one escrow service, and drops the entropy requirement of the root keys from 512 bits to 256 bits. The apparent reason for the long-term nature of these keys is that they are updated manually.

exceed the limits of this paper. Briefly put, TI consists of a shared DMZ that parties like insurance providers and healthcare providers connect to through a VPN. At the client location, usually an individual doctor's office or a hospital, this VPN connection is terminated by a specialized VPN appliance named "Konnektor" that simultaneously acts as a trusted component inside the client network hosting some software for purposes such as authentication. The Konnektor contains several smart cards that store keys used for authentication. Konnektor devices are offered by several vendors and healthcare providers like doctor's offices are indivudally responsible for purchasing and maintaining a Konnektor.

Every person enrolled in the system as well as every healthcare professional providing services under it is issued an ID card that contains a smart card that contains keys used to authenticate towards the central infrastructure. The primary use of these smart cards up to now is that when someone visits a healthcare provider, they will insert their ID card into a terminal so the healthcare provider can automatically fetch their personal information such as name, birth date, address and enrollment status from their insurance provider.

ePA is implemented inside the TI system. Its centralized services are accessed by healthcare providers through the TI's VPN. Patient records are encrypted and decrypted inside TI's backend systems. Smart cards authenticate parties and hardware devices to each other. Each insurance provider picks one of several implementations of ePA's server-side infrastructure to run for its clients. Currently, there are two approved implementations of this server-side infrastructure.

With the current version of the specificatoin, the overall architecture of ePA heavily relies on Trusted Execution Environments (TEEs). Data processing on the server side is done in plaintext inside TEEs, with some cryptographic key management delegated to a Hardware Security Module. While attacks on the TEEs are considered in the system, the HSMs are assumed to be perfectly secure, and the system does not include mitigations for a compromised HSM. The primary motivation for plaintext processing seems to be to enable large-scale data analysis for research purposes without requiring consent or cooperation of the people whose records are being processed.

The primary services offered by the server side are authentication services, key escrow, and a database storing the encrypted records themselves. Records are symmetrically encrypted with keys that are derived from system-wide secrets inside an HSM. The primary motivation behind the use of a key escrow service seems to be to enable the creation of a duplicate patient ID smartcard in case a person looses theirs. While the current version of the standard is unclear on the exact mechanism of key derivation, in previous versions of the standard, the escrow service's root key, a random salt, and the healthcare ID number of the person owning the record was used in SHA256-HKDF. The specification requires that a new root key is generated once a year, but as far as we can tell, record key rollover is not done automatically but is only meant to be done when the *user* requests it, and old root keys must be retained forever to ensure old records can be accessed.

3 Related Work

The state-owned company specifying the system commissioned several security assessments of the system relating to the key escrow service. Fischlin [7] focuses on the cryptographic dimension of the key escrow service used in an older version of the standard, and is now obsolete. Slany [18] approaches the system at a higher level, and focuses on the cryptography of the inner protocol layers spoken between the system's components. Industry research organization Fraunhofer SIT was comissioned for a structured, theoretical assessment of attack paths to the system [8]. We are not currently aware of independent academic security research on the system.

The design and operation of the system have been independently described in detail by civil society activists, who have demonstrated several successful attacks on the system. Tschirsich, Brodowski, and Zilch [19] demonstrated how they could trivially acquire each of the smartcards as well as the Konnektor necessary for accessing the system. Tschirsich and Kastl [20] summarize the history of attacks demonstrated on the system and show multiple practical attacks on various parts of the system's implementation.

4 Concerning Cryptographic Engineering Choices

In this paper, we aim to highlight some of the design choices in the system that we believe stray from current best practice. This is by no means an exhaustive list, and is only meant to underscore why we believe the system deserves more scrutiny.

4.1 Use of Key Escrow

First, the system's general approach of using a key escrow service instead of securely storing the keys inside the system's already existing smart card infrastructure is concerning, given that this key escrow service poses a centralized security risk. The system's designers made this decision since it was deemed important that access to an encrypted record can be restored quickly after an insurance ID card is lost, without requiring the cooperation of the healthcare providers holding the primary copies of the person's medical records.

While key escrow services have been a topic of political debate in decades past, in the cryptographic community, consensus generally is that they are a bad idea since they pose a centralized target for attack, and increase attack surface [3–5].

4.2 Cryptographic Design

The system's overall cryptographic design is intentionally kept simple. The standard explicitly mentions that symmetric primitives have been preferred over asymmetric primitives in the core key escrow functions due to the risk of an attack on asymmetric primitives in the long term. Notably, other advanced cryptographic techniques such as secret sharing schemes, oblivious pseudo-random functions, or multiparty computation that could help with the security and privacy of the key escrow service by reducing trust placed in any single component of the service are also absent while the system relies extensively on the engineering-based security guarantees of TEEs and HSMs. Given that the ePA system trusts its HSMs as unconditionally secure, it is unclear what purpose the manual yearly root key renewal serves, especially absent an automatic way to roll over the wrapped record keys.

A consequence of the systems' simple cryptographic design is that the system trusts its components to a large degree. For instance, the system leaks a person's insurance ID number to the key escrow HSM every time record keys are requested. Along with the timing and frequency of these requests, this leaks information on the person's condition to the key escrow service in an identifiable way.

4.3 A Realistic Attacker Model

We observe that the system as a whole does not appear to be designed to defend against well-resourced adversaries. The series of practical attacks that have been demonstrated on the system confirm this impression. In Tschirsich and Kastl [20] summarize a series of successful attacks. Attacks include social engineering resulting in access to copies of smartcards enabling accessing patient records, using misconfigured Konnektor VPN appliances with their LAN DMZ and authentication interface exposed on the public internet, circumventing video-based authentication processes resulting in duplicate file keys being provided, classis SQL injection on a backend service maintaining an authentication database, accessing all national patient records through brute-force enumeration of weak identifiers, and several more.

We believe that a system like this must be designed to withstand well-resourced adversaries such as enemy secret services, since the medical data stored in such as information on chronic illness, sexually transmittable disease or severe food allergies has intelligence value. Repeated breaches of national digital infrastructure such as the 2015 breach of the US Office of Personnel Management [6] or the 2024 compromise of US telecommunications wiretapping systems [17] demonstrate that such state-sponsored attacks on national digital infrastructure are a realistic concern. A possible scenario in the ePA system would be an enemy secret service gaining access to one of the HSMs storing the systems' root secrets, extracting the root secret by an advanced physical attack, then being able to decrypt captured encrypted health records at will. Similarly, a nation-state adversary might have access to an exploit allowing the compromise of the system's TEEs, which would enable the extraction of any patient records being processed in plaintext inside these TEEs.

4.4 Physical Security

Physical security has received some consideration in the system's specification. First, smart cards are used extensively for authentication. Second, Hardware Security Modules are used in key locations of the system to process some cryptographic secrets. The core of the system's key escrow service is implemented inside an HSM. However, it is notable that the actual security level required for this HSM is only FIPS 140-2 level 3 [1]. Not only has FIPS 140-2 been superseded by FIPS 140-3 since 2019 [2], its security level 3 mostly provides logical separation of cryptographic functions from other logic and is not very meaningful in the context of physical attacks. The only physical requirement of FIPS 140-2 level 3 is that the HSM has a hard, opaque coating. This coating is specified to be tamper-evident, but notably no active tamper detection or response features are required by this standard. In contrast to the newer FIPS 140-3 standard and the related ISO/IEC 19790 [14] as well as ISO/IEC 24759 [15] standards, FIPS 140-2 does not make any particular requirements regarding resistance to side-channel attacks. The lack of tamper response, unspecified resistance to side-channel attacks and the fact that the ePA specification only requires the long-lived key escrow root key inside the HSM to have 256 bits of entropy lead to an unsatisfactory overall constellation.

5 Conclusion

In conclusion, we observe that in Germany's ePA national medical record database, despite the decade-long standardization and implementation process, several cryptographic compromises ended up in the system's final deployment. Even assuming that nation-scale key escrow is a good idea, the implementation of this key escrow system seems to stray from current best practice. The system uses a secret key with only 256 bits of entropy to derive highly sensitive secret keys for potentially tens of millions of people sharing an insurance provider. The cryptographic design of this escrow system is unsophisticated, ignoring the past three decades in cryptographic developments particularly in multiparty computation (MPC) and other secret sharing techniques in favor of an engineering approach. In the engineering dimension, the system's physical security is only held to the basic level 3 of the obsolete FIPS 140-2 standard, which is considerably less secure than an average credit card payment terminal. The system's root keys are only protected by a "hard, opaque potting material" and no tamper detection and response is required. We estimate that the system poses an attractive and soft target to nation-state adversaries. The system's shortcomings are made more severe by the fact that the system disproportionally affects the lives of people with low income.

References

1. (US) National Institute of Standards and Technology, Security Requirements for Cryptographic Modules, U.S. Department of Commerce (2002). https://csrc.nist.gov/pubs/fips/140-2/upd2/final. https://doi.org/10.6028/NIST.FIPS.140-2. Accessed 08 Apr 2025
2. (US) National Institute of Standards and Technology, Security Requirements for Cryptographic Modules, U.S. Department of Commerce (2019). https://csrc.nist.gov/pubs/fips/140-3/final. https://doi.org/10.6028/NIST.FIPS.140-3. Accessed 15 May 2025
3. Abelson, H., et al.: The risks of key recovery, key escrow, and trusted third-party encryption. World Wide Web J. **2**(3), 241–257 (1997)
4. Abelson, H., et al.: Keys under doormats. Commun. ACM **58**(10), 24–26 (2015). https://doi.org/10.1145/2814825
5. Anderson, R.: Security Engineering: A Guide to Building Dependable Distributed Systems. Wiley, Hoboken (2020)
6. Barrett, D., Yadron, D., Paletta, D.: U.S. suspects hackers in China breached about 4 million people s records, officials say. Wall Street J. (2015). http://www.wsj.com/articles/u-s-suspects-hackers-in-china-behind-government-data-breach-sources-say-1433451888. Accessed 15 May 2025
7. Fischlin, M.: Kryptographische Analyse Spezifikation Schl sselgenerierungsdienst ePA, Technische Universit t Darmstadt (2021). https://www.gematik.de/media/erezept/SGD_Analyse_2021.pdf. Accessed 15 May 2025
8. Fraunhofer SIT, Abschlussbericht Sicherheitsanalyse Des Gesamtsystems ePA F r Alle (2024). https://www.sit.fraunhofer.de/fileadmin/dokumente/studien_und_technical_reports/Abschlussbericht_Sicherheitsanalyse_ePA_fuer_alle_Fraunhofer_SIT.pdf. Accessed 16 May 2025
9. gematik, Spezifikation Aktensystem ePA f r alle v1.4.1 (2025). https://gemspec.gematik.de/docs/gemSpec/gemSpec_Aktensystem_ePAfueralle/latest/. Accessed 16 May 2025
10. gematik, Spezifikation Schl sselgenerierungsdienst ePA v1.6.0 (2023). https://gemspec.gematik.de/downloads/gemSpec/gemSpec_SGD_ePA/gemSpec_SGD_ePA_V1.6.0.pdf. Accessed 26 May 2025
11. gematik, bergreifende Spezifikation Verwendung Kryptographischer Algorithmen in Der Telematikinfrastruktur v2.28.1 (2024). https://gemspec.gematik.de/downloads/gemSpec/gemSpec_Krypt/gemSpec_Krypt_V2.28.1.html. Accessed 16 May 2025
12. gematik, bergreifende Spezifikation Verwendung kryptographischer Algorithmen in der Telematikinfrastruktur v2.40.0 (2025). https://gemspec.gematik.de/downloads/gemSpec/gemSpec_Krypt/gemSpec_Krypt_V2.40.0.pdf
13. Github Repository: eRP-FD/Vau-Hsm. https://github.com/eRP-FD/vau-hsm/tree/master. Accessed 16 May 2025
14. ISO/IEC 19790:2025, ISO. https://www.iso.org/standard/82423.html. Accessed 15 May 2025
15. ISO/IEC 24759:2025, ISO. https://www.iso.org/standard/82424.html. Accessed 08 Apr 2025
16. Koch, M.-C.: More and more experts warn against electronic patient records. Heise online. (2025). https://www.heise.de/en/news/More-and-more-experts-warn-against-electronic-patient-records-10235907.html. Accessed 26 May 2025

17. Menn, J.: Chinese Government Hackers Penetrate U.S. Internet Providers to Spy, The Washington Post (2024). https://www.washingtonpost.com/technology/2024/08/27/chinese-government-hackers-penetrate-us-internet-providers-spy/. Accessed 15 May 2025
18. Slany, W.: Sicherheitsanalyse zur Sicherheit der kritischen Komponenten der elek tronischen Patientenakte nach §291a SGB V (2020). https://www.gematik.de/media/gematik/Medien/Newsroom/Presse/Dokumente/Sicherheitsanalyse_TU_Graz_zur_ePA_mit_Vorwort_der_gematik.pdf. Accessed 15 May 2025
19. Tschirsich, M., Brodowski, C.-D.M.C., Zilch, D.A.: "Hacker Hin Oder Her": Die Elektronische Patientenakte Kommt!, (01:00:00 +0100). https://media.ccc.de/v/36c3-10595-hacker_hin_oder_her_die_elektronische_patientenakte_kommt. Accessed 15 May 2025
20. Tschirsich, M., Kastl, B.: Konnte Bisher Noch Nie Gehackt Werden : Die Elek tronische Patientenakte Kommt- Jetzt F r Alle!, (00:00:00 +0100). https://media.ccc.de/v/38c3-konnte-bisher-noch-nie-gehackt-werden-die-elektronische-patientenakte-kommt-jetzt-fr-alle. Accessed 15 May 2025

Hardware Performance Counters for Anomaly Detection in Embedded Devices

Victor Breux(✉) and Pierre-Henri Thevenon

Univ. Grenoble Alpes, CEA, Leti, 38000 Grenoble, France
{victor.breux,pierre-henri.thevenon}@cea.fr

Abstract. Cyber threats are increasing on a continuous basis, and the Internet of Things (IoT) and embedded devices are also increasingly exposed to attackers. Given the critical nature of these devices in Industrial Control Systems (ICS), the implementation of an Intrusion Detection System (IDS) is necessary. In particular, current researches focus on Host-Intrusion Detection Systems (H-IDS) which leverage signals from the device to detect attacks and intrusions before their impacts become devastating. This paper presents an H-IDS solution that relies on Hardware Performance Counters (HPC) and Machine Learning (ML) anomaly detection to raise alarms when an attack is detected on an embedded device. The proposed solution collects HPCs at the kernel level of the device and uses a remote computer to extract statistical features from the HPC values, then makes a decision with a ML model. An experimental platform simulating an Industrial Control System is presented with a simulated hydroelectric physical process and a hardware emulation of the Programmable Logic Controller managing sensors and actuators logic. The platform also contains 6 typical attacks that often target embedded devices, such as a ransomware, flooding on a communication protocol, SSH bruteforce, malicious data transfers and intensive CPU resources. This setup enables the evaluation of our H-IDS solution under both normal and malicious conditions. Results show that our solution has low CPU and memory footprint on the embedded device and is able to detect critical attacks without raising false alarm.

Keywords: HPCs · machine learning · intrusion detection system · embedded systems · cybersecurity

1 Introduction

As the number of cyberattacks continues to rise, especially in embedded systems, the exclusive use of traditional preventative defences such as root of trust, memory protection or access protection is rarely sufficient. Modern security strategies increasingly integrate Intrusion Detection Systems (IDS) as a complementary tool to detect, in real time, any abnormal behavior that may indicate a compromise in the system. In particular, Host-based Intrusion Detection Systems

R. Laborde et al. (Eds.): ESORICS 2025 Workshops, LNCS 16233, pp. 378–396, 2026.
https://doi.org/10.1007/978-3-032-16165-9_23

(H-IDS) have shown considerable promise due to their ability to monitor internal activities during runtime in order to provide fine-grained analysis of the system behavior.

Unlike network-based IDS (N-IDS), which monitor network traffic to detect a compromise, H-IDS are deployed directly on the host to detect suspicious or unauthorized behavior. H-IDS can be used as a complement of N-IDS to focus on a specific device and to allow the detection of cyberattacks targeting the internal behavior of the device without altering its network interactions. Two approaches are mainly proposed for H-IDS [28]. **Signature-based Detection** method involves identifying known patterns of malicious activity by comparing system information such as byte codes, text strings or instruction sequences with signatures of known attacks stored in their databases. While effective against known threats, this kind of solution is limited in detecting new, modified or obfuscated attack vectors. **Anomaly-based Detection** approach establishes a baseline of normal system behavior and identifies deviations from this reference as potential cyberattacks. By dynamically analyzing the internal system state using internal signals such as log files, system calls, resource usage or even hardware-level measurements, an anomaly-based H-IDS provides unique visibility into the execution of malicious softwares on the target and can detect most attacks such as privilege escalation or code injection. It is particularly suitable for detecting zero-day attacks based on unknown vulnerabilities. A significant challenge in anomaly-based detection is minimizing false alerts while accurately identifying a majority of true threats.
For H-IDS, one emerging reliable data source is Hardware Performance Counters (HPCs). Available in most modern processors (such as Intel, AMD, ARM, RISC-V), HPC registers can be used to measure the number of occurrences of hardware units usage within the processor core. They provide information about the low-level behavior of the processor and count events during process execution related to instructions (e.g. instruction retired, CPU cycles), memory accesses (e.g. cache hits or misses, main memory hits or misses) and the execution behavior on the CPU pipeline, among others. Although modern processors may support monitoring dozens or even hundreds of such events (e.g., 84 on ARM Cortex-A72, 62 on Cortex-A53), a key hardware limitation is that only a limited number (typically between 2 and 8) can be monitored simultaneously as only a limited number of CPU registers are allocated for HPC monitoring. This limitation requires a careful selection of HPC.

Originally designed for performance profiling and debugging, HPCs have been leveraged in recent years for security purposes, particularly for anomaly detection. Some studies demonstrated the efficiency of HPCs in detecting microarchitectural attacks [20,21,25,26], control flow hijacking attacks [10,12,24,35,38], rootkits [30,34], malwares [15,19,27,29] and some specific malwares types such as ransomwares [8,23,36,37] or DDoS [22]. H-IDS solution based on HPCs have been criticized because of the non determinism of HPC registers [11], however they are suited for embedded systems, such as Programmable Logic Controllers (PLC) or Industrial IoT (I-IoT) gateways, where the normal behavior is usually deterministic, not too complex and well defined.

Contributions: In this paper, we provide an innovative solution leveraging HPCs for H-IDS on embedded systems. Our contributions are as follows:

1. We present a novel H-IDS for embedded systems, using HPCs to detect malicious behavior in an embedded device. Our approach combines statistical features extraction with a reconstruction-based AI model.
2. We implement a complete and operational prototype on an ARM-based embedded device integrating custom kernel module for HPC extraction and offloading the anomaly detection process to a remote server.
3. We design a realistic hardware-in-the-loop experimental platform comprising embedded systems (PLC and I-IoT gateway) that are representative of an hydroelectric industrial control system. This testbed allows the execution of both benign and malicious behaviors and serves for the dataset generation. We also define and implement a representative set of attacks commonly targeting embedded systems.
4. We thoroughly evaluate the performance overhead introduced by our solution by analysing its impact on the CPU usage, the memory consumption, the network traffic and the inference duration.

Outline: The rest of the paper is organized as follows. Section 2 provides a detailed description of the complete solution and its implementation. Section 3 then focus on describing the methodology used to identify the best HPCs, the extraction of features and the machine learning model for anomaly detection. Section 4 introduces a dedicated tested with different malware behaviors and evaluates the solution. Section 5 reviews the state-of-the-art of H-IDS based on HPCs for embedded systems. Finally, Sect. 6 concludes with a summary and future directions.

2 Proposed Solution

As illustrated in Fig. 1, the proposed solution described in this section is a countermeasure designed to monitor and detect abnormal behaviors in an embedded device using HPCs. It is based on a centralized architecture, where the storage and analysis of the raw data extracted from all embedded devices is handled on a remote server ensuring easier management and scalability. The target device is equipped with a kernel module and a dedicated application to extract HPC data in real-time, while the remote server is responsible for analyzing these data, calculating anomaly scores through the machine learning (ML) model, and displaying the results via a comprehensive dashboard.

2.1 Embedded Solution

The target device integrates the two main components required for HPC extraction and transmission: a kernel module and a user-space application.

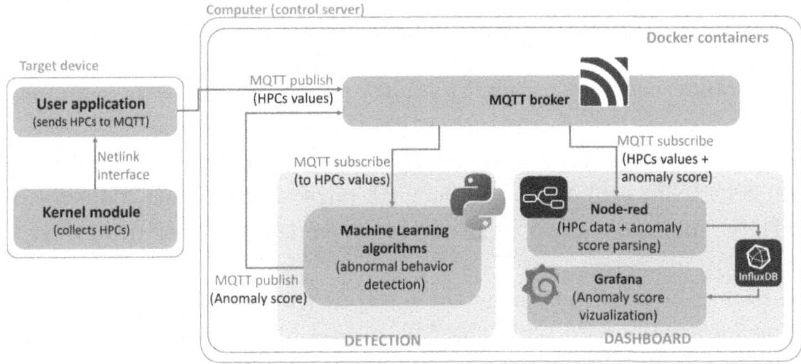

Fig. 1. Architecture of the solution

The kernel module is designed to interact directly with the registers of the Hardware Performance Counters to periodically extract low-level statistics in each core of the processor using assembly code. For each specific counter, its global value is obtained by summing the measurements from all cores. By reading these counter values, the kernel module captures real-time data about the system's resources usage, thus enabling an understanding of its hardware behavior. Compared to a user-space application for HPC extraction, the kernel-level extraction mechanism limits the impact of system load and scheduling for real-time monitoring and allows us to collect HPC raw values at 100 Hz (every 10 ms). We chose 100 Hz as a good trade-off between a sufficiently high sampling rate and a low overhead induced by the extraction.

The user space application aggregates the raw data, formats them and prepares them for a transmission to the centralized remote server. The application communicates with the kernel module through Netlink, a communication protocol to exchange data between kernel and user space through a low latency channel. The processed data are sent to the centralized served through MQTT (Message Queuing Telemetry Transport), a lightweight protocol allowing communications with limited bandwidth.

2.2 Remote Server: Data Analysis and Client Application

The function of the remote server is to receive, analyze and visualize data transmitted from the embedded device. The client application is at the core of this component, which analyzes the incoming raw HPC data, preprocesses them to compute statistical features and finally calculates the anomaly scores using the trained ML model. These algorithms are designed to detect subtle deviations in the target system's behavior, which may indicate a malfunction or a potential security threat. A dashboard also allows to visualize both the detection results (anomaly scores) and HPC values.

The server's architecture relies on a network of Docker containers deployed on the client machine to provide a modular and scalable environment and facilitate the setup of the solution. The components deployed in each container are described below:

- to facilitate the communication between the embedded devices(s) and the remote server, the system is based on MQTT protocol. The Mosquitto **MQTT broker** acts as an intermediary to collect published messages from multiple devices and transmits them to their subscribers.
- the **Node-RED server** subscribes to MQTT services and process incoming data packets from embedded devices. It parses these data packets into individual HPC register values in order to write them in an InfluxDB database for further analysis.
- the **client** application performs the computation of statistical features, computes the anomaly score with the ML model and publishes it on the MQTT channel.
- **InfluxDB** is a time-series database and serves as a central repository for HPC raw values and the calculated anomaly scores, providing an easy-to-query backend for data analysis or display.
- A **Grafana dashboard** is used to visualize the anomaly scores computed by the ML model and sorted in the InfluxDB database.

3 Anomaly Detection Methodology

An overview of the methodology is described in Fig. 2. First, relevant HPCs were selected and their signals were preprocessed. Then, on those preprocessed signals, features were computed on sliding time windows and used as inputs for the ML anomaly detection model.

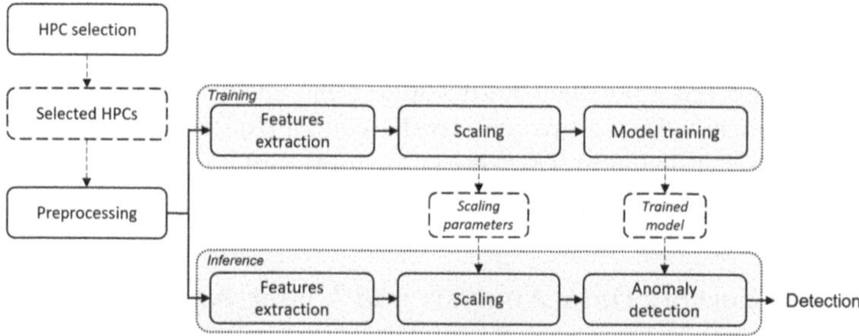

Fig. 2. Overall methodology pipeline

3.1 HPCs Selection and Preprocessing

From all the HPCs available on a processor, only a limited number (let say m) can be monitored concurrently. A first step of HPC selection was thus required to select these m HPCs. Our selection method relied on mutual information [14]. Mutual information between two random variables is a measure from the information theory that quantifies the dependency between them. A higher mutual information value represents higher dependency.

To select the best m HPCs, several datasets were generated (see Sects. 4.1 and 4.2), each comprising m HPCs with HPC sets differing across datasets, allowing to have recordings for all available HPCs. Based on these recordings, the mutual information between each HPC and the ground-truth label (0 for benign and 1 for an attack) was computed with a non-parametric method relying on entropy estimation from k-nearest neighbors [17]. This approach gave us the value of mutual information for all HPCs available on the processor. We finally selected the m non-correlated HPCs with the highest mutual information value and a final dataset with this set of HPCs was generated and used for the rest of the study. The corresponding signals were then preprocessed with two additional steps:

- resampling: the signals were resampled to match the 100 Hz sampling frequency of the HPC extraction. The missing values induced by the resampling were filled with the value following the gap evenly distributed on it. This step is necessary to ensure a constant time gap between consecutive values for correct features computation, and to ensure that no accumulation of HPC values occurs if some time slots were missing.
- smoothing: Exponentially-Weighted Moving Average (EWMA) technique was applied on the signals to smooth them and remove noise. The weighting parameter was arbitrarily set to $\frac{2}{9}$ (corresponding to a span of 8 for the filtering).

These preprocessed signals were used for the next steps of features computation and anomaly detection model.

3.2 Features Computation

After selecting the HPCs and preprocessing the signals, a set of statistical features was computed. For each HPC, a sliding window of 1 s (i.e. 100 measurements) was moved along the signals and features were computed on each window. On each window, and for each HPC, two signals were considered for features computation:

- raw signal : HPC signal after the preprocessing step
- derivative signal: derivative of the HPC signal, computed using the second order central differences

On both the raw signal and its derivative, for each time window and each HPC, the following features were computed: mean, standard deviation, minimum, median, maximum, root mean square, median absolute deviation from the median, kurtosis, skewness and coefficient of variation.

In total, on each time window, $20 \times m$ features were computed (10 on the signal and 10 on its derivative for each of m HPC) to represent the trend and the variation of the signals and their derivative and to capture distribution information over 1 s time windows [13]. Computed features were then scaled with a Min-max scaling to ensure they were all in comparable ranges before being fed to the ML model.

3.3 ML Anomaly Detection Model

For anomaly detection we chose to use a one-class anomaly detection model based on machine learning. The anomaly detection model was trained only on the features from the normal behavior of the system and any deviation from this behavior should be detected as an anomaly.
Our method was based on a reconstruction method with an autoencoder (AE) and is described in Fig. 3.

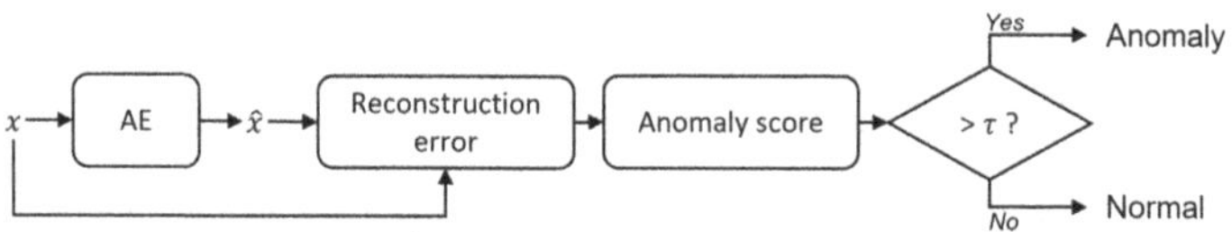

Fig. 3. Reconstruction-based anomaly detection with an autoencoder (AE) and a threshold τ

An autoencoder is a neural network architecture whose aim is to reconstruct the input (mimic the identity function) from a compression (or latent vector) of the input. After training, the reconstruction error of x, $r(x)$, was computed as the L2-distance between x and its reconstruction by the autoencoder.

The autoencoder was trained to reconstruct data from the normal behavior in the training set. Therefore a data not coming from the training distribution would be poorly reconstructed with a high reconstruction error.
A soft-decision anomaly score s was computed with the sigmoid function σ and the relative difference between the reconstruction error $r(x)$ and t, the maximum of the reconstruction errors on the training set:

$$s(x) = \sigma\left(2 * \frac{r(x) - t}{t}\right) \tag{1}$$

The higher the reconstruction error, the higher the anomaly score; and reconstruction errors greater than t gave anomaly scores above 0.5. This anomaly score is between 0 and 1 and can be interpreted as the probability of the vector x to be an anomaly with respect to the training set distribution.

Finally, a predefined threshold $\tau \in [0, 1]$ was used on the anomaly score to have a binary decision (1 being the anomaly label and 0 the normal label) :

$$A(x) = \begin{cases} 1, & \text{if } s(x) \geq \tau. \\ 0, & \text{otherwise.} \end{cases} \tag{2}$$

Increasing τ would decrease false alarms as higher deviation from the maximum reconstruction error on the training set would be needed to be detected as an anomaly.

4 Experimental Results

4.1 Evaluation Platform

Our experimental platform in Fig. 4 is mainly based on the STMicroelectronics evaluation board STM32MP157F-DK2 [5] running an embedded Buildroot distribution with a SLTS (Super Long Term Support) Linux kernel 6.1. Its processor is widely used in embedded devices with high resources requirements, such as I-IoT gateways or PLC, and has two ARM Cortex-A7 cores running at 800 MHz. Each core of the processor provides 42 HPCs and enables the extraction of measurements from four registers simultaneously, in addition to CPU cycles register. As discussed in Sect. 2, we extracted measurements from the HPC registers every 10 ms using a dedicated kernel module to extract the values and to limit the performance overhead.

We implemented software scripts on this platform to reproduce the internal behavior of off-the-shelf industrial embedded systems. In our case, I-IoT and PLC functionalities were considered as the normal behavior of the system. The PLC abstraction executes control logic using OpenPLC [7] to drive a hydroelectric simulated physical process using Modbus TCP protocol; it also communicates with a SCADA server that displays the state of each sensors and actuators. The I-IoT gateway extracts data sensors from a Raspberry Pi Sense HAT add-on board using I^2C communication bus and sends the values to an I-IoT server.

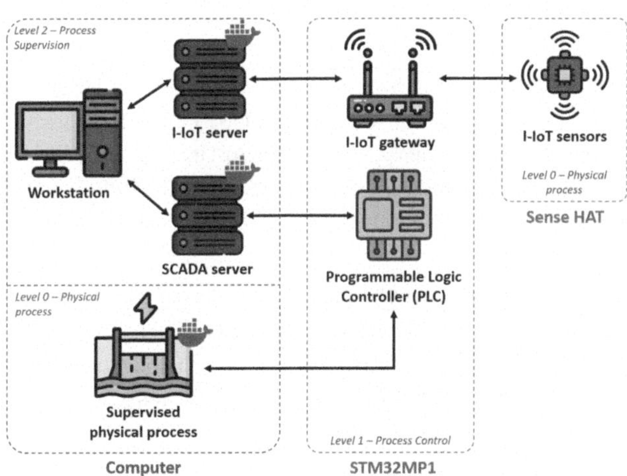

Fig. 4. Evaluation platform

The goal of our detection solution is to detect malicious modifications of the system and/or malicious applications aiming at disrupting the availability, integrity or confidentiality/privacy of target applications and their data. Applicative malwares were developed to stress the target system and to evaluate the detection mechanisms, and were written from scratch so they could be updatable and expandable.

Even if I-IoT devices or PLC are not connected to the Internet, they are connected to Information Technology (IT) systems or supervision computers within an internal network. The attacker can gain access to the IT systems thanks to vulnerabilities or misconfigured network defenses that then allows connecting to the internal network, and thus to the target device. However in this work, we mainly focused on the main impacts of a malicious behavior on the device, so we considered that the attacker is already connected to the target system with super-user privileges.

*Malware 1 - Data transfer to attacker (**M1**):* This malware aims to mimic the attacker sending a memory dump with potentially confidential data to its attacker's server. It is based on a FTP client that sends all files from a defined folder to the FTP server.

*Malware 2 - Task execution with data leakage (**M2**):* This malware aims at running a heavy resource consuming application on the target system. We chose a cryptocurrency mining use-case as such malwares were infecting many real embedded devices in the past years. The mining is performed by cpuminer software [1] on the target system and a Stratum server.

*Malware 3 - Cryptolocker (**M3**):* This malware aims at mimicking the behavior of a classic cryptolocker, a type of ransomware that encrypts either a file or a directory making its content inaccessible. This malware connects to the target system via SSH and then encrypts the target directory using ccrypt, a Linux utility for file encryption and decryption.

*Malware 4 - Modbus TCP flooding (**M4**):* A significant threat to industrial control systems (ICS) is the denial-of-service (DoS) attack on industrial communication protocols, which can lead to the disruption or corruption of the associated physical processes. One such attack involves Modbus flooding, where the attacker sends a high volume of requests to a Modbus TCP server, overwhelming its capacity.

*Malware 5 - SSH bruteforce (**M5**):* Dictionary based attacks on telnet or SSH services are one of the most common vectors of attacks in I-IoT devices. The implemented attack is based on Hydra [2], a widely used password-cracking tool that can perform brute-force or dictionary-based attacks.

*Malware 6 - Communication DoS (**M6**):* This malware aims at blocking communications between the application OpenPLC running on the target to execute control logic and the rest of its environment (namely the SCADA server and the physical process simulator). We add an iptables rule on the target system that blocks incoming and outgoing communication on TCP port associated with Modbus TCP.

Evasivity: Strategies to soften the impact of the malwares on the device were also developed and are presented in Table 1. Malwares **M4** and **M6** do not integrate such strategies. These strategies allow to lower the visibility of the malwares by detection mechanisms.

Table 1. Evasivity of malwares

Malware	Name	Evasivity
M1	Data transfer to attacker	Files are transferred in decreasing order of size
M2	Task execution with data leakage	Ten executions of cpuminer with evasivity parameter from 0 to 100 for the last execution
M3	Cryptolocker	Files are encrypted in decreasing order of size with a sleeping time in between
M5	SSH bruteforce	Hydra is executed with a decreasing number of threads

4.2 Dataset

Applications: The dataset with the selected HPCs contained executions of several applications:

- Normal behavior (**N**): nominal and safe behavior of the system with OpenPLC application handling the PLC logic of the physical process. Data from this application were labelled as 0 (benign state) and represented a recording of 1 h.
- Succession of malware applications: all malwares described in Sect. 4.1 were sequentially executed on top of the normal behavior. Data obtained during malware executions were labelled as 1 (anomaly state). Some malwares were executed with evasivity strategies as described in Table 1.

Training and Evaluation Split for ML Model: The dataset was divided into 2 parts for the training and the evaluation of the ML anomaly detection model respectively. The training set contained only data from the benign state of the system, so that the model could learn the nominal distribution and detect any deviation from it as an anomaly. This set was used to train the anomaly detection model and was made of the first 80% of the normal behavior recording (corresponding to a contiguous recording of 2880 s).

Conversely, the goal of the evaluation set (also called test set) was to evaluate the trained detection model on new data that were not seen during training. This allowed assessing model's performances and its ability to generalize on new data. Evaluation metrics (see Sect. 4.3) were computed on this set. The remaining 20% of the normal behavior recording was incorporated into the test set (corresponding to a contiguous recording of 720 s), in conjunction with all entire malware recordings.

4.3 Anomaly Detection Results

As explained in Sect. 3.1, we selected HPCs based on mutual information with the label. The five selected HPCs, that had the highest dependency with the label, were:

- DATA_WRITE_INSTR: Counts the number of data write instructions accepted by the Load Store Unit.
- Data Memory Access: Counts the number of read or write instructions in the data memory.
- Bus access write: Counts the number of bus accesses for write instructions.
- Bus Cycles: Counts the number of clock cycles used for write or read instructions on bus.
- CPU cycles: Counts the number of clock cycles of the CPU.

Selected HPCs signals were resampled and smoothed as discussed in Sect. 3.1. A sliding window of 100 timesteps was then used to extract 1 s time windows and compute features (see Sect. 3.2). On the training set, the sliding window moved with a step of 1 to augment the number of windows during training. However, the window moved with a step equal to the window size on the test set to have non-overlapping windows for the evaluation resembling a real-time scenario. On each window, 20 features were computed for each of the 5 HPC, resulting in features vectors with 100 components.

The encoder and the decoder of the AE model both had 3 fully-connected hidden layers (with Exponential Linear Unit activation) with 128, 64 and 32 units for the encoder and 32, 64, 128 for the decoder. The output layer of the encoder had 16 units (with *tanh* activation) and the output of the decoder had 100 units (=size of the features vectors). Dropout regularization was also used during training with a rate of 0.2. The AE model was trained on the scaled features vectors from the training set during 50 epochs on batches of size 512 using Adam optimizer and Mean-Squared Error loss function.

Evaluation Metrics. We evaluated the binary detection with True Positive Rate (TPR) and False Positive Rate (FPR) metrics computed on the test set. These two metrics represent respectively the proportion of time windows from malware executions correctly labelled as anomalies by the model and the proportion of time windows from the benign application misclassified as anomalies. TPR should be maximized, whereas FPR should be as low as possible. In our use case, decreasing the FPR is crucial because a detection system with too many false alarms would be unusable.

We also evaluated the model by computing the detection accuracy on each application (Acc_a for application a) in the test dataset. Accuracy is the proportion of time windows correctly classified by the model. In our case, accuracy on an application is the proportion of the application execution time correctly predicted.

Table 2. Evaluation of anomaly detection model on the test set

	TPR	FPR	Acc_{M1}	Acc_{M2}	Acc_{M3}	Acc_{M4}	Acc_{M5}	Acc_{M6}
$\tau = 0.4$	42.04 %	0.14 %	2.07 %	73.18 %	22.57 %	100 %	41.46 %	0.83 %
$\tau = 0.5$	41.19 %	0.14 %	1.67 %	70.25 %	18.96 %	100 %	41.33 %	0.83 %
$\tau = 0.6$	40.35 %	0 %	1.67 %	67.32 %	16.49 %	100 %	41.03 %	0.56 %

Results. The binary decision computed by the model with Eq. (2) was evaluated for 3 values of threshold τ: 0.4, 0.5 and 0.6. Values of the metrics for those 3 thresholds are given in Table 2.

Anomaly scores computed by the model on the test set, using Eq. (1), for each application are shown in Fig. 5.

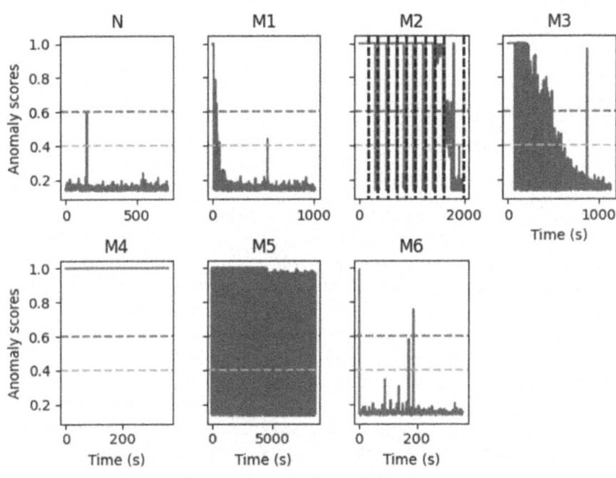

Fig. 5. Anomaly scores on the test set for each application (vertical dashed lines in **M2** separate different executions of the same application). Orange line indicates the warning threshold and red line the alert threshold

The results in Table 2 show that increasing the threshold reduced the FPR from 0.14% with a threshold of 0.4 to 0% with a threshold of 0.6. TPR was slighlty reduced when increasing the threshold: from 42.04% with 0.4 to 40.35% with 0.6.

The low TPR and accuracy values on malware could be explained because a malware execution does not contain only malicious portions. Indeed, a malware could also perform safe operations in addition to its malicious payload. Detecting the entire execution of an attack as abnormal is not necessary, we only need the model to detect at least one portion (even small) of the attack execution to consider it as detected. Therefore the TPR and the accuracy on malwares can be low without affecting the model capacity of raising alarms during attacks.

For our solution, we chose to use 0.4 as a warning threshold (in orange on Fig. 5) that indicated when something needed attention without necessarily being detected as an attack; and 0.6 as the alert threshold (in red on Fig. 5).

Based on results from Table 2 and Fig. 5, we can give more details on the model's detection performance on each malicious application:

- data transfer (**M1**): only the beginning of the attack where larger files were sent raised an alarm. The evasivity strategy of the attack allowed it to bypass the detection by not raising alarms when smaller files were being sent.
- CPU miner attack (**M2**): The model detected anomalies in each of the 10 executions (separated by the black-dashed lines on Fig. 5) of this attack (with 67.32% detection). As explained before and since at least one portion in each execution raised an alarm, we consider this attack as well detected by the model.
- Cryptolocker (**M3**): 16.49% of the attack execution was detected as abnormal by the model and Fig. 5 shows that the anomaly scores decreased during the execution. As for the data transfer attack, dealing with small files did not raise alarm and bypassed the model.
- Modbus TCP flooding (**M4**): this attack execution was entirely detected, with 100% accuracy and anomaly scores constantly above the alert threshold.
- SSH bruteforce (**M5**): almost half of the attack execution was detected (41.03%). The model raised alarm during this attack making it well detected.
- Communication DOS (**M6**): only a poor proportion of the attack execution was detected, however the model still raised some alarms during the execution.

4.4 Overhead Results

In this section, we evaluated the performance overhead introduced by our solution, focusing on memory usage, CPU consumption and network traffic. Understanding these impacts on an embedded device is mandatory for determining the feasibility of deploying such solution in a resource-constrained environment.

Impact on the Memory and CPU Resources: To measure the overhead on resource consumption, global memory and CPU consumption were continuously monitored on the platform over two-hour periods, both in the presence and absence of the detection solution. The memory and CPU usage remained stable and comparable to that of the reference consumption. This indicates that our solution did not introduce significant additional memory demands, making it suitable for systems with limited memory resources.

Impact on the Network: Our embedded solution transmitted raw HPC to the control server at a rate of 2976 bytes per second using MQTT protocol. These 2976 bytes corresponded to the MQTT frame used to transmit one hundred sets of five 32-bit HPC registers and 64-bit timestamp value. This transmission rate is manageable for most network infrastructures; however, in bandwidth-constrained environments, this could contribute to network congestion.

Anomaly Detection Inference Time: We evaluated the time to make an inference on a 1 s HPC time window. The inference time comprised the preprocessing of the signals, the features computation and the detection by the ML model. Evaluated on a Intel Core i5-1235U with 10 cores at 1.3 GHz, the mean inference time for one inference was about 73 ms (with a standard deviation of 23 ms).

In summary, our anomaly detection solution demonstrated a low memory and CPU footprint and a manageable network usage. These findings suggests that the solution is viable for deployment in embedded systems with limited resources. However, for applications with stricter performance and real-time requirements, further optimizations may be necessary. One solution would be to implement the ML model in the embedded device to reduce the network bandwidth usage; however, this approach would result in increased CPU and memory consumption.

5 Related Works and Discussions

Numerous approaches were proposed in the state-of-the-art to detect and mitigate attacks targeting embedded devices such as PLC or I-IoT gateway. Main characteristics of these approaches are summarized in Table 3, with a comparison to our proposed solution.

As illustrated in Table 3, two different approaches were adopted in the scientific literature. The first approach involved the use of numerous real-world malwares, taken from public malwares library, and benign samples to measure the accuracy of their detection algorithms. The second approach involved forged attacks to mimic potential impacts of an attack in order to detect all deviations from the reference behavior of the system. If the first approach evaluated the solution with a greater library of normal and malicious executables, each sample was evaluated individually in a sandbox, which was not an accurate representation of a real-life scenario. At the opposite, forged attacks added more realism in the malwares impacts as they were specifically developed to target a real-life scenario such as the behavior of a PLC or a data gateway.

Another important consideration in evaluating anomaly detection methods is the granularity of analysis of the samples. Some approaches operated without appropriate timing windows, triggering alerts for each individual extracted sample or for short timing windows. While these solutions offer a better sensitivity and detection speed, they also increased the potential number of false alarms. For example, a seemingly low FPR of 0.1% may become problematic when applied at high detection rate such as 10ms as it would introduce a potential false alert every 10 s making the solution unusable. Conversely, solutions with equivalent FPR yet with suitable timing windows yield a reduced frequency of false alarms. Identifying the best compromise between detection accuracy, overhead and the number of false alerts is crucial before deploying such detection solution in real use-cases. In our solution, we chose a sampling rate of 100 Hz and a timing window of 1 s (i.e. 100 measurements) which seemed the best compromise between these metrics.

Table 3. State-of-the-art of H-IDS based on HPC for embedded devices

Method	Sampling rate [window]	HPC extractor	Target	Attacks	Overhead	Detection
[18]	1kHz [250ms]	PAPI	PLC Wago Raspberry Pi	forged (6,no)	CPU: 10% Mem: 5%	Off
[9]	0.2Hz [1800s]	kernel module	Raspberry Pi 3b	forged (8,no)	N/A	On, R
[19]	1kHz [5-45 ms]	perf	Raspberry Pi 3b	malwares	N/A	Off
[31]	N/A	perf	Raspberry Pi 3b+	forged (1,no)	N/A	Off
[33]	1kHz	perf & simperf	Google Pixel 4	malwares	execution time: 3.2%	On, L
[16]	1kHz [0.25s]	PAPI	Raspberry Pi	forged (3,no)	N/A	Off
[6]	1kHz	perf	Raspberry Pi 2b	malwares	N/A	Off
[32]	1kHz [100ms]	hardware	Xilinx ARTIX-7	forged (7,no)	hardware implementation	On, R
Our method	**100Hz [1s]**	**kernel module**	**STM32MP1**	**forged (6,yes)**	**0%**	**On, R**

Sampling rate [window]: sampling rate and timing window used by the solution
HPC extractor: method used to extract the HPC values
Target: target device used for the evaluation
Attacks: type of attacks with the number of attacks and the consideration of evasiveness for forged attacks
Overhead: performance overhead on the target device
Detection: Online (On) represents a real-time detection and Offline (Off) a detection at a later time. Local (L) means a detection on the targeted device and Remote (R) on a distant server
N/A: no information provided by the authors

Evasive attacks, which are designed to bypass detection systems by lowering their impact on the target, were rarely integrated to evaluate the accuracy of a detection method in the literature. In our evaluation, we proposed different evasive strategies such as increasing the sleep time between task execution or decreasing the file size for a datalogger or a cryptolocker attacks. Our results highlighted the difficulty to detect correctly an attack if its malicious payload was hidden between the normal process of the system.

Despite significant progress in the field of attack detection using hardware performance counters, very few papers proposed a comprehensive and real-time solution. Most of the solution described in the state-of-the-art were based on tools to extract the raw HPC values such as PAPI Library [3] or perf [4] that seem not appropriate for a real solution. Our solution was based on dedicated kernel module to extract HPC data and all firmware to send these data from the kernel space to a remote server in order to compute the anomaly score. Using a kernel module enhances security and reduces overhead compared to user-space solution but it reduces portability across different CPU architectures.

6 Conclusion

In this work, we proposed a novel H-IDS leveraging Hardware Performance Counters (HPCs) for anomaly detection on embedded devices. Our system extracts HPC values at the kernel level and processes them using statistical features on 1-second time windows. An autoencoder-based model is then used to identify deviations from the learned normal behavior of the system.

To support the evaluation of our approach, we introduced a realistic experimental platform simulating a physical process controlled by OpenPLC. This setup allowed us to emulate industrial control systems and to test the robustness of our H-IDS against a set of common and evasive attacks targeting embedded devices. Our results demonstrate that the proposed method achieves low overhead and no false alarm, while successfully detecting various types of attacks, such as Modbus TCP flooding, SSH brute-force, and CPU miner activity. However, some highly evasive attacks, such as data exfiltration and cryptolockers, were able to evade detection, highlighting current limitations of the solution.

Future work will focus on expanding the attack set and improving the realism of the adversarial behaviors by integrating more advanced evasiveness parameters. Additionally, we plan to embed the ML model directly into the monitored device to remove the remote communication. This would reduce network impact but introduce new challenges related to resource usage and potential self-interference, as the monitoring process itself may affect the HPCs. We also envision enhancing the anomaly detection capabilities by incorporating complementary signals, such as system call traces, to provide a more holistic view of system behavior.

Acknowledgements. This work was supported by the French National Research Agency in the framework of the "Investissements d'avenir" program (IRT Nanoelec, ANR-10-AIRT-05) and under the France 2030 label (Superviz ANR-22-PECY-0008). The views reflected herein do not necessarily reflect the opinion of the French government.

References

1. Cpuminer-multi. https://github.com/tpruvot/cpuminer-multi. Accessed 25 Apr 2025
2. Hydra. https://www.kali.org/tools/hydra/. Accessed 25 Apr 2025
3. PAPI: the performance application programming interface. https://hpc.llnl.gov/software/development-environment-software/papi-performance-application-programming-interface. Accessed 25 Apr 2025
4. perf: Linux profiling with performance counters. https://perfwiki.github.io/main/. Accessed 25 Apr 2025
5. STM32MP157F-DK2 - DISCOVERY KIT WITH STM32MP157F MPU. https://www.st.com/en/evaluation-tools/stm32mp157f-dk2.html. Accessed 21 Jan 2025
6. Adhikari, S., Asad, H., Jones, K.: Enhancing IoT security: novel mechanisms for malware detection using HPCs and neural networks. In: 2023 IEEE 22nd International Conference on Trust, Security and Privacy in Computing and Communications (TrustCom), pp. 1455–1463. IEEE, Exeter (2023). 10.1109/TrustCom60117.2023.00199
7. Alves, T.R., Buratto, M., de Souza, F.M., Rodrigues, T.V.: OpenPLC: an open source alternative to automation. In: IEEE Global Humanitarian Technology Conference (GHTC 2014), pp. 585–589 (2014). 10.1109/GHTC.2014.6970342
8. Anand, P.M., Charan, P.V.S., Shukla, S.K.: HiPeR - early detection of a ransomware attack using hardware performance counters. Dig. Threats **4**(3), 1–24 (2023). 10.1145/3608484
9. Bourdon, M., et al.: Hardware-performance-counters-based anomaly detection in massively deployed smart industrial devices. In: 2020 IEEE 19th International Symposium on Network Computing and Applications (NCA), pp. 1–8. IEEE, Cambridge (2020). 10.1109/NCA51143.2020.9306726
10. Das, S., Chen, B., Chandramohan, M., Liu, Y., Zhang, W.: ROPSentry: runtime defense against ROP attacks using hardware performance counters. Comput. Secur. **73**, 374–388 (2018). 10.1016/j.cose.2017.11.011
11. Das, S., Werner, J., Antonakakis, M., Polychronakis, M., Monrose, F.: SoK: the challenges, pitfalls, and perils of using hardware performance counters for security. In: 2019 IEEE Symposium on Security and Privacy (SP), pp. 20–38 (2019). 10.1109/SP.2019.00021
12. Demme, J., et al.: On the feasibility of online malware detection with performance counters. ACM SIGARCH Comput. Architect. News **41**(3), 559–570 (2013). 10.1145/2508148.2485970
13. Fulcher, B.D.: Feature-based time-series analysis (2017). 10.48550/arXiv.1709.08055
14. Guyon, I., Elisseeff, A.: An introduction to variable and feature selection. J. Mach. Learn. Res. **3**(null), 1157–1182 (2003)
15. Kadiyala, S.P., Jadhav, P., Lam, S.K., Srikanthan, T.: Hardware performance counter-based fine-grained malware detection. ACM Trans. Embed. Comput. Syst. **19**(5), 1–17 (2020). 10.1145/3403943
16. Konstantinou, C., Wang, X., Krishnamurthy, P., Khorrami, F., Maniatakos, M., Karri, R.: HPC-based malware detectors actually work: transition to practice after a decade of research. IEEE Design Test **39**(4), 23–32 (2022). 10.1109/MDAT.2022.3143438
17. Kraskov, A., Stögbauer, H., Grassberger, P.: Estimating mutual information. Phys. Rev. E, Statist., Nonlinear, Soft Matter Phys. **69**(6 Pt 2), 066138 (2004). 10.1103/PhysRevE.69.066138

18. Krishnamurthy, P., Karri, R., Khorrami, F.: Anomaly detection in real-time multi-threaded processes using hardware performance counters. IEEE Trans. Inf. Forensics Secur. **15**, 666–680 (2020). 10.1109/TIFS.2019.2923577
19. Kuruvila, A.P., Karmakar, S., Basu, K.: Time series-based malware detection using hardware performance counters. In: 2021 IEEE International Symposium on Hardware Oriented Security and Trust (HOST), pp. 102–112. IEEE, Tysons Corner (2021). 10.1109/HOST49136.2021.9702291
20. Kuruvila, A.P., Meng, X., Kundu, S., Pandey, G., Basu, K.: Explainable machine learning for intrusion detection via hardware performance counters. IEEE Trans. Comput.-Aided Des. Integr. Circ. Syst. **41**(11), 4952–4964 (2022). 10.1109/TCAD.2022.3149745
21. Mushtaq, M., Akram, A., Bhatti, M.K., Chaudhry, M., Lapotre, V., Gogniat, G.: Nights-watch: a cache-based side-channel intrusion detector using hardware performance counters. In: Proceedings of the 7th International Workshop on Hardware and Architectural Support for Security and Privacy, pp. 1–8 (2018)
22. Nascimento, P.P.D., Pereira, P., Mialaret, J.M., Ferreira, I., Maciel, P.: A methodology for selecting hardware performance counters for supporting non-intrusive diagnostic of flood DDoS attacks on web servers. Comput. Secur. **110**, 102434 (2021). 10.1016/j.cose.2021.102434
23. Olani, G., Wu, C.F., Chang, Y.H., Shih, W.K.: DeepWare: imaging performance counters with deep learning to detect ransomware. IEEE Trans. Comput., 1–1 (2022). 10.1109/TC.2022.3173149
24. Omotosho, A., Welearegai, G.B., Hammer, C.: Detecting return-oriented programming on firmware-only embedded devices using hardware performance counters. In: Proceedings of the 37th ACM/SIGAPP Symposium on Applied Computing, pp. 510–519. ACM, Virtual Event (2022). 10.1145/3477314.3507108
25. Oshana, R., Thornton, M.A., Larson, E.C., Roumegue, X.: Real-time edge processing detection of malicious attacks using machine learning and processor core events. In: 2021 IEEE International Systems Conference (SysCon), pp. 1–8. IEEE, Vancouver (2021). 10.1109/SysCon48628.2021.9447078
26. Polychronou, N.F., Thevenon, P.H., Puys, M., Beroulle, V.: A hybrid solution for constrained devices to detect microarchitectural attacks. In: 2023 IEEE European Symposium on Security and Privacy Workshops (EuroS&PW), pp. 259–269 (2023). 10.1109/EuroSPW59978.2023.00033
27. Pundir, N., Tehranipoor, M., Rahman, F.: RanStop: a hardware-assisted runtime crypto-ransomware detection technique (2020). 10.48550/arXiv.2011.12248
28. Satilmiş, H., Akleylek, S., Tok, Z.Y.: A systematic literature review on host-based intrusion detection systems. IEEE Access **12**, 27237–27266 (2024). 10.1109/ACCESS.2024.3367004
29. Sayadi, H., et al.: Towards accurate run-time hardware-assisted stealthy malware detection: a lightweight, yet effective time series CNN-based approach. Cryptography **5**(4), 28 (2021). 10.3390/cryptography5040028
30. Singh, B., Evtyushkin, D., Elwell, J., Riley, R., Cervesato, I.: On the detection of kernel-level rootkits using hardware performance counters. In: Proceedings of the 2017 ACM on Asia Conference on Computer and Communications Security, pp. 483–493. ACM, Abu Dhabi United Arab Emirates (2017). 10.1145/3052973.3052999
31. Singh, Y., Kuruvila, A.P., Basu, K.: Hardware-assisted detection of malware in automotive-based systems. In: 2021 Design, Automation & Test in Europe Conference & Exhibition (DATE), pp. 1763–1768. IEEE, Grenoble (2021). 10.23919/DATE51398.2021.9474053

32. Thevenon, P., et al.: iMRC: integrated monitoring & recovery component, a solution to guarantee the security of embedded systems. J. Internet Serv. Inf. Secur. 12(2), 70–94 (2022). 10.22667/JISIS.2022.05.31.070
33. Wang, H., Sayadi, H., Pudukotai Dinakarrao, S.M., Sasan, A., Rafatirad, S., Homayoun, H.: Enabling micro AI for securing edge devices at hardware level. IEEE J. Emerg. Sel. Top. Circuits Syst. **11**(4), 803–815 (2021). 10.1109/JETCAS.2021.3126816
34. Wang, X., Karri, R.: NumChecker: detecting kernel control-flow modifying rootkits by using hardware performance counters. In: Proceedings of the 50th Annual Design Automation Conference, DAC '13. Association for Computing Machinery, New York (2013). 10.1145/2463209.2488831
35. Wang, X., Karri, R.: Reusing hardware performance counters to detect and identify kernel control-flow modifying rootkits. IEEE Trans. Comput.-Aided Des. Integr. Circuits Syst. **35**(3), 485–498 (2016). 10.1109/TCAD.2015.2474374
36. Woralert, C., Liu, C., Blasingame, Z.: HARD-Lite: a lightweight hardware anomaly realtime detection framework targeting ransomware. IEEE Trans. Circuits Syst. I: Regul. Pap. **70**(12), 5036–5047 (2023). 10.1109/TCSI.2023.3299532
37. Woralert, C., Liu, C., Blasingame, Z., Yang, Z.: A comparison of one-class and two-class models for ransomware detection via low-level hardware information. In: 2023 Asian Hardware Oriented Security and Trust Symposium (AsianHOST), pp. 1–6. IEEE, Tianjin (2023). 10.1109/AsianHOST59942.2023.10409333
38. Zhou, H., Wu, X., Shi, W., Yuan, J., Liang, B.: HDROP: detecting ROP attacks using performance monitoring counters. In: Information Security Practice and Experience, vol. 8434, pp. 172–186. Springer International Publishing, Cham (2014). https://doi.org/10.1007/978-3-319-06320-1_14. series Title: Lecture Notes in Computer Science

Semantic-Aware Provenance-Based Intrusion Detection for Edge Systems

Qingyu Zeng(✉), Songxuan Liu, Yu Wu, and Yuko Hara

Institute of Science Tokyo, Tokyo 152-8550, Japan
{qyzeng,hara}@cad.ict.e.titech.ac.jp, liu.s.au@m.titech.ac.jp, wu.y.e989@m.isct.ac.jp

Abstract. As cyberattacks targeting edge devices become increasingly sophisticated, detecting intrusion behaviors becomes increasingly difficult, demanding effective intrusion detection systems (IDS) tailored for resource-constrained environments. Existing provenance-based IDSs show a promising ability to detect benign and attack behaviors, but require a lot of computing resources to build provenance graphs, which is not conducive to edge deployment. To address this gap, we propose a semantic-aware provenance-based IDS, which constructs provenance graphs and prioritizes security-critical events using semantic roles. Through structural and semantic analysis on the DARPA Engagement 3 (CADETS) dataset, we show that role-annotated subgraphs exhibit measurable divergence b etween benign and attack activities, with certain roles (e.g., `binary-execution`) appearing over 3× more frequently in attack traces, demonstrating the feasibility of semantic priors for lightweight intrusion detection.

Keywords: Intrusion detection · Provenance graph · Semantic aware

1 Introduction

The proliferation of edge computing devices, ranging from smart gateways to industrial controllers, has significantly expanded the attack surface of modern cyber-physical systems. These devices, often deployed in uncontrolled environments and lacking comprehensive security infrastructure, are increasingly targeted by adversaries for persistent surveillance, lateral movement, and sensitive data exfiltration [5]. The constrained nature of edge platforms, however, poses fundamental challenges for deploying effective intrusion detection systems (IDS) that are both precise and lightweight [8].

Recent advances in provenance-based security monitoring have demonstrated the effectiveness of system-level event graphs in capturing causal dependencies between entities such as processes, files, and network flows [9]. Provenance graphs offer a holistic and high-fidelity view of system behavior, enabling accurate detection and forensic traceability of complex attack chains [7]. However, most existing provenance-based IDS frameworks assume access to abundant computational

R. Laborde et al. (Eds.): ESORICS 2025 Workshops, LNCS 16233, pp. 397–406, 2026.
https://doi.org/10.1007/978-3-032-16165-9_24

resources and rely on heavyweight graph analytics, rendering them unsuitable for edge deployment [3].

In this work, we explore the feasibility of integrating semantic-awareness into provenance graphs as part of an ongoing effort. We present a preliminary modular framework that constructs, filters, and analyzes provenance subgraphs. Our key idea is to associate system events with high-level *semantic roles* (e.g., `binary-execution`) and leverage these roles during training to differentially weight behavior based on its security relevance. This enables a tunable trade-off between accuracy and efficiency, while enhancing the interpretability of alerts. To evaluate our design, we conduct a preliminary analysis using the CADETS dataset, which includes detailed system call-level traces and ground truth. Our results indicate that role-annotated subgraphs exhibit measurable divergence between benign and attack activities. To the best of our knowledge, this is the first work that introduces semantic role annotation into provenance-based intrusion detection system in edge computing scenarios.

The remainder of this paper is organized as follows. Section 2 briefly reviews prior work on provenance-based intrusion detection systems. Section 3 presents the overview of our proposed system architecture. Section 4 presents the semantic-aware provenance graph modeling. Section 5 presents preliminary results. Section 6 concludes our work and discusses future research directions.

2 Related Work

Provenance-based IDSes leverage data provenance, which records the origin and transformation processes of data within a system, to detect malicious activities more effectively than traditional host-based IDSes. Unlike traditional intrusion detection methods that primarily analyze system events in isolation, Provenance-based IDS provide richer semantic context by constructing provenance graphs–directed acyclic graphs recording causal relationships among system entities and events. These systems typically include modules for data collection, graph summarization, intrusion detection, and benchmarking datasets.

Figure 1 illustrates a benign scenario: a common debugging workflow using `LD_PRELOAD`. A user connects to the system via `SSH` and writes a custom shared library, `my_debug_hooks.so`, containing specific debugging code. Subsequently, the `LD_PRELOAD` environment variable is configured with the path of the custom library. Then, the target application (`test`) is launched. Because of the `LD_PRELOAD` setting, the operating system loads the custom library into the application's memory first. Finally, the custom library's code intercepts function calls from the `test` process and writes diagnostic data to a log file (`/tmp/app_debug.log`). This is a routine, non-intrusive debugging practice.

Provenance-based methods can broadly be categorized into anomaly-based, rule-based, and tag-propagation-based approaches. Anomaly-based systems [1] identify intrusions by detecting deviations from established normal behaviors, rule-based methods [6] utilize predefined rules and signatures, and tag-propagation methods assign and propagate trustworthiness or risk labels through the provenance graph to highlight suspicious activities.

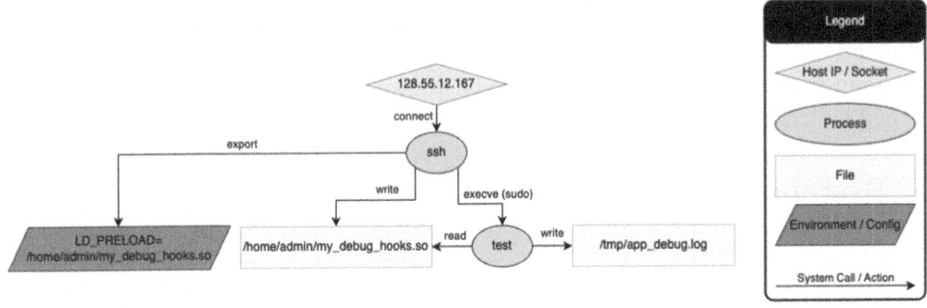

Fig. 1. Illustrative provenance graphs of a benign administrative activity.

ALASTOR [1] is a provenance-based IDS framework leveraging graph embedding techniques under the anomaly-based category, tailored specifically for serverless computing environments. Traditional provenance approaches face challenges in these environments due to ephemeral function lifetimes and container reuse, which attackers can exploit to conceal malicious activities from detection. To overcome these limitations, ALASTOR captures detailed provenance data at both the system and application layers, tracing interactions such as system calls and network requests within each serverless function instance. These fine-grained events are aggregated into global provenance graphs, enabling precise reconstruction and analysis of intrusion scenarios. ALASTOR was evaluated through implementation on the OpenFaaS platform, testing complex intrusion scenarios targeting serverless applications. The results indicated that ALASTOR reconstructed detailed attack paths that traditional monitoring methods and several commercially available tools failed to detect.

CAPTAIN [6] is another adaptive provenance intrusion detection framework. Different from ALASTOR, CAPTAIN employs a rule-based approach. Specifically designed to overcome the limitations of traditional static-rule provenance systems, it utilizes a differentiable rule-configuration method based on gradient descent algorithms to dynamically adjust system parameters, including tag initialization, tag propagation rates, and alarm generation thresholds. In contrast to conventional rule-based provenance intrusion detection systems that rely on manually configured static rules, CAPTAIN automatically adjusts these parameters using benign training data, effectively reducing false alarms while preserving detection accuracy against malicious activities. Experimental evaluations conducted on datasets from DARPA Engagements and datasets generated from simulated environments demonstrated substantial performance improvements, including over 90% reduction in false alarms compared with traditional rule-based methods.

Both ALASTOR and CAPTAIN represent significant advancements in the provenance-based intrusion detection. However, these systems are facing limitations in lightweight security for edge devices. Thus, there is an urgent need of lightweight provenance-based intrusion detection system optimized specifically for the resource-constrained edge environments. This could include reducing the overhead associated with provenance data collection and analysis, simplifying provenance graphs, and optimizing graph summarization without compromising critical security insights.

3 System Design

In this work, we introduce the semantic-aware method into provenance-based intrusion detection, specifically optimizing the graph construction phase through semantic-aware filtering.

Goal. This work aims to enhance provenance-based intrusion detection by introducing semantic-awareness into graph construction. We assign high-level semantic roles to system events, focusing on security-critical behaviors.

Assumptions. Provenance traces contain a large volume of semantically irrelevant events, and that meaningful roles can be assigned using rules.

3.1 Architecture Overview

Figure 2 illustrates the architecture of the proposed system. The system operates on a stream of low-level system audit events and produces alerts corresponding to anomaly signatures. It consists of the following main components:

1. **Event Parser:**
   The event parser processes raw system logs from the widely acknowledged public datasets provided by DARPA Engagement, where each line contains a single event record with detailed information about system activities such as file operations, process executions, network communications, and memory operations. The parser extracts key components from these logs including subjects (processes), objects (files, network flows, memory), and events (read, write, execve, clone, etc.), then standardizes them into a unified format that can be used to construct provenance graphs.
2. **Graph Constructor:**
   The graph constructor uses data processed by the event parser to generate a provenance graph. The graph nodes represent the system entities: Subject nodes capture process information including PID, PPID, command line, process name, and parent relationships, while Object nodes represent files, network flows, memory regions, and other system resources with their respective attributes like file paths, IP addresses, and memory addresses. The edges between nodes represent the events and operations that occurred between subjects and objects, each edge containing metadata such as timestamp, event type, and operation parameters. The system maintains a node buffer to track entity states and handles node updates when entity properties change over time. The final graph is serialized into JSON format with separate files for nodes, edges, and principals, creating a comprehensive provenance graph that captures the complete system execution history and can be used for intrusion detection through graph-based analysis and rule-based analysis.

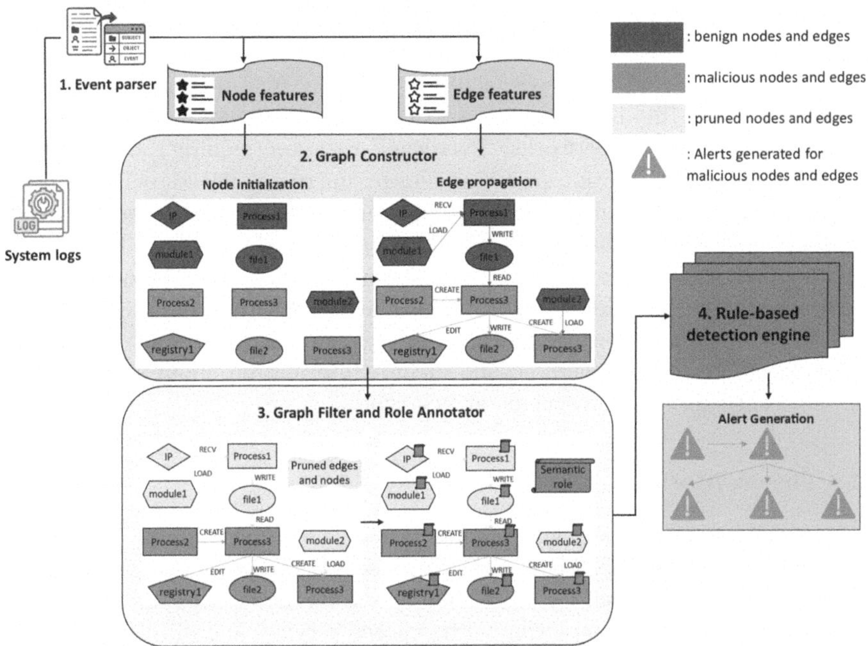

Fig. 2. Architecture overview of the proposed IDS.

3. **Graph Filter and Role Annotator:**
   The original provenance graph generated by the graph generator contains a large number of edges and nodes that represent low-risk operations. These routine operations in the provenance graph take up a lot of memory, making them unsuitable for edge environments to process. The idea is to apply graph filters and eliminate redundant events, focusing attention on security-critical behaviors. The graph filter prunes the edges representing these low-risk operations, which not only reduces memory usage but also improves the clarity of the risk operations in the provenance graph.
   A role annotator is applied to assign high-level semantic roles that capture the potential impact of each event on system security. We define a set of deterministic mappings based on file paths, system call types, and access patterns. For example, any execution of a binary via `execve`, such as launching tools in `/usr/bin`, is categorized as `binary-execution`, while read operations from low-sensitivity sources like `/dev/tty` are labeled as `routine-read`.
4. **Detection Engine:**
   The detection engine combines rule-based analysis with the Adam optimizer. The detection engine uses a tag-based propagation system. These tags are initialized based on predefined rules (e.g., untrusted files have lower label vector values) and then propagated through the graph as events occur. The detection engine works by continuously processing system events and updating the value

of the tags of each node. After an event happens, the detection engine compares the tag values with learned thresholds to identify attacks. The system can detect various attack types including FileExec (executing untrusted files), FileCorruption (modifying high-integrity files), DataLeak (sending confidential data to untrusted networks), PrivilegeEscalation (gaining root privileges), and MaliciousFileCreation (creating files by untrusted processes). The detection engine uses Adam optimizer to optimize the propagation strength and detection threshold parameters based on benign training data. The training process minimizes false positives by adjusting these parameters to ensure that normal system behavior doesn't trigger alarms while maintaining sensitivity to actual attacks. After comparing the tag values with the detection rules, the alarms would be generated and include information about the suspicious events, entities, and the specific attack type.

3.2 Threat Model

We consider a threat model where edge devices, including smart gateways and industrial controllers, operate in environments that are network-untrusted. The adversary can be local, with remote shell access to the device, and adjacent on the network, capable of interacting with exposed services and injecting traffic. In either case, the attacker can execute code, exploit software vulnerabilities, and misuse legitimate tools.

The attacker aims to execute malicious binaries and perform write operations. We assume that the attacker has no prior control over the monitoring agent and cannot tamper with the system audit logs. The logging mechanism is trusted.

The malicious activity, depicted in the Fig. 3, is based on an attack scenario from the DARPA Engagement 5 dataset. The attack sequence demonstrates a classic post-exploitation pattern. It begins with the attacker connecting to the system via `ssh` using stolen credentials. The attack then uses `scp` to upload a malicious toolset, including a client named `mchk` for privilege escalation. After establishing a foothold, the `mchk` client is executed, which employs a local privilege-escalation technique, and leverages `memfd_create` to map an anonymous, in-memory payload before invoking it, while avoiding on-disk detection. Operating with full administrative control, the attacker then proceeds to exfiltrate critical system files, including `/etc./passwd` and `/etc./shadow`, as well as sensitive user documents like `/home/admin/biol`, back to the remote socket.

4 Semantic-Aware Provenance Graph Modeling

System behavior is modeled using a directed provenance graph $G = (V, E, T)$, where V includes heterogeneous entities (e.g., process, files, and network sockets); E encodes interactions between entities (e.g., *read-from*, *write-to*, and *executes*); and T preserves temporal ordering of events. The graph structure captures causal relationships between system activities and forms the basis of behavioral analysis [4].

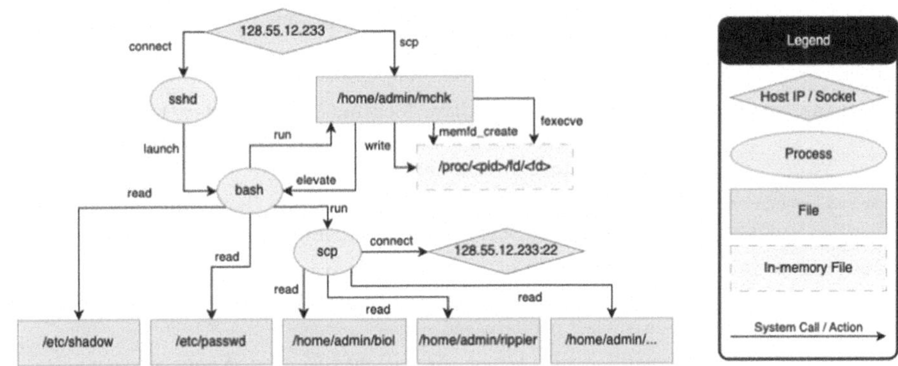

Fig. 3. Illustrative provenance graphs of a multi-stage malicious attack.

4.1 Provenance Graph Semantics and Role Annotation

While many provenance systems treat audit events as atomic interactions, this work augments each event with a high-level *semantic role* that captures its functional intent and potential security relevance. These roles are derived using lightweight, rule-based heuristics that analyze object paths, file types, and system call contexts.

Given the volume and redundancy of system-level provenance data, this work focuses on high-value behavioral features.

- **Edge Filtering:** Routine interactions, such as reading configuration files and writing logs, are prevalent in both benign and malicious sessions. We filter edges that correspond to known low-risk actions (e.g., `read-from` on `/etc./motd`) to reduce graph clutter without losing detection sensitivity.
- **Role Annotation:** We apply deterministic labeling rules to assign each event a semantic role, as shown in Table 1. These annotations serve dual purposes: (i) they filter out low-risk behavior during graph construction, and (ii) they modulate loss weights during model training. For instance, misclassifying a `binary-execution` or `staging-write` event may incur a higher penalty than a benign `routine-read`.

4.2 Role-Weighted Training Objective

To reflect the varying semantic importance of different events, we introduce a *role-weighted loss* scheme that scales each event's loss contribution based on its semantic role. Formally, for each event e with associated role $r \in \mathcal{R}$, the final loss is computed as:

$$\mathcal{L}_{\text{total}} = \sum_{e \in \mathcal{E}} w_r \cdot \mathcal{L}(e), \tag{1}$$

where $\mathcal{L}(e)$ is the base loss (e.g., reconstruction error), and w_r is the role weight assigned to semantic role r.

Table 1. Semantic Role Definitions

Role	Definition
`routine-read`	Reads from non-sensitive locations such as `/dev/tty`, temporary user files, or other benign sources. Common in routine system interactions
`privileged-read`	Read access to sensitive credentials files, including `/etc./shadow`, SSH private keys, and password files
`staging-write`	Writes directed at temporary or staging directories, e.g., `/tmp`, `/var/tmp`. Often used for staging payloads and served as attacker preparation zones
`binary-execution`	Execution of a binary file, as captured by `execve` system calls and equivalent process launch events
`neutral`	Events that do not match any defined semantic rules. These are often low-risk actions not indicative of security-critical behavior. Used as the default role when no semantic annotation applies

5 Preliminary Evaluation

5.1 Experimental Setup

All offline experiments are conducted on a machine equipped with an Intel Xeon(R) Silver 4410Y and 256 GB RAM. We conduct evaluations on the DARPA Engagement 3 dataset, specifically focusing on the CADETS scenario. This dataset is part of DARPA's Transparent Computing program and was collected from a real-world enterprise environment under controlled attack conditions. It offers system-level event traces in the common data model format, including both benign and malicious activities.

The CADETS trace contains detailed logs of system calls. Each event is timestamped and linked [6], making it suitable for constructing temporal provenance graphs. The dataset includes several realistic attack campaigns such as reverse shell injection, credential scraping, and privilege escalation, embedded within multi-day traces.

5.2 Semantic Subgraph Analysis

To evaluate the feasibility of our approach, we analyzed provenance subgraphs derived from benign and malicious activity windows. We compute a set of structural and semantic metrics on each subgraph to investigate whether malicious behaviors exhibit statistically distinct topological patterns. This allows us to answer the core question: *does the role-annotated subgraph itself encode enough information to separate benign from attack behavior?*

Table 2 compares the proportion of semantically annotated nodes in benign vs. attack subgraphs. We observe that `binary-execution` and `staging-write`

Table 2. Structural comparison of benign vs. attack subgraphs. (mean ± std.)

Metric	Benign	Attack
% of `routine-read` nodes	6.59 ± 16.91%	0.70 ± 5.89%
% of `privileged-read` nodes	0.01 ± 0.57%	0.00 ± 16.10%
% of `binary-execution` nodes	1.49 ± 8.49%	4.93 ± 14.91%
% of `staging-write` nodes	0.03 ± 1.26%	0.70 ± 5.89%

Table 3. Comparison of training efficiency between w/o and w/ role-weighted loss.

Metric	w/o Role-Weighted	w/ Role-Weighted
Epochs to Reach Loss < 10	33	**26**
Epochs to Reach Loss < 1	79	**45**
Min Final Loss (after 100 epochs)	0.00	**0.00**
Avg. Loss (Epochs 20–40)	23.23	**6.71**

roles are more prevalent in attack graphs, reflecting typical behaviors like launching malicious payloads and staging operations in temporary storage. In contrast, `routine-read` appears more in benign traces, consistent with normal startup and interactive operations. This distinction validates the design intuition behind our semantic annotation: although individual events may not be malicious in isolation, their elevated presence in attack subgraphs provides valuable priors for learning. Consequently, assigning higher weights to such roles during training can help amplify model sensitivity to stealthy but structurally deviant behaviors.

5.3 Training Efficiency Comparison

To evaluate the efficiency of our semantic-aware training strategy, we compare the convergence behavior of models trained with and without role-weighted loss. We introduce a semantic-aware loss weighting scheme, where each role is assigned a fixed importance weight reflecting its potential security impact. For example, `binary-execution` and `staging-write` are considered more critical than routine operations.

Our role-weighted loss improves convergence speed by emphasizing security-critical semantic roles and down-weighting routine events during training. Table 3 compares the training efficiency with and without role-weighted loss. The role-weighted model achieves faster convergence, reaching critical loss thresholds significantly earlier than without role-weighted.

Summary. Preliminary results show that semantic role annotations help distinguish attack behaviors through structural patterns and improve model training efficiency when used in loss weighting. These findings highlight the potential of semantic-aware provenance analysis and provide a promising foundation for future development.

6 Discussion and Future Work

In this work, we introduce a semantic-aware, provenance-based IDS optimized for edge computing environments. By incorporating semantic role annotation, this work aims to balance detection fidelity, interpretability, and resource efficiency. Our current prototype focuses on offline analysis using the CADETS dataset. The results demonstrate that role-annotated subgraphs exhibit measurable structural divergence between benign and attack behavior, validating the effectiveness of our semantic modeling approach.

Several directions remain open for future exploration: 1) Deploying the proposed IDS on actual edge platforms will allow us to evaluate system behavior under real workload conditions. This includes assessing runtime performance, memory usage, and detection latency. 2) Rule-based IDS are lightweight and interpretable, making them well-suited for constrained edge environments. However, their reliance on predefined rules limits their ability to detect zero-day attacks. As part of future work, we plan to integrate lightweight graph neural network (GNN)-based detection models that can identify anomalous provenance graphs. To maintain resource efficiency, we will explore GNN architectures such as GraphSAGE [2] or spatio-temporal GNNs with pruning.

Acknowledgment. This work is supported by JST SPRING, Grant Number JPMJSP2180 and JSPS KAKENHI Grant Numbers JP23H00464, JP24KK0184, and JP25K03091.

References

1. Datta, P., et al.: ALASTOR: reconstructing the provenance of serverless intrusions. In: 31st USENIX Security Symposium, pp. 2443–2460 (2022)
2. Hamilton, W., Ying, Z., Leskovec, J.: Inductive representation learning on large graphs. In: Advances in Neural Information Processing Systems, vol. 30 (2017)
3. Han, X., Pasquier, T., Seltzer, M.: Provenance-based intrusion detection: opportunities and challenges. In: 10th USENIX Workshop on the Theory and Practice of Provenance (2018)
4. Mei, J., Moura, J.M.: Signal processing on graphs: causal modeling of unstructured data. IEEE Trans. Signal Process. **65**(8), 2077–2092 (2016)
5. Siwakoti, Y.R., et al.: Advances in IoT security: vulnerabilities, enabled criminal services, attacks, and countermeasures. IEEE Internet Things J. **10**(13), 11224–11239 (2023)
6. Wang, L., et al.: Incorporating gradients to rules: towards lightweight, adaptive provenance-based intrusion detection. arXiv preprint arXiv:2404.14720 (2024)
7. Xie, Y., et al.: Pagoda: a hybrid approach to enable efficient real-time provenance based intrusion detection in big data environments. IEEE Trans. Dependable Secure Comput. **17**(6), 1283–1296 (2018)
8. Zarpelão, B.B., et al.: A survey of intrusion detection in internet of things. J. Netw. Comput. Appl. **84**, 25–37 (2017)
9. Zipperle, M., et al.: Provenance-based intrusion detection systems: a survey **55**(7), 1–36 (2022)

Inter-Device PUFs: A Novel Paradigm for Physical Unclonable Functions

Emiliia Geloczi(✉) and Stefan Katzenbeisser

University of Passau, Innstr. 43, 94036 Passau, Germany
{emiliia.geloczi,stefan.katzenbeisser}@uni-passau.de

Abstract. A Physical Unclonable Function (PUF) is a promising concept for device authentication, as it can be extracted from existing device components and enables the generation of unique, device-specific keys. However, existing PUF-based approaches often require prior distribution of these keys during an enrolment phase, require persistent storage or transmission of sensitive data, and are vulnerable to different attacks. To address these limitations, we propose a novel approach to using PUFs. While PUFs are typically employed by leveraging the inherent uniqueness of their responses, our approach instead focuses on their similarities, exploiting matching segments of two distinct PUFs. This enables the identification of a PUF that is unique per-device-pair, termed Inter-Device PUF (ID-PUF), which links two devices and serves as the basis for a shared secret key. This key can be independently generated on both devices, eliminating the need for its prior distribution and persistent storage, thus making an ID-PUF well-suited for application in lightweight symmetric cryptographic schemes. The feasibility of an ID-PUF is demonstrated through statistical analysis and experimental evaluation on several devices. Furthermore, to illustrate its application, we present a novel ID-PUF-based mutual authentication protocol (ID-PUMA) and analyse its security.

Keywords: PUF · ID-PUF · Mutual Authentication · ID-PUMA

1 Introduction

The number of Internet of Things (IoT) devices is rapidly increasing, currently estimated at around 23.15 billion and projected to reach 39.65 billion by 2028 [40]. During operation, devices generate, process and transfer large amounts of data, which can be critical in certain contexts, becoming attractive targets for adversaries [30]. Despite many existing security measures [31], the rise in newly discovered vulnerabilities and attacks [11], combined with the heterogeneous and resource-constrained nature of IoT systems, requires the continuous evolution of security solutions [45].

In order to secure an IoT system, solutions should not only guarantee compliance with the fundamental security principles known as the CIA Triad (confidentiality, integrity, and availability) [39], but also ensure privacy, auditability,

R. Laborde et al. (Eds.): ESORICS 2025 Workshops, LNCS 16233, pp. 407–427, 2026.
https://doi.org/10.1007/978-3-032-16165-9_25

non-repudiation, and trust [25]. In particular, authentication plays a critical role in IoT [28], as it establishes mutual trust between system parties and, hence, facilitates many security properties, thereby reducing overall security risks [2].

For lightweight devices, Physical Unclonable Functions (PUFs) have been proposed as a promising means of authentication. A PUF is an intrinsic device fingerprint [21], unique for each device and unclonable due to minor deviations of the hardware components [1], which cannot exactly be reproduced, even by the manufacturer. PUFs can be extracted from components already present in a device, such as memory modules [8], thereby eliminating the need for additional hardware. Moreover, they can serve as the basis for device-specific keys that are generated on demand, thus removing the requirement for persistent key storage. Despite these advantages, existing PUF-based authentication solutions often rely on a prior key exchange during the enrolment phase, require persistent storage or transmission of sensitive data, and remain vulnerable to known attacks [28].

In this paper, we propose a novel approach to applying PUFs that addresses the listed limitations while preserving the advantages of PUF-based security. Traditional PUF-based solutions typically rely on the uniqueness of PUF responses to distinguish between devices and verify their identities. In contrast, we explore the potential of leveraging matching segments of PUFs from two devices to form a unique characteristic related to both, allowing their inter-device association. We name this characteristic an Inter-Device PUF (ID-PUF). An ID-PUF enables the generation of a shared key that is unique for the device pair, thus facilitating the use of lightweight symmetric cryptography. Since this key can be independently reproduced on both devices on demand, there is no need for it to be distributed during enrolment. To demonstrate the possible application of ID-PUFs, we also introduce a novel mutual authentication protocol based on this concept. The results of our statistical and security analyses confirm the feasibility and advantages of using ID-PUFs as a foundation for authentication solutions, particularly in terms of resistance to common attacks.

In summary, we present the following two key **contributions**:

- *ID-PUF:* A novel paradigm for PUFs that leverages matching segments from two different PUFs to generate a shared key that is unique per-device-pair. It preserves PUF advantages while addressing common limitations of traditional PUF-based solutions, making it a robust foundation for symmetric cryptographic schemes and mutual device authentication.
- *Mutual Authentication Protocol:* A novel lightweight ID-PUF-based protocol (ID-PUMA) demonstrating the concept's applicability and enhanced security over existing solutions.

The rest of the paper is organised as follows. Section 2 provides general background information on PUFs. Section 3 introduces the proposed ID-PUF concept. The mutual authentication protocol is described in Sect. 4, followed by its security analysis in Sect. 5. Section 6 offers an overview of related work and their comparison with our approach. In Sect. 7, we discuss potential challenges in the application of ID-PUFs. Finally, Sect. 8 concludes the paper and outlines directions for future research.

2 Background: Physical Unclonable Functions

During the manufacturing of electronic devices, variations in the characteristics of their components naturally occur. Even devices originating from the same production series exhibit slight differences in their physical properties [28]. While these variations do not impact functionality or reliability, they can be used to create a unique fingerprint for a device. Such a fingerprint is known as a Physical Unclonable Function (PUF), a function embedded in a physical object that receives a challenge c and generates a response r, forming a challenge-response pair [21]. Ideally, PUF should exhibit the following properties [18]:

- *Unclonability:* A PUF should not be physically reproducible or clonable, even by its manufacturer.
- *Unpredictability*: It should be impossible to predict the response r for a new challenge c, even if other challenges and corresponding responses have been previously observed.
- *Reproducibility:* The same challenge c should consistently produce the same response r on the same physical object.
- *Tamper-Evidence*: Any physical tampering with a PUF should significantly alter its response.

PUFs can be extracted from various device components and characteristics, such as memory modules or signal timing patterns [8]. In our work, we use a start-up Static Random Access Memory (SRAM) PUF [19], which exhibits a limited number of challenge-response pairs [38], demonstrating that our approach can also be applied to so-called "weak" PUFs. Additionally, SRAM is present in most devices, not easily accessible externally, and relatively stable [44].

Due to slight variations in transistor properties at power-up, SRAM modules generate bit patterns that appear random but are stable and unique to each module. These patterns can serve as a distinct fingerprint of a device. In the case of SRAM PUFs, a memory address serves as a challenge c while its corresponding uninitialised value, read out immediately after power-up, represents a response r. Multiple challenge-response pairs constitute the challenge set $C := \{c_i\}$ and the corresponding response set $R := \{r_i\}$ ($\forall i = 0, \ldots, n$), together forming the set of challenge-response pairs $CRP := (C, R)$. It is important to note that the number of challenge-response pairs (n) may vary depending on the application requirements. Furthermore, a single PUF can produce many distinct $CRPs$.

3 Inter-Device PUF

Due to the uniqueness of PUF responses [24], device-specific cryptographic keys and robust device identification can be achieved. Typically, $CRPs$ from a PUF are collected during an enrolment process, and one of them is later used for authentication or key generation. We propose an alternative to this canonical use of PUFs. Instead of relying on a single device's uniqueness, our approach leverages matching response segments from the PUFs of two devices to identify a device-pair-specific PUF, termed an Inter-Device PUF (ID-PUF), which enables inter-device association.

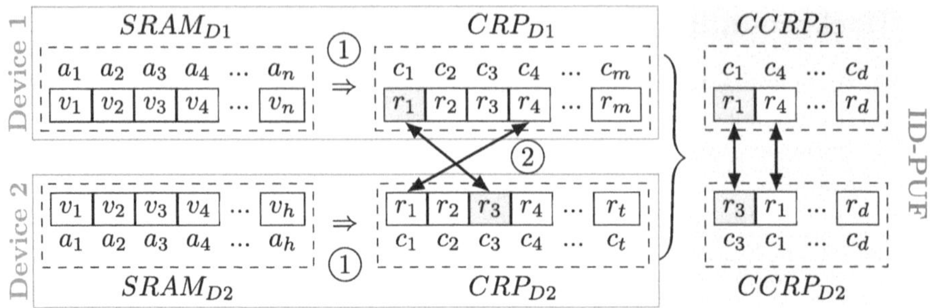

Fig. 1. Identification procedure of an SRAM-based ID-PUF.

3.1 ID-PUF Identification

In this section, we detail an ID-PUF identification process, consisting of two phases: ① PUF Initialisation and ② Collision Search (see Fig. 1).

① PUF Initialisation

Consider two devices $D1$ and $D2$, each equipped with an SRAM module. These modules contain n and h addresses (a) with corresponding values (v), respectively. Hence, the total memory available on each device is $SRAM_{D1} := \{(a_i, v_i)|\forall i = 1, \ldots, n\}$ and $SRAM_{D2} := \{(a_j, v_j)|\forall j = 1, \ldots, h\}$.

The first phase is dedicated to selecting combinations (a, v) that are suitable to serve as a PUF. Their number depends on the size of the SRAM module, its stability, and PUF-metric thresholds applied during selection. These PUF-suitable combinations form the device-specific CRP, where a corresponds to the challenge c, and v corresponds to the response r, i.e., $(a, v) \rightarrow (c, r)$. In our case, this results in two sets: $CRP_{D1} := \{(c_i, r_i)|\forall i = 0, \ldots, m\}$ and $CRP_{D2} := \{(c_j, r_j)|\forall j = 0, \ldots, t\}$. To identify these $CRPs$, all (a, v) combinations unsuitable for use as a PUF are filtered out. This requires evaluation of potential responses (v), which can be done using the following PUF metrics [24]:

- The *uniformity* of v is evaluated using the fractional Hamming Weight $HW(v)$. The closer $HW(v)$ is to the ideal value of 0.5, the more uniform v is.
- The *reliability* of v is evaluated using the fractional intra-device Hamming Distance $HD_{intra}(v, v')$, which reflects the difference between multiple responses to the same corresponding challenge on a single device. A lower HD_{intra} indicates a more stable response; hence, the ideal value is 0.
- The *uniqueness* of v is evaluated using fractional inter-device Hamming Distance $HD_{inter}(v_1, v_2)$, which measures the difference between responses to the same challenge across different memory modules, indicating the ability of a PUF to produce unique responses and ideally tends to 0.5.

Thus, combinations (a, v) that eventually form the $CRPs$ and become (c, r) are selected such that the corresponding r values meet predefined thresholds for each metric.

② Collision Search

After performing PUF initialisation, we obtain two sets CRP_{D1} and CRP_{D2} that are used to further identify Collision $CRPs$ ($CCRPs$) for the device pair $D1$ and $D2$. To achieve this, we need to select pairs $(c_i, r_i) \in CRP_{D1}$ and $(c_j, r_j) \in CRP_{D2}$, where collisions of responses occur, i.e., $r_i = r_j$ and $c_i \neq c_j$, thereby forming $CCRP_{D1}$ and $CCRP_{D2}$ related to the ID-PUF of the devices:

$$CCRP_{D1} := \{(c_i, r_i)\},\ CCRP_{D2} := \{(c_j, r_j)\},\ \forall i, j = 0, \ldots, d.$$

For each $CCRP$, the sets of included challenges c and their corresponding responses r are referred to as the collision challenge set CC and the collision response set CR, respectively. Thus, for devices $D1$ and $D2$:

$$CCRP_{D1} := \{CC_{D1}, CR_{D1}\},\ CCRP_{D2} := \{CC_{D2}, CR_{D2}\}.$$

Given that $CR_{D1} = CR_{D2} = CR$, we can rewrite $CCRPs$ as:

$$CCRP_{D1} := \{CC_{D1}, CR\},\ CCRP_{D2} := \{CC_{D2}, CR\}.$$

Both identified $CCRPs$ contain an identical set of responses CR that can be used to generate a shared key for the two devices. However, using the entire set at once would allow for the creation of only a single key for the device pair. In practice, though, there may be a need to generate multiple keys, e.g., to support multi-channel communication. To address this, various subsets of CR can be selected for key generation, enabling the creation of multiple unique keys.

3.2 Statistical Analysis

The uniqueness property seems to contradict the concept of an ID-PUF. Still, in this section, we demonstrate that, in theory, a sufficient number of response collisions can be found in SRAM PUFs of realistic size to enable key generation.

Assume that there are two devices $D1$ and $D2$ with corresponding CRP sets of sizes m and t, identified in ① PUF initialisation step:

$$CRP_{D1} := \{(c_i, r_i) | \forall i = 0, \ldots, m\}, CRP_{D2} := \{(c_j, r_j) | \forall j = 0, \ldots, t\}.$$

Due to uniformity, a response r is a w-bit random-looking value drawn from a discrete set of 2^w possible values. Responses are independent and may recur within the same CRP.

Probability of Collision Occurrence. To calculate the probability $P(COL)$ that at least one response collision ($r_i = r_j$, $c_i \neq c_j$) occurs between CRP_{D1} and CRP_{D2}, we apply the complementary event approach [9]. Thus, $P(COL)$ can be expressed as 1 minus the probability that no response collision between two $CRPs$ exists. Additionally, in our case, $m \times t \gg 2^w$, indicating that the values involved are relatively large. We can then employ the first-order exponential approximation $(1 - x)^y \approx e^{-xy}$ [4]. Consequently, the probability of a collision can be approximated by

$$P(COL) \approx 1 - e^{-\frac{mt}{2^w}}. \qquad (1)$$

Therefore, to expect collisions, the probability $P(COL)$ must approach 1.

Expected Number of Collisions. To calculate the expected number of collisions $E[X]$, we first define an indicator random variable $X_{i,j}$ for each pair of responses $r_i \in CRP_{D1}$ and $r_j \in CRP_{D2}$ [37]:

$$X_{i,j} = \begin{cases} 1, & \text{if } r_i = r_j, \\ 0, & \text{if } r_i \neq r_j. \end{cases}$$

The total number of collisions is then given by $X = \sum_{i=1}^{m} \sum_{j=1}^{t} X_{i,j}$. Finally, by applying the linearity of expectation [13], we can express $E[X]$ as:

$$E[X] = \sum_{i=1}^{m} \sum_{j=1}^{t} E[X_{i,j}].$$

Since $X_{i,j} = 1$ with the probability that a response $r_i \in CRP_{D1}$ matches a specific response $r_j \in CRP_{D2}$, we have $E[X_{i,j}] = \frac{1}{2^w}$. Thus, the total expected number of collisions can be calculated using the formula:

$$E[X] = \sum_{i=1}^{m} \sum_{j=1}^{t} \frac{1}{2^w} = \frac{mt}{2^w}. \tag{2}$$

Number of Keys. As mentioned in Sect. 3.1, using different subsets of the collision response set $CR := \{r_i \mid \forall i = 0, \dots, d\}$, which is identical for both devices, enables the generation of multiple distinct keys for a single device pair. Hence, to estimate the number of keys of varying lengths that can be generated from CR, we count the total number of unique subsets of CR of a specified length, taking into account the order of the included responses r. For clarity, we refer to this number of subsets as the number of potential keys. The calculations use the formulas for permutations with (NK_{WR}) and without (NK_{NR}) repetitions [36], depending on whether repeated responses are allowed:

$$NK_{WR} = P'(d, l) = d^l, \;\; NK_{NR} = P(d, l) = \frac{d!}{(d-l)!}, \tag{3}$$

where d is the cardinality of the collision response set CR, and l is the number of w-bit responses needed to construct a key of a length k, i.e., $l \times w = k$.

Estimation Results. Figure 2 shows estimations of $P(COL)$, $E[X]$, NK_{NR} and NK_{WR} for various response lengths w (8, 16 and 32 bit) and different cardinalities of $CRPs$ from two devices. For simplicity, we assume that $|CRP_{D1}| = |CRP_{D2}| = |CRP_D|$, i.e., $CRPs$ consist of the same number of (c, r) pairs (e.g., $2^{13}, \dots, 2^{22}$).

As shown in Fig. 2a, collisions are guaranteed to happen for relatively short response lengths. However, this is not the case for 32-bit responses, where the probability approaches 1 only when more than 2^{17} responses are available. Similarly, Figure 2b shows that the expected number of collisions is relatively high for 8 and 16-bit response lengths; in contrast, for 32-bit responses, the expected

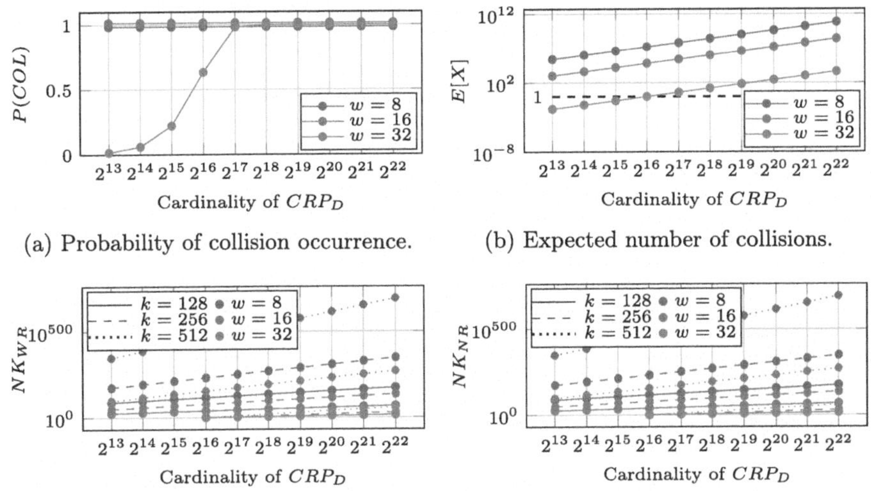

(a) Probability of collision occurrence.

(b) Expected number of collisions.

(c) Number of possible distinct keys allowing repetitions of r.

(d) Number of possible distinct keys without repetitions of r.

Fig. 2. Theoretical estimations of $P(COL)$, $E[X]$, NK_{WR} and NK_{NR}; w denotes the response length (in bits), k denotes the key length (in bits).

number of collisions is significantly lower, often less than one, meaning that in some cases, no collisions are expected at all.

Based on the estimated expected number of collisions, we then calculated the number of distinct keys of varying lengths (k) that can potentially be generated. Figure 2c shows the number of keys that allow repetitive responses. It can be observed that a large number of keys of all considered lengths can be constructed from 8- and 16-bit responses. However, in the case of 32-bit responses, where fewer collisions are expected, keys can only be generated if the cardinalities of $CRPs$ are at least 2^{16}. Similar results are observed for keys that contain no repeated responses (see Figure 2d). Although their total number is slightly lower than that of keys allowing repetition, it remains large enough that the difference is negligible given the magnitude of the values.

The results of our statistical analysis indicate that it is theoretically possible to identify ID-PUFs for device pairs, even when the devices have short PUF segments, i.e., relatively limited SRAM.

3.3 Experimental Implementation

To validate the estimates presented in the previous section in practice, we performed the ID-PUF identification on four existing development boards listed in Table 1. Since five instances of each board type were used, the results in this section represent average values. For instance, when analysing the probability of collisions between boards I and II, the reported value represents the average across the results obtained for all 25 possible instance combinations (5×5).

Table 1. Development boards selected for the ID-PUF identification.

№	Board's Name	SRAM		Amount
		Initial	PUF-suitable	
I	ESP32-S3 [14]	416 kB	188 kB	5
II	ESP8266EX [15]	50 kB	23 kB	5
III	Arduino Nano 33 (internal SRAM) [3]	200 kB	102 kB	5
IV	Arduino Nano 33 (external SRAM) [3,29]	512 kb	266 kb	5

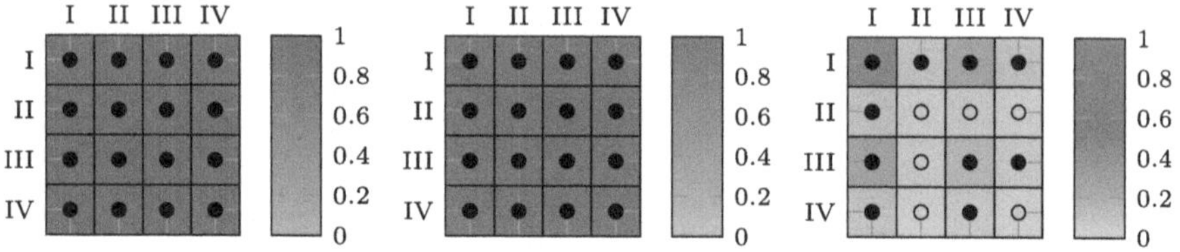

(a) 8-bit response (b) 16-bit response (c) 32-bit response

Fig. 3. Theoretical probability of collision occurrence (heat map) and experimental validation (● – at least one collision is observed, ○ – no collisions were observed) between ESP32-S3 (I), ESP8266EX (II), and Arduino Nano 33 with internal (III) and external SRAM (IV).

During ① PUF initialisation, we selected (a, v) that satisfied the following conditions: $HW(v), HW_{inter}(v_1, v_2) \in [0.4; 0.6]$ and $HD_{intra}(v, v') \leq 10\%$. As a result, on average, 50% of each device's memory was identified as PUF-suitable and was used for ② collision search (see Table 1). Since all boards support 8/16/32-bit word sizes, collisions were searched for across these response lengths.

Probability of Collision Occurrence. First, we used Eq. 1 to theoretically calculate the probability of collision occurrence $P(COL)$ for all combinations of the selected boards. The results are presented in Fig. 3 as a heat map. Additionally, in order to reflect experimental findings, we marked the board combinations where at least one collision was observed with ●, and if no collisions were found with ○. It can be seen that collisions are theoretically guaranteed, and confirmed experimentally, for 8- and 16-bit responses. In contrast, for 32-bit responses, the probabilities are significantly lower due to limited memory on the boards. Nevertheless, despite the low theoretical probability, some collisions were still observed in practice.

Expected Number of Collisions. First, we calculated the expected number of potential collisions using Eq. 2. Then, we experimentally tested our boards to verify whether the observed number of collisions aligns with the theoretical prediction. The results, presented in Fig. 4, show that the number of detected collisions closely matches the theoretical assessment. Additionally, it is visible that the number of collisions for 8- and 16-bit responses is significantly higher than for 32-bit responses. In the case of 32-bit responses, the theoretical prediction

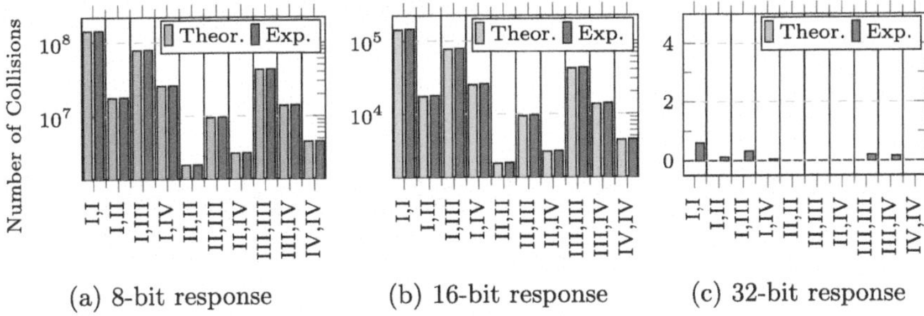

Fig. 4. Number of collisions, both theoretically predicted and experimentally detected, between ESP32-S3 (I), ESP8266EX (II), and Arduino Nano 33 with internal (III) and external SRAM (IV).

indicates no collisions; however, in practice, a few collisions were still observed among board combinations with the largest available memory. As illustrated in Fig. 4c, the average number of detected collisions per combination remains below one, indicating that, despite the theoretical prediction, one or two collisions occasionally occurred.

Number of Keys. As mentioned earlier in Sect. 3.2, to determine the number of distinct keys that can be generated from the collision response set CR, which is shared by both devices, we count the number of possible subsets of CR, as each subset serves as a seed for one cryptographic key. Additionally, we assume that each subset used for key generation has the same length as the resulting key. Figure 5 presents the results of our assessment of the potential number of distinct keys. For the theoretical calculations, we used the expected number of collisions as the cardinality of CR while for the real-world assessment, we used the actual number of detected collisions (see Fig. 4). Due to an insufficient number of collisions for 32-bit responses, the results are presented only for 8- and 16-bit responses.

In our experiment, we count the number of keys of lengths k equal to 128, 256, and 512 bits under two scenarios: with (NK_{WR}) and without (NK_{NR}) including repeated responses (see Eq. 3). The results show that the theoretical predictions closely match the actual observed values, appearing nearly identical given the magnitude of the values. Regarding the difference between NK_{WR} and NK_{NR}, we can see that although NK_{WR} is consistently higher than NK_{NR}, it is almost indistinguishable due to the scale of the values. Overall, the potential number of distinct keys is extremely large. Even for boards with the smallest available memory (e.g., II, II), it exceeds 10^{14}.

The results of the statistical analysis and experimental implementation demonstrate that the existence of collisions, and thus the feasibility of ID-PUFs, can be guaranteed, even when only relatively limited PUF-suitable memory is available. For example, using Eq. 1, it can be calculated that to ensure the presence of collisions ($P(COL) \approx 1$), each device must have at least 280 bit/8.6

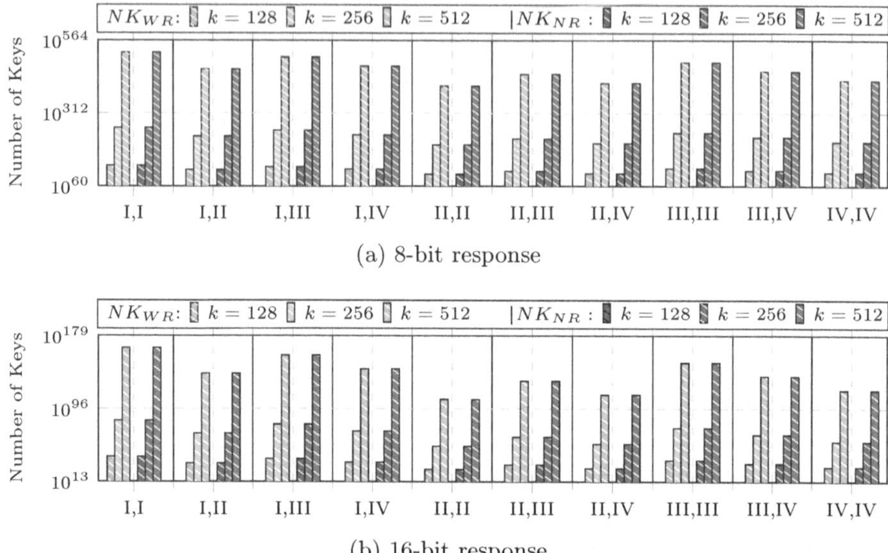

(a) 8-bit response

(b) 16-bit response

Fig. 5. Number of distinct keys of various lengths (k-bit) that can be generated from theoretically estimated (colored) and experimentally observed (patterned) collisions between ESP32-S3 (I), ESP8266EX (II), and Arduino Nano 33 with internal (III) and external SRAM (IV).

kb/550 kB of PUF-suitable memory for 8/16/32-bit words, respectively, which is significantly less than what is typically available. Furthermore, the quantity of collisions is sufficient to generate thousands of distinct keys of any recommended lengths for both symmetric (from 128-bit) and asymmetric (to 4096-bit) encryption schemes [16,32].

4 Mutual Authentication Protocol Based on ID-PUF

In this section, we present a novel ID-PUF-based Mutual Authentication protocol (ID-PUMA) that enables an inter-device association mechanism without the need for a prior distribution of a secret key, its persistent storage, and transmission of sensitive data.

ID-PUMA involves three parties: two devices ($D1$ and $D2$), each equipped with SRAM, and a manager M. Initially, $D1$ and $D2$ initialise their PUFs, and then M performs a collision search to identify ID-PUF (see Sect. 3.1). If both devices originate from the same manufacturer, it serves as M; otherwise, a user-side application may fulfil this role.

In describing the protocol workflow, we do not revisit the ID-PUF identification procedure, as it has already been detailed in Sect. 3.1. We assume that the manager M has already completed this process: derived a shared collision response CR and the corresponding collision challenges CC_{D1} and CC_{D2}, and

Table 2. Symbols used for the protocol description.

Symbol	Description
$D1$, $D2$	Devices participating in mutual authentication
M	Manager responsible for ID-PUF identification
ID_{D1}, ID_{D1}	Unique identifiers of the devices $D1$ and $D2$
CC_{D1}, CC_{D2}	Collision challenges embedded in the corresponding devices
CR	Collision response derived from devices' SRAMs using CC_{D1} or CC_{D2}
SK	Secret shared key generated on demand using CR_x
N_{D1}, N_{D2}	Nonces generated by the devices
$Encr_{SK}(\ldots)/Decr_{SK}(\ldots)$	Encryption/decryption functions using SK
$E_{SK}(\ldots)$	Value encrypted using SK
$FindCC(ID_x)$	Function to retrieve the CC associated with ID_x
$DeriveCR(CC_x)$	Function to derive CR from CC_{D1} or CC_{D2}
$KeyGen(CR_x)$	Function to generate a secret key SK based on CR
$GenerateNonce()$	Function to generate a random nonce
$Hash(\ldots)$	One-way hash function used to create a hash value
$H(\ldots)$	Hash value produced using the function $Hash(\ldots)$

embedded these challenges into the respective devices. While the challenges are public, the response CR is considered secret and is never persistently stored or transmitted between system parties. Additionally, M distributes the identifiers of the devices involved in the protocol, ID_{D1} and ID_{D2}. The symbols used for the protocol description are listed in Table 2, followed by a detailed explanation of the workflow that is also illustrated as a sequence diagram in Fig. 6.

Assume that $D1$ initiates mutual authentication with $D2$. In the first step (1), $D1$ identifies CC_{D1} associated with $D2$ using ID_{D2}. Based on CC_{D1}, $D1$ then derives the corresponding CR that is used to generate a shared secret key SK. Next, $D1$ generates a random nonce N_{D1} and encrypts it using SK, resulting in $E_{SK}(N_{D1})$. Finally, $D1$ computes $H_1(ID_{D2}, N_{D1})$. In the second step (2), $D1$ sends to $D2$ its identifier ID_{D1}, the previously computed $H_1(ID_{D2}, N_{D1})$, and the encrypted nonce $E_{SK}(N_{D1})$. Upon receiving the message from $D1$, $D2$ identifies CC_{D2} associated with $D1$ using ID_{D1}, derives CR corresponding to CC_{D2} and generates the shared secret key SK. Using this SK, $D2$ decrypts the nonce received from $D1$ and obtains N'_{D1} (3).

Next, the first comparison step, denoted as $(C.I)$, is performed. $D2$ computes the hash value H'_1 of its identifier ID_{D2} and the decrypted nonce N'_{D1}. The computed hash value is then compared with the hash H_1 received from $D1$. To proceed with the mutual authentication process, these values must match; otherwise, the authentication fails and is terminated.

If authentication proceeds, $D2$ initiates the next step (4). First, $D2$ generates a nonce N_{D2} and encrypts it using SK generated during step (3). Then, $D2$ computes a hash value H_2 based on both device identifiers ID_{D1} and ID_{D2}, as well as the two nonces: the decrypted nonce N'_{D1} received from $D1$ in step (3), and the previously generated N_{D2}. Finally, $D2$ sends H_2 and the encrypted nonce $E_{SK}(N_{D2})$ to $D1$ (5). Upon receiving the message from $D2$, $D1$ proceed

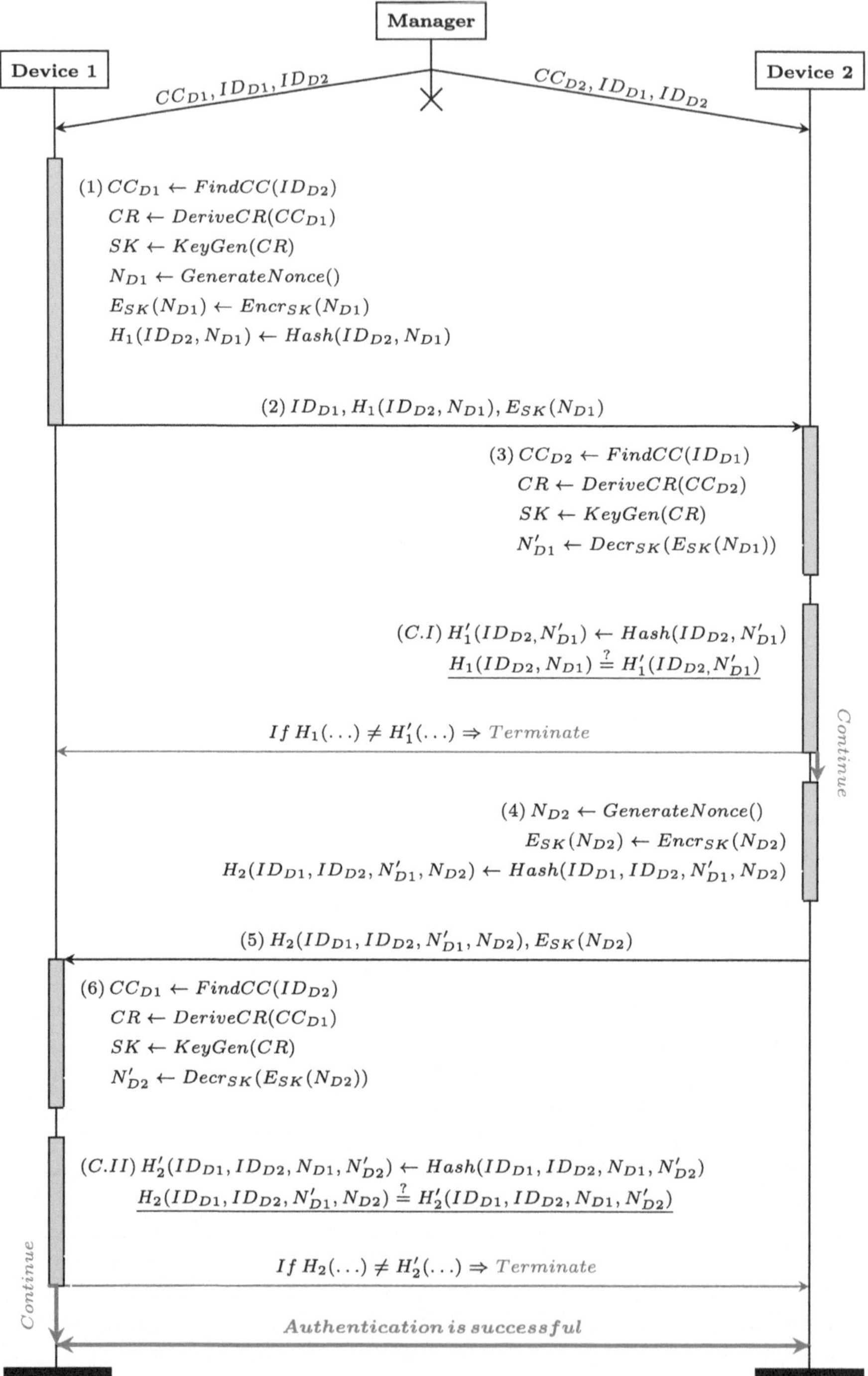

Fig. 6. Workflow of the proposed ID-PUMA protocol.

to step (6), where similarity to step (1), $D1$ generates the shared secret key SK and uses it to decrypt $E_{SK}(N_{D2})$, obtaining N'_{D2}.

Next, $D1$ performs the second comparison step $(C.II)$. It computes the hash value H'_2 based on both device identifiers ID_{D1} and ID_{D2}, as well as the two nonces: N_{D1}, generated in step (1), and N'_{D2}, obtained in step (6). This H'_2 is then compared with the value H_2 received from $D2$. If these values do not match, the authentication is terminated; otherwise, the authentication is successful.

It is important to note that SK and CR do not need to be stored permanently in the device memory, as they are derived on demand and can be deleted immediately after use.

5 Security Analysis

In this section, we perform a security analysis of the proposed mutual authentication protocol ID-PUMA. First, we describe the system and adversary models, then we discuss the feasibility of potential attacks against the protocol.

5.1 System Model

The system consists of legitimate and trusted protocol parties (devices $D1$ and $D2$, a manager M) and an adversary $\mathcal{A}$. $D1$ and $D2$ are engaged in the mutual authentication protocol, in which M is not directly involved. Instead, M is responsible solely for the secure preparatory phase that includes ID-PUF identification and the distribution of the associated collision challenges (CCs) and device identifiers (IDs) used later for secret key generation. In addition, we assume that only strong cryptographic schemes, primitives, or random number generation functions are employed within the system [7].

5.2 Adversary Model

The adversary $\mathcal{A}$ aims to disrupt the mutual authentication between $D1$ and $D2$ by performing attacks within their capabilities and limitations. We adapt the Dolev-Yao model [12], under which $\mathcal{A}$ has full control over the communication between $D1$ and $D2$. Accordingly, $\mathcal{A}$'s capabilities include intercepting, injecting, and manipulating any transmitted message; establishing a connection with any party; and impersonating any party within the system. However, $\mathcal{A}$ has limited capabilities regarding cryptographic primitives and, therefore, cannot perform the following actions: guess or generate nonces identical to legitimate ones; correctly decrypt or encrypt messages without possessing the secret key SK; break or forge hash values. Additionally, we assume that $\mathcal{A}$ does not collaborate with any of the protocol parties to deceive the other one, nor with M to obtain any information, e.g., SRAM or ID-PUF.

5.3 Analysis of the Protocol's Resistance to Attacks

In the following, we analyse the resistance of the ID-PUMA (see Sect. 4) to nine common attacks [23,28], based on the system and adversary models introduced in Sects. 5.1 and 5.2.

Eavesdropping Attack: $\mathcal{A}$ eavesdrops on communication between $D1$ and $D2$ to extract information for future attacks. In our protocol, $\mathcal{A}$ can capture ID_{D1} (2), which is public; encrypted nonces $E_{SK}(N_x)$ (2, 5), which cannot be decrypted without SK; and $H_x(\ldots)$ (2, 5), which $\mathcal{A}$ cannot break. Furthermore, none of these items provides sufficient information to facilitate other attacks.

Replay Attacks: $\mathcal{A}$ intercepts and retransmits messages in an attempt to impersonate $D1$ or $D2$. Although the intercepted ID_{D1} can be reused, successful authentication requires encrypting a fresh nonce with SK, which $\mathcal{A}$ cannot perform. Consequently, the attack fails when $D2$ attempts to decrypt $E_{SK}(N_{D1})$ in step (3) or verify the hash in step ($C.I$). Reusing of encrypted nonces or hashes would also fail due to nonce freshness.

Man-in-the-Middle (MitM) Attack: $\mathcal{A}$ intervenes the communication, causing the devices interact with $\mathcal{A}$ instead of each other. During attack in step (2)/(5), $\mathcal{A}$ can replace the legitimate N_x with $N_{\mathcal{A}}$ encrypted with their own key $E_{SK_{\mathcal{A}}}(N_{\mathcal{A}})$. However, this yields no meaningful result, as the probability of $SK_{\mathcal{A}}$ matching the actual SK is negligible. Consequently, any tampering would be detected in the next comparison step ($C.I$) or ($C.II$).

Impersonation Attack: $\mathcal{A}$ attempts to impersonate a device using fabricated data. For example, to impersonate $D1$, $\mathcal{A}$ can reuse ID_{D2} intercepted via eavesdropping, generate a nonce $N_{\mathcal{A}}$, encrypt it with $SK_{\mathcal{A}}$, and create $H_{\mathcal{A}}(ID_{D2}, N_{\mathcal{A}})$. However, without SK, $\mathcal{A}$ cannot perform correct encryption. As a result, $D2$ cannot decrypt the message, and authentication fails at step ($C.I$). The same applies if $\mathcal{A}$ attempts to impersonate $D2$.

Sybil Attack: $\mathcal{A}$ forges a device identity to bypass the authentication. Similar to impersonation, this may involve reusing intercepted IDs and fabricating other data, but it fails due to the absence of a valid SK. $\mathcal{A}$ may also attempt to flood $D2$ with requests, overloading the system and potentially causing unintended information leaks. However, our protocol prevents this by avoiding persistent storage or transmission of sensitive data and minimising its processing time.

Brute-Force and Forging Attacks: Guessing or forging protocol items can facilitate MitM or impersonation attacks. However, the ability to generate sufficiently secure keys enabled by an ID-PUF, combined with the use of strong cryptographic primitives (see Sect. 5.1), prevents $\mathcal{A}$ from successfully performing such actions, and thus from successful subsequent attacks.

Side-Channel Attack: $\mathcal{A}$ analyses information unintentionally leaked during protocol operation, e.g., power consumption. In such cases, security depends on the implementation of the underlying mechanisms and algorithms. According to the system model, ID-PUMA includes only strong security mechanisms; therefore, we believe it remains secure against such attacks under the defined conditions.

Cloning Attack: $\mathcal{A}$ creates an exact copy or model of a device, e.g., using Machine Learning (ML), to mimic its identity and behaviour. It is assumed that $\mathcal{A}$ cannot access the device's SRAM but can obtain CC and the key generation algorithm. However, due to the unclonability that ID-PUF inherits from PUF, the resulting $CR_{\mathcal{A}}$ and $SK_{\mathcal{A}}$ would differ from the original, making cloning attempts ineffective.

Our security analysis shows that the proposed ID-PUMA protocol is resistant to nine known attacks. Its robustness relies on strong cryptographic primitives, freshly generated nonces, the inherent unclonability of ID-PUFs, and the ID-PUF-enabled elimination of permanent storage or transmission of the secret key.

6 Related Work

Most existing PUF-based authentication protocols follow a standard approach to PUF usage [17,22,26,34,35,43,46], relying on challenge-response pairs from a single PUF. Therefore, in this section, we focus instead on approaches that employ alternative techniques, which we consider more relevant to our research.

Paral *et al.* [33] introduce a reverse paradigm for PUFs where responses are public and their starting indices, serving as challenges, are secret. This scheme resists modelling attacks due to limited CRP exposure and is lightweight, requiring only basic hardware components.

A lightweight mutual authentication protocol using a challenge-challenge approach is proposed in [20], where both parties share access to the same PUF. The prover sends challenges c_{i1} and c_{i2} such that $r_{i1} \oplus r_{i2} = r_i$, enabling for the verifier (with c_i) validation via XOR. The protocol supports unlimited mutual authentications and resists guessing, challenge collection and correlation attacks.

Wang *et al.* [41] present an authentication protocol based on a modified arbiter PUF. During enrolment, the server stores only a configuration signal L received from the device. In the authentication phase, both parties generate response sequences using the exchanged nonces and L: the device via its PUF, the server via the PUF model. Authentication is performed by matching the indices of the response sequences. The protocol resists common ML attacks, including deep neural networks and logistic regression.

Majzoobi *et al.* [27] follow a similar matching approach in their Slender PUF authentication protocol. However, they use a standard arbiter PUF without modifications, relying on static PUF responses, in contrast to the dynamic approach of Wang *et al.* [41]. Despite this, the Slender protocol remains resilient to different ML attacks while maintaining low overhead.

Barbareschi *et al.* [5,6] introduce a Physical Hardware-Enabled Mutual Authentication Protocol (PHEMAP). By representing CRP of recursively invoking a device's PUF as a graph, the authors use a simple path to form a chain of values, ensuring synchronisation between communicating parties throughout the authentication process. Evaluation results show that PHEMAP is resistant to MitM and differential power analysis attacks.

Xu *et al.* [42] propose a PUF matching security platform based on Programmable Delay Lines (PDL), to provide a primitive that enables low-energy and low-latency execution of multi-party communication, encryption/decryption, and authentication protocols. Using a four-step process that applies PDL to tune and modify the delays of each segment in a standard Arbiter PUF, the authors identify PUFs with identical CRP mapping functions. This allows multiple devices with such PUFs to communicate securely without prior key exchange.

Chatterjee *et al.* [10] propose a Physical Related Function (PReF), an abstraction of a strong PUF, based on fully correlated $CRPs$ on two devices (i.e., $HD_{inter} \rightarrow 0$) that are typically excluded in traditional PUF use. They introduce a PReF-based key-exchange protocol that outperforms many existing PUF-based schemes in storage, computation, communication, and hardware efficiency.

The overview of related work shows that alternative approaches to PUF usage differ fundamentally from the ID-PUF concept, resulting in notable differences between our ID-PUMA and other existing protocols. To highlight these distinctions, we compare our protocol with other solutions based on both standard and non-traditional PUF utilisation techniques across four key characteristics and resistance to nine attack types, as shown in Table 3.

Analysis shows that most existing protocols rely on large numbers of $CRPs$, thus requiring "strong" PUFs [6,20], while only a few support "weak" PUFs [26,43,46]. In contrast, our protocol can seamlessly use both types, demonstrating flexibility and a broader application scope; however, this remains a topic for future research. In this work, we present only a pilot version of the ID-PUF-based protocol using SRAM PUF, which is typically present in devices and does not require any enhancement or adjustments [41,42]. Additionally, unlike other protocols, ID-PUF enables the application of lightweight symmetric cryptography while eliminating the need for prior key exchange or transmission of secrets between protocol parties [34,35]. Although this paper does not detail the proof-of-concept prototype of the ID-PUMA protocol, as the main focus is on the novelty of the ID-PUF mechanism, our implementation and statistical analysis of ID-PUFs (see Sects. 3.2 and 3.3) show that ID-PUF identification is feasible even on resource-constrained devices. This indicates that our ID-PUF-based protocol can be considered lightweight. Moreover, the results of the performed security analysis (see Sect. 5) demonstrate that ID-PUMA can resist nine known attacks, outperforming comparable protocols.

Table 3. Comparison of our protocol with existing solutions.

Protocol	Characteristics				Attacks								
	PT	**CT**	**PK**	**L**	**EA**	**RA**	**MM**	**IA**	**SA**	**BF**	**FA**	**SC**	**CA**
Protocols based on non-trivial PUF utilisation techniques													
Barbareschi *et al.* [6]	S	–	–	–	–	✓	✓	✓	–	–	✓	✓	–
Chatterjee *et al.* [10]	S	A/S	N	✓	–	✓	–	✓	–	–	–	✓	✓
Idriss *et al.* [20]	S	–	–	✓	–	–	–	–	–	✓	✓	–	–
Majzoobi *et al.* [27]	S	–	–	✓	✓	✓	–	–	–	✓	–	–	✓
Paral *et al.* [33]	S	A	–	✓	–	–	–	–	–	–	–	–	✓
Wang *et al.* [41]	S	–	–	–	–	–	–	–	–	✓	–	–	✓
Xu *et al.* [42]	S	S	N	✓	–	–	–	–	–	–	–	–	–
Protocols based on standard PUF utilisation techniques													
Garg *et al.* [17]	–	A	Y	✓	✓	✓	✓	✓	✓	–	–	–	–
Khatua *et al.* [22]	S	S	Y	✓	–	✓	✓	–	–	–	–	–	–
Mahalat *et al.* [26]	S/W	–	Y	✓	✓	✓	✓	✓	–	–	–	✓	✓
Pham *et al.* [34]	S	S	Y	✓	✓	✓	✓	✓	✓	–	✓	–	–
Raj *et al.* [35]	S	S	Y	✓	–	✓	✓	–	–	–	–	–	–
Yoon *et al.* [43]	W	S	–	✓	–	✓	✓	✓	–	✓	–	–	✓
Zhu *et al.* [46]	W	–	Y	✓	–	✓	✓	✓	✓	–	✓	–	✓
ID-PUMA	S/W	S	N	✓	✓	✓	✓	✓	✓	✓	✓	✓	✓

Characteristics: PT: Type of used PUF (S-strong, W-weak); CT: Type of involved cryptographic mechanism (A-asymmetric, S-symmetric); PK: The need for pre-shared keys (Y-yes, N-no); L: Lightweightness of the protocol.
Attack Abbreviations: EA: Eavesdropping; RA: Replay; MM: Man-in-the-Middle; IA: Impersonation; SA: Sybil; BF: Brute-Force; FA: Forging; SC: Side-Channel; CA: Cloning.
Symbols: ✓: The protocol is resistant to the attack; –: The protocol is vulnerable to the attack or it is not mentioned in the paper.

7 Challenges

Despite the advantages of using ID-PUFs, certain challenges may arise that can impact the real-world deployment of any ID-PUF-based protocol.

PUF Selection: Several factors should be considered during the selection of a PUF type for an ID-PUF-based protocol. First, key generation mechanisms vary depending on PUF type, e.g., SRAM PUFs generate keys only at memory power-up, which may influence protocol design. Second, some PUFs, such as DRAM PUFs, are relatively slow, which may affect performance. Finally, not all PUFs provide the stability needed for reliable key generation.

Scalability: Initially, devices are paired ($D1$ and $D2$), each containing logic for its partner. The setup can scale by adding new partners, e.g., $D3$ to $D2$, requiring $D2$ to support multiple logics and increasing resource usage. Alternatively, all three devices can be mutually associated, requiring only storage of additional IDs and CCs. Thus, the number of associated devices is scalable, though constrained by the computational and memory resources of the devices involved.

Different Manufacturers of the Devices: If the devices originate from different manufacturers, ID-PUF identification would need to be performed by a user-side application. This introduces development challenges due to the variety of devices and security risks if the user's system is compromised. Therefore, additional security measures are required on the user side.

8 Conclusions and Future Work

In this paper, we propose a novel PUF paradigm called Inter-Device PUF (ID-PUF), which leverages matching segments between two PUFs to form a shared and unique per-device-pair PUF. An ID-PUF enables devices to independently generate a shared key on demand, thereby facilitating the use of lightweight symmetric cryptography without requiring key transfer, distribution or storage. Our statistical analysis and prototype implementation confirm the feasibility of ID-PUFs on memory-constrained devices and the capability to generate a large number of unique keys. Additionally, to demonstrate the applicability of ID-PUFs, we introduce an ID-PUF-based mutual authentication protocol named ID-PUMA. Our analysis shows that it is conceptually distinct, lightweight, and offers robust security against nine known attacks, outperforming existing solutions.

Promising directions for future work include evaluating the protocol's robustness against a broader range of attacks, as well as assessing its practical feasibility across diverse device and PUF combinations.

Acknowledgments. This work has been funded by the Bavarian State Ministry of Science and Arts (BayStMWK), under Project "ForDaySec: Security in Everyday Use of Digital Technologies (fordaysec.de)" of the Bavarian Research Association.

Disclosure of Interests. The authors have no competing interests to declare that are relevant to the content of this article.

References

1. Al-Meer, A., Al-Kuwari, S.: Physical unclonable functions (PUF) for IoT devices. ACM Comput. Surv. **55**(14s) (2023). https://doi.org/10.1145/3591464
2. Andrea, I., Chrysostomou, C., Hadjichristofi, G.: Internet of things: security vulnerabilities and challenges. In: 2015 IEEE Symposium on Computers and Communication (ISCC), pp. 180–187 (2015). https://doi.org/10.1109/ISCC.2015.7405513
3. Arduino: Nano 33 BLE Rev2 Documentation. Arduino Documentation. https://docs.arduino.cc/hardware/nano-33-ble-rev2/
4. Arfken, G.B., Weber, H.J.: Mathematical Methods for Physicists. Academic Press, Orlando (1972)
5. Barbareschi, M., De Benedictis, A., La Montagna, E., Mazzeo, A., Mazzocca, N.: A PUF-based mutual authentication scheme for cloud-Edges IoT systems. Futur. Gener. Comput. Syst. **101**, 246–261 (2019). https://doi.org/10.1016/j.future.2019.06.012
6. Barbareschi, M., De Benedictis, A., Mazzocca, N.: A PUF-based hardware mutual authentication protocol. J. Parallel and Distrib. Comput. **119**, 107–120 (2018). https://doi.org/10.1016/j.jpdc.2018.04.007

7. Barker, E.B., Roginsky, A.L.: Transitioning the Use of Cryptographic Algorithms and Key Lengths. Technical report NIST SP 800-131A Rev. 3, National Institute of Standards and Technology (NIST), Gaithersburg, MD (2024). https://doi.org/10.6028/NIST.SP.800-131Ar3.ipd
8. Böhm, C., Hofer, M., Pribyl, W.: A microcontroller SRAM-PUF. In: 2011 5th International Conference on Network and System Security, pp. 269–273 (2011). https://doi.org/10.1109/ICNSS.2011.6060013
9. Borovkov, A.: Probability Theory. Taylor & Francis (1999)
10. Chatterjee, D., Boyapally, H., Patranabis, S., Chatterjee, U., Hazra, A., Mukhopadhyay, D.: Physically related functions: exploiting related inputs of PUFs for authenticated-key exchange. IEEE Trans. Inf. Forensics Secur. **17**, 3847–3862 (2022). https://doi.org/10.1109/TIFS.2022.3214089
11. CVE Details: Number of common IT security vulnerabilities and exposures (CVEs) worldwide from 2009 to 2024 YTD. Graph (2024). https://www.statista.com/statistics/500755/worldwide-common-vulnerabilities-and-exposures/
12. Dolev, D., Yao, A.: On the security of public key protocols. IEEE Trans. Inf. Theory **29**(2), 198–208 (1983). https://doi.org/10.1109/TIT.1983.1056650
13. Durrett, R.: Probability: Theory and Examples, vol. 49. Cambridge University Press, Cambridge (2019)
14. Espressif Systems: ESP32-S3-DevKitC-1 Documentation. Espressif Documentation. https://docs.espressif.com/projects/esp-dev-kits/en/latest/esp32s3/esp32-s3-devkitc-1/index.html
15. Espressif Systems: ESP8266-DevKitC Getting Started Guide. PDF Documentation. https://www.espressif.com/sites/default/files/documentation/ESP8266-DevKitC_getting_started_guide__EN.pdf
16. Federal Office for Information Security (BSI): BSI Technical Guideline TR-02102-1: Cryptographic Mechanisms and Key Lengths. Technical Guideline (2025). https://www.bsi.bund.de/SharedDocs/Downloads/EN/BSI/Publications/TechGuidelines/TG02102/BSI-TR-02102-1.pdf?__blob=publicationFile&v=10
17. Garg, S., Kaur, K., Kaddoum, G., Choo, K.K.R.: Toward secure and provable authentication for internet of things: realizing Industry 4.0. IEEE Internet Things J. **7**(5), 4598–4606 (2020). https://doi.org/10.1109/JIOT.2019.2942271
18. Grubel, B.C., et al.: Silicon photonic physical unclonable function. Opt. Express **25**(11), 12710–12721 (2017). https://doi.org/10.1364/OE.25.012710
19. Guajardo, J., Kumar, S.S., Schrijen, G.-J., Tuyls, P.: FPGA intrinsic PUFs and their use for IP protection. In: Paillier, P., Verbauwhede, I. (eds.) CHES 2007. LNCS, vol. 4727, pp. 63–80. Springer, Heidelberg (2007). https://doi.org/10.1007/978-3-540-74735-2_5
20. Idriss, T., Bayoumi, M.: Lightweight highly secure PUF protocol for mutual authentication and secret message exchange. In: 2017 IEEE International Conference on RFID Technology & Application (RFID-TA), pp. 214–219 (2017). https://doi.org/10.1109/RFID-TA.2017.8098893
21. Katzenbeisser, S., Schaller, A.: Physical unclonable functions: Sicherheitseigenschaften und Anwendungen. Datenschutz und Datensicherheit - DuD **36**(12), 881–885 (2012). https://doi.org/10.1007/s11623-012-0295-z
22. Khatua, M., Das, S., Rana, P.M.: PUF-based lightweight mutual authentication scheme for IoT-based smart grids. In: 2024 IEEE International Conference on Advanced Networks and Telecommunications Systems (ANTS), pp. 1–6 (2024). https://doi.org/10.1109/ANTS63515.2024.10898763

23. Kumar, A., Saha, R., Conti, M., Kumar, G., Buchanan, W.J., Kim, T.H.: A comprehensive survey of authentication methods in Internet-of-Things and its conjunctions. J. Netw. Comput. Appl. **204**, 103414 (2022). https://doi.org/10.1016/j.jnca.2022.103414
24. Kumar, R., Burleson, W.: On design of a highly secure PUF based on non-linear current mirrors. In: 2014 IEEE International Symposium on Hardware-Oriented Security and Trust (HOST), pp. 38–43 (2014). https://doi.org/10.1109/HST.2014.6855565
25. Lin, J., Yu, W., Zhang, N., Yang, X., Zhang, H., Zhao, W.: A survey on internet of things: architecture, enabling technologies, security and privacy, and applications. IEEE Internet Things J. **4**(5), 1125–1142 (2017). https://doi.org/10.1109/JIOT.2017.2683200
26. Mahalat, M.H., Karmakar, D., Mondal, A., Sen, B.: PUF-based secure and lightweight authentication and key-sharing scheme for wireless sensor network. J. Emerg. Technol. Comput. Syst. **18**(1) (2021). https://doi.org/10.1145/3466682
27. Majzoobi, M., Rostami, M., Koushanfar, F., Wallach, D.S., Devadas, S.: Slender PUF protocol: a lightweight, robust, and secure authentication by substring matching. In: 2012 IEEE Symposium on Security and Privacy Workshops, pp. 33–44 (2012). https://doi.org/10.1109/SPW.2012.30
28. Mall, P., Amin, R., Das, A.K., Leung, M.T., Choo, K.K.R.: PUF-based authentication and key agreement protocols for IoT, WSNs, and smart grids: a comprehensive survey. IEEE Internet Things J. **9**(11), 8205–8228 (2022). https://doi.org/10.1109/JIOT.2022.3142084
29. Microchip Technology Inc.: 23A512 - 512 Kbit SPI Serial SRAM (2025). https://www.microchip.com/en-us/product/23a512
30. Miorandi, D., Sicari, S., De Pellegrini, F., Chlamtac, I.: Internet of things: vision, applications and research challenges. Ad Hoc Netw. **10**(7), 1497–1516 (2012). https://doi.org/10.1016/j.adhoc.2012.02.016
31. Mohamad Noor, M.B., Hassan, W.H.: Current research on internet of things (IoT) security: a survey. Comput. Netw. **148**, 283–294 (2019). https://doi.org/10.1016/j.comnet.2018.11.025
32. National Institute of Standards and Technology (NIST): NIST Special Publication 800-78-5: Cryptographic Algorithms and Key Sizes for PIV. NIST Special Publication (2025). https://nvlpubs.nist.gov/nistpubs/SpecialPublications/NIST.SP.800-78-5.pdf
33. Paral, Z., Devadas, S.: Reliable and efficient PUF-based key generation using pattern matching. In: 2011 IEEE International Symposium on Hardware-Oriented Security and Trust, pp. 128–133 (2011). https://doi.org/10.1109/HST.2011.5955010
34. Pham, H.L., Tran-Thi, T.Q., Bui, D.H., Tran, X.T.: Novel PUF-based authentication protocol for IoT devices with secure boot and fuzzy matching. In: 2023 International Conference on Advanced Technologies for Communications (ATC), pp. 78–83 (2023). https://doi.org/10.1109/ATC58710.2023.10318908
35. Raj, K., Bodapati, S., Chattopadhyay, A.: PUF-based lightweight mutual authentication protocol for internet of things (IoT) devices. In: 2024 IEEE International Symposium on Circuits and Systems (ISCAS), pp. 1–5 (2024). https://doi.org/10.1109/ISCAS58744.2024.10558672
36. Rosen, K.H., Krithivasan, K.: Discrete Mathematics and its Applications, vol. 6. McGraw-Hill, New York (1999)
37. Ross, S.: A First Course in Probability, vol. 2. Macmillan, New York (1976)

38. Rührmair, U., Busch, H., Katzenbeisser, S.: Strong PUFs: Models, Constructions, and Security Proofs, pp. 79–96. Springer, Heidelberg (2010). https://doi.org/10.1007/978-3-642-14452-3_4
39. Samonas, S., Coss, D.: The CIA strikes back: redefining confidentiality, integrity and availability in security. J. Inf. Syst. Secur. **10**(3) (2014)
40. Statista: Internet of Things - Market Outlook Report. Statista. https://de.statista.com/statistik/studie/id/109209/dokument/internet-der-dinge-market-outlook-report/
41. Wang, Y., Wang, C., Gu, C., Cui, Y., O'Neill, M., Liu, W.: A dynamically configurable PUF and dynamic matching authentication protocol. IEEE Trans. Emerg. Top. Comput. **10**(2), 1091–1104 (2022). https://doi.org/10.1109/TETC.2021.3072421
42. Xu, T., Gu, H., Potkonjak, M.: An ultra-low energy PUF matching security platform using programmable delay lines. In: 2016 11th International Symposium on Reconfigurable Communication-centric Systems-on-Chip (ReCoSoC), pp. 1–8 (2016). https://doi.org/10.1109/ReCoSoC.2016.7533899
43. Yoon, S., Han, S., Hwang, E.: Joint heterogeneous PUF-based security-enhanced IoT authentication. IEEE Internet Things J. **10**(20), 18082–18096 (2023). https://doi.org/10.1109/JIOT.2023.3279847
44. Zhang, Y., Ge, Y.: Evaluation of microcontroller-based SRAM PUF and the authentication scheme. In: Proceedings of the 4th International Conference on Computer, Internet of Things and Control Engineering. CITCE 2024, pp. 79–86. Association for Computing Machinery, New York (2025). https://doi.org/10.1145/3705677.3705691
45. Zhang, Z.K., Cho, M.C.Y., Wang, C.W., Hsu, C.W., Chen, C.K., Shieh, S.: IoT security: ongoing challenges and research opportunities. In: 2014 IEEE 7th International Conference on Service-Oriented Computing and Applications, pp. 230–234 (2014). https://doi.org/10.1109/SOCA.2014.58
46. Zhu, Y., Guan, Z., Wang, Z., Li, D., Wang, Y., Xu, M.: SRAM-PUF based lightweight mutual authentication scheme for IoT. In: 2021 IEEE Internationall Conference on Parallel ISPA/BDCloud/SocialCom/SustainCom, pp. 806–813 (2021). https://doi.org/10.1109/ISPA-BDCloud-SocialCom-SustainCom52081.2021.00115

Mitigation of the Impact of Virtual Machine Introspection Pauses on Multi-core Virtual Machines

Léo Cosseron[1(✉)], Louis Rilling[2], and Martin Quinson[1]

[1] Univ. Rennes, Inria, CNRS, IRISA, Rennes, France
{leo.cosseron,martin.quinson}@irisa.fr
[2] DGA, Rennes, France
louis.rilling@irisa.fr

Abstract. Virtual machine introspection (VMI) is a class of monitoring techniques used by malware analysis sandboxes to analyze the behavior of malware samples. VMI introduces execution pauses that can be detected within the virtualized environment, revealing the usage of a sandbox. Thus, many sandboxes implement countermeasures to conceal VMI pauses from the guest However, these countermeasures have limitations on multi-core guests.

We propose several metrics to characterize the side effects caused by a VMI monitor in multi-core guests. We introduce a new strategy to conceal VMI pauses in multi-core guests, and assert its performance compared to the regular approaches used by sandboxes. Our results show that this new strategy improves the stealthiness of VMI pauses on a multi-core system for some metrics, but it still has shortcomings that should be addressed in future work.

Keywords: Virtualization · Virtual machine introspection · Hypervisor introspection

1 Introduction

Malware analysis sandboxes can leverage CPU support for machine virtualization to stay stealth and securely isolated from malware samples [12]. However, whereas sandboxes use Virtual Machine Introspection (VMI) [8] to analyze malware behavior, *Hypervisor introspection* [16,23,25] allows malware to leverage side-channels from the virtual machine (VM) perspective (e.g. cache misses, execution delays) to detect whether it is being inspected.

Typical examples of execution delays that can thus be observed from inside the VM are the execution pauses caused by VMI procedures. Such pauses last long enough to be attributed to VMI activity rather than to usual execution on top of a hypervisor [25].

To prevent evasive malware from observing VMI pauses, some sandboxes leverage CPU support for clock virtualization to adjust the virtual clock of

R. Laborde et al. (Eds.): ESORICS 2025 Workshops, LNCS 16233, pp. 428–447, 2026.
https://doi.org/10.1007/978-3-032-16165-9_26

the analysed VM and pretend that the clock is stopped during the whole VMI pause [11]. It is even possible to synchronize the clock of a fake network environment with the clock of the analysis VM to hide VMI pauses while showing realistic network performance metrics [6].

Such clock manipulation techniques have to assume that either time-based evasion techniques do not involve network communications or that the sandbox runs in a closed environment in which the whole network is controlled [11,19]. These assumptions are different but necessary trade-offs that are adapted to different analysis constraints [26].

The stealthiness of clock manipulation is significantly more limited in the case of multi-core VMs [6,13]. A first solution to hide such VMI pauses consists in independent modifications of the virtual core-local clocks to conceal the pauses. This unfortunately induces virtual core clocks desynchronizations that can be detected by malware. Alternatively, the VMI pauses can be concealed by pausing some virtual cores while the virtual clocks remain unchanged, but malware can then detect that paused virtual cores execute fewer instructions than the other ones.

In this paper, we present three contributions to hide VMI pauses in multi-core analysis VMs:

- We introduce time-related observable phenomena and example algorithms that allow malware to detect VMI in multi-core VMs.
- We propose a strategy for an analysis sandbox to reduce the ability of malware to detect VMI in a multi-core VM. Our implementation on Xen is open-source [2].
- We evaluate the proposed strategy against the observable phenomena introduced and with the VMI plugins of the DRAKVUF analysis sandbox [12]. This evaluation shows the limitations of stealth analysis with the hardware support in modern CPUs and allows us to suggest research directions to improve this support.

This paper is organized as follows. In Sect. 2 we present the threat model and technical background about VMI. In Sect. 3 we detail the issue of hiding VMI pauses in multi-core VMs and introduce the observable phenomena allowing malware to detect VMI. In Sect. 4 we present a strategy to reduce the observability of VMI on multi-core VMs. An evaluation of this strategy in the DRAKVUF sandbox is presented in Sect. 5. Related work is presented in Sect. 6 and Sect. 7 concludes the paper.

2 Context

Using VMI triggers execution pauses that can be detected by an attacker thanks to *hypervisor introspection*. Section 2.1 presents the threat model while Sect. 2.2 details the operation of VMI pauses in `libVMI`, including in multi-core VMs settings.

2.1 Threat Model

In this work, we focus solely on detecting the use of VMI-related tools by the Virtual Machine Monitor (VMM or hypervisor). Our threat model assumes that the attacker has root and kernel rights in the VM, and has access to high-resolution timers. However, the attacker has neither access to the host nor to the VMM, which are assumed to be isolated from the VMs.

We consider the following techniques to be out of scope: the detection of virtualization, access to co-resident VMs, and access to the host or the VMM.

Moreover, the attacker's main objective is to remain undetected during the attack. The attacker will thus prefer improved stealthiness over increased introspection detection accuracy. This may restrict the hypervisor introspection techniques available to the attacker despite their root and kernel privileges in the VMs.

2.2 VMI Pauses

We now present the general behavior of a VMI program or *monitor*, including how it induces execution pauses. Our focus is on `libVMI` [1,18], which is one of the most popular open-source VMI library. A VMI monitor uses `libVMI` to access information about the execution of a monitored VM. `libVMI` interacts with the VMM to retrieve the relevant information.

`libVMI` enables two types of VMI requests that can eventually trigger execution pauses. *VMI commands* are issued immediately to the target VM or virtual CPU (vCPU) by the VMM. Examples include operations such as pausing a VM or accessing its memory. *VMI events* are callbacks that are triggered by specific actions of the VMs. When such an event occurs, the VMM is configured to trigger a transition from the guest to the VMM (VM Exit on Intel CPUs). If required, the vCPU is paused while handling the event. VMI events can be used to monitor a memory area or the usage of instructions such as `MOV to CR3`. A VMI event callback can affect future VMI events, because it is possible to configure new or existing VMI events from a callback.

In addition, `libVMI` is compatible with multi-core VMs. VMI events only occur on individual vCPUs but can occur concurrently on multiple vCPUs. In `libVMI`, events are processed through a VM-specific ring structure in FIFO order. Additionally, some VMI commands can affect multiple (usually all) vCPUs, such as `vmi_pause_vm`.

3 Usage of VMI on Multi-core VMs

Similarly to single-core VMs, VMI pauses can also be detected in multi-core VMs, although new metrics should be used. Section 3.1 discusses in-VM observable phenomena resulting from VMI usage on a multi-core VM. To our knowledge, previous works having studied strategies to conceal the impact of VMI pauses do not address multi-core VMs [6,13]. These limitations are discussed in Sect. 3.2 and experimental insight is provided in Sect. 3.3.

3.1 Detecting Local VMI Pauses in a Multi-core VM

Many hypervisor introspection strategies depend on an accurate clock source for detecting inconsistencies induced by VMI pauses. On Intel x86 CPUs, the most accurate clock source is the TSC (Time Stamp Counter), which is a 64-bit counter register that continuously increments at a constant, high frequency. In VMs, the guest TSC is an affine function of the host TSC. It is computed from the host TSC and two parameters (`TSC-offset` and `TSC-multiplier`). The used formula according to Intel [10] is ($\gg$ is the bitwise right shift operator):

$$TSC_{guest} = (\texttt{TSC-multiplier} \times TSC_{host}) \gg 48 + \texttt{TSC-offset}$$

These two parameters are set in the Virtual Machine Control Structure (VMCS). On standard VMMs such as Xen and KVM, each vCPU has a dedicated VMCS, enabling independent values of these parameters for each vCPU.

As for single-core VMs, VMI execution pauses can be detected from the vCPU that was paused by observing gaps in the clock flow of the paused vCPU. The frequency and duration of these gaps are key metrics to infer the usage of a VMI tool [25]. In multi-core VMs, VMI pauses may occur on all or only a subset of vCPUs, making a VMI pattern more difficult to identify using the approaches from single-core VMs.

From in-VM observable phenomena, we propose two new time-related metrics to detect the presence of VMI on multi-core VMs. Indeed, VMI usage has two low-level time-related effects. First, a vCPU in a VMI pause cannot produce in-VM side effects based on clocks, like writing timestamps in a shared memory. Second, a paused vCPU cannot produce side effects based on work done, like writing results of computations in a shared memory.

For clock-based side effects, we propose a *timing metric* based on the key property of the guest TSC that it is synchronized across all the vCPUs. A simple algorithm measures the TSC simultaneously on each vCPU, and stores the results in a shared array. By repeating this process many times and comparing the difference between the highest and lowest TSC measurements from each iteration, it is possible to infer the usage of VMI. On a system without VMI, these differences will usually be very small, with occasional outliers due to a VM Exit or a NMI (Non-Maskable Interrupt). A VM Exit happens when the VMM traps the guest to perform a privileged operation, while a NMI is issued by the hardware and cannot be ignored. To the opposite, the number of outliers likely increases significantly when VMI is used. Indeed, VMI pauses are often longer than regular VM Exits, as they they are typically handled in userspace while most VM Exits are handled directly in the VMM.

For work-done-based side effects, we propose a *performance metric* that measures the loss of performance caused by VMI pauses. During a VMI pause, the vCPU thread is not scheduled, but its clock continues to tick. We measure the quantity of work that each vCPU can achieve during a given amount of time, and compare the results. This can be done by incrementing a counter within a dedicated thread for each vCPU. On a system without VMI, we can expect to observe similar results for each vCPU since each thread is scheduled for roughly the same amount of time. However, if a VMI monitor is active, the paused vCPUs likely achieve less work than others. By observing a large decrease in performance or a high disparity between the results of each vCPU, an attacker can detect the usage of VMI. This approach can be extended to heterogeneous processors by either comparing only cores with the same specifications or determining the relative speed of different cores.

In addition to these two low-level metrics, higher-level phenomena can be observed in the execution environment in the VM. In Linux-based VMs, an example is the clock stability checking logic of the kernel, which regularly checks that the currently used clock source (usually the TSC) is synchronized across cores and runs at a constant speed [3,4].

3.2 Limitations of Existing Strategies to Hide VMI Pauses

Previous works have proposed solutions to hide the impact of VMI pauses, but these solutions are only applicable to either single-core VMs or to VMI pauses affecting the entire VM (e.g. a VM pause) [6,25]. In the following, we focus on the TSC clock, as it is the primary clock source on Intel x86 processor. The logic is also mostly valid for other clock sources. The main strategy is to roll back the guest TSC, after a VMI pause, to its value before the pause. This strategy can almost completely hide VMI pauses in single-core VMs. This idea was first proposed to tackle hypervisor introspection in [25], and implemented in a few works [6,11]. In the rest of the paper, we call this strategy the `Naive` approach.

In a multi-core VM, each vCPU has its own TSC counter, `TSC-offset` and `TSC-multiplier` registers. That way, any clock adjustment can be done either on all vCPUs at once, or only on a subset of vCPUs. After a VMI pause on a single vCPU, the `Naive` approach may adjust only the TSC clock of the paused vCPU. But this will introduce clock-based side-effects, as the TSC clocks will no longer be synchronized across all vCPUs, as shown on Fig. 1. Adjusting the TSC clocks of all the vCPUs after a VMI pause regardless of if they were paused will instead introduce work-done-based side effects, as the vCPUs that were not paused will have more CPU time than the others. In addition, for unpaused vCPUs, this would create clock rollbacks observable from the TSC clock local to the vCPU. In Sect. 3.3, the `Naive` approach is extended to multi-core VMs by adjusting the clock of paused vCPUs only and independently from each other.

An appealing approach would be to pause all vCPUs each time a VMI pause is triggered. Then, by performing a global TSC rollback, the clock would stay consistent between the vCPUs and there would be no clock-based or work-done-based side effects observable from within the VM. However, this idea is impracticable because it goes against the design of VMI tools like `libVMI`, and it could interfere with dependencies between VMI events. Furthermore, there could be concurrent VMI pauses on different vCPUs, while this cannot be handled with this approach. It would also introduce a very high performance penalty.

Hypervisor introspection will thus always be possible on a multi-core VM, although it can be made harder by limiting observable work-done and clock related side effects.

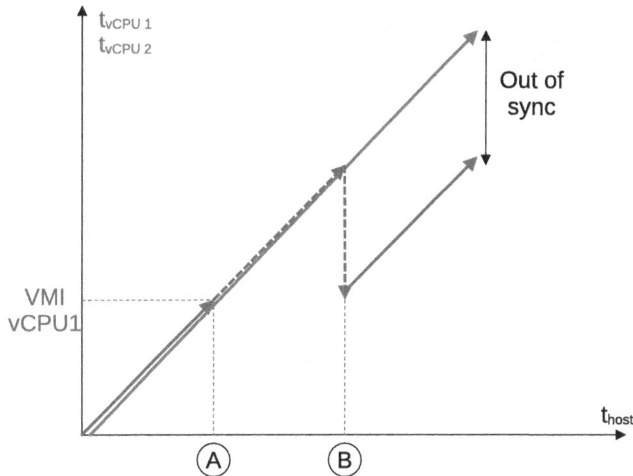

Fig. 1. Illustration of the shortcoming of the `Naive` single-core strategy to hide VMI pauses on a VM with 2 vCPUs. The X axis represents host time, the Y axis virtual time. Both vCPUs clocks are synchronized until (A), where $vCPU_1$ is paused by VMI. At (B), $vCPU_1$ is adjusted to hide the duration of the VMI pause. From this moment on, $vCPU_1$ and $vCPU_2$ clocks are out of sync.

3.3 Evaluation of the `Naive` strategy to hide VMI pauses

We now experimentally evaluate how both metrics introduced in 3.1 can detect in a multi-core setting the `Naive` approach that is classically used to conceal VMI pauses on single-core VMs. To that extent, we use two baselines. `NoAnalysis` constitutes a classic VM setup with no introspection while `Baseline` adds a VMI script to the VM (no attempt is made to conceal the VMI pauses in this case). We opted for DRAKVUF [12], an open-source Xen sandbox based on the `libVMI` library. We used the default DRAKVUF configuration, which traces the execution of the guest operating system. As the guest OS idles and the vCPUs are running on dedicated CPU cores, DRAKVUF mostly traces the execution of the metrics scripts.

The goal of evasive malware is to detect the VMI analysis, so a technique to conceal VMI pauses is effective if the measurement with this technique cannot be distinguished from the `NoAnalysis` measurements. The more a concealing technique differs from `NoAnalysis` on a given metric, the more detectable it is with this metric, and thus the less it is effective.

All experiments in this paper are executed on an Intel i7-1165G7 CPU (4.70 GHz max CPU frequency), in the Xen 4.17 VMM, with a Debian 11 guest. The VM is configured with 8 GB of RAM and 4 vCPUs. Xen was configured to allocate 4 CPU cores exclusively to the VM, to limit potential noise caused by the dom0 OS.

Figure 2 shows the distribution of the results for the clock-based side effects metric, while the values are detailed in Table 1. Symmetrically, Fig. 3 shows the distribution of the results for the work-done-based side effects metric, while Table 2 details values.

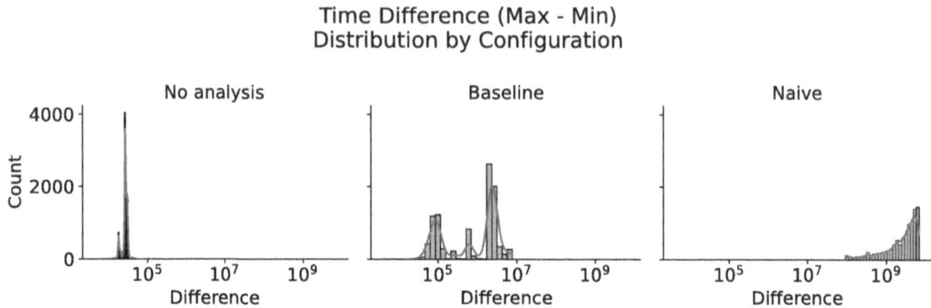

Fig. 2. Histogram of the distribution of the maximum observed time gap between vCPUs for the `NoAnalysis`, `Baseline` and `Naive` approaches, for the clock-based side effects metric. The difference unit are TSC ticks, with a logarithmic scale. For each iteration, we measure the difference between the highest and lowest TSC timestamps taken by all the vCPUs. We cut values above the 99th percentile to filter outliers (Caused by NMIs for instance). We observe 3 different distributions for each approach. With `NoAnalysis`, the differences between the measurements of TSC are small, between 1×10^4 and 4×10^4. With the `Baseline` VMI script we observe a first peak around the values of the `NoAnalysis`, and a second peak around 2.5×10^6 TSC ticks of difference. This value very likely corresponds to the average duration of a VMI pause. Finally, with the `Naive` approach, we have yet another distribution, which goes up to 7×10^9 TSC ticks of difference, which is about 2.5 s on the Intel i7-1165G7 CPU. This is because the vCPUs clocks are out of sync, and drift from each other as time passes.

Table 1. Summary of time differences (Max - Min per measurement) over 10,000 measurements. Unit: TSC ticks. We can see that the values differ by orders of magnitude between the configurations, so this metric can indeed be used to discriminate between the `NoAnalysis` and a tampered multi-core configuration, even if the `Naive` approach is used.

Config	Min	Q1	Median	Q3	Max	Mean	Std
`NoAnalysis`	9.28×10^3	2.59×10^4	2.69×10^4	2.91×10^4	6.06×10^5	2.72×10^4	1.26×10^4
`Baseline`	4.26×10^3	9.95×10^4	2.13×10^6	2.38×10^6	2.10×10^7	1.67×10^6	1.66×10^6
`Naive`	9.17×10^7	1.57×10^9	3.43×10^9	5.24×10^9	7.04×10^9	3.40×10^9	2.09×10^9

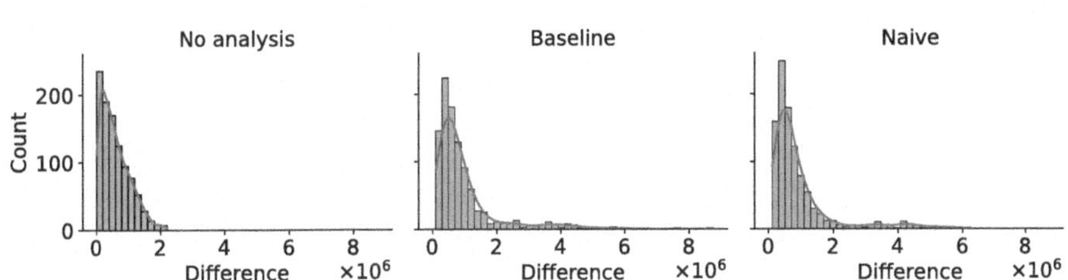

Fig. 3. Histogram of the distribution of the maximum observed performance difference between vCPUs for the `NoAnalysis`, `Baseline` and `Naive` approaches, for the work-done-based side effects metric. For each iteration, we measure the difference between the highest and lowest counter value computed by each vCPU. With `NoAnalysis`, we observe most difference values are below 2×10^6. With the `Baseline` VMI script, the distribution is slightly shifted to the right, and has a longer tail, with many values between 2×10^6 and 5×10^6, indicating more discrepancies in the performance achievable by each vCPU. We observe similar results with the `Naive` approach.

Table 2. Summary of performance differences (Max - Min per measurement) over 1,000 measurements, with 10ms per iteration. Unit: N/A. We can see that `Baseline` and `Naive` results are similar. Compared to the `NoAnalysis`, the standard deviation and mean are noticeably higher, showing more spread out and overall larger performance differences between vCPUs in these configurations.

Config	Min	Q1	Median	Q3	Max	Mean	Std
`NoAnalysis`	3.89×10^3	2.25×10^5	4.79×10^5	8.69×10^5	2.21×10^6	5.90×10^5	4.52×10^5
`Baseline`	9.73×10^4	3.83×10^5	6.40×10^5	1.04×10^6	8.75×10^6	9.72×10^5	1.05×10^6
`Naive`	1.11×10^5	3.87×10^5	5.97×10^5	9.96×10^5	6.25×10^6	9.25×10^5	9.89×10^5

4 Strategy to Hide VMI Pauses on Multi-core VMs

This section discusses a strategy to synchronize the different TSC clocks while hiding VMI pauses, with the goal of performing better than the `Naive` approach, that is minimizing the opportunities for an attacker to observe out of sync clocks. Section 4.1 introduces our design principle. Section 4.2 details our proposed `Acceleration` strategy, which accelerates the clocks of late vCPUs. Section 4.3 presents implementation details on the Xen hypervisor.

4.1 Design Approach

As discussed in Sect. 3.2, designing a strategy to mitigate time-based hypervisor introspection implies a trade-off. Rollbacks of the VM clock are ruled out, because they would likely introduce execution bugs in guest applications and kernel services that often assume the clock to be monotonic. Instead, we propose a strategy that authorizes temporarily desynchronization between vCPUs during VMI pauses and then progressively resynchronizes the clocks.

The strategy is designed by assuming that VMI pauses concerning only subsets of vCPUs are likely to be short and last a few milliseconds at most before either ending the pause or having all vCPUs paused by VMI. Thus, we disregard edge cases such as very long VMI pauses on only a subset of vCPUs, which are irrelevant for any real-world VMI script.

Another important design choice is that when a vCPU is stopped by a VMI pause, we let the other vCPUs continue their execution. Doing otherwise could result in deadlocks when the VMI script expects a VMI pause to occur on multiple vCPUs.

4.2 Adjusting the Execution Speed of vCPUs

Algorithm 1. Setup of the `TSC-multiplier` after a VMI pause. `current` is the current vCPU. `get_guest_tsc_at` provides the TSC date of a vCPU at a specific host TSC date, while taking into account the state of the vCPU.

```
Initialize Δ
if VMI pause is over then
    pause_duration ← current.tsc − current.vmexit_tsc
    current.tsc_offset ← current.tsc_offset − pause_duration
    current.synchronized ← false
    now_current ← current.tsc
    now ← rdtsc()
    target_tsc ← 0
    for all v ∈ vCPUs ≠ current do
        target_tsc ← max(target_tsc, get_guest_tsc_at(v, now + Δ))
    end for
    tsc_multiplier ← default_multiplier
    if target_tsc > now_current then
        tsc_multiplier ← (target_tsc − now_current) × (default_multiplier/Δ);
        if tsc_multiplier exceeds 16 bits then
            tsc_multiplier ← max_multiplier
        end if
    end if
    current.tsc_multiplier ← tsc_multiplier
    Update current.tsc_offset so that current.tsc = now_current
    Setup a timer to expire at target_tsc
end if
```

Algorithm 2. Timer expiration handling.

```
current.tsc_multiplier ← default_multiplier
current.synchronized ← true
tsc_offset ← −1
for all v ∈ vCPUs ≠ current do
    if v.sychronized then
        tsc_offset ← v.tsc_offset
    end if
end for
if tsc_offset = −1 then
    Update current.tsc_offset so that current.tsc is the timer expiration date
else
    current.tsc_offset ← tsc_offset
end if
```

Algorithm 3. VMI Pause handling. This algorithm is executed between the VM Exit that triggered the VMI pause and the actual handling of the VMI pause.

```
current.vmexit_tsc ← current.tsc                  ▷ Immediately after the VM Exit
...
current.synchronized ← false                       ▷ Handling of the VMI pause
if current.tsc_multiplier ≠ default_multiplier then
    current.tsc_multiplier ← default_multiplier
    now_current ← current.tsc
    if now_current > current.vmexit_tsc then
        delta_tsc = now_current − current.vmexit_tsc
        current.tsc_offset ← current.tsc_offset − delta_tsc
    else
        delta_tsc = current.vmexit_tsc − now_current
        current.tsc_offset ← current.tsc_offset + delta_tsc
    end if
end if
```

We propose a new `Acceleration` strategy to synchronize the TSC clocks of each vCPU while hiding VMI pauses on each vCPU by taking advantage of the `TSC-multiplier` VMCS field. By default, the guest TSC clocks run at the rate of the host TSC clock. However, by using the `TSC-multiplier`, it is possible to accelerate or slow down the guest TSC clock.

With the `Acceleration` strategy, the synchronization of each TSC clock is triggered unconditionally when a vCPU resumes from a VMI pause. As depicted in Fig. 4, the main idea is to accelerate the vCPU clock by increasing the `TSC-multiplier` field, until it catches up with the most advanced TSC clock.

The `Acceleration` strategy is implemented within the VMM, between the code handling the completion of the VMI pause and the resuming of the vCPU. It begins by locally hiding the vCPU pause, by subtracting the duration of the pause to the vCPU `TSC-offset`, similarly to the `Naive` approach presented in Sect. 3.2. The vCPU is then flagged as not synchronized.

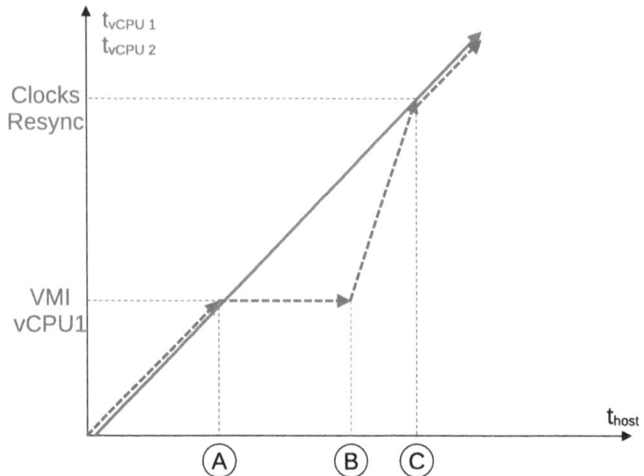

Fig. 4. Illustration of the `Acceleration` strategy to hide VMI pauses with 2 vCPUs. The X axis represents host time, the Y axis virtual time. Both vCPUs clocks are synchronized until (A), where $vCPU_1$ is paused by VMI. When it resumes at (B), its `TSC-multiplier` is set so that its clock runs faster until (C), when it catches up with $vCPU_2$ and the clocks are synchronized.

The default value of the `TSC-multiplier` field is 2^{48}, so we have $TSC_{guest} = TSC_{host} +$ `TSC-offset`. As the `TSC-multiplier` is a 64 bits field, we can write down $TSC_{guest} = m \times TSC_{host} +$ `TSC-offset`, where m is a 16 bits integer with a default value of 1. To accelerate the clock, we set $m = \frac{D-T}{\Delta}$, with Δ the duration of the synchronization process, T the TSC clock at VMI pause resume time, and D the targeted TSC clock of the most advanced vCPU at the end of the synchronization.

The computation of D depends on the status of the most advanced vCPU, which can be in one of three states: synchronized, paused, or in the synchronization process. In case m exceeds 16 bits, we set it to $2^{16} - 1$ to avoid an overflow of the `TSC-multiplier` field, although it is unlikely to ever happen with typical VMI pauses duration. The setup of the `TSC-multiplier` is detailed in Algorithm 1.

Then, we set up a timer to interrupt the accelerated vCPU once it reaches the end of the synchronization process. Algorithm 2 presents the handling of the timer expiration. We check if there is another vCPU which has a synchronized clock. If there is one, we reset m to 1 and adjust the `TSC-offset` to match the one from a synchronized vCPU. In the edge case of a `TSC-multiplier` equal to the maximum, this might cause a time jump in the future. Otherwise, if no vCPU is flagged as synchronized, it means that all others vCPUs are paused by VMI, or in the synchronization process. In this case, we reset m to 1 and adjust the `TSC-offset` so that TSC_{guest} is equal to the end date of the synchronization process. In both cases, once the timer expires, the vCPU is flagged as synchronized.

Finally, we detail what happens if a vCPU is interrupted due to a VMI pause in Algorithm 3. The vCPU is flagged as not synchronized anymore. In case the vCPU was in the synchronization process, we reset m to 1, and adjust its `TSC-offset` so that TSC_{guest} is equal to its value at the beginning of the VMI pause.

4.3 Implementation on Xen

In this section, we present how we implemented the `Acceleration` strategy on the Xen VMM. `libVMI` supports both the KVM and Xen VMM. We opted for Xen because `libVMI`'s support for it is more mature than for KVM. As KVM, Xen is a mature, open source VMM that is commonly used in computer science research [12,18,19,21,23]. Complex VMI programs based on `libVMI` such as the DRAKVUF sandbox only support Xen.

`libVMI` uses Xen's *VM event* system to perform VMI. We identified that all VMI events are processed by the `monitor_traps` function, which takes an argument to flag if the vCPU must be paused or not. That way, we can identify which VM Exits correspond to a VMI pause, and perform clock adjustments accordingly. To do so, we take a TSC timestamp as soon as possible after a VM Exit.

Moreover, the `Acceleration` strategy mandates the use of an accurate timer to interrupt accelerated vCPUs at a precise end-of-synchronization date, when the accelerated TSC catches up with the most advanced vCPU. We opted for the VMX Preemption Timer, which is specific to Intel x86 processors. It consists of a register counter that counts down at a rate proportional to the host TSC only when the corresponding vCPU is being executed in guest mode. When it reaches 0, a VM Exit is triggered. It is suited for our purpose because it has a high accuracy and handles the interruption of vCPUs. Besides, it is not otherwise used by Xen. It is possible to use other timers, such as Xen's software timer, but doing so will likely be detrimental to the accuracy. This could be due to the timer's inherent low accuracy, the timer being based on host time rather than on guest time or having to trigger the VM Exit on the target vCPU from another hardware core because of lack of control on which hardware core executes the timer handler at expiration time.

Nothing in our implementation relies on Xen-specific mechanisms, so the `Acceleration` strategy should be portable to other VMMs supporting VMI, such as KVM.

5 Evaluation

This section evaluates the efficiency of the proposed `Acceleration` strategy. To that extent, we use the metrics introduced in Sect. 3.1 to assert if the proposed strategy is able to conceal VMI pauses from an attacker performing hypervisor introspection, and discuss how this strategy performs compared to the other configurations. We use the same experimental setup as in Sect. 3.3.

We do not evaluate here the ability of the `Acceleration` strategy to hide VMI pauses from time measurements that are local to a single vCPU, because it is not the focus of this paper. Our implementation is a port of the VMI concealment strategy presented in [6] from KVM to Xen, extended to include the `Acceleration` strategy. VMI pause local concealment is enabled in the `Acceleration` configuration.

First, we compare the results of both the performance and timing metrics between the configurations of `NoAnalysis` and analysis with the `Acceleration` strategy. Figure 5 shows that the `Acceleration` strategy performs similarly to the `Baseline` setup for the performance metric. While the `Acceleration` only provides an illusion of continuous time to a paused vCPU, it does not change the actual CPU time allocated to the VM. Consequently, the CPU time spent in a VMI pause is stolen from the vCPU, similarly to the `Baseline` configuration. This leads to more performance differences between each vCPU over a fixed period of time. These differences can be caused by either a subset of paused vCPUs having less available CPU time, or by the vCPU monitoring the duration of the measurement being paused, which gives more time to the other vCPUs.

Next, Fig. 6 shows that the `Acceleration` strategy performs differently from both `NoAnalysis` and `Baseline` configurations for the timing metric. According to the design of the `Acceleration` strategy, we must allow out-of-sync vCPUs to run concurrently. Thus, as expected, we can observe timing differences across concurrent vCPUs two order of magnitudes greater than in the `NoAnalysis` configuration, so the usage of VMI could still be detected with a well chosen threshold.

We also observe that the median difference value with the `Acceleration` strategy is 2 times lower than the one from the `Baseline` scenario. This improvement can be explained by the fact that accelerating the TSC clock can partially conceal the duration of the VMI pause before the TSC timestamp is taken by the metric script. By adjusting the duration of Δ (synchronization process duration) in the `TSC-multiplier` computation, it could be possible to conceal this pause duration even more, although reducing Δ too much would make the strategy nearly identical to `Baseline`.

Another observation is that the observable drift between TSC clocks is much lower than that from the `Naive` approach. Indeed, while the clock drift grows over time in the `Naive` approach (see Fig. 6), the drift is bounded by the duration of a VMI pause with the `Acceleration` strategy. It makes `Acceleration` more stealthy regarding this metric.

Finally, we assess the stealthiness of the strategy against high-level time-based phenomena by checking the behavior of the Linux kernel `clocksource` watchdog [4]. As introduced in Sect. 3.1, Linux provides a watchdog kernel thread that can assess the TSC stability. This watchdog performs time measurements with the TSC, and compares the results to an alternate clock source,

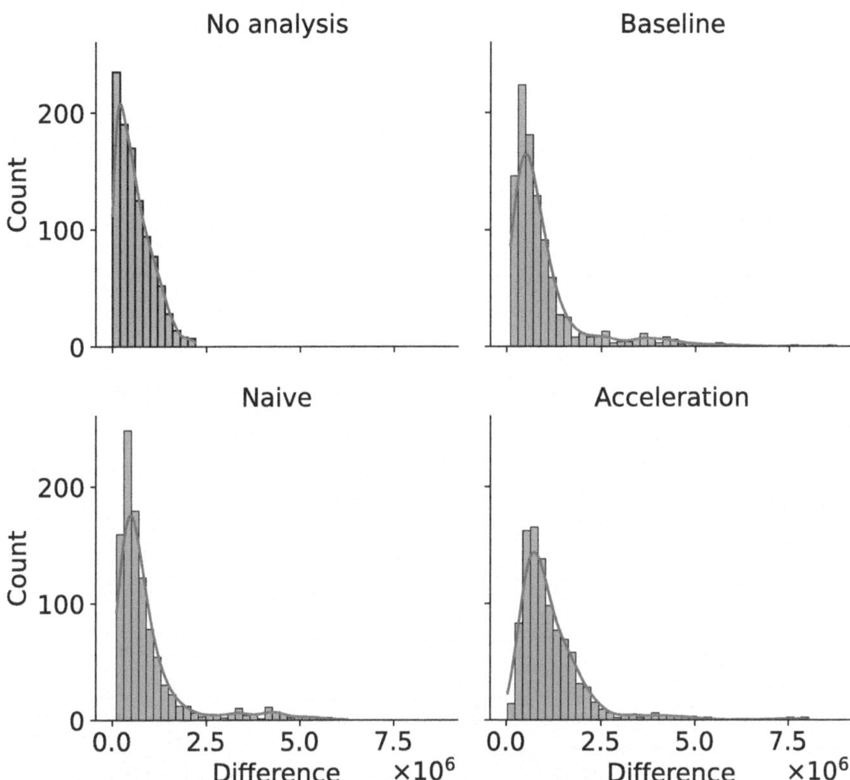

Fig. 5. Histogram of the distribution of the maximum observed performance difference between vCPUs for the `Acceleration`, `NoAnalysis`, `Baseline` and `Naive` configurations. We can see that the `Acceleration` strategy results are close the `Baseline` and `Naive` results, and thus are still noticeably different from the `NoAnalysis`. This can be explained by the fact that the `Acceleration` strategy only accelerates the TSC clock and not the actual CPU speed. The CPU time spent in a VMI pause is not compensated by this strategy.

usually the HPET, considered to be less accurate but more stable. If there is a noticeable drift between both clocksources, the TSC is flagged as unstable and the Linux kernel switches to a more stable clocksource such as the HPET. The threshold to mark the clocksource as unstable is usually rather large, typically in tens of milliseconds. Furthermore, the watchdog also checks if the clocksource remains synchronized across all CPUs [3]. To do so, it performs three clock measurements. A clock measurement is done on a tested vCPU between two measurements on the current vCPU. It then asserts that the three measurements

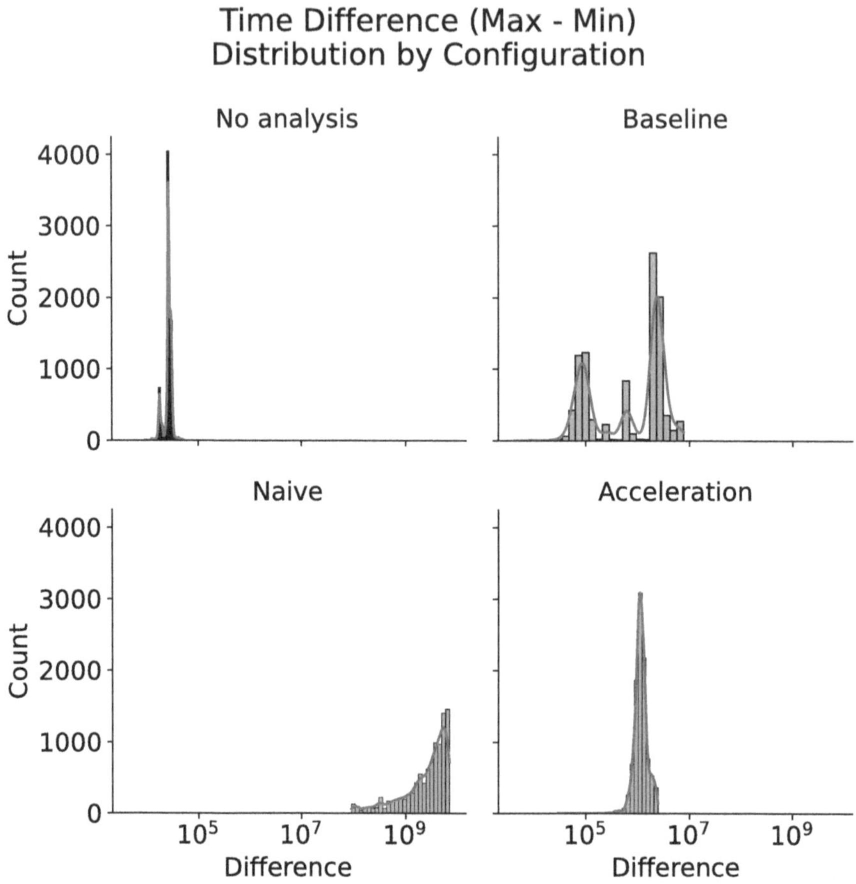

Fig. 6. Histogram of the distribution of the maximum observed time gap between vCPUs for the `Acceleration`, `NoAnalysis`, `Baseline` and `Naive` configurations. The differences unit are TSC ticks. We cut values above the 99th percentile to filter outliers (caused by NMIs for instance). As expected, the `Acceleration` strategy values are far from the `NoAnalysis` configuration, because the strategy allows out of sync vCPUs to run concurrently. Nevertheless, the drift between the TSC clocks of each vCPU is much more limited than the `Naive` approach, with most differences values below 3×10^6 (About 1ms of drift on the Intel i7-1165G7 CPU).

are in order, otherwise the vCPUs are flagged as out of sync and the clocksource marked as unstable.

We configured the guest OS to activate the watchdog, and summarized the results in Table 3 after a short run of DRAKVUF (except for `NoAnalysis`). A first observation is that the watchdog is not triggered in the `Baseline` scenario, because the average duration of VMI pauses is lower than the clock skew threshold of the watchdog. We can see that the watchdog is triggered both for the `Naive` and `Acceleration` approach, although for different reasons. Note that it

Table 3. Summary of Linux TSC `clocksource` Watchdog behavior under different setups.

Setup	Watchdog Behavior
`NoAnalysis`	Not triggered
`Baseline`	Not triggered
`Naive`	Triggered (Clock skew too large compared to HPET)
`Acceleration`	Triggered (CPU clocks out of sync)

cannot be ruled out that the watchdog could be triggered by each configuration for the reported reason only. Thus, both approaches introduce side-effects to the virtual TSC clocks that can be detected from the Linux kernel.

Table 4. Summary of VMI detection techniques on a multi-core VM. ✓: Unaffected; ✗: Affected; $\sim$: Depends on the detection script (see footnotes).

Detection technique	`NoAnalysis`	`Baseline`	`Naive`	`Acceleration`
Local to a single vCPU time gaps	3	✗	3	3
Performance difference between vCPUs	3	✗	✗	✗
Clock synchronization between vCPUs	3	$\sim^{a}$	✗	$\sim^{b}$
TSC clock kernel watchdog	3	3	✗	✗

[a] The clocks are synchronized, but concurrent measurements can be affected by VMI pauses. The observable delay is bounded by the duration of a VMI pause.
[b] The clocks are out of sync, but the maximum difference is bounded by the strategy.

As summarized in Table 4, these results show shortcomings of the `Acceleration` vCPU synchronization strategy, although this strategy offers improvements compared to the `Naive` and `Baseline` approaches in terms of stealthiness.

6 Related Work

6.1 Hypervisor Introspection

It is a well known problem that VMI pauses can be exploited to perform hypervisor introspection [6,16,17,23,25], and many countermeasures have been studied [6,7,11,13,24]. However, the proposed countermeasures are either limited to single-core VMs [6], or disregard new timing attacks introduced by the countermeasure's side effects when used on multi-core VMs [11].

Countermeasures that introduce alternative virtual clocks have the same limitations. For example, StopWatch [13] proposes replacing the clock with a virtual clock that counts the number of instructions executed in the VM. The authors explain that their design is incompatible with multi-core VMs because the scheduling of instructions across all cores is non-deterministic.

Approaches that skew the clock by adding randomized delay or degrading its resolution [15,24] can be extended to multi-core VMs if the clock adjustments are well-balanced across all cores. However, these methods introduce undesirable side effects and the degraded timer resolution may still be sufficient to detect VMI pauses.

In [23], the authors mention that a resilient strategy for performing hypervisor introspection in a multi-threaded environment is to use parallel loops that count the number of iterations. This reuses an approach first proposed to detect the usage of virtualization on a multi-core system [22]. We used a similar method for the work-done-based metric. In [14], the authors highlight multiple side channels to detect the presence of a sandbox in multi-core environments, mostly related to the scheduling of virtual cores. In this paper, we mitigated most of these attacks by properly dedicating a CPU core to each vCPU.

Many sandboxes are still configured as single-core VMs [5]. Limiting sandboxes to single-core configurations has been discussed [14], but in addition to the large performance penalty, this makes it easy for evasive malware to detect such sandboxes because most systems, even virtualized, are multi-core [14,17].

6.2 Time Dilation

The strategy we proposed in this work to synchronize the vCPUs clocks is similar to *time dilation* [9] techniques. Time dilation involves scaling the rate at which time and system resources run by a constant factor. In TimeSync [21], this constant factor is updated regularly to synchronize a VM with a network simulator. In this work, we also use a dynamic factor to modify the virtual clock speed. However, TimeSync only slows down virtual time, so that the network simulator running its nominal speed can keep up with the execution of the VMs. To produce the opposite effect, distem [20], a network emulation tool, can throttle some CPU cores to create the illusion to the others that they can achieve better performance than in reality. In this paper, we accelerate the clock speed to produce an effect similar to distem's, but without introducing CPU throttling.

7 Conclusion and Future Work

In this paper, we introduced two new metrics to characterize the usage of VMI on a multi-core VM. We have shown that both work-done-based and clock-based side effects occur after a VMI pause, and can be observable by an attacker within the VM. Furthermore, the metrics classically used to detect the usage of VMI on single-core VM are also applicable in multi-core settings.

We proposed a new VMI pause concealing strategy named `Acceleration` that takes advantage of Intel's virtualization of the TSC clock source. When evaluated in multi-core VMs, this strategy outperforms the ones used in current sandboxes for some metrics, but still has numerous shortcomings, especially regarding work-done based side effects, as they are not taken into account in the strategy design.

As future work, we plan to conduct a more thorough evaluation of the impact of each DRAKVUF plugin on each studied metric. This will require adjusting the workload in the guest VM, in order to significantly stimulate most DRAKVUF plugins.

A better strategy than `Acceleration` would have to take into account the CPU time in addition to the clock time, in order to better conceal VMI pauses across all cores. This could be achieved by balancing the runtime of each vCPU of a VM over a certain period of time. Another idea similar to the `Acceleration` strategy would be to control the CPU frequency of each vCPU core, to balance the average CPU frequency despite VMI pauses. However, without specific hardware support, this would likely require patching the guest OS, which would degrade the stealthiness of the approach.

Hardware extensions to better control the vCPUs clocks and speed from the VMM would help implementing flexible strategies to reduce observable time-based side-effects of VMI in multi-core VMs. Similarly to the VMX preemption timer, such extensions would likely be the most helpful if their effect is enabled only while the CPU is in guest mode. For instance, having guest TSC clocks that stop running on a VM-Exit would make VMI hiding simpler (no need to measure the VMI pause durations) and thus more accurate. Similarly, such extensions would allow the VMM to slow down a vCPU without intervention of the guest OS and keeping the guest TSC running at a speed looking constant from the guest kernel point of view on the vCPU.

References

1. Libvmi: simplified virtual machine introspection (2010). https://github.com/libvmi/libvmi
2. Xen artifacts, TANSIV project (2025). https://gitlab.inria.fr/tansiv/xen/-/tree/HS3-Xen-Artifact?ref_type=tags
3. Bootlin: clocksource_verify_percpu identifier (2025). https://elixir.bootlin.com/linux/v6.15.2/A/ident/clocksource_verify_percpu
4. Bootlin: clocksource_watchdog identifier (2025). https://elixir.bootlin.com/linux/v6.15.2/A/ident/clocksource_watchdog
5. Brengel, M., Backes, M., Rossow, C.: Detecting hardware-assisted virtualization. In: Caballero, J., Zurutuza, U., Rodríguez, R.J. (eds.) Detection of Intrusions and Malware, and Vulnerability Assessment - 13th International Conference, DIMVA 2016, San Sebastián, Spain, July 7-8, 2016, Proceedings. Lecture Notes in Computer Science, vol. 9721, pp. 207–227. Springer (2016). https://doi.org/10.1007/978-3-319-40667-1_11
6. Cosseron, L., Rilling, L., Simonin, M., Quinson, M.: Simulating the network environment of sandboxes to hide virtual machine introspection pauses. In: Proceedings of the 17th European Workshop on Systems Security, EuroSec 2024, Athens, Greece, 22 April 2024, pp. 1–7. ACM (2024). https://doi.org/10.1145/3642974.3652280
7. Dinaburg, A., Royal, P., Sharif, M.I., Lee, W.: Ether: malware analysis via hardware virtualization extensions. In: Ning, P., Syverson, P.F., Jha, S. (eds.) Proceedings of the 2008 ACM Conference on Computer and Communications Security, CCS 2008, pp. 51–62. ACM (2008). https://doi.org/10.1145/1455770.1455779

8. Garfinkel, T., Rosenblum, M.: A virtual machine introspection based architecture for intrusion detection. In: Proceedings of the Network and Distributed System Security Symposium, NDSS 2003. The Internet Society (2003)
9. Gupta, D., Vishwanath, K.V., Vahdat, A.: Diecast: testing distributed systems with an accurate scale model. In: Crowcroft, J., Dahlin, M. (eds.) 5th USENIX Symposium on Networked Systems Design & Implementation, NSDI 2008, April 16-18, 2008, San Francisco, Proceedings, pp. 407–422. USENIX Association (2008)
10. Intel: Intel® 64 and IA-32 architectures software developer's manual volume 3 (3A, 3B, 3C & 3D): System programming guide (2021). https://www.intel.com/content/www/us/en/developer/articles/technical/intel-sdm.html
11. Karvandi, M.S., et al.: Hyperdbg: reinventing hardware-assisted debugging. In: Yin, H., Stavrou, A., Cremers, C., Shi, E. (eds.) Proceedings of the 2022 ACM SIGSAC Conference on Computer and Communications Security, CCS 2022, Los Angeles, CA, USA, November 7-11, 2022, pp. 1709–1723. ACM (2022). https://doi.org/10.1145/3548606.3560649
12. Lengyel, T.K., Maresca, S., Payne, B.D., Webster, G.D., Vogl, S., Kiayias, A.: Scalability, fidelity and stealth in the DRAKVUF dynamic malware analysis system. In: Jr., C.N.P., Hahn, A., Butler, K.R.B., Sherr, M. (eds.) Proceedings of the 30th Annual Computer Security Applications Conference, ACSAC 2014, pp. 386–395. ACM (2014). https://doi.org/10.1145/2664243.2664252
13. Li, P., Gao, D., Reiter, M.K.: Mitigating access-driven timing channels in clouds using stopwatch. In: 2013 43rd Annual IEEE/IFIP International Conference on Dependable Systems and Networks (DSN), pp. 1–12. IEEE Computer Society (2013). https://doi.org/10.1109/DSN.2013.6575299
14. Lusky, Y., Mendelson, A.: Sandbox detection using hardware side channels. In: 22nd International Symposium on Quality Electronic Design, ISQED 2021, Santa Clara, April 7-9, 2021, pp. 192–197. IEEE (2021). https://doi.org/10.1109/ISQED51717.2021.9424260
15. Martin, R., Demme, J., Sethumadhavan, S.: Timewarp: rethinking timekeeping and performance monitoring mechanisms to mitigate side-channel attacks. In: 39th International Symposium on Computer Architecture (ISCA 2012), pp. 118–129. IEEE Computer Society (2012). https://doi.org/10.1109/ISCA.2012.6237011
16. Mishra, P., Pilli, E.S., Varadharajan, V., Tupakula, U.K.: Intrusion detection techniques in cloud environment: a survey. J. Netw. Comput. Appl. **77**, 18–47 (2017). https://doi.org/10.1016/J.JNCA.2016.10.015
17. Nance, K.L., Hay, B., Bishop, M.: Investigating the implications of virtual machine introspection for digital forensics. In: Proceedings of the The Forth International Conference on Availability, Reliability and Security, ARES 2009, March 16-19, 2009, Fukuoka, pp. 1024–1029. IEEE Computer Society (2009). https://doi.org/10.1109/ARES.2009.173
18. Payne, B.D.: Simplifying virtual machine introspection using libvmi. Tech. rep., Sandia National Laboratories (SNL), Albuquerque, NM, and Livermore, CA (2012)
19. Proskurin, S., Lengyel, T.K., Momeu, M., Eckert, C., Zarras, A.: Hiding in the shadows: empowering ARM for stealthy virtual machine introspection. In: Proceedings of the 34th Annual Computer Security Applications Conference, ACSAC 2018, San Juan, December 03-07, 2018, pp. 407–417. ACM (2018). https://doi.org/10.1145/3274694.3274698
20. Sarzyniec, L., Buchert, T., Jeanvoine, E., Nussbaum, L.: Design and evaluation of a virtual experimental environment for distributed systems. In: 2013 21st Euromicro International Conference on Parallel, Distributed, and Network-Based Processing, pp. 172–179 (2013). https://doi.org/10.1109/PDP.2013.32

21. Sultan, F., et al.: Timesync: enabling scalable, high-fidelity hybrid network emulation. In: Zomaya, A.Y., Landfeldt, B., Prakash, R. (eds.) The 15th ACM International Conference on Modeling, Analysis and Simulation of Wireless and Mobile Systems, MSWiM '12, pp. 185–194. ACM (2012). https://doi.org/10.1145/2387238.2387271
22. Thompson, C., Huntley, M., Link, C.: Virtualization detection: new strategies and their effectiveness. Univ. of Minn, Minneapolis (2010)
23. Tuzel, T., Bridgman, M.P., Zepf, J., Lengyel, T.K., Temkin, K.J.: Who watches the watcher? detecting hypervisor introspection from unprivileged guests. Digit. Investig. **26**(Supplement), S98–S106 (2018). https://doi.org/10.1016/j.diin.2018.04.015
24. Vattikonda, B.C., Das, S., Shacham, H.: Eliminating fine grained timers in xen. In: Cachin, C., Ristenpart, T. (eds.) Proceedings of the 3rd ACM Cloud Computing Security Workshop, CCSW 2011, pp. 41–46. ACM (2011). https://doi.org/10.1145/2046660.2046671
25. Wang, G., Estrada, Z.J., Pham, C.M., Kalbarczyk, Z.T., Iyer, R.K.: Hypervisor introspection: a technique for evading passive virtual machine monitoring. In: Francillon, A., Ptacek, T. (eds.) 9th USENIX Workshop on Offensive Technologies, WOOT '15. USENIX Association (2015)
26. Wong, M.Y., Landen, M., Antonakakis, M., Blough, D.M., Redmiles, E.M., Ahamad, M.: An inside look into the practice of malware analysis. In: Kim, Y., Kim, J., Vigna, G., Shi, E. (eds.) CCS '21: 2021 ACM SIGSAC Conference on Computer and Communications Security, Virtual Event, Republic of Korea, November 15 - 19, 2021, pp. 3053–3069. ACM (2021). https://doi.org/10.1145/3460120.3484759

International Workshop on Mobile and IoT Security Technologies (MIST 2025)

Streamlining Security Patches and Remote Attestations for the Internet of Things

Konrad-Felix Krentz(✉)

Siemens AG, FT RPD CED SSI-DE, Schuckertstraße 2, 91058 Erlangen, Germany
konrad-felix.krentz@siemens.com

Abstract. Internet of things (IoT) devices without Trusted Platform Modules (TPMs) usually suffer from two limitations. First, such devices resort to store preloaded keying material in software-accessible memory. This necessitates rekeying when fixing software vulnerabilities that might have caused the preloaded keying material to leak. Second, such devices cannot attest their software integrity to a remote verifier. The Device Identifier Composition Engine (DICE) approaches both these limitations through a layered boot process, where a device-specific secret remains within the confines of a trusted first-stage bootloader. Subsequent boot layers derive asymmetric key pairs and build a certificate chain, which includes evidence for remote attestations. Alternatively, subsequent boot layers may avoid asymmetric cryptography. However, that mode of DICE presumes trust in remote verifiers, thereby limiting application scenarios. Thus, asymmetric cryptography is often inevitable, which renders DICE quite communication and processing intensive for low-power IoT devices. In this paper, we propose TinyDICE and the Implicit Remote Attestation Protocol (IRAP). TinyDICE aligns DICE's asymmetric mode with low-power IoT devices by swapping its explicit certificates for implicit certificates, as well as by compressing certificates. These measures reduce certificate sizes by one order of magnitude and validation times by half compared to the Open Profile for DICE. IRAP, in turn, performs remote attestations with TinyDICE certificates and Fully Hashed Menezes-Qu-Vanstone (FHMQV). Compared to the recent Tiny Remote Attestation Protocol (TRAP), IRAP further reduces communication traffic by 14.9% and processing times by 18.9% in our experiments, while overcoming practical limitations of TRAP, too.

Keywords: Remote attestation · Key exchange · Rekeying · Implicit certificate · Menezes–Qu–Vanstone · Attested channel · OSCORE · CoAP

1 Introduction

Cost pressure hinders equipping Internet of things (IoT) devices with Trusted Platform Modules (TPMs). Hence, IoT devices commonly store their preloaded keying material in software-accessible memory, which carries the risk that malware may leak this preloaded keying material. Therefore, whenever fixing software vulnerabilities that might have caused leakage of preloaded keying material,

R. Laborde et al. (Eds.): ESORICS 2025 Workshops, LNCS 16233, pp. 451–471, 2026.
https://doi.org/10.1007/978-3-032-16165-9_27

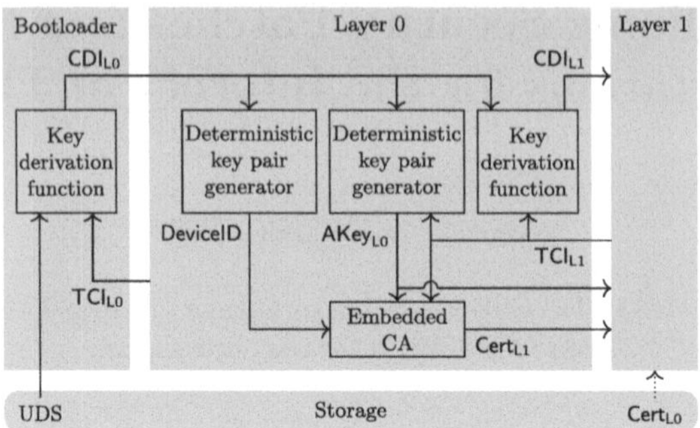

Fig. 1. The DICE layering architecture.

rekeying is advisable. Moreover, the lack of TPMs inhibits straightforward remote attestations [51]. A remote attestation is the process of convincing a remote verifier that an attester runs trustworthy software. In the IoT, remote attestations are, e.g., useful for establishing trust in sensor readings, control commands, or enclaves, also known as trusted execution environments (TEEs).

The Device Identifier Composition Engine (DICE) tackles both these issues as shown in Fig. 1 [2]. A first-stage bootloader has exclusive access to a Unique Device Secret (UDS). At start up, the first-stage bootloader determines the so-called Trusted Computing Base (TCB) Component Identifier (TCI) of Layer 0, denoted by $\mathsf{TCI}_{\mathsf{L0}}$. A TCI is a digest over a layer's software at load time and optionally over system settings, too. Then, the first-stage bootloader derives the Compound Device Identifier (CDI) for Layer 0, denoted by $\mathsf{CDI}_{\mathsf{L0}}$, from the UDS and $\mathsf{TCI}_{\mathsf{L0}}$. Eventually, the first-stage bootloader passes control to Layer 0. In DICE's more versatile mode with asymmetric cryptography, Layer 0 derives two public/private key pairs named $\mathsf{DeviceID}$ and $\mathsf{AKey}_{\mathsf{L0}}$. The $\mathsf{DeviceID}$ usually does not change during a device's life cycle. Remote verifiers either know the public portion of the $\mathsf{DeviceID}$ or manufacturers preload a certificate $\mathsf{Cert}_{\mathsf{L0}}$ for the $\mathsf{DeviceID}$. In the latter case, it suffices for remote verifiers to possess the public key of the root certificate authority (CA). $\mathsf{AKey}_{\mathsf{L0}}$, by contrast, changes with every software update of Layer 1 as it depends on $\mathsf{TCI}_{\mathsf{L1}}$. Layer 0 issues a certificate $\mathsf{Cert}_{\mathsf{L1}}$ for $\mathsf{AKey}_{\mathsf{L0}}$ and signs $\mathsf{Cert}_{\mathsf{L1}}$ with the private portion of the $\mathsf{DeviceID}$. Crucially, $\mathsf{Cert}_{\mathsf{L1}}$ contains $\mathsf{TCI}_{\mathsf{L1}}$ and possibly other *evidence* for remote attestations. $\mathsf{AKey}_{\mathsf{L0}}$, $\mathsf{Cert}_{\mathsf{L1}}$, and $\mathsf{Cert}_{\mathsf{L0}}$ (if preloaded) allow Layer 1 to authenticate to remote verifiers, as well as to attest software integrity to remote verifiers. Besides, Layer 1 may use $\mathsf{CDI}_{\mathsf{L1}}$ to stack up further layers in an analogous manner.

Yet, DICE suggests using X.509 certificates, which mismatch low-power IoT devices [29]. For one, validating X.509 certificates is time and hence energy consuming on low-power IoT devices, even with hardware acceleration for signature verifications. For another, X.509 certificates grow large, incurring long airtimes and thus a high energy consumption. As a remedy, the Internet Engineering Task Force put forward Concise Binary Object Representation (CBOR)-encoded X.509 certificates [41]. Similarly, the Open Profile for DICE (herein abbreviated as OpenDICE) encodes DICE certificates as signed CBOR Web Tokens [7]. Indeed, CBOR saves communication overhead, but there remains a signature and a public key per certificate, which quickly adds up in a certificate chain.

Owing to the high resource requirements of traditional, i.e., explicit certificates, Elliptic Curve Qu-Vanstone (ECQV) certificates are gaining attention in the IoT [1,5,8,26,40,44,48]. ECQV certificates neither carry an entity's public key nor a CA's signature. Instead, an ECQV certificate contains data to reconstruct the certified public key. The validation of an ECQV certificate then happens implicitly during usage as a wrong public key will be reconstructed if an ECQV certificate is invalid. Also, ECQV saves processing time since the reconstruction of a public key works about twice as fast as a signature verification [40].

To compress ECQV certificates even more, Malik et al. proposed a CBOR format called L-ECQV [40]. However, L-ECQV is incompatible with DICE since L-ECQV drops support for extensions. Extensions attach extra information to a certificate, which DICE uses extensively to track evidence. Similarly, Ford et al. conceived a compact certificate format with support for ECQV [21]. Their format, on the other hand, is susceptible to Curveball+ attacks, which trick vulnerable remote verifiers into accepting forged key pairs [53]. Other ECQV formats specifically target vehicular networks [4,5]. In sum, none of these ECQV formats is readily applicable to DICE. After all, none of these ECQV formats leverages opportunities for further compression in the specific context of DICE.

As for remote attestations, DICE does not specify a protocol. Instead, DICE certificates are intended to replace ordinary ones in existing key exchange protocols, such as Datagram Transport Layer Security (DTLS) or Ephemeral Diffie-Hellman Over CBOR Object Signing and Encryption (EDHOC) [45,49]. In addition to the normal DTLS or EDHOC processing, a remote verifier just has to check the evidence contained in an attester's DICE certificates. After such a key exchange, the remote verifier is not only sure of the software integrity of the attester, but also possesses an *attested channel* with the attester.

However, Diffie-Hellman (DH)-based remote attestations cause unnecessary overhead. In fact, the Tiny Remote Attestation Protocol (TRAP) proofed to reduce communication traffic and processing times by replacing DH with Fully Hashed Menezes-Qu-Vanstone with Confirmation (FHMQV-C) [34,46]. This is because FHMQV-C has mutual authentication built-in, whereas DH requires extra measures for mutual authentication, e.g., signatures in SIGn-and-MAc (SIGMA) variants [33]. But, TRAP is subject to five practical limitations. First, TRAP only allows Keystone TEEs to act as attesters [36]. Second, TRAP lacks support for mutual remote attestations. Third, TRAP identifies clients based on their IP address, which conflicts with both proxies and dynamic IP addresses. Forth, TRAP requires providing each remote verifier and attester with the static public keys of their peers. Finally, TRAP cannot accept alternative TCIs, as would be useful while rolling out a new software version.

In this paper, we make two main contributions:

- First, we propose TinyDICE. TinyDICE replaces DICE's explicit certificates with ECQV certificates and encodes them in a compact DICE-specific CBOR

format. These changes significantly reduce certificate sizes and verification times. Also, TinyDICE adopts countermeasures against Curveball+ attacks.
- Second, we propose the Implicit Remote Attestation Protocol (IRAP), a TinyDICE- and FHMQV-based remote attestation protocol. Unlike TRAP, IRAP obviates signatures entirely, which reduces communication traffic and processing times. Also, IRAP overcomes TRAP's five practical limitations.

The rest of this paper is organized as follows. Section 2 defines our threat model. Section 3 introduces TinyDICE. Section 4 elaborates on IRAP. Section 5 gives implementation details. Section 6 evaluates TinyDICE and IRAP. Section 7 completes our discussion of related work. Section 8 concludes and suggests directions for future research. Finally, Appendix A details data formats.

2 Threat Model

Throughout, we assume (i) a probabilistic polynomial time attacker, (ii) a trusted root CA, (iii) the validity of all preloaded public keys, and (iv) implementations to protect their elliptic curve cryptography (ECC) against side-channel attacks.

TinyDICE particularly presumes a trusted first-stage bootloader with exclusive access to a UDS. Upper layers, by contrast, may contain vulnerabilities, which may cause their secrets to leak. Fixing their vulnerabilities is always possible. Even Layer 0 is updateable, but doing so necessitates issuing a new $\mathsf{Cert}_{\mathsf{L0}}$ or, if $\mathsf{Cert}_{\mathsf{L0}}$ is not preloaded, conveying a new $\mathsf{DeviceID}$ public key to remote verifiers. Hence, Layer 0 should only comprise minimal functionality to make Layer 0 updates rare. Rekeying is unnecessary when updating any Layer $i \geq 1$, but entails conveying a new $\mathsf{TCI}_{\mathsf{L}i}$ to remote verifiers. When chaining three or more certificates, TinyDICE requires a curve of higher order to prevent generalized birthday attacks [14]. Lastly, TinyDICE thwarts Curveball+ v1 and v2 attacks [53]. Both variants depend on the ability to tamper with the curve parameters of an ECQV certificate. Curveball+ v1 attacks additionally depend on a victim to look up cached certificates by matching public key reconstruction data. Ultimately, a Curveball+ v1 attack tricks such a victim into accepting a forged certificate. Curveball+ v2 attacks, on the other hand, target a victim who neglects if the same curve parameters are used across an ECQV certificate chain. A Curveball+ v2 attack tricks such a victim into accepting a forged signature.

IRAP assumes an attacker who can sniff, inject, modify, block, and delay any message. In the event that the attacker blocks, modifies, or delays messages, IRAP contents itself with not completing successfully. Likewise, the injection of plenty of messages may defer IRAP's completion indefinitely. Furthermore, IRAP tackles amplification and denial-of-service attacks [45]. In an amplification attack, an attacker injects user datagram protocol (UDP) datagrams with the source IP address of a victim host. If this triggers responses that are longer than the injected UDP datagrams, this will amplify the attacker's bandwidth. Besides, as IRAP involves processing-intensive cryptographic operations, denial-of-service attacks become a threat. In such attacks, an attacker initiates several protocol runs, e.g., with the goal of depriving low-power IoT devices from

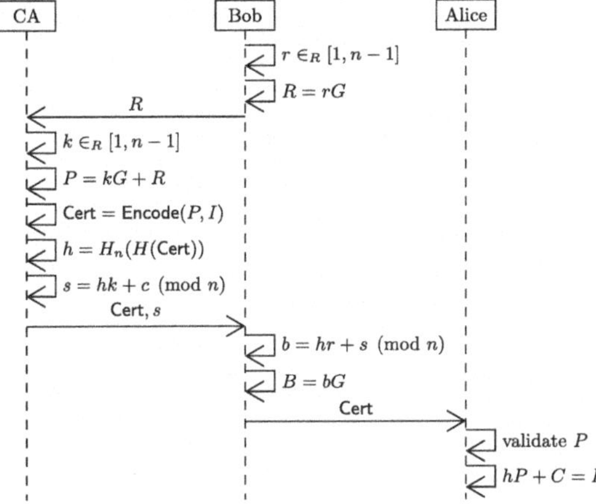

Fig. 2. Issuance of an ECQV certificate and reconstruction of the certified public key.

entering energy-saving sleep modes. On the other hand, IRAP settles for attesting software integrity at load time. This excludes Time-Of-Check Time-Of-Use (TOCTOU) attacks, where software manipulations happen at runtime [28]. Also, IRAP inherits FHMQV's privacy issue of revealing endpoint identities.

3 TinyDICE

TinyDICE has two novelties. First and foremost, TinyDICE integrates DICE and ECQV. Second, TinyDICE uses a concise DICE-specific format for ECQV certificates. This format conjoins various existing ideas. Specifically, TinyDICE adopts CBOR for encoding [40], the inheritance of values from superior certificates [21], the omission of certificate entries in transit [22], as well as countermeasures against Curveball+ attacks [53]. Below, we first outline ECQV.

3.1 ECQV: Elliptic Curve Qu-Vanstone

The issuance of an ECQV certificate works like shown in Fig. 2 [14]. Fix an elliptic curve over the finite field $\mathbb{F}_p$. We denote the curve's generator point by G and G's order by n. Further, let H be a cryptographic hash function and H_n be a function that reduces digests of H to integers in $[0, n-1]$. Initially, Bob generates a public/private key pair R/r, which we refer to as *proto-key pair*. Next, Bob passes R to the CA over an authenticated channel. Upon reception, the CA draws k randomly from the range $[1, n-1]$ and computes public key reconstruction data $P = kG + R$. Then, the CA encodes Bob's certificate Cert. Cert contains P and additional information I. Thereafter, the CA computes integer $h = H_n(H(\mathsf{Cert}))$ and private key reconstruction data $s = hk + c \pmod{n}$, where c is the CA's private key. As Bob gets back Cert and s over an authenticated channel, he computes its actual public/private key pair B/b. When Alice receives Cert over

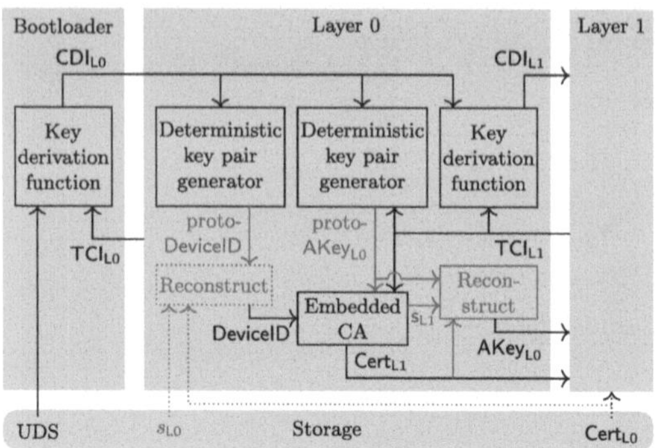

Fig. 3. The DICE layering architecture with TinyDICE's changes highlighted in blue.

an unauthenticated channel, she first validates if the contained P lies on the curve. If so, Alice uses the CA's public key C to reconstruct B as

$$hP + C = h(k + r)G + cG = (hr + hk + c)G = (hr + s)G = bG = B. \quad (1)$$

3.2 Integration

TinyDICE adapts DICE's layered boot process in three regards, as shown in Fig. 3:

1. If a manufacturer preloads $\mathsf{Cert}_{\mathsf{L0}}$, Layer 0 only derives a proto-$\mathsf{DeviceID}$ from $\mathsf{CDI}_{\mathsf{L0}}$. The public portion of the actual $\mathsf{DeviceID}$ could be reconstructed from the preloaded $\mathsf{Cert}_{\mathsf{L0}}$ like Alice does in Fig. 2. However, to reconstruct the private portion of the actual $\mathsf{DeviceID}$, manufacturers must also preload the private key reconstruction data s_{L0} associated with $\mathsf{Cert}_{\mathsf{L0}}$. Fortunately, s_{L0} is not confidential and can be stored alongside the Layer 0 software.
2. Layer 0 only derives a proto-$\mathsf{AKey}_{\mathsf{L0}}$ from $\mathsf{CDI}_{\mathsf{L0}}$ and $\mathsf{TCI}_{\mathsf{L1}}$. When the embedded CA of Layer 0 issues $\mathsf{Cert}_{\mathsf{L1}}$ using the actual $\mathsf{DeviceID}$, it also produces private key reconstruction data s_{L1}. s_{L1} serves to compute the actual $\mathsf{AKey}_{\mathsf{L0}}$.
3. Like in DICE, Layer 0 passes $\mathsf{CDI}_{\mathsf{L1}}$ to Layer 1, where it may serve to stack up more layers. In this case, Layer 1 uses $\mathsf{AKey}_{\mathsf{L0}}$ and $\mathsf{CDI}_{\mathsf{L1}}$ in the same manner as Layer 0 uses the actual $\mathsf{DeviceID}$ and $\mathsf{CDI}_{\mathsf{L0}}$, respectively.

3.3 ECQV Format

TinyDICE encodes ECQV certificates with CBOR. While a tailored binary format is even more compact, the use of CBOR opens up synergy effects since CBOR is commonplace in the IoT. The top type of a TinyDICE certificate is a CBOR map with integers as keys, as specified in Appendix A. A CBOR map takes more space than a CBOR array, yet provides for extensions. Also, it enables eliding entries that are known from the context, which is useful to save bytes in transit. The following entries can appear in a TinyDICE certificate:

- The `subject` entry identifies the device to which the certificate was issued. In transit, this entry is left optional as it is often known implicitly. In particular, since a chain of TinyDICE certificates always pertains to a single device, an inferior certificate inherits the `subject` entry from its superior certificate.
- In a root certificate, the `issuer` entry identifies ECQV's cryptographic hash function H with an ID. Allowable cryptographic hash functions and their IDs are defined in Section C.2 of [14]. If a root certificate lacks an `issuer` entry, TinyDICE defaults to SHA-256 because low-power IoT devices commonly have hardware acceleration for this hash algorithm [31]. In an inferior certificate, the value of the `issuer` entry is the digest of the superior certificate. Hence, in inferior certificates, the `issuer` entry is omissible in transit.
- The `curve` entry specifies the employed curve with an ID. Again, allowable curves and their IDs are defined in Section C.2 of [14]. `curve` entries must only appear in root certificates and apply to all inferior certificates. If no `curve` entry is present in a root certificate, TinyDICE defaults to P-256 since low-power IoT devices often have hardware acceleration for P-256 [31].
- The `reconstruction-data` entry contains ECQV's public key reconstruction data. As this data constitutes a point on the employed curve, the point is compressible through public-key compression. For encoding compressed points, TinyDICE adopts the binary format specified in Sect. 2.3.3 of [12].
- The `tci` entry either carries a TCI in-line or a version number. $\mathsf{Cert}_{\mathsf{L0}}$ certificates always contain version numbers as they are shorter and accessible at the time of issuing such certificates. When Layer 0 issues a $\mathsf{Cert}_{\mathsf{L1}}$ certificate, one option is to include $\mathsf{TCI}_{\mathsf{L1}}$ in-line. In transit, $\mathsf{TCI}_{\mathsf{L1}}$ may be compressed to a version number if both sides can map the version number to the original $\mathsf{TCI}_{\mathsf{L1}}$. Another option is for Layer 0 to certify the version number of $\mathsf{TCI}_{\mathsf{L1}}$ directly. This obviates mappings, but Layer 0 must then ensure the version number's authenticity. To do so, a manufacturer may sign the Layer 1 software together with its version number so that Layer 0 can check it. However, this will decelerate Layer 0 and increase the TCB, unless Layer 0 checks the authenticity of the Layer 1 software anyway. The same trade-off arises in upper layers.

Note that TinyDICE certificates lack an expiry date. Instead, the expiry of $\mathsf{Cert}_{\mathsf{L}i}$ coincides with the time when all remote verifiers became aware of an outdated $\mathsf{TCI}_{\mathsf{L}i}$. In such cases, remote verifiers clear each cached certificate $\{\mathsf{Cert}_{\mathsf{L}j}\}_{j \geq i}$ pertaining to the affected devices, as well as break ongoing communication with the affected devices. If $i = 0$ and once there is an update for Layer 0, remote verifiers should either be informed of the new version number of Layer 0 or, when not preloading $\mathsf{Cert}_{\mathsf{L0}}$, of the new $\mathsf{DeviceID}$ public keys of the affected devices. On the other hand, if $i \geq 1$ and once there is an update for Layer i, remote verifiers should be informed of the new version number of Layer i and, if Layer $i - 1$ does not certify version numbers directly, of the new $\mathsf{TCI}_{\mathsf{L}i}$, too.

3.4 Security Analysis

Prior work found ECQV secure in our threat model with two caveats [13,53]. First, when composing ECQV with itself or other cryptographic schemes, vulnerabilities may arise. For example, chains of three or more ECQV certificates are vulnerable to generalized birthday attacks, unless using curves of higher order as per our threat model [14]. Also, ECQV is incompatible with certain signature schemes, but its composition with MQV is deemed secure [13–15]. Second, ECQV is susceptible to Curveball+ attacks. TinyDICE's basic defense against Curveball+ attacks is to only offer a choice between predefined curves, all of which the Standards for Efficient Cryptography Group (SECG) approved for use with ECQV [14]. Of course, remote verifiers may choose to only accept a subset. Additionally, by identifying issuers by the digests of their certificates, TinyDICE inclines implementations to securely look up cached certificates by their digests rather than matching public key reconstruction data [53]. Lastly, TinyDICE's ECQV format excludes the possibility to mix curves in a chain of TinyDICE certificates, thus removing a prerequisite for Curveball+ v2 attacks.

DICE's security hinges on the exclusive access of each layer to its secrets, as detailed by England et al. [20]. We skip over their security arguments as TinyDICE only affects the detection of outdated and invalid certificates. Specifically, recall that TinyDICE's ECQV format introduces the possibility of compressing TCIs to version numbers. This actually eases the detection of outdated certificates. In fact, let us consider what happens when a remote verifier is presented with an outdated $\mathsf{Cert}_{\mathsf{L}i}$. If $i = 0$, $\mathsf{Cert}_{\mathsf{L}0}$ contains a certified version number. Thus, the remote verifier can immediately recognize an outdated $\mathsf{Cert}_{\mathsf{L}0}$. If $i \geq 1$ and $\mathsf{Cert}_{\mathsf{L}i}$ contains a version number, the remote verifier can recognize that $\mathsf{Cert}_{\mathsf{L}i}$ is outdated, too. Similarly, if $\mathsf{Cert}_{\mathsf{L}i}$ contains $\mathsf{TCI}_{\mathsf{L}i}$ in-line, it is obvious to the remote verifier that $\mathsf{Cert}_{\mathsf{L}i}$ is no longer acceptable. Besides, ECQV defers the validation of certificates. For instance, suppose an attacker compromised Layer i, yet not any Layer $j < i$. Further, assume that a remote verifier became aware of a new $\mathsf{TCI}_{\mathsf{L}i}$. An idea to trick the remote verifier into accepting an outdated $\mathsf{Cert}_{\mathsf{L}i}$ anyway is to tamper with the `tci` entry. However, this will cause the remote verifier to reconstruct another public key than the originally certified one. Since the attacker has not compromised any Layer $j < i$, the attacker cannot forge a valid $\mathsf{Cert}_{\mathsf{L}i}$ efficiently either. Eventually, the remote verifier detects an invalid certificate because subsequent communication appears inauthentic.

4 IRAP: Implicit Remote Attestation Protocol

TinyDICE's layered boot process yields a certificate chain containing TCIs. IRAP leverages this output to attest the software integrity of all layers to a remote verifier. Additionally, IRAP can attest the software integrity of a TEE that runs on top of the last layer to a remote verifier. IRAP even supports mutual remote attestations if both sides implement TinyDICE. Conversely, IRAP degenerates into a key exchange protocol if neither side implements TinyDICE. In the following, we will first give an overview of IRAP.

4.1 Protocol Overview

IRAP comprises three request-response pairs between a client and a server:

1. The initial /kno request-response is part of IRAP's protection against amplification and denial-of-service attacks.
2. The subsequent /reg request-response performs an FHMQV key exchange and optionally the TinyDICE-based remote attestation.
3. The final request-response pair serves for key confirmation and can carry end-to-end-secured application data already.

All messages are sent as Constrained Application Protocol (CoAP) messages [50], usually but not necessarily over UDP. CoAP and TinyDICE match well since both target low-power IoT devices. For securing CoAP traffic, IRAP uses Object Security for Constrained RESTful Environments Next-Generation (OSCORE-NG) since it fixes vulnerabilities of IPsec, DTLS, and OSCORE [35].

As its key exchange protocol, IRAP uses FHMQV, which is the most secure iteration of the seminal MQV key exchange protocol [46]. FHMQV derives a shared secret σ not only from ephemeral key pairs like DH but also static key pairs. From σ, a variant called FHMQV-C derives the symmetric keys K and K_{HMAC}. K_{HMAC} serves to generate two hash-based message authentication codes (HMACs) for mutual key confirmation. FHMQV is a simpler variant that works without HMACs and only derives K. Regardless, parties can confirm to each other that they possess K by authenticating a message with K like IRAP does.

4.2 Protocol Design

Figure 4 shows the protocol details. Either side can act as attester, remote verifier, or both. If a client or server runs in a TEE, the highest boot layer m or n acts on behalf of the client or server, respectively. Otherwise, the client or server is a subprocess of Layer m or n, respectively.

① A client initiates a protocol run by sending a /kno request containing padding bytes so that the /kno request is at least as long as a /kno response. The server replies with a cookie c, which has to be presented in the second request. The server calculates c as $c = \mathsf{HMAC}(r, a) \| i$, where r is a random key that changes at regular intervals, a is the client's IP address, and i is the least significant bit of the current interval. Appending i allows the server to accept old cookies for a transition period.

② Upon reception of a /kno response, the client generates FHMQV's ephemeral public/private key pair E/e and sends a /reg request. The format of /reg requests is specified in Appendix A. At minimum, the /reg request imparts E. In this basic case, the server cannot assess the software integrity of the client side. Also, the server must have the public portion D of a static key pair D/d of Layer m. If the client side implements TinyDICE, the client includes its chain of TinyDICE certificates. This chain implicitly certifies $\mathsf{AKey}_{\mathsf{L}m-1}$. $\mathsf{AKey}_{\mathsf{L}m-1}$ constitutes the static key pair D/d of Layer m if the client side implements TinyDICE. If the client side implements TinyDICE and the client runs in a

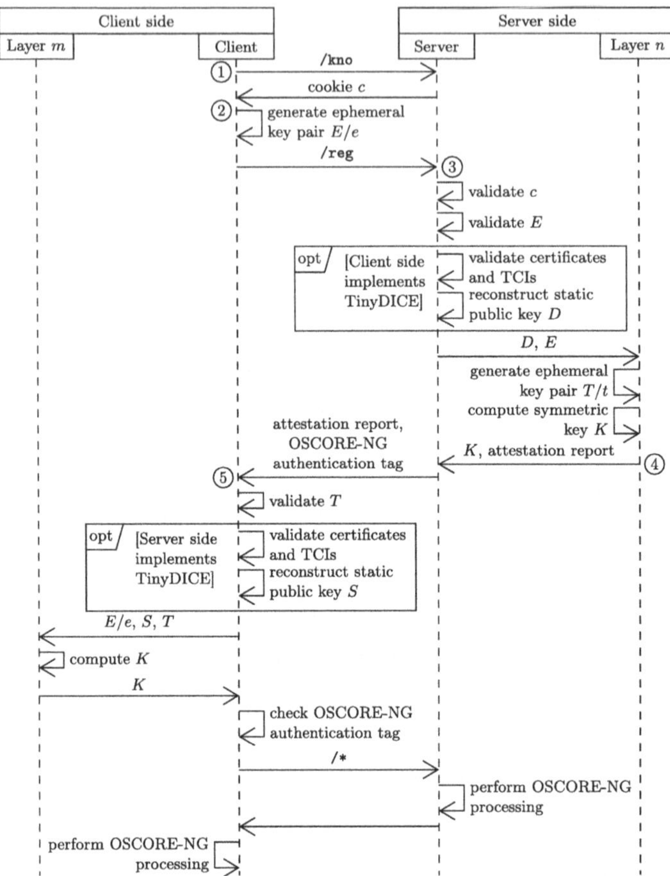

Fig. 4. Operation of IRAP.

TEE, the client adds the TCI of its TEE to the `/reg` request, too. That TCI may be either carried in-line or compressed to a version number.

To obviate IP address-based identification, the CoAP header of `/reg` requests contains an OSCORE-NG option that states the client's ID. This ID could have been placed in the payload of `/reg` requests, as well. Yet, the advantage of an OSCORE-NG option is that CoAP proxies can process the OSCORE-NG option as usual and insert information required for authenticating `/reg` responses.

③ Upon reception of the `/reg` request, the server checks the received cookie c and the received ephemeral public key E. If TinyDICE certificates are present, the server validates their public key reconstruction data and TCIs. If the TCI of the client's TEE is present, the server checks if that TCI is acceptable, too. Also, the server reconstructs the public portion D of $\mathsf{AKey}_{\mathsf{L}m-1}$. Next, Layer n generates FHMQV's ephemeral public/private key pair T/t. If the server side does not implement TinyDICE, Layer n has a static key pair S/s and the public portion S is known to the client. Else, $\mathsf{AKey}_{\mathsf{L}n-1}$ constitutes the static key pair S/s of Layer n. Then, Layer n generates a shared secret σ using S/s, T/t, D, and E as per FHMQV. Subsequently, Layer n derives the symmetric key K from σ. A salt to the derivation of K is the concatenation of the TCI of the client's TEE (if any), and the TCI of the server's TEE (if any). In salts, it is possible to leave the TCI of the server's or client's TEE compressed to a version number if Layer m or n checks the authenticity of the TEE's version number, respectively.

④ Layer n returns K and an attestation report, whose format is specified in Appendix A. At minimum, it includes T. If the server side implements TinyDICE, the attestation report also contains the TinyDICE certificate chain that certifies $\mathsf{AKey}_{\mathsf{L}n-1}$. If the server side implements TinyDICE and the server runs in a TEE, that TEE's TCI appears in the attestation report either in-line or as a version number, too. The attestation report and an authentication tag form the payload of the `/reg` response. For generating the authentication tag, IRAP lets OSCORE-NG authenticate the `/reg` response with K.

⑤ Upon reception of the `/reg` response, the client validates if T lies on the curve. If present, the client also validates the contained TinyDICE certificate chain by inspecting public key reconstruction data and TCIs. If successful, the client reconstructs the static public key S. Next, Layer m generates a shared secret σ using D/d, E/e, S, and T as per FHMQV. Then, Layer m derives K from σ. Again, a salt to the derivation of K is the concatenation of the TCI of the client's TEE (if any), and the TCI of the server's TEE (if any). K serves to check the OSCORE-NG authentication tag of the `/reg` response, as well as to secure subsequent communication with OSCORE-NG. To allow the server to distinguish concurrent protocol runs, the OSCORE-NG option of the third request contains leading bytes of the client's ephemeral public key.

4.3 Security Analysis

From DTLS and TRAP, IRAP adopts the use of a cookie c to combat amplification and denial-of-service attacks. c complicates amplification attacks as an attacker must first proof address ownership. Off-path attackers are left with the possibility to inject `/kno` requests, which are longer than `/kno` responses due to padding bytes. Thus, `/kno` responses cannot serve for amplifying an attacker's bandwidth. Furthermore, c enables rate-limiting IP addresses from which many remote attestation requests originate. Yet, like in DTLS and TRAP, legitimate clients may get rate-limited when an on-path attacker spoofs their IP address.

IRAP then follows FHMQV to establish K. FHMQV was individually proven secure in our threat model [46]. On the other hand, a security analysis of the composition of FHMQV and ECQV was not yet performed to the best of our knowledge. For the scope of this paper, we rely on conjectures that this composition is secure [13–15]. A tweak to FHMQV is the use of the TCIs of TEEs (if any) as salts. This ensures the integrity of these TCIs since changes result in unequal values for K (if the TCIs are acceptable at all) and eventually in unfinished protocol runs due to inauthentic authentication tags.

More specifically, K serves as a Master Secret in OSCORE-NG. The role of OSCORE-NG is to ensure the authenticity, confidentiality, and freshness of CoAP messages between the client and the server beginning with the deliberately unencrypted `/reg` response. To authenticate and encrypt messages, OSCORE-NG uses a replaceable Authenticated Encryption with Associated Data (AEAD) algorithm. To detect duplicate messages, OSCORE-NG keeps short-term anti-replay data. To detect delayed messages, OSCORE-NG performs a Secure Pairwise Synchronization (SPS) during the first three message flights in an OSCORE-NG session [24]. During SPS, OSCORE-NG uses full timestamps to measure the delay of the second and third message. If the second or third message exceeds an acceptable delay OSCORE-NG will discard it. Until a resynchronization is due, OSCORE-NG truncates timestamps in subsequent messages. Receivers restore full timestamps using their measured clock offsets. Crucially, this restoration fails if and only if a message is delayed by longer than the deduplication window, which causes delayed messages to appear inauthentic.

5 Implementation

We implemented TinyDICE and IRAP as follows. On the client side, our target IoT devices run the Contiki-NG operating system (OS) and use CC2538 System-on-Chips (SoCs) [54]. CC2538 SoCs feature hardware acceleration for P-256 and SHA-256, which we leverage for executing ECQV and FHMQV. To enable comparisons, we also implemented ECQV and FHMQV in software by expanding micro-ecc, a fast, side-channel attack-resistant implementation of ECC for embedded devices [39,42]. Furthermore, we integrated IRAP's protocol logic into libcoap and use that version of libcoap instead of Contiki-NG's CoAP implementation. A work in progress is to integrate TinyDICE into MCUboot. On the server side, we integrated TinyDICE into Keystone by splitting Keystone's bootloader in two boot stages [36]. The first one generates $\mathsf{CDI}_{\mathsf{L0}}$. The second one implements Layer 0. Layer 1 constitutes the Keystone security monitor (SM), which launches an untrusted Linux OS, as well as Keystone TEEs upon request. Based on this implementation of TinyDICE, we enabled a Keystone TEE to engage in protocol runs of IRAP via a host app in the untrusted Linux OS. While the Keystone TEE performs security checks and keeps secrets, the host app takes care of CoAP communication. For executing ECQV and Fully Hashed Menezes-Qu-Vanstone (FHMQV), the server side uses our adapted version of micro-ecc, too. Our source code is available at https://github.com/kkrentz/contiki-ng.

6 Evaluation

In this section, we show the certificates of TinyDICE to be far more compact than those of OpenDICE. Next, we quantify the boot delay incurred by TinyDICE. Lastly, we demonstrate IRAP to reduce communication traffic and processing times compared to both TRAP and a SIGMA-based counterpart of TRAP.

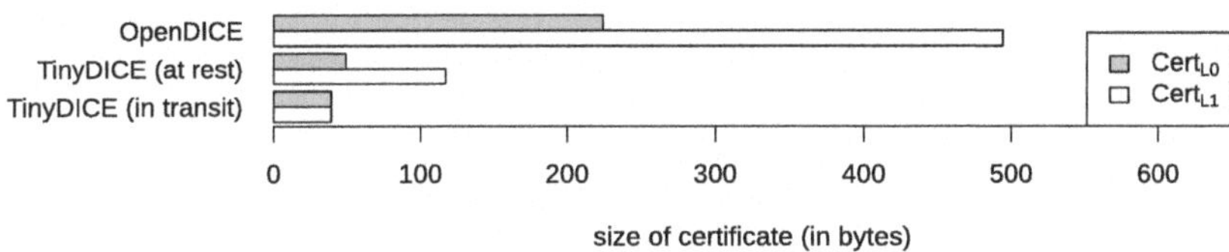

Fig. 5. Sizes of exemplary OpenDICE and TinyDICE certificates.

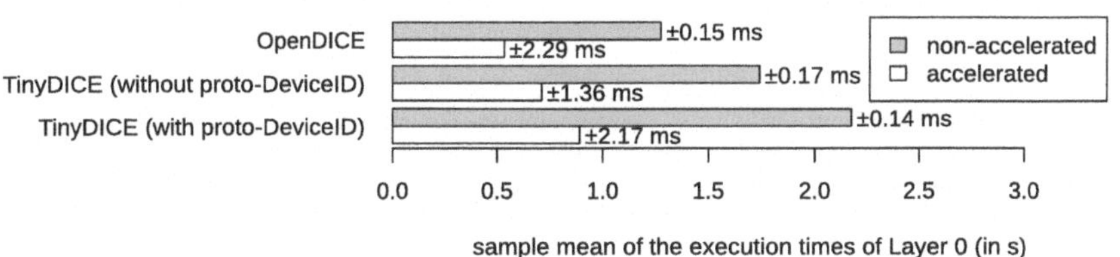

Fig. 6. Execution times of OpenDICE's and TinyDICE's Layer 0. Behind each bar, we report on the 99% confidence interval.

6.1 Comparison of OpenDICE and TinyDICE

To compare the sizes of OpenDICE and TinyDICE certificates, exemplary $\mathsf{Cert}_{\mathsf{L0}}$ and $\mathsf{Cert}_{\mathsf{L1}}$ certificates were generated in both formats. Throughout, P-256 and SHA-256 were used. As for OpenDICE, only mandatory fields were populated and the $\mathsf{Cert}_{\mathsf{L0}}$ certificate had an 8-byte issuer name. As for TinyDICE, 8-byte subject names were used and $\mathsf{Cert}_{\mathsf{L1}}$ had an in-line $\mathsf{TCI}_{\mathsf{L1}}$. Furthermore, one experimental run measured sizes at rest, i.e., without eliding any entries. Another experimental run measured sizes when compressing all possible entries.

Figure 5 shows the results. Though OpenDICE also uses CBOR, its certificates are much bigger. For one, OpenDICE mandates multiple 64-byte digests to communicate evidence. TinyDICE, by contrast, uses a single combined 32-byte TCI and even allows compressing it to a version number in transit. For another, OpenDICE uses explicit certificates, which is why a public key and signature are present in each certificate. Moreover, OpenDICE does not compress public keys. By contrast, a TinyDICE certificate only contains public key reconstruction data, which TinyDICE compacts through public-key compression.

To compare the boot times of OpenDICE and TinyDICE, the steps of Layer 0 were executed on a CC2538-based IoT device using the same certificates like in the above experiment at a clock frequency of 32 MHz. The time to obtain TCIs was excluded. This experiment was repeated with and without hardware acceleration for P-256 and SHA-256, as well as with and without reconstructing the actual DeviceID from a proto-DeviceID. The sample size was 30 per configuration.

Figure 6 shows the results. Accordingly, OpenDICE boots faster. This is because TinyDICE's Layer 0 performs two time-consuming operations, namely the issuance of $\mathsf{Cert}_{\mathsf{L1}}$ and the reconstruction of the actual $\mathsf{AKey}_{\mathsf{L0}}$. Moreover, when a manufacturer preloads $\mathsf{Cert}_{\mathsf{L0}}$, Layer 0 needs to reconstruct the actual DeviceID, too. We note, however, that caching can speed up reboots [20, 37].

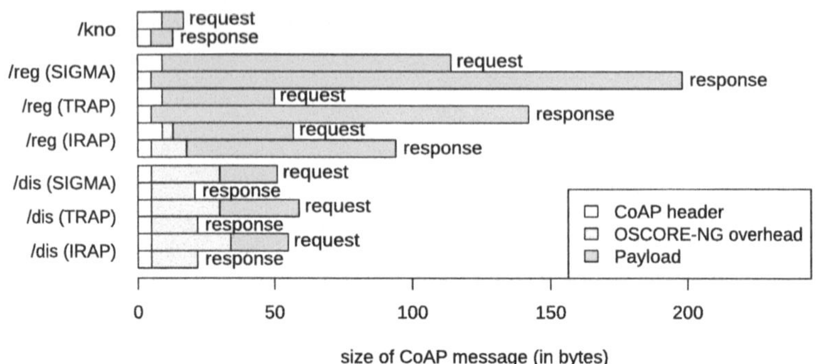

Fig. 7. Communication traffic of IRAP, TRAP, and a SIGMA-based counterpart.

Furthermore, processing implicit certificates only takes about half as long [40], which reduces the processing time per each remote attestation, as we see shortly.

6.2 Comparison of IRAP, TRAP, and a SIGMA-Based Counterpart

To compare the communication overhead of IRAP, TRAP, and a SIGMA-based counterpart of TRAP [34], their three request-response pairs were captured during protocol runs. Throughout, the attesting server ran in a Keystone TEE, whereas the verifying client neither ran in a TEE nor acted as attester itself. This scenario was chosen because it is the only one that all three protocols support. The third request was always sent to the path `/dis` with 16 bytes of data. As for IRAP, Layer 0 lacked the optional $\mathsf{Cert}_{\mathsf{L0}}$. Thus, the client used a preloaded public key to check the server's authenticity in all three protocols.

Figure 7 shows the results. The length `/kno` requests and responses is equal across all three protocols. `/reg` requests and responses are longest when using SIGMA. This is because SIGMA uses two 64-byte signatures for mutual authentication. Specifically, `/reg` requests contain a signature that signs the client's ephemeral public key and the server's cookie. `/reg` responses, on the other hand, contain a signature over (i) the ephemeral public keys of both sides and (ii) the TCI of the Keystone TEE. TRAP and IRAP obviate these two signatures via FHMQV-C and FHMQV, respectively. Additionally, TinyDICE frees Keystone's bootloader from signing an "SM report" (equivalent to $\mathsf{Cert}_{\mathsf{L1}}$) for the Keystone SM. This further shortens IRAP's `/reg` responses since they no longer carry that 64-byte signature either. IRAP's `/reg` requests are a bit longer due to using CBOR rather than a custom binary format, as well as due to inserting an OSCORE-NG option with the client's 2-byte ID. TRAP and its SIGMA-based counterpart identify clients based on their IP address. This saves communication overhead, yet conflicts with both proxies and dynamic IP addresses. As for `/dis` requests, they are longest when using TRAP due to conveying FHMQV-C's HMAC. Instead, IRAP relies on OSCORE-NG to authenticate `/dis` requests.

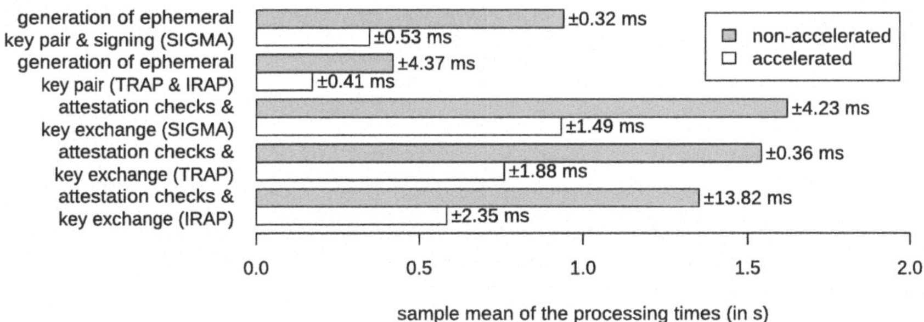

Fig. 8. Processing times of the cryptographic operations of IRAP, TRAP, and a SIGMA-based counterpart. Behind each bar, we report on the 99% confidence interval.

To measure the processing times of cryptographic operations, the above experiment was repeated with a CC2538-based IoT device acting as client with and without hardware acceleration. The sample size was 30 per configuration. Throughout, the CC2538-based IoT device ran at a clock frequency of 32 MHz.

The results are shown in Fig. 8. SIGMA performs worst due to involving three signatures. TRAP reduces processing times by obviating two signatures. IRAP dispenses with signatures entirely, which further reduces processing times.

7 Related Work

Generally, one distinguishes between software-based, hardware-based, and hybrid remote attestation. Software-based remote attestation dispenses with hardware support altogether, but is very susceptible to attacks [16]. Hardware-based remote attestation, on the other hand, typically relies on relatively expensive TPMs [51]. To reduce costs, hybrid attestation uses a hardware-software co-design [43]. DICE is hardware-based, yet, uncommonly, builds upon a minimal set of commonly available hardware features [2,20], as originally proposed by Francillon et al. [23]. Specifically, DICE depends on (i) an uninterruptable immutable first-stage bootloader, and (ii) secure storage to prevent access to the UDS by subsequent boot layers. Many embedded devices come with a memory protection unit (MPU), which helps satisfy both requirements [32]. Alternatively, an MPU can be implemented in software at the cost of runtime overhead [10,25].

DICE offers two modes, one of which uses asymmetric cryptography and the other of which solely uses symmetric cryptography. In asymmetric mode, DICE suggests generating an X.509 certificate chain with evidence contained in X.509 extensions during boot. DICE certificates are akin to Entity Attestation Tokens (EATs) [38]. An EAT contains evidence, a nonce from a remote verifier, and a signature over these contents. A main drawback of EATs is that they do not provide for establishing an attested channel, as opposed to DICE. In symmetric mode, DICE derives symmetric keys from the UDS during boot [3]. The symmetric mode enables very lightweight remote attestation protocols [30], but presumes trust in remote verifiers. In fact, compromises of remote verifiers are severe. To this end, Chi et al. complemented DICE's symmetric mode with key revocation and rekeying functionality [18]. Alternatively, Schulz et al. proposed a trusted mediator, which solves the issue, but involves asymmetric cryptography [47].

There have been many proposals for improving DICE's security. For example, to protect the UDS against physical attacks, a physically unclonable function may serve to store the UDS [7]. Further, with minor additions, DICE may not only ensure software but also hardware integrity [30]. Also, DICE was hardened against attacks through formal methods [52], and a more secure implementation design [6]. Lastly, Xu et al. added mechanisms to enforce software updates [55].

An immanent limitation of DICE is that it cannot detect runtime alterations to the attested software. This leaves DICE vulnerable to TOCTOU attacks [28]. A mitigation is to ask Layer 0 to generate a fresh certificate chain on request at runtime [27]. However, this mitigation fails to detect malware that hides itself during remote attestations [17]. To detect such malware, one may enforce a reboot after changes to program memory [51], or use special hardware [11,19].

Another limitation regarding DICE's asymmetric mode is that it only lends itself to attesting individual devices one by one. This renders the attestation of a whole IoT network inefficient. In symmetric mode, the overhead is reducible through swarm attestation, also called collective attestation [9], where a whole network of IoT devices attests to a remote verifier at once [56].

8 Conclusion and Future Work

Software updates are a timely issue due to the impending Cyber Resilience Act (CRA). In the IoT, a concern with security fixes, in particular, is that preloaded keying material might have leaked already. This is because low-power IoT devices cannot typically afford TPMs. DICE resolves this issue, but some of its design choices mismatch the resource constraints of low-power IoT devices. We have therefore proposed a lightweight version of DICE called TinyDICE. Besides, the CRA mandates ensuring security across a device's life cycle, part of which should be remote attestations of a device's software integrity. To do so on low-power IoT devices, we have proposed IRAP. IRAP improves on TRAP by resting on the platform-independent TinyDICE, supporting mutual remote attestations, as well as obviating IP address-based identification. Furthermore, in IRAP, either side may only need the public key of a root CA and remote verifiers may choose to accept multiple TCIs while transitioning to a new software version. This is in contrast to TRAP, where either side needs the other side's static public key and only one TCI is acceptable at a time. Beyond that, IRAP involves less communication traffic and less computational effort than TRAP. Nonetheless, remote attestations remain time-consuming on low-power IoT devices. Prospective optimizations include certificate caches, session resumption mechanisms, and precomputations of FHMQV steps.

Acknowledgments. This study was funded by BMBF (grant number 16ME0270K).

A Concise Data Definition Language (CDDL) Descriptions

Listing A.1. CDDL description of the format of TinyDICE certificates. Most entries are omissible in transit as their contents are often known implicitly. Receivers need to insert missing entries so as to obtain the same digest as the issuing CA.

```
certificate-chain = [ + certificate ]
certificate = {
  ? subject => bstr / tstr,
  ? issuer => uint / digest,
  ? curve => uint,
  reconstruction-data => compressed-point,
  tci => digest / version,
  * int => any, ; future extensions
}

subject = 0
issuer = 1
curve = 2
reconstruction-data = 3
tci = 4

compressed-point = bstr
digest = bstr
version = uint
```

Listing A.2. CDDL description of the format of `/reg` request payloads and attestation reports in IRAP.

```
reg-request-payload = [ ; CBOR Sequence of:
  cookie : bstr,
  ~attestation-report,
]

attestation-report = [ ; CBOR Sequence of:
  ephemeral-public-key : compressed-point,
  ? certificates : certificate-chain,
  ? tee-tci : digest / version,
]
```

References

1. Zigbee smart energy standard (2017). version 1.4
2. DICE layering architecture. TCG Specification (2020). version 1.0
3. Symmetric identity based device attestation. TCG Specification (2020). version 1.0
4. Intelligent Transport Systems (ITS); Security; Security header and certificate formats; Release 2. ETSI TS 103 097 (2021)
5. IEEE Standard for Wireless Access in Vehicular Environments (WAVE) – Certificate Management Interfaces for End Entities. IEEE 1609.2-2022 (2022)
6. DICE protection environment. TCG Specification (2023). version 1.0
7. Open profile for DICE. v2.5 (2023)
8. Almuhaideb, A.M., Algothami, S.S.: ECQV-based lightweight revocable authentication protocol for electric vehicle charging. Big Data Cogn. Comput. **6**(4) (2022). https://doi.org/10.3390/bdcc6040102
9. Ambrosin, M., Conti, M., Lazzeretti, R., Rabbani, M.M., Ranise, S.: Collective remote attestation at the Internet of things scale: state-of-the-art and future challenges. IEEE Commun. Surv. Tutor. **22**(4), 2447–2461 (2020). https://doi.org/10.1109/COMST.2020.3008879
10. Ammar, M., Crispo, B., Jacobs, B., Hughes, D., Daniels, W.: Sμv-the security microvisor: a formally-verified software-based security architecture for the Internet of things. IEEE Trans. Dependable Secure Comput. **16**(5), 885–901 (2019). https://doi.org/10.1109/TDSC.2019.2928541
11. Arkannezhad, F., Feng, J., Sehatbakhsh, N.: IDA: hybrid attestation with support for interrupts and TOCTOU. In: Proceedings of the NDSS 2024. Internet Society (2024). https://doi.org/10.14722/ndss.2024.23059
12. Brown, D.R.L.: SEC 1: Elliptic curve cryptography. Standards for Efficient Cryptography, Version 2.0 (2009)
13. Brown, D.R.L., Gallant, R., Vanstone, S.A.: Provably secure implicit certificate schemes. In: Syverson, P. (eds.) Financial Cryptography. FC 2001. LNCS, vol. 2339, pp. 156–165. Springer, Berlin, Heidelberg (2002). https://doi.org/10.1007/3-540-46088-8_15
14. Campagna, M.: SEC 4: Elliptic curve Qu-Vanstone implicit certificate scheme (ECQV). Standards for Efficient Cryptography, Version 1.0 (2013)
15. Campagna, M., Stebila, D.: ECMQV_ECQV Cipher Suites for Transport Layer Security (TLS). draft-campagna-tls-ecmqv-ecqv (2010)
16. Castelluccia, C., Francillon, A., Perito, D., Soriente, C.: On the difficulty of software-based attestation of embedded devices. In: Proceedings of the CCS '09, pp. 400–409. ACM (2009). https://doi.org/10.1145/1653662.1653711
17. Castelluccia, C., Francillon, A., Perito, D., Soriente, C.: On the difficulty of software-based attestation of embedded devices. In: Proceedings of the CCS '09, pp. 400–409. ACM (2009). https://doi.org/10.1145/1653662.1653711
18. Chi, H., Jakielaszek, L., Du, X., Paul Ratazzi, E.: DICE-enabled distributed security schemes for the air force Internet of things. In: Proceedings of the ICC '22, pp. 2212–2217. IEEE (2022). https://doi.org/10.1109/ICC45855.2022.9838675
19. De Oliveira Nunes, I., Jakkamsetti, S., Rattanavipanon, N., Tsudik, G.: On the TOCTOU problem in remote attestation. In: Proceedings of the CCS '21, pp. 2921–2936. CCS '21, ACM (2021). https://doi.org/10.1145/3460120.3484532
20. England, P., Marochko, A., Mattoon, D., Spiger, R., Thom, S., Wooten, D.: RIoT-a foundation for trust in the Internet of things. Technical report. MSR-TR-2016-18 (2016)

21. Ford, W., Poeluev, Y.: The Machine-to-Machine (M2M) Public Key Certificate Format. draft-ford-m2mcertificate (2015)
22. Forsby, F., Furuhed, M., Papadimitratos, P., Raza, S.: Lightweight X.509 digital certificates for the Internet of things. In: Fortino, G., et al. (eds.) Interoperability, Safety and Security in IoT. InterIoT SaSeIoT 2017 2017. LNICS, Social Informatics and Telecommunications Engineering, vol. 242, pp. 123–133. Springer, Cham (2018). https://doi.org/10.1007/978-3-319-93797-7_14
23. Francillon, A., Nguyen, Q., Rasmussen, K.B., Tsudik, G.: A minimalist approach to remote attestation. In: Proceedings of the DATE '14, pp. 1–6. IEEE (2014). https://doi.org/10.7873/DATE.2014.257
24. Ganeriwal, S., Pöpper, C., Capkun, S., Srivastava, M.B.: Secure time synchronization in sensor networks. ACM Trans. Inf. System Secur. (TISSEC) **11**(4), 23:1–23:35 (2008). https://doi.org/10.1145/1380564.1380571
25. Grisafi, M., Ammar, M., Roveri, M., Crispo, B.: PISTIS: trusted computing architecture for low-end embedded systems. In: Proceedings of the USENIX Security '22, pp. 3843–3860 (2022)
26. Ha, D.A., Nguyen, K.T., Zao, J.K.: Efficient authentication of resource-constrained IoT devices based on ECQV implicit certificates and datagram transport layer security protocol. In: Proceedings of the SoICT '16, pp. 173–179. ACM (2016). https://doi.org/10.1145/3011077.3011108
27. Hristozov, S., Heyszl, J., Wagner, S., Sigl, G.: Practical runtime attestation for tiny IoT devices. In: Proceedings of the DISS '18 (2018). https://doi.org/10.14722/diss.2018.23011
28. Hristozov, S., Wettermann, M., Huber, M.: A TOCTOU attack on DICE attestation. In: Proceedings of the CODASPY '22, pp. 226–235. ACM (2022). https://doi.org/10.1145/3508398.3511507
29. Hummen, R., Ziegeldorf, J.H., Shafagh, H., Raza, S., Wehrle, K.: Towards viable certificate-based authentication for the Internet of things. In: Proceedings of the HotWiSec '13, pp. 37–42. ACM (2013). https://doi.org/10.1145/2463183.2463193
30. Jäger, L., Lorych, D.: Remote attestation extended to the analog domain. In: Proceedings of the ARES '21. ACM (2021). https://doi.org/10.1145/3465481.3465762
31. Kietzmann, P., Boeckmann, L., Lanzieri, L., Schmidt, T.C., Wählisch, M.: A performance study of crypto-hardware in the low-end IoT. In: Proceedings of the EWSN '21, pp. 79–90. Junction (2021)
32. Kohnhäuser, F.: Advanced Remote Attestation Protocols for Embedded Systems. Ph.D. thesis, Technische Universität Darmstadt (2019)
33. Krawczyk, H.: SIGMA: the 'SIGn-and-MAc' approach to authenticated Diffie-Hellman and its use in the IKE protocols. In: Advances in Cryptology - CRYPTO 2003. CRYPTO 2003. LNCS, vol. 2729, pp. 400–425. Springer, Cham (2003). https://doi.org/10.1007/978-3-540-45146-4_24
34. Krentz, K.F., Voigt, T.: Reducing trust assumptions with OSCORE, RISC-V, and layer 2 one-time passwords. In: Jourdan, GV., Mounier, L., Adams, C., Sèdes, F., Garcia-Alfaro, J. (eds.) Foundations and Practice of Security. FPS 2022. LNCS vol. 13877, pp. 389–405. Springer, Cham (2023). https://doi.org/10.1007/978-3-031-30122-3_24
35. Krentz, K.F., Voigt, T.: More lightweight, yet stronger: revisiting OSCORE's replay protection. In: Proceedings of the SDIoTSec'24. Internet Society (2024). https://doi.org/10.14722/sdiotsec.2024.23003
36. Lee, D., Kohlbrenner, D., Shinde, S., Asanović, K., Song, D.: Keystone: an open framework for architecting trusted execution environments. In: Proceedings of the EuroSys '20. ACM (2020). https://doi.org/10.1145/3342195.3387532

37. Lorych, D., Jäger, L., Fuchs, A.: Acceleration of DICE key generation using key caching. In: Proceedings of the ARES '24. ACM (2024). https://doi.org/10.1145/3664476.3670869
38. Lundblade, L., Mandyam, G., O'Donoghue, J., Wallace, C.: The Entity Attestation Token (EAT). draft-ietf-rats-eat-31 (2024)
39. Luo, C.: Novel Side-Channel Attacks on Emerging Cryptographic Algorithms and Computing Systems. Ph.D. thesis, Northeastern University (2018). https://doi.org/10.17760/D20316363
40. Malik, M., Kamaldeep, Dutta, M., Granjal, J.: L-ECQV: lightweight ECQV implicit certificates for authentication in the Internet of things. IEEE Access 35517–35540 (2023). https://doi.org/10.1109/ACCESS.2023.3261666
41. Mattsson, J.P., Selander, G., Raza, S., HÖglund, J., Furuhed, M.: CBOR Encoded X.509 Certificates (C509 Certificates). draft-ietf-cose-cbor-encoded-cert-13 (2024)
42. MÖssinger, M., et al.: Towards quantifying the cost of a secure IoT: overhead and energy consumption of ECC signatures on an ARM-based device. In: Proceedings of the WoWMoM 2016, pp. 1–6 (2016). https://doi.org/10.1109/WoWMoM.2016.7523559
43. Nunes, I.D.O., Eldefrawy, K., Rattanavipanon, N., Steiner, M., Tsudik, G.: VRASED: a verified Hardware/Software Co-Design for remote attestation. In: Proceedings of the USENIX Security 19, pp. 1429–1446. USENIX (2019)
44. Park, C.S., Park, W.S.: A group-oriented DTLS handshake for secure IoT applications. IEEE Trans. Autom. Sci. Eng. **15**(4), 1920–1929 (2018). https://doi.org/10.1109/TASE.2018.2855640
45. Rescorla, E., Tschofenig, H., Modadugu, N.: The Datagram Transport Layer Security (DTLS) Protocol Version 1.3. RFC 9147 (2022). https://doi.org/10.17487/RFC9147
46. Sarr, A.P., Elbaz-Vincent, P., Bajard, J.C.: A secure and efficient authenticated Diffie-Hellman Protocol. In: Martinelli, F., Preneel, B. (eds.) Public Key Infrastructures, Services and Applications. EuroPKI 2009. LNCS, vol. 6391, pp. 83–98. Springer, Berlin, Heidelberg (2010). https://doi.org/10.1007/978-3-642-16441-5_6
47. Schulz, S., Schaller, A., Kohnhäuser, F., Katzenbeisser, S.: Boot attestation: secure remote reporting with off-the-shelf IoT sensors. In: Foley, S., Gollmann, D., Snekkenes, E. (eds.) Computer Security – ESORICS 2017. ESORICS 2017. LNCS, vol. 10493, pp. 437–455. Springer, Cham (2017). https://doi.org/10.1007/978-3-319-66399-9_24
48. Sciancalepore, S., Capossele, A., Piro, G., Boggia, G., Bianchi, G.: Key management protocol with implicit certificates for IoT systems. In: Proceedings of the 2015 Workshop on IoT Challenges in Mobile and Industrial Systems (IoT-Sys '15), pp. 37–42. IoT-Sys '15, ACM (2015). https://doi.org/10.1145/2753476.2753477
49. Selander, G., Mattsson, J.P., Palombini, F.: Ephemeral Diffie-Hellman Over COSE (EDHOC). RFC 9528 (2024). https://doi.org/10.17487/RFC9528
50. Shelby, Z., Hartke, K., Bormann, C.: The Constrained Application Protocol (CoAP). RFC 7252 (2014). https://doi.org/10.17487/RFC7252
51. Tan, H., Hu, W., Jha, S.: A TPM-enabled remote attestation protocol (TRAP) in wireless sensor networks. In: Proceedings of the PM2HW2N '11, pp. 9–16. ACM (2011) https://doi.org/10.1145/2069087.2069090
52. Tao, Z., Rastogi, A., Gupta, N., Vaswani, K., Thakur, A.V.: DICE*: a formally verified implementation of DICE measured boot. In: Proceedings of the USENIX Security '21, pp. 1091–1107 (2021)

53. Teng, Y., et al.: Curveball+: exploring curveball-like vulnerabilities of implicit certificate validation. In: Tsudik, G., Conti, M., Liang, K., Smaragdakis, G. (eds.) Computer Security – ESORICS 2023. ESORICS 2023. LNCS, vol. 14345, pp. 212–234. Springer, Cham (2024).https://doi.org/10.1007/978-3-031-51476-0_11
54. Texas Instruments: CC2538 SoC for 2.4-GHz IEEE 802.15.4 & ZigBee/ZigBee IP Applications User's Guide (Rev. C), SWRU319C
55. Xu, M., et al.: Dominance as a new trusted computing primitive for the Internet of things. In: Proceedings of the S&P 2019, pp. 1415–1430 (2019). https://doi.org/10.1109/SP.2019.00084
56. Yu, F., Huang, Y.: SDATA: symmetrical device identifier composition engine complied aggregate trust attestation. Symmetry **16**(3) (2024). https://doi.org/10.3390/sym16030310

Lightweight IoT Intrusion Detection with Hybrid Feature Selection and CNN-Driven Image Transformation

Negar Mansouri[1], Seyedeh Leili Mirtaheri[2(✉)], Seyyed Amir Asghari[1], and Andrea Pugliese[2]

[1] Department of Electrical and Computer Engineering, Kharazmi University, Tehran, Iran

[2] Department of Informatics, Modeling, Electronics and System Engineering (DIMES), University of Calabria, Rende, Italy

leili.mirtaheri@dimes.unical.it

Abstract. The increasing prevalence of IoT devices introduces unique cybersecurity challenges due to their limited computational resources and exposure to dynamic threats. This paper proposes an intrusion detection framework that integrates random forest-based feature selection and deep learning techniques. Network traffic is transformed into RGB images using clustering-based feature grouping, enabling the application of convolutional neural networks (CNNs) for accurate detection. Our evaluation on two public datasets (N-BaIoT and IoT-23) shows that the proposed pipeline achieves high detection performance, with accuracies up to 99.96%, while remaining efficient for edge deployment. While our method combines established techniques, its strength lies in the integration of lightweight preprocessing and visual modeling tailored to the IoT context.

Keywords: IoT Security · Intrusion Detection System (IDS) · Traffic Visualization · Convolutional Neural Networks (CNNs)

1 Introduction

The Internet of Things (IoT) has become an important part of modern digital platforms. It makes it possible for everything to be connected and automated, from smart cities [24] and healthcare [14] to industrial systems [23]. The collected big data can help to extract valuable insights and support decision-making through advanced analytics [18,19]. IoT devices with sensors, processors, and communication modules have changed the way real-time tracking and control work [8]. However, as IoT becomes more common, it receives more cybersecurity threats, especially from botnets [28].

Botnets are considered dangerous because they usually exploit IoT devices to perform large-scale hacks like distributed denial-of-service (DDoS) attacks

R. Laborde et al. (Eds.): ESORICS 2025 Workshops, LNCS 16233, pp. 472–485, 2026.
https://doi.org/10.1007/978-3-032-16165-9_28

[11,25]. Traditional intrusion detection systems (IDS), which are mostly rule-based and centralized, have a hard time keeping up with IoT environments, which are flexible, decentralized, and limited in resources. Machine learning (ML) and deep learning (DL) techniques, especially convolutional neural networks (CNNs) [4,9] have been proposed to deal with the IoT security issues. Similar AI-driven approaches have also been applied to other cybersecurity challenges, such as automated vulnerability scoring using large language models and deep learning architectures [20–22]. This is because they can correctly identify abnormal network behavior patterns. In parallel, advances in network representation learning, clustering optimization, and active learning have enhanced the capability to model complex relationships and extract meaningful patterns from data [10,15,16,27]. CNN-based networks can quickly and accurately find and classify cyber threats, especially when they are combined with visual representations of network traffic data [13]. However, it's still hard to put these complicated models straight on IoT devices because CNN-based methods are computationally expensive and IoT environments don't have large memory or processing power.

This paper presents an optimized and lightweight botnet detection framework specifically tailored for IoT environments, which integrates advanced network traffic visualization techniques with CNN-based classification. While this work is rooted in deep learning, it is motivated by the constraints of real-world IoT deployments. These environments are often characterized by limited CPU, memory, and energy resources. As such, we prioritize models with reduced parameter sizes, streamlined inference, and high throughput. Furthermore, the traffic data used reflect the types of threats typically encountered in smart home and industrial IoT settings. This practical orientation ensures that our system remains viable for edge deployment in resource-constrained scenarios, bridging the gap between theoretical detection frameworks and operational IoT systems.

The core contributions of this research are:

- A novel traffic-visualization approach: We transform network traffic data into intuitive, image-like representations that capture important patterns for detecting botnet activities. This method improves the classification accuracy while simplifying the detection process.
- Optimized CNN architectures: We discuss lightweight, edge-friendly convolutional networks that enable high-precision detection for various IoT botnets. By balancing accuracy and computational cost, we address the real-time performance on resource-limited devices.
- Extensive experiments: Leveraging two leading IoT security datasets (N-BaIoT and IoT-23), we show that our framework consistently outperforms common baselines—such as deep neural networks (DNNs) and autoencoders (AEs)—in both detection accuracy and inference speed.

While several machine learning approaches have been proposed for network intrusion detection, many fail to consider the specific limitations of IoT environments. Our work focuses on resource awareness, using dimensionality reduction and image-based transformation to enable CNN usage on edge-constrained devices. By tailoring the preprocessing pipeline and using compact model designs, the framework supports real-time operation under memory and energy constraints typical of IoT gateways. Furthermore, the datasets used in this study represent common botnets targeting consumer and industrial IoT, improving the relevance of our evaluation.

This paper is structured as follows: Sect. 2 reviews existing studies, while Sect. 3 presents the details on the proposed pipeline for transforming network traffic data into visual formats. This section also presents the evaluated CNN, DNN, and AE architectures. Section 4 presents the experimental outcomes and compares the performance of our proposed framework against a recent existing method presented in [5]. Finally, Sect. 5 concludes the paper, highlighting our findings and addressing future research directions.

2 Related Works

Researchers have explored numerous methods to detect and prevent cyberattacks, leveraging deep learning approaches [6]. This section reviews several recent studies focusing on IoT security and anomaly detection.

Abbasi et al. [1] investigated DNN approaches to detect botnet activities in IoT networks. Their study utilized dimensionality reduction and feature selection techniques to optimize classifier performance, achieving a high accuracy of 99.9% with reduced computational complexity. Among the tested methods, CNN and multilayer perceptrons (MLP) showed better performance. Wang et al. [26] compared Long Short-Term Memory (LSTM) and CNN models for IoT botnet detection, reporting accuracies of 99.13% for LSTM and 98.92% for CNN. The study demonstrated that dimensionality reduction significantly reduced processing time by approximately 35% without significantly compromising detection accuracy. In another study, the authors introduced ELBA-IoT, an ensemble learning model combining Random Forest (RF), Gradient Boosting (GB), and Decision Trees (DT), achieving a detection accuracy of 97.8% [3]. The ensemble learning approach notably enhanced system performance while reducing false alerts. Douiba et al. [7] proposed an anomaly detection model using a combination of decision trees and gradient boosting decision trees (GBDT), which achieved a 95.4% accuracy rate. Their research demonstrated that combining tree-based models with optimization techniques significantly improves detection accuracy. Abdalgawad et al. [2] use generative deep learning methods like adversarial autoencoders (AAE) and bidirectional genetic adversarial networks (BiGAN) for intrusion detection in IoT networks, achieving an F1 score of 0.99.

Autoencoders have gained attention due to their efficiency in detecting deviations from typical network behavior. Such models encode normal network patterns into a lower-dimensional space, with anomalies detected based on increased reconstruction error. These models are advantageous in reducing false alarms and enhancing the accuracy of threat detection. For instance, Meidan et al. [17] used autoencoders effectively for detecting botnets within IoT networks. Kalidindi et al. [12] used CNN fused with deep stacked autoencoder (CNN-FDSA) for botnet attack detection. The CNN-FDSA achieved recall, precision, f-measure, and accuracy of 93.3%, 91.6%, 91.9%, and 92.4%, with the lowest false positive rate (FPR) of 8.2%.

Prior research, and in particular the work presented in [5] illustrate the advantages of CNN-based traffic visualization. They show that the accuracy of multi-class classification is limited by more fundamental feature extraction methods. This paper fills the gap by including improved data preprocessing and advanced visualization approaches to enhance detection effectiveness for various IoT botnets. While image-based representations of data have been effectively used in domains such as healthcare diagnostics, financial fraud detection, and industrial control systems, their application in intrusion detection for IoT networks remains relatively underexplored. For instance, CNN-driven image classification has demonstrated strong performance in identifying anomalies in electrocardiogram (ECG) patterns and financial transactions. By drawing inspiration from these domains, our approach adapts the traffic visualization paradigm to suit the unique characteristics and constraints of IoT environments. A comparative study of these approaches in Sect. 4 further highlights the novelty and domain-specific optimization of our model.

3 Proposed Architectures

To provide a clearer understanding of the framework's design, we first outline the interconnection between its components. The system starts with data acquisition and preprocessing using random forest and clustering-based methods to extract the most relevant features. These features are then transformed into RGB image representations, which serve as input to various deep learning models. The CNN model, in particular, processes these images to learn spatial hierarchies corresponding to attack patterns. The output is a multi-class classifier that flags malicious activity. This modular yet interlinked architecture allows flexible optimization at both preprocessing and classification stages, ensuring adaptability across different IoT scenarios.

3.1 Preprocessing

Transforming tabular network data into images may seem counterintuitive at first; however, this approach leverages CNNs' strength in learning spatial hierarchies. While raw features lack natural ordering, our clustering-based method groups semantically related attributes (e.g., entropy, packet count, jitter) into fixed image positions. This artificial spatial structure helps CNNs recognize co-occurrence and intensity patterns indicative of specific attacks. To enhance interpretability and performance, we transform selected network traffic features into image-like representations. Unlike conventional traffic matrices or flow charts, our method generates RGB-encoded visualizations where clusters of features are mapped spatially into a 2D grid. Figure 1 and Fig. 2 illustrate the resulting transformation for a sample data point, demonstrating how correlated features are grouped visually. This transformation enables CNNs to exploit spatial patterns in network behavior, such as coordinated port scans or volumetric attacks, which are often difficult to capture in tabular format.

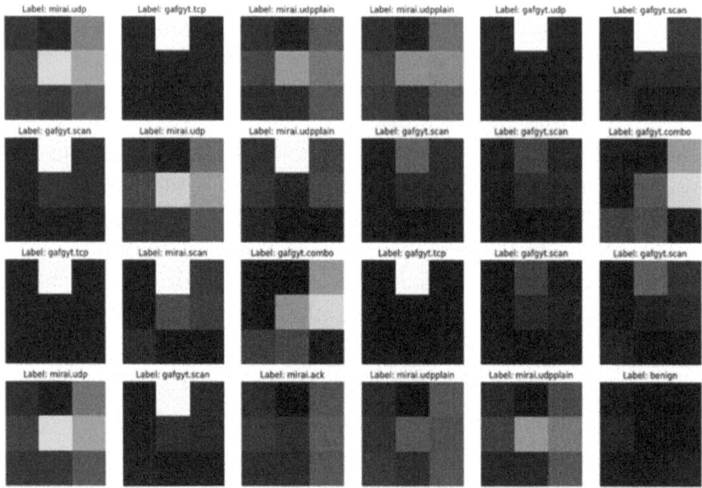

Fig. 1. Example of an RGB image generated from clustered and scaled features of network traffic from the N-BaIoT dataset.

We consider the Random Forest (RF) algorithm for filtering the datasets and feature selection. We compute the features from the trained RF on the dataset and select the important ones based on a predefined threshold. This filtering process improves model efficiency by reducing noise and computational complexity due to the selection of only important features. These selected features represent diverse aspects of network traffic behavior, including entropy, mutual information, jitter, and weighted values. Their selection is based on their strong correlation with identifying attacks and distinguishing normal traffic patterns. These features are then encoded to deal with categorical labels besides the numerical values. Feature values are standardized, ensuring that values are scaled with a mean of zero and a standard deviation of one. This normalization step optimizes model performance by eliminating disparities in feature magnitude. The processes for the two considered real-world datasets (N-BaIoT[1], IoT-23[2]) are presented in the following. After standardizing, we employ the KMeans clustering, and the output clusters are mapped onto an RGB image. The generated images serve as inputs for deep learning models. These steps include:

RGB Image Generation for N-BaIoT Dataset.

- Feature Scaling: Normalize feature values to $[0, 255]$ using "MinMaxScaler".

[1] https://www.kaggle.com/datasets/mkashifn/nbaiot-dataset.
[2] https://www.kaggle.com/datasets/astralfate/iot23-dataset.

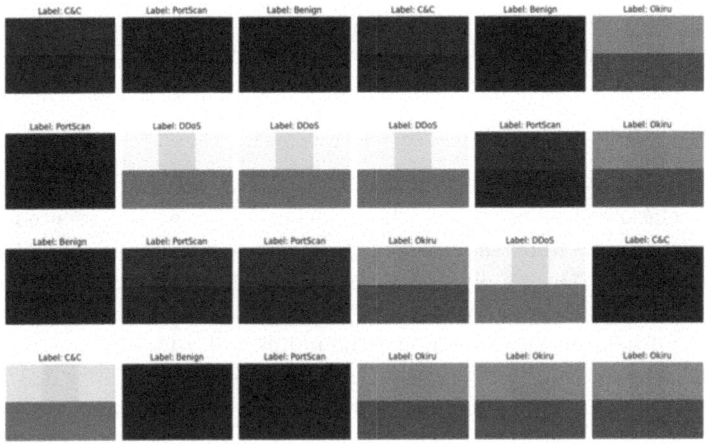

Fig. 2. Example of an RGB image generated from clustered and scaled features of network traffic from the IoT-23 dataset.

- Clustering: Apply KMeans ($k = 9$) clustering to group features based on similarity.
- Feature-to-Image Mapping: Initialize a $3 \times 3 \times 3$ RGB image for each data point. Assign feature values to different grid positions based on cluster assignments.

RGB Image Generation for IoT-23 Dataset.

- Feature Scaling: normalizing feature values to $[0, 255]$ using "MinMaxScaler".
- Clustering: dividing the features into six clusters using agglomerative clustering, each mapped to an RGB channel.
- Feature-to-Image Mapping: transforming each sample into a 2×3 RGB image, with clusters assigned to different color channels.

The rationale for using image-based transformation lies in enabling spatial feature extraction through CNNs. While tabular network data lacks natural spatial correlation, clustering-based grouping of features simulates structural locality. This design allows CNNs to capture correlations between semantically related features, such as timing jitter, entropy, and flow counts, which often co-occur in coordinated attacks. We acknowledge that this transformation introduces a degree of abstraction, but it is justified by prior works [5] and future work will explore more principled embedding strategies to enhance interpretability.

3.2 Evaluated Models

This section presents the optimized deep learning-based models incorporating DNN, CNN, and AE. Each model is designed to optimize accuracy, computational efficiency, and anomaly detection capabilities in IoT botnet classification.

We implemented these models using *PyTorch*, which provides flexibility and efficiency, especially when handling large datasets and complex architectures.

3.3 DNN Model

The DNN model consists of four layers and employs non-linear transformations to improve classification accuracy. The model architecture is presented in Fig. 3. The input layer aims to extract features from the N-BaIoT and IoT-23 datasets. The hidden layers (three fully connected) are followed by a `Tanh` function to introduce non-linearity and enhance the learning capability. In the output layer, the number of neurons should support the number of attack classes that is realized by `Softmax` activation to convert the outputs into probability distributions. To enhance model performance, several optimization techniques were applied. The `CrossEntropyLoss` is utilized to ensure its suitability for multi-class problems. L1 regularization is considered to prevent overfitting by reducing model complexity and encouraging sparsity in learned weights. The `AdamW` optimizer is employed for weight optimization, offering adaptive learning rate adjustments and improved generalization. To prevent overfitting, training is stopped when validation performance is satisfactory over multiple consecutive epochs.
The optimized network structure is as follows:

- Layer 1: Input $\rightarrow$ 115 neurons, Activation: `Tanh`, Regularization: $L1$
- Layer 2: 115 $\rightarrow$ 64 neurons, Activation: `Tanh`, No Regularization
- Layer 3: 64 $\rightarrow$ 32 neurons, Activation: `Tanh`, No Regularization
- Layer 4: 32 $\rightarrow$ Output neurons, Activation: `Softmax`

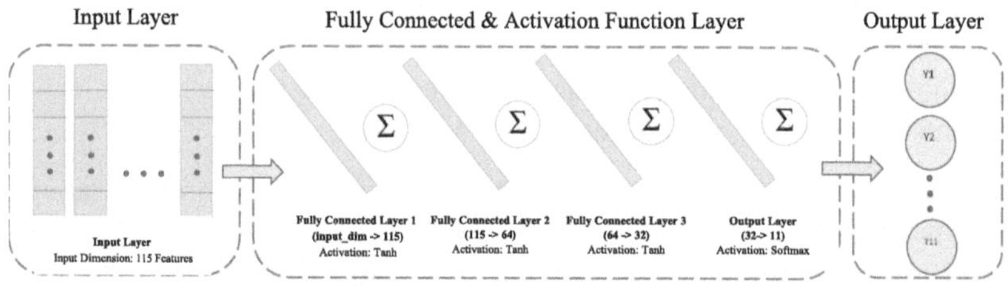

Fig. 3. Optimized DNN architecture for IoT intrusion detection.

3.4 CNN Model

The optimized CNN consists of three convolutional layers to extract hierarchical spatial patterns from network images. To stabilize training and accelerate convergence, we apply *batch normalization* after each convolutional layer. The `ReLU` activation function is used to introduce non-linearity and enhance network capacity. The utilized Global Average Pooling (GAP) reduces feature dimensions efficiently while preserving critical information. Flattened feature maps are passed through two fully connected layers for classification. Finally, the `dropout` is applied to mitigate overfitting by randomly deactivating neurons during training. The details of the optimized CNN, shown in Fig. 4, are listed in the following.

- Layer 1: Conv (3 → 16 filters), Kernel: 3, Activation: `ReLU`, Batch Normalization
- Layer 2: Conv (16 → 32 filters), Kernel: 3, Activation: `ReLU`, Batch Normalization
- Layer 3: Conv (32 → 64 filters), Kernel: 3, Activation: `ReLU`, Batch Normalization
- Layer 4: Global Average Pooling
- Layer 5: Fully Connected (64 → 128 neurons), Activation: `ReLU`, Dropout: 0.4
- Layer 6: Fully Connected (128 → num_classes), Output Layer

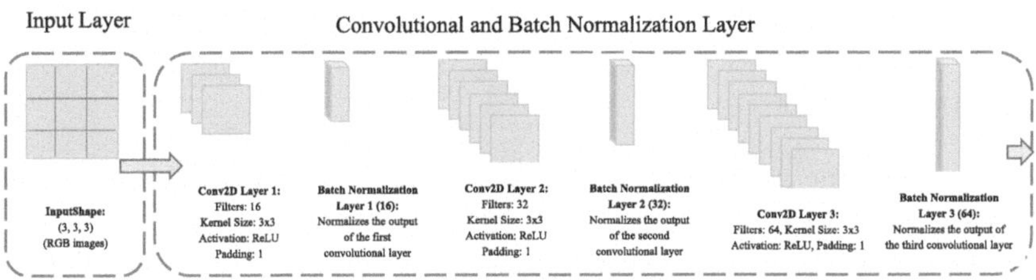

Fig. 4. Optimized CNN architecture for IoT intrusion detection.

3.5 Autoencoder

Autoencoders are applied for unsupervised learning to reconstruct input data and detect anomalies by analyzing reconstruction errors. The autoencoder consists of an encoder-decoder structure. In the encoder, three convolutional layers are used to reduce input dimensions while preserving key information. This is followed by fully connected layers to extract high-level feature representations before classification. Finally, the decoder reconstructs the original input from compressed representations by transposing the convolutional layers. The AE architecture is presented in Fig. 5.

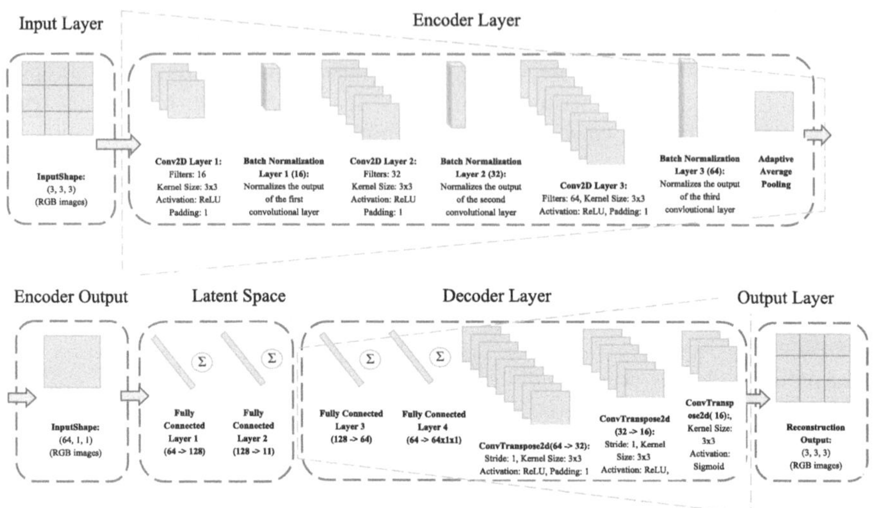

Fig. 5. Optimized AE architecture for IoT intrusion detection.

4 Experiments

After balancing the datasets, we split them randomly into training, validation, and testing sets with proportions of 60%, 20%, and 20%, respectively. For autoencoder and CNN models, the data is converted into images for training, validation, and testing. The DNN is considered the baseline model; therefore, no preprocessing was applied in our experiments. We consider accuracy, precision, recall, and F1-score as our evaluation metrics. The software packages and datasets used in this paper are publicly available[3].

4.1 Multi-class Performance

The IoT-23 dataset consists of 5 attack classes, while the N-BaIoT dataset includes 11 classes. We implemented and evaluated the optimized models on both datasets for multi-class classification. The results are presented in Table 1. Additionally, Table 2 provides the comparison results with the baseline [5]. The results show that the AE achieved the highest classification accuracy, followed by CNN and DNN for the N-BaIoT dataset. In the case of the IoT-23 dataset, the DNN model shows superior performance compared to AE and CNN. To address potential class imbalance in both datasets, we expand our evaluation to include precision, recall, and F1-score for each class, along with macro and weighted averages. These metrics offer a more nuanced view of model performance, particularly for underrepresented classes. Table 2 presents this detailed breakdown, showing that the DNN model achieves balanced precision-recall tradeoffs, especially in the IoT-23 dataset. Such comprehensive analysis ensures that our evaluation is not solely reliant on accuracy, which may be misleading in imbalanced settings.

[3] https://github.com/ShahbazianR/IoT_Intrusion_CNN.

Table 1. Performance of Optimized CNN, DNN, and AE Models Over N-BaIoT and IoT-23 datasets.

Dataset	Model	Accuracy (%)	Precision (%)	Recall (%)	F1-score (%)
N-BaIoT	AE	90	86	91	88
	DNN	89	85	90	87
	CNN	90	93	91	88
IoT-23	AE	89	90	89	88
	DNN	98	98	98	98
	CNN	88	89	88	87

Table 2. Comparison of Proposed and Baseline Model Accuracy

Dataset	Model	Optimized Accuracy (%)	Baseline Accuracy (%) [5]
N-BaIoT	AE	89.89	66.87
	DNN	88.74	78.74
	CNN	89.85	69.29
IoT-23	AE	88.94	66.80
	DNN	99.64	72.22
	CNN	88.27	76.31

As shown in Fig. 6, the CNN model does not precisely distinguish between Gafgyt UDP and Gafgyt Combo attacks in the N-BaIoT dataset. Similarly, both the autoencoder and DNN models have difficulty in differentiating between Gafgyt UDP and Gafgyt TCP attacks within the N-BaIoT dataset.

Figure 7 indicates that the CNN and autoencoder models have difficulties in distinguishing between benign and port scan activities in the IoT-23 dataset. A closer examination suggests that these two attack types share similar characteristics. This visual similarity is likely the primary reason behind the misclassifications. In contrast, the DNN model demonstrates strong performance in distinguishing different attack types within the IoT-23 dataset.

Since IoT devices have limited storage capacity, DL models must maintain high accuracy while utilizing the minimum possible memory. For edge deployment on IoT devices, reducing the number of parameters leads to faster processing and lower resource consumption. Therefore, there is a need to balance accuracy and model complexity, considering the hardware limits. The number of trainable parameters for the optimized model and the baseline model are given in Table 3. These results indicate that our optimized autoencoder model reduces the number of parameters. However, the optimized CNN model requires more parameters compared to the baseline due to the added complexity in the proposed architecture. The *throughput* refers to the number of data packets processed per second and can be calculated as presented in (1). Optimizing computational efficiency directly impacts real-time performance.

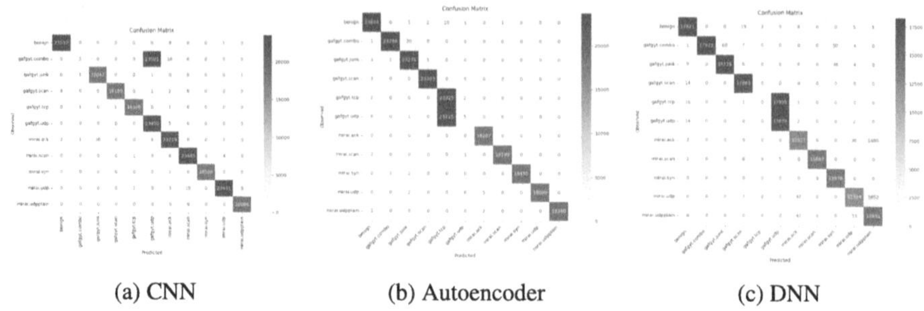

(a) CNN (b) Autoencoder (c) DNN

Fig. 6. Confusion matrices for CNN, autoencoder, and DNN models on the N-BaIoT dataset.

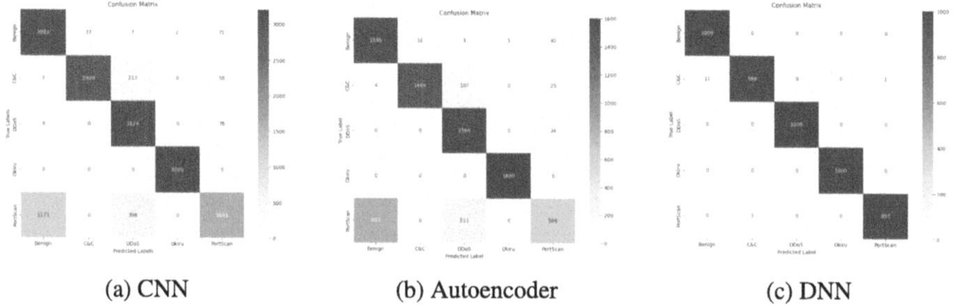

(a) CNN (b) Autoencoder (c) DNN

Fig. 7. Confusion matrices for CNN, autoencoder, and DNN models on the IoT-23 dataset.

$$\text{Throughput} = \frac{\text{Total Packets Processed}}{\text{Total Inference Time (seconds)}} \quad (1)$$

Although our CNN model achieves superior accuracy, we recognize the increase in parameter count relative to the baseline. The proposed model prioritizes detection accuracy under constrained conditions, and we strike a balance by optimizing the CNN depth and applying GAP and dropout layers to reduce inference time. Table 3 illustrates this trade-off. Nonetheless, we acknowledge that alternative methods such as boosting-based models offer attractive efficiency profiles. These will be incorporated in future comparative studies to assess where CNN-based models provide irreplaceable benefits. Table 3 shows the throughput of the optimized DNN and CNN models compared with the baseline models [5]. The AE requires both a generator and a classifier for each class and can perform in sequential or parallel mode. This leads to inconsistent throughput measurements.

Although our experiments primarily focus on the N-BaIoT and IoT-23 datasets, the proposed framework is inherently scalable. The feature selection and clustering modules do not rely on dataset-specific structures and can be extended to other labeled or semi-labeled datasets. Moreover, the image-based

Table 3. Comparison of optimized models and the baseline model [5] on IoT-23 and N-BaIoT datasets over throughput and number of parameters.

Dataset	Model	Throughput	Throughput [5]	# Parameters	# Parameters [5]
IoT-23	AE	–	–	48549	–
	DNN	20661	–	13317	–
	CNN	15506	–	26437	–
N-BaIoT	AE	–	–	69582	189756
	DNN	38947	7000	23207	23207
	CNN	45770	17000	33547	18231

transformation abstracts raw traffic into a uniform format, enabling the CNN to generalize across traffic sources. Future work will include validation across additional public and proprietary datasets to assess broader applicability and domain independence.

5 Conclusions and Future Work

This paper presented a lightweight yet effective intrusion detection framework that integrates advanced feature selection and deep learning techniques. By transforming network traffic into image-based representations, our CNN-driven approach achieves high accuracy in identifying malicious activities. The experiment results demonstrate significant improvements over traditional methods, particularly in handling complex attack patterns in real-world IoT-23 and N-BaIoT datasets. We considered the computational efficiency to provide compatibility with resource-constrained IoT devices. The comparison with existing models confirms the effectiveness of our optimized preprocessing pipeline and CNN-based architectures. While our work builds on existing techniques such as feature selection, autoencoders, and CNNs, the contribution lies in their integration into a lightweight, image-driven IDS pipeline optimized for IoT. Unlike traditional methods, we explore a clustering-based visual encoding of traffic features and analyze its trade-offs.

Future work will explore further optimizations for deployment on ultra-low-power devices and adaptation to emerging attack patterns. Additionally, integrating explainable AI (XAI) techniques could enhance the trustworthiness of intrusion detection models. Although deep learning-based intrusion detection is an active research area, our contribution lies in bridging feature selection and image-based representation to enhance detection in IoT environments. The proposed framework is not merely another neural network model but a composite system optimized for edge scenarios and validated across multiple datasets. We acknowledge that generative tools assisted in improving writing clarity, but every technical decision and experimental result is original and rigorously tested. We hope this work contributes practically to the growing need for lightweight, real-time IoT security solutions.

Acknowledgment. We acknowledge that two authors of this paper (S.L.M. and A.P.) received financial support from the PNRR MUR project *SERICS* (PE00000014).

Declaration of Generative AI. During the preparation of this work, the authors used ChatGPT-4 and QuillBot in order to assist in paraphrasing, grammar correction, and rewording complex sentences for enhanced readability. After using these tools, the author(s) reviewed and edited the content as needed and take full responsibility for the content of the publication.

References

1. Abbasi, F., Naderan, M., Alavi, S.E.: Anomaly detection in internet of things using feature selection and classification based on logistic regression and artificial neural network on n-baiot dataset. In: 2021 5th International Conference on Internet of Things and Applications (IoT), pp. 1–7. IEEE (2021)
2. Abdalgawad, N., Sajun, A., Kaddoura, Y., Zualkernan, I.A., Aloul, F.: Generative deep learning to detect cyberattacks for the IoT-23 dataset. IEEE Access **10**, 6430–6441 (2021)
3. Abu Al-Haija, Q., Al-Dala'ien, M.: Elba-IoT: an ensemble learning model for botnet attack detection in IoT networks. J. Sens. Actuator Netw. **11**(1), 18 (2022)
4. Alshehri, M.S., Ahmad, J., Almakdi, S., Al Qathrady, M., Ghadi, Y.Y., Buchanan, W.J.: Skipgatenet: a lightweight CNN-LSTM hybrid model with learnable skip connections for efficient botnet attack detection in IoT. IEEE Access (2024)
5. Arnold, D., Gromov, M., Saniie, J.: Network traffic visualization coupled with convolutional neural networks for enhanced IoT botnet detection. IEEE Access (2024)
6. Bahşi, H., Nõmm, S., La Torre, F.B.: Dimensionality reduction for machine learning based IoT botnet detection. In: 2018 15th International Conference on Control, Automation, Robotics and Vision (ICARCV), pp. 1857–1862. IEEE (2018)
7. Douiba, M., Benkirane, S., Guezzaz, A., Azrour, M.: An improved anomaly detection model for IoT security using decision tree and gradient boosting. J. Supercomput. **79**(3), 3392–3411 (2023)
8. Dui, H., Zhang, S., Liu, M., Dong, X., Bai, G.: IoT-enabled real-time traffic monitoring and control management for intelligent transportation systems. IEEE Internet Things J. **11**(9), 15842–15854 (2024)
9. Yamani, E.L., Y., Baddi, Y., EL Kamoun, N.: A survey on the contribution of ml and dl to the detection and prevention of botnet attacks. J. Reliable Intell. Environ. **10**(4), 431–448 (2024)
10. Flesca, S., Mandaglio, D., Scala, F., Tagarelli, A.: A meta-active learning approach exploiting instance importance. Expert Syst. Appl. **247**, 123320 (2024). https://doi.org/10.1016/j.eswa.2024.123320
11. Gelgi, M., Guan, Y., Arunachala, S., Samba Siva Rao, M., Dragoni, N.: Systematic literature review of IoT botnet ddos attacks and evaluation of detection techniques. Sensors **24**(11), 3571 (2024)
12. Kalidindi, A., Arrama, M.B.: Feature selection and hybrid CNNF deep stacked autoencoder for botnet attack detection in IoT. Comput. Electr. Eng. **122**, 109984 (2025)
13. Kharoubi, K., Cherbal, S., Mechta, D., Gawanmeh, A.: Network intrusion detection system using convolutional neural networks: NIDS-DL-CNN for IoT security. Clust. Comput. **28**(4), 219 (2025)

14. Li, C., Wang, J., Wang, S., Zhang, Y.: A review of IoT applications in healthcare. Neurocomputing **565**, 127017 (2024)
15. Mandaglio, D., Tagarelli, A., Gullo, F.: In and out: optimizing overall interaction in probabilistic graphs under clustering constraints. In: Proc. KDD Conf, pp. 1371–1381 (2020). https://doi.org/10.1145/3394486.3403190
16. Mandaglio, D., Tagarelli, A., Gullo, F.: Correlation clustering with global weight bounds. In: Proc. ECML PKDD Conf. vol. 12976, pp. 499–515 (2021). https://doi.org/10.1007/978-3-030-86520-7_31
17. Meidan, Y., Bohadana, M., Mathov, Y., Mirsky, Y., Shabtai, A., Breitenbacher, D., Elovici, Y.: N-baiot–network-based detection of iot botnet attacks using deep autoencoders. IEEE Pervasive Comput. **17**(3), 12–22 (2018)
18. Mirarab, A., Mirtaheri, S.L., Asghari, S.A.: Value creation with big data analytics for enterprises: a survey. TELKOMNIKA (Telecommun. Comput. Electron. Control) **17**(6), 2790–2802 (2019)
19. Mirarab, A., Mirtaheri, S.L., Asghari, S.A.: A model to create organizational value with big data analytics. Comput. Syst. Sci. Eng. **35**(2), 69–79 (2020)
20. Mirtaheri, S.L., Pugliese, A.: Leveraging generative ai to enhance automated vulnerability scoring. In: 2024 IEEE Conference on Dependable, Autonomic and Secure Computing (DASC), pp. 57–64. IEEE (2024)
21. Mirtaheri, S.L., Pugliese, A., Movahed, N., Shahbazian, R.: A comparative analysis on using GPT and Bert for automated vulnerability scoring. Intell. Syst. Appl. **26**, 200515 (2025)
22. Mirtaheri, S.L., Pugliese, A., Movahedkor, N., Majd, A.: Advanced automated vulnerability scoring: Improving performance with a fine-tuned Bert-CNN model. In: 2024 11th International Symposium on Telecommunications (IST), pp. 109–113. IEEE (2024)
23. Mu, X., Antwi-Afari, M.F.: The applications of internet of things (Iot) in industrial management: a science mapping review. Int. J. Prod. Res. **62**(5), 1928–1952 (2024)
24. Nassereddine, M., Khang, A.: Applications of internet of things (Iot) in smart cities. In: Advanced Iot Technologies and Applications in the industry 4.0 Digital Economy, pp. 109–136. CRC Press (2024)
25. Sharma, A., Babbar, H.: Iot-pot: machine learning-based detection of mirai botnet attacks in Iot. In: 2024 First International Conference on Innovations in Communications, Electrical and Computer Engineering (ICICEC), pp. 1–6. IEEE (2024)
26. Wang, H., Guo, D., Wei, J., Li, J.: A method of classifying Iot devices based on attack sensitivity. J. Inf. Secur. Appl. **82**, 103751 (2024)
27. Zangari, L., Mandaglio, D., Tagarelli, A.: Link prediction on multilayer networks through learning of within-layer and across-layer node-pair structural features and node embedding similarity. In: Proc. WWW Conf, pp. 924–935 (2024). https://doi.org/10.1145/3589334.3645646
28. Zhukabayeva, T., Zholshiyeva, L., Ven-Tsen, K., Adamova, A., Mardenov, Y., Karabayev, N.: Enhancing Iot security: effective botnet attack detection through machine learning. Procedia Comput. Sci. **241**, 421–426 (2024)

Function-Level Syscall Fingerprinting for IoT Malware Capability Classification

Yutaro Osako[1,4(✉)], Hayato Hamano[1], Yuto Aono[1], Toshihiro Yamauchi[2], Katsunari Yoshioka[3], Takahiro Kasama[4], Takuya Fujihashi[1], and Shunsuke Saruwatari[1]

[1] The University of Osaka, Osaka, Japan
[2] Okayama University, Okayama, Japan
[3] Yokohama National University, Yokohama, Japan
[4] National Institute of Information and Communications Technology, Tokyo, Japan
osako.yutaro@ist.osaka-u.ac.jp

Abstract. This paper presents a function-level syscall fingerprinting approach for cross-architecture Internet of Things (IoT) malware capability profiling. Our method extracts syscall patterns from malware functions across MIPS, PowerPC, and i586 architectures, generating normalized syscall fingerprints that enable immediate capability assessment without requiring family-based classification or dynamic execution. Cross-architecture consistency evaluation using Mirai, Lizkebab, and Bashlite demonstrates reliable normalization effectiveness, with PowerPC-i586 pairs achieving the strongest similarity, while capability profiling evaluation shows effective inference for unknown Lizkebab functions against Mirai and Bashlite reference databases. Performance analysis confirms linear scaling with an average processing time of 7.3 s, while case studies demonstrate effective capability inference for unknown functions. The approach enables rapid, architecture-agnostic malware analysis suitable for heterogeneous IoT environments where traditional approaches face scalability limitations.

Keywords: IoT malware · function-level fingerprinting · cross-architecture compatibility · capability profiling · system call

1 Introduction

The IoT ecosystem has experienced unprecedented growth in recent years, embedding connected devices across domains ranging from smart homes to critical infrastructure. Unlike traditional x86 environments, IoT devices employ heterogeneous CPU architectures spanning diverse instruction sets and calling conventions across different embedded platforms. This widespread proliferation, combined with inherent security weaknesses, has created a vast attack surface that enables large-scale botnet recruitment and facilitates devastating

R. Laborde et al. (Eds.): ESORICS 2025 Workshops, LNCS 16233, pp. 486–502, 2026.
https://doi.org/10.1007/978-3-032-16165-9_29

Distributed Denial of Service (DDoS) attacks. Modern IoT malware can compromise thousands of devices within hours, making rapid analysis a critical operational requirement.

Effective cross-architecture IoT malware analysis requires satisfying three fundamental requirements: **R1. Cross-architecture compatibility**: Analysis must work consistently across diverse CPU architectures without platform-specific adaptations. **R2. Immediate capability profiling**: The approach must identify *what* malware can do rather than *which family* it belongs to, enabling rapid incident response. **R3. Lightweight static analysis**: The pipeline must operate with minimal computational overhead suitable for resource-constrained environments.

Current approaches have limitations in simultaneously satisfying these requirements. Hash-based methods [1] provide fast analysis but lack cross-architecture compatibility and cannot profile unknown variants. Graph-based approaches [2,3] address cross-architecture challenges but require pre-trained family patterns and substantial computational resources. Dynamic analysis faces scalability limitations in resource-constrained IoT environments. Existing approaches have difficulty combining all three requirements in a unified framework.

This paper proposes a function-level syscall fingerprinting approach that addresses all three requirements. Our method extracts function call graphs from malware binaries across diverse CPU architectures, generating unique fingerprints based on normalized system call patterns. Cross-architecture normalization maps architecture-specific implementations to common functional semantics, enabling immediate capability profiling without dynamic execution while maintaining computational efficiency.

Our key contributions include:

- A function-level syscall fingerprinting methodology that generates consistent signatures across MIPS, PowerPC, and i586 architectures through semantic normalization, enabling immediate capability profiling without requiring family-based classification
- Comprehensive evaluation using Mirai, Lizkebab, and Bashlite demonstrating reliable cross-architecture consistency
- Performance validation using 50 IoT malware samples confirming linear scaling characteristics with mean processing time of 7.3 s.

2 Related Work

This section examines existing malware analysis approaches through the lens of the three fundamental requirements established in Sect. 1.

2.1 Cross-Architecture Compatibility (R1)

The first requirement, cross-architecture compatibility, demands analysis techniques that function consistently across diverse CPU architectures without platform-specific adaptations.

Several approaches have achieved cross-architecture compatibility through different methodologies. Su et al. [4] propose converting binary code into grayscale images for CNN-based classification, achieving consistent representation across MIPS, ARM, and x86 platforms by eliminating instruction-level dependencies. Their approach demonstrates effective cross-architecture malware family classification through image-based feature extraction. Deng et al. [3] develop Enimanal, using attributed system call graphs with graph neural networks to handle architectural differences in IoT malware. Their framework achieves effective performance across ARM, MIPS, and x86 architectures through graph-level feature extraction that abstracts from architecture-specific implementations. Lee et al. [5] utilize printable string information as architecture-agnostic features, demonstrating effective cross-platform analysis for IoT malware classification across heterogeneous architectures.

Building upon the concept of architectural abstraction, several approaches have explored intermediate representation (IR) based methods for achieving cross-architecture compatibility. Greco et al. [6] propose a cross-architecture malware detection method using intermediate representations to normalize instruction-level differences, achieving consistent analysis across diverse CPU architectures through compiler-independent semantic modeling. Similarly, Song et al. [7] introduce Inter-bin, an interaction-based framework that leverages behavioral patterns and control flow interactions to establish semantic equivalence across different instruction sets for IoT binary similarity comparison. Extending this IR-based approach, Collyer et al. [8] develop FASER for binary code similarity search, enabling function-level cross-architecture matching through semantic abstraction rather than syntactic instruction patterns. While these IR-based approaches demonstrate promising directions for cross-architecture analysis and successfully address architectural compatibility challenges, they typically focus on similarity detection and family classification rather than capability profiling, and require substantial preprocessing and compilation-level transformations that may impact deployment efficiency in resource-constrained IoT environments.

2.2 Capability Profiling of Unknown Malware (R2)

The second requirement, capability profiling of unknown malware, demands identifying functional capabilities of previously unseen malware variants without relying on family-based classification.

Several research efforts have addressed capability profiling through various methodologies. Vasan et al. [9] present DEEPCAPA, a deep learning approach for identifying malicious capabilities in Windows malware that automatically learns capability signatures from large-scale datasets. Their framework achieves automated capability identification through neural network-based pattern recognition, demonstrating effective capability detection for previously unseen malware samples. Chen et al. [10] develop semantic-aware detection methods that focus on behavioral patterns rather than signature-based identification, enabling cross-architecture analysis of IoT malware variants. Their framework provides functional insights for malware analysis across diverse embedded architectures including ARM, MIPS, and x86 platforms. Saha et al. [11] propose MalXCap, a multi-label classification approach for malware capability extraction that automatically identifies specific malicious functionalities from binary samples. Their method employs machine learning techniques to map malware behaviors to predefined capability categories, enabling systematic capability profiling for security analysis and threat assessment.

2.3 Fast and Lightweight Analysis (R3)

The third requirement, fast and lightweight analysis, demands techniques with minimal computational overhead suitable for resource-constrained IoT environments.

Farfoura et al. propose a lightweight machine learning framework that converts binaries into down-sampled byte-images and classifies them into multiple families on embedded boards with minimal processing time and compact model parameters [12]. Wang et al. introduce an LMDNet model, which distils features to a compact network that assigns samples to known families with fast inference times [13]. Although these studies satisfy the computational constraints of R3 and extend beyond mere binary detection to provide family-level output, they neither normalise across architectures (R1) nor infer fine-grained capabilities required by R2.

2.4 Research Positioning and Novelty

The analysis of existing work reveals that while individual research efforts successfully address specific requirements, no current approach simultaneously satisfies all three fundamental requirements for comprehensive IoT malware analysis.

The fundamental challenge lies in the inherent trade-offs between these requirements: achieving cross-architecture compatibility often requires complex processing that violates lightweight constraints, while capability profiling approaches typically focus on single-architecture scenarios and lack computational efficiency evaluation.

Our research addresses this gap through function-level syscall fingerprinting that integrates semantic cross-architecture normalization for R1, capability-focused analysis independent of family classification for R2, and static analysis suitable for lightweight deployment for R3. This integrated approach enables practical capability profiling of unknown malware variants across heterogeneous architectures while maintaining computational efficiency.

3 Proposed Approach

3.1 Function-Level Syscall Fingerprinting Overview

Our function-level syscall fingerprinting approach consists of six main stages that enable capability profiling of unknown malware variants by leveraging fingerprint patterns observed in known samples as shown in Fig. 1. The approach begins with (1) function extraction and disassembly, where static analysis using radare2 identifies function boundaries and extracts disassembly code for each function across MIPS, PowerPC, and i586 architectures. The pipeline then performs (2) architecture-specific syscall identification through pattern matching to identify system call invocations within each function, accounting for architecture-specific calling conventions and instruction patterns. To enable cross-platform consistency, the approach implements (3) cross-architecture normalization, mapping architecture-specific system call numbers and mechanisms to unified semantic labels for consistent fingerprint generation across different CPU architectures. The normalized syscall patterns are then processed through (4) fingerprint generation, creating functional fingerprints for each function represented as binary vectors encoding syscall presence. These individual fingerprints contribute to (5) reference database construction, building a comprehensive database of function fingerprints from known malware samples with labeled capabilities and metadata across multiple architectures. Finally, the approach enables (6) similarity-based matching and capability inference, comparing unknown malware fingerprints against the reference database using Jaccard similarity to infer functional capabilities through nearest neighbor matching.

This end-to-end pipeline enables immediate capability identification for unknown malware variants by leveraging fingerprint patterns observed in known samples, without requiring family-based classification or dynamic execution environments.

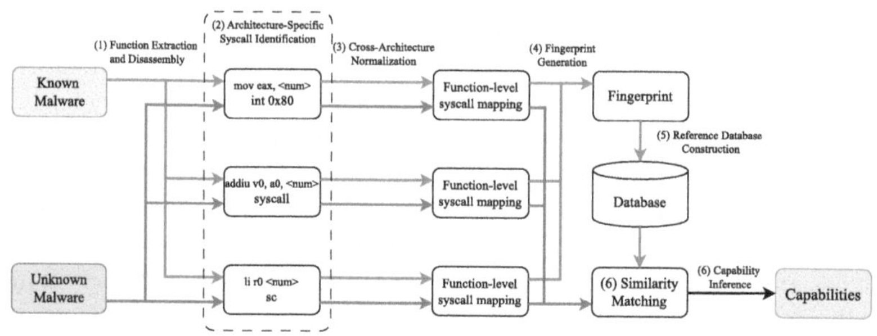

Fig. 1. System overview of the function-level syscall fingerprinting pipeline.

3.2 Function Extraction and Architecture-Specific Syscall Identification

We utilize radare2's static analysis capabilities [14] through r2pipe to identify function boundaries using call/return patterns, jump targets, and symbol information. For each function f_i, we establish boundaries $[\text{addr}_{\text{start}}, \text{addr}_{\text{end}}]$ for precise syscall attribution.

System call identification varies across architectures due to different calling conventions. MIPS uses `syscall` instruction with syscall number in `$v0`. PowerPC employs `sc` instruction with number in `r0`. i586 uses `int 0x80` interrupt with number in `eax`, plus modern `sysenter`/`syscall` variants. For each function f_i, this generates raw syscall set $S_i = \{s_1, s_2, ..., s_k\}$.

3.3 Cross-Architecture Normalization

To enable consistent fingerprint generation across heterogeneous IoT architectures, we implement a comprehensive normalization framework that addresses three primary challenges: syscall number mapping, library function resolution, and semantic consistency.

Syscall Number to Name Mapping. System calls exhibit significant variation patterns that extend beyond simple numerical differences across architectures. Table 1 illustrates the key variant normalization challenges addressed by our approach.

Table 1. System call variant normalization examples

Raw System Call	Variant Type	Normalized
socketcall+socket	i586 unified interface	socket
socketcall+recv	i586 unified interface	recv
socketcall+send	i586 unified interface	send
time32	32-bit compatibility	time
clock_getres_time32	32-bit compatibility	clock_getres
fcntl64	64-bit variant	fcntl
fstat64	64-bit variant	fstat
old_mmap	Legacy interface	mmap
mmap2	Page-offset interface	mmap
sys_pipe	Architecture naming	pipe
sysm_pipe	Architecture naming	pipe

We maintain architecture-specific mapping tables $M_{\text{arch}} : \mathbb{N} \rightarrow \mathcal{S}$ derived from Linux kernel system call definitions, where $\mathcal{S}$ represents the set of standardized syscall names. These mappings transform raw syscall sets S_i into normalized sets $\tilde{S}_i = \{M_{\text{arch}}(s_1), M_{\text{arch}}(s_2), ..., M_{\text{arch}}(s_k)\}$.

System Call Variant Normalization. Cross-architecture normalization addresses multiple patterns of system call variation that arise from architectural differences, implementation choices, and compatibility requirements.

System calls with identical functionality may have different names across architectures due to implementation-specific conventions. For example, `sys_pipe` in MIPS and PowerPC corresponds to `sysm_pipe` in i586, requiring name-based normalization to establish functional equivalence. Many system calls also exist in multiple variants to support different data sizes or maintain backward compatibility. Time-related system calls exemplify this pattern: `sys_clock_getres_time32` represents the 32-bit variant while `sys_clock_getres` provides 64-bit support. Similarly, file control operations use `sys_fcntl` for basic functionality and `sys_fcntl64` for 64-bit file operations. Our normalization maps these variants to their base functional categories such as clock operations and file control while preserving capability semantics.

Architectures also maintain both legacy and modern interfaces for compatibility, such as `sys_mmap` versus `sys_old_mmap`, both providing memory mapping functionality. The normalization process consolidates these variants into unified capability representations. Socket operations demonstrate the most complex normalization pattern. i586 architectures employ a unified `sys_socketcall` system call with function codes to dispatch individual socket operations, while MIPS and PowerPC architectures implement separate system calls for each operation including `sys_socket`, `sys_recv`, `sys_send`, and `sys_sendto`. Our framework decomposes `sys_socketcall` invocations into their constituent operations, enabling consistent network capability representation.

High-level library functions compile to different syscall sequences across architectures and implementations. Our approach traces library function calls to their underlying syscall implementations through symbolic function resolution.

Semantic Consistency Framework. The normalization process ensures that functionally equivalent operations across architectures generate identical normalized representations. This enables a function implementing file I/O operations to produce consistent fingerprints regardless of whether it executes on MIPS networking equipment or PowerPC industrial controllers.

The normalized syscall set $\tilde{S}_i$ serves as the foundation for architecture-independent fingerprint generation, enabling capability profiling that transcends implementation-specific details.

3.4 Function-Level Fingerprint Generation

Syscall Set Encoding. For each function f_i with normalized syscall set $\tilde{S}_i = \{s_1, s_2, ..., s_k\}$, we generate a binary fingerprint F_i that captures the presence of system calls using a bag-of-words approach.

We employ a binary vector representation:

$$F_i = \boldsymbol{v}_i \in \{0, 1\}^{|\mathcal{S}|} \tag{1}$$

where $\boldsymbol{v}_i$ is a binary presence vector indicating whether each standardized syscall appears within function f_i.

Binary Vector Generation. The binary vector $\boldsymbol{v}_i \in \{0,1\}^{|S|}$ indicates the presence or absence of each standardized syscall within function f_i:

$$\boldsymbol{v}_i[j] = \begin{cases} 1 & \text{if } \text{syscall}_j \in \tilde{S}_i \\ 0 & \text{otherwise} \end{cases} \tag{2}$$

This bag-of-words representation enables identification of functions with similar syscall usage patterns, such as network communication functions consistently utilizing `socket`, `bind`, `listen`, and `accept` calls, regardless of the frequency or order of these calls within the function. The binary encoding approach simplifies the fingerprint representation while maintaining the essential information needed for capability profiling, as the mere presence of specific syscalls often indicates functional capabilities more reliably than their frequency or temporal arrangement.

3.5 Capability Profiling and Malware Functionality Identification

Fingerprint Database Construction Our approach constructs a reference database of function-level fingerprints from known malware samples across multiple architectures. For each analyzed malware sample, we extract all function fingerprints F_i and store them along with their corresponding metadata including source malware family, architecture, and function context. This creates a comprehensive fingerprint database $\mathcal{D} = \{(F_i, \text{metadata}_i) : i = 1, 2, ..., n\}$ where each entry represents a function's syscall pattern and its associated characteristics.

Similarity-Based Function Matching. When analyzing an unknown malware sample, we extract function fingerprints using the same normalization pipeline and perform nearest neighbor search against the fingerprint database. For each function f_{unknown} with fingerprint F_{unknown}, we compute similarity scores against all database entries using the Jaccard index, which measures the proportion of shared syscalls and is well-suited for binary feature vectors:

$$\text{similarity}(F_{\text{unknown}}, F_i) = \frac{|F_{\text{unknown}} \cap F_i|}{|F_{\text{unknown}} \cup F_i|} \tag{3}$$

The most similar function fingerprint from the database is identified as:

$$F_{\text{match}} = \arg\max_{F_i \in \mathcal{D}} \text{similarity}(F_{\text{unknown}}, F_i) \tag{4}$$

Capability Inference Framework. Capability profiling is performed through inference from the matched functions in the fingerprint database. When a function from unknown malware matches a function from known malware with high similarity, we infer that the unknown function likely exhibits similar capabilities to the matched function. This similarity-based inference framework enables capability estimation without requiring predefined capability categories or direct functional analysis.

The approach provides a foundation for understanding unknown malware functionality by leveraging patterns observed in known samples, while acknowledging that capability inference is probabilistic rather than deterministic. Unlike family-based approaches where taxonomic classification does not guarantee functional equivalence due to variant evolution and feature drift within malware lineages, our function-level syscall fingerprinting enables capability inference based on actual syscall usage patterns rather than genealogical relationships.

4 Evaluation

4.1 Experimental Setup

Our evaluation examines three IoT malware families: Mirai, Lizkebab, and Bashlite. Mirai represents the archetypal IoT botnet focused on DDoS attacks, Lizkebab demonstrates advanced persistence and communication capabilities, while Bashlite exhibits comprehensive remote shell and command execution functionality.

We selected MIPS, PowerPC, and i586 architectures based on several technical considerations: these architectures are among the primary targets for IoT malware cross-compilation and are provided as pre-built toolchains in the uClibc distribution. While ARM is also prevalent in IoT environments, we excluded it from this evaluation due to Application Binary Interface (ABI) variations and multiple architecture versions that would introduce additional complexity beyond the scope of cross-architecture normalization assessment.

The fingerprinting system is implemented in Python utilizing radare2 for binary analysis and static system call extraction. The experimental pipeline processes each binary through automated architecture detection, function extraction, syscall identification, and fingerprint generation stages. All experiments were conducted on a computer with Intel Core i9-10850K CPU (10 physical cores, 20 logical cores), 128 GB RAM, running Ubuntu 22.04.5 LTS.

4.2 Cross-Architecture Consistency

We evaluate cross-architecture compatibility using consistency metrics that measure how similarly our approach generates fingerprints for functionally equivalent malware across different CPU architectures. For this evaluation, we utilize malware binaries compiled from the ifding/iot-malware open-source repository [15], cross-compiled for MIPS, PowerPC, and i586 architectures using architecture-specific GCC toolchains with uClibc 0.9.33.2, ensuring identical source code across all architectures for precise consistency measurement.

We measure how consistently our approach generates fingerprints for the same malware across different architectures. For each malware sample compiled for MIPS, PowerPC, and i586, we compute pairwise Jaccard similarity between architecture variants:

$$\text{Consistency}_{\text{arch}} = \frac{1}{|\mathcal{P}|} \sum_{(a_i, a_j) \in \mathcal{P}} \text{Jaccard}(F_{a_i}, F_{a_j}) \quad (5)$$

where $\mathcal{P}$ represents all architecture pairs and F_{a_i} is the fingerprint set for architecture a_i.

Figure 2 presents the cross-architecture consistency results, demonstrating substantial variation across different architecture combinations, with PowerPC-i586 pairs achieving the highest consistency scores.

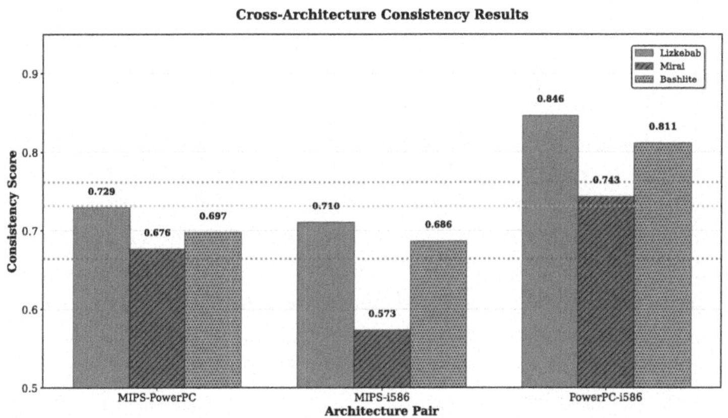

Fig. 2. Cross-Architecture Consistency Results. The chart shows consistency scores for each architecture pair across malware samples. PowerPC-i586 pairs achieve the highest consistency, while MIPS-i586 pairs show the lowest performance across all evaluated samples.

The results reveal significant patterns in cross-architecture consistency performance, with notable variation across different architecture combinations. PowerPC-i586 pairs consistently achieve the highest similarity scores with mean consistency of 0.800, while MIPS-i586 pairs show the lowest performance at mean 0.656.

The cross-architecture analysis demonstrates that our normalization framework performs differently across architecture pairs, with PowerPC-i586 combinations showing particularly strong performance due to similar compilation characteristics and system call mapping compatibility. MIPS-i586 pairs face greater challenges, likely reflecting fundamental differences in instruction set architectures and calling conventions that impact syscall pattern generation.

While the mean consistency of 0.719 indicates reasonable normalization effectiveness for operational deployment scenarios, the substantial range between best and worst cases suggests that library implementation variations and compilation differences significantly impact fingerprint consistency, necessitating careful consideration of architecture-specific factors in deployment environments, as detailed in our Discussion analysis (Sect. 5).

4.3 Capability Profiling Through Unknown Malware Analysis

To demonstrate the practical effectiveness of our capability profiling approach, we conducted a comprehensive case study using unknown malware binaries analyzed against our reference database constructed from known samples. This evaluation directly reflects the operational deployment scenario where analysts encounter previously unseen malware variants and require immediate capability assessment.

Our capability profiling evaluation employs a realistic unknown malware analysis scenario. We construct a reference database containing function-level syscall fingerprints from known Mirai and Bashlite malware families across MIPS, PowerPC, and i586 architectures, totaling 1,294 labeled functions with their associated capability metadata. For unknown malware analysis, we utilize Lizkebab samples that were excluded from the database construction, simulating the scenario where analysts encounter a completely unknown malware family.

Each unknown function generates a syscall fingerprint using our normalization pipeline, which is then compared against all database entries using Jaccard similarity. The system returns the Top-K most similar functions along with their similarity scores, enabling analysts to infer capabilities based on the matched functions' known behaviors.

Case Study: Unknown Lizkebab Function Analysis. We present a detailed case study analyzing the `StartTheLelz` function from a Lizkebab MIPS binary, treating it as unknown malware to demonstrate realistic capability profiling. This function serves as the main coordination routine for botnet operations and exhibits a comprehensive syscall pattern: `socket, connect, send, recv, select, getsockopt, fcntl, close, write, brk, getrlimit, time`. The analysis utilizes a reference database constructed from Mirai and Bashlite families, with Lizkebab excluded to simulate the scenario where analysts encounter a previously unknown malware family.

Table 2 presents the Top-5 similarity matches returned by our system, demonstrating the effectiveness of our similarity-based matching approach.

The case study demonstrates the effectiveness of our capability inference approach through systematic analysis of the unknown function's syscall pattern. The comprehensive syscall signature `socket, connect, send, recv, select, getsockopt, fcntl, close, write, brk, getrlimit, time` enables our system to infer network communication and coordination capabilities without prior knowledge of the function's actual purpose.

Based on the Top-5 similarity matches, our approach infers the following capabilities: (1) network socket establishment and management from `socket,`

Table 2. Case Study: Top-5 Similarity Matches for Unknown Lizkebab StartTheLelz Function

Rank	Matched Function	Source Family	Similarity
1	`StartTheLelz`	Bashlite-MIPS	1.000
2	`sendJUNK`	Bashlite-MIPS	0.833
3	`sendHOLD`	Bashlite-MIPS	0.750
4	`processCmd`	Bashlite-MIPS	0.667
5	`initConnection`	Bashlite-MIPS	0.500

`connect, getsockopt` patterns, (2) bidirectional communication functionality from `send, recv` operations, (3) connection multiplexing capabilities from `select` usage, and (4) coordination and timing functionality from `time, getrlimit` patterns. These inferred capabilities accurately correspond to the actual function behavior as the main botnet coordination routine, validating our syscall-based capability profiling approach.

The similarity match with Bashlite's equivalent function confirms that our normalization framework successfully identifies functionally equivalent implementations across different malware families, demonstrating the practical utility of syscall fingerprinting for unknown malware analysis. It also highlights the effectiveness of our approach in enabling analysts to rapidly infer capabilities from unknown malware samples based on observed syscall patterns, without requiring prior knowledge of the specific malware family or dynamic execution environments.

4.4 Computational Performance

We conducted comprehensive performance measurements across end-to-end pipeline execution using real malware binaries from the IoTPOT Dataset A [16,17], which contains real-world malware captured from IoT honeypots. Our performance evaluation randomly selected 50 IoT malware samples from successfully analyzed binaries in this dataset, with multiple independent measurement trials per binary to ensure statistical reliability, measuring complete pipeline execution including binary analysis, function extraction, syscall identification, normalization, fingerprint generation, and similarity matching.

Figure 3 illustrates the relationship between function count and execution time across the 50 randomly selected IoT malware samples.

The performance analysis confirms strong linear scaling behavior (correlation coefficient: 0.851) without exponential performance degradation, even for binaries containing up to 1,638 functions. With an average processing time of 7.3 s across diverse real-world samples and a maximum observed time of 18.4 s, our approach maintains operational efficiency suitable for rapid incident response scenarios where immediate malware characterization is essential.

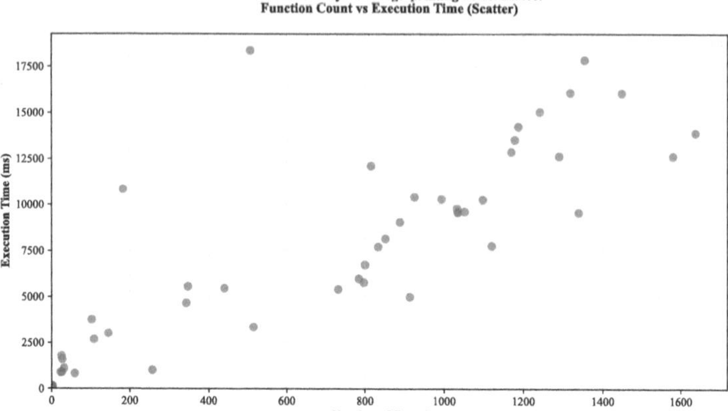

Fig. 3. Performance Scalability Analysis. The analysis of 50 randomly selected IoT malware samples from IoTPOT Dataset A demonstrates strong linear scaling characteristics between function count and execution time (correlation coefficient: 0.851), with an average processing time of 7.3 s for binaries containing an average of 672 functions.

While the overall trend demonstrates linear scaling, individual binaries occasionally exhibit elevated processing times that deviate from the general pattern. These performance variations reflect the influence of function complexity characteristics including control flow intricacy, syscall density, and binary structure complexity beyond simple function count. Binaries with highly complex control flow patterns or dense syscall usage may require additional processing time for accurate function boundary detection and syscall identification. Despite these variations, the consistent linear relationship between function count and execution time demonstrates that our approach avoids computational bottlenecks that could impede practical deployment in time-sensitive security operations.

5 Discussion

5.1 Current Limitations and Technical Challenges

Our comprehensive experimental evaluation reveals three fundamental limitations that significantly impact the accuracy and operational applicability of our function-level syscall fingerprinting approach.

Cross-Architecture Normalization Challenges. The most significant limitation manifests in substantial performance variations across CPU architecture pairs due to fundamental architectural incompatibilities. Different architectures implement distinct syscall numbering schemes requiring complex mapping tables that may not capture semantic equivalence accurately, while architecture-specific calling conventions alter how function parameters are passed and syscalls are invoked, creating architecturally-dependent fingerprint variations. Furthermore, underlying instruction set differences create cascading effects through compilation, affecting syscall pattern extraction and creating architecture-specific signatures that resist normalization efforts across diverse CPU architectures.

Library Implementation Dependencies. Our analysis reveals a fundamental dependency on specific C library implementations that significantly constrains the generalizability of our approach. The uClibc environment employed in our evaluation provides multiple memory allocation implementations (malloc, malloc-simple, malloc-standard), each generating distinct syscall patterns for functionally equivalent operations. Different malloc implementations within the same library version produce different sets of system calls for memory allocation requests, where the malloc-standard implementation utilizes sophisticated heap management with pre-allocation strategies, generating complex syscall patterns involving multiple `mmap()` calls, while malloc-simple employs direct `brk()` system calls for each allocation request. This implementation variance directly explains the low consistency scores observed in our cross-architecture evaluation, particularly the 0.656 consistency achieved by MIPS-i586 pairs where different malloc implementations were inadvertently used during cross-compilation.

The normalization framework demonstrates strong performance within the uClibc ecosystem but faces fundamental challenges when extended to other C library implementations such as glibc or musl, where each library ecosystem implements different internal calling conventions, error handling mechanisms, and optimization strategies that alter the resulting syscall patterns in ways that cannot be easily normalized through simple mapping approaches. This cross-library incompatibility significantly constrains the operational applicability of our approach in heterogeneous environments where different malware samples may be compiled against different library versions or implementations.

Static Analysis Limitations and Evasion Resilience. Our approach relies exclusively on static analysis for syscall extraction, which provides computational efficiency but introduces fundamental limitations in handling advanced malware evasion techniques. Modern malware increasingly employs sophisticated evasion strategies that specifically target static analysis approaches, including code obfuscation techniques such as control flow flattening, instruction substitution, and function inlining that can significantly alter the apparent syscall patterns without changing the underlying malicious functionality. Static analysis also inherently cannot capture runtime-dependent behaviors that are only observable during execution, where malware samples may employ dynamic syscall generation, runtime library loading, or self-modifying code that present particular challenges for our fingerprinting approach. Polymorphic malware variants may introduce dummy syscalls, reorder syscall sequences, or employ conditional execution paths that make static syscall extraction incomplete or misleading, while our current approach cannot distinguish between genuine functional calls and decoy operations introduced for evasion purposes.

Design Trade-offs in Binary Vector Representation: The binary vector representation of syscall presence represents a deliberate design choice that involves trade-offs between analytical precision and cross-architecture robustness. The binary encoding discards crucial context information about syscall usage patterns, frequency, and sequencing, where functionally different behaviors may generate identical fingerprints. However, this abstraction provides significant advantages for cross-architecture consistency by normalizing implementation variations across different compiler optimizations and architectures. This design choice prioritizes functional capability identification over behavioral intensity quantification, making the approach suitable for initial threat classification rather than detailed behavioral analysis.

While these limitations constrain the applicability of our approach against sophisticated evasion techniques, our evaluation demonstrates effectiveness against common IoT malware families where such advanced techniques are less prevalent, making the approach suitable for initial threat assessment and large-scale automated analysis scenarios.

5.2 Future Research Directions

The limitations identified in our evaluation suggest several promising research directions that could significantly enhance the effectiveness and applicability of function-level syscall fingerprinting.

Enhanced Normalization Frameworks: Future work should explore machine learning-based normalization approaches that can automatically discover semantic equivalence patterns across architectures rather than relying on static mapping tables. Deep learning approaches trained on large datasets of cross-compiled binaries might identify subtle patterns that enable more accurate cross-architecture normalization.

Additionally, investigating hybrid normalization approaches that combine static analysis with limited dynamic analysis could provide more accurate understanding of functional equivalence while maintaining computational efficiency suitable for operational deployment.

Library-Agnostic Analysis: Developing library-agnostic analysis techniques that can distinguish between application-specific functionality and library implementation details represents a critical research direction. This might involve creating abstraction layers that normalize library-specific syscall patterns to functional semantics independent of specific implementations.

Research into automatic library identification and version detection could enable context-aware normalization that adapts to specific library environments while maintaining cross-library compatibility.

Advanced Static Analysis Techniques: Future research should explore advanced static analysis techniques that can better handle obfuscated and optimized binaries. This includes investigating symbolic execution approaches for resolving dynamic syscall patterns and developing more sophisticated control flow analysis that can handle complex calling mechanisms.

Integration with binary rewriting or instrumentation techniques might enable hybrid approaches that combine the efficiency of static analysis with the completeness of dynamic analysis for critical functionality identification.

6 Conclusion

This paper presents a function-level syscall fingerprinting approach for cross-architecture IoT malware capability profiling that addresses three critical requirements: cross-architecture compatibility, immediate capability profiling, and lightweight static analysis. Our six-stage pipeline including function extraction, syscall identification, cross-architecture normalization, fingerprint generation, database construction, and similarity-based matching enables immediate capability assessment of unknown malware variants without requiring family-based classification or dynamic execution environments.

Comprehensive evaluation across three malware families and three CPU architectures demonstrates substantial cross-architecture consistency and operational efficiency. The semantic normalization framework successfully abstracts architectural differences, enabling effective capability inference and accurate similarity-based matching for immediate capability assessment.

The proposed methodology advances the state-of-the-art in IoT security by enabling rapid, architecture-agnostic malware analysis suitable for operational deployment in heterogeneous IoT environments where traditional analysis approaches face scalability and compatibility limitations. However, our evaluation reveals key limitations including architecture-specific consistency variations, dependency on symbol information for accurate function boundary detection, and challenges with library implementation differences across compilation environments. Future research should prioritize development of library function signature databases for stripped binary analysis, extension to broader library ecosystems beyond uClibc, and integration with lightweight dynamic analysis techniques to address static analysis limitations while maintaining operational efficiency requirements.

Acknowledgments. This work was supported by JSPS KAKENHI Grant Number JP25K22803, JST ASPIRE Grant Number JPMJAP2432, and NEC Corporation, Japan.

References

1. Bak, M., Papp, D., Tamás, C., Buttyán, L.: Clustering IoT malware based on binary similarity. In: NOMS 2020 - 2020 IEEE/IFIP Network Operations and Management Symposium, pp. 1–6. IEEE Press (2020)
2. Wu, C.Y., Ban, T., Cheng, S.M., Takahashi, T., Inoue, D.: IoT malware classification based on reinterpreted function-call graphs. Comput. Secur. **125**, 103060 (2023)

3. Liting, D., Hui, W., Mingfeng, X., Hong, L., Zhiwen, P., Limin, S.: Enimanal: augmented cross-architecture IoT malware analysis using graph neural networks. Comput. Secur. **132**, 103323 (2023)
4. Su, J., Vasconcellos, D.V., Prasad, S., Sgandurra, D., Feng, Y., Sakurai, K.: Lightweight classification of IoT malware based on image recognition. In: 2018 IEEE 42nd Annual Computer Software and Applications Conference (COMPSAC), vol. 02, pp. 664–669 (2018)
5. Lee, Y.T., et al.: Cross platform IoT-malware family classification based on printable strings. In: 2020 IEEE 19th International Conference on Trust, Security and Privacy in Computing and Communications (TrustCom), pp. 775–784 (2020)
6. Greco, C., Ianni, M.: A cross-architecture malware detection approach based on intermediate representation. J. Inf. Secur. Appl. **93**, 104117 (2025)
7. Song, Q., Zhang, Y., Wang, B., Chen, Y.: Inter-BIN: interaction-based cross-architecture IoT binary similarity comparison. IEEE Internet Things J. **9**(20), 20018–20033 (2022)
8. Collyer, J., Watson, T., Phillips, I.: FASER: binary code similarity search through the use of intermediate representations. In: CEUR Workshop Proceedings, vol. 3652, pp. 193–202 (2023)
9. Vasan, S., et al.: DEEPCAPA: identifying malicious capabilities in windows malware. In: 2024 Annual Computer Security Applications Conference (ACSAC), pp. 826–842 (2024)
10. Chen, X., Liu, M., Wang, Y., Li, Z.: Semantic-aware cross-architecture IoT malware detection. In: 32nd USENIX Security Symposium, pp. 1823–1840. USENIX Association (2023)
11. Saha, B., Rani, N., Shukla, S.K.: MalXCap: a method for malware capability extraction. In: Information Security Practice and Experience: 18th International Conference. ISPEC 2023, Copenhagen, Denmark, August 24–25, 2023, Proceedings, pp. 230–249. Springer-Verlag, Berlin, Heidelberg (2023)
12. Farfoura, M.E., Mashal, I., Alkhatib, A., Batyha, R.M., Rosiyadi, D.: A Novel lightweight machine learning framework for IoT malware classification based on matrix block mean downsampling. Ain Shams Eng. J. **16**(1), 103205 (2025)
13. Wang, C., Ma, Z., Li, Q., Zhao, D., Wang, F.: A lightweight IoT malware detection and family classification method. J. Comput. Commun. **12**(4), 201–227 (2024)
14. Radare2 Team: Radare2 GitHub repository (2017). https://github.com/radare/radare2
15. Fei, D.: IoT Malware (2017). https://github.com/ifding/iot-malware
16. Pa, Y.M.P., et al.: IoTPOT: Analysing the rise of IoT compromises. In: Proceedings of the USENIX Workshop on Offensive Technologies (USENIX WOOT'15) (2015)
17. Yokohama National University: IoT honeypot: Malware binaries dataset A. https://sec.ynu.codes/iot/available_datasets#1

Policy Enforcement Protocols with Split Keys

Gizem Akman[1,2(✉)], Philip Ginzboorg[3,4], Sampo Sovio[5], and Valtteri Niemi[1,2]

[1] University of Helsinki, Helsinki, Finland
{gizem.akman,valtteri.niemi}@helsinki.fi
[2] Helsinki Institute for Information Technology (HIIT), Espoo, Finland
[3] Aalto University, Espoo, Finland
philip.ginzboorg@aalto.fi
[4] South-Eastern Finland University of Applied Sciences (XAMK), Kotka, Finland
[5] Huawei Technologies, Helsinki, Finland
sampo.sovio@huawei.com

Abstract. Policy enforcement is crucial to ensure secure data transfer between systems. We introduce a Mutual Policy Enforcement (MPE) protocol, where policy enforcement is carried out by dedicated controller devices after the message exchange between two primary devices. Our approach integrates secret sharing to maintain policy integrity, ensuring that a compromise of one device does not lead to unauthorized message approval. A successful run of the protocol ensures that the controllers of both primary devices have verified the messages. We propose two variants of the mutual enforcement protocol: MPE-SIGN, which relies on digital signatures, and MPE-MAC, which uses message authentication codes. We define use cases in which MPE can be applied, set security goals for the protocol, and analyze the performance of the protocol considering communication and computational overhead. We discuss the impact of compromises and perform security analysis. We also formally model our protocols in ProVerif and verify their security properties.

Keywords: policy enforcement · secret splitting · ProVerif

1 Introduction

Policy enforcement is a process of network management that follows the rules for application connectivity, access, and use [10]. Transferring data between different systems with different security and privacy policies induces security and privacy risks, which policy enforcement helps to mitigate. Policy enforcement mechanisms apply filtering, inspection, and sanitation rules before the transfer of data to different domains. Such rules include restricting transfers, verifying write permissions, enforcing one-way flows through hardware, and implementing trustworthy regrading processes to adjust security or privacy attributes [19].

R. Laborde et al. (Eds.): ESORICS 2025 Workshops, LNCS 16233, pp. 503–523, 2026.
https://doi.org/10.1007/978-3-032-16165-9_30

Secret splitting allows dividing the secret into shares and distributing these shares to multiple hosts without disclosing the whole secret. This method is useful in cases where the secret is supposed to be shared with untrusted parties or the secret is sent over untrusted networks [29]. The compromise of one party does not reveal the whole secret. A party is considered compromised if, e.g., its secret key is leaked, if it intentionally fails to follow the protocol, or if it intentionally acts against policy.

In this paper, we introduce a mutual policy enforcement protocol, in which the policy enforcement is applied by the controller devices after the messages are exchanged between two primary devices; refer to Sect. 3 for a detailed description of the system model. A successful run of the protocol means that the exchanged messages have been authorized by both controller devices according to their respective policies.

The secret is shared between the primary and controller devices to ensure the integrity of policy enforcement. We aim to prevent cases where the compromise of a party or parties causes wrong messages to pass the policy enforcement or wrong claims of successful policy enforcement, where the result should have been a failure. For example, if one primary device is compromised, then the controller devices or the other primary device should be able to detect the compromise. The impact of compromises is discussed in Sect. 8.

There are several use cases that can utilize our mutual policy enforcement protocol, such as parental control, where parents check their kids' messages for their policy rules, e.g., kids do not use profanity or insult each other, and communication with smart devices, e.g., autonomous cars. The use cases are discussed further in Sect. 5.

Our contributions are as follows: We (1) propose two variants of the mutual policy enforcement (MPE) protocol: signature-based (MPE-SIGN) and MAC-based (MPE-MAC) protocols, (2) identify several use cases where the MPE protocol can be applied, and (3) implement the models of MPE-SIGN and MPE-MAC in ProVerif and formally verify their security properties.

The paper continues with the background and related work in Sect. 2. We define the system model in Sect. 3 and set the security goals in Sect. 4. We describe several use cases in Sect. 5. Then, in Sect. 6, we have the description of mutual policy enforcement (MPE) protocols, where we introduce signature-based MPE (MPE-SIGN) and discuss MAC-based MPE (MPE-MAC). We continue with formal verification of the protocols in Sect. 7, security analysis in Sect. 8, and performance analysis in Sect. 9. We finalize the paper with a discussion and conclusion in Sect. 10. Appendix A provides the details of MPE-MAC, and Appendix B includes the explanation of the construction of the model described in Sect. 7 and its results.

2 Background and Related Work

In this section, we review the background and related work in the areas of security policy enforcement, secret splitting, and formal verification.

Security Policy Enforcement: In RFC 2196, Fraser et al. [15] define security policy as a formal statement of the rules by which people who are given access to an organization's technology and information assets must abide.

Security policies consist of several components, such as authentication, accountability, audit, managing policies, access control, and administration functions. Access control policies ensure that authorized users can perform the tasks that they are authorized to do, and access requests are granted only to those who comply with the definition of the security policy [22,28].

A generic security policy enforcement model includes the following: (1) Policy Enforcement Point (PEP) forwards requests to PDP and enforces the decisions made by the PDP; (2) Policy Decision Point (PDP) evaluates requests against the security policies and decides to accept or reject; (3) Policy Information Point (PIP) collects and stores attribute information related to the system and provides them to PDP; (4) Policy Administration Point (PAP) manages and stores policies and makes them available for PDP; and (5) Policy Refinement Point (PRP) refines policies at runtime and updates PAP [26,28,32].

In relation to our use cases, Sicari et al. [31] design a framework for policy enforcement in the IoT domain aimed at healthcare applications. Neisse et al. [23] provide an efficient policy enforcement system for IoT devices. Smart contracts-based policies for the IoT domain have been studied by Puri et al. [27]. Buccafurri et al. [8] introduce a framework to formalize authentication policies and interactions among systems and a protocol that ensures dependencies in the system do not weaken security policies. Varadharajan et al. [34] propose a policy-based security architecture and discuss its use in scenarios that involve communications with Software-Defined Networking (SDN) controllers. Farahmandian et al. [14] study a policy-based interaction model to manage security in cloud computing environments using SDN and Network Function Virtualization (NFV). Sicari et al. [32] introduce a security enforcement framework, integrated within a distributed IoT middleware platform. Hamlen et al. [17] provide a general policy enforcement framework for cloud data management and discuss different policy types applicable for cloud environments.

We require that policy enforcement by the controller devices takes place during the run of our protocol, but we keep the details of policy checking and the question of what kind of policies are enforceable out of scope.

Secret Splitting: Cryptographic secret keys stored on a device may be vulnerable to exposure, e.g., if an attacker gets physical access to the device. Splitting the secret across several devices and requiring their cooperation to use the secret is one of the ways to reduce the risk and provide an additional level of control over the secret.

Secret splitting is an established concept for authentication, e.g., multi-factor authentication [30] and authentication with biometrics [35]. Splitting a secret key into several pieces and storing them in different devices requires cooperation to utilize the whole secret, such as splitting the keys at different source nodes [9]. This split-key setting can be applied to key agreement [4].

In this paper, we consider a split-key setting for the digital signature scheme implemented in one of the variants of our mutual policy enforcement protocol, assuming that the initial agreement on session keys between the parties has already happened.

Formal Verification: Automated formal analysis tools have been used for the analysis of cryptographic protocols to detect whether an attacker can prevent the protocol from achieving the security goals [33]. ProVerif [7] and Tamarin-Prover [5] are state-of-the-art tools used for formal verification and security protocol analysis. Both tools assume the Dolev-Yao adversary model.

ProVerif uses applied pi-calculus as a formal language, translates the protocol into a set of Horn clauses, and considers an unbounded number of sessions and an unbounded message space for the protocol analysis. ProVerif is able to provide formal proofs of security properties. The tool can also detect attacks; if a protocol property cannot be proven, ProVerif attempts to construct an execution trace that contradicts that property. We utilize ProVerif to model our protocols and to formally verify their security properties.

3 System Model

We base our system model on an abstract scenario in which Alice and Bob are communicating with each other. Communication is carried out through the primary devices, while authentication and policy verification are done through the two controller devices, so that the messages sent and received are verified according to their policies. Therefore, we have four parties in our system model: Alice1 (primary device of Alice), Alice2 (controller device of Alice), Bob1 (primary device of Bob), and Bob2 (controller device of Bob). The visualization of the system model is shown in Fig. 1. It is also possible that the primary device and the controller device are used by different entities (e.g., a child and a parent), but these two are closely related to each other.

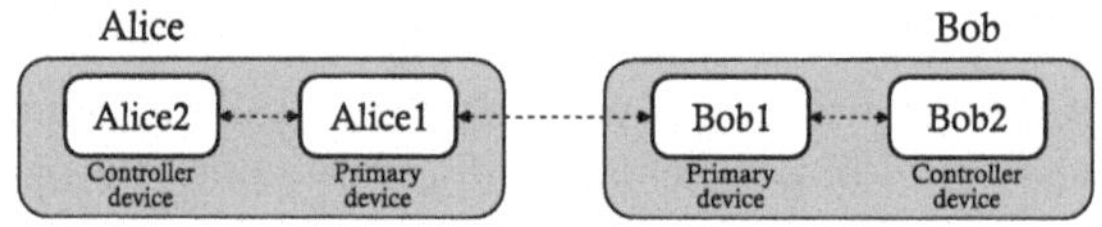

Fig. 1. Illustration of system model.

We include controller devices to actively participate in the protocol during the communication of the primary devices. In this way, the controller devices, Alice2 and Bob2, can ensure that the primary devices, Alice1 and Bob1, behave according to the controller device policies. The proposed protocol would be part of a system that needs to take care of, among other things, key management and secure distribution, protecting the keys, pre-establishing secure channels, handling software and policy updates, and ensuring scalability to accommodate large numbers of primary and controller device pairs.

4 Security Goals

Next, we define the adversary model and the security goals of our system.

We assume that the participants of the protocol, Alice1, Alice2, Bob1, and Bob2, are *honest-but-curious* as adversaries. This type of adversary is a legitimate party in a protocol that faithfully follows the protocol, but still tries to learn as much as possible from legitimately received messages [25]. We also assume the *extended Canetti-Krawczyk (eCK)* adversary model for compromised participants. A participant can be compromised, e.g., by the adversary gaining physical access to the device or infecting the device with malware [20,33]. Two or more participants can be compromised, and they can also collude for an attack.

We assume outsiders, i.e., any entity other than the participants, to be *Dolev-Yao* adversaries. An attacker, as a Dolev-Yao adversary, can see the messages sent during the protocol and manipulate the messages by modifying, replaying, inserting, and deleting them, e.g., such an adversary can carry out Man-in-the-Middle attacks [16]. In addition, they can be a legitimate user of the network and exchange messages with the participants in the protocol, so that they can initiate a session or reply to messages intended for another participant [11,33].

Finally, we assume perfect cryptographic primitives so that the hash functions are one-way and collision-resistant, and the encrypted messages can be decrypted (resp., digital signatures can be created) only if the corresponding secret keys are possessed.

The main goal of our protocol is to achieve mutual policy enforcement: a successful run of the protocol means that both controller devices have done a policy check. We have the following security goals that support achieving the main goal: (i) authentication and authorization of the parties, (ii) replay protection, and (iii) integrity of protocol messages. Detailed definitions of security properties and related proofs are given in Sects. 7 and 8.

Note that confidentiality of protocol messages is not a goal because it is not necessary for achieving the main goal of policy enforcement. However, confidentiality can be added as an extension because we assume that the parties have the keys needed for secure communication before our protocol starts.

5 Use Cases

We will now give examples of use cases where the mutual policy enforcement (MPE) protocol can be applied. We denote the messages as m_1, m_2 exchanged by the primary devices in each use case, and the results of the policy check on these messages by the controller devices as $Success$ or $Failure$.

UC1 Communicating Smart Devices. We have divided this use case further into three subcases that have some relevant differences between themselves from the point of view of policies.

UC1.1. Alice1 and Bob1 are two cars in traffic, while Alice2 and Bob2 are applications on the drivers' phones. The two cars exchange data that is relevant locally, but they should not communicate without the approval of the applications. One car asks for information from the other car. The other car replies with an answer. The application on both sides checks whether the question and the answer are according to the policies. If the policy check results in a *Failure*, then the exchanged information is deleted in a controlled manner. As a concrete example, consider a flexible parking space for residents in a neighborhood where the number of parking spots is limited. Alice1 looks for free parking spots in the neighborhood and asks Bob1, who is coming from the neighborhood, if there are free parking slots around (m_1). Bob1 informs Alice1 about the free parking spots (m_2). Alice2 checks if the information received about parking spots can be considered reliable, while Bob2 checks if it is appropriate to share this information with a car like Alice1. If any of the two policy checks fails, the provided information is requested to be ignored and deleted.

UC1.2. Alice1 and Bob1 are drones that communicate with each other, whereas Alice2 and Bob2 are the corresponding ground stations or the leaders of two drone swarms. For example, Alice1 wants to get photos of the surroundings, so she wants to ask Bob1 to share the photos that Bob1 may have taken. First, Alice1 sends a communication request by providing the basic information about itself (m_1). Bob1 replies, also including similar information about itself (m_2). Alice2 and Bob2 then check if sharing further information with the other party is acceptable. If the policy check succeeds, Alice1 continues communicating by requesting photos of the surroundings. Further policy checks may verify the validity of the photos.

UC1.3 Alice1 and Bob1 are IoT devices in a smart environment (e.g., smart home or smart factory) that communicate with each other. Alice2 and Bob2 are controlled by the owners of the smart devices, the environment, or the server to which the devices are connected. For example, Bob is the owner of a smart home, and Alice is a visitor. Alice owns a health tracking device, e.g., a smartwatch or a ring. The device tracks Alice's health because Alice has asthma. If the condition of Bob's home is not suitable for Alice's health, the device communicates with Bob's smart home, and requests a change (m_1), e.g., adjusting air conditioning, temperature, or humidity. Smart home returns the parameters as a response (m_2). Alice2, the application on Alice's mobile phone, checks if the parameters are compliant with her policy (i.e., good for Alice's health). Bob2, the application on Bob's mobile phone, checks whether the parameter proposal is according to Bob's policy, i.e., whether such changes are acceptable for the other people in the household. The changes apply after the success messages are received from Alice2 and Bob2.

UC2 Simple IoT Devices that Collect Data. Alice1 and Bob1 are IoT devices that report their consumption of, e.g., energy, and Alice2 and Bob2 verify the reported consumption. For example, Alice and Bob are neighbors and both have solar panels on their roofs. Alice1 and Bob1 are the electricity storage systems of these houses. Alice2 and Bob2 are the applications on the mobile phones of their respective owners. If Alice1 runs out of energy, it sends a request to Bob1 for additional energy (m_1). Then, Bob1 replies to Alice1 with its additional capacity (m_2). Alice2 checks if the offer is acceptable for Alice, based on her policy; Bob2 accepts or rejects the delivery of the energy.

UC3 Ensuring Honest-but-Curious Behavior of Participants in Multi-party Computation. Alice1 and Bob1 run a multi-party computation (MPC) protocol. Alice2 and Bob2 check the content of the MPC protocol messages and verify that Alice1 and Bob1 behave according to the protocol. Instead of being dependent on a Trusted Third Party (TTP), Alice2 (resp., Bob2) ensures to the other communicating party that the messages Alice1 (resp., Bob1) sends are formed properly and according to the protocol. For example, Alice1 and Bob1 run 1–2 Oblivious Transfer [13]. Alice1 sends two random variables (x_1, x_2) to Bob1 (m_1). Bob1 replies with v to Alice1 (m_2). Alice2 and Bob2 ensure that the computations are done and the variables are generated according to the protocol.

UC4 Machine to Machine (M2M) Contract Negotiation. Alice1 and Bob1 are negotiating a smart contract; Alice2 and Bob2 are checking the contract conditions. For example, Alice1 has digital artwork and intends to tokenize it as a Non-Fungible Token (NFT), and Bob1 is the platform for tokenizing the digital artwork. Alice1 provides her digital artwork to Bob1 (m_1), and Bob1 sends the instructions to Alice1 (m_2). Alice2 verifies that her application is done according to the instructions, and Bob2 checks whether the artwork is up to the rules and regulations of the platform. If Alice2 and Bob2 both receive the *Success* messages, then Alice1 can receive the NFT for her digital artwork.

UC5 Parental Control. Alice1 and Bob1 are underage children with mobile devices, and Alice2 and Bob2 are parents monitoring the actions of their children. For example, Alice1 and Bob1 chat online and exchange messages (m_1, m_2). Alice2 and Bob2 check their child's messages and verify that the messages are according to their policies, e.g., they do not insult each other or use profanity. If Alice2 and Bob2 allow, by sending *Success* message, Alice1 and Bob1 can continue their communication. Otherwise, Alice2 and Bob2 may want to take action offline, e.g., warning the children and talking with the other parent. In another example, Bob is a content provider. The child's device Alice1 sends the message m_1 to Bob1 asking him to watch a particular video. Bob1 replies with m_2, allowing the request, with the provision that Alice2 approves it as well.

The above use cases have different characteristics, e.g., time sensitivity, non-repudiation, and repetition. We will discuss this further in Sect. 10.

6 Mutual Policy Enforcement Protocol

We propose a protocol that provides secure communication between two communicating parties, Alice1 and Bob1, but which also includes active controller devices, Alice2 and Bob2. We assume that Alice1 and Bob1 have already agreed on a shared key, K, e.g., using split-key protocols proposed by Akman et al. [4], and the communication between them is protected by K. We further assume that Alice1 and Alice2 share a key K_a and Bob1 and Bob2 share a key K_b to protect communication between parties in each pair.

The controller devices check the messages for compliance with their policy, which is set for the communication on each side. Note that the key agreement protocol is run once, while the proposed protocol can be run several times during the communication after that key agreement.

We propose two variants for the mutual policy enforcement (MPE) protocol: signature-based (MPE-SIGN) and MAC-based (MPE-MAC). The signature-based protocol utilizes public keys and the corresponding private keys, which are split between the controller and primary devices. The contributions of both devices are necessary to sign a message so that other parties can verify it. The MAC-based protocol utilizes symmetric keys shared by a pair of participants.

Now, we present a signature-based mutual policy enforcement protocol (MPE-SIGN). Each communicating party and the corresponding controller device have split private keys that correspond to a public key. For example, Alice has a private key sk_a. Alice1 keeps the private split-key sk_{a_1}, and Alice2 keeps private split-key sk_{a_2}, where $\textit{Split-Key}(sk_a) = (sk_{a_1}, sk_{a_2})$ and *Split-Key* is a function that splits the private key. The corresponding public key for sk_a is pk_a. Bob's key distribution is similar to Alice's.

The same private and public key pairs can be used to agree on K and to compute digital signatures in the proposed protocol. However, it is recommended to use a different split of sk for each purpose. Note that there can be several splits for sk that correspond to the same pk [12].

Figure 2 presents the communication flow in the protocol. Note that the protocol halts if any verification or policy check fails.

Signature-based Mutual Policy Enforcement (MPE-SIGN) Protocol

---

Setup: Alice1 and Alice2 split a secret key sk_a, corresponding to pk_a, and each has sk_{a_1} and sk_{a_2}, respectively. Similarly, Bob1 and Bob2 split a secret key sk_b, corresponding to pk_b, and each has sk_{b_1} and sk_{b_2}, respectively. The message integrity between Alice1 and Bob1, between Alice1 and Alice2, and between Bob1 and Bob2 is protected with the keys K, K_a, and K_b, respectively, which they shared before this protocol run.

Remark: All parties verify MACs of the messages they receive, computed with the keys K, K_a, and K_b, in each step, except for Steps 2 and 3, before they continue with the protocol. If the MAC verification fails, the protocol does not continue unless another message is received before the connection times out. The description of the protocol below gives the case of a successful result from all other verifications and checks (Steps 6(a), 8(c), 10, 12(a), 12(b), 14(c), 16, 18).

Protocol description: (cf. Figure 2.)

1. Alice1 sends her message m_1, a freshly generated random r_{a_1}, and $MAC_K(m_1, r_{a_1})$ to Bob1.
2. Bob1 sends his freshly generated random r_{b_1} to Bob2.
3. Bob2 sends his freshly generated random r_{b_2} back to Bob1.
   Assume $T = (m_1, r_{a_1}, m_2, r_{b_1})$ for simplicity.
4. Bob1 sends his message m_2 along with the randoms, r_{b_1} and r_{b_2}, and $MAC_K(T, r_{b_2})$ to Alice1.

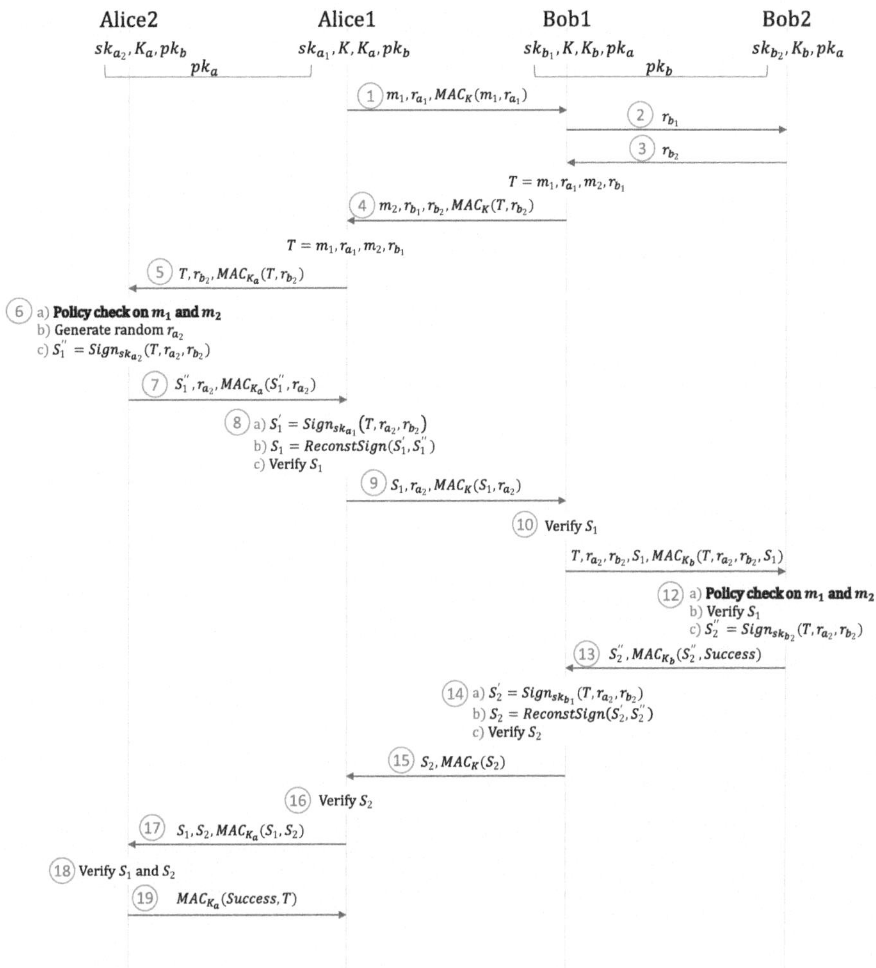

Fig. 2. Communication flow of the signature-based protocol (MPE-SIGN).

5. Alice1 forwards the exchanged messages, m_1 and m_2, and generated randoms, r_{a_1}, r_{b_1}, and r_{b_2}, and $MAC_{K_a}(T, r_{b_2})$ to Alice2.
6. **(a)** Alice2 checks the messages, m_1 and m_2, whether they are compliant to Alice's policy.
   (b) If the messages are according to the policy, Alice2 generates a fresh random r_{a_2}.
   (c) Alice2 computes the split signature using her split key sk_{a_2} including all the messages and randoms: $S_1'' = Sign_{sk_{a_2}}(T, r_{a_2}, r_{b_2})$.
7. Alice2 sends the split signature S_1'', her random r_{a_2}, and $MAC_{K_a}(S_1'', r_{a_2})$ to Alice1.

8. (a) Alice1 computes the split signature using her split key sk_{a_1} including all the messages and randoms: $S'_1 = Sign_{sk_{a_1}}(T, r_{a_2}, r_{b_2})$.
   (b) Alice1 reconstruct the signature using both split signatures: $S_1 = ReconstSign(S'_1, S''_1)$.
   (c) Alice1 verifies S_1 before sending it to Bob1 to make sure that Alice2 provided a correct split signature.
9. Alice1 sends the reconstructed signature S_1, Alice2's random r_{a_2}, and $MAC_K(S_1, r_{a_2})$ to Bob1.
10. Bob1 verifies Alice's signature S_1.
11. Bob1 sends the messages, the signature, and randoms, $(T, r_{a_2}, r_{b_2}, S_1)$, and $MAC_K(T, r_{a_2}, r_{b_2}, S_1)$ to Bob2.
12. (a) Bob2 checks the messages, m_1 and m_2, whether they are compliant to Bob's policy.
   (b) Bob2 verifies Alice's signature S_1.
   (c) Bob2 computes the split signature using his split key sk_{b_2} including all the messages and randoms: $S''_2 = Sign_{sk_{b_2}}(T, r_{a_2}, r_{b_2})$.
13. Bob2 sends the split signature S''_2 and $MAC_K(S''_2, Success)$ to Bob1.
14. (a) Bob1 computes the split signature using his split key sk_{b_1} including all the messages and randoms: $S'_2 = Sign_{sk_{b_1}}(T, r_{a_2}, r_{b_2})$.
   (b) Bob1 reconstruct the signature using both split signatures: $S_2 = ReconstSign(S'_2, S''_2)$.
   (c) Bob1 verifies S_2 before sending it to Alice1 to make sure that Bob2 provided a correct split signature.
15. Bob1 sends the reconstructed signature S_2 and $MAC_K(S_2)$ to Alice1.
16. Alice1 verifies Bob's signature S_2.
17. Alice1 sends the signatures, (S_1, S_2), and $MAC_{K_a}(S_1, S_2)$ to Alice2.
18. Alice2 verifies both Alice's and Bob's signatures S_1 and S_2, respectively.
19. Alice2 sends a $MAC_{K_a}(Success, T)$ as a *Success* message to Alice1.

Next, we introduce another variant, the MAC-based mutual policy enforcement protocol (MPE-MAC). This protocol is similar to MPE-SIGN, with the usage of MAC on the messages instead of signing them. So, the parties do not use asymmetric keys as in MPE-SIGN, but use symmetric keys that should have been agreed on before the protocol starts. These keys are K_{11} between Alice1 and Bob1, K_{21} between Alice2 and Bob1, K_{12} between Alice1 and Bob2, and K_{22} between Alice2 and Bob2. Differences in MPE-MAC compared to MPE-SIGN can be observed in the communication flow in Fig. 5 in Appendix A.

After the protocol ends, the communication continues based on the *Success* message. Alice1 and Bob1 can continue the communication. This protocol can be repeated as long as the parties communicate.

In case of a failure in verifications, e.g., policy check failure, signature verification failure, and MAC verification failure, the participant should inform the other participant that there is a failure. However, we do not want the outsider to know what kind of failure has occurred. Thus, to inform the failure and its type, where the types are pre-saved constants or codes that participants have, the participant computes the MAC of the failure type along with

T using the MAC keys used for integrity protection. For example, Bob2 would send $MAC_{K_b}(PoliceCheckFail, T)$ to Bob1. Bob1 tries to compute the MAC with different failure types and determines the correct one. The outsider can understand that there is a failure because the communication halts, but only Bob1 can verify the MAC.

7 Formal Verification

The description of how we model our protocol with ProVerif is given in Appendix B.1, and the code is available on GitHub [3]. Next, we first discuss correspondence queries and authentication, authorization, and replay protection, and then we continue with how compromised parties impact these security properties. In Sect. 8, we analyze the results of the formal verification and show how these provide formal proofs for the security properties.

Correspondence Queries. We define `events` to mark specific milestones in the protocol. With the reachability queries, we can learn if the events can occur, which means that the protocol was run successfully up to that point. With correspondence queries, we can ensure that the events have happened in a desired relationship to each other, e.g., in a specific order and with specific data.

In ProVerif [7], authentication is checked by defining the correspondence of two milestone events (`E1` and `E2`), such that the occurrence of `event(E2)` implies that `event(E1)` has previously occurred (`event(E2)==>event(E1)`). If the number of occurrences of `event(E1)` is always greater than or equal to `event(E2)`, then the correspondence is injective. This property proves the authentication and replay protection in the protocol.

We want to investigate the authentication, authorization, and replay protection for each participant. We achieve this by building a query where one party has finished the run of the protocol, then the other parties must have finished their run of the protocol, and the controller parties must have done the policy check, and they agreed on the same variables. For example, the query for how Alice1 authenticates the others is as follows:

```
query a1:host,a2:host,b1:host,b2:host,m1:bitstring, m2:bitstring;
inj-event(Alice1FINISHED(a1,b1,m1,m2))
    ==>inj-event(Bob1FINISHED(a1,b1,m1,m2))
    && inj-event(Alice2FINISHED(a2,a1,m1,m2))
    && inj-event(Bob2FINISHED(b2,b1,m1,m2))
    && inj-event(Alice2PolicyCheck(a2,a1,m1,m2))
    && inj-event(Bob2PolicyCheck(b2,b1,m1,m2)).
```

Examples in this section are for MPE-SIGN. The event and variable names may vary from the corresponding ones in MPE-MAC. Complete code and the full list of queries can be found in the GitHub repository [3].

When we run the ProVerif code of the models of our protocols, all authentication queries turn *true*. Figure 3 shows a screenshot of the results of these

```
Query inj-event(Alice1FINISHED(a1,b1,m1,m2)) ==> inj-event(Bob1FINISHED(a1,b1,m1,m2)) && inj-event(Alice2FINISHED(a2,a1,m1,m2)) &&
 inj-event(Bob2FINISHED(b2,b1,m1,m2)) && inj-event(Alice2PolicyCheck(a2,a1,m1,m2)) && inj-event(Bob2PolicyCheck(b2,b1,m1,m2)) is t
rue.

Query inj-event(Bob1FINISHED(a1,b1,m1,m2)) ==> inj-event(Alice1sendS1(a1,b1,m1,m2)) && inj-event(Alice2START(a2,a1,m1,m2)) && inj-
event(Bob2FINISHED(b2,b1,m1,m2)) && inj-event(Alice2PolicyCheck(a2,a1,m1,m2)) && inj-event(Bob2PolicyCheck(b2,b1,m1,m2)) is true.

Query inj-event(Alice2FINISHED(a2,a1,m1,m2)) ==> inj-event(Alice1verifyS2(a1,b1,m1,m2)) && inj-event(Bob1FINISHED(a1,b1,m1,m2)) &&
 inj-event(Bob2FINISHED(b2,b1,m1,m2)) && inj-event(Alice2PolicyCheck(a2,a1,m1,m2)) && inj-event(Bob2PolicyCheck(b2,b1,m1,m2)) is t
rue.

Query inj-event(Bob2FINISHED(b2,b1,m1,m2)) ==> inj-event(Alice1sendS1(a1,b1,m1,m2)) && inj-event(Alice2START(a2,a1,m1,m2)) && inj-
event(Bob1sendS1(a1,b1,m1,m2)) && inj-event(Alice2PolicyCheck(a2,a1,m1,m2)) && inj-event(Bob2PolicyCheck(b2,b1,m1,m2)) is true.
```

Fig. 3. Authentication queries.

queries of the MPE-SIGN protocol. We also have similar results with the MPE-MAC protocol. This means that we proved that all parties authenticated and authorized other parties that are part of the protocol, and they complete the run of the protocol with the same variables. Furthermore, with injectivity, we prove that the messages cannot be replayed by the attacker, so each session of the protocol run is unique.

The policy check is not modeled explicitly in ProVerif. However, the ProVerif tool inherently allows processes to stop running at any time. Therefore, a failed policy check is covered by a discontinued process, while a successful policy check is covered by a continuing process.

In real-world deployments, policies can be described using a suitable policy specification language, e.g., Datalog [18] or SecPAL [6]. Any policy mechanism that produces a Boolean (yes-no) result is compatible with our protocol.

Compromised Parties. We want to prove the authentication, authorization, and replay protection in the protocol, even if one of the parties is compromised, which means that its secret keys and identities are made available to the attacker. We have maintained that by including `(event compromise(Alice1); out(internet,(ska1,K,Ka,Success))` in the main process and repeating similar events and actions for all parties in the protocol.

In each run of the ProVerif protocol model, we have compromised one party. Next, we will discuss the example of Alice1's compromise in the MPE-SIGN protocol. The results of the other single-party compromises in MPE-SIGN are given in Appendix B.2. The ProVerif code of the compromise cases for both MPE-SIGN and MPE-MAC can be found in the GitHub repository [3].

Figure 4 shows the results of the queries when Alice1 is compromised. The results with "`true`" mean that even if Alice1 is compromised, (i) Alice1 maintains authentication of the Bob's side, (ii) Alice2, Bob1, and Bob2 can authenticate each other and agree on the same messages, (iii) if the non-compromised parties have successfully run the protocol, then the attacker did not interrupt and intercept messages. The results are similar for other parties' compromises as well, as can be seen in Appendix B.2.

```
Query inj-event(Alice1FINISHED(a1,b1,m1,m2)) ==> inj-event(Bob1FINISHED(a1,b1,m1,m2)) && inj-event(Bob2FINISHED(b2,b1,m1,m2))
&& inj-event(Bob2PolicyCheck(b2,b1,m1,m2)) is true.

Query inj-event(Bob1FINISHED(a1,b1,m1,m2)) ==> inj-event(Alice2START(a2,a1,m1,m2)) && inj-event(Bob2FINISHED(b2,b1,m1,m2)) &&
inj-event(Alice2PolicyCheck(a2,a1,m1,m2)) && inj-event(Bob2PolicyCheck(b2,b1,m1,m2)) is true.

Query inj-event(Bob2FINISHED(b2,b1,m1,m2)) ==> inj-event(Alice2START(a2,a1,m1,m2)) && inj-event(Bob1sendS1(a1,b1,m1,m2)) && in
j-event(Alice2PolicyCheck(a2,a1,m1,m2)) && inj-event(Bob2PolicyCheck(b2,b1,m1,m2)) is true.

Query inj-event(Alice2FINISHED(a2,a1,m1,m2)) ==> inj-event(Bob1FINISHED(a1,b1,m1,m2)) && inj-event(Bob2FINISHED(b2,b1,m1,m2))
&& inj-event(Alice2PolicyCheck(a2,a1,m1,m2)) && inj-event(Bob2PolicyCheck(b2,b1,m1,m2)) is true.
```

Fig. 4. Authentication queries of compromised Alice1.

8 Security Analysis

As discussed in Sect. 4, the main goal of mutual policy enforcement is supported by (i) authentication and authorization of the parties, (ii) replay protection, and (iii) integrity of protocol messages.

With authentication queries, explained in Sect. 7, we have formally proved with ProVerif that for all parties, when one party (A) ends the protocol, the other parties (B, C, and D) have previously been running the protocol and agree on the messages (m_1, m_2), and each run of A corresponds to unique runs of B, C, and D. This means, according to Lowe's authentication hierarchy [21], that the protocol guarantees injective agreement for all parties, i.e., it provides the strongest form of authentication. In addition, our positive result for the injective agreement guarantees replay protection. Furthermore, the injective agreement on (m_1, m_2) proves that the integrity of these messages is protected.

Furthermore, Steps (6.a) and (12.a) are dedicated to policy checking for Alice2 and Bob2, respectively, both in MPE-SIGN and MPE-MAC. In this setting, if the policy check fails, the protocol halts and does not continue. As explained earlier, ProVerif models this case by a discontinued process. On the other hand, when the process continues in ProVerif, this models the successful policy check. We obtain the authorization property through these policy checks.

We do not set confidentiality as the security goal, as it is not necessary for enforcing policies. However, our protocols utilize shared symmetric keys to check the integrity of the messages by computing their MAC. These MAC-related keys can be used to secure the channel if confidentiality is required.

We evaluate the impact of an attacker compromising one or more participants by adopting the extended Canetti-Krawczyk (eCK) adversary model for compromised participants. We have shown using ProVerif (see Sect. 7) that when at most one party is compromised, the non-compromised parties, which have successfully completed their part in the protocol run, obtain the following assurances: if the compromised participant is on the Alice's side, then the Bob's side gets assurance that one of the following is true: the message m_1 is indeed sent by Alice1 (in the case Alice2 is compromised), or m_1 is at least according to Alice's side policies (in the case Alice1 is compromised). Respectively, if the compromise is on Bob's side, then Alice's side gets assurance that either message m_2 is sent by Bob1 or at least the reply m_2 is according to Bob's side policies.

When considering two-party compromises, we first note that if both devices on the same side, e.g., Alice1 and Alice2, are compromised, then the other side cannot get any assurances. Otherwise, we have three cases: (i) if Alice1 and Bob1 are compromised, they could communicate between themselves without involving the controller devices at all, (ii) if Alice2 and Bob2 are compromised, they could reject messages that are according to the policy or they could accept messages that are not according to the policy, while the primary devices may be unaware of this, and (iii) if Alice1 and Bob2 or Alice2 and Bob1 are the two compromised parties, the compromised controller device could accept the messages that are not acceptable according to their policies but acceptable for the other side. The case (i) cannot be prevented by our protocol. The case (ii) could be mitigated if the primary devices are also aware of the policy rules, but the compromised controller devices could still stop acceptable message exchanges. The case (iii) could be mitigated if both sides (Alice and Bob) adopt the same security policies.

In summary, our protocols mitigate quite well the impacts of one compromised party among four. Some of the combinations of two corrupted parties are also mitigated to some extent, but our protocols cannot protect against the case where both the controller and the primary device on the same side are compromised. As a consequence, our protocol cannot protect against more than two compromised parties.

9 Performance Analysis

We have proposed two variants of a policy-checking protocol in Sect. 6: signature-based (MPE-SIGN), shown in Fig. 2, and MAC-based (MPE-MAC), shown in Fig. 5 in Appendix A. Now, we discuss the communication and computational cost of the two protocols and also compare them.

We start with the communication cost. Both protocols start similarly, such as sending (m_1, m_2), randoms, and MACs of every message sent between the parties. The differences are observed in later steps: MPE-SIGN includes signatures in the messages, while MPE-MAC includes MACs instead.

The primary devices, Alice1 and Bob1, exchange two messages, m_1 and m_2, whose content depends on the use case. In our protocol, these two messages are also included in the transcript T sent from Alice1 to Alice2 in Steps 5 and 11 (of both protocol variants): messages m_1 and m_2 that are exchanged between the primary devices are also sent by the primary device to its controller. Therefore, the additional communication overhead of our protocol includes $2 \cdot (|m_1| + |m_2|)$, where $|m_i|$ denotes the length of the i-th message.

In order to estimate the communication costs of MPE-SIGN and MPE-MAC, we have chosen two algorithms for the digital signature scheme: Elliptic Curve Digital Signature Algorithm (ECDSA) and Module-Lattice-Based Digital Signature Algorithm (ML-DSA). ECDSA produces 64 bytes of signature with curve P-256 [1] and ML-DSA-44 [2] produces 2420 bytes of signature. Then, we have chosen HMAC-SHA-1-96 to compute MACs in the protocol; therefore, the output of the MAC is 12 bytes. We also assume that the randoms created in the protocol are 16 bytes. Table 1 summarizes the communication overhead of two protocols, including the number of signatures and MACs, and the length of these messages depending on the different choices of algorithms.

Table 1. Summary of communication costs of MPE-SIGN and MPE-MAC

	Total communicated	Total length (bytes)
MPE-SIGN	$3(m_1, m_2)$, 14 randoms, 7 Signatures, 10 MACs	$3(\|m_1\| + \|m_2\|)$ + 792 bytes (ECDSA P-256)
		$3(\|m_1\| + \|m_2\|)$ + 17347 bytes (ML-DSA-44)
MPE-MAC	$3(m_1, m_2)$, 14 randoms, 28 MACs	$3(\|m_1\| + \|m_2\|)$ + 560 bytes (SHA-1-96)

We can conclude from Table 1 that the communication overhead in MPE-SIGN is larger than the communication overhead in MPE-MAC. The choice of algorithms affects the difference between the two protocols.

Next, we continue with the computational overhead. Both MPE-SIGN and MPE-MAC have policy checks, MAC computations, and random generation as common computations. They differ when MPE-SIGN has additional signatures and signature verification operations. We do not include signature reconstruction in the computational cost.

Table 2 presents the summary of the computational costs and computation time of MPE-SIGN and MPE-MAC. As can be observed in the table, 11 public key operations (signing and signature verification) in MPE-SIGN are replaced with 16 symmetric key operations (MAC computation). Considering that computations of public key operations are heavier than symmetric key operations, we can conclude that MPE-SIGN is computationally heavier than MPE-MAC.

In order to determine the computation time of the MPE protocols, we investigated the computation times of cryptographic primitives using OpenSSL 3.0.2

Table 2. Summary of computational costs of MPE-SIGN and MPE-MAC. CT: Computation Time

Computations	MPE-SIGN	CT of MPE-SIGN (μs)	MPE-MAC	CT of MPE-MAC (μs)
Policy Check	2	~1000	2	~1000
Signing	4	85.80	–	–
Verification	7	450.38	–	–
Random Gen.	4	3.08	4	3.08
MAC	20	6.20	36	11.16
Total		~1545		~1014

on a workstation with a processor Intel(R) Core(TM) Ultra 5 125U @ 1.30 GHz. According to this investigation, signing a signature with ECDSA P-256 takes 21.45 microseconds (μs) and verification of this signature takes 64.34 μs. MAC computation with HMAC-SHA-1-96 for 16-byte input takes 0.31 μs. In our protocol, we use a 12-byte input; therefore, we can assume that the computation time for MAC computation would be less than this value. The random generation of a 16-byte value takes 0.77 μs. Since we do not specify the details of the policy check in our protocols, we will use an approximation of 500 μs for policy check [24]. As also shown in Table 2, the computation time of the complete MPE-SIGN is around 1.5 ms, and the MPE MAC is around 1.1 ms.

In summary, the MPE-SIGN has more communication and computational overhead compared to the MPE-MAC. On the other hand, MPE-MAC requires heavier key agreement procedures than MPE-SIGN, considering the computations of the shared keys for MAC. If a secure key-sharing protocol, e.g., split-key protocols proposed in [4], is used to share a key for the MAC keys, then MPE-MAC needs to run the protocol four times, while MPE-SIGN does not require additional protocols.

Note that we do not count K, K_a, and K_b for the comparison above. This is because, first, both protocols require these keys; second, in reality, it is likely that these parties have their channels secured, e.g., by TLS 1.3, which would result in sharing such keys.

10 Discussion and Conclusion

We have introduced a mutual policy enforcement protocol with two variants: signature-based (MPE-SIGN) and MAC-based (MPE-MAC). A successful run of the protocol means that the exchanged messages have been authorized by the controller devices on the initiating and responding sides according to their respective policies. The results of formal verification, as discussed in Sect. 7, show that both variants satisfy the security goals, such as providing authentication of the parties and replay protection, as well as the integrity of the messages.

Performance analysis in Sect. 9 shows that both protocols are efficient. Furthermore, MPE-MAC is more efficient than MPE-SIGN.

In Sect. 5, we have defined use cases for MPE protocols. The use cases can be characterized on the basis of their time sensitivity, the need for non-repudiation, and the need for repetition. For example, UC1.2, communicating drones, is time-sensitive, whereas UC3, multi-party computation, is not time-sensitive. Another example is that UC4, smart contract negotiation, needs non-repudiation, whereas UC1.1, communicating cars, does not need it. As a final example, UC5, parental control, requires repetition such that the protocol would be run several times while the kids are talking to each other or using streaming services. However, our example for UC1.3, communicating smart devices, does not require repetition, since continuation of the communication is not needed.

We assume that the keys are shared between the participants before the protocol starts. Considering the different characteristics of the use cases and the performance analysis, we can conclude the following. If the use case is time-sensitive or requires repetition, the MPE-MAC protocol would be more suitable to use because it would incur less computational and communicational costs. On the other hand, MPE-SIGN would be more suitable for use cases that require non-repudiation because the signature is involved.

Future work includes the addition of details of policy checking to the formal model of our protocol. It may also include prototyping the protocol and working further with each use case.

Acknowledgements. We would like to thank Mohamed Taoufiq Damir, Aleksi Peltonen, and Tuomas Aura for many helpful discussions.

A Protocol Flow of MPE-MAC

The communication flow of the MPE-MAC protocol is illustrated in Fig. 5.

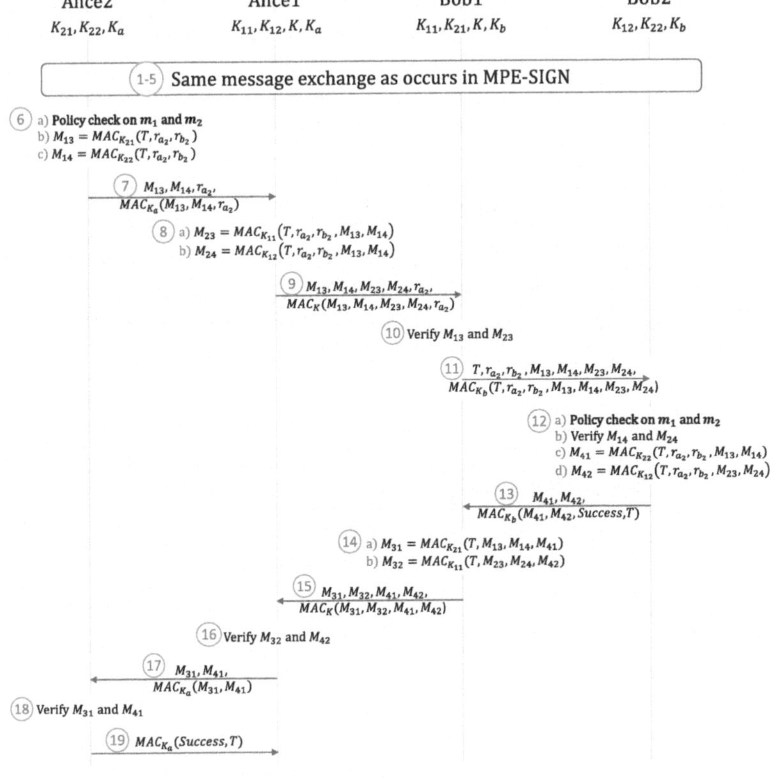

Fig. 5. Communication flow of MAC-based protocol (MPE-MAC).

B ProVerif Construction and Results

In this chapter, we explain how we model the protocol and provide the results of ProVerif queries for the compromised cases explained in Sect. 7.

B.1 Modeling the Protocol

We start by defining four public (unsecured) channels: `chAA` between Alice1 and Alice2, `chAB` between Alice1 and Bob1, `chBB` between Bob1 and Bob2, and `internet` for sending messages to the public network.

Next, we model the subprocesses and the main process. We define one subprocess for each party: `processAlice1`, `processAlice2`, `processBob1`, and `processBob2`. Each subprocess describes the actions of each party, i.e., generating new nonces, sending messages to other parties, and receiving messages.

For simplicity, we create the identifiers, public-private key pairs, split keys, integrity keys, and certificates for the public keys in the main process instead of modeling a separate subprocess for the certificate authority (CA). This is because we assume that the certificates and the keys are shared before the protocol starts.

We introduced an exclamation mark for some parts of the code in the main process. In this way, we can have an unbounded number of parallel sessions, and each session also runs an unbounded number of times. For all parties, their identifiers and shared keys are renewed in different sessions.

B.2 Queries for the Compromised Cases

Here we give only the rest of the result of the ProVerif model of the MPE-SIGN protocol (Fig. 6), since the case of the compromise of Alice1 is explained in Sect. 7. We do not separately include the ProVerif results of the MPE-MAC protocol because they are similar to the MPE-SIGN protocol.

Only Bob1 is compromised:

```
Query inj-event(Bob1FINISHED(a1,b1,m1,m2)) ==> inj-event(Alice1sendS1(a1,b1,m1,m2)) && inj-event(Alice2START(a2,a1,m1,m2)) &&
inj-event(Bob2FINISHED(b2,b1,m1,m2)) && inj-event(Alice2PolicyCheck(a2,a1,m1,m2)) && inj-event(Bob2PolicyCheck(b2,b1,m1,m2)) i
s true.

Query inj-event(Alice1FINISHED(a1,b1,m1,m2)) ==> inj-event(Alice2FINISHED(a2,a1,m1,m2)) && inj-event(Bob2FINISHED(b2,b1,m1,m2)
) && inj-event(Alice2PolicyCheck(a2,a1,m1,m2)) && inj-event(Bob2PolicyCheck(b2,b1,m1,m2)) is true.

Query inj-event(Alice2FINISHED(a2,a1,m1,m2)) ==> inj-event(Alice1verifyS2(a1,b1,m1,m2)) && inj-event(Bob2FINISHED(b2,b1,m1,m2)
) && inj-event(Alice2PolicyCheck(a2,a1,m1,m2)) && inj-event(Bob2PolicyCheck(b2,b1,m1,m2)) is true.

Query inj-event(Bob2FINISHED(b2,b1,m1,m2)) ==> inj-event(Alice1sendS1(a1,b1,m1,m2)) && inj-event(Alice2START(a2,a1,m1,m2)) &&
inj-event(Alice2PolicyCheck(a2,a1,m1,m2)) && inj-event(Bob2PolicyCheck(b2,b1,m1,m2)) is true.
```

Only Alice2 is compromised:

```
Query inj-event(Alice2FINISHED(a2,a1,m1,m2)) ==> inj-event(Bob1FINISHED(a1,b1,m1,m2)) && inj-event(Bob2FINISHED(b2,b1,m1,m2))
&& inj-event(Alice2PolicyCheck(a2,a1,m1,m2)) && inj-event(Bob2PolicyCheck(b2,b1,m1,m2)) is true.

Query inj-event(Alice1FINISHED(a1,b1,m1,m2)) ==> inj-event(Bob1FINISHED(a1,b1,m1,m2)) && inj-event(Bob2FINISHED(b2,b1,m1,m2))
&& inj-event(Bob2PolicyCheck(b2,b1,m1,m2)) is true.

Query inj-event(Bob1FINISHED(a1,b1,m1,m2)) ==> inj-event(Alice1sendS1(a1,b1,m1,m2)) && inj-event(Bob2FINISHED(b2,b1,m1,m2)) &&
 inj-event(Bob2PolicyCheck(b2,b1,m1,m2)) is true.

Query inj-event(Bob2FINISHED(b2,b1,m1,m2)) ==> inj-event(Alice1sendS1(a1,b1,m1,m2)) && inj-event(Bob1sendS1(a1,b1,m1,m2)) && i
nj-event(Bob2PolicyCheck(b2,b1,m1,m2)) is true.
```

Only Bob2 is compromised:

```
Query inj-event(Bob2FINISHED(b2,b1,m1,m2)) ==> inj-event(Alice1sendS1(a1,b1,m1,m2)) && inj-event(Alice2START(a2,a1,m1,m2)) &&
inj-event(Alice2PolicyCheck(a2,a1,m1,m2)) && inj-event(Bob2PolicyCheck(b2,b1,m1,m2)) is true.

Query inj-event(Alice1FINISHED(a1,b1,m1,m2)) ==> inj-event(Bob1FINISHED(a1,b1,m1,m2)) && inj-event(Alice2FINISHED(a2,a1,m1,m2)
) && inj-event(Alice2PolicyCheck(a2,a1,m1,m2)) is true.

Query inj-event(Bob1FINISHED(a1,b1,m1,m2)) ==> inj-event(Alice1sendS1(a1,b1,m1,m2)) && inj-event(Alice2START(a2,a1,m1,m2)) &&
inj-event(Alice2PolicyCheck(a2,a1,m1,m2)) is true.

Query inj-event(Alice2FINISHED(a2,a1,m1,m2)) ==> inj-event(Alice1verifyS2(a1,b1,m1,m2)) && inj-event(Bob1FINISHED(a1,b1,m1,m2)
) && inj-event(Alice2PolicyCheck(a2,a1,m1,m2)) is true.
```

Fig. 6. Authentication queries of MPE-SIGN when Bob1, Alice2, and Bob2 are compromised.

References

1. Digital Signature Standard (DSS). Standard NIST FIPS 186-5, National Institute of Standards and Technology (NIST), Washington, D.C. (2023). https://doi.org/10.6028/NIST.FIPS.186-5
2. Module-lattice-based digital signature standard. Standard NIST FIPS 204, National Institute of Standards and Technology (NIST), Washington, D.C. (2024). https://doi.org/10.6028/NIST.FIPS.204
3. Akman, G.: ProVerif Implementation of Mutual Enforcement Policy (MPE) Protocols (2025). https://github.com/gizem-akman/MutualEnforcementPolicy
4. Akman, G., Taoufiq Damir, M., Ginzboorg, P., Sovio, S., Niemi, V.: Split keys for station-to-station (STS) protocols. J. Surveill., Secur. Saf. **4**(3), 62–93 (2023). https://doi.org/10.20517/jsss.2023.16
5. Basin, D., Cremers, C., Dreier, J., Meier, S., Sasse, R., Schmidt, B.: Tamarin-prover manual: security protocol analysis in the symbolic model. User Manual and Tutorial (2022)
6. Becker, M.Y., Fournet, C., Gordon, A.D.: SecPAL: Design and Semantics of a Decentralized Authorization Language. Technical Report, Microsoft Research (2010)
7. Blanchet, B., Smyth, B., Cheval, V., Sylvestre, M.: ProVerif v2.05: Automatic Cryptographic Protocol Verifier, User Manual and Tutorial. Inria (2023)
8. Buccafurri, F., De Angelis, V., Lazzaro, S., Pugliese, A.: Enforcing security policies on interacting authentication systems. Comput. Secur. **140**, 103771 (2024). https://doi.org/10.1016/j.cose.2024.103771
9. Choi, S., Sun, K., Eom, H.: Resource-efficient multi-source authentication utilizing split-join one-way key chain. In: Emerging Trends in ICT Security, pp. 267–279. Elsevier (2014). https://doi.org/10.1016/B978-0-12-411474-6.00017-7

10. Darling, D.: What is policy enforcement? (2022). https://www.quest.com/learn/what-is-policy-enforcement.aspx. Accessed 03 Sep 2025
11. Dolev, D., Yao, A.: On the security of public key protocols. IEEE Trans. Inf. Theory **29**(2), 198–208 (1983). https://doi.org/10.1109/TIT.1983.1056650
12. Ebina, M., Mita, J., Shikata, J., Watanabe, Y.: Efficient threshold public key encryption from the computational bilinear Diffie-Hellman assumption. In: Proceedings of the 8th ACM on ASIA Public-Key Cryptography Workshop, pp. 23–32. ACM, Virtual Event Hong Kong (2021). https://doi.org/10.1145/3457338.3458296
13. Even, S., Goldreich, O., Lempel, A.: A randomized protocol for signing contracts. Commun. ACM **28**(6), 637–647 (1985). https://doi.org/10.1145/3812.3818
14. Farahmandian, S., Hoang, D.B.: A policy-based interaction protocol between software defined security controller and virtual security functions. In: 2020 4th Cyber Security in Networking Conference (CSNet), pp. 1–8. IEEE, Lausanne, Switzerland (2020). https://doi.org/10.1109/CSNet50428.2020.9265460
15. Fraser, B.: Site Security Handbook. Tech. Rep. RFC2196, RFC Editor (1997). https://doi.org/10.17487/rfc2196
16. Halpern, J.Y., Pucella, R.: Modeling adversaries in a logic for security protocol analysis. In: Formal Aspects of Security, vol. 2629, pp. 115–132. Springer, Berlin, Heidelberg (2003). https://doi.org/10.1007/978-3-540-40981-6_11
17. Hamlen, K.W., Kagal, L., Kantarcioglu, M.: Policy enforcement framework for cloud data management. Bull. IEEE Comput. Soc. Techn. Committee Data Eng. (2013)
18. Johnston, S.K.: DATALOG-TEXT: Datalog Text Representation V1.0. Specification (2022)
19. Joint Task Force: Security and Privacy Controls for Information Systems and Organizations. Tech. rep., National Institute of Standards and Technology (2020). https://doi.org/10.6028/NIST.SP.800-53r5
20. LaMacchia, B., Lauter, K., Mityagin, A.: Stronger security of authenticated key exchange. In: Susilo, W., Liu, J.K., Mu, Y. (eds.) ProvSec 2007. LNCS, vol. 4784, pp. 1–16. Springer, Heidelberg (2007). https://doi.org/10.1007/978-3-540-75670-5_1
21. Lowe, G.: Breaking and fixing the Needham-Schroeder public-key protocol using FDR. In: Margaria, T., Steffen, B. (eds.) TACAS 1996. LNCS, vol. 1055, pp. 147–166. Springer, Heidelberg (1996). https://doi.org/10.1007/3-540-61042-1_43
22. Macfarlane, R., Buchanan, W., Ekonomou, E., Uthmani, O., Fan, L., Lo, O.: Formal security policy implementations in network firewalls. Comput. Secur. **31**(2), 253–270 (2012). https://doi.org/10.1016/j.cose.2011.10.003
23. Neisse, R., Steri, G., Baldini, G.: Enforcement of security policy rules for the Internet of Things. In: 2014 IEEE 10th International Conference on Wireless and Mobile Computing, Networking and Communications (WiMob), pp. 165–172. IEEE, Larnaca (2014). https://doi.org/10.1109/WiMOB.2014.6962166
24. Olivier, A.: Why low latency is important in authorization (2024). https://www.cerbos.dev/blog/low-latency-in-authorization. Accessed 15 June 2025
25. Paverd, A., Martin, A., Brown, I.: Modelling and Automatically Analyzing Privacy Properties for Honest-but-Curious Adversaries. Technical Report (2014)
26. Pendarakis, D., Yavatkar, D.R., Guerin, D.R.: A framework for policy-based admission control. Request for Comments RFC 2753, IETF (2000). https://doi.org/10.17487/RFC2753
27. Puri, V., Priyadarshini, I., Kumar, R., Van Le, C.: Smart contract based policies for the Internet of Things. Clust. Comput. **24**(3), 1675–1694 (2021). https://doi.org/10.1007/s10586-020-03216-w

28. Ragothaman, K., Wang, Y., Rimal, B., Lawrence, M.: Access control for IoT: a survey of existing research, dynamic policies and future directions. Sensors **23**(4), 1805 (2023). https://doi.org/10.3390/s23041805
29. Rijmenants, D.: Secret Splitting (2004). https://www.ciphermachinesandcryptology.com/en/secretsplitting.htm. Accessed 09 Mar 2025
30. Shah, R.H., Salapurkar, D.P.: A multifactor authentication system using secret splitting in the perspective of Cloud of Things. In: 2017 International Conference on Emerging Trends & Innovation in ICT (ICEI), pp. 1–4. IEEE, Pune (2017). https://doi.org/10.1109/ETIICT.2017.7977000
31. Sicari, S., Rizzardi, A., Grieco, L., Piro, G., Coen-Porisini, A.: A policy enforcement framework for Internet of Things applications in the smart health. Smart Health **3–4**, 39–74 (2017). https://doi.org/10.1016/j.smhl.2017.06.001
32. Sicari, S., Rizzardi, A., Miorandi, D., Cappiello, C., Coen-Porisini, A.: Security policy enforcement for networked smart objects. Comput. Netw. **108**, 133–147 (2016). https://doi.org/10.1016/j.comnet.2016.08.014
33. van Tilborg, H.C.A., Jajodia, S. (eds.): Encyclopedia of Cryptography and Security. Lecture Notes in Computer Science. Springer, Boston (2011). https://doi.org/10.1007/978-1-4419-5906-5
34. Varadharajan, V., Karmakar, K., Tupakula, U., Hitchens, M.: A policy-based security architecture for software-defined networks. IEEE Trans. Inf. Forensics Secur. **14**(4), 897–912 (2019). https://doi.org/10.1109/TIFS.2018.2868220
35. Wang, P., Ku, C., Wang, T.C.: A new fingerprint authentication scheme based on secret-splitting for cloud computing security. In: Recent Application in Biometrics, pp. 183–196. InTech (2011). https://doi.org/10.5772/18135

Breaking the Silence: Fuzzing LTE-M and NB-IoT Protocols

Ilja Siroš[1(✉)], Rafael Cavalcanti[2], Dave Singelée[1], and Bart Preneel[1]

[1] COSIC, KU Leuven, Leuven, Belgium
{ilja.siros,dave.singelee,bart.preneel}@esat.kuleuven.be
[2] CSG, Keysight Technologies, Leuven, Belgium
rafael.cavalcanti@keysight.com

Abstract. The rise of Internet of Things (IoT) devices has significantly expanded the need for secure communication networks. While security testing for these protocols is crucial, there has been limited research in fuzzing cellular IoT protocol implementations. This paper presents the first framework for fuzz-testing the LTE-M and NB-IoT protocol implementations in IoT devices. Our approach focuses on testing the LTE-M and NB-IoT *Attach procedure*. It adapts an existing cellular protocol fuzzing framework for the specific requirements of LTE-M and NB-IoT. The framework's effectiveness is validated through testing of four commercially deployed LTE-M/NB-IoT modems, leading to the discovery of 25 new vulnerabilities in two of the modems. This work underscores the importance of security testing emerging IoT technologies and demonstrates the potential of fuzzing to identify vulnerabilities in LTE-M and NB-IoT devices.

Keywords: Fuzzing · LTE-M · NB-IoT

1 Introduction

In recent years, the rise of the Internet of Things (IoT) has spurred the development of various communication technologies designed to support many low-power, low-data-rate devices. Among these, Long Term Evolution for Machines (LTE-M) and Narrowband Internet of Things (NB-IoT) have emerged as two prominent protocols, both belonging to the broader category of cellular IoT standards developed by the 3rd Generation Partnership Project (3GPP) [1]. These technologies are specifically designed to support massive IoT deployments with long battery life, low cost, and extended coverage in challenging environments such as basements or rural areas. According to Ericsson [8], by the end of 2024, cellular IoT connections reached approximately 4 billion worldwide, projected to reach 7 billion by 2030.

As the adoption of IoT devices accelerates, the security of these communication protocols becomes increasingly critical. Given the potential for vulnerabilities in constrained IoT environments, comprehensive security testing, including

R. Laborde et al. (Eds.): ESORICS 2025 Workshops, LNCS 16233, pp. 524–543, 2026.
https://doi.org/10.1007/978-3-032-16165-9_31

fuzzing techniques, is essential to identify and mitigate risks that could compromise the reliability, privacy, and safety of IoT networks. However, there has been limited research on security testing for LTE-M and NB-IoT, and no prior work has used fuzzing techniques to test the security of implementations of LTE-M and NB-IoT protocols in IoT devices. Fuzzing cellular protocol implementations is challenging due to the nature of baseband processors, which operate separately from the main application processor. Extracting any form of feedback from the baseband is difficult, often making black-box fuzzing techniques the only suitable approach.

In this paper, we aim to address the research gap by introducing a fuzzing framework that can be used to test the LTE-M and NB-IoT protocols. Rather than developing novel fuzzing techniques, we opted to leverage on existing fuzzing methods to evaluate the security of IoT devices that support these protocols. Specifically, in this work, we selected an existing fuzzing framework originally designed for 4G LTE and 5G NR (hereafter referred to as 4G and 5G) testing and extend its capabilities to support fuzzing of LTE-M and NB-IoT protocols. We also describe the technical challenges encountered when adapting the framework, as well as the differences in fuzzing approaches between 4G/5G and LTE-M/NB-IoT protocols. To evaluate our framework, we tested it on four LTE-M/NB-IoT modems commonly found in IoT devices worldwide.

The contributions of this paper can be summarized as follows:

- We present the extended fuzzing framework for IoT devices supporting LTE-M or NB-IoT. To the best of our knowledge, this is the first work that applies fuzz testing to the LTE-M and NB-IoT protocol implementations in IoT devices, filling a gap in security research.
- We evaluate our framework by testing it on four LTE-M/NB-IoT modems commonly found in IoT devices worldwide. In total, we discovered 25 new vulnerabilities that led to crashes in two out of four tested modems, highlighting the need for security testing of LTE-M and NB-IoT protocols.

Responsible Disclosure. As part of our responsible disclosure procedure, we have notified the relevant modem manufacturers regarding our findings.

2 Background

Understanding the context of this study requires basic knowledge of cellular protocols and fuzzing. This section first provides an overview of cellular protocols, explaining key concepts and the high-level architecture. It then introduces fuzzing as a testing technique and describes the challenges of applying fuzzing to wireless protocol implementations in embedded devices.

2.1 Cellular Protocols

Overview. Cellular protocols have evolved from the early 2G networks, which mainly supported voice and basic text messaging, to the high-speed, data-rich

4G and, most recently, 5G networks. Each generation brought advancements in data capacity, speed, and reliability to meet the increasing demands of modern applications like streaming and cloud-based services. With the growth of the IoT, specialized protocols like LTE-M and NB-IoT emerged within the 4G and 5G standards to address the unique needs of low-power, low-data-rate devices. These protocols are optimized for extended battery life, robust connectivity in difficult locations, and the ability to support large-scale deployments.

Architecture. Cellular networks have three main components: User Equipment (UE), the Radio Access Network (RAN), and the Core Network (CN). The UE, such as a smartphone or IoT device, connects wirelessly to the RAN to access services like data, voice, or messaging. The RAN includes base stations (eNodeBs for 4G/LTE-M/NB-IoT and gNodeBs for 5G) that manage radio signals, resource allocation, and mobility. Uplink (UL) refers to transmissions from UE to RAN/CN, and downlink (DL) is the reverse. The RAN links to the CN, which manages subscriber authentication, session control, and traffic routing to external networks like the Internet.

Cellular networks are divided into the control and user planes: the control plane manages signaling tasks like connection setup and mobility, while the user plane handles actual user data traffic. Our framework targets the *Attach procedure*, so it focuses exclusively on the control plane.

Control Plane Stack. The control plane protocol stack is composed of multiple layers, as illustrated in Fig. 2 in the Appendix, each contributing to the overall functionality of cellular networks.

Layer 1 (Physical Layer) transmits data over the air, linking MAC transport channels to the physical medium.

Layer 2 consists of the Medium Access Control (MAC), Radio Link Control (RLC), and Packet Data Convergence Protocol (PDCP). MAC and RLC handle scheduling, error correction, and packet segmentation, while PDCP manages header compression, encryption, and integrity protection.

Layer 3 includes the Radio Resource Control (RRC) and Non-Access Stratum (NAS) layers. RRC oversees radio connection setup, maintenance, and measurement reporting, while NAS enables UE-Core Network communication and manages sessions.

Attach Procedure. Cellular standards define numerous procedures, the *Attach procedure*, which is a focus of our study, being a central one. It initiates a device's connection by registering with and authenticating to the Core Network, ultimately setting up a secure bearer for data transmission. The *Attach procedure* is an appealing target for security testing as the early stages of the *Attach procedure* lack security protection, making them vulnerable to potential attacks before encryption is established.

The normal *Attach procedure* flow for LTE-M and NB-IoT is depicted in Fig. 3 in the Appendix. Note that during fuzzing, other messages may also appear in the

Attach procedure. In our experiments, all downlink messages exchanged during the *Attach procedure* were subjected to fuzzing.

Comparing 4G LTE and LTE-M/NB-IoT. In our study, we extend an existing 4G/5G fuzzing framework to support LTE-M/NB-IoT. Therefore, it is crucial to understand the similarities and differences between these protocols. Since 4G LTE, LTE-M, and NB-IoT all fall under the 4G 3GPP standard, here we compare 4G LTE with LTE-M and NB-IoT.

Both 4G LTE and its low-power variants, LTE-M and NB-IoT, are cellular technologies based on the LTE standard. They share a common network architecture and adhere to a similar protocol stack structure.

Despite their architectural similarities, LTE-M and NB-IoT differ from standard 4G LTE in several key aspects. They utilize distinct lower layer configurations, operating on significantly narrower bandwidths and optimizing power consumption and efficient data transmission. Furthermore, their *Attach procedure* involve modified signaling, with differences in message structures and fields tailored for reduced overhead and enhanced efficiency in IoT applications. These differences prevent the direct application of the existing 4G/5G fuzzing framework to LTE-M and NB-IoT devices.

2.2 Fuzzing

Fuzzing, first introduced by Miller et al. [17], is a well-established software testing technique aimed at uncovering vulnerabilities in systems by subjecting them to random or malformed inputs and monitoring their behavior. By generating unexpected data and observing how a program or device reacts—whether it crashes, hangs, or exposes security flaws—fuzzing has proven effective in identifying weaknesses that might otherwise go unnoticed. This approach has become a cornerstone of security testing across a wide range of software applications.

A well-known tool in the fuzzing ecosystem is American Fuzzy Lop (AFL) [41], a coverage-guided fuzzer that leverages coverage instrumentation and address sanitization of the target program. Coverage instrumentation helps to extract the coverage data from the target, which is then leveraged during input mutation to maximize the coverage of the target throughout the fuzzing process. Address sanitization helps to detect memory vulnerabilities that may arise during program execution. AFL's techniques have become foundational in the fuzzing community, inspiring many subsequent fuzzers built upon its principles.

While fuzzing is relatively straightforward for software applications, it becomes significantly more complex when applied to embedded devices. These devices often cannot be easily instrumented, leading to difficulties in obtaining meaningful feedback during fuzzing. Furthermore, detecting memory corruption vulnerabilities can be challenging due to the nondeterministic nature of their consequences [18].

Fuzzing wireless protocols, the focus of this paper, introduces additional challenges. These protocols often enforce strict message formats, incorporating checksums, encryption, and other integrity mechanisms that complicate mutation-based testing. Additionally, they are inherently stateful, meaning packets must be sent at precise moments when the device is in a state that allows processing them. This significantly increases the difficulty of generating valid inputs that the target will accept. Furthermore, transmitting fuzzed packets requires utilizing a complete protocol stack, extending down to the physical layer, just to deliver the mutated data, adding another layer of complexity to the fuzzing process.

3 Related Work

Recent years have seen extensive research on wireless protocol fuzzing. Studies have used fuzzing techniques to target various wireless protocols such as Bluetooth [10–12,23,24,28], Wi-Fi [4,9,29], Zigbee [26,27,31,39]. Among the cellular protocol fuzzing, notable works include LTEFuzz [15], BERSEKER [25], CovFuzz [32], and part of U-Fuzz [31] each targeting the security of 4G or/and 5G components and proposing frameworks to uncover flaws within these network implementations.

Nevertheless, research on LTE-M and NB-IoT fuzzing remains limited. To date, Liu et al. [16] have conducted the only known study addressing fuzzing in NB-IoT environments. Their work, HFuzz, focused on core network protocol implementations for NB-IoT, specifically targeting vulnerabilities within the GPRS Tunneling Protocol. However, to the best of our knowledge, no studies have been published on fuzzing LTE-M or NB-IoT at the end-device level, marking a gap in security research for these protocols, which we aim to bridge in the current research.

4 Selection of the Fuzzing Framework

Given our aim to leverage existing fuzzing techniques for testing LTE-M and NB-IoT protocols, we determined that extending an existing fuzzing framework would be more efficient than building one from scratch. Since both LTE-M and NB-IoT are cellular protocols, we concentrated our search on fuzzing frameworks specifically designed for cellular protocol testing. After reviewing the available open-source frameworks, we identified two options that support cellular protocol fuzzing: U-Fuzz [31] and CovFuzz [32].

U-Fuzz is a versatile framework for CoAP, Zigbee, and 5G protocols, while CovFuzz is designed specifically for 4G and 5G protocols. We ultimately selected CovFuzz for its compact codebase, straightforward setup, and flexible architecture, which make it an ideal foundation for our LTE-M and NB-IoT fuzzing framework. Following previous cellular fuzzing studies, we focus on the *Attach procedure* during testing.

Building upon CovFuzz, our fuzzing framework retains the same core architecture but has been adapted to support the fuzzing of LTE-M and NB-IoT protocols. In the next sections, we provide a high-level overview of CovFuzz framework, challenges in adapting it for fuzzing LTE-M and NB-IoT devices, followed by a description of our extensions and modifications.

5 Overview of the CovFuzz Framework

The CovFuzz framework consists of several main components, briefly described below. Here, we focus only on the functionalities that are important for the current work. For a more detailed explanation of each component as well the additional information, we refer the reader to the CovFuzz paper [32].

5.1 Protocol Stack Implementation

The *protocol stack implementation* is responsible for generating benign packets, which are intercepted and then manipulated during the fuzzing. The CovFuzz framework leverages the open-source srsRAN 4G [35], srsRAN Project [34], and Open5GS [22] to generate 4G and 5G packets, respectively.

To enable packet interception, software hooks are inserted at key points within the protocol stack code, allowing the framework to capture packets at various protocol layers. In CovFuzz, there are interception points on RRC and MAC layers. As the encryption happens on PDCP layer, having two interception points is enough to be able to mutate the fields on all the layers of the protocol stack except layer one.

After the packet is intercepted, the normal flow of the protocol stack is temporarily paused, transferring the packet via shared memory to the *Fuzzing Controller*. After the *Fuzzing Controller* returns a manipulated packet, the flow resumes, sending the fuzzed packet to the *DUT*.

5.2 DUT

The *DUT* serves as the fuzzing target and can be any device that supports at least one of the protocols implemented by the *protocol stack implementation*, i.e., 4G and/or 5G in CovFuzz. Vast majority of the 4G and 5G modems expose the virtual serial interface which can be used for communicating with the modem using the AT commands, which CovFuzz primarily relies on. In case of Android smartphones, that do not support direct AT commands, the modem can be controlled via the Android Debug Bridge (ADB) [2], which is also leveraged in CovFuzz.

5.3 Fuzzing Controller

The *Fuzzing Controller* manages the core fuzzing operations, including packet manipulation and the coordination of the entire fuzzing process. It consists of the following sub-components.

Dissector *Dissector* identifies the type of the intercepted packet and extracts the information about its fields. The *Dissector* used in a CovFuzz framework is a custom C++ library build on top of the Wireshark [40]. This ensures comprehensive support for all the dissection features available in Wireshark, including detailed protocol analysis and packet field extraction. The same library was also used in [31].

Coordinator *Coordinator* handles the lifecycle of fuzzing iterations by initiating and terminating test cycles. It also monitors the status of the *protocol stack implementation* and the *DUT*. In case of anomalies or crashes, the *Coordinator* ensures the fuzzing process is restarted promptly.

Fuzzer *Fuzzer* manipulates the packet based on a given fuzzing strategy. In CovFuzz, two packet manipulation strategies are supported: *Replay* and *Mutation*.

Replay replaces the intercepted packet with a previously captured one, which may come from either the current or a previous fuzzing iteration.

Mutation alters the values of specific fields within the intercepted packet. Every field in the packet gets assigned a mutation probability, calculated as follows:

$$p_f = \frac{k}{|F_P|}$$

where:

- p_f is a probability of mutating a given field
- $|F_P|$ is the total number of fields in the packet
- k is a hyperparameter representing the average number of mutated fields per packet

This approach ensures that the probability is evenly distributed across all fields in a packet, and the average number of mutated fields per packet remains the same among all the intercepted packets.

5.4 Fuzzing Flow

In the CovFuzz framework, one fuzzing iteration corresponds to a single attempt to execute an *Attach procedure*. During this process, all the downlink packets are fuzzed.

On a high level, the fuzzing flow consists of the following steps:

1. *Coordinator* sends an AT command (or an ADB command) to the *DUT*, instructing it to connect to the network.
2. *DUT* initiates the *Attach procedure*, during which messages are intercepted, dissected and then fuzzed according to the user-defined strategies.

3. Once the *Attach procedure* completes, whether successful or not, the *Coordinator* verifies that both *DUT* and *protocol stack implementation* are still alive. If either component is unresponsive, it is restarted and all the packets sent during the last iteration are saved for the later inspection. Additionally, when available, the *Coordinator* collects coverage data from both the *DUT* and the *protocol stack implementation*. This data is used to guide subsequent fuzzing iterations and assess the fuzzer's overall effectiveness.

6 Extension of CovFuzz Framework for Fuzzing LTE-M&NB-IoT

Before discussing the extension of CovFuzz framework, it is worth noting why CovFuzz framework cannot be directly applied to fuzzing LTE-M and NB-IoT protocols. Below, we outline the key reasons for this limitation and the challenges that must be addressed.

Challenge 1 (C1): Lack of LTE-M and NB-IoT Support in the *protocol stack implementation*.
As discussed in Sect. 5.1, CovFuzz relies on srsRAN as its *protocol stack implementation*. However, at the time of the research, srsRAN does not support LTE-M or NB-IoT, making it impossible to communicate with LTE-M/NB-IoT-compliant devices. Furthermore, to the best of our knowledge, there are no open-source LTE-M and NB-IoT *protocol stack implementations*, posing a significant research challenge.

Challenge 2 (C2): Lack of Support for *DUTs* Without a Direct Access to the AT Commands.
As discussed in Sect. 5.2, CovFuzz primarily uses AT commands to communicate directly with the modem. These commands allow the CovFuzz framework to initiate the *Attach procedure* at the start of a fuzzing iteration and verify the modem's status after fuzzing is complete. However, many IoT devices do not expose AT commands directly, making it difficult to trigger the *Attach procedure* and check device status during fuzzing. Developing an alternative method for interacting with such devices is another key research challenge. It is important to note that this limitation applies only to the fuzzing stage and does not occur during the exploitation stage.

To overcome these challenges, we introduced several key modifications to adapt CovFuzz for LTE-M and NB-IoT fuzzing.

First, we integrated a *protocol stack implementation* capable of generating LTE-M and NB-IoT packets, addressing **C1**. Additionally, for devices that do not support direct AT command communication, we developed custom firmware and modified the *Coordinator* to enable alternative methods for monitoring the *DUT*, addressing **C2**. The architecture of the extended CovFuzz framework for fuzzing LTE-M and NB-IoT is shown in Fig. 1. This section details these enhancements and their implementation.

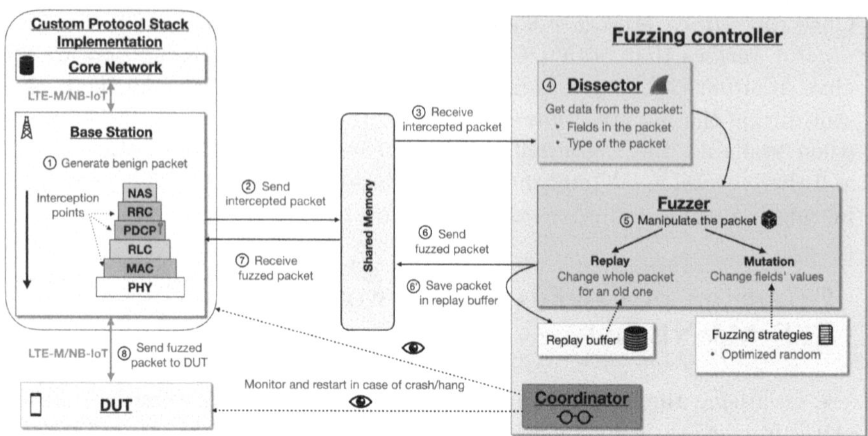

Fig. 1. The illustration of the extended CovFuzz fuzzing framework architecture for LTE-M/NB-IoT fuzzing. The figure is adapted from [32]. The steps shown in the figure outline the fuzzing flow for one packet.

6.1 Protocol Stack Implementation

Generating LTE-M and NB-IoT Packets. Given the lack of open-source LTE-M and NB-IoT *protocol stack implementations*, we utilized a closed-source, custom-built pre-commercial prototype of an eNB/gNB emulator. The emulator was provided to us through a research collaboration with Keysight [13]. However, as part of the agreement, we were not granted access to its source code. This emulator supports LTE-M and NB-IoT alongside 4G and 5G, ensuring compliance with 3GPP Release 16 standards. Additionally, it enables connectivity validation under real-world-like network conditions.

The emulator provides extensive capabilities across the physical (PHY) and upper protocol layers (MAC, RLC, PDCP, and RRC). On the PHY layer, it supports configurations such as Frequency Division Duplex (FDD), Time Division Duplex (TDD), bandwidths from 1.4 MHz to 20 MHz, MIMO (up to 4x2), Positioning Reference Signals (PRS), and Channel State Information-Reference Signals (CSI-RS). These features allow precise emulation and rigorous performance testing.

Notably, the emulator goes beyond just implementing the protocol stack for the above-mentioned protocols. It also incorporates the built-in software hooks on RRC, PDCP, and MAC layers that allow for the interception and manipulation of the downlink messages and the observation of the uplink ones. These software hooks are designed to facilitate targeted test scenarios, such as positive and negative tests, making the emulator an essential component of the fuzzing framework discussed in this work.

However, the closed-source nature of the *protocol stack implementation* (which we could only use as precompiled binaries) introduces two limitations, which are discussed in Sects. 6.1 and 6.3.

Avoiding the Lightweight *Attach procedure*. The lightweight *Attach procedure* occurs when a Core Network recognizes a device from a previous connection attempt, streamlining the *Attach procedure* by skipping NAS message exchanges. This optimization reduces signalling overhead in standard network operations but is less suitable for fuzzing research. The omission of NAS messages decreases the number of packets available for fuzzing, thereby narrowing the testing surface.

In CovFuzz, the authors addressed this by modifying the Core Network implementations, ensuring that the network "forgets" the device after each iteration. This feature ensures that all the NAS messages are present during every *Attach procedure*. In our case, the *protocol stack implementation* does not support the "forgetting" feature mentioned above, and due to its closed-source nature, we cannot integrate this functionality ourselves. However, we identified an alternative approach to achieve the same result.

We observed that the lightweight *Attach procedure* only occurs after the device has successfully completed a full attach process. To prevent this, our strategy is to ensure that an initial successful attach never takes place. This is accomplished by introducing a targeted mutation that halts the *Attach procedure* before it completes. Ideally, this mutation should be applied to a packet near the end of the *Attach procedure* to maximize the number of messages available for fuzzing.

Through our research, we identified such mutations with ease. By applying them in every fuzzing iteration (if this message is reached), we can effectively prevent a successful attach from occurring, thereby eliminating lightweight *Attach procedures* throughout the fuzzing process.

To extend fuzzing beyond this stage, targeted fuzzing campaigns can be conducted, focusing exclusively on these messages. As these messages occur after the NAS phase, the lightweight nature of the *Attach procedure* will no longer impose limitations.

6.2 DUT

The *DUT* in our setup can be any IoT device supporting LTE-M or NB-IoT protocols.

To address **C2**, for devices that do not provide direct access to AT commands, we deployed a custom firmware that interacts with the device's modem via the available API calls. Additionally, a watchdog mechanism ensures automatic restarts in case of unexpected crashes or system hangs.

A pseudocode representation of this firmware is provided in Algorithm 1. To initiate a connection attempt—i.e., the *Attach procedure*—an API call instructs the modem to connect to the network. The process then follows one of two outcomes: either the modem successfully establishes a connection and the function returns, or the modem fails to connect, terminating the function after a predefined, device-specific timeout. This timeout is carefully calibrated to ensure that the *Attach procedure* is triggered exactly once per iteration while minimizing unnecessary waiting time in case of failure.

Next, the modem's status is verified to confirm that it remains alive and responsive. The response is transmitted to the fuzzer via the device's serial interface. If a crash is detected, the modem is restarted before proceeding to the next fuzzing iteration.

6.3 Fuzzing Controller

As described in Sect. 5.3, the main sub-components of *Fuzzing controller* are *Dissector*, *Fuzzer* and *Coordinator*. Here, we describe the extensions made to those sub-components.

Dissector. Since the *Dissector* component leverages Wireshark libraries for packet dissection, it can analyze any protocol supported by Wireshark. In our case, because Wireshark natively supports LTE-M and NB-IoT, no modifications were required to the *Dissector* apart from specifying the appropriate protocol name (LTE-M/NB-IoT instead of 4G/5G) during the dissection process.

Fuzzer. The CovFuzz framework implements multiple fuzzers, including the optimized *Random fuzzer*, the *Grey-box fuzzer*, and the *Black-box fuzzer*. The *Grey-box fuzzer* is guided by code coverage from the *DUT*, while the *Black-box fuzzer* relies on code coverage from the *protocol stack implementation*. In contrast, the optimized *Random fuzzer* operates without any guiding feedback during fuzzing.

However, in our case, code coverage information is unavailable from both the *DUT* and the *protocol stack implementation*. As a result, we use the optimized *Random fuzzer* for our experiments. Instead of feedback-driven guidance, it relies on empirically chosen hyperparameters to maximize performance. Following the recommendations from the CovFuzz paper, we set the parameter $k = 0.5$, ensuring an average of 0.5 mutated fields per intercepted packet, which was shown to yield optimal results for downlink 4G fuzzing.

Coordinator. As discussed before, in CovFuzz framework the *Coordinator* mostly uses AT commands to initiate and terminate fuzzing iterations, as well as to monitor the state of the *DUT*.

In our framework, for IoT devices that support direct AT commands, the *Coordinator* continues to use them to control the fuzzing flow.

However, for devices running custom firmware (as discussed in Sect. 6.2), the *Coordinator* acts more like an observer - it monitors the data transmitted by the *DUT* over the serial interface after each fuzzing iteration. Using this data, the *Coordinator* collects statistics and stores the seeds that trigger crashes.

Algorithm 1. Pseudocode of a firmware running in the IoT device that does not expose AT command interface

```
Input:
    max_i                                  ▷ Total number of fuzzing iterations
    max_timeout                            ▷ Maximum duration of one iteration

▷ Procedure is triggered when the watchdog timeouts
procedure WATCHDOG_CALLBACK()
    ▷ Report a restart to the fuzzer via serial output
    SERIAL.WRITE("dut restart")
    ▷ Now device resets and starts the main procedure
end procedure

▷ Main code of the program
procedure MAIN()
    ▷ Set timeout value to watchdog
    WATCHDOG.INIT(max_timeout)
    ▷ Initialize the modem
    MODEM.INIT()
    for i in 1, 2, ..., max_i do
        ▷ Restart the watchdog's internal timer
        WATCHDOG.FEED()
        ▷ Trigger the Attach procedure
        MODEM.CONNECT()
        ▷ Check if the modem has crashed
        res ← MODEM.IS_ALIVE()
        ▷ Report the result to fuzzer via serial output
        SERIAL.WRITE(res)
        if not res then
            ▷ Modem has crashed -> Restart it
            MODEM.RESTART()
            ▷ Initialize the modem to continue fuzzing
            MODEM.INIT()
        else
            ▷ Disconnect the modem from the network
            MODEM.DISCONNECT()
        end if
    end for
end procedure
```

7 Evaluation

7.1 Experimental Setup

All fuzzing experiments were conducted on a machine running the *protocol stack implementation*, specifically the custom eNB/gNB emulator, alongside the *Fuzzing Controller*. The machine was equipped with an Intel Core i7-9700 CPU (8 cores, 3 GHz) and 32 GB of RAM.

For the *DUTs*, we tested four IoT development kits, each having a built-in LTE-M/NB-IoT modem. To ensure diversity, we chose kits from different manufacturers with distinct modems. Development kits were preferred over commercial devices to simplify fuzzing by offering greater control. Since these modems are widely deployed in commercial products—ranging from smart lockers and tracking devices to medical equipment and EV charging stations [5,20,33,37]—any vulnerabilities discovered impact those as well.

For each *DUT*, we performed 25000 fuzzing iterations, meaning the *Attach procedure* was triggered 25000 times. The duration of these experiments ranged from 50 to 150 hours, depending on the target. Some modems required longer wait times to reliably initiate the *Attach procedure*, increasing the overall runtime for those specific targets.

To ensure ethical compliance and prevent unintended RF emissions, all fuzzing experiments were conducted in a cabled environment.

Table 1 summarizes the *DUT*s tested, their modem versions, whether AT commands are directly exposed via serial interface and the results obtained. Two of the *DUT*s supported sending the AT commands directly via the serial interface and for other two we prepared the custom firmware, as described in Sect. 6.2. Three of the tested *DUT*s successfully detected our custom network in both LTE-M and NB-IoT modes, allowing them to be tested across both protocols. However, the other *DUT* could only connect to our custom network in only one of the two modes despite showing successful connectivity in the other. Similar connectivity issues with mobile devices connecting to custom networks have been observed in previous research, as noted in [32] and [14].

Table 1. List of tested *DUTs*

DUT	Modem	Firmware version	AT support	LTE-M	NB-IoT
Arduino MKR NB 1500 [3]	UBlox SARA R410M [38]	L0.0.00.00.05.12	No	V	T
DIGI XBIB-CU-TH [7]	DIGI XBee 3 Global [6]	1161C	Yes	T	T
NRF9160 DK [30]	NRF9160 [21]	1.3.5	No	V	V
STM32L462RE [36]	LBAD0XX1SC-DM [19]	RK.03.00.00.00.04121.001	Yes	NC	T

NC - No Connection (we could not connect *DUT* to our network)
V - Vulnerabilities were found during the fuzzing tests
T - Tested and no vulnerabilities were found

7.2 Results

As shown in Table 1, among the four *DUT*s tested, we identified vulnerabilities in two: the Arduino MKR NB 1500 (while fuzzing LTE-M) and the NRF9160 DK module (while fuzzing both LTE-M and NB-IoT). Table 2 lists all the distinct vulnerabilities discovered, detailing the affected *DUT*, relevant protocol, packet type, and the manipulations needed to trigger the vulnerability. All found vulnerabilities are caused by the malformed packets on the RRC layer. Each of these vulnerabilities caused the modem in the *DUT* to crash, resulting in a complete loss of cellular connectivity. Furthermore, Table 2 includes the information about the underlying causes of these vulnerabilities where possible. Notably, only the NRF9160 DK provides a specific error code indicating the modem's crash reason. Understanding the reasons behind vulnerabilities can provide insights into the potential for escalating the impact of the vulnerabilities, which is critical for assessing their security implications comprehensively. However, without an access to the source code of the modem, doing that would require reverse engineering the firmware, which lies out of the scope of the current work.

Table 2. List of vulnerabilities found during fuzzing

DUT	Protocol	Packet type	Manipulation of the packet	Reason
Arduino MKR NB 1500	LTE-M	RRCConnectionSetup	Set *lte-rrc.sr_PUCCH_ResourceIndex* field to 2047	Unknown
			Set *lte-rrc.cqi_PUCCH_ResourceIndex* field to 1053	
		RRCConnectionReconfiguration Attach accept	Set *lte-rrc.cqi_PUCCH_ResourceIndex_r10* field to 958	
		RRCConnectionReconfiguration	Fuzz multiple fields[a]	
		RRCConnectionReestablishment[b]	Set *lte-rrc.sr_PUCCH_ResourceIndex* field to 2047	
NRF9160 DK	LTE-M	RRCConnectionSetup	Set *lte-rrc.cqi_pmi_ConfigIndex* field to 1023	Fault usage
			Set 6th *per.extension_bit* field to 1	Reachable assertion
			Set 8th *per.choice_index* field to 1	
			Set *lte-rrc.retxBSR_Timer* field to 7	
			Set 41st *per.optional_field_bit* field to 1	
			Set *lte-rrc.srb_Identity* field to 1	
			Set 42nd *per.optional_field_bit* field to 1	
			Set 9th *per.enum_index* field to 1	
			Set *per.bit_string_length* field to 31	
			Set 5th *per.choice_index* and 2nd *per.optional_field_bit* fields to 1	
			Set *lte-rrc.sr_PUCCH_ResourceIndex* field to 1705	
			Set 43rd *per.optional_field_bit* field to 1	
		RRCConnectionReconfiguration Attach accept	Set *lte-rrc.cqi_PUCCH_ResourceIndex_r10* field to 2047	
	NB-IoT	RRCConnectionSetup-NB	Set 3rd *per.choice_index* field to 1	Memory fault
			Set 4th *per.choice_index* field to 1	
			Set *lte-rrc.retxBSR_Timer_r13* field to 7	Reachable assertion
			Set 4th *per.enum_index* field to 7	
		DLInformationTransfer-NB EMM information	Set 2nd *per.choice_index* field to 2	
		RRCConnectionRelease-NB	Set 1st *per.enum_index* field to 2	
			Set *lte-rrc.releaseCause_r13* field to 2	

[a]Set *lte-rrc.pollByte* field to 15 and 2nd *per.extension_present_bit* and 35th *per.optional_field_bit* fields to 1

[b]Note that RRCConnectionReestablishment does not naturally happen during the *Attach procedure* flow. However, it can be easily triggered, for example, by setting the 1st *per.optional_field_bit* field to 1 in Security Mode Command

7.3 Attack Scenario and Impact of the Vulnerabilities

To exploit the vulnerabilities described in our paper, an attacker must first deploy a malicious base station—commonly referred to in the literature as a fake base station—and induce the targeted device to initiate an attach procedure. This can occur in several ways. First, if the modem is not currently connected to any network, it will perform a full network scan and may attempt to connect to the malicious base station. Alternatively, the attacker can transmit a stronger signal while spoofing the identifier of a legitimate network, causing the modem to preferentially attach to the attacker-controlled station. In either case, the *Attach procedure* is initiated, during which the malicious packet is delivered, thereby triggering the vulnerability.

The impact of vulnerabilities depends on two key factors. The first factor is whether the vulnerability can be triggered before or after the authentication step. Vulnerabilities happening before authentication allow attacks with any SIM card in the target device, making them significantly more accessible and impactful. In contrast, post-authentication vulnerabilities require the attacker to possess specific cryptographic keys associated with the network to pass the authentication stage successfully and reach a point in the *Attach procedure* when the malicious packet can be sent. As shown in Table 2, most vulnerabilities occur after the reception of the RRC Connection Setup packet—one of the first packets in the *Attach procedure*—indicating they occur prior to authentication and, therefore, are more impactful.

The second factor is the nature of the crash: whether it results in a denial-of-service (DoS) condition or has the potential to escalate to remote code execution (RCE). Table 2 reveals that most crashes are triggered by reachable assertions, limiting their impact to DoS attacks. However, two crashes were caused by memory faults, which hold the potential for escalation to RCE. An RCE vulnerability significantly heightens the risk, as it could allow an attacker to gain complete control over the affected device.

8 Discussion

In this section, first, we compare our results with CovFuzz. Then, we outline some limitations of our fuzzing framework and mention potential directions for future improvements.

8.1 Comparing Results with CovFuzz

Both, our framework and CovFuzz, identified vulnerabilities exclusively through fuzzing packets at the RRC layer. However, among the mutations that triggered crashes in our *DUT*s, only one manipulation overlapped with CovFuzz's findings. Specifically, CovFuzz reported that setting the *lte-rrc.sr_PUCCH_ResourceIndex* field to its maximum value 2047 in the RRC Connection Setup message led to crashes in certain 4G and 5G modems. We observed the same behavior with the Arduino MKR NB 1500.

8.2 Limitations and Future Work

Fuzzing only the *Attach procedure*. Our framework focuses solely on fuzzing the *Attach procedure*, which is straightforward to trigger in a lab environment. We argue that vulnerabilities in this phase—especially before authentication—are more impactful. However, expanding fuzzing efforts to other procedures in future work could uncover additional security risks.

Mutation-Based Fuzzing. We use mutation-based fuzzing, allowing modification of existing field values but not adding optional fields absent from the original *protocol stack* packet. This limitation restricts the attack surface our framework can explore. Future work could involve generating packets from protocol specifications rather than relying on the *protocol stack implementation*.

Lack of Feedback for Guiding the Fuzzer. CovFuzz utilizes coverage feedback from either the *DUT* or the *protocol stack implementation* to guide fuzzing, demonstrating improved performance compared to an optimized *Random fuzzer*. In contrast, our framework lacks access to coverage information from both the *DUT* and the closed-source *protocol stack implementation*. Consequently, we relied on an optimized *Random fuzzer*. Future work could explore alternative feedback mechanisms to enhance IoT fuzzing effectiveness.

9 Availability of the Code

To ensure transparency and reproducibility, the code is available at https://github.com/KULeuven-COSIC/Fuzzing_LTE-M_and_NB-IoT/. Due to licensing, the *protocol stack implementation* is omitted; users must integrate their own at the designated interception points.

10 Conclusion

In this paper, we introduced the first systematic framework for fuzz-testing LTE-M and NB-IoT protocol implementations in end-devices. Building on the existing 4G/5G fuzzing framework CovFuzz, we adapted our approach to specifically test LTE-M and NB-IoT implementations during the *Attach procedure*. The framework proved effective, uncovering 25 new vulnerabilities in two of four tested LTE-M/NB-IoT modems, and underscoring the urgency of security testing in these emerging communication technologies.

Acknowledgments. This work was supported in part by CyberSecurity Research Flanders with reference number VR20192203, the European Union's Horizon Research and Innovation program TELEMETRY (grant agreement No. 101119747) and VLAIO in the context of the CS-ICON project IDIoTS.

Disclosure of Interests. The authors have no competing interests.

Appendix

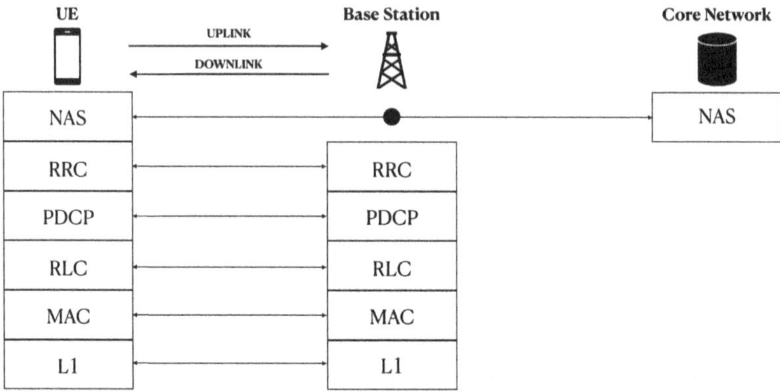

Fig. 2. Control-plane stack for cellular networks. The figure is adapted from [32].

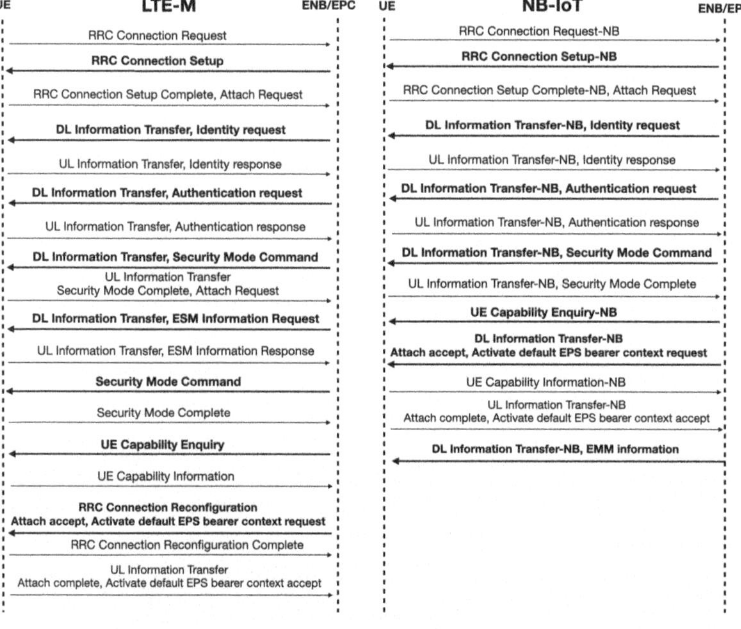

Fig. 3. Attach procedure in LTE-M and NB-IoT. Packets in bold represent downlink messages, which are the focus of fuzzing in our framework.

References

1. 3GPP: 3GPP – The Mobile Broadband Standard. https://www.3gpp.org/. Accessed 27-06-2025
2. Android: Android Debug Bridge (ADB). https://developer.android.com/tools/adb. Accessed 27-06-2025
3. Arduino: MKR NB 1500 | Arduino Documentation. https://docs.arduino.cc/hardware/mkr-nb-1500/. Accessed 27-06-2025
4. Cao, H., Huang, L., Hu, S., Shi, S., Liu, Y.: Owfuzz: discovering WI-FI flaws in modern devices through over-the-air fuzzing. In: Proceedings of the 16th ACM Conference on Security and Privacy in Wireless and Mobile Networks. p. 263–273. WiSec '23, Association for Computing Machinery, New York, NY, USA (2023). https://doi.org/10.1145/3558482.3590174
5. Digi: Digi international exhibits innovative IoT solutions at CES 2025. https://www.digi.com/company/press-releases/2025/digi-exhibits-innovative-iot-solutions-at-ces-2025. Accessed 27-06-2025
6. Digi: Digi XBee 3 global and low-power LTE-M/NB-IoT | digi international. https://www.digi.com/products/embedded-systems/digi-xbee/cellular-modems/digi-xbee-3-global-cellular-cat-1. Accessed 27-06-2025
7. Digi: XBIB-CU-TH - development board - XBee 3, USB-C, through-hole sockets | Digi international. https://www.digi.com/products/models/xbib-cu-th. Accessed 27-06-2025
8. Ericsson: IoT connections forecast – Ericsson mobility report. https://www.ericsson.com/en/reports-and-papers/mobility-report/dataforecasts/iot-connections-outlook. Accessed 27-06-2025
9. Garbelini, M., Wang, C., Chattopadhyay, S.: Greyhound: directed greybox Wi-Fi fuzzing. IEEE Trans. Dependable Sec. Comput. **PP**, 1–1 (2020). https://doi.org/10.1109/TDSC.2020.3014624
10. Garbelini, M.E., Bedi, V., Chattopadhyay, S., Sun, S., Kurniawan, E.: BrakTooth: causing havoc on Bluetooth link manager via directed fuzzing. In: 31st USENIX Security Symposium (USENIX Security 22). pp. 1025–1042. USENIX Association, Boston, MA (2022). https://www.usenix.org/conference/usenixsecurity22/presentation/garbelini
11. Garbelini, M.E., Wang, C., Chattopadhyay, S., Sun, S., Kurniawan, E.: Sweyntooth: unleashing mayhem over bluetooth low energy. In: Proceedings of the 2020 USENIX Conference on Usenix Annual Technical Conference. USENIX ATC'20, USENIX Association, USA (2020)
12. Jang, M., Hwang, Y., Kwon, Y., Kim, H.: Btfuzzer: a profile-based fuzzing framework for Bluetooth protocols. In: Seo, H., Kim, S. (eds.) Information Security and Cryptology - ICISC 2023, pp. 20–38. Springer Nature Singapore, Singapore (2024)
13. Keysight: Keysight: design, emulate, and test to accelerate innovation. https://www.keysight.com/be/en/home.html. Accessed 11-08-2025
14. Syed, K., et al.:: Astra-5g: automated over-the-air security testing and research architecture for 5G SA devices. In: Proceedings of the 17th ACM Conference on Security and Privacy in Wireless and Mobile Networks. p. 89–100. WiSec '24, Association for Computing Machinery, New York, NY, USA (2024). https://doi.org/10.1145/3643833.3656141
15. Kim, H., Lee, J., Eunkyu, L., Kim, Y.: Touching the untouchables: dynamic security analysis of the LTE control plane. In: Proceedings of the IEEE Symposium on Security & Privacy (SP). IEEE (2019)

16. Liu, X., Cui, B., Fu, J., Ma, J.: Hfuzz: Towards automatic fuzzing testing of NB-IoT core network protocols implementations. Futur. Gener. Comput. Syst. **108**, 390–400 (2020)
17. Miller, B.P., Fredriksen, L., So, B.: An empirical study of the reliability of Unix utilities. Commun. ACM **33**(12), 32–44 (1990). https://doi.org/10.1145/96267.96279
18. Muench, M., Stijohann, J., Kargl, F., Francillon, A., Balzarotti, D.: What you corrupt is not what you crash: challenges in fuzzing embedded devices. In: Network and Distributed System Security Symposium (2018). https://api.semanticscholar.org/CorpusID:267919144
19. Murata Manufacturing: Type 1SC (LBAD0XX1SC) | LPWA Products | Murata Manufacturing Co., Ltd. https://www.murata.com/products/connectivitymodule/lpwa/overview/lineup/type-1sc. Accessed 27-06-2025
20. Nordic Semiconductor: Cellular IoT and Bluetooth LE smart locker device offers secure parcel drop-off and pick-up solution. https://www.nordicsemi.com/Nordic-news/2024/10/Jetbeep-employs-Nordic-nRF5340-SoC-and-nRF9160-SiP. Accessed 27-06-2025
21. Nordic Semiconductor: nRF9160. https://www.nordicsemi.com/Products/nRF9160. Accessed 27-06-2025
22. Open5Gs: A C-language Open Source implementation for 5G Core and EPC. https://github.com/open5gs/open5gs. Accessed 27-06-2025
23. Park, H., Nkuba, C.K., Woo, S., Lee, H.: L2fuzz: Discovering bluetooth l2cap vulnerabilities using stateful fuzz testing. In: 2022 52nd Annual IEEE/IFIP International Conference on Dependable Systems and Networks (DSN), pp. 343–354 (2022). https://doi.org/10.1109/DSN53405.2022.00043
24. Pferscher, A., Aichernig, B.K.: Stateful black-box fuzzing of Bluetooth devices using automata learning. In: Deshmukh, J.V., Havelund, K., Perez, I. (eds.) NASA Formal Methods, pp. 373–392. Springer International Publishing, Cham (2022)
25. Potnuru, S., Nakarmi, P.K.: Berserker: ASN.1-based fuzzing of radio resource control protocol for 4G and 5G. In: 2021 17th International Conference on Wireless and Mobile Computing, Networking and Communications (WiMob), pp. 295–300 (2021). https://doi.org/10.1109/WiMob52687.2021.9606317
26. Ren, M., Ren, X., Feng, H., Ming, J., Lei, Y.: Z-fuzzer: device-agnostic fuzzing of Zigbee protocol implementation. In: Proceedings of the 14th ACM Conference on Security and Privacy in Wireless and Mobile Networks, pp. 347–358. WiSec '21, Association for Computing Machinery, New York, NY, USA (2021). https://doi.org/10.1145/3448300.3468296
27. Ren, M., Zhang, H., Ren, X., Ming, J., Lei, Y.: Intelligent Zigbee protocol fuzzing via constraint-field dependency inference. In: Tsudik, G., Conti, M., Liang, K., Smaragdakis, G. (eds.) Computer Security - ESORICS 2023, pp. 467–486. Springer Nature Switzerland, Cham (2024)
28. Ruge, J., Classen, J., Gringoli, F., Hollick, M.: Frankenstein: advanced wireless fuzzing to exploit new Bluetooth escalation targets. In: 29th USENIX Security Symposium (USENIX Security 20), pp. 19–36. USENIX Association (2020). https://www.usenix.org/conference/usenixsecurity20/presentation/ruge
29. Schepers, D., Vanhoef, M., Ranganathan, A.: A framework to test and fuzz Wi-fi devices. In: Proceedings of the 14th ACM Conference on Security and Privacy in Wireless and Mobile Networks, pp. 368–370. WiSec '21, Association for Computing Machinery, New York, NY, USA (2021). https://doi.org/10.1145/3448300.3468261
30. Semiconductor, N.: nRF9160 DK. https://www.nordicsemi.com/Products/Development-hardware/nRF9160-DK. Accessed 27-06-2025

31. Shang, Z., Garbelini, M.E., Chattopadhyay, S.: U-fuzz: Stateful fuzzing of IoT protocols on cots devices. In: 2024 IEEE Conference on Software Testing, Verification and Validation (ICST) (2024)
32. Siroš, I., Singelée, D., Preneel, B.: CovFUZZ: Coverage-based fuzzer for 4G&5G protocols (2024). https://arxiv.org/abs/2410.20958
33. Skylo Team: Murata and Skylo Simplify NTN Device Development. https://www.skylo.tech/newsroom/murata-and-skylo-simplify-ntn-device-development. Accessed 27-06-2025
34. SRS: A complete 5G RAN solution, featuring an ORAN-native CU/DU developed by SRS. https://github.com/srsran/srsRAN_Project. Accessed 27-06-2025
35. SRS: An open source 4G software radio suite developed by SRS. https://github.com/srsran/srsRAN_4G. Accessed 27-06-2025
36. STMicroelectronics: STM32L462RE - Ultra-low-power with FPU Arm Cortex-M4 MCU 80 MHz with 512 kbytes of Flash memory, USB Device, AES-256, DFSDM - STMicroelectronics. https://www.st.com/en/microcontrollers-microprocessors/stm32l462re.html. Accessed 27-06-2025
37. u-blox: Digital Matter: battery-powered, IP67 tracking device. https://www.u-blox.com/en/casestudies/digital-matter-battery-powered-ip67-tracking-device. Accessed 27-06-2025
38. U-BLOX: SARA-R4 series | U-BLOX. https://www.u-blox.com/en/product/sara-r4-series. Accessed 27-06-2025
39. Wang, J., Yu, L., Luo, X.: Llmif: Augmented large language model for fuzzing IoT devices. In: 2024 IEEE Symposium on Security and Privacy (SP), pp. 881–896. IEEE Computer Society, Los Alamitos, CA, USA (2024). https://doi.org/10.1109/SP54263.2024.00211
40. Wireshark: Wireshark: The world's most popular network protocol analyzer. https://www.wireshark.org/. Accessed 27-06-2025
41. Zalewski, M.: Technical whitepaper for AFL-FUZZ. https://lcamtuf.coredump.cx/afl/technical_details.txt. Accessed 27-06-2025

Permission Granted? How Android's App List Protection Fails in Practice

Julian Gagel, Kris Heid(✉), and Jens Heider

Fraunhofer SIT, Rheinstraße 75, 64295 Darmstadt, Germany
{julian.gagel,kris.heid,jens.heider}@sit.fraunhofer.de

Abstract. A substantial volume of private data resides on smartphones, necessitating robust operating system protections. The prevalence of advertising and tracking libraries has significant business for such personally identifiable information (PII), including the list of installed apps—a PII type (previously) often exploited by trackers and advertisers. Recent Android versions have sought to restrict access to such data, notably through the high-risk `QUERY_ALL_PACKAGES` permission, which is now tightly regulated through Google Play. However, our responsibly disclosed alternative method for querying installed apps intentionally remains unrestricted, undermining these protective measures. Our analysis of the top 2,000 Google Play apps reveals that 21.6% already exploit this loophole to access the user's installed app lists.

1 Introduction

The Android operating system handles most of its app security and privacy via permissions. The permission system was introduced very early in the history of Android versions, and it was constantly enhanced and expanded throughout the years. All permissions an app wants to access have to be defined in the Android Manifest during the development process. This allows users and Google Play to categorize an app and judge the appropriateness of the intended permissions. Applying this security and privacy concept, an app that wants to access sensitive user data needs permission and a reason to do so. Therefore, the proper implementation of permissions in the Android API is critical to the operating system.

It was observed that many advertisement and tracking libraries vastly use PII [12,17] such as IMEI, MAC address, build numbers or installed applications as one integral part of their user categorization and identification mechanism. Thus, Android 11 introduced the `QUERY_ALL_PACKAGES` permission, among other mechanisms such as limited access to device identifiers like IMEI, MAC etc. or resettable Advertisement ID which all aim at restricting such practices. This work especially focuses on `QUERY_ALL_PACKAGES` permission which should restrict the app's ability to list all installed apps. The permission is flagged as high-risk by Google, and Google Play requires special justification and checking if an app with this permission should be published.

R. Laborde et al. (Eds.): ESORICS 2025 Workshops, LNCS 16233, pp. 544–557, 2026.
https://doi.org/10.1007/978-3-032-16165-9_32

Since apps are sometimes legitimately required to interoperate and communicate with one another, a query mechanism was introduced in the app's manifest file to, for example, find installed apps that can view PDF files or share pictures. However, the query allows for very open filter rules, making it possible to create a pass-through filter, which in turn delivers all installed applications. This query mechanism is under no restrictions through permissions and can thus be easily exploited by tracking and advertisement libraries to collect PII.

The remainder of the paper is structured as follows: Sect. 2 elaborates the newly introduced OS restrictions and the query bypass in more detail. Section 3 highlights related work about this topic. Our methodology how we analyze if an app uses this bypass is described in Sect. 4 and the evaluation results of the top 2,000 apps on Google Play are laid out in Sect. 5. A discussion in Sect. 6 elaborates the resulting privacy threats and resolution as well as protection strategies. It also contains our arguments for the responsible disclosure to Google and their response. Our results are concluded in Sect. 7 where also ideas for future work presented.

2 Background

2.1 Android Package Visibility

According to Google's app architecture design guidelines [7], the full list of installed applications on a device is categorized as sensitive data:

> When an app targets Android 11 (API level 30) or higher and queries for information about the other apps that are installed on a device, the system filters this information by default. This filtering behavior means that your app can't detect all the apps installed on a device, which helps minimize the potentially sensitive information that your app can access but doesn't need to fulfill its use cases.
> Moreover, filtered package visibility helps app stores like Google Play assess the privacy and security that your app provides for users. For example, Google Play considers the list of installed apps to be personal and sensitive user data.

Protecting this data was the main motivation for the introduction of package visibility filtering in Android 11. Before then, every app could access information about all other applications on that device using the functions provided by the Package Manager API. By default, package visibility filtering will only allow an app to access system packages and certain other interacting apps [6].

If an app needs access to all other installed applications (e.g. for security apps or custom launchers) it should request the permission `QUERY_ALL_PACKAGES`. This permission is classified as a high-risk or sensitive permission and apps requesting it are therefore subject to approval when publishing to Google Play. An app must only use this information according to Google's permitted uses and comply with user data, disclosure and consent policies. [9] This level of review and approval forces developers to consider if full access to installed applications is necessary or if they can implement their app's functionality while protecting the users' privacy.

To achieve interactions with other applications, e.g. sharing text or images, developers can declare the targeted app packages explicitly in the Android manifest. This will expand their app's access to include information about the declared packages and applications. If the interaction should accommodate certain functionality, rather than targeting each application individually, the developer should make use of Intent Action queries. These queries allow developers to specify that their app wants to interact with all other apps that provide a specific functionality. The package visibility system allows access to information about target apps that provide the requested functionality while protecting the users data privacy as much as possible. However, this presents a problem similar to that of permission system. Allowed queries need to be broad enough to accommodate most use cases of most apps while still being specific enough to provide actual protection of the user's privacy.

2.2 Permission Bypass

In its current implementation it is possible to define `android.intent.action.MAIN` as an Intent Action query as shown in Listing 1.1 without requesting any permission.

Listing 1.1. Contents of `AndroidManifest.xml` to implement the pass-through filter

```
<manifest>
  <queries>
    <intent>
      <action android:name="android.intent.action.MAIN"/>
    </intent>
  </queries>
  [...]
</manifest>
```

This allows an application to access information about all apps that provide a `MAIN` Intent. All user-facing apps that are launchable via an icon also provide this Intent. By using this method, it is possible to get information about all user installed apps on a device without requesting the intended permission, effectively bypassing the permission `QUERY_ALL_PACKAGES` and the required review and approval process when publishing to Google Play. This bypass method will also be referred to as a pass-through filter.

2.3 Proof of Concept

To demonstrate the extent of the access achieved via the bypass method a proof of concept app was designed. This app attempts to access all Package Manager functions that retrieve information about other installed applications on the device. It was then built in three variants: One with the permission `QUERY_ALL_PACKAGES`, one without the permission but implementing the pass-through filter and one without the permission or pass-through filter. The last variant should return a baseline of an app that has no special access within the package visibility system.

The purpose of package visibility filtering can be observed when comparing the filtered app list to the app list acquired with the permission in Table 1. Comparing the filtered result on a test device to the app list acquired with the permission, demonstrates the intended functionality of the package visibility system. The permissionless app could retrieve information about 352 installed packages, while the app with the permission had access to all 696. When retrieving the same list using the pass-through filter, a list of 606 packages was returned. The 90 packages that were not shared are exclusively Android, Samsung, and Google system packages. Therefore, all user installed applications retrieved using the permission are also visible when using the pass-through filter. Reasons for this being problematic are further discussed in Sect. 6.

Table 1. Number of retrieved apps on a test device using the three implemented test apps: using package manager API in case of being limited by package visibility filtering, requesting the permission or using the pass-through filter

	Specific filter	Permission	pass-through filter
Apps queried	595	959	959
Apps listed	352	696	606

3 Related Work

As this work focuses on a single specific contradiction between app abilities and the permissions intended to protect them, there is no directly related work. Thus, we categorize the related work in two categories: publications about Android's permission system and papers covering the privacy implications of the data that is accessible through this loophole.

3.1 Android Permission System

Several studies have analyzed the limitations of Android's permission system. Early work by Felt et al. [4] criticized the coarse-grained control and the difficult management of permissions for developers, marketers, and end-users. Stowaway [5] highlighted that many apps are overprivileged, often requesting more permissions than necessary. PScout [1] performed a comprehensive analysis of the Android permission model using static analysis, already noting its complexity in

Android 4, a problem which has only worsened in later versions. Similarly, Wei et al. [18] observed that the set of permissions has grown over time, not towards finer granularity, but to accommodate new hardware features. The study also found that both popular and vendor-preinstalled apps tend to be overprivileged, which increases security and privacy risks. Other research [13] quantified the privacy impact of individual and combined permissions, noting that many free apps request unnecessary permissions to collect user data. While context-aware models [14] have been proposed to address these issues, the current Android implementation still relies on relatively coarse-grained control.

3.2 PII Usage for User Tracking

As direct access to unique device identifiers (such as IMEI or MAC address) has been restricted in recent Android versions, tracking and advertisement libraries have shifted towards alternative fingerprinting methods, including the use of, for example, installed applications as identifiers [12,17]. The publications by Heid et al. [11,12] explicitly list the installed apps on the user phone as one data source of device fingerprinting, a method to uniquely identify devices and therewith users. Studies on taint analysis [15,16] have been used to track privacy leaks in apps. Book et al. [3] performed a longitudinal analysis of advertising libraries, showing that these increasingly leverage the permissions of host apps for data collection, a trend further explored for newer Android versions by Backes et al. [2]. Grace et al. [10] analyzed a large corpus of apps and advertising libraries, identifying privacy and security threats not only from explicit permission use but also from API calls that do not require permissions.

4 Method

To perform the quantitative analysis in Sect. 5 a robust and scalable app analysis framework is required. A reliable method of detecting requested permissions and the implementation of the pass-through filter is created using a static application analysis approach. This approach is chosen for its global view on an applications source code and its scalability when testing multiple applications. Because this method relies on the availability of an applications source code, an open source decompilation tool for Android applications is used. To achieve scalability when performing tests on multiple applications a Google Play interface is created that automates the download process. The app analysis framework is shown in Fig. 1.

4.1 The App Analysis Framework

The framework will perform automated testing on multiple applications given a list of the applications' package names in Google Play. The analysis flow manager is responsible for coordinating the testing of multiple applications by dispatching the corresponding workers and managing the interim findings and result data flows for each tested application.

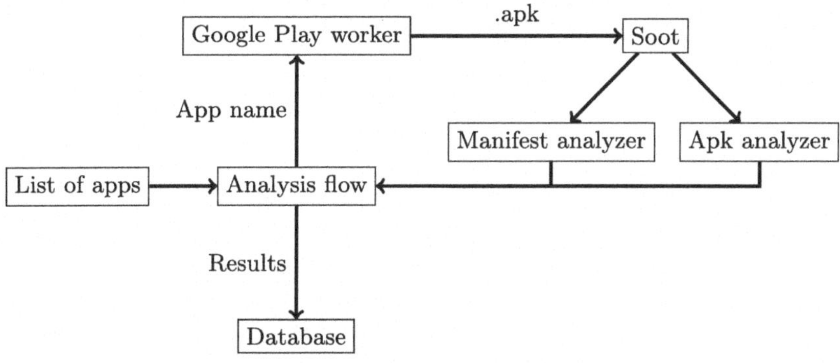

Fig. 1. App analysis framework.

When an analysis starts, the app's package name is passed on to the Google Play worker. This worker is responsible for retrieving the application's APK-file from Google Play. This file gets passed on to the Soot[1] framework which handles the decompilation process.

The manifest analyzer checks the application's `AndroidManifest.xml` for the presence of the pass-through filter as shown in Listing 1.1. Additionally, the manifest file is checked for a request of the permission `QUERY_ALL_PACKAGES`.

The decompiled source code is used by the apk analyzer to check for method signatures of Package Manager functions. In particular the functions `getInstalledApplications`, `getInstalledPackages` and `queryIntentActivities` allow for the retrieval of lists of all installed applications on a device.

Based on these test results, every app is categorized by its permission type and its access method respectively.

5 Results

To gain an insight into the prevalence of the pass-through filter in common Android apps, a representative study has to be performed. The goal of this study is to gain an understanding of how widespread the usage is and how applications access the corresponding user data. To do so, a selection of apps is tested for the implementation of the bypass. It is examined whether they request the proper permission and the apps' usage of the Package Manager API is checked. This information is used to determine if and how an application accesses the list of installed applications. The top 2,000 apps from the Google Play[2] are selected to be analyzed by the framework described in Sect. 4.

[1] https://github.com/soot-oss/soot.
[2] https://42matters.com/top-charts-explorer/android.

5.1 Access Level

First, the manifest analyzer determined the application's access level. Apps that have no special access and use intent action queries as intended with package visibility filtering fall into the category of *Specific filter*. Apps that requested the permission to query all packages make up the category *Permission*. Apps in this category are assumed to be legitimate use cases since they must have passed the Google Play review process before being published. Apps that do not request the proper permission but implement the pass-through filter represent the problematic *pass-through filter* category. These apps either knowingly circumvent the permission system to get around the review and approval process, or they unknowingly created the possibility to expose sensitive user data to libraries and third parties.

Table 2. App count based on permission type and detected access method

Permission type	Apps listed	Apps queried	No access detected	**Total**
Specific filter	308	1,182	16	**1,506**
Permission	58	13	2	**73**
Pass-through filter	273	160	2	**435**

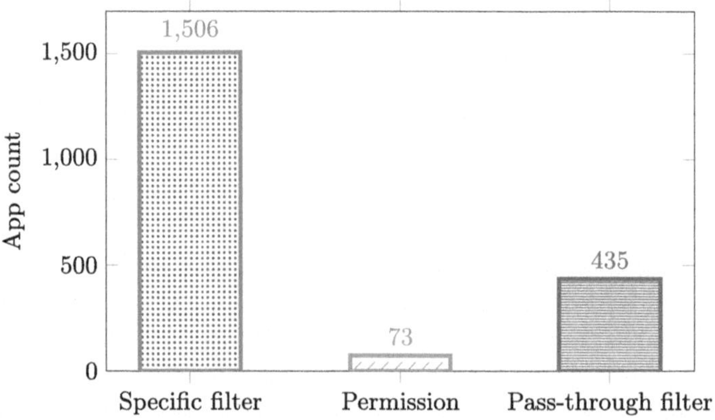

Fig. 2. Apps categorized by their access level to information about installed applications (column *Total* in Table 2).

Figure 2 shows that 21.6% of the 2,014 tested applications make use of the pass-through filter. These apps have not requested the permission to query all packages but have access to all installed applications on a device as demonstrated in Sect. 2.3. This indicates that the bypass usage is preferably used compared to the 3.62% that did use the proper permission. Possible reasons for this widespread usage are further examined in Sect. 6.1.

5.2 Access Type

While the manifest analyzer is responsible for categorizing the access level to information about installed applications, the apk analyzer determines how that information was accessed. Which Package Manager functions were used by an application determines what kind of information they receive. Functions that are intended to retrieve full lists of all installed applications fall into the category *Apps listed.* These can be adjusted to also include uninstalled applications or to only retrieve system apps, but they typically return a list of all applications or packages on the device. Apps in the category *Apps queried* perform an intent action query on installed applications. This is typically used to implement specific interactions with other apps, but it can be used to retrieve information about most installed applications by querying apps with a MAIN intent. Apps that did not have detectable method signatures of these Package Manager functions make up the category of *No access detected.*

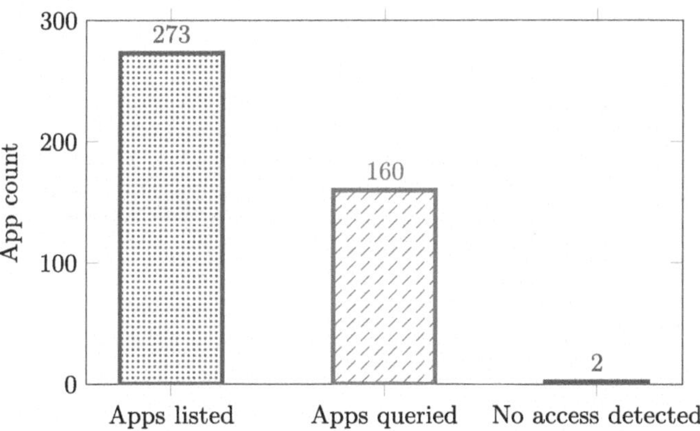

Fig. 3. Methods used by apps with permission bypass (row *Pass-through filter* in Table 2).

Figure 3 shows that 63%, of the total 435 applications that use the pass-through filter, retrieved a full list of installed apps (and possibly uninstalled apps that kept some data on the device). 37% perform a query on installed applications which can be used to retrieve lists of most installed applications or to retrieve a list of applications providing specific functionality like PDF viewers. In the latter case the application should have specified the Intent Action query related to the functionality in its android manifest instead of using the pass-through filter.

5.3 No Access Detected

In case the apk analyzer does not find any method signature of the relevant Package Manager functions, the app is categorized as *No access detected.* Applications that do not access any information about other installed apps on the device are contained within this category. Interestingly, Table 2 shows that there were four cases with broad package visibility but without detectable access to that information. In two cases the app requested the permission to access all packages and two cases implemented the pass-through filter. This would indicate that the applications gain elevated access to installed packages but do not interact with that information.

Further analysis of these cases revealed that some applications use sophisticated obfuscation methods with Java reflection to decrease the chance of detecting method signatures within the decompiled code.

Listing 1.2. Code snippet obfuscating the call to Package Manager functions

```
PackageManager packageManager = context.getPackageManager();
if (packageManager != null) {
    [...]
    Method method = cls.getMethod(C0383.m13387("\b\u0007\u0017d\
        u0015\u0016\u0013\u0011\f\u000b\u001f\u0015\u001c\u001cw
        \u001e\u0017!", (short) (C0241.m13047() ^ 12213)),
        clsArr);
    try {
        method.setAccessible(true);
        ApplicationInfo applicationInfo = (ApplicationInfo)
            method.invoke(packageManager, objArr2);
        if (applicationInfo != null && (bundle = applicationInfo
            .metaData) != null && bundle.containsKey(str)) {
            return Boolean.valueOf(applicationInfo.metaData.
                getBoolean(str));
        }
    } catch (InvocationTargetException e) {
        throw e.getCause();
    }
}
```

Listing 1.3. Code snippet of C0383.m13387(String, short) generating the name of the method to call

```
public static String m13387(String str, short s) {
    int[] iArr = new int[str.length()];
    C0314 c0314 = new C0314(str);
    int i = 0;
    while (c0314.m13220()) {
        int m13219 = c0314.m13219();
        AbstractC0305 m13215 = AbstractC0305.m13215(m13219);
        iArr[i] = m13215.mo12979(m13215.mo12980(m13219) - ((s &
            i) + (s | i)));
        i++;
    }
    return new String(iArr, 0, i);
}
```

Listing 1.4. Code snippet of C0314.m13219() manipulating individual characters of the stored string

```
public int m13219() {
    char charAt = this.f380.charAt(this.f381);
    this.f381++;
    return (1729690436 | 1729627323) & ((~1729690436) |
        (~1729627323)) & charAt;
}
```

One obfuscation example shown in Listing 1.2 uses reflection to invoke a Package Manager function in line 7. The result is converted to the Package Manager class `ApplicationInfo` and therefore contains information about an installed application on the device. The creation of the method reference in line 4 passes a string of characters to the method in Listing 1.3. There the initial string is stored in an object c0314 in line 3 and in line 6 the characters of that string are retrieved individually. Listing 1.4 shows the method manipulating individual characters before returning them.

All of this computation overhead is done to prevent the created method signature from being visible in the source code, thereby obfuscating the usage of the called Package Manager function.

Therefore, there is a slight uncertainty in 20 out of the 2014 tested applications categorized as access type *No access detected*. 16 of these cases do not possess any elevated access to information about installed applications and therefore are not a threat to user privacy regardless of the presence of obfuscation techniques. The remaining 4 applications, or 0.2% of tested applications, where no access was detected, but elevated access is obtained (*Pass-through filter* or *Permission* in Table 2) possibly use obfuscation techniques to avoid the detection of used method signatures in a manner that is relevant to the user's privacy. The detection of any application's access level (shown in Fig. 2) remains reliable since its implementation is in plain text in the app's Android manifest at compile time.

6 Discussion

Among other things, the Android permission system is responsible for protecting the user's privacy. Many of the disclosure systems that tell users which apps use what types of data also rely on the supposed robustness of the permission system. Therefore, allowing developers to bypass the use of proper permissions also means allowing them to bypass the data transparency systems. To a privacy conscious user looking into the permissions and data access of an app before downloading it from Google Play, it looks like 3.62% of apps have access to all of their other installed applications. In reality the 21.6% of apps that do not declare their interest in accessing that sensitive information, but still do so, are not only bypassing the permission but also bypassing the privacy disclosure system alongside it.

6.1 Possible Reasons

It is important to mention that not all the applications that use the bypass method can be accused of ill intent. Often, it might stem from a failure to follow best practices leading to the possibility of exposing personal user data.

When it comes to implementing interactions between apps a trivial approach is to let the app access all other applications, get a full list and keep the ones that provide the desired functionality. But in following, this bad practice allows the app to access more personal information than necessary to fulfill its core-functionality. Even if the app developers themselves do not abuse or sell this information, external libraries could still profit from the app's overprivileged state.

Responsible Disclosure. This issue is further complicated by the fact that Google does not acknowledge this permission bypass as a threat to the user's privacy. After discovering the bypass method it was reported via the Google BugHunters platform[3]. The reviewers concluded that "[...]this is not a security vulnerability. Querying packages via an action in an intent element is working as intended[...]" before closing the issue. This implies that by Google's definition using Intent Action queries to bypass the permission `QUERY_ALL_PACKAGES`, and the additional review and approval process, is part of the system's intended functionality. This does raise the question of why the permission alongside the package visibility system was introduced in the first place.

Irresponsible Privacy. When reviewing the development guidelines for the Google ads library, it was noted that they provide example applications[4] that developers can use as a starting point or integration reference. These examples implement the pass-through filter in the Android manifest, thereby leading developers to adopt this bad practice and creating applications that possibly expose sensitive user data.

Additionally, Google states within their guidelines on sensitive permissions [8]:

> Use of alternative methods to approximate the broad visibility level associated with `QUERY_ALL_PACKAGES` permission are also restricted to user-facing core app functionality and interoperability with any apps discovered via this method.

Thereby stating that bypassing the permission is within the guidelines as long as the data is not used beyond the stated purpose. But the intention of the review and approval process when requesting the proper permission is to force developers to reflect on what data they truly need to access to fulfill their apps core functionality while still protecting the user's privacy. The additional hurdles

[3] https://bughunters.google.com/report.
[4] https://github.com/googleads/googleads-mobile-android-examples.

of the process should incentivize developers to follow best practices and protect user data. Allowing developers to circumvent the permission and approval system is providing developers with a method to fully ignore the user privacy aspect of the package visibility system without repercussions.

6.2 Threat to Privacy

Even though there are legitimate use cases for accessing all installed applications on a device, protecting this data is essential. In a scenario where users do not willingly share device identifiers with service providers, any device-specific information can be used as an additional factor in fingerprinting. Furthermore, knowing which apps are installed on user's devices could be used to build a rather indicative interest profile. Especially tracking changes within that list over time is a simple way of identifying newly installed and removed applications. This could yield valuable information about a user's changing habits and interests which could be of high value to advertisement providers and data brokers at the expense of the user's privacy.

6.3 Resolutions

The introduction of package visibility filtering forced developers to confront the privacy question in the first place. Allowing developers a way to work around this system allows them work around this confrontation.

In case of package visibility, Google needs to remove the possibility of applying such broad Intent Action queries. If acquiring such broad access through the proper permission entails review, approval and privacy protection then any other method of acquiring similar broadness of access should entail the same level of protection. Therefore, the possibility of gaining this access level without the proper permission needs to be revoked. This would force developers to consider if they truly need full access for the core-functionality of their application or if they can work within the privacy limitations of the package visibility system.

6.4 Protection Strategies

Because bypassed permissions are not explicitly declared and therefore not disclosed to users it is difficult to judge whether to trust an application from a consumer's perspective. Until the Package Manager's permissions and privacy disclosure policies are improved, users do not have a simple way of assessing an application's privacy via Google Play.

As shown in this work it is possible to analyze applications for their potential impact on user privacy beyond the information shared by Google Play. Third-party institutes that provide app analysis services for businesses could test for the presence of such permission bypasses and possibly provide further analysis of data handling within an application. These results allow businesses to create customized block- and allow-lists for the installation of applications on company devices. The framework presented in this paper is in use as one of many tests in the Fraunhofer SIT's Appicaptor software[5].

7 Conclusion

In this work, we have demonstrated a significant loophole in the Android permissions system: although access to the list of installed apps is ostensibly protected by the strongly regulated `QUERY_ALL_PACKAGES` permission, we have shown that the same information can be obtained through a bypass that does not require any permission. Google currently does not acknowledge this bypass as privacy-relevant, which undermines the intended purpose of the permission model and renders the `QUERY_ALL_PACKAGES` permission largely ineffective. Our analysis of the top 2,000 apps on Google Play reveals that this bypass is extremely widespread, with 21% of the evaluated apps implementing it. In fact, more apps use the bypass than the official permission, thereby avoiding potential obstacles during Google Play publication. This widespread use highlights the urgent need for Google to reconsider its stance and address this privacy gap. Moreover, we have emphasized the serious privacy implications of leaking the list of installed apps. This information can be exploited for device fingerprinting, making user tracking trivial and providing valuable insights into user interests, especially for advertising companies. Through this publication, we aim to raise awareness and draw attention, once again alerting Google and urging it to acknowledge and fix this flaw.

Future work could address a deeper examination of the package manager API with a dynamic analysis or taint checking methods. Libraries with supposed interest in this data, like advertisement or tracking libraries, could be examined in more detail for access and handling of this information. Furthermore, the usefulness of tracking user's app lists over time to build interest profiles could be evaluated and compared to other user profiling algorithms to further assess the risk associated with the lacking protection of this data.

References

1. Au, K.W.Y., Zhou, Y.F., Huang, Z., Lie, D.: PScout: analyzing the android permission specification. In: Proceedings of the 2012 ACM Conference on Computer and Communications Security, CCS '12, pp. 217–228. Association for Computing Machinery, New York (2012). https://doi.org/10.1145/2382196.2382222
2. Backes, M., Bugiel, S., Derr, E., McDaniel, P., Octeau, D., Weisgerber, S.: On demystifying the android application framework: Re-Visiting android permission specification analysis. In: USENIX Security, pp. 1101–1118. Austin, TX (2016). https://www.usenix.org/conference/usenixsecurity16/technical-sessions/presentation/backes_android
3. Book, T., Pridgen, A., Wallach, D.S.: Longitudinal analysis of android ad library permissions (2013). arXiv:1303.0857

[5] https://www.sit.fraunhofer.de/en/appicaptor/.

4. Fang, Z., Han, W., Li, Y.: Permission based android security: issues and countermeasures. Comput. Secur. **43**, 205–218 (2014). https://doi.org/10.1016/j.cose.2014.02.007
5. Felt, A.P., Chin, E., Hanna, S., Song, D., Wagner, D.: Android permissions demystified. In: Proceedings of the 18th ACM Conference on Computer and Communications Security, CCS '11, pp. 627–638. Association for Computing Machinery, New York (2011). https://doi.org/10.1145/2046707.2046779
6. Google: Know which packages are visible automatically. https://developer.android.com/training/package-visibility/automatic
7. Google: Package visibility filtering on Android. https://developer.android.com/training/package-visibility
8. Google: Permissions and APIs that Access Sensitive Information. https://support.google.com/googleplay/android-developer/answer/9888170
9. Google: Use of the broad package (App) visibility (QUERY_ALL_PACKAGES) permission. https://support.google.com/googleplay/android-developer/answer/10158779?sjid=16774600286025479966-EU
10. Grace, M.C., Zhou, W., Jiang, X., Sadeghi, A.R.: Unsafe exposure analysis of mobile in-app advertisements. In: ACM WiSec, pp. 101–112 (2012)
11. Heid, K., Andrae, V., Heider, J.: Towards detecting device fingerprinting on iOS with API function hooking. In: Proceedings of the 2023 European Interdisciplinary Cybersecurity Conference, EICC '23, pp. 78–84. Association for Computing Machinery, New York (2023). https://doi.org/10.1145/3590777.3590790
12. Heid, K., Heider, J.: Haven't we met before? - detecting device fingerprinting activity on android apps. In: Proceedings of the 2024 European Interdisciplinary Cybersecurity Conference, EICC '24, pp. 11–18. Association for Computing Machinery, New York (2024). https://doi.org/10.1145/3655693.3655695
13. Khatoon, A., Corcoran, P.: Android permission system and user privacy — a review of concept and approaches. In: 2017 IEEE 7th International Conference on Consumer Electronics - Berlin (ICCE-Berlin), pp. 153–158 (2017). https://doi.org/10.1109/ICCE-Berlin.2017.8210616
14. Kumar, S., Shanker, R., Verma, S.: Context aware dynamic permission model: a retrospect of privacy and security in android system. In: 2018 International Conference on Intelligent Circuits and Systems (ICICS), pp. 324–329 (2018). https://doi.org/10.1109/ICICS.2018.00073
15. Li, L., et al.: I know what leaked in your pocket: uncovering privacy leaks on android apps with static taint analysis (2014). https://arxiv.org/abs/1404.7431
16. Mann, C., Starostin, A.: A framework for static detection of privacy leaks in android applications. In: Proceedings of the 27th Annual ACM Symposium on Applied Computing, SAC '12, pp. 1457–1462. Association for Computing Machinery, New York (2012). https://doi.org/10.1145/2245276.2232009
17. Stevens, R., Gibler, C., Crussell, J., Erickson, J., Chen, H.: Investigating user privacy in android ad libraries. In: Workshop on Mobile Security Technologies (MoST), vol. 10, pp. 195–197 (2012). https://api.semanticscholar.org/CorpusID:18944389
18. Wei, X., Gomez, L., Neamtiu, I., Faloutsos, M.: Permission evolution in the android ecosystem. In: Proceedings of the 28th Annual Computer Security Applications Conference, ACSAC '12, pp. 31–40. Association for Computing Machinery, New York (2012). https://doi.org/10.1145/2420950.2420956

Revisiting the Effectiveness of Jailbreak Detection

Muhammad Irfan[1] and Nelson Uto[2(✉)]

[1] Nagarro AS, Kongens gate 14, 0153 Oslo, Norway
muhammad.irfan@nagarro.com, muhammad.irfan.raja@proton.me

[2] Noroff University College, Tordenskjolds gate 9, 4612 Kristiansand, Norway
nelson.uto@noroff.no

Abstract. This study evaluates the effectiveness of jailbreak detection in iOS banking apps, particularly how new "rootless" jailbreaks can circumvent the majority of Apple's improved security measures, notably the Signed System Volume (SSV) and the Secure Page Table Monitor (SPTM). Building upon earlier findings that showed banking apps were easily bypassed, this research investigates whether detection methods have improved or if developers still depend mainly on operating system security. A total of 489 iOS applications, including 52 renowned banking apps, were collected and tested on two jailbroken environments. The research shows that 72% of all tested applications did not detect a jailbreak in a rootful environment, and 92% did not detect in a rootless environment. Although banking applications did show somewhat better rootful detection than other categories, most still struggled to identify a rootless environment. Additionally, those that detected it could be bypassed with very simple methods. These findings highlight a security gap in modern iOS banking applications as jailbreak techniques continue to evolve away from system-volume exploits. This study provides evidence that rootless jailbreaking is largely undetectable. It illustrates the necessity for more customizable and behaviour-based detection approaches that no longer strictly rely on static file paths or library checks.

Keywords: Jailbreak · iOS · Rootful · Rootless · Application security

1 Introduction

Mobile security has become an increasingly critical concern in recent years, especially with the growing reliance on these devices. A study by Mohd Saudi *et al.* [1] highlighted the shifted focus of malware developers towards iOS. Malware like `Pegasus` and `YiSpecter` easily bypassed security mechanisms like sandboxing and entitlements restrictions, which seriously threatened sensitive user data.

Furthermore, a report by Yaswant *et al.* [2] highlighted a 200% yearly increase in malware families targeting banking applications, rising from 10 to 29 families and affecting over 1,800 apps worldwide. The report highlighted the growing threat cybercriminals posed to mobile banking applications, particularly when

R. Laborde et al. (Eds.): ESORICS 2025 Workshops, LNCS 16233, pp. 558–577, 2026.
https://doi.org/10.1007/978-3-032-16165-9_33

combined with jailbreaking. As per Statista, almost 7 billion devices were utilized worldwide. Many of these devices contained sensitive data, such as banking transaction information [3].

Jailbreaking bypasses the security measures imposed by Apple on iOS, allowing unauthorized escalation of privileges within the system [4]. For example, it turns off code signing mechanisms to enable a device to run applications not officially approved by Apple [5, p. 9]. There have been multiple jailbreak detection mechanisms, such as monitoring whether child processes are spawned, reading file paths outside the sandbox, and checking loaded libraries and their names. These methods have been frequently implemented to prevent applications from running in unsafe environments, but [5, pp. 9–10] argued that most of the techniques were flawed and could easily be circumvented.

Despite the critical nature of mobile devices and the sensitive data they carry, such as personal and banking information [6], research on the effectiveness of jailbreak detection methods remains surprisingly limited [7]. In comparison, Android has seen more research, with several studies exploring advanced techniques to identify and counteract rooting [8,9]. Research by Zhang, She, and Qian [10] has explored the Android root ecosystem and examined how root exploits can be both a tool for legitimate control and a serious security risk when misused. This has shown the proactive approach adopted by researchers to comprehend and address such vulnerabilities in the Android domain.

The remainder of this paper is organized as follows: Sect. 2 covers jailbreaks and techniques for jailbreak detection; Sect. 3 describes the primary dataset and how it was collected; the methodology is described in Sect. 4 and the results, in Sect. 5; limitations are presented in Sect. 6; finally, the conclusions are drawn in Sect. 7.

2 Background

This section presents the types of jailbreaks, including the new type called rootless, and the most common techniques used to detect a jailbroken device.

2.1 Jailbreaks

Jailbreaking is the process of escalating privileges on an iOS device from a `mobile` user to a root user. It is often achieved by exploiting some serious vulnerability in the iOS operating system. On the Android OS, such a process is called rooting. [4]. The only difference is that on Android, users can get the possibility of rooting, called hard rooting, from some mobile manufacturers [10]. When Apple launched its first iPhone, it had an operator lock, which caused serious frustrations among users and led to an unending race on jailbreaking [11]. Despite Apple's efforts to counter these modifications, the practice continued, leading to an ongoing challenge for the company.

The jailbreaking community continued to evolve, and, on July 19, 2008, `PwnageTool` [12] jailbreaking tool was released. It supported the iPhone 3G

Table 1. Types of Jailbreaks adapted from Kellner *et al.* [4].

Types	Jailbreak	Reboot Support	Permanent Modification	Distinction Rootless/Rootful
Tethered	External	×	✓	Rootful
Semi-tethered	External	✓	×	Rootful
Untethered	App	×	✓	Rootful
Semi-untethered (Rootful)	App	✓	×	Rootful
Semi-untethered (Rootless)	App	✓	×	Rootless

and, for the first time, began installing `Cydia` [13], an open-source alternative to Apple's App Store, which was used to install applications and jailbreak tweaks. It quickly became popular, and by August 2009, it was installed on over 10 percent of Apple devices, as claimed by Jay Freeman (Saurik), its creator [11].

There are five primary types of jailbreaks, as shown in Table 1. Each variant is distinguished by whether it requires an external device to reboot the target device and whether the jailbreak is persistent across reboots. Recent developments have introduced new categories of jailbreaks: **rootful** and **rootless**. The rootless jailbreaks avoid modifying the system volume by redirecting jailbreak installation to a different Apple File System (APFS) volume, preventing conflicts with SSV. The primary difference between rootful and rootless jailbreaks is the level of system access. In rootful jailbreaks, users can access the root volume, meaning they can modify or install files directly on the core operating system. In rootless jailbreaks, such access is not available, and it only allows changes to files in `/var` and `/private/preboot` volumes [14]. Despite this restriction, users can still become root users and modify anything other than the root volume [15].

Tethered Jailbreak. A tethered jailbreak permanently grants elevated privileges on an iOS device, but requires re-tethering through a jailbreak tool after every reboot to reload the jailbreak. Once the device is powered off or the battery runs out, the system cannot complete its boot cycle without being reconnected to a computer running a jailbreak tool via a physical cable and ends up in recovery mode [16]. This dependency makes tethered jailbreaks less user-friendly. Famous examples include `blackra1n` [17] and `orangesn0w` [18].

Semi-tethered Jailbreak. The device can reboot back into the stock OS in a semi-tethered jailbreak. However, the jailbreak functionality, such as extensions and tweaks, will not load until the device is connected to a computer and the jailbreak tool is rerun. This balances usability and flexibility, as the device can still function [16]. Famous examples are `Checkra1n` and `Palera1n`, based on `Checkm8` boot ROM exploit [19], which support older devices up to iPhone X.

Untethered Jailbreak. This jailbreak remains active after reboots without reactivation [20], but it is rare and very difficult, as it often requires a powerful exploit [4]. A notable example of an untethered jailbreak is the Pangu9 [21].

Semi-untethered Jailbreak. A semi-untethered jailbreak allows the device to complete a boot cycle without needing a computer. However, the jailbreak extensions do not load automatically after a reboot. Instead, the user must open a jailbreak app (installed on the device) to re-enable jailbreak functionality. This jailbreak is convenient for daily users, as it can be reactivated without external tools. Famous examples of this jailbreak include `Dopamine2` (rootless) [22,23], and `UncOver` [24], which allow jailbreaking through an app on the device itself.

2.2 Jailbreak Detection

Implementing jailbreak detection mechanisms is vital for mobile applications, especially those dealing with sensitive data. Effective jailbreak detection can prevent an app from launching if it detects that the operating system's underlying security protocols have been bypassed. Data security cannot be guaranteed on jailbroken devices. This section will explore some standard techniques modern iOS applications employ to detect jailbroken devices.

Jailbreak File Path Checks. Jailbreak detection mechanisms often check for specific files and directories commonly created or installed during jailbreaking. For example, the presence of apps like `Cydia` and `apt`, directories such as `/Applications/Cydia.app`, or system modifications like `/bin/bash` can indicate a jailbreak. Detection routines for file path check typically use system calls like `stat`, `fopen`, and `access`, or, in many implementations with Swift, a `fileExists(atPath:isDirectory:)` method is also utilized to check if these files exist at a specific path [25,26].

Suspicious Dynamic Library Detection. Jailbreaks introduce custom libraries like `MobileSubstrate.dylib`, designed to modify system behavior by loading custom code into official applications [4]. To detect such unauthorized changes, systems can examine the app's memory space for these libraries using dynamic linker functions or scanning app binaries for linked libraries.

For example, one can use the function `_dyld_image_count()` to determine the number of dynamic libraries currently loaded in the process. It then employs `_dyld_get_image_name()` to retrieve the file path of each library. These paths are checked against a list of library names commonly associated with jailbreak tools, such as Frida and Cydia Substrate [27]. The function then flags the environment as potentially compromised if a match is found.

URL Scheme Handling. For inter-app communication, iOS initially allowed apps to register individual URL schemes. This feature permitted apps to load on an iOS device using custom URL schemes and share information with other apps. However, this was susceptible to attacks, as iOS allowed a single URL Scheme to be claimed by multiple apps. This led to privacy leaks where applications could easily steal authentication tokens with the usage of URL schemes and replay attacks where attackers could capture legitimate URL scheme requests (such as login or payment requests) and reuse them to perform unauthorized actions [28,29]. Apple introduced universal links in 2015 [30], which offered a more secure way to handle links that need to open directly in a corresponding app.

Despite these advancements, jailbroken devices may still have apps using custom URL schemes (e.g., `cydia://`). Detection can attempt to open these custom URLs with system APIs like `canOpenURL:`, to see if any app responds, which would suggest the presence of jailbreak-related applications [4,26].

File System Write Permissions. The file system is carefully partitioned on non-jailbroken devices in user and iOS system partitions. Applications are restricted to their designated storage areas inside the former, and any attempt to write outside these sandboxed directories – particularly to system-protected paths such as `/`, `/root/`, `/private/`, or `/jb/` – is prevented by default [31]. One effective method to detect jailbreaks based on this structure is to attempt to write in restricted directories. If a test file is successfully created in a restricted path, it likely indicates a jailbroken environment [26].

Symbolic Link Verification. Jailbreaks often alter iOS's standard file system structure by overwriting the system partition and relocating system data to the larger, writable user partition. To maintain access to relocated system files and settings, jailbreaks create symbolic links from original system paths to new locations in the user partition [32]. Therefore, symbolic links for system directories are a significant hint for a jailbroken device.

Other Methods. Frida is a dynamic instrumentation toolkit often used for runtime analysis and manipulation in jailbroken environments. It allows injecting custom scripts into an application to monitor or alter its behavior [33]. Detection mechanisms might look for signs of Frida's server (e.g., checking open ports or active processes) or, more generally, checking for active debugging interfaces [27].

The `ptrace` system call is primarily designed for process tracing, but it includes a specific request called `PT_DENY_ATTACH` that can be used to prevent any debugging attempts on an application. It can indirectly indicate a jailbroken environment, as process hooking will not be able to break the sandbox unless it is on a jailbroken device [34]. Other methods include system calls like `fork` to create a child process [26,34], which is impossible to happen if sandbox security is not compromised [7]. The `system` function call returns true if the device is jailbroken [32]. The `getppid` is also utilized in some cases to check the parent Process ID (PID), and if the parent PID is not equal to 1 [35], it indicates the process is not started by `launchd` [36].

Open Source Solutions. Mobile developers often use open-source jailbreak detection frameworks to implement standard jailbreak checks. However, their effectiveness varies widely based on how they are used, maintained, and then updated in the face of jailbreak evolutions.

`JailMonkey` is an open-source library for jailbreak detection in React Native developed applications, which uses simple static checks. For example, it looks for known file paths or known system directories. It has been updated to support rootless jailbreaks [37], and despite being updated, its detection logic is relatively simple and thus sometimes easily bypassed.

`iOS Security Suite` is a Swift-based library that supports checks for many security measures. It has detection logic for rootless jailbreaks and uses a modular design that allows developers to decide which checks to include [26]. However, its effectiveness depends on the quality of integration and any custom checks.

`Bugsnag` is a much broader framework that also includes jailbreak detection. Their implementation checks for four key indicators: the ability to create files in the protected `/tmp` directory, existence of `MobileSubstrate` library (used for tweaks), presence of `/etc/apt` directory, and environment variables containing `DYLD_INSERT_LIBRARIES` directives (used to override functions). To prevent bypass techniques, `Bugsnag` uses direct syscalls on supported architectures rather than standard library functions, which could be more easily patched or hooked, thus providing sufficient protection against general jailbreak detection [38].

3 Dataset Collection

This research focused on iOS-based banking apps collected directly from the iTunes/App Store using the iTunes search API. If the App was not automatically installed on the devices by the collection script, it was downloaded manually on the device and later dumped from the device to compose the dataset. Apps were chosen based on availability on the Norwegian App Store and the possibility of installing on iOS 14.4 and 15.7.

3.1 The Primary Dataset

The dataset consisted of 489 applications, including 105 financial applications, of which 52 were explicitly identified as banking apps based on the recognized names of financial institutions. The remaining 384 applications were selected from the following categories: *business* (80), *education* (99), *medical* (97), *productivity* (90), and *games* (18). To support focused comparative analysis, the dataset was divided into banking apps, financial (non-banking) apps, and other category apps, following an approach similar to that of Kellner *et al.* [4].

3.2 Collection Automation

The collection process was inspired by Orikogbo, Büchler, and Egele [39] approach, which was customized according to project needs and was divided into three stages: (i) Creation of applications lists. (ii) Automated downloading of applications from iTunes. (iii) Installation of applications.

The first stage utilized the approach outlined by Tang *et al.* [40] to compile a list of applications. The iTunes Search API provides relevant data about each application in a JSON key-value format. Within this data, the key `trackViewUrl` contains the URL for downloading the application. To achieve this, a Python script was developed to access the iTunes Search API through the following URL: https://itunes.apple.com/search?term=finance&country=no&media=software&limit=100. The script generated multiple text files that organized all the URLs and replaced the "https" with "itms" according to their respective categories. The second part extracted the `trackName` along with its `version`, and created a second set of files.

In the second stage, a Python script was implemented to automate the iTunes download process on a Windows 10 virtual machine using the libraries `pyautogui`, `pygetwindow`, and `webbrowser`. The `pygetwindow` library was used to activate the iTunes window, ensuring that it was at the forefront of automation. Meanwhile, `pyautogui` recorded the coordinates of the download button manually and simulated a user click to initiate the download. To implement this automation successfully, it was necessary to use iTunes version 12.6.5, the last version that allowed users to download applications. Both iOS devices were configured to automatically download applications. This setup enabled downloads to both devices whenever applications were downloaded from iTunes.

Downloading 100 applications took approximately two hours, and the duration varied depending on the size of the iOS App Store Package (IPA) files. In addition, a reserve account was also created in case the primary account got banned. Unlike earlier pipelines that decrypted every IPA as soon as it was downloaded [39,40], this workflow delayed decryption until an application could not be bypassed with dynamic evasion techniques. This decrypt-on-demand strategy removed roughly 80% of otherwise unnecessary dump operations while still decrypting the entire banking subset for deep static analysis.

Removal of Applications. The devices in use had limited storage, so the apps were installed in phases and removed before installing the next batch. For bulk deletion, `imazing` [41] was used. Once an iOS device was connected to a Mac, multiple installed applications could be selected and removed with a single click from inside `imazing`'s connected devices section.

System Setup and Configuration. iTunes was configured to never prompt for a password login for purchases to ensure uninterrupted automated downloads during data collection. This was done to disable the default 15-min password prompt, which allowed the data collection scripts to run without interruption. iTunes was run as an administrator to avoid the error `5105` on some applications.

In total, 111 applications on rootless and 190 on rootful devices could not be installed due to operating system incompatibility and were omitted from further analysis. As a result, 378 and 299 applications were actually tested in the rootless and rootful environments, respectively.

4 Testing Methodology

This study was inspired by methodologies used by D'Orazio *et al.* [42] and Kellner *et al.* [4]. Before collecting applications, an iPhone 12 (iOS 15.6.1) was jailbroken with the `Dopamine2-roothide` [43] rootless jailbreak, and an iPad 3 with `checkRa1n` [44]. Both test devices were prepared with the necessary tools for the experiments. The rootful device was installed with `Shadow` [45] and `A-Bypass` [46], while `Roothide` [47] tweak was installed on the rootless device. A `Frida server` and the `Flex 3 beta` [48] tweaks were installed on both devices.

As illustrated in Fig. 1, the jailbreak detection process was divided into several sequential phases, as outlined below:

1. In the initial testing, each application was opened separately on both rootful (iPad 3) and rootless (iPhone 12) jailbroken devices to observe if it detected the jailbreak environment. Applications were then categorized based on whether or not they detected the jailbreak.
2. In the next stage, the above-mentioned Cydia/Sileo tweaks were utilized to bypass jailbreak detection.
3. After that, Frida's script was used to bypass the remaining applications.
4. Finally, any applications that could not be bypassed with Frida were decrypted and downloaded for static analysis using `frida-ios-dump` [49] or `bagbak` [50] on a MacBook and later analyzed with Ghidra or Hopper.
5. For detailed banking applications analysis, all the banking applications were dumped from a rootless[1] device and statically tested with the steps outlined in Fig. 1: (i) Applications were decrypted and dumped. (ii) A custom script checked a specified list of strings against all the applications. (iii) Applications were reverse engineered with `radare2`.

String Checker Script. The script for static application analysis had been created with three functions, and only did string-based checks. The first function would analyze the binaries with the `strings` command, and store the output in a variable. Then, it was cross-matched against predefined jailbreak patterns that utilized regular expressions. This function would return the string matches whenever it was called on a binary that clearly had strings. The second function, named `find_binary`, would find the main executable of the app bundle by navigating the iOS application. The only way it matched this was using the `file` command and confirming `Mach-O` was present. The last function worked like a coordinator function; it orchestrated the workflow, pulling the IPA file from the temporary directory, locating the binaries, analyzing the binaries, and returning the detection effectiveness. The main execution block was intended to work with IPA files placed in the target directory, as it sent each binary to the `process_ipa` function. In doing this, it produced simple, unencoded strings to completion without modifying the binary itself.

[1] This environment was chosen due to the possibility of dumping most applications.

5 Results

This section presents the results obtained by applying the methodology described in Sect. 4 and compares them to previous work, such as Kellner *et al.* [4].

5.1 Manual Testing

In the initial phase, applications were launched on jailbroken devices (both rootful and rootless environments) to observe jailbreak detection, as shown in Table 2. Among the 299 applications tested in the rootful environment, 84 (approximately 28%) detected a jailbreak. In contrast, 32 of the 378 applications (only 8%) in the rootless environment detected a jailbreak, indicating a significantly lower detection rate under the rootless environment.

Table 2. Rootless vs. rootful jailbreak detection.

Category	Rootless			Rootful		
	Detected	Not Detected	Grand Total	Detected	Not Detected	Grand Total
Banking	20	25	45	31	15	46
Business	0	49	49	1	22	23
Education	1	85	86	3	84	87
Finance	9	38	47	43	9	52
Game	0	18	18	1	16	17
Medical	1	65	66	4	31	35
Productivity	1	66	67	1	38	39
Grand Total	**32**	**346**	**378**	**84**	**215**	**299**

Considering banking applications only, 20 out of 45 (approximately 44%) detected a jailbreak in the rootless environment, compared to 31 out of 46 (roughly 67%) in the rootful environment, as shown in Table 2. However, when financial applications were analyzed, only 9 out of 47 detected jailbreak in rootless, while 43 out of 52 applications detected in rootful. Finally, when all other application categories[2] were compared, only 3 out of 286 (roughly 1%) detected jailbreak in the rootless environment. In contrast, in the rootful environment, 10 out of 201 (around 5%) had active jailbreak detection mechanisms.

5.2 Dynamic Testing

In the next phase, applications that initially detected jailbreak were run through `Cydia/Sileo` tweaks[3] to determine how many applications could easily be

[2] Business, education, medical, productivity, and games.

[3] `Shadow, A-Bypass, Flex, and Roothide.`

bypassed with `Cydia` tweaks. As shown in Table 3, 26 applications out of 31 (approximately 84%) were bypassed with a simple `roothide` tweaker. In contrast, in the rootful environment, only 40 out of 82 applications (roughly 49%) were bypassed. These results suggest that rootful apps generally exhibit stronger resistance against tweak-based evasion. In contrast, rootless jailbreak evasion tweaks remain highly effective, making it difficult for applications to prevent bypass attempts in the rootless scenario.

Table 3. Applications that detected jailbreak and are bypassed by Cydia tweaks.

Category	Rootless			Rootful		
	Bypassed	Not Bypassed	Grand Total	Bypassed	Not Bypassed	Grand Total
Banking	15	5	20	9	22	31
Business	0	0	0	0	1	1
Education	1	0	1	0	2	2*
Finance	8	0	8*	31	11	42*
Game	0	0	0	0	1	1
Medical	1	0	1	0	4	4
Productivity	1	0	1	0	1	1
Grand Total	**26**	**5**	**31**	**40**	**42**	**82**

*Apps that only showed jailbreak notification messages without enforcing any restriction were excluded from this table (Rootless: Kraken; Rootful: Kraken, Pregnancy +).

Finally, the remaining applications were hooked through a Frida script that looked for the following functionalities: (1) Jailbreak file paths (2) Dynamic libraries (3) URL scheme verifiers (4) System and runtime function detectors (5) Symbolic link checker. The script modified the return values when they matched known jailbreak indicators, allowing Frida to simulate a non-jailbreak state. In the rootful environment, the script successfully bypassed detection in 4 out of 42 applications; however, for two of these applications, the script had to be used alongside `Shadow` to achieve successful bypass. In contrast, none of the five remaining applications in the rootless environment could be bypassed.

These results show a major flaw in the implementation approach. Although the detection employed in banking and financial applications was slightly improved in rootful environments compared to the earlier studies, these detections were still less effective against rootless jailbreak. This output suggests that the current detection methods, which are mainly static and apply system-based checks, are inferior to a rapidly evolving jailbreak landscape. There is a need for more robust, dynamic, and diversified detection approaches that are secure regardless of whether a device is jailbroken through traditional or rootless means.

5.3 Static Analysis

The static analysis was divided in two phases. The first part focused on the applications that were able to detect a jailbroken environment and could not be bypassed, while the second analyzed all banking applications.

Applications Not Bypassed. As shown in Table 3, only five applications – all from the banking category – required static testing in the rootless case. For that reason, they were moved to the next phase of testing, where only banking applications were statically tested for detailed mapping of detection mechanisms implemented in those applications. In the rootful case, out of the 38 applications that could not be bypassed, 13 of them could not be dumped, 8 showed no indicators of detectors, and 17 contained indicators of detection mechanisms.

Banking Applications. In this phase, forty-four applications were decrypted and dumped from the rootless environment, manually checked for any name discrepancies, and later tested. The initial testing focused mainly on string-based detections using a custom script designed to search for common jailbreak detection strings that were also used in the Frida script. This way, a baseline was created, which was later analyzed with multiple tools, including `radare2`, `nm`, and `strings`, to identify and evaluate jailbreak detection mechanisms.

Applications were first unzipped, and binaries were looked for inside the application and framework[4] directories. Strings were then checked, symbols were analyzed with the `nm` tool, and finally `radare2` was utilized to decrypt and decompile the applications and analyze them. The findings were then categorized according to the detection techniques explained in Sect. 2.2. The categories were assigned based on file paths, dynamic libraries, and URL schemes. Filesystem permissions were analyzed with the Swift API (`FileExistsAtPaths`) and then categorized accordingly. Additionally, system runtime functions (`fork`, `syscall`, `system`) were checked and categorized. Anti-debugging techniques ("debug", "`ptrace`", "isdebugged"), sandboxing ("isSandboxed", "sandbox"), and symbolic link ("readlink", "symlink", "`destinationOfSymbolicLinkAtPath`") were also evaluated and categorized.

Table 4 presents a summary of the static analysis findings with respect to the detection technique implemented. The results show that overall, 36 applications showed some form of jailbreak-related code. Twenty-four showed straightforward implementation of jailbreak path checks, and 25 showed dynamic libraries checks. Only 14 showed URL Scheme-based check. Eighteen applications showed evidence of sandbox escape checks (write and read permissions), and 15 applications showed Symbolic link-based checks. Interestingly, no application showed any form of rootless checks, such as "dopamine" and "xinaA15".

Table 5, in turn, presents the number of detection indicators identified in each application. The results reveal a paradox in jailbreak detection: several applications with extensive detection indicators (e.g., all Nordea applications with 52

[4] frameworks were not analyzed with `radare2`.

Table 4. Summary of jailbreak detection implementations.

Detection Mechanism	Implementation Rate
Jailbreak Function/Class	36/44 (81.8%)
File Path Checks	24/44 (54.5%)
Dynamic Libraries	25/44 (56.8%)
URL Schemes	14/44 (31.8%)
Sandbox Violation Check	18/44 (40.9%)
Symbolic Links	15/44 (34.1%)
Rootless Jailbreak Strings	0/44 (0.0%)

indicators, Storebrand Mobilbank, ASBank, and Facit Bank with 64 indicators each) failed to detect jailbroken environments, especially in the rootless context. Contrarily, some applications that initially showed few or no detection indicators in the string-based checks (such as Both DNB, SpareBank1, Sbanken, Eika bank og Kreditt application, Coop Bank, SAS Mastercard, BN Bank Bedrift, Santander Consumer Bank PL, Swedbank, ABBank Business, Aani, Santander UK, AB Direct, and SEB) were later confirmed, through in-depth static analysis, to implement sophisticated jailbreak detection mechanisms. Notably, in the rootless case, only one application (Starling Bank UK) could not be dumped and was therefore excluded from static testing.

Table 5. Detection indicators in banking applications.

Detection Level	Apps Count	Percentage	List of Applications
50+ indicators	11	25.0%	TF Bank (65), Aasen Mobilbank (64), Storebrand Mobilbank (64), 4 Nordea Bank Applications(52), ActivoBank (51), FP mobilbank (64), Facit Bank NO Mobilbank (64), ASbank (64)
10–30 indicators	6	13.6%	Lunar (20), AJIB Mobile (20), AB Ditizen (22), CitiManager (10), 365.bank (25), ABA Mobile (19)
1–9 indicators	4	9.1%	Bank Norwegian (3), Resurs (2), SantanderConsumerNO (1), DanskebankenMobilbank (2)
No Indicators*	23	52.3%	Sparebank1Mobilbank, Spink, SEB, DNB, Santander Consumer BankPL, EikaMobilbank, ActivoBank PL, ABDirect, BN Bank Bedrift, Swedbank, DNB Spare, Aani, SAS Mastercard, Coop Bank, ABBANK Business, Mitt Kort, Bulder, Sbanken, SantanderUK, SparebankVestMobilbank, SparebankVestBedrift, SantanderPL, Handelsbanken

*No Indicators: Applications with no jailbreak detected signatures (either no detection or advanced bypass).

Danskebanken initially showed some jailbreak indicators, but during the detailed analysis, none of the detected indicators could be connected to any specific functions. This way, false positives were avoided. In total, eight applications – Bulder, Sparebank Vest Bedrift, Handelsbanken, Swedbank, SEB, Spink BarneBank, AB Direct, and Danske Bank – showed no signs of implementing jailbreak detection. This overall behavior confirms that these applications did not actively attempt to detect jailbreak. An exception was observed with AB Direct, which showed the iOS Security Suite-related framework during the dynamic analysis. However, detailed static analysis did not find any corresponding jailbreak-related functions. This suggests that although the framework exists, it may not be implemented out-of-the-box, or it could be updated or encoded in a way that prevents it getting detected through simple string-based static analysis.

5.4 Rootful vs. Rootless Jailbreak Detection Comparison

Based on Table 2, one can verify that 28% of applications in the rootful environment successfully detected jailbreak versus 8% in the rootless scenario. This implies that most iOS banking and non-banking apps rely on root-level checks, which fail under rootless jailbreak conditions. These numbers change when only banking applications are in focus, as many detect jailbreaks in both environments. Yet, only five required static testing under rootless conditions, whereas twenty did so in rootful environments (Table 3).

Table 2 also shows that 38 out of 47 financial applications (approximately 81%) failed to detect a jailbreak in the rootless environment, versus 9 out of 52 (roughly 17%) in the rootful environment. This suggests that even within financial apps, reliance on root-level detection is predominantly implemented. In dynamic testing, only five applications could resist the `Roothide` bypasser in rootless cases. In rootful cases, 32 applications could be bypassed with simple Cydia Tweaks. This indicates that even financial applications implementing jailbreak detection have not adopted a comprehensive approach, leaving them vulnerable to straightforward evasion techniques in rootful cases.

In contrast, the remaining categories consistently showed extremely low detection rates under both testing devices. As indicated in Table 2, nearly all applications in non-financial categories failed to detect a jailbreak in the rootless environment, and nine detected jailbreaks in rootful, out of which none could be bypassed.

Another perspective consists in comparing how the same application performs in both rootless and rootful environments. In a comparative analysis in all categories, 11 applications not easily bypassed on a rootfull jailbreak environment did not detect jailbreak in the rootless case. On the other hand, 18 applications could not be bypassed in a rootful environment, but could be easily bypassed on a rootless device. These results show a strong indication of an application that has not implemented a dynamic jailbreak detection. Even if these have a good jailbreak detection strategy for a rootful environment, they fail to detect jailbreaks in a rootless case.

These results suggest that: (1) Financial and banking apps are much more effective at detecting a jailbreak in rootful environments than rootless ones. (2) There is a clear divergence between banking, financial, and non-banking apps. Most apps do not detect rootless jailbreak, even if the application handles sensitive data, such as medical applications. (3) Dynamic testing revealed that while 83% of the detected cases in the rootless environment were bypassed with a simple tweak, only 51% could be bypassed in the rootful environment. These results suggest that rootful apps generally exhibit stronger resistance against tweak-based evasion, whereas rootless jailbreak evasion techniques remain highly effective. (4) Rootless environments affect traditional jailbreak detection, and even when a jailbreak is detected, it has become very easy to bypass with trivial means. The contrast in results suggests that most checks depend on root-level filesystem indicators that do not apply to rootless jailbroken devices.

5.5 Comparison with Prior Research

This research can partially be compared with past work. Very few studies have focused on the impact of jailbreak on banking applications, and that focus was primarily on rootful jailbreaks – no work has addressed the challenges posed by rootless jailbreaks to the best of our knowledge. Kellner *et al.* [4] looked closely at many iOS applications to check how many implemented and detected jailbreaking. In their work, many applications did not include any jailbreak detection, and most that did detect relied on straightforward file or process checks that could be bypassed easily with common tweaks or hooking frameworks. Their work only focused on rootful jailbreaking detection and evasion. Since that time, Apple has implemented multiple new security measures, and due to that, new jailbreaking methods have emerged, which laid the ground for this research.

Table 6 compares the current findings to the Kellner *et al.* [4] study of 34 banking apps. In their dataset, slightly over half (53%) attempted jailbreak detection, yet nearly all of those (94%) were trivially bypassed with simple evasion techniques. By contrast, 67% of the 46 banking apps tested in a rootful environment included some form of detection, and only 35% of those were easily bypassed. This suggests a moderate improvement in detection compared to the earlier study, where major banking apps were trivially bypassable. In Kellner *et al.* [4], research focused on intercepting users' data, which was not the objective of this research and hence not tested.

Table 6. Comparison of jailbreak detection in banking apps (rootful vs. rootless vs. Kellner *et al.*)

Study	Banking Apps	Jailbreak Detection	Easily Bypassed
Kellner *et al.*	34	18 (≈53%)	17 of 18 (≈94%)
This work (Rootful)	46	31 (≈67%)	11 of 31 (≈35%)
This work (Rootless)	45	20 (≈44%)	15 of 20 (75%)

However, when focusing in rootless jailbreaks, detection rates drop to 44%, and evasion techniques bypass 75% of those detections. This indicates that while detection appears stronger in a rootful setting than in Kellner *et al.* [4]'s results, the advent of rootless jailbreaks is a new challenge that needs to be addressed. The outcomes from static analysis land on the same conclusion as the previous studies' findings that the majority of apps rely on root-level filesystem checks, but such applications are less equipped to handle a jailbreak installed outside the system partition and do not apply diverse jailbreak detection mechanisms.

The comparison shows progress in jailbreak detection for banking apps since previous studies. Still, it underscores how a new rootless jailbreak undermines existing detection strategies and will require a new approach. This comparative view suggests that while banking apps may have improved in a rootful environment and there is a shift in awareness, as more banks have applied security measures against jailbreaking, the advent of rootless jailbreaks negates much of this progress. Developers relying primarily on system partition-level checks must focus on runtime-based or system-API-based checks to avoid new jailbreak implementations.

Compared with previous findings, static analysis reveal notable changes in the implementation of foreign files (path-based detection) and file system checks (sandbox violation). For example, `Applications/Cydia.app` was previously detected in 15% of applications; in the current research, it is present in 43% of applications. In contrast, reliance on a file system check for `/private/jailbreak.txt` has decreased – from 27% to 23%. However, although sandbox-violation-based checks have improved in comparison to previous studies, the focus has shifted toward the implementation of multiple different checks, and reliance on a single `/private/jailbreak.txt` check has decreased. In total, 18 (40%) banking applications showed some form of sandbox violation-based checks.

Additionally, platform functionality checks have changed; only one application looked for `system` function, while in Kellner *et al.* [4] findings, 63% utilized this functionality. The focus for `cydia://` has increased as 32% of applications utilized this for jailbreak detection, compared to only 15% of applications in the past that made use of this.

Overall, the results show a slight improvement in jailbreak detection for rootful applications. Many applications in the finance and banking sector have taken iOS application security more seriously and have started implementing jailbreak detection. The improvement has focused heavily on system-based detection, which is not applicable for rootless applications, as these applications do not utilize the system volume. Hence, there is a need for improved jailbreak detection for rootless.

6 Limitations

This work has some limitations that can be addressed in future research:

- A significant portion of the original dataset was excluded due to OS incompatibility, which may have reduced the representativeness of the study.
- Static analysis was limited to the banking apps, but expanding it to all categories could enhance the study.
- Static analysis based on string matching is ineffective for obfuscated code or dynamically generated strings.
- Unlike previous studies, data interception was excluded from the scope.
- The paper does not address countermeasures or propose improved detection mechanisms.

7 Conclusions

This study revisited the effectiveness of jailbreak detection in iOS applications, with an emphasis on the emerging challenges posed by rootless jailbreaks. The findings demonstrate a similar profile of detection failures for both the financial and non-financial applications, particularly in the rootless contexts. Of the 378 apps explored in a rootless setup, 346 (approximately 92%) failed to detect the jailbreak. Similarly, in the rootful environment, 215 out of 299 applications (approximately 72%) failed.

Banking applications, although slightly better in detection, still exhibited significant weaknesses. In the context of rootless testing, 25 out of 45 apps (56%) did not detect jailbreak; similarly, in the case of rootful testing, 15 out of 46 (33%) did not detect the jailbroken environment. Additionally, financial applications (non-banking) showed particularly weak detection in the rootless context, with 38 out of 47 apps (81%) not detecting jailbreak.

Dynamic evasion analysis revealed that 26 out of 31 applications initially detecting jailbreak in rootless could be bypassed with simple tweaks, confirming the ease of circumvention. Static analysis of 44 banking apps revealed that while 82% included some form of jailbreak-related strings or logic, none showed rootless-specific detection strings. Additionally, eight banking apps did not appear to contain any relevant jailbreak detection at all.

These results reinforce the notion that detection continues to rely heavily on static file paths and system-level checks methods that are fundamentally ineffective against rootless jailbreaking. While there has been a moderate increase in detection capacity in rootful contexts since the previous studies, the rootless model exposes a major security blind spot. As jailbreaks continue to evolve away from system volume tampering, detection strategies must similarly evolve toward dynamic, behavior-based methods. Without this transition, iOS applications, even those in sensitive areas such as banking, will remain vulnerable to simple bypass methods and runtime evasion.

Acknowledgments. The first author wants to thank **David Hilmarsson** of **Nagarro** for encouraging and motivating him to contemplate – and ultimately pursue – Apple Security. He also acknowledges **Nagarro** for providing the tools and collaborative environment that made this project possible. Finally, he would like to extend his gratitude to all his colleagues, friends, and family for their unwavering support and encouragement throughout this journey.

Disclosure of Interests. The authors have no competing interests to declare that are relevant to the content of this article.

A Testing Methodology

Figure 1 illustrates the phases of the jailbreak detection testing.

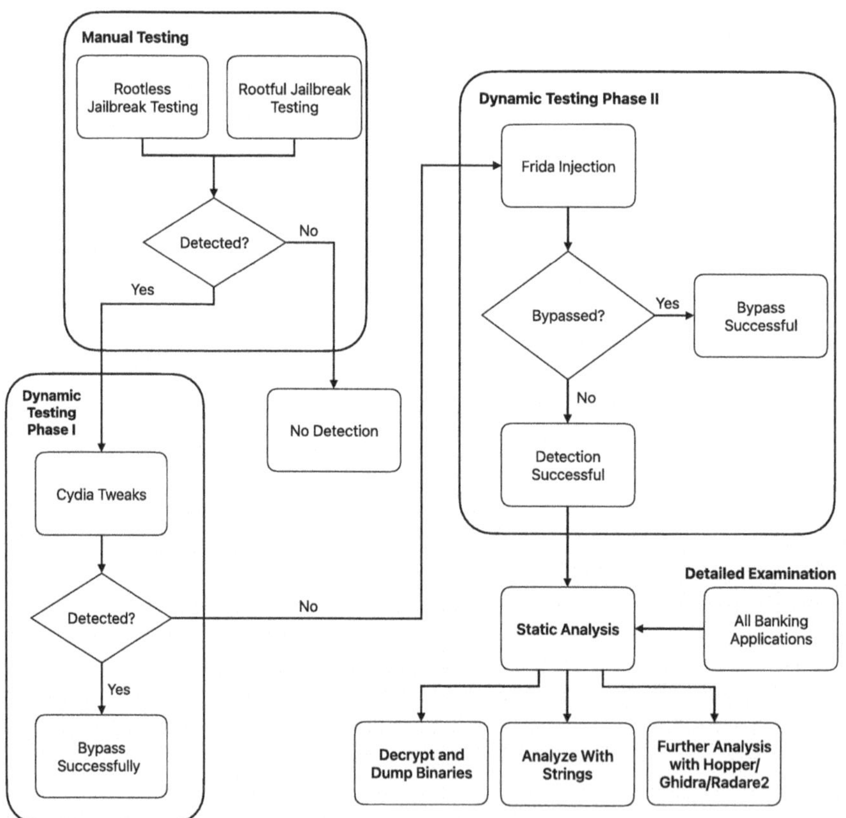

Fig. 1. Jailbreak detection testing phases.

References

1. Mohd Saudi, M., Husainiamer, M.A., Ahmad, A., Idris, M.Y.I.: iOS mobile malware analysis: a state-of-the-art. J. Comput. Virol. Hacking Tech. (2023). https://doi.org/10.1007/s11416-023-00477-y. Accessed 09 Dec 2024
2. Yaswant, A., Bertona, F., Braga, G., Chiaraviglio, N., Pratapagiri, V.: 2023 mobile banking heists report. Technical report, p. 35. Zimperium Inc. (2023). Accessed 13 Sept 2024
3. Statista, Mobile network subscriptions worldwide 2028 | Statista (2024). https://www.statista.com/statistics/330695/number-of-smartphone-users-worldwide/. Accessed 13 Sept 2024
4. Kellner, A., Horlboge, M., Rieck, K., Wressnegger, C.: False sense of security: a study on the effectivity of jailbreak detection in banking apps. In: 2019 IEEE European Symposium on Security and Privacy (EuroS&P), pp. 114. IEEE, Stock holm (2019). https://doi.org/10.1109/EuroSP.2019.00011. Accessed 10 Aug 2024
5. Thiel, D.: iOS Application Security: The definitive Guide for Hackers and Developers. No Starch Press, San Francisco (2016)
6. Wu, F., Chen, C.-H., Clarke, D.: Sensitive data protection on mobile devices. Int. J. Adv. Comput. Sci. Appl. **5**(9) (2014). https://doi.org/10.14569/IJACSA.2014.050907. Accessed 14 Sept 2024
7. Han, J., et al.: Launching generic attacks on iOS with approved third-party applications. In: Jacobson, M., Locasto, M., Mohassel, P., Safavi-Naini, R. (eds.) ACNS 2013. LNCS, vol. 7954, pp. 272–289. Springer, Heidelberg (2013). https://doi.org/10.1007/978-3-642-38980-1_17
8. Sun, S.-T., Cuadros, A., Beznosov, K.: Android rooting: methods, detection, and evasion. In: Proceedings of the 5th Annual ACM CCS Workshop on Security and Privacy in Smartphones and Mobile Devices, pp. 314. ACM, Denver (2015). https://doi.org/10.1145/2808117.2808126. Accessed 19 Sept 2024
9. Soewito, B., Suwandaru, A.: Android sensitive data leakage prevention with rooting detection using Java function hooking. J. King Saud Univ.- Comput. Inf. Sci. **34**(5), 19501957 (2022). https://doi.org/10.1016/j.jksuci.2020.07.006. Accessed 15 Sept 2024
10. Zhang, H., She, D., Qian, Z.: Android root and its providers: a double-edged sword. In: Proceedings of the 22nd ACM SIGSAC Conference on Computer and Communications Security, pp. 10931104. ACM, Denver (2015). https://doi.org/10.1145/2810103.2813714. Accessed 15 Sept 2024
11. Key, D.: The history of iOS jailbreaking (2014). https://medium.com/@dannykey/the-history-of-ios-jailbreaking-d1a42f48e462. Accessed 27 Oct 2024
12. AppleWiki, PwnageTool (2024). https://theapplewiki.com/wiki/PwnageTool. Accessed 26 Oct 2024
13. Freeman, J.: Bringing debian apt to the iPhone (2008). https://www.saurik.com/telesphoreo.html. Accessed 26 Oct 2024
14. AppleWiki, Filesystem:/private/preboot/boot-manifest-hash/procursus (2024). https://theapplewiki.com/wiki/Filesystem:/private/preboot/ash
15. Bouchard, A.: What a rootless iOS 15+ jailbreak means for you (2023). https://www.idownloadblog.com/2022/05/13/f-a-q-rootless-ios-15-jailbreak/. Accessed 13 Sept 2024
16. Bouchard, A.: Understanding untethered, semi-untethered, semi-tethered, and tethered jailbreaks (2019). https://www.idownloadblog.com/2019/11/21/types-of-jailbreaks/. Accessed 26 Oct 2024

17. AppleWiki, blackra1n Jailbreak- The Apple Wiki (2024). https://theapplewiki.com/wiki/Blackra1n. Accessed 27 Oct 2024
18. AppleWiki, Jailbreak- The Apple Wiki (2024). https://theapplewiki.com/wiki/Jailbreak. Accessed 01 Oct 2024
19. Newman, L.H.: Unfixable exploit is the latest Apple Security Upheaval (2019). https://www.wired.com/story/ios-exploit-jailbreak-iphone-ipad/. Accessed 25 Oct 2024
20. AppleWiki, Untethered jailbreak- The Apple Wiki (2024). https://theapplewiki.com/wiki/Untethered_jailbreak. Accessed 18 Oct 2024
21. AppleWiki, Pangu9- The Apple Wiki (2024). https://theapplewiki.com/wiki/Pangu9. Accessed 28 Oct 2024
22. Fröder, L.: Dopamine jailbreak (2023). https://ellekit.space/dopamine/. Accessed 27 Oct 2024
23. AppleWiki, Dopamine- The Apple Wiki (2024). https://theapplewiki.com/wiki/dopamine. Accessed 28 Oct 2024
24. unc0ver-team, unc0ver (2018). https://unc0ver.dev/. Accessed 27 Oct 2024
25. AppleDevelopers, fileExists(atPath:isDirectory:) | Apple Developer Documentation, (2024). https://developer.apple.com/documentation/foundation/filemanager/1410277-fileexists. Accessed 01 Nov 2024
26. Reguła, W.: securing/IOSSecuritySuite: iOS platform security & anti-tampering Swift library (2020). https://github.com/securing/IOSSecuritySuite. Accessed 01 Nov 2024
27. Yegorov, V.: Jailbreak detection The modern way (2020). https://github.com/vadim-a-yegorov/Jailbreak-detection-The-modern-way. Accessed 01 Nov 2024
28. Wu, L., Zhou, Y., Li, M.: IOS URL scheme susceptible to hijacking (2019). https://web.archive.org/web/20191030235352/https://blog.trendmicro.com/trendlabs-security-intelligence/ios-url-scheme-susceptible-to-hijacking/. Accessed 01 Nov 2024
29. Bisson, D.: Threat actors could abuse iOS URL scheme to undermine user privacy (2019). https://securityintelligence.com/news/threat-actors-could-abuse-ios-url-scheme-to-undermine-user-privacy/. Accessed 01 Nov 2024
30. Lindemann, W.: IOS 9.2 update: the fall of URI schemes and the rise of universal links (2015). https://www.branch.io/resources/blog/uri-schemes-and-universal-links-for-ios/. Accessed 01 Nov 2024
31. Apple, Apple Platform Security 2024. Technical report, Apple (2024). https://help.apple.com/pdf/security/en_GB/apple-platform-security-guide-b.pdf. Accessed 13 Sept 2024
32. Trustwave, Jailbreak detection methods (2014). https://www.trustwave.com/en-us/resources/blogs/spiderlabs-blog/jailbreak-detection-methods/. Accessed 01 Nov 2024
33. Ravnås, O.A.V.: Frida • A world-class dynamic instrumentation toolkit | Ob serve and reprogram running programs on Windows, macOS, GNU/Linux, iOS, watchOS, tvOS, Android, FreeBSD, and QNX (2014). https://frida.re/. Accessed 14 Sept 2024
34. Geist, D., Geist, D., Nigmatullin, M., Nigmatullin, M., Bierens, R.: Jailbreak/root detection evasion study on iOS and android. MA thesis, SNE-Universitetiet van Amsterdam (2016). https://rp.os3.nl/2015-2016/p51/report.pdf
35. OWASP-MASTG, iOS Anti-Reversing Defenses-OWASP Mobile Application Security (2021). https://mas.owasp.org/MASTG/0x06j-Testing-Resiliency-Against-Reverse-Engineering. Accessed 03 Nov 2024

36. Levin, J.: Mac OS X and iOS Internals: To the Apple's Core. Wiley, Wrox (2013)
37. Laborde, G.: GantMan/jail-monkey: a React Native library for identifying if a phone is rooted or mocking locations (2019). https://github.com/GantMan/jail-monkey . Accessed 02 Nov 2024
38. Bugsnag, Bugsnag Framework Cocoapods (2012). https://github.com/bugsnag/bugsnag-cocoa. Accessed 09 Apr 2025
39. Orikogbo, D., Büchler, M., Egele, M.: CRiOS: toward large-scale iOS application analysis. In: Proceedings of the 6th Workshop on Security and Privacy in Smart phones and Mobile Devices, p. 3342. ACM, Vienna (2016). https://doi.org/10.1145/2994459.2994473. Accessed 17 Oct 2024
40. Tang, Z., Tang, K., Tian, Y., Ikram, M., Zhu, H.: iOS, Your OS, Everybody's OS: Vetting and Analyzing Network Services of iOS Applications (2020)
41. DigiDNA, IMazing: IPhone, iPad and iPod Manager for mac and PC (2008). https://imazing.com/. Accessed 06 Mar 2025
42. D'Orazio, C.J., Lu, R., Choo, K.-K.R., Vasilakos, A.V.: A Markov adversary model to detect vulnerable iOS devices and vulnerabilities in iOS apps. Appl. Math. Comput. **293**, 523544 (2017). https://doi.org/10.1016/j.amc.2016.08.051. Accessed 31 Aug 2024
43. Roothide-team, Roothide/Dopamine2-Roothide: Dopamine is a semi-untethered jailbreak for IOS 15 and 16 (2024). https://github.com/roothide/Dopamine2-roothide. Accessed 07 Mar 2025
44. Todesco, L.: Checkra1n (2019). https://checkra.in/. Accessed 07 Mar 2025
45. jjolanos, jjolano/shadow: a jailbreak detection bypass for modern iOS jailbreaks. (2019). https://github.com/jjolano/shadow. Accessed 07 Nov 2024
46. Appie, B.: Download a-bypass (2022). https://repo.co.kr/package/com.rpgfarm.a-bypass. Accessed 07 Nov 2024
47. Roothide, Developer/roothide.md at main- roothide/Developer (2024). https://github.com/roothide/Developer/blob/main/roothide.md. Accessed 02 Nov 2024
48. DXcool223, DXCOOL223 REPO (2013). https://dxcool223-repo.github.io/repo/. Accessed 07 Mar 2025
49. AloneMonkey, AloneMonkey/frida-iOS-dump: pull decrypted IPA from jailbreak de vice (2017). https://github.com/AloneMonkey/frida-ios-dump. Accessed 15 Nov 2024
50. ChiChou, ChiChou/bagbak: Yet another frida based iOS dumpdecrypted. Also decrypts app extensions (2020). https://github.com/ChiChou/bagbak. Accessed 15 Nov 2024

PIM: A Metric to Empower Mobile App Users in Privacy Management

Amador Aparicio[1(✉)], M. Mercedes Martínez-González[1], Alejandro Pérez-Fuente[1], and Pablo-Abel Criado-Lozano[1,2]

[1] Privacy Engineering Research Group (IngPriv), University of Valladolid, Valladolid, Spain
{amador,mercedes}@infor.uva.es, alejandro.perez.fuente@uva.es

[2] Miguel de Cervantes European University, Valladolid, Spain
pacriado@uemc.es

Abstract. Despite growing privacy concerns, many mobile app users are unaware of how the permissions they grant affect their privacy. One reason for this is the lack of understandable tools to help them interpret how this impact varies according to their choices in device settings. As far as we know, there are no tools that quantify this impact from the user's perspective. This paper presents the Privacy Impact Metric (PIM), a tool aimed at empowering users to manage their privacy when using mobile applications. PIM provides quantitative values that reflect the impact that an application has on the user's privacy. This quantification allows users to compare applications, anticipate risks and make informed decisions about granting permissions. The metric is based on permission groups, the only mechanism Android provides for managing privacy after installation. This structure allows the granting or revoking of permissions to be simulated and observing the resulting impact to be observed. Another contribution of the work is the grouping of permissions, extracted directly from the Android source code, as this information is not officially documented by Google. This classification facilitates the validation of research that uses categories other than those defined by Android.

Keywords: Privacy · Android Permissions · Privacy Metrics · Permission Groups

1 Introduction

According to the Android security model [34,35], applications must request permissions to access device resources [50]. However, many applications request more than necessary, compromising user privacy. This, understood as the right to confidentiality of personal information [22], requires the access to and use of data by applications and third parties to be controlled. Although concern for privacy is increasing [12], many users are unaware of how the permissions they grant affect their security and privacy [38], and they do not understand what

R. Laborde et al. (Eds.): ESORICS 2025 Workshops, LNCS 16233, pp. 578–598, 2026.
https://doi.org/10.1007/978-3-032-16165-9_34

data they are sharing or what granting those permissions entails, which can lead them to allow unnecessary access [51].

On Android, critical permissions are grouped into categories visible in the system settings, such as camera, location, or microphone. Once an application is installed, users manage permissions only through these groups [5,26]. Granting a group does not imply authorizing all its permissions, but only those declared by the developer. With each new Android API[1], Google updates both the permissions and their grouping [23].

Given this situation, this work poses the following research question: ***RQ: Is it possible to design an understandable tool that helps users make informed decisions about their privacy when using Android mobile applications?***

To answer this question, PIM (*Privacy Impact Metric*) is proposed as user oriented tool that allows users to understand the impact of applications on their privacy, comprehend the causes, and make informed decisions to reduce the said impact. PIM has been successfully validated technically, demonstrating consistency with external sources. Furthermore, preliminary validation is being conducted with users through workshops, where they interact with a web service that displays the impact, explains its factors, and allows the simulation of permission granting or revocation. This environment enables an assessment of PIM's usefulness and its acceptability as a tool to support informed decision-making.

The main contributions of this work are:

1. Metric, *Privacy Impact Metric* (PIM), which quantifies the impact of mobile applications on user privacy. It is based on the grouping of permissions, allowing the metric to reflect how this impact varies depending on user actions when granting or denying permissions. This approach has the advantage that the values generated by the metric align with real user behavior.
2. The classification of permissions into groups, obtained from the source code since it is not available in the official documentation, is necessary to construct the PIM and provides a consistent basis for comparison with other works, even if they follow different criteria.

The remainder of the paper is organized as follows: Sect. 2 presents the Android permission system. Section 3 reviews related work. Section 4 describes the methodology used to develop and validate the proposed metric. Section 5 outlines the formulation of PIM. Section 6 validates the metric using recognized sources. Section 7 discusses the results obtained and their implications. Finally, Sect. 8 concludes the paper and outlines future research directions. The appendices include information on statistical validation and permission classification.

[1] The Android platform provides an API with a set of functions that allow applications to interact with the operating system. The API level is an integer value that identifies the version of said API. https://developer.android.com/guide/topics/manifest/uses-sdk-element?hl=es-419.

2 Android Permission System

2.1 Protection Levels

Android classifies permissions into five categories[2] based on their risk to device security and data privacy. *Normal* permissions are granted automatically due to their minimal risk. *Signature* and *knownSigner* permissions are also granted at install time: the former to apps from the same developer, and the latter if signed with a previously authorized certificate. *SignatureOrSystem*, now obsolete, were used by system-integrated apps. *Dangerous* permissions, which allow access to sensitive data, may compromise user privacy and are the only ones manageable by users post-installation via permission groups.

2.2 Permission Groups

Permission groups logically organize *dangerous* permissions with similar functionalities, allowing users to manage their privacy from the device settings [11]. This management involves granting or denying an application access to all the permissions within the group declared in its manifest file. Figure 1 illustrates this process for the SMS group: when access is granted to an application, Android automatically enables all permissions in the group, applying the decision at the group level rather than individually.

Fig. 1. Authorization of SMS group permissions following an application's request.

This example illustrates that Android permissions are granted at the group level. Granting access to one function (e.g., sending SMS) also authorizes related ones (e.g., reading or receiving SMS), potentially compromising privacy. This has been exploited in attacks to intercept OTP codes sent via SMS [6].

3 Related Work

Permission Analysis in Android. Numerous studies have addressed privacy analysis in Android applications based on the permissions declared in the *AndroidManifest.xml* file. Some examine the evolution of the operating system and the complexity introduced by new versions [4,7]. Others use this information to

[2] Types of Android permissions: https://developer.android.com/guide/topics/manifest/permission-element?hl=es-419.

detect malicious applications [3,42,43] or to generate informed recommendations for users [28,46]. Permission analysis has also been linked to educational initiatives focused on self-management of privacy [25,60], although these efforts often lack user-friendly, quantitative metrics that end users can easily understand.

Restricting the analysis to dangerous permissions may exclude other categories (normal or signature) with privacy implications. Even seemingly safe permissions can be exploited through side channels or alternative uses [15,33,40]. However, users can only manage permission groups, which do not include normal or *signature* permissions, limiting their protection. Moreover, many tools rely on concepts beyond users' control, hindering effective self-protection [32].

Permission Groups and Evaluation. Several studies propose grouping permissions to simplify privacy management, either through visualizations or justification messages [25,29], by functionality to assess privacy impact [28,57], or through risk models categorizing critical areas [19,58]. However, these approaches do not follow Android's official classification, limiting their real-world applicability.

Malware and Privacy in Android. Recent studies have shown that malware in the Android ecosystem poses not only a security threat to the device but also a significant risk to user privacy. Several works highlight how malicious applications actively seek to access personal information by exploiting system permissions to obtain sensitive data without the user's knowledge [27,61]. Additionally, other studies propose detection mechanisms that aim to preserve user privacy during malware analysis [10,16].

Visual Privacy Indicators. These visual indicators alert users about access to sensitive data, such as the microphone or camera icon in Android [18]. More visible alternatives have also been proposed, such as an animated ring at the top of the screen, evaluated through *eye tracking* techniques [17]. Both studies assess whether these indicators truly fulfill their role: the former measures their ability to convey useful information, while the latter analyzes how users perceive them during interaction. They agree that the presence of an indicator alone does not ensure user understanding or influence on decision-making.

Dynamic Privacy Indicators Based on Observed Leaks. Some studies rely on dynamic analysis of app behavior to detect data exfiltration. Tools like *MobHide* intercept and anonymize outgoing data [8], while others analyze third party SDK patterns [36], network traffic, or execution flows [44,63]. Several works also question the reliability of privacy indicators, showing how they can be hidden [9], or detect undeclared sensitive accesses like background sensor use [52,54]. However, these approaches often require modified environments or elevated privileges, and their results are not always presented as user-friendly metrics. As highlighted in [41], some SDKs act as massive data collectors, reinforcing the need for tools that alert users to the indirect impact of granting permissions.

Hybrid Metrics for Estimating Privacy Risk. Several studies combine static and dynamic analysis to build privacy metrics. Some validate statically detected leaks through execution [56], or trace sensitive data paths with different granularity levels [53,62]. Others combine theoretical and executed paths to calculate risk [47]. Together, these works aim to represent privacy impact quantitatively. However, static analysis depends on access to source code or effective reverse engineering, which may be limited by obfuscation techniques.

Analysis and Visualization Tools. Services like *Exodus Privacy* [21,24,30] have been used to identify risks and trackers in mobile apps. Meanwhile, *ToS;DR* [2,39,48,49] provides collaborative summaries of privacy policies, combining declared terms with real world implications and offering a structured basis for assessing privacy impact. In addition, [14] analyze how apps and services structure access to personal data, creating opaque dynamics that hinder informed user decisions.

4 Methodology

The methodology is based on Marono et al. [31], who propose a quantitative approach for developing and validating privacy metrics in mobile applications. It therefore includes the elaboration and validation phases of PIM.

4.1 Elaboration

PIM is based on *dangerous* permissions, the only ones that Android allows users to manage after installation through the permission group mechanism. The development of the metric is built upon this structure.

1. **Retrieve the set of Android permissions**. A comprehensive set of all Android permissions is obtained[3], including their API level and *protection level.*
2. **Filter user manageable permissions.** Permissions that cannot be managed by the user are excluded, retaining only those that can be administered during app usage. These correspond to *dangerous* permissions.
3. **Assign an impact value to user manageable permissions.** Since user manageable permissions represent a potential privacy risk, as acknowledged in Google's official documentation[4], each of the permissions obtained in step 2 is assigned a value that quantifies its impact on privacy.
4. **Retrieve permission groups.** The updated Android permission groups are obtained from the official documentation provided by Android developers[5].
5. **Classify permissions within permission groups.** The permissions from step 2 are assigned to the groups obtained in step 4, following the functional classification extracted from the Android source code.

[3] All Android permissions: https://developer.android.com/reference/android/Manifest.permission.

[4] https://developer.android.com/guide/topics/manifest/permission-element?hl=en-419.

[5] https://developer.android.com/reference/android/Manifest.permission_group.

6. **Define PIM based on the obtained parameters.** The PIM metric is defined by integrating the results obtained in the previous steps. For each user-manageable permission (step 2), its assigned impact value (step 3) and the permission group it belongs to (steps 4 and 5) are taken into account.
7. **Normalize the values provided by PIM.** The values generated by the PIM metric are normalized within a common range to facilitate interpretation and enable comparison between different applications in terms of their impact on privacy.

4.2 Validation

Once PIM has been defined, an external validation is conducted to verify its consistency with other sources focused on the impact of applications on user privacy.

1. **Select validation sources**. Sources are selected that: adopt a user centered approach, are based on privacy analysis, and provide scores that allow comparison with PIM results.
2. **Select the validation method**. A method is selected that enables comparison between the results provided by PIM and those obtained from external validation sources, with the aim of analyzing whether both metrics produce consistent values for the same set of applications.
3. **Select a dataset**. A random set of applications is selected that meets two conditions: they must be evaluable using PIM and must have quantifiable information available from the chosen validation sources.
4. **Apply the validation method**. For the selected set of applications, the values obtained through PIM are compared with those extracted from the validation sources.
5. **Analyze the results**. The results obtained after applying the validation method are analyzed to identify whether there are significant differences between the values generated by PIM and those obtained from external sources.

5 Development of PIM

PIM is based on the analysis of permissions declared in the *AndroidManifest.xml* file and on three principles: (1) only *dangerous* permissions require user intervention [35]; (2) these permissions are grouped according to similar levels of risk [35]; and (3) *malware* typically requests more *dangerous* permissions than legitimate apps [7,13].

5.1 Retrieval of Android Permissions

The permissions specified by Google for Android are obtained from its official page[6]. All the permissions defined by Google for Android and used in this study are available for download and analysis at the following link: https://zenodo.org/records/15031554.

[6] Source: https://developer.android.com/reference/android/Manifest.permission.

5.2 Filtering User Manageable Permissions

Permissions manageable by the user are selected, specifically those whose protection level is *dangerous*. Table 1 shows the first 10 *dangerous* permissions listed in API 33 (Android 13).

Table 1. First 10 *dangerous* permissions in API 33 (Android 13).

Permission	
ACCESS_FINE_LOCATION	READ_CONTACTS
ACCESS_COARSE_LOCATION	WRITE_CONTACTS
READ_EXTERNAL_STORAGE	GET_ACCOUNTS
WRITE_EXTERNAL_STORAGE	READ_MEDIA_IMAGES
ACCESS_MEDIA_LOCATION	READ_MEDIA_VIDEO

5.3 Assignment of an Impact Value to User Manageable Permissions

To assign impact values to the identified *dangerous* permissions, we adopt the ranking proposed in [59], shown in Table 2, which lists the most frequently exploited permissions by *malware* with their normalized values in the [0,1] range. This ranking, based on the assumption that exploited permissions are often linked to personal data and critical device functions, serves as an indicator of potential privacy impact. Although derived from technical studies on *malware* [59], the frequency with which permissions are exploited is used as a proxy for privacy risk, since it reveals those most likely to enable unauthorized access to personal data [10,16,27,61]. This provides an objective and quantifiable basis for assigning weights in the metric.

Table 2. Ranking of most exploited *dangerous* permissions by *malware* along with their privacy impact value.

Permission	Impact	Permission	Impact
READ_PHONE_STATE	0.488382	RESTART_PACKAGES	0.188282
READ_SMS	0.456050	WRITE_APN_SETTINGS	0.185852
SEND_SMS	0.433686	WRITE_CONTACTS	0.178911
WRITE_SMS	0.395856	GET_TASKS	0.164140
RECEIVE_SMS	0.352381	MOUNT_UNMOUNT_FILESYSTEMS	0.145570
READ_CONTACTS	0.203704	CALL_PHONE	0.192382

5.4 Dangerous Permissions Not Included in the Ranking of Most Exploited by Malware

Not all *dangerous* permissions appear in the ranking in Table 2. Table 3 lists those not identified as frequently exploited by *malware*. According to the official Android documentation [1], *dangerous* permissions grant access to sensitive data or critical device functions. Consequently, they are considered to pose a potential privacy risk and must therefore receive an impact value in PIM. Permissions not included in the ranking are assigned a residual value of $\frac{1}{|P_D|} \approx 0.0256$, where $|P_D| = 39$ represents the number of *dangerous* permissions identified in our reference set, obtained from the *Android Open Source Project* (AOSP) code[7]. This value is lower than the minimum impact in the ranking, enabling a clear distinction between the most exploited permissions and the rest.

Table 3. Dangerous permissions outside the ranking of most exploited by *malware*.

Permission	
ACCESS_BACKGROUND_LOCATION	ACCESS_COARSE_LOCATION
ACCESS_FINE_LOCATION	ACCESS_MEDIA_LOCATION
ACTIVITY_RECOGNITION	ADD_VOICEMAIL
ANSWER_PHONE_CALLS	BLUETOOTH_ADVERTISE
BLUETOOTH_CONNECT	BLUETOOTH_SCAN
BODY_SENSORS	BODY_SENSORS_BACKGROUND
NEARBY_WIFI_DEVICES	POST_NOTIFICATIONS
READ_PHONE_NUMBERS	RECEIVE_MMS
RECEIVE_WAP_PUSH	RECORD_AUDIO
WRITE_CALENDAR	

5.5 Retrieval of Permission Groups

The permission groups defined by Google for Android are obtained[8]. Table 4 presents these groups, along with the API level at which they were introduced and a brief description of their function.

At the time of this work, the most recent version of the Android API that defines the latest permission groups is API level 33[9], corresponding to Android 13. With each update, Android has introduced new permission groups to strengthen security and enhance user privacy management.

[7] AOSP source code: https://android.googlesource.com/platform/frameworks/base/+/refs/heads/master/core/res/AndroidManifest.xml.

[8] Source: https://developer.android.com/reference/android/Manifest.permission_group.

[9] Available at: https://zenodo.org/records/14944161.

Table 4. Android permission groups and their corresponding API levels.

API Level	Permission Groups	Description
1	LOCATION	Access to precise and approximate device location
4	STORAGE	Read and write access to shared storage
17	ACTIVITY_RECOGNITION	Detect and recognize user activity, such as walking or driving
17	CALENDAR	Read and write access to the user's calendar events
17	CAMERA	Capture photos and videos using the device's camera
17	MICROPHONE	Record audio through the device's microphone
23	CONTACTS	Access and modify contacts stored on the device
23	PHONE	Manage phone calls, read phone state, and interact with telephony services
23	SENSORS	Access to body and environmental sensors
23	SMS	Send and receive SMS and MMS messages
28	CALL_LOG	Read and write access to the call history log
31	NEARBY_DEVICES	Discover, connect, and communicate with nearby devices
33	NOTIFICATIONS	Manage the ability to post and control notifications
33	READ_MEDIA_AURAL	Read audio media files from shared storage
33	READ_MEDIA_VISUAL	Read image and video files from shared storage

5.6 Classification of Dangerous Permissions Into Permission Groups

The next step is to classify the *dangerous* permissions into groups. Since Google's documentation does not provide this, a limitation for *PIM*, the classification was obtained directly from the Android source code in the official GitHub repository[10]. Table 5 presents a subset of these permissions, grouped by API level and exemplified through WhatsApp, as detailed in Sect. 5.8.

Table 5. Grouping of dangerous permissions into permission groups.

API Level	Permission Groups	Permissions
1	LOCATION	ACCESS_FINE_LOCATION ACCESS_COARSE_LOCATION
4	STORAGE	READ_EXTERNAL_STORAGE WRITE_EXTERNAL_STORAGE
...	...	...
17	CONTACTS	READ_CONTACTS WRITE_CONTACTS GET_ACCOUNTS
...	...	...
33	READ_MEDIA_VISUAL	READ_MEDIA_IMAGES READ_MEDIA_VIDEO ACCESS_MEDIA_LOCATION

[10] Android Open Source Project: https://github.com/aosp-mirror/platform_frameworks_base/blob/master/core/res/AndroidManifest.xml.

The complete classification of all dangerous permissions and their mapping to the respective groups is available in the repository at https://zenodo.org/records/15290288.

5.7 Formulation of PIM

PIM is presented as a simple and flexible solution for assessing the impact of permissions on user privacy. Its design allows the simulation of permission granting and revocation, and its normalization on a scale from 0 to 1 facilitates interpretation. The configurable assignment of weights per group enables adaptation to new permissions, and the sum-based representation helps identify which groups pose the highest privacy risk.

The formulation of PIM is defined as:

$$PIM(app) = \frac{\sum_{i=1}^{n}(e_i \sum_{j=1}^{m_i} p_{ij})}{maxI}$$

where:

- $PIM(app)$: is the metric that quantifies the privacy impact of the *app*. Its value lies between 0, indicating no impact on privacy, to 1, which represents the maximum possible impact.
- *app*: is the application for which the privacy impact value on users is to be determined.
- n: is the number of permission groups used by the application *app*.
- e_i: is the state of the ith permission group, $e_i \in \{0, 1\}$. A value of 0 indicates that the ith permission group is revoked, and 1 indicates it is granted.
- m: is the number of permissions within a permission group used by the application *app*.
- p_{ij}: is the impact value of the jth permission within the ith permission group used by the application *app*. The impact values p_{ij} are assigned as described in Sect. 5.3.
- max_I: reference value for normalization, obtained as the sum of the impact values in Tables 2 and 3. Its value (4.1468) corresponds to the worst-case scenario, where all *dangerous* permissions are granted, giving full control over sensitive data and functions. This reference allows any partial combination of permissions to be normalized.

5.8 Example of PIM Usage

A practical case is presented for evaluating privacy impact using PIM, applied to the application *WhatsApp* (version *2.23.24.20*, downloaded from *Google Play*). Table 6 lists the *dangerous* permissions used, organized by group, along with their respective privacy impact values.

Table 6. Privacy impact of the *WhatsApp* application, including a detailed breakdown of the impact of each permission and permission group.

Permission Group	Impact	Permissions and Individual Impact
Impact of permission groups	**2.1456**	
CAMERA	0.0256	CAMERA (0.0256)
CONTACTS	0.415	READ_CONTACTS (0.204) WRITE_CONTACTS (0.179) GET_ACCOUNTS (0.032)
LOCATION	0.0512	ACCESS_FINE_LOCATION (0.0256) ACCESS_COARSE_LOCATION (0.0256)
MICROPHONE	0.0256	RECORD_AUDIO (0.0256)
NEARBY_DEVICES	0.1024	BLUETOOTH_SCAN (0.0256) BLUETOOTH_CONNECT (0.0256) BLUETOOTH_ADVERTISE (0.0256) NEARBY_WIFI_DEVICES (0.0256)
NOTIFICATIONS	0.0256	POST_NOTIFICATIONS (0.0256)
PHONE	0.520	READ_PHONE_STATE (0.488) READ_PHONE_NUMBERS (0.032)
READ_MEDIA_AURAL	0.0256	READ_MEDIA_AUDIO (0.0256)
READ_MEDIA_VISUAL	0.0768	READ_MEDIA_VIDEO (0.0256) READ_MEDIA_IMAGES (0.0256) ACCESS_MEDIA_LOCATION (0.0256)
SMS	0.786	SEND_SMS (0.434) RECEIVE_SMS (0.352)
STORAGE	0.0512	READ_EXTERNAL_STORAGE (0.0256) WRITE_EXTERNAL_STORAGE (0.0256)
Impact of permission groups	**2.1456**	

Applying PIM, the privacy impact of the WhatsApp app is obtained as follows:

$$PIM(\textit{WhatsApp}) = \frac{\underbrace{1 \cdot 0.0256}_{\text{CAMERA}} + \underbrace{1 \cdot 0.415}_{\text{CONTACTS}} + \cdots + \underbrace{1 \cdot 0.0512}_{\text{STORAGE}} + \underbrace{1 \cdot 0.786}_{\text{SMS}}}{4.1468} = 0.5172$$

The maximum impact on the privacy of the application's users is quantified at a value of 0.5172. This value corresponds to the scenario in which the user has granted all permissions requested by the application, belonging to the CAMERA, CONTACTS, LOCATION, and STORAGE groups.

If a user were to disable the CAMERA, CONTACTS and SMS permission groups, the impact of the app on users' privacy would be as follows:

$$PIM(WhatsApp) = \frac{\underbrace{\mathbf{0} \cdot 0.0256}_{\text{CAMERA}} + \underbrace{\mathbf{0} \cdot 0.415}_{\text{CONTACTS}} + \cdots + \underbrace{1 \cdot 0.0512}_{\text{STORAGE}} + \underbrace{\mathbf{0} \cdot 0.786}_{\text{SMS}}}{4.1468} = 0.2823$$

Note: Bold zeros indicate permission groups not granted.

Disabling the permissions CAMERA, CONTACTS and SMS reduces the privacy impact from 0.5172 to 0.2823, a decrease of 45.4%. This decrease provides a clear visualization of how certain user decisions can mitigate the exposure of their personal information.

6 PIM Validation

6.1 Selection of Validation Sources

Although *ToS;DR* and PIM stem from different foundations—legal textual analysis and technical permission inspection, respectively—both aim to assess the extent to which mobile applications respect user privacy. *ToS;DR* evaluates the intrusiveness of legal terms and conditions, while PIM measures potential exposure of sensitive data through system-level permissions. Despite this difference, both yield interpretable values aligned with privacy impact, making their comparison meaningful for checking whether technical configurations (captured by PIM) match the guarantees or risks described in legal documents (captured by *ToS;DR*). Given the lack of open repositories for large-scale privacy evaluations, *ToS;DR* is considered the closest available reference, widely recognised and based on user assessments of transparency, which justifies its joint use in the validation framework [20].

Building on this alignment, *ToS;DR*[11][12] is selected as a validation source because it is recognised, accessible, widely covering applications, oriented to user perception, and provides structured ratings. It assesses privacy impact collaboratively, with users and experts labelling clauses by intrusiveness, classifying apps from Class A (respectful) to Class E (highly intrusive) [55]. The quantitative mapping of these classes is obtained via the *App-PIMD* repository, which transforms A–E into a numerical scale (0, 2.5, 5, 7.5, 10) [37]. This preserves category order and enables direct comparison with the proposed metric. Table 7 lists applications (*App*), their PIM scores (*PIM*), the original *ToS;DR* category (*ToS;DR*), and the derived numerical value from *App-PIMD* (*App-PIMD*).

In Table 7, several cases illustrate the relation between *ToS;DR*, App-PIMD, and PIM. Apps like ProtonMail and Free Sticker Maker are rated Class A (*App-PIMD* = 0.0), denoting excellent terms; however, ProtonMail shows a PIM of

[11] Terms of Service; Didn't Read: https://tosdr.org/en.

[12] The ToS;DR category corresponds to the official classification available at https://tosdr.org, and the numerical value has been obtained from the *App-PIMD* repository [37].

Table 7. Privacy impact scores based on PIM, ToS;DR, and App-PIMD.

App	PIM	ToS;DR	App-PIMD
ProtonMail	0.221	A	0.0
Vik Lymphome	0.527	C	5.0
coins.ph	0.953	E	10.0
Free Sticker Maker	0.000	A	0.0
CBC News	0.000	E	10.0
Bíobla	0.449	B	2.5

0.221, reflecting minimal data collection, while Free Sticker Maker remains consistent (PIM = 0.0). Conversely, coins.ph and CBC News fall in Class E (*App-PIMD* = 10.0). For coins.ph, PIM = 0.953 confirms high privacy impact due to extensive dangerous permissions, whereas CBC News scores PIM = 0.000, showing no sensitive permissions but revealing intrusive terms. Intermediate situations are also observed: Vik Lymphome (PIM = 0.527, Class C, *App-PIMD* = 5.0) exhibits medium impact on both dimensions, while Bíobla (PIM = 0.449, Class B, *App-PIMD* = 2.5) reflects moderate permission use with relatively benign terms.

6.2 Selection of the Validation Method

First, we will study the possible relationships between PIM and ToS;DR graphically. If a relationship is found, a non parametric approach will be chosen, since ToS;DR uses an ordinal scale and PIM produces continuous values without guaranteed normality. The Spearman correlation coefficient will be applied, as it is suitable for assessing the strength of monotonic relationships between ranked variables. According to Schober et al., this method is particularly appropriate for ordinal, non-normally distributed data, or when outliers are present [45].

6.3 Dataset

Table 8 shows the dataset used, which consists of 44 mobile applications[13]. Each app was evaluated using the proposed metric (PIM) and the external classification provided by ToS;DR, with numerical values obtained from the App-PIMD repository. The application set corresponds to the first 44 results returned by the App-PIMD repository, which provides both PIM and ToS;DR values. This approach ensures consistency and reproducibility.

[13] According to Statistics Solutions, for $\rho \approx 0.34$ and $\alpha = 0.05$, 44 samples provide sufficient statistical power https://www.statisticssolutions.com/wp-content/uploads/wp-post-to-pdf-enhanced-cache/1/spearman-correlation-2-tailed.pdf.

Table 8. "Subconjunto de 44 aplicaciones: App, PIM y ToS;DR."

App	PIM	ToS;DR	App	PIM	ToS;DR
Lock	0.410	7.500	Opera Mini (beta)	0.650	2.500
Lwp Plus	0.019	5.000	Booksy Biz	0.804	0.000
Darby	0.039	5.000	Adobe Digital Editions	0.019	5.000
App	0.117	5.000	Amazon Seller	0.039	5.000
Invitation Maker by Desygner	0.078	0.000	Google Wallet	0.631	7.500
Talkingflashcards New	0.039	5.000	Streetmall	0.000	5.000
Ultra	0.039	5.000	TodoTest	0.019	5.000
Galaxyshooter	0.000	5.000	Worldtriger	0.429	5.000
Gotyew	0.260	5.000	Meta Business Suite (Pages)	0.843	7.500
Coders	0.000	0.000	App	0.117	5.000
Memo	0.000	0.000	Gifgoodevening collection	0.039	7.500
Shoot	0.000	5.000	RTVE Play (tablet)	0.000	5.000
Wear OS by Google	1.593	7.500	Increase Height Weight	0.019	0.000
DeepL Translate	0.058	2.500	Viaggiintrenofast	0.019	5.000
Moovle	0.097	7.500	MyToyota	0.689	5.000
Bounty Pregnancy	0.039	5.000	Centr (Fitness)	0.019	5.000
Kia Connect	0.271	5.000	Ebook0	0.019	0.000
Wildcoyote	0.019	10.000	Raider	0.986	10.000
Market	0.058	0.000	Dynamite	0.221	7.500
Language	0.039	5.000	Urdu	0.039	10.000
Meetings	0.232	7.500	Ebok	0.039	5.000
English Words	0.000	5.000	Game	0.000	0.000

6.4 Application of the Validation Method

To evaluate the relationship between the privacy impact values obtained through the PIM metric and those assigned by *ToS;DR*, the Spearman correlation coefficient was calculated using the dataset shown in Table 8. This non-parametric method is suitable for comparing ordinal data (such as *ToS;DR*) with continuous data (such as PIM), especially in the absence of normality and in the possible presence of outliers. The result was a Spearman correlation coefficient of $\rho = 0.343$, with a p-value of 0.024.

6.5 Analysis of the Results

The Spearman correlation analysis reveals a positive monotonic relationship of weak to moderate magnitude ($\rho = 0.343, p = 0.024$) between the privacy impact values obtained through PIM and those assigned by *ToS;DR*. This statistically significant result ($\alpha = 0.05$) suggests consistency and partial alignment between both metrics, despite their different perspectives.

Figure 2 displays a scatter plot of the 44 evaluated applications, with PIM scores (0–10) on the X-axis and *ToS;DR* scores (0–10) on the Y-axis. The dashed blue line marks perfect agreement, while the shaded orange band indicates a ± 2 point tolerance margin.

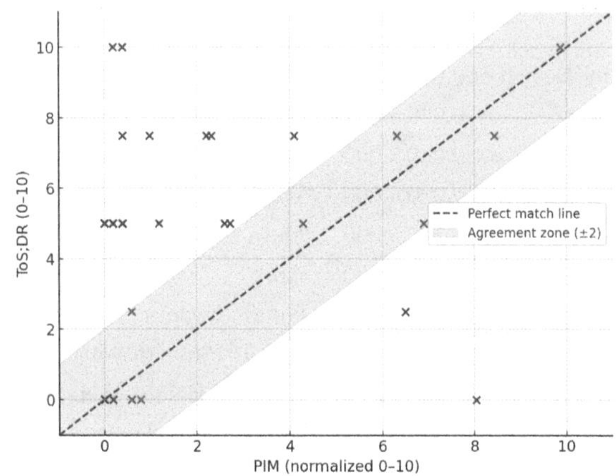

Fig. 2. Comparasion between PIM and ToD;DR scores.

Figure 2 shows the distribution of the original metric values, supporting the observed consistency. Most applications fall within the ± 2 point margin, though some outliers diverge, underscoring the complementary nature of both metrics.

7 Discussion

The validation of PIM has demonstrated its value as a tool for quantifying the privacy impact of mobile applications. Its design enables the generation of easily interpretable numerical values, facilitating app comparison and supporting users in making informed decisions. Technical validation against external sources, such as ToS;DR, and the application of Spearman correlation analysis confirm that PIM captures patterns consistent with established privacy evaluation approaches. In extreme cases, consistency is observed: for example, coins.ph shows both a high PIM score and a poor ToS;DR rating, while ProtonMail exhibits the opposite. This suggests that low transparency often accompanies higher privacy impact, although the opposite may also occur (many permissions with high transparency).

Nevertheless, PIM has some limitations. It treats dangerous permission groups uniformly, without distinguishing perceived risk levels. This can introduce bias into the impact calculation, since permissions such as `MICROPHONE` or `CAMERA` may be perceived as more intrusive than others like `CALENDAR`. Moreover, PIM excludes normal or signature-level permissions, even though some of them, such as `signatureOrSystem`, can compromise privacy, particularly in health-related contexts. Another limitation is that PIM depends on the set of dangerous permissions defined by each Android API level. As a result, PIM scores should be compared within the same API level, or normalized when comparing different versions of the same app across Android releases.

The current weighting of permissions, based on their frequency of exploitation by malware, captures potential technical risks but simplifies reality and does not always reflect user perceptions. This criterion was chosen because malware remains a primary concern for a general audience that is often unfamiliar with advanced privacy issues. Future refinements should consider alternative weightings, including the type of personal data exposed and users' subjective perception of intrusiveness.

Regarding validation, the Spearman correlation between PIM and ToS;DR assesses their overall alignment. Both metrics address privacy from different perspectives: ToS;DR is based on expert analysis of legal documents, while PIM focuses on system-level permissions accessible to users. Despite this methodological difference, both metrics aim to quantify the privacy impact of apps. The scatter plot analysis shows that most applications cluster at low PIM values, consistent with limited use of dangerous permissions. However, discrepancies arise in apps with high ToS;DR ratings but minimal permission requests, highlighting the complementary nature of both approaches.

Finally, while PIM does not analyze the dynamic use of permissions, its value lies in enabling users to make informed decisions based on information available in the manifest. Rather than detecting all potential leaks, PIM seeks to empower users and complement technical and regulatory approaches. A pending research direction is the evaluation of cases where PIM may overestimate or underestimate privacy risks compared to actual app behavior, as such contrasts would be essential to strengthen practical trust in the metric.

8 Conclusions and Future Work

The results of this study show that PIM is a viable metric for representing the privacy impact of the permissions requested by mobile applications in a technical and interpretable way. Its correlation with user-oriented evaluations, such as *ToS;DR*, highlights its value as a complementary tool, even though both metrics address different dimensions of privacy.

Future work will focus on refining the weighting of permissions by integrating users subjective perceptions, since perceived intrusiveness varies across groups. It is also relevant to extend the metric to other categories of sensitive data, such as health-related information.[14] Another key direction is user-centered validation: beyond statistical evidence, studies with real users are required to examine how PIM influences decision making and whether it reveals scenarios where consent

[14] Android Health Permissions: https://developer.android.com/reference/android/health/connect/HealthPermissions.

is not freely given, for instance when functionality depends on accepting all permissions.

A broader evaluation including more applications and users is under development to confirm whether the correlation between PIM and *ToS;DR* strengthens with a larger dataset. Finally, a research line is proposed to combine PIM with dynamic analysis techniques capable of detecting hidden data flows and undeclared behaviors, and to integrate the metric into automated analysis platforms to facilitate its adoption in privacy audits by developers and end users.

Acknowledgements. This work is included in the activities of the strategic Cybersecurity project "App-PI (App Privacy Impact): An ecosystem for the evaluation of the impact of apps for mobile devices on the privacy and security of their users" (C120.23_UVa), which is carried out under a collaboration agreement between the University of Valladolid and the Spanish National Institute of Cybersecurity (INCIBE) for the promotion of strategic Cybersecurity projects in Spain, within the framework of the Recovery, Transformation and Resilience Plan funds, financed by the European Union (Next Generation).

References

1. Android developers - app permissions overview. https://developer.android.com/guide/topics/permissions/overview. Accessed April 2025
2. Deliberately confusing language in terms of service and privacy policy agreements. Issues In Information Systems (2022). https://api.semanticscholar.org/CorpusID:252322031
3. Akbar, F., Hussain, M., Mumtaz, R., Riaz, Q., Wahab, A.W.A., Jung, K.: Permissions-based detection of android malware using machine learning. Symmetry **14**(4), 718 (2022). https://doi.org/10.3390/SYM14040718
4. Almomani, I.M., Al Khayer, A.: A comprehensive analysis of the android permissions system. IEEE Access **8**, 216671–216688 (2020)
5. Android Open Source Project: AndroidManifest.xml (sf). https://github.com/aosp-mirror/platform_frameworks_base/blob/master/core/res/AndroidManifest.xml. recuperado 15 de febrero de 2025
6. Aparicio, A., Martínez-González, M.M., Cardeñoso-Payo, V.: App-based detection of vulnerable implementations of OTP SMS APIs in the banking sector. Wirel. Networks **30**(7), 6451–6464 (2024). https://doi.org/10.1007/S11276-023-03455-W
7. Calciati, P.: Understanding the Evolution of Android Applications. Ph.D. thesis, Technical University of Madrid, Spain (2019). https://oa.upm.es/57886/
8. Caputo, D., Pagano, F., Bottino, G., Verderame, L., Merlo, A.: You can't always get what you want: towards user-controlled privacy on android. IEEE Trans. Dependable Secur. Comput. **20**(2), 975–987 (2023). https://doi.org/10.1109/TDSC.2022.3146020
9. Choe, Y., Yu, H., Kim, T., Lee, S., Lee, H., Kim, H.: (in)visible privacy indicator: Security analysis of privacy indicator on android devices. In: Zhou, J., Quek, T.Q.S., Gao, D., Cárdenas, A.A. (eds.) Proceedings of the 19th ACM Asia Conference on Computer and Communications Security, ASIA CCS 2024, Singapore, 1–5 July 2024. ACM (2024). https://doi.org/10.1145/3634737.3645014

10. D'Angelo, G., Farsimadan, E., Ficco, M., Palmieri, F., Robustelli, A.: Privacy-preserving malware detection in android-based IoT devices through federated Markov chains. Future Gener. Comput. Syst. **148**, 93–105 (2023). https://doi.org/10.1016/J.FUTURE.2023.05.021
11. Developers, A.: Android permission groups (2025). https://developer.android.com/reference/android/Manifest.permission_group
12. European Commission: Eurobarometer: Europeans show support for digital principles. Press release (2021). https://ec.europa.eu/commission/presscorner/api/files/document/print/en/ip_21_6462/IP_21_6462_EN.pdf. disponible en línea
13. Feal, Á., Calciati, P., Vallina-Rodriguez, N., Troncoso, C., Gorla, A.: Angel or devil? A privacy study of mobile parental control apps. Proc. Priv. Enhancing Technol. (2020)
14. Flensburg, S., Lai, S.S.: Datafied mobile markets measuring control over apps, data accesses, and third-party services (2021). https://api.semanticscholar.org/CorpusID:242048476
15. Fratantonio, Y., Qian, C., Chung, S.P., Lee, W.: Cloak and dagger: from two permissions to complete control of the UI feedback loop. In: 2017 IEEE Symposium on Security and Privacy, SP 2017, San Jose, CA, USA, 22–26 May 2017, pp. 1041–1057. IEEE Computer Society (2017). https://doi.org/10.1109/SP.2017.39
16. Gálvez, R., Moonsamy, V., Díaz, C.: Less is more: a privacy-respecting android malware classifier using federated learning. Proc. Priv. Enhancing Technol. **2021**(4), 96–116 (2021). https://doi.org/10.2478/POPETS-2021-0062
17. Guerra, M., Milanese, R., Deodato, M., Perozzi, V., Fasano, F.: Visual attention and privacy indicators in android: Insights from eye tracking. In: Lenzini, G., Mori, P., Furnell, S. (eds.) Proceedings of the 10th International Conference on Information Systems Security and Privacy, ICISSP 2024, Rome, Italy, 26–28 February 2024, pp. 320–329. SCITEPRESS (2024). https://doi.org/10.5220/0012437600003648
18. Guerra, M., Scalabrino, S., Fasano, F., Oliveto, R.: An empirical study on the effectiveness of privacy indicators. IEEE Trans. Software Eng. **49**(10), 4610–4623 (2023). https://doi.org/10.1109/TSE.2023.3308392
19. Hamidreza, A., Mohammed, N.: Permission-based analysis of android applications using categorization and deep learning scheme. In: MATEC Web of Conferences, vol. 255, p. 05005. EDP Sciences (2019)
20. Hashmi, S.S., Waheed, N., Tangari, G., Ikram, M., Smith, S.: Longitudinal compliance analysis of android applications with privacy policies. In: Hara, T., Yamaguchi, H. (eds.) Mobile and Ubiquitous Systems: Computing, Networking and Services - 18th EAI International Conference, MobiQuitous 2021, Virtual Event, 8–11 November 2021, Proceedings. Lecture Notes of the Institute for Computer Sciences, Social Informatics and Telecommunications Engineering, vol. 419, pp. 280–305. Springer (2021). https://doi.org/10.1007/978-3-030-94822-1_16,
21. Hazim, A.: Privacy visualizations: introducing an interactive visualization of privacy indicators based on exodus privacy to F-Droid (2023)
22. International Electrotechnical Commission: IEC 60050 - International Electrotechnical Vocabulary - Details for IEV number 871-04-23: Privacy (sf). https://www.electropedia.org/iev/iev.nsf/display?openform&ievref=871-04-23. recuperado 11 de febrero de 2022
23. yung Kim, J., Yoon, Y., Yi, K.: Static analyzer for detecting privacy leaks in android applications (2012). https://api.semanticscholar.org/CorpusID:267870077
24. Lai, S.S., Flensburg, S.: A proxy for privacy uncovering the surveillance ecology of mobile apps. Big Data Soc. **7** (2020). https://api.semanticscholar.org/CorpusID:225640889

25. Lavranou, R., Karagiannis, S., Tsohou, A., Magkos, E.: Unraveling the complexity of mobile application permissions: strategies to enhance users' privacy education. Eur. J. Eng. Technol. Res., 87–95 (2023)
26. Li, L., et al.: I know what leaked in your pocket: uncovering privacy leaks on android apps with static taint analysis (2014). ArXiv: abs/1404.7431
27. Lim, J.G.Q., et al.: A-COPILOT: android covert operation for private information lifting and OTP theft: a study on how malware masquerading as legitimate applications compromise security and privacy. In: Vilela, J.P., Schulmann, H., Li, N. (eds.) Proceedings of the Fourteenth ACM Conference on Data and Application Security and Privacy, CODASPY 2024, Porto, Portugal, 19–21 June 2024, pp. 155–157. ACM (2024). https://doi.org/10.1145/3626232.3658638
28. Liu, M., Wang, Q.: Research on android user privacy permission analysis and protection mechanism under big data environment. In: MATEC Web of Conferences (2024). https://api.semanticscholar.org/CorpusID:269854220
29. Liu, X., Leng, Y., Yang, W., Wang, W., Zhai, C., Xie, T.: A large-scale empirical study on android runtime-permission rationale messages. 2018 IEEE Symposium on Visual Languages and Human-Centric Computing (VL/HCC), pp. 137–146 (2018). https://api.semanticscholar.org/CorpusID:51917470
30. Mann, H., Wigren, A.: Risk assessment of managed smartphones using MDM: an automated approach to security and privacy analysis (2024)
31. Marono, J., Silva, C., Barraca, J.P., Cunha, V.A., Salvador, P.: Assessing mobile application privacy: a quantitative framework for privacy measurement. CoRR abs/2311.00066 (2023). https://doi.org/10.48550/ARXIV.2311.00066
32. Martínez-González, M.M., Aparicio, A., Pérez Fuente, A., Criado Lozano, P.A., Gonzalo Tasis, M., Moro, Q.I., et al.: Marco para una autoprotección eficaz de la privacidad en entornos móviles. XVIII Reunión Española sobre Criptología y Seguridad de la Información: XVIII RECSI, León 23–25 octubre 2024, pp. 237–242
33. Mavroudis, V., Hao, S., Fratantonio, Y., Maggi, F., Vigna, G., Kruegel, C.: Talking behind your back: attacks and countermeasures of ultrasonic cross-device tracking. Black Hat Europe, London, UK **109** (2016)
34. Mayrhofer, R., Stoep, J.V., Brubaker, C., Kralevich, N.: The android platform security model. ACM Trans. Priv. Secur. (TOPS) **24**, 1–35 (2021)
35. Mayrhofer, R., et al.: The android platform security model (2023). Tech. rep., Cornell University (2023). https://arxiv.org/pdf/1904.05572/1000.pdf
36. Meng, M.H., et al.: A large-scale privacy assessment of android third-party SDKs. CoRR abs/2409.10411 (2024). https://doi.org/10.48550/ARXIV.2409.10411
37. Pérez-Fuente, A., Martínez-González, M.M., Aparicio, A., Moro, Q.I.: A data warehouse for mobile application privacy and security study. Tech. rep. (2024)
38. Peruma, A.S., Palmerino, J., Krutz, D.E.: Investigating user perception and comprehension of android permission models. In: 2018 IEEE/ACM 5th International Conference on Mobile Software Engineering and Systems (MOBILESoft), pp. 56–66 (2018)
39. Picalho, A.C., de Oliveira Lucas, E.R.: "li e aceito os termos de uso": iniciativas de auxílio ao usuário em meio ao que pode ser uma das maiores mentiras da internet. AWARI **3**, 1–7 (2022). https://doi.org/10.47909/awari.152
40. Preda, M.D., Greco, C., Ianni, M., Lupia, F., Pugliese, A.: Light sensor based covert channels on mobile devices. Inf. Sci. **690**, 121581 (2025). https://doi.org/10.1016/J.INS.2024.121581

41. Pybus, J., Coté, M.: Super SDKs: tracking personal data and platform monopolies in the mobile. Big Data Soc. **11**(1) (2024). https://doi.org/10.1177/20539517241231270
42. Quattrone, A., Kulik, L., Tanin, E., Ramamohanarao, K., Gu, T.: PrivacyPalisade: evaluating app permissions and building privacy into smartphones. In: 10th International Conference on Information, Communications and Signal Processing, ICICS 2015, Singapore, 2–4, December 2015, pp. 1–5. IEEE (2015). https://doi.org/10.1109/ICICS.2015.7459926
43. Rathore, H., Sahay, S.K., Rajvanshi, R., Sewak, M.: Identification of significant permissions for efficient android malware detection. CoRR abs/2103.00643 (2021). https://arxiv.org/abs/2103.00643
44. Ren, J., Rao, A., Lindorfer, M., Legout, A., Choffnes, D.R.: ReCon: revealing and controlling PII leaks in mobile network traffic. In: Balan, R.K., Misra, A., Agarwal, S., Mascolo, C. (eds.) Proceedings of the 14th Annual International Conference on Mobile Systems, Applications, and Services, MobiSys 2016, Singapore, 26–30 June 2016, pp. 361–374. ACM (2016). https://doi.org/10.1145/2906388.2906392
45. Schober, P., Boer, C., Schwarte, L.A.: Correlation coefficients: appropriate use and interpretation. Anesthesia Analg. **126**(5), 1763–1768 (2018)
46. Sokolova, K., Lemercier, M., Perez, C.: Android permission usage: a first step towards detecting abusive applications. PATTERNS **2015**, 10 (2015)
47. Son, H.X., Carminati, B., Ferrari, E.: A risk estimation mechanism for android apps based on hybrid analysis. Data Sci. Eng. **7**(3), 242–252 (2022). https://doi.org/10.1007/S41019-022-00189-1
48. Soneji, S., Panda, S., Neve, S., Dodge, J.: Signed, sealed,... confused: Exploring the understandability and severity of policy documents (2025). ArXiv: abs/2502.08743. https://api.semanticscholar.org/CorpusID:276318061
49. Srinath, M., Venkit, P.N., Badillo, M., Schaub, F., Giles, C.L., Wilson, S.: Automated detection and analysis of data practices using a real-world corpus. In: Annual Meeting of the Association for Computational Linguistics (2024). https://api.semanticscholar.org/CorpusID:267751256
50. Stach, C.: How to assure privacy on android phones and devices? In: 2013 IEEE 14th International Conference on Mobile Data Management, vol. 1, pp. 350–352. IEEE (2013)
51. Stevens, R., Gibler, C., Crussell, J., Erickson, J., Chen, H.: Investigating user privacy in android ad libraries. In: Workshop on Mobile Security Technologies (MoST), vol. 10, pp. 195–197 (2012)
52. Sun, X., et al.: Demystifying hidden sensitive operations in android apps. ACM Trans. Softw. Eng. Methodol. **32**(2), 1–30 (2023). https://doi.org/10.1145/3574158
53. Sun, X., Chen, X., Liu, K., Wen, S., Li, L., Grundy, J.: Characterizing sensor leaks in android apps. In: 2021 IEEE 32nd International Symposium on Software Reliability Engineering (ISSRE), pp. 498–509. IEEE (2021)
54. Sun, X., Chen, X., Liu, K., Wen, S., Li, L., Grundy, J.C.: Characterizing sensor leaks in android apps. CoRR abs/2201.06235 (2022). https://arxiv.org/abs/2201.06235
55. Terms of Service; Didn't Read: ToS;DR: Analyzing Terms of Service and Privacy Policies (2025). https://tosdr.org/. Accessed 20 Apr 2025
56. Tuan, L.H., Cam, N.T., Pham, V.: Enhancing the accuracy of static analysis for detecting sensitive data leakage in android by using dynamic analysis. Clust. Comput. **22**(Suppl 1), 1079–1085 (2019). https://doi.org/10.1007/S10586-017-1364-8
57. Tuncay, G.S.: Android permissions: evolution, attacks, and best practices. IEEE Secur. Priv. **22**(6), 40–49 (2024). https://doi.org/10.1109/MSEC.2024.3461629

58. Tyagi, V., Singh, R., Tripathi, A., Agarwal, V., Pandey, S.: An android app permission analysis for user privacy and security. In: Futuristic Trends for Sustainable Development and Sustainable Ecosystems, pp. 89–103. IGI Global (2022)
59. Upadhayay, M., Sharma, A., Garg, G., Arora, A.: RPNDroid: android malware detection using ranked permissions and network traffic. In: 2021 Fifth World Conference on Smart Trends in Systems Security and Sustainability (WorldS4), pp. 19–24 (2021)
60. Wijesekera, P., Baokar, A., Hosseini, A., Egelman, S., Wagner, D.A., Beznosov, K.: Android permissions Remystified: a field study on contextual integrity. In: Jung, J., Holz, T. (eds.) 24th USENIX Security Symposium, USENIX Security 15, Washington, D.C., USA, 12–14 August 2015, pp. 499–514. USENIX Association (2015). https://www.usenix.org/conference/usenixsecurity15/technical-sessions/presentation/wijesekera
61. Wu, Y., et al.: TraceDroid: aetecting android malware by trace of privacy leakage. In: Wang, L., Segal, M., Chen, J., Qiu, T. (eds.) Wireless Algorithms, Systems, and Applications - 17th International Conference, WASA 2022, Dalian, China, 24–26 November 2022, Proceedings, Part I. Lecture Notes in Computer Science, vol. 13471, pp. 466–478. Springer (2022). https://doi.org/10.1007/978-3-031-19208-1_38
62. Yang, Z., et al.: FSAFlow: lightweight and fast dynamic path tracking and control for privacy protection on android using hybrid analysis with state-reduction strategy. In: 2022 IEEE Symposium on Security and Privacy (SP), pp. 2114–2129 (2022). https://api.semanticscholar.org/CorpusID:251140982
63. Zhou, Y.: An automated pipeline for privacy leak analysis of android applications. In: ASE 2021, pp. 1048–1050. IEEE (2021). https://doi.org/10.1109/ASE51524.2021.9678875

Correction to: An Explainable Multimodal Framework for Phishing Attack Detection

Shokooh Khandan, Mohammadreza Tabatabaei, Ifeanyi Bryan Uzoatu, Olamide Jogunola, Yakubu Tsado, and Tooska Dargahi

Correction to:
Chapter 5 in: R. Laborde et al. (Eds.): ***Computer Security. ESORICS 2025 International Workshops*****, LNCS 16233, https://doi.org/10.1007/978-3-032-16165-9_5**

The original version of chapter 5 was inadvertently published with the incorrect author's name, which have now been corrected (Ifeanyi Bryan Uzoatu). The corrections to the book have been updated with the changes.

The updated version of this chapter can be found at
https://doi.org/10.1007/978-3-032-16165-9_5

R. Laborde et al. (Eds.): ESORICS 2025 Workshops, LNCS 16233, p. C1, 2026.
https://doi.org/10.1007/978-3-032-16165-9_35

Author Index

R. Laborde et al. (Eds.): ESORICS 2025 Workshops, LNCS 16233, pp. 599–600, 2026.
https://doi.org/10.1007/978-3-032-16165-9

The manufacturer's authorised representative in the EU is Springer Nature Customer Service Centre GmbH, Europaplatz 3, 69115 Heidelberg, Germany. If you have any concerns regarding our products, please contact ProductSafety@springernature.com

Printed and bound by CPI Group (UK) Ltd, Croydon, CR0 4YY
07/07/2026
02160906-0016